TRUTH WORTH TELLING

TRUTH WORTH TELLING

A REPORTER'S SEARCH FOR MEANING
IN THE STORIES OF OUR TIMES

SCOTT PELLEY

HANOVER
SQUARE
PRESS

**HANOVER
SQUARE
PRESS**

Recycling programs
for this product may
not exist in your area.

ISBN-13: 978-1-335-99914-6

Truth Worth Telling

HanoverSqPress.com
BookClubbish.com

Printed in U.S.A.

To the men and women of CBS News who gave me a career.

To Jane, Reece and Blair, who gave me a life.

TABLE OF CONTENTS

In these times, don't ask the meaning of life.
Life is asking,
What's the meaning of *you*?

From the author's essay,
the *CBS Evening News with Scott Pelley*,
November 18, 2015, after the ISIS attack on Paris.

Free Speech
Free Press

"The only effectual guardian of every other right."

—James Madison, 1800

WHAT THIS BOOK IS ABOUT

A Search for Meaning

I was looking forward to the twenty-first century. To me, the arrow of time was aimed in the direction of wonder. But, as soon as it began, the twenty-first became the century of serial shock. It started with the first election in 112 years in which the runner-up became president. Next came 9/11, then war in Afghanistan and war in Iraq. These were followed by an economic calamity that threated to be the worst in history. Now, in the second decade, we have a second election in which the people's choice for president was defeated. Institutions that have made America the envy of history are under relentless attack by our own leaders.

Perhaps because of a new, violent, political rhetoric, we have witnessed an attack on congressmen playing baseball, a politically motivated mailbomb campaign and massacres in our houses of worship. Finally, just when social media became our indispensable connection with one another, we learn it can't be trusted. If you're anxious and confused, I have written this book for you.

In these pages you will find one truth that has not changed in the twenty-first century nor in any other—values matter—and it is up to each of us, as individuals, to own that truth.

This idea of individual triumph in the face of uncertain times crystalized for me in November 2015 after I hurried to Paris on a tragically unlucky Friday the 13th. Terrorists who called themselves ISIS or Islamic State attacked a soccer stadium, a rock concert and sidewalk cafés. One hundred and thirty innocent people were shot to death. As darkness descended on the City of Light I watched Parisians offer candles to a makeshift street memorial. Pallid flames glazed cobblestones and exposed emotions of loss and bewilderment. As I searched their faces, it struck me that I'd seen these mourners before. I had met the same questioning faces in 1993 at the World Trade Center in New York City; in 1995 at the Murrah Federal Building in Oklahoma City; in 2001 at Ground Zero in Manhattan; in 2012 outside an elementary school in Newtown, Connecticut; and among the dispossessed striving against famine and war in Afghanistan, Syria, Iraq, Somalia and Sudan.

For me, that moment of recognition in Paris added the final weight to a critical mass of understanding. In every language, in every heritage, in every time, the longing question is the same: What is the meaning of life?

Earlier that morning, I had noticed an open letter by Antoine Leiris in a Paris newspaper. His wife, whom he described as the love of his life, was among the murdered. Leiris addressed his letter to the terrorists, writing on behalf of himself and his seventeen-month-old son. "You will not have my hatred," Leiris wrote. "This little boy will insult you by being happy and free." His words reminded me instantly of Viktor Frankl, the Austrian psychiatrist who endured three years in Nazi death camps including Auschwitz. The love of *his* life was murdered in Bergen-Belsen. Frankl's landmark 1946 philosophical memoir was published in English under the title *Man's Search for Meaning*. Frankl wrote, "Everything can be taken from a man but one thing, the last of the human freedoms…to choose one's attitude." That is the truth that no century can change.

That fall night in Paris was cool and damp. I anchored the *CBS Evening News* from the granite sidewalk of the Pont Notre Dame bridge overlooking the 670-year-old Gothic cathedral. London plane trees, relatives of the American sycamore, were sacrificing the last of their color to the Seine. To my right, a clock high on a lamppost reached toward 1:00 a.m.—six hours ahead of New York and near the end of our broadcast. I closed our report with images of the mourners in the candlelight vigil and an essay describing Leiris's letter and Viktor Frankl's insight. The essay ended with this:

The search for an explanation leaves us with silence until we search inside.
Don't ask the meaning of life.
Life is asking,
What's the meaning of *you*?

A year later, another night would fill many Americans with a similar sense of bewilderment. On November 8, 2016, I was on the air trying to explain a presidential election that carried us into uncertainty. That's not a partisan shot, both Hillary Clinton and Donald Trump were the most unpopular candidates ever to win their party's nomination. Many voters held their nose with one hand and tossed the dice with the other. There was already more than enough anxiety before we learned there was a third campaign in the running—the Russian disinformation campaign designed to upend our democracy. On Inauguration Day, nearly three months later, America itself seemed unfamiliar as Donald

J. Trump began his presidency with a speech that did not appeal to aspiration but instead described "American carnage." In his first years as president, he tore at the Constitution he had sworn to "preserve, protect and defend." The American system of justice was "a joke" and "a laughingstock" in the president's estimation. Americans working in journalism were described by President Trump as the "enemy of the American people." Imagine what citizens of Russia and China would give for independent, generally reliable information and for courts that are among the most transparent and least corrupt in the world. Even Mr. Trump's supporters admitted many of his attacks and aspirations were untethered to reality. Mr. Trump was the first presidential candidate to take advantage of the great paradox of the information age: never in human history has more information been available to more people, but it's also true that never in history has more *bad* information been available to more people. What to believe? Whom to believe *in*? Viktor Frankl's answer, restated seventy years later by Antoine Leiris, is to believe in our ability as individuals to triumph over fate. As Leiris put it in his open letter, "We are two, my son and I, but we are stronger than all the armies of the world."

I have discovered that strength in extraordinary people I have met while traveling in a world of inspiration. You'll meet them in each chapter of the book. Some are famous—most are not— but all discovered the meaning of their lives in moments of great challenge. Most of the chapters are titled for virtues I have witnessed, including gallantry, devotion, audacity, self-sacrifice and authenticity. Of course, human nature being what it is, not everything I've witnessed has fallen on the side of the angels so I've included cautionary tales of the failure of virtue when the powerful succumb to deceit and hubris. Covering the great stories of our times has taught me about the inescapable sovereignty of character. As the English statesman Henry Bolingbroke put it in 1735, "History is philosophy teaching by example."[1]

As you make your way through these short stories on character, you'll discover small tales of insight drawn from my field notes. Later, the book leads to where we are today and how we can chart the way ahead in uncertain times.

Reporting is the world's greatest continuing education program. I have had the privilege of exploring the Arctic Circle, the Antarctic Circle and nearly everywhere in between. This collection of short stories is based on my experiences, my research, my notes, video recordings and the best of my recollection. For better or worse, I have written every word. Errors are my responsibility alone.

If you are looking for a partisan point of view, stop here. No sense wasting time. I praise what is worthy of praise and criticize what is worthy of criticism. Liberals and conservatives appear abundantly deserving of both. The conclusions I draw are mine alone and do not reflect the views of CBS News nor the CBS Corporation. You have not heard me express opinion on CBS. You will not hear my opinion on CBS in the future. I have strived to reach the conclusions in this book through a nonpartisan assessment of fact. I have no interest in deepening the political fault lines in my beloved America. Journalism is a quest to open minds, not close them.

It has taken me forty-five years—in war and peace, at home and abroad—to collect these stories of triumph, failure, gallantry and hope. I hope you find these examples as vibrant as I have as you continually calibrate "the meaning of you."

CHAPTER ONE

Gallantry
The FDNY

That morning in early September struck me as the most beautiful I had ever seen in New York City. My 7:00 a.m. run through Central Park began with more habit than awareness until my heart rose above 125 beats per minute. "Blood to the brain," I muttered as I awakened on the road, slipping past lethal bike racers and into the pack of strangers pounding a beat to the Reservoir. The palette of the park dripped early autumn. Rust was forming in red maples. Misnamed redbuds were rioting pink. Sixty-five degrees, a breath of a breeze and a sky that pilots call "clear and a million." Transparent. Sapphire. Vision for a million miles. "God, what a beautiful day," I whispered as I huffed along the park's West Drive, dodging hills of black granite sequined with mica. So beautiful. Clear and a million. September 11, 2001.

★ ★ ★

As I ran, a silver Boeing 767-200ER—striped in red, white and blue—rose from the runway at Boston Logan International Airport. American Airlines Flight 11 was on a "milk run" to Los Angeles International. Passengers settled. Announcements were made. In coach, flight attendants Betty Ong and Amy Sweeney began the prep for breakfast. Fifteen minutes into the trip there was a burst of violence in first class.[1] Ong quietly used a radiotelephone to call her company's Southeastern Reservations Office in North Carolina.[2] The twenty-five-minute call was recorded. "Okay, my name is Betty Ong. I'm [flight attendant] number three on Flight 11. The cockpit is not answering their calls...we can't breathe in business class. Somebody's got mace or something. Our number one got stabbed. Nobody knows who stabbed who and we can't even get up to business class because nobody can breathe." Minutes later Ong reported, "the first-class galley flight attendant and our passenger is [sic] stabbed. We can't get to the cockpit; the door won't open." Amy Sweeney was on the other end of coach on another of the plane's radiotelephones. She reached American's Boston base station. The call was not recorded but Sweeney reported the seat numbers of four of the hijackers. American's Boston station manager asked Sweeney to look out the window for landmarks. He told the FBI that Sweeney replied, "I see water and buildings. Oh my God! Oh my God!"[3] About this time, Betty Ong asked the American Airlines managers who had assembled on her line to "please pray for us."[4]

In Manhattan, about fourteen blocks from the World Trade Center, firefighters from downtown's Battalion 1 were checking a routine natural gas leak at the intersection of Lispenard and Church Streets.[5][6] At 8:46 a.m., their curiosity turned to the roar of two General Electric CF-6 turbofan engines furiously compressing the autumn sky into 100,000 pounds of thrust.[7] A camera crew shooting a documentary about the life of a rookie in the Fire Department of the City of New York caught the men as their eyes rose the length of the World Trade Center's north tower and intersected with the fireball that consumed Betty Ong, Amy Sweeney and eighty-five other innocent souls on the plane. American Flight 11, traveling at approximately 440 miles an hour, gouged through half the width of the tower and blasted a hole, vertically, from the 93rd to the 99th floor.[8] "Holy shit!" one fireman yelled.[9] On FDNY radio channel 15, at 8:47 a.m., Battalion 1's chief, Joseph Pfeifer, made the first call to the Manhattan Fire Dispatch Operations Center located in Central Park. "We just had a plane crash into the upper floors of the World Trade Center. Transmit a second alarm and start relocating companies into the area."[10] Seconds later, Battalion 1's Engine 10 radioed, "Engine 1-0, World Trade Center, *10-60!*"

"10-60" is FDNY code for a catastrophe. The voice from Engine 10 shouted, "Send every available ambulance, everything you've got, to the World Trade Center *now!*"

I was in New York City by happenstance. My home was outside Washington, DC, but I did my writing and editing at the *60 Minutes* offices in a high-rise near the Hudson River on Manhattan's West 57th Street. I was preparing a story on Bovine Spongiform Encephalopathy, which seemed, at the time, an urgent public health risk. But soon, Mad Cow Disease would be the furthest thing from my mind. Our world, and my life, changed as I prepared to leave my hotel room on Central Park South. I aimed the TV remote control for a parting shot at CBS's morning news. The remote dropped slowly to my side when I noticed a Special Report and live pictures of smoke erupting from One World Trade Center. Early word was a small plane hit the building. That didn't seem likely to me. It was clear and a million.

Battalion Chief Pfeifer's truck pulled into the shadow of the wounded tower. His next call to Manhattan Dispatch was meant to remove any doubt about what he witnessed. "We have a number of floors on fire," Pfeifer radioed. "It looked like the plane was *aiming* toward the building."[11] Within three minutes, fire units that had not been assigned to the World Trade Center began raising their hands. "Do you want us to bring the high-rise unit?" one station asked. The dispatcher replied, "Bring everything you got!"[12] One of the department's elite rescue trucks called dispatch. "Rescue 2 to Manhattan...are we assigned to any of your boxes in lower Manhattan?"

"10-4, Rescue 2," the dispatcher replied. "Start out to Box 8087."

The box numbers marked fire alarm stations the public could use to call for help. On the organizational maps of the FDNY every address was assigned a box number. Box 8087 marked One World Trade Center.

Peter J. Ganci Jr. was supposed to have jury duty that day but he convinced himself he didn't have time. The highest-ranking uniformed officer in the FDNY decided to make good with the court another day. Ganci had devoted most of his adult life to the department—thirty-three years. He had served in the army with the 82nd Airborne and joined the FDNY as soon as he came home.[13] Ganci began as a probationary firefighter and rose through all eight ranks, but he was no bureaucrat. In 1982, when Ganci was a young lieutenant in command of Ladder 124, he crawled into an inferno to save a five-year-old girl. The department's investigation found that Ganci shimmied on his hands and knees into the burning apartment, pushed flaming furniture out of his way and crawled out with the girl while giving her mouth-to-mouth resuscitation. The department citation for gallantry noted that the child certainly would have died had Ganci not acted "with disregard for his own life."[14] No wonder Ganci's two sons followed him into the FDNY. Ganci's daughter married a fireman.

Now, at the age of fifty-four, Ganci's starched white shirt

collar was pierced by a pentagon of stars. His helmet shield was gold and read Chief of Department. Behind the shield, the formerly white helmet was gray with years and indelibly smudged with soot. Halfway up the crown was a ring of yellow reflective triangles. Ganci had tied the chin strap behind the crown to get the damn thing out of his way. There were dents in his headgear and in some spots the paint was worn to bare metal. The helmet was a metaphor for the man. Ganci was visibly tough and handsome. Not tall, but trim. If he'd been an actor, he would have been cast to play the chief of department. Ganci's soft blue eyes were framed by deep, radiating wrinkles. His hair was charcoal with faint streaks of ash. Ganci was friendly, sociable, even more so when armed with his preferred scotch. He was sometimes profane and always trying to quit smoking. Maybe he wasn't your first choice for a guest at a tea party. But in a service that was all about saving lives from the horror of fire, no one would quite equal his experience or dedication. Peter J. Ganci Jr. was the indispensable man.

The office of the Chief of Department looked out on Manhattan from the higher floors of headquarters in Brooklyn. Ganci had a grand view across the East River. He was taking in the beauty of the day when he witnessed American Flight 11 ripping through 1 WTC. Ganci shouted to his second in command, Chief of Operations Daniel Nigro, "Look out your window! A plane just hit the World Trade Center."[15] Several staff chiefs ran into the boss's office. A few thought he was joking.[16]

Ganci, Nigro and Ganci's executive officer, Steven Mosiello, headed down to the garage on level C-1 and piled into Ganci's car.[17] Mosiello slid in behind the wheel. The chief's top aide was a close friend. In the Long Island suburb of Massapequa, Ganci and Mosiello lived across the street from one another. Most days, by sunrise, they drove to headquarters together. As they raced over the Brooklyn Bridge, Ganci assessed the burning tower and radioed to Manhattan Dispatch, "Car 3 [Ganci] to Manhattan,

K. Car 3 and Car 4 [Nigro] are arriving together responding down. Transmit a fifth alarm for this box. Get us a staging area somewhere on West Street, K."[18] On the radio, the use of the letter *K* was a throwback to the days of the telegraph when *K* was transmitted to signal the end of a message. In the twentieth century, when the FDNY began using radios, it kept the *K*. At the dawn of the twenty-first century, firefighters spoke it, unconsciously, as terminal punctuation. Ganci's "fifth alarm" order automatically summoned twenty-two engine companies and fourteen ladder companies. Before the morning was out, four additional five-alarm responses would be called to the World Trade Center. Speeding over the bridge, Chief of Operations Dan Nigro measured the enormity of the fire and knew there was no way to put it out. The FDNY had never faced an inferno across that many floors in a high-rise. Raising his voice above the siren, Nigro told Ganci, "This is going to be one of the worst days of our careers."[19]

"Hi, honey. It's me. A plane hit the building. Um, I'm okay. The building's on fire. We're trying to get out. I love you. I'll see you later."[20] Frank Spinelli, forty-four, hated to leave the message for his wife, Michelle. Now she was going to worry and he didn't want to put her through that. He'd spent twenty years on Wall Street as a foreign exchange trader. Seven months before 9/11 he won a new job at the trading firm Cantor Fitzgerald on the 105th floor of One World Trade Center. Each morning, Spinelli rose long before dawn to commute from Short Hills, New Jersey, to catch the end of the trading day in overseas markets. The focus of his life was Michelle and their three children: Nicole, eighteen; Christopher, fourteen; and Danielle, eight. Nicole Spinelli told me, "He would kiss us goodbye in the morning and it was just one of those things that you'd maybe roll over and just be, like, 'Dad, it's too early.' But he told me one time, 'Nikki, I kiss you and your brother and sister goodbye in the morning to let you know that, if anything ever happened to me at work, you would always know that I loved you.'"[21] Cantor Fitzgerald's five floors began at floor 101, two stories above the grotesque gash in the tower. Spinelli and more than 650 Cantor co-workers were trapped.

Sirens split the morning. Pedestrians cringed as powerful air horns packed a physical punch. The FDNY's armada of engines, ladders and specialty trucks rolled at the sound of a woman's voice on the dispatch frequency ordering seemingly endless lists of divisions, battalions and companies. Half of the city's 281 firehouses emptied. In Manhattan, the Bronx, Queens, Brooklyn and Staten Island, firefighters writhed into worn black flame-resistant bunker coats. Yellow-and-silver reflective stripes orbited the chest, arms and waist. On the back, "F.D.N.Y." stood across the shoulders in yellow capitals. Near the bottom and just above the hem, the last name of the firefighter was lettered: Ryan, Feinberg, Jovic, Mercado, Freund, Vega, Sweeny, O'Rourke, Regan. The Irish were overrepresented because of the potato famine in 1845 that pushed an immigrant wave into New York Harbor. In the Civil War, thousands of Irishmen formed their own units in the Union Army. When the modern FDNY was organized in 1865, the year after the war's end, returning Irish troops filled its roster. Even today, the tradition of service is passed down through fathers, sons and brothers. So, if a captain yelled "Mulligan" or "O'Hagan" in a firehouse, he might get more than one answer.

Racing to the battlefield were 121 engine companies, 62 ladder companies and 100 ambulances. Boastful rigs—labeled The Pride of Hell's Kitchen, The Pride of Midtown—trailed the stars and stripes from their decks. Many firefighters tightened their grip on unfamiliar handholds because the rigs labored under twice the normal crew. Firehouses were changing shifts at 9:00 a.m. At many or most, both shifts answered the call. One thousand firefighters, paramedics and emergency medical technicians were in pursuit. The most senior among the uniformed firefighters, sixty-three-year-old Joseph Angelini Sr. had forty years on the job, but he still preferred to "ride the back step" of Rescue 1. His son, Joe Jr., thirty-eight years old, was aboard Ladder 4. The youngest was twenty-two-year-old Michael Cammarata with Ladder Company 11. He had scored a perfect 105 on the FDNY entrance exam. This was his fifth month on the job. He hadn't attended his official graduation yet. Cammarata was a thoughtful son. As he answered the alarm, he called his father's voice mail. "I am going to the World Trade Center. A plane just hit it. Just tell everyone I'm alright," he said. A thousand names were lettered on a thousand bunker coats, but each firefighter knew the other by only one. It is a carefully observed tradition in the FDNY that firefighters call one another "brother."

Chief Albert Turi's staff car came to a stop on the east side of the burning tower. He hurried to the trunk and shoved his arms into his bunker coat which read "F.D.N.Y. Chief of Safety." In the hierarchy, Deputy Assistant Chief Turi reported directly to the chief of department. But the organizational chart wasn't the reason Turi had Pete Ganci's ear. They were close friends who had risen together from the time they were probationary firefighters. Turi was in Ganci's wedding party.[22] It was Turi's job to analyze the danger and safeguard the brothers as best he could. Dozens of firefighters were already scaling the stairwells to rescue the wounded and the trapped. Turi was facing the most hazardous calamity of his career but as he pulled on his boots, his attention was seized by a deafening roar.[23]

"Holy shit! What's going on with the flight patterns?" firefighter Scott Holowach said to the fireman next to him. Chief of Department Ganci was standing nearby. "Chief, there is a second plane that hit the other tower!" Holowach reported.

"No, no, no," Ganci replied. "It's another explosion." Ganci assumed the blast he heard was a secondary eruption in the already burning 1 WTC.

"Chief, I *witnessed* it," Holowach protested.

"Are you sure?" Ganci asked.

"Chief, I'm 100 percent positive I watched a plane hit the other tower."[24]

Others had seen it too. "Marine 6 to Manhattan, urgent!"

At 9:03 a.m., seventeen minutes after the first impact, an FDNY fireboat called dispatch. "Urgent" was an official understatement used on the radio rarely and carefully. It signaled the highest priority, a call that must be handled before all others.

"Marine 6, go," answered the dispatcher.

"You have a *second* plane into the other tower of the Trade Center! Major fire!"

"Mayday! Mayday!" An unidentified engine company exploded onto the frequency. "Another plane hit the second tower! K!"

United Airlines Flight 175, another Boeing 767-200 scheduled from Boston to Los Angeles, vaporized into Two World Trade Center at 540 miles an hour.[25] The south tower was lacerated from floor 77 through 85.[26] The plane's right engine passed entirely though the building and landed more than a quarter mile away near the corner of Murray and Church Streets.[27] In the first attack, on 1 WTC, American Flight 11 severed all three emergency stairwells. But in 2 WTC, United Flight 175 just missed a corner of the building's central core.[28] One stairway to the top survived.[29]

Eight miles north, on the south end of Central Park, I hurried out of my hotel and waved down a taxi. "World Trade Center," I said. The cabbie, listening to the news on the radio, shrugged, "They ain't going to let you near it."

"Well, get as far as you can," I urged.

I started flipping through my memories of the Trade Center. This wasn't my first rush to the twin towers. In February 1993, a frantic CBS News National Desk assistant sent me to what was reported to be a subway accident in the World Trade Center's extensive underground transit hub. There's a maxim in journalism: "First reports are always wrong." That would be true enough on that day. In 1993, I wouldn't have expected to be sent to such a big story. I had been with CBS News only four years, not even a start at an organization where the contributions of correspondents were metered in decades. But the New York correspondent on duty had misplaced her pager. I was the only guy the desk could find. This would be the beginning of my education into the fanatics who hijacked one of the great religions of Abraham and their obsession with the dual symbols of American economic might.

The twin towers began to rise from lower Manhattan in 1968. They were meant to make a statement. Each, at the time, was the tallest building in the world and the Port Authority of New York and New Jersey was building *two* of them. Ayn Rand's fictional architect, Howard Roark, would have admired the simplicity: austere aluminum-sheathed columns soaring 110 stories as though they were needed to hold up the sky. They'd been drafted in the mind of Japanese American architect Minoru Yamasaki, but the genius behind the construction was a thirty-four-year-old structural engineer named Leslie Robertson. His innovation created open floor plans by almost eliminating interior columns. Each tower was built around a core of steel—this much was typical. But Robertson took the load that would normally be supported by interior columns and moved it to the outside—to the facade. Half the weight of the buildings was carried at the core; half was distributed to the exterior.[30] The two load-bearing systems multiplied their strength when they were bolted together by the floors.[31] Additional strength was added by a steel structure at the top of each tower. The so-called "hat truss" encompassed the top four floors and was intended to support the weight of a rooftop mast and television antenna.[32] Both towers wore a hat truss but only 1 WTC lofted a mast. Robertson's ingenious arrangement saved everything that mattered: money, weight and time.[33] The towers were over-engineered to survive hurricanes and one other force that had never been contemplated before. Opponents of the project argued that the towers, at 1,368 feet and 1,362 feet respectively, were too tall. They might be hit by a plane lost in fog. In the late 1960s, critics took out a full-page ad in the *New York Times* with an artist's impression of an airliner approaching the towers. Robertson took this seriously. He was also mindful of the foggy day in 1945 when a B-25 Mitchell bomber collided with the 78th and 79th floors of the Empire State Building.[34] The World Trade Center towers became the first skyscrapers in history designed with an airliner collision in mind.[35] The engineering analysis imagined the impact of one of the larger planes of the day: a Boeing 707.

In February 1993, I could see the buildings were strong. I pulled up at 1 WTC to find smoke raging from the entrance of the parking garage. Firefighters emerged as black silhouettes except for the oval where their Scott Air-Pak facemasks shielded them from brow to chin. I knew enough to look for a white helmet among all the black: a chief officer.

"What do you have down there?" I asked.

"A bomb," the chief said.

I was stunned and pretty sure he must be wrong. Remember, it was 1993. It would be another two years before I would find myself standing before the ruined Murrah Federal Building in Oklahoma City. "Bomb" was not an answer I had imagined nor one I was eager to stick my neck out reporting. "Gas main?" I offered. "Maybe a transformer?" The white helmet with the gold shield announcing "Chief, Battalion," panned slowly left and right. "There's nothing down there that could do *this*," he emphasized. "There's a huge hole blown through five floors of the parking structure."

The blast propelled smoke up all 110 floors. Power was out, elevators dead. Office workers felt their way down blackened stairwells and emerged into light snow, their faces layered with soot. Depending on their altitude and abilities, it took evacuees between one and nine hours to descend.[36] Six people were killed, more than one thousand were injured.

That night, we set up a "live truck" to report from the scene for the *CBS Evening News with Dan Rather.* Shortly before air, at 6:30 p.m. Eastern Standard Time, one of our producers with deep contacts at the FBI called to tell me the bureau was confirming a bomb. That fulfilled my need for two independent sources of information. Before I broke the news to the nation, there was one person I wanted to report to first. I called home. I was so heartsick that someone would try to kill so many innocents that I shared the news with my wife, Jane. I needed to hear her strength.

The investigation of the bombing would reveal that a Sunni Islamic extremist named Ramzi Yousef had engineered a 1,310-pound homemade bomb inside a rental van. The FBI made its first arrest when one of Yousef's co-conspirators reported the truck stolen and *went back to the rental office to get his $400 deposit.*[37] I thought, with enemies like these, we might not have much to worry about. Yousef was captured in Pakistan in 1995. No one understood at that time that Ramzi Yousef had a Pakistani uncle who was angry, ambitious and patient. Yousef took up residence in the "Supermax" federal prison on the plains of South-Central Colorado. His uncle, Khalid Sheikh Mohammed, would never see his nephew again and would never take his eyes off the World Trade Center. Yousef's failure set in motion his uncle's plan to ensure the destruction of the twin towers eight years later. That night, in February 1993, on the *Evening News*, I included a fact that I found astounding. On any given day, forty-thousand people worked in the twin towers.[38]

The bombing was my first experience with the Fire Department of the City of New York. In 2001, the department was the second largest in the world after Tokyo. Eleven thousand uniformed firefighters and four thousand paramedics answered about one-and-a-half-million calls each year.[39] The annual budget is nearly $2 billion.

The Fire Department of the City of New York is so singular, so storied, that no one thinks it odd that it places its name *before* the name of the city it serves, leading to the somewhat backward acronym, FDNY. Its shield, the department symbol, is a stylized version of the Maltese Cross, an eight-pointed star. The cross originated nearly one thousand years ago when the Knights of St. John became the first organized firefighters. During the first Crusade, Muslim Saracens defended their occupation of the Holy Land with a new type of bomb composed of naphtha in a glass jar. Hurled from a castle wall, the bomb set attacking crusaders ablaze. The Knights of St. John specialized in dousing the flames with blankets and evacuating the wounded. Their cross became the international symbol of firefighters.

Two towers burned above Chief Peter Ganci as he waved his arms in the middle of West Street. "Gary!" Ganci yelled. "Right here." Ganci was flagging down the department's Field Communications Unit, known as Field Com. "Right here" was where Ganci wanted his incident command post. It was directly across from 1 WTC, roughly where the command post had been after the bombing in 1993. "Set it up right here," Ganci told Field Com Lieutenant Gary Gates.[40] Field Com was the central nervous system of Ganci's command. Firefighters trained in communications kept track of the incoming rigs and their assignments. Lieutenant Gates set up an aluminum stand with what looked like a metal suitcase on top. This was the Command Board on which each fire unit was recorded with color-coded magnetic nameplates. Engines were noted in black, ladders in red, battalions in gold. Unit numbers were written on the plates with a marker. Ganci's incident command post oversaw three other command posts: one in the lobby of each tower and another in the Marriott Hotel which stood between them. Ganci ordered West Street cleared of fire trucks. He intended to use the six-lane road for ambulances. To organize communications, he assigned unique radio channels to each building.[41] But the feeble handheld radios that the department called "handie-talkies" tormented him. He looked at his black radio wrapped in a fake leather case and shouted, "Goddamn it! The radios aren't working!"[42][43][44] After the bombing in 1993, the FDNY discovered the signal of its handheld radios couldn't ascend the vertical expanse of the Trade Center. A "repeater" system was installed to boost the signal. But on 9/11 the repeater wasn't working in One World Trade Center.[45][46] Firefighters rising toward the inferno were cut off from their officers and each other. Off-duty firefighters who wedged themselves onto rigs at shift change didn't have radios at all.

Even when the radios worked, Ganci faced a shortage of facts and a surplus of rumors. Word spread from law enforcement that another plane was inbound. There was no third plane targeting Manhattan, but after the warning, Ganci tried to stop the upward flow of firefighters. "There's another plane in the air," he radioed. "I don't want anybody to go into the towers. Everybody stay put." Ganci wondered aloud why the military was not yet shooting down hijacked airliners. He told the assembled chiefs at the command post, "Make sure no companies go in right now. There's another plane up in the air. We don't know what's going on."[47]

At the command board, Chief of Safety Al Turi turned to

Ganci. "Pete, we're going to lose some people here. It's inevitable. It's too tremendous." Ganci said nothing. He simply nodded in agreement. In his head, Turi estimated as many as a dozen firefighters could be killed.[48]

Across the East River in Brooklyn Heights, the Maltese Cross was embroidered with the words *Engine 205* and *118 Truck*.

"Truck" is what fire companies call their ladder rigs. A brass plaque on the narrow red-brick building at 74 Middagh Street informed passersby that the firehouse had been built in 1929 under the administration of Mayor James "Jimmy" Walker. Walker was a character from a colorful day. He was a notoriously corrupt womanizer. During the days of prohibition, Walker's police department often found his honor enjoying a refreshing beverage in a speakeasy. To the right of the plaque, the red overhead door was open. Engine 205's side of the house was empty. The men of 205 rolled when the first plane hit. The crew of Ladder 118 was left behind to cover Brooklyn until the second attack. L–118 lumbered onto Middagh Street, shooing pedestrians with its air horn. She was an older truck, a 1991 Seagrave Tractor Drawn Aerial—a "tiller rig"—that looked something like an eighteen-wheeler. In three quick turns, L–118 mounted the Brooklyn Bridge. There is an iconic photo of the burning towers taken from Brooklyn. Black smoke engulfs the top third of each building. On the bridge, in the center lane, you can make out 118.

Leon "Express" Smith Jr., forty-eight, tightened his grip on the steering wheel. Smith, the "chauffeur" in fire department lingo, was a member of the Vulcan Society, the FDNY's association of black firefighters. People who met him could not forget his face, which was dominated by a remarkably generous mustache that flowed far beyond the corners of his smile. Smith liked internal combustion engines. He liked building them, overhauling them, and he knew how to coax compression out of the Detroit Diesel thundering behind his seat. His nickname, "Express," had been earned over nineteen years. Somehow, he always seemed to be the first to arrive at a fire. The rig's ladder could reach one hundred feet into the air. But because she was so long, 118 had a second driver riding high astern—"the tiller"—who guided the rear end around tight Brooklyn corners. Up front in the cab, next to Smith, rode Lieutenant Robert "Bobby" Regan, also forty-eight years old. Regan was the officer in charge. His name was the first listed on the green chalkboard mounted in the firehouse's white-tile garage. Across the top of the board the chalk noted "Date: 9/11. L-118. Lt. Regan— officer." The rest of 118's crew continued down the column: "Smith, Cherry, Vega, Davidson, Agnello." Lieutenant Regan was nicknamed "Dizzy Dean" after the hall of fame pitcher. In his off-hours, he coached Little League. Over the summer, Regan's team won the district championship by one run. The run had been batted in on a single off the bat of twelve-year-old Brendan Regan, the coach's hero and his son.

The span of the 118-year-old Brooklyn Bridge shortened before them. Smith and Regan could see black clouds rolling furiously from the towers. Three firefighters in the back of the tractor would have to twist and shoulder each other for a look. Pete Vega had the best view. The sight of the catastrophe from his tiller cab would have made any firefighter curse the distance. On the radio, Lieutenant Regan received orders to evacuate 3 WTC, the Marriott Hotel. The night before, the twenty-two-story hotel had been nearly sold out. In 825 rooms, there were more than 1,000 guests.

To those on the Brooklyn Bridge, Ladder 118 began to blur under the demanding foot of "Express" Smith. On the outside of the tractor, on Bobby Regan's door, they might have made out the FDNY's modern logo featuring the New York City skyline dominated by austere twin towers.

★ ★ ★

My taxi came up short, nosing into blue NYPD sawhorse barricades that severed the West Side Highway along the Hudson River. The barricade was superfluous. All eight lanes were jammed with thousands of people trudging north, shoulder to shoulder. Their eyes projected disbelief and the dawning realization they had escaped downtown. I bailed out of the taxi and ran against the current. "Sorry! Sorry! Sorry!" I repeated as I stumbled through the crowd. I figured I had two miles to run before I reached the towers. Small obstacles littered the roadway. They felt like stones spilling at my feet left and right. The crowd was so tight, I couldn't see what they were. After a few blocks, there was a parting of the pack and I saw what was tripping me: high heels, hundreds of pairs of women's shoes, abandoned for speed.

I reached the Tribeca neighborhood, a few blocks from the towers, running as I had an hour before in idyllic Central Park. My right thumb flipped open my Motorola cell phone. I called the CBS News National Desk to find out what we knew. By then, the newsroom was crowded with producers, reporters and photographers who rushed to work without being called. Dan Rather was on the air, anchoring continuously. The desk assistant told me, "The Pentagon is on fire."

American Airlines Flight 77, a Boeing 757, had left Washington Dulles International Airport bound for LA at 9:37 a.m. Thirty-seven minutes after the second tower was struck in New York, American Flight 77 exploded into the west wall of the Pentagon in Arlington County, Virginia. The impact, at 530 miles an hour, killed fifty-nine passengers and crew along with five hijackers.[49] In the military headquarters, 125 lost their lives.[50]

The National Desk continued to fill me in, "There's been a car bomb reported at the State Department and a plane has crashed into the president's compound at Camp David in Maryland." That last one struck me as odd. President George W. Bush was in Florida. Remember what reporters say about "first reports." We would soon find out neither the State Department nor Camp David had been attacked. But with the Pentagon ablaze, the scope of 9/11 was greater than I had been capable of imagining. Now I was thinking about my wife and our young son and daughter. Our home and their schools were a few miles from the Pentagon. Nothing seemed beyond the reach of the unfolding catastrophe. Everything I loved—my country, my wife, my son and my daughter—seemed held at risk by a force we did not know.

A traffic jam of fire equipment hardened around the World Trade Center. Firefighters bailed out of their trucks to pursue the FDNY doctrine known as "aggressive interior attack." Fighting fire from the inside is the only way given a skyline no escalade can reach. Ganci's hope was to evacuate everyone below the impact zones and use handheld hoses connected to the buildings' standpipes to cut a path through burning stairwells for survivors trapped on the higher floors.[51] There had been 198 elevators in the two towers. Now, only one was operating in each. In 1 WTC the lone elevator rose from the lobby to the 16th floor.[52] In 2 WTC the surviving elevator climbed to the 40th.[53] Firefighters heaved fifty pounds of protective gear plus another fifty pounds of equipment.[54] When smoke in the stairwell grew heavy, each lowered his face into the Plexiglas mask of an Air-Pak and pulled the elastic straps over his head. Reaching behind with his right hand, he pushed in, then rotated a knob that opened the flow of compressed air into the regulator near his mouth. There would have been a quick, sharp *chirp, chirp, chirp* from a device called a Personal Alert Safety System. The chirp assured the firefighter that his PASS alarm had been armed automatically by the pressurized air. If the fireman was motionless for thirty seconds, the PASS would erupt into a piercing ninety-five-decibel wail. Firefighters drop everything at the call of the PASS to rush to the aid of a downed brother.

Ganci learned the rumor of a third plane targeting New York was false. He ordered reinforcements up the stairwells. One of the early engine companies at 1 WTC reached the 54th floor in forty-five minutes.[55] But the ascending legion did not know that American Flight 11 destroyed the fire sprinkler system and severed all three emergency stairwells.[56] [57] [58] Above the 92nd floor, 1,355 people had only one way out.[59]

The first member of the FDNY to lose his life was killed at 9:32 a.m. near West and Liberty Streets. Firefighter Daniel "Danny" Suhr, thirty-seven, was struck by a fellow human being hurtling to earth at approximately seventy miles an hour.[60] Many victims above the burning floors leaned through smashed windows and clung to the outside of the towers. At least 111 fell or jumped.[61] One anonymous couple held hands as they tumbled through the last moments of their lives. A fire marshal reported that a body hit every thirty to forty seconds.[62] Firefighter Richard Boeri was in the soaring lobby of 1 WTC preparing to start his climb, when he was rendered immobile by the sight of jumpers disintegrating on the plaza. "I think we saw like eighteen people jump," Boeri recalled. Then, one of the officers in the lobby said, "Turn around. Let's concentrate on who we *can* save. We can't save those people anymore."[63] Outside the entrance of 1 WTC, a firefighter bent his neck skyward to watch for desperate souls in flight. In the breaks between jumps—like a traffic cop—he signaled people waiting in the lobby. "Stop! Stop! Stop!" he yelled until the next falling victim hit the plaza. "Come on! Run! Run! Run!" was the signal to those in the lobby that it was momentarily safe to escape with their lives.[64] [65] One plunging soul caught the eye of Mayor Rudy Giuliani. The mayor raised his hand to his mouth and recoiled. Giuliani rushed to the FDNY incident command post on West Street as soon as his police detail told him about the first plane. Ganci had moved the command post from its first location in the middle of the street. Chief of Safety Al Turi insisted on shifting it twenty yards farther from the World Trade Center to the entrance of an underground parking garage. There, two wide lanes ducked beneath the American Express building. The garage could be a refuge, Turi reasoned, if falling windows began to shoot shards of glass into the command post. Giuliani asked Chief Ganci if helicopters could rescue victims from the roof. "My guys can save everyone *below* the fire,"[66] Ganci said. Giuliani understood the implication. Flying helicopters through the flames was not an option. Giuliani recalled saying, "God bless you, Pete." The mayor told reporters that the number of souls lost that day would be "more than any of us can bear."

Ganci believed he had time to work with. No steel high-rise in the history of the world had ever fully collapsed because of fire.[67] None of Ganci's chief officers at the incident command post expressed concern about a total collapse as company after company of "brothers" heaved up smoky stairwells.[68] [69] The chiefs estimated they had twelve hours before a partial collapse of some of the floors. For planning, Chief Turi cut the estimate in half. Based on a maximum time of six hours, he recommended to Ganci that all FDNY personnel be clear of the towers in two hours. Then the inferno would be left to burn itself out. The plan was tried and true. Other high-rise fires had been dealt with in the same way. Ganci agreed to Turi's timeline.

His tactics might have been different had he known that each of the 300,000-pound airplanes blasted away the spray-on fire resistant foam applied to both buildings' steel during construction.[70] A subsequent study by the National Institute of Standards and Technology concluded that both buildings would have survived the impact of the aircraft and the heat of the fires had it not been for the loss of the thermal insulation.[71] In 1968, the requirements of the city's building code relied on two assumptions: the fireproofing would always remain intact and the sprinkler system would work. Now, neither was true. Structural steel begins to lose significant strength and stiffness at 1,112 degrees Fahrenheit.[72] In some locations, the jet fuel infernos raged at 1,832 degrees.[73]

In stratospheric offices the sun was extinguished by rising smoke. Operators for 9-1-1 received 130 pleas for help from inside the towers. The recordings tell us what little is known about the fight to survive. An unnamed 9-1-1 operator tells a caller, "Alright. Hold one second, sir. Try to stay calm okay? I know— is there any towels in the area? Okay, listen, everybody, wet the towels. Listen. Lie on the floor. Everybody wet the towels, put it over your head, lie on the floor, okay?" The 9-1-1 recordings were released by court order five years after the attack. In respect for the dead, the judge redacted the words of the callers, leaving only the reaction of the emergency operators.

"Okay, listen please do not break the window," one operator urges. "Don't break the windows because there's too much smoke outside. If you break the window, you guys won't be able to breathe." In another recording we can infer the caller's plea to 9-1-1: "We are," the operator says. "We're trying to get up there, sir. Like you said, the stairs are collapsed, okay? Put the wet towels over your head and lie down. Okay, listen. Listen. Listen to me. Listen to me. Okay? Listen, don't—try not to panic. You can save your air supply by doing that, okay?"

Manhattan Dispatch noted each caller's location and reported to Ganci's command post.

"Manhattan calling Field Com, K."

"Field Com, go ahead Manhattan."

"Alright Field Com, you ready to write? I got...building one and building two, everything we have up to now."

"Give me building one."

The list of the survivors' locations revealed the immensity of the vertical battlefield. Tearful prayers were reduced to numbered targets.

"Okay, building one: 9-2 floor; the 106th floor; the 89th floor; 104th floor; the 100th floor, the northeast side; the 8-8 floor; the 8th floor, east side; the 105th floor; the 68th floor; 106th floor, northwest; 103rd floor, room 1-0-3; 83rd floor, room 8-3-11. Let me know when you are ready for building two."

Field Com replied, "Proceed with building two."

"Okay, the 82nd floor, west side; the 88th floor; 89th floor; 73rd floor, west side; 105th floor, east side; 104th floor, east side; 47th floor; 73rd floor, west office; 83rd floor, room 8-3-0-0 and 80th floor, northwest. That is what we have at this time."

"Field Com received."

One of the calls from that 83rd floor of Two World Trade Center was from Melissa "Missy" Doi, a thirty-two-year-old financial analyst. The only child of a single mother, Doi had dreamed of being a ballerina. She graduated from the prestigious all-girl Spence School in Manhattan, which boasted alumnae including Gwyneth Paltrow, Kerry Washington and daughters of the Carnegie, Post and Astor families. Later, after graduating from Northwestern, she returned to her native New York City seeking fortune more than fame. Doi brightened and lightened every meeting at IQ Financial Systems—a firm creating software for Wall Street. Her complexion was light brown. Her hair was absolute black, pulled back in a tight, professional style. But the feature no one could fail to notice was her illuminating smile that tickled her eyes to laughter. At the moment the 9-1-1 operator answered her call, Doi can be overheard nearing the end of the Hail Mary prayer: "Holy Mary mother of God, pray for us sinners, now and at the hour of our death."

"9-1-1 operator, good day."[74]

"I'm on the 83rd floor! I'm on the 83rd floor!" Doi shouted into the phone. The nose of United Flight 175 had hit two floors below her. Part of the right wing ripped into Doi's 83rd floor.[75] The twenty-four-minute conversation between Melissa Candida Doi and a 9-1-1 operator is among the few in which we have the caller's words. The recording was entered into evidence in the 2006 federal trial of Zacarias Moussaoui, a Frenchman, who ultimately pleaded guilty to conspiring with the 9/11 hijackers. Moussaoui will spend the rest of his days in the federal Supermax prison in Colorado.

"Ma'am, how you doin'?" The operator speaking to Missy Doi was a woman. Listening to the recording, I suspect she's middle-aged and experienced. Her voice is earnest and empathetic.

"Are you going to be able to get somebody up here?" Doi asked. I'm struck by the youth in Doi's pleading soprano.

"Of course, ma'am, we're coming up to you."

"Well there's no one here yet and the floor is completely engulfed. We're on the floor and we can't breathe. And it's very, very, very *hot*!"

The operator was right, there was a firefighter rising toward Doi. Chief Orio Palmer of Battalion 7 was well-known for his unusual first name which, of course, earned him the moniker "Cookie." Palmer shared something in common with Doi, the once aspiring ballerina. He loved to dance, albeit to rock. Palmer was so devoted to the classics (Led Zeppelin in his case), his three young children called him "the music man."

Chief Palmer had rushed into the lobby of 2 WTC precisely ten minutes after the plane hit. He took the working elevator as far as it would go. Palmer radioed, "This is Battalion 7, on floor 40 in tower 2. We've got one elevator working up to the 40th floor staffed by a member of Ladder 1-5, K."[76] Palmer headed up the stairwell with six men from Ladder Company 15 trailing behind. No one who heard Palmer's voice on the radio was surprised he was leading the charge. How could it have been otherwise? At age forty-five, Palmer was known as the fittest man in the department. He was an accomplished marathon runner who had won the FDNY's annual fitness medal repeatedly. Palmer's gallantry and leadership that morning remained unknown until nearly a year after 9/11. The only audio recording of his radio transmissions was lost in the labyrinthine bureaucracy of the Port Authority of New York and New Jersey. When the CD was discovered in 2002, the audio revealed that Palmer and others had climbed far higher than anyone had known.

Palmer was rising toward Missy Doi at a rate of one floor a minute. At 9:42 a.m., a fellow FDNY officer, Battalion 9 Chief Edward Geraghty, radioed Palmer. "Orio, I couldn't find a [elevator] bank to bring me up any higher. I'm on the 40th. What can I do for you?"

"You're going to have to hoof it up," Palmer replied.[77] "I'm on 69 now."

Palmer was the advance scout, telling firemen on the floors below how to navigate the best route and sending survivors to the 40th floor where they could find the working elevator. At 9:47 a.m., Palmer radioed to Ladder 15, "I'm standing in 'Boy' stairway on the 74th floor, no smoke or fire problem. The walls are breached so be careful."

"10-4, I saw that on 68," Ladder 15 replied. "We're on 71. We're coming up behind ya."

Palmer was now nine floors below Missy Doi and rising fast.

"Are the lights still on?" the 9-1-1 operator asked Doi.

"The lights are on, but it's very *hot! Very hot!* We are all the way on the other side of Liberty [Street] and it's very, very hot!" The fire below Doi was raging at a little over one thousand degrees Fahrenheit. On the east and south sides of 2 WTC the floor trusses were failing. The steel, robbed of its fireproof insulation by the impact of United Flight 175, began to sag. On one end, the weakening trusses were pulling the load-bearing columns of the facade inward; on the other end, they were straining their connections to the central core.[78] With the weight of one third of the tower above them, the trusses would last fifty-six minutes.

"I don't see any *air* anymore. All I see is smoke," Doi reported to 9-1-1.

"Okay, dear. I'm so sorry. Hold on. Stay calm with me, stay calm."

Doi begged, "Please!" The earnestness in her voice broke. It is unclear whether the gasps between her words were forced through smoke or tears.

"What floor you on, Orio?" radioed a fireman assigned to Ladder 15.

"Stairway on 75," Palmer replied. "Go to the south stairway and continue up." On his pathfinding ascent, Orio Palmer ran into another fireman. Ron Bucca, forty-six, was pretty fit himself. He was a twenty-nine-year military vet who still served in the Army Reserve as a Special Forces intelligence officer working in counterterrorism. In 1986, Bucca earned the nickname "the flying fireman" after he fell five stories from a tenement fire escape. It took him a year to recover, but he did—with an intense physical fitness regimen. Bucca had climbed all seventy-five flights. He hadn't known about the working elevator to the 40th floor. In truth, Bucca didn't have to be there at all. Years earlier, he had been promoted to Fire Marshal. His job was investigating fires, not fighting them. Still, he came, to challenge the largest inferno of his life. Bucca and Palmer directed injured survivors to follow the vertical trail they had cleared. From his radio transmissions, we know Palmer reached the 78th floor, the bottom of the gash blasted into the tower by the 767. "Ladder 1-5," Palmer called. "We've got two to three pockets of fire. We should be able to knock it down with two lines [fire hoses]." After thirty-seven flights of stairs, Palmer was finally out of breath. The horror of the 78th floor added an edge to his voice. Palmer keyed his mic to request that his next message be passed on to the incident command post. "Radio…" *gasp*, "Radio that…" *gasp*, "78th floor, numerous 10-45 Code Ones." Fatalities, more than he could count, were strewn across the 78th floor. The four floors above 78 were heavily damaged. The nearest survivors to Palmer were likely five floors above him on 83—including Missy Doi and her five co-workers.

"I'm going to die, aren't I?" Doi said to the operator.

"No, no, no, no, no, no, say your—"

"I'm going to die."

"Ma'am, ma'am, ma'am, say your prayers," the operator counseled.

"I'm going to die," Doi repeated. In the recording, I do not hear panic. Her voice sounds as though she had come to a realization. "I'm going to die," was self-empathy reconciling with the inevitable. The two women on the telephone line—strangers who would never meet—formed an intimate bond. "We've gotta think positive," the operator urged. "Because we have to help each other get off this floor. Stay calm. Stay calm. Stay calm."

"Please God!" Doi called out.

"You're doing a good job ma'am—you're doing a good job..."

"It's so hot! I'm burning up!" Doi said. Then she asked whether her mother could be patched into the call. The operator explained she had no way of making a third-party connection.

Five floors below, Orio Palmer began directing the firefighting attack. He radioed the men of Ladder 15 who were still headed up. "I'm going to need your firefighters, 'Adam' stairway, to knock down two fires. Get a house line [connection to a building standpipe] stretched. We can get some water on it and knock it down, K." Palmer had discovered the only stairwell that was intact above the point of impact. If he could extinguish the fire in stairway A, more than six hundred people would have a way out.[79] Ladder 15 replied, "Alright, 10-4, we're coming up the stairs. We're on 77 now on the B stair. We'll be right to ya." Before this recording was discovered, investigators estimated that firefighters reached no higher than fifty stories.

"Battalion 9, I need ya on the floor above 79," Palmer advised his fellow chief. "We have access stairs going up to 79, K."

"Alright, I'm on my way up, Orio," Battalion 9 responded. At 9:57 a.m. it appears the one elevator stopped working. A member of Ladder 15 radioed, "Trapped in the elevator in the elevator shaft. You're gonna have to get a different elevator. We're chopping through the wall to get out." Other members of Ladder 15 were stuck in a stairwell. "Orio," one of them called on the radio, "we're on 78 but we're in the B stairway, trapped in here, we've got to put out some fire to get to ya."

"Wait! Wait! We hear voices!" Melissa Doi reported to her 9-1-1 operator. "Hello! Help!" she shouted into the burning room. Then she screamed, "HELLP! HELLP!" Doi asked the operator, "Can you find out if there's anybody on the 83rd floor? We think we heard somebody!" What Doi heard is unknown. But based on the records I have studied, it is plausible that Orio Palmer, Ron Bucca and perhaps some of the men of Ladder 15 continued climbing the intact Stairway A, fighting the fire as they rose.

Having received no answer, Doi returned to the call. "Can you…can you stay on the line with me, please? I feel like I'm dying."

"Are they inside with you yet, dear?" the operator asked.

"No," Doi said. "Can you find out where they are? Can…"

That was Missy Doi's last word. By my count, the operator called her name without response more than sixty times over the next thirteen minutes. "Melissa! Do not give up, please! Do not give up, Melissa! Oh, my God. Melissa! Melissa!"

A structural engineer working in the city's Office of Emergency Management foresaw what no one could imagine. The OEM happened to be headquartered in 7 World Trade Center, across the street from the towers. The engineer warned EMS Division Chief John Peruggia that both buildings could falter at any moment. Peruggia sent a runner to the incident command post about two blocks away. "You see Chief Ganci and

Chief Ganci *only*," Peruggia told Emergency Medical Technician Richard Zarrillo. "Tell him the building integrity is severely compromised and they believe the building is in imminent danger of collapse."[80]

"Who the fuck told you that?" Ganci fired back at the messenger. Ganci's expression was a mix of determination and fear.[81][82] "Listen, I was just at OEM," Zarrillo repeated. "The message I was given was that the buildings are going to collapse; we need to get our people out."[83] Zarrillo had hardly stopped speaking when a roar and seismic tremor overwhelmed the command post. "What the fuck is this!" Ganci yelled.[84][85]

At same instant, Battalion Chief Orio Palmer keyed the mic on his handheld radio, still directing the firefighting and rescue, "Battalion 7 to Ladder 15…" There was no time for a reply. At 9:58 a.m. the exterior columns along the east wall buckled. The failure raced around the corners to the north and south faces. Two WTC tilted to the southeast and foundered on the floors where Orio Palmer was climbing toward Missy Doi.[86] The south tower, which was built over the course of three and a half years, was gone in five seconds. The building had burned for seventy-three minutes.

"…to Manhattan, urgent!" An unidentified firefighter began shouting before he keyed his mic.

"Go ahead, K."

"One of the buildings, the entire building has collapsed, major collapse in one of the towers!"

"Which tower? K."

"Tower 2! Tower 2! The entire tower, major collapse!"

The dispatcher radioed Ganci's incident command post. "Manhattan to Field Com."

"Manhattan to Field Com."

"Manhattan to Field Com, K."

"Manhattan to Field Com."

"Manhattan to Field Com, K."

An unidentified screaming voice broke in on the frequency, "Have them mobilize the *army*! We need the *army* in Manhattan!" The dispatcher replied, composed, steady, "All units stand by. Everybody try to calm down. Manhattan to Field Com, K."

"Manhattan to Division."

"Manhattan to Car 9 [borough commander of Queens], urgent."

"Manhattan to *any unit* operating at the fifth alarm, West Street and Liberty, for tower 2. Any unit, K."

Silence spoke of inconceivable loss.

About sixty officers and firefighters were standing at the incident command post as the tower fell before them.[87] Chief Ganci, Chief Turi and the rest dove into the adjacent parking garage that Turi had imagined as an emergency shelter. They managed only fifteen to twenty steps before they were overwhelmed by a cascade of choking dust that blotted out the sun.[88] The dust was so dense the men felt they were drowning with their last breath stuck in their throats. Some who had Air-Paks shared their masks with those who did not. Darkness was total. When the roar subsided, survivors slowly rose from the ramp. They were coated in gray like victims felled by the ash of a volcanic eruption. Some reached for flashlights which feebly failed to penetrate the fog. Chief Turi could not see the hand in front of his face. He moved by memory up the ramp toward West Street. After a few yards he walked headlong into a tree. The startling collision was a relief. In the blackness, the feel of bark told Turi he'd made it outside. "My God," Turi thought to himself. "We just lost two hundred-fifty men." Chief Ganci stumbled out of the garage disoriented, choked and nearly blinded by ash.[89] The staff chiefs gathered, looking like they had been shaken in a bag of flour. "Pete, get everyone, everybody out of the north tower," Chief Turi urged Ganci. "If it happened there [2 WTC], it's going to happen here [1 WTC]. We've got to get everybody out." With his hand radio, Ganci immediately and repeatedly ordered the evacuation of all FDNY from 1 WTC. I have not found any evidence that Ganci's order was heard by Manhattan Dispatch nor anyone else.

Among those missing after the first collapse were "Express" Smith, "Dizzy Dean" Regan and all the men of Ladder 118. Regan had been leading his men up the floors of the Marriott in search of civilians who were trapped or disabled. They reported by radio they were on the 15th floor and working their way up.[90] Moments later 2 WTC crushed the hotel. Manhattan Dispatch could offer only information and for a time, the dispatcher broadcast into silence. "Be advised in the area at the Marriott Hotel, receiving reports of firefighters trapped and down." There was no response on the radio.

Firefighter Mike Brennan burst onto the frequency, "4 Truck OV. Mayday! Mayday! I've fallen several floors." Firefighters identify themselves by their rig and their job. "OV" stands for Outside Vent, the ladder company fireman who uses tools to break open ventilation from the outside of a burning building. "4 Truck OV. Mayday! Mayday! I'm running out of air!" Pete Ganci overheard Brennan's distress call on his hand radio. Just then, another truck company called to Brennan, "Hey, brother. We gotcha. We gotcha. Turn on your PASS [alarm]. We got a roof rope. We'll come and get you."[91][92] Many other mayday calls were going unanswered. Ganci could hear them—dozens of his men pleading for help.

Turi, chief of safety, wanted everyone three blocks north. He grabbed a bullhorn and herded survivors up West Street. Ganci gave orders to set up a new command post in the direction Turi felt was secure. Then the chief of department gave his officers and friends their orders. Chief of Operations Nigro was to head north and inspect the far side of the still standing 1 WTC. Executive Officer Mosiello was ordered to head north and organize search and rescue teams. North was the direction of safety. The more dangerous assignment was to head

south to track down the mayday calls in the twisted steel. Pete
Ganci gave that assignment to himself. With First Deputy Fire
Commissioner William Feehan at his side, Ganci turned and
headed toward the collapse.[93] "Chief, where are you going?"
Steve Mosiello asked Ganci.

"Steve, I'm going to take a walk down here. Get me two
trucks."[94] "Two trucks" was a request for two ladder companies—
twelve firefighters. A few minutes later, having assessed the catastrophe, Ganci called Mosiello on the radio. "Steve, I want
two of my *best* trucks. Rescue squads, two of my best trucks."
The rescue firefighters were assembled. Ganci radioed, "Steve,
I want you to bring those two trucks to me. Stay on the west
side of West Street. I'm south of our last command post."

"Okay," Mosiello replied. "I have the trucks coming. I'll be
there in a couple of minutes."[95]

As I ran toward the World Trade Center, the West Side Highway became West Street. Dazed firefighters, covered in gray and
streaked in blood, were laboring north. Fresh companies hurried
south in clean black bunker gear. Because of other skyscrapers,
I had lost sight of the towers until I was nearly on them. I was
awed by the sight of smoke raging from 1 WTC. Endless black
clouds were borne on an easterly wind and rose over the harbor to Brooklyn and beyond. Still, my immediate emotion was
something like joy. I assumed the north tower was blocking my
view of its twin. Amid the smoke and chaos, I did not recognize
that 2 WTC was gone. I imagined the forty thousand people I
expected in both towers had a chance.

Inside 1 WTC, firefighters were also unaware of the collapse.
A chief crackled onto Tactical Frequency 1. "Command to all
units in One World Trade Center, evacuate the building!" Few
heard the order. The signal wasn't getting through. A chief on
the 35th floor grabbed a bullhorn: "All FDNY, get the fuck
out!"[96] Many followed the order, but others refused to aban-

don the wounded and the disabled. One company of firefighters who were obeying the evacuation order discovered forty to sixty disabled civilians lying on the 12th floor. The civilians had been told to wait there because their immobility was blocking the evacuation routes. The firefighters stopped their descent and began lifting each individual down the stairwell.[97] Other firefighters refused to leave while there were still brothers on the floors above. Captain Patrick "Paddy" Brown, forty-eight, of Ladder Company 3, was leading his men up from the 35th floor. Brown was a Marine Corps veteran who came to the FDNY after two tours in Vietnam.[98] Brown radioed, "This is 3 Truck and we're still heading up..." His voice, which had inspired a generation of young firefighters, would never be heard again.

I could see West Street was filled with debris. A fire truck I noticed appeared to be cut in half by a collapsed pedestrian bridge. My eyes rose the height of 1 WTC, past the burning floors, to the mast and TV antenna projecting from the roof. Odd, I thought. The mast seemed to be swaying slightly like a metronome—left, right, left—nearly imperceptible. I made sense of it as an illusion conjured by the heat tormenting the air. I was wrong. The upper third of the tower was tilting to the south. The steel was weakening under the relentless heat.[99] One World Trade Center was losing its will to survive.

You've heard people describe terror as unfolding somehow in slow motion. I can tell you it is true. As I squinted at the wavering mast, the collapse of the north tower began. The failure started at the hideous wound gouged by the initial impact. It appeared to me that the top third of the building fell one story then paused. It seemed to drop another floor and pause. Then, another. But the stop-action pace was entirely in my mind. The floors were pancaking with heartbreaking acceleration. In a person's limitless ability to fool himself, I thought it would stop. Just a few more floors. Surely it would stop. But the reality that viewers of television saw was the sixth tallest building in the world thundering to earth as its twin sister had twenty-nine minutes before. Someone behind me and on my right screamed, "God! *Nooooooo!*" with such force, he seemed to be trying, with breath alone, to reverse the weight of gravity and the course of history. Entirely on instinct, before I realized what I was doing, I felt my knees hit the pavement. My vision blurred with tears as I reached out to God in prayer for the people in the tower. "Take them, Lord," I said. "Take them all with *no pain!*" I believed I had just witnessed the deaths of as many as forty thousand people—their souls rising in ash that exploded into the sky. Standing before the collapse was the most wrenching experience of my life. As I write, eighteen years later, tears still come. If you were there, you know the feeling; the horror—the enduring disbelief, even now, that such a catastrophe was possible. I still feel something like a fist squeezing the blood from my heart and the air from my lungs. For me, a new emotion was composed in the moment—a combined sense of fragility and overwhelming loss—hollowness. Nothing I've seen since— combat in Afghanistan and Iraq; the 2011 tsunami in Japan; war in Somalia, South Sudan and Congo—has recalled the feeling of tipping backward into an abyss. For anyone on that corner, at that moment, it seemed the end of time.

Near the center of the human brain, there is a pair of primitive, almond-shaped, structures called the amygdalae. They process fear and are designed to save your life. The amygdalae are faster than conscious thought. They're the reason you leap back to the curb *before* you think "That bus almost killed me!" And so, I have no memory of rising from my knees, just an awareness, milliseconds later, that I was in motion, sprinting from a hurricane of ash, ten stories high, roaring through the canyons of lower Manhattan and enveloping the world.

"Three-three to Manhattan, urgent!"

"Three-three."

"The other tower just collapsed! Major collapse! Major collapse!"

A second voice broke in on the dispatch frequency.

"Urgent! Urgent!"

"Unit calling Urgent, K."

"We had a collapse of the second tower. Everybody's running from there. This is…" The transmission ends.

FDNY paramedic Karen Lamanna survived the first collapse, sheltering inside her ambulance. Now, she was trapped on the street watching the second tower cascade toward her. "I couldn't see, I couldn't hear, I couldn't breathe," she remembered. "I'm going to die here alone," Lamanna said to herself. "It felt like forever and every once in a while, I would squeak out, *help!* just so I could hear a human voice."[100]

The shudder of the earth blurred my vision. I could hear steel colliding with the street. The air thickened to paste. Somewhere behind me, Chief Albert Turi was among those running north. Unable to breathe, he dropped to the ground near a young firefighter and covered their heads with his bunker coat. "We're going to die here!" the fireman said. "We're going to die, I can't breathe."

Turi replied, "I just went through this twenty minutes ago. We're not dead yet."[101]

The hurricane struck with such fury it blew away any thought of survival. Then…there was silence. No sirens. No screaming. Stillness descended like the calm after a heavy snow. Gray ash swirled in the streets and climbed into drifts. I walked among survivors in shock. They stumbled aimlessly, blinded by dust, camouflaged in ash. Color was gone; skin color, hair color, clothing—all were gray. The living looked like ghosts and the dead had disappeared. I turned and headed back toward what would come to be known as Ground Zero. In the middle of Greenwich Street, I found a jet engine. It was small, not like the big turbines that lifted the wings of the airliners. I recognized it as an auxiliary power unit that had been housed in the tail of one of the planes. My eye was drawn to a flash of yellow—a crushed taxi—not much more than a foot tall. Around me, engines, trucks and ambulances were flattened or incinerated. The department would later count ninety-one vehicles destroyed. A black, two-door Mercedes sedan had landed, upside down, on top of one engine.

A hysterical voice, gasping for air, broke onto the frequency. "Can anybody hear me?"

Manhattan Dispatch replied, "Go ahead."

"I'm a civilian. I'm trapped inside one of your fire trucks. I can't breathe much longer. Save me!"

"Unit transmitting a mayday. Where are you? K."

"It's north of the World Trade Center. I was on the street. Please, help me!"

The voice seemed to be a man's although some firefighters thought they heard a woman. That was the last transmission.

I came to Ground Zero at Vesey Street. Wreckage burned across sixteen acres. White smoke swelled from a mountain of broken steel beams and twisted rebar, but I was more surprised by what I *did not* see. There were no bodies on my approach. No sign of humanity. No sign of our modern world. Imagine what filled the towers, the desks, phones, computers, filing cabinets, carpets and drapes. *None* of that was apparent. There was only powder, swirling, sticking to windows, lampposts, people and the sky. Out of this cloud fell one thing that had survived—paper—millions of pages, wheeling down one thousand feet. The flurries lasted for hours; stock receipts, pages from desk calendars, greeting cards, memos written with great urgency before 8:48:40 a.m. I noticed a loose picture lying in the ash. It was a family on vacation. Dad. Children. Someplace warm. Someplace safe.

The FDNY dispatcher tried to reach Chief Ganci or any of

his top officers. "Manhattan announcing. Any division or any staff chief at the scene of the World Trade Center? K."

Silence.

"Any division chief or any staff chief at the scene of any of the World Trade Centers? K."

Silence.

"Manhattan to Mobile Command Center, K."

Silence.

Then, a voice from Ground Zero replied, "Mobile Command Center to Manhattan, K."

"Mobile Command Center, what chief do you have at your Mobile Command Center? K."

"Negative on any chief, K. Right now, we're all alone. The second building came down. I can't see. So, we have no contact with anybody at this time, K."

I flipped open my phone, but the cell system had crashed with the buildings. I found myself living what had been a recurring nightmare that had awakened me for years. In my dream, I witness an enormous event but I have no way to report the story. Every phone I try is dead. Looking up from my useless Motorola, I noticed an ash-shrouded pay phone. "No way," I muttered. With the advent of cell phones, I had stopped carrying change. So, even if the pay phone did work, I'd be separated from the newsroom by the width of a quarter. I swept the dense ash off the chrome and picked up the receiver. Dial tone. I learned later the phone company had a standing emergency plan to switch pay phones to coin-free mode in case of emergency. I started punching buttons.

The phone rang at my home outside Washington, DC. My wife, Jane, lifted the receiver. The caller was one of my producers, who came to the point. "Have you heard from Scott? Do you know where he is?"

The producer who was near the collapse was searching for

me and sensibly assumed I would have called my wife. The fact that I *had not* is something of which I'm occasionally reminded.

"No, I haven't heard," Jane replied.

With no thought of reassurance, the producer continued, "The buildings collapsed. The cops told everyone to run for the [Hudson] river; we can't find him."

Jane is a former award-winning reporter. She was once one of my competitors and a formidable one. Later, she built a successful advertising agency, starting with nothing but a desk and a phone. Jane is not easily shaken nor given to worst-case thinking.

"Let me know what you hear," she said. The receiver found its way back into its cradle.

I punched the last digits on the pay phone to ring the CBS News National Desk. Bill Felling, the national editor, picked up. "Bill, I'm at the World Trade Center, do you need me to file a report?" I imagined there might be several correspondents at the scene. Maybe some had "live trucks" and were already on the air. I could hear shouting in the newsroom and the steady roar of a powerful organization pulling together every resource it had in the world. In the tumult, Felling missed what I had said. "How far are you from the World Trade Center? We don't have contact with *anyone* downtown."

"Bill," I repeated, "I'm *at* the World Trade Center. I can reach out and touch it." He patched me through to the television and radio networks and I began to describe the collapse, the devastated cityscape and the firefighters scaling broken steel in the search for survivors. CBS News was on the air for ninety-three hours—no commercials, no breaks. Hundreds of men and women worked to exhaustion to separate fact from rumor and present solid information and analysis when America needed it most. It had been sixty-three years since CBS's Edward R. Murrow invented broadcast news, painting vivid images of history as the Nazis seized Austria. All that Murrow started, all that we had become, prepared us for this day. In the storied history of CBS News—this was our finest hour.

The American people needed pictures, interviews and first-hand reporting. Accurate information is the lifeblood of a democracy in crisis. I discovered the mistaken report that a plane hit Camp David had been passed from sources in Washington after this radio exchange between the FAA and the Air Force Northeast Air Defense Sector:

"United 93, have you got information on that yet?" NEADS asked.

The FAA controller responded, "Yeah, he's down."

"When did he land?"

"He did not land."

"Oh, he's *down*, down?" NEADS asked.

"Yes. Somewhere up northeast of Camp David."

United Flight 93 was the fourth plane in the attack. It had been delayed at the international airport in Newark, New Jersey.[102] For reasons we do not know, it flew much longer than the other hijacked airliners toward its intended destination, San Francisco, before the terrorists turned toward the East Coast.[103] The delays gave at least five of the passengers time to learn, by phone, about the attacks on the World Trade Center. Unlike the other three hijacked planes, the cockpit voice recorder on Flight 93 survived. The 757, with forty passengers and crew plus four hijackers, was twenty minutes away from its target, either the White House or the US Capitol.[104] Microphones in the cockpit picked up passengers ramming what sounds like a service cart into the cockpit door. A hijacker at the controls rocked the plane violently to throw the passengers off their feet. One passenger is heard saying "...in the cockpit. If we don't, we'll die."[105] Apparently, the passengers were close to breaking through. One hijacker said in Arabic, "Is that it? I mean, shall we put it down?" Another replied, "Yes, put it in and pull it down." There were shouts of "Allah is the greatest!" as the aircraft rolled onto its back. It was diving at 580 miles per hour when it disintegrated, nose first, in an empty field outside Shanksville, Pennsylvania.

In Manhattan, 10 million square feet of American ambition and audacity had towered over one of the world's greatest cities. Now, 1.8 million tons of ruins filled the basement floors of the World Trade Center and hulked above ground in a mountain of misery.

Chief Albert Turi organized two ladder companies to search for Chief Ganci and Deputy Commissioner Feehan who had gone in search of victims of the first collapse.[106] But another search party with a rescue dog named "Bear" was already walking over the jumble of steel. Bear pawed at an opening with his right foot. The firefighters saw nothing but Bear insisted. They dug through the metal until they found a bunker coat labeled "F.D.N.Y. Chief of Dept. Ganci."

It was apparent that Ganci died instantly. FDNY Lieutenant John Mendez witnessed the recovery of the chief's body as it was carried into a building across West Street. Mendez told investigators, "We ended up in the back of the atrium as they were pulling his body out. A fireman was carrying his remains down the stairs—his head—and the other firefighters were carrying the rest of his body in a [rescue] basket. Chief Turi was there. We started crying. They placed his body on the ground and we all kneeled around it and prayed."[107] Ganci was carried to an ambulance guarded by a chief and a captain. "I told you I wouldn't leave here without Pete," Chief Turi said, breaking the news to Ganci's chief of staff, Steven Mosiello. "He's in the ambulance—dead."[108] Mosiello was handed Ganci's gold helmet shield which read Chief of Department. It had been found near the body.[109] A few hours later the body of First Chief Deputy Feehan was pulled from the wreckage. He was laid in the ambulance next to Ganci.[110] Feehan—who was said to know the location of every fire hydrant in the city by heart—was two weeks shy of his seventy-second birthday.

When Ganci and Feehan set out from the parking garage, they knew total collapse of 1 WTC was likely imminent. Yet, they turned their backs on safety because no cry for help could go unanswered.

Turi and Mosiello took a police car to Massapequa on the south shore of Long Island to tell Ganci's wife, Kathleen, that the chief was gone.[111] Mosiello turned down an offer of a helicopter. He needed a long drive to think of what to say.[112]

By midday, I stood before tall remnants of Minoru Yamasaki's design. Part of the facade at the base of one of the towers was standing. Shards of aluminum rose about ten stories like spires from a netherworld. They were jagged at the top. Their neo-Gothic arches at the bottom were the only hint of what had stood here half an hour before. To my right I could see Seven World Trade Center was burning. It had been shot through with shrapnel. On the far side of the debris pile, to the south, another high-rise was ablaze. I shouted to a police captain leading officers into the devastation. "What about casualties? What have you seen?"

"Uncountable!" he yelled, as he rallied his men. "Let's go! Let's go!"

The air swelled with the wailing, undulating cry of high-pitched electronic alarms. They were all the same, rising up the scale of notes and down the other side—*Wheeeee-hooo, Wheeeee-hooo, Wheeeee-hooo*—overlapping, out of sync, like crickets on a summer night. They were the Personal Alert Safety System (PASS) alarms of more than three hundred firefighters. Cries for help from dead men would wail three hours, then fade one by one as the batteries were exhausted.

Surviving firefighters dug for their brothers with their hands. "Indescribable," one firefighter told me. "We're standing on the *roof*, digging down. There's stuff and people everywhere." Civilian volunteers poured onto the site. Men under hard hats, who had been on a construction job nearby, arrived in military formation. "What do you hope to do here?" I asked Fred Clark, a carpenter who helped build the towers in the '60s. "I'm here to find somebody still alive," he said without breaking stride. Another firefighter told me, "Everybody's working together, the whole city is trying to get people out."

I ran into the superb CBS News producer Janet Klein and CBS News cameraman Brian Nolan. Brian was carrying several industrial dust masks, the paper kind strung on an elastic band. A quick-thinking desk assistant in the newsroom sent the masks because the ash in the air was a hazard, a greater hazard than we knew at the time. I wasn't entirely happy to see Brian. He was battling lung cancer and there was no way the ash was going to help. I said, "You shouldn't be here, man, you don't have to do this. There's plenty to do uptown." With weary eyes and irony in his smile, he silently made it clear I could stop wasting words and time. "Let's start shooting," Brian said. It would be the biggest story of his career and the last full year of his life.

Fresh ambulances rushed in but I noticed they did not rush out. "You can read a couple of things into that," Dr. Lincoln Cleveland told me. He ran to the scene from New York University Hospital. "Either people are buried and they're going to start bringing out the wounded, or just everybody died," he said. Doctors from the FDNY Bureau of Health Services broke into a drugstore adjacent to the World Trade Center and set up an emergency surgical center. The number of survivors was so small, they never saw a patient. One firefighter used an ax to cut himself out of a collapsed stairwell. Two Port Authority cops used pistols to shoot out a window that held up their escape.[113] The survivor who was trapped the longest was Port Authority Police Sergeant John McLoughlin. He was discovered the next day.

I returned to Ground Zero every day for two weeks to watch

thousands of rescue workers from throughout the United States climb the mountain and burrow in. Motivated by hope of a miracle, they worked in shifts all day, all night, for weeks. But no one was found alive after the first thirty hours.

Late in the afternoon, a sudden roar behind me triggered an instinctive cringe. I hunched the muscles in my back and squeezed my eyes shut. Jet engines, too low, too close. "Shit! Another one," I shouted. My eyes followed the roar toward the Hudson River where two US Air Force F-15 Eagles streaked like arrowheads toward the sea. They wheeled left, past the Statue of Liberty, around the tip of Manhattan, then left again up the East River. I could make out air-to-air missiles slung under their wings. In a couple of minutes, they were back. I had seen this pattern a hundred times, in Iraq, during the war in 1990/91, but I never imagined I would see fighters flying combat air patrol over an American city.

In the early evening, two firefighters marched past me with an American flag draped from a pole. I had no idea where they found it. They climbed a dozen feet up the pile, planted the Stars and Stripes, stepped back, drew themselves to attention and snapped a salute. The surrendering sun cast an orange glare and firefighters wept into the twilight's last gleaming.

Across Vesey Street, opposite Ground Zero, 7 World Trade Center had been burning furiously for hours. This office building, clothed in red granite, was "only" forty-seven stories tall. It had been added to the complex in 1985. At the base of the building, I spotted a half-dozen firemen. They too had collapsed, exhausted, heartbroken, taking a minute before going back into hell. They didn't seem concerned that heavy panes of glass were popping out of window frames hundreds of feet above and disintegrating nearby in the street. I was interviewing them when a police officer ran up, waving his arms at the burning building. "This one's coming down. Get out of here, NOW!" I said what reporters always say in moments like this: "Okay, officer, we'll just be another minute." Instead of arguing, the cop sprinted away without another word—unusual in my experience. The firefighters, accustomed to following orders, rose as one body and scuffed their boots up the street. It was almost time to broadcast the *CBS Evening News*, so I followed them out in the direction of a "live truck" a couple of blocks away. When I arrived, a producer was shouting, "We need you on the air now! Seven World Trade collapsed and we're going live!"

"No, it didn't," I told him. "I just came from there."

"It collapsed!" he insisted. "We're going to you live."

"I'm *telling* you," I said, raising my voice. "I was there ninety seconds ago. It's standing!" The engineer operating the truck turned to me with no expression. "Look," he said. His fingertips twisted a large black rubber knob counterclockwise, rewinding a cassette in a videotape machine. He jabbed at the controls and the white "play" button illuminated. On the screen, 7 World Trade Center buckled. All forty-seven stories dropped like someone pulled the corner from a house of cards. *Okay, officer, we'll just be another minute*, I remembered saying. If I *had* been another minute, I wouldn't be here now. Engineers had been watching the four corners of the roof of 7 World Trade Center through spotting scopes. They'd seen it sagging on its way to imminent collapse. The officer hadn't been speculating that the tower *might* go. He was telling me it *was* going—right then. I went on the air.

By evening, the last plaintive PASS alarm fell silent. The remains of the department's eldest firefighter, sixty-six-year-old Joseph Angelini Sr., were found with the men of Rescue 1. His son, Joe Jr., was killed with the crew of Ladder 4. The youngest in the FDNY, twenty-two-year-old Michael Cammarata, who left the reassuring phone message for his dad, died with the men of Ladder 11. Battalion 1 Chief, Joseph Pfeifer, had been among the first on the scene after witnessing the beginning of the attack. Within minutes, he ran into Lieutenant Kevin Pfeifer, in the lobby of 1 WTC. He watched his younger brother head up the stairs. They would never meet again.[114] In 2018, Joseph Pfeifer became the last of the surviving 9/11 chiefs to retire. Steve Mosiello, who brought the heartbreaking news to Chief Ganci's wife, survived but did not escape. Ten years after 9/11 he lost his life to esophageal cancer believed to have been triggered by the toxic dust at Ground Zero.

That morning, I was privileged to witness the greatest act of gallantry ever granted to an American city. How small the firefighters looked to me as each stood for a moment taking the measure of the inferno. Then, having assessed the odds, the meaning of their lives was plain. Fear did not bind them. Love of family did not hold them fast to safety. Long ago they had decided what they would do on this day. Each placed his life in trade for the mere chance of saving another.

Four weeks after September 11, twelve-year-old Brendan Regan accepted the championship award for his Floral Park, New York, Little League team. His father, Lieutenant Bobby Regan of Ladder 118, had not been found. He would have admired his son's brave face beaming under a weary and frayed New York Yankees 1999 championship cap. A few days after the ceremony, I met Brendan and his sister, sixteen-year-old Caitlin, at their Long Island home. Buzz-cut, lanky and freckled, you've seen Brendan before. He's in every Little League scene Norman Rockwell ever painted. We talked about the hit that won the championship that summer. I wondered about his dad's reaction. "What did he say?" I asked. Sweet memory pulled a grin across Brendan's face. "Nice hit," he quoted. Caitlin wore a maturity beyond her years. I had the sense she had tried it on only recently. Her memories were of her dad's firefighter schedule, often twenty-four hours on and forty-eight off. "I was really happy that he was around," she told me. "I notice a lot of my friends' dads work into the night. I was always really thankful that my dad was around a lot and he spent a lot of time with us." I asked Brendan what he would say to his dad if he could. I immediately regretted the question. I'd gone too far. Darkness crossed his innocence. He struggled silently with all the things he could have said, would have said, still wanted to say. He settled on a message: "We have practice tonight."

A little more than two months later, New Year's Day 2002, Lieutenant Regan's body was discovered. He was wearing a medallion of Saint Florian, the patron saint of chimney sweeps and firefighters. Engraved on the back were the words "We love you, Caitlin, Brendan and Donna."[115] All six men of Ladder 118 were killed. But their Brooklyn firehouse roommates on Engine 205 survived.

The body of Frank Spinelli, the currency trader who left the calm, reassuring message for his wife, was found two weeks after 9/11. It was a few days before his forty-fifth birthday. His wife, Michelle Spinelli, and their eight-year-old daughter, Danielle, baked his birthday cake anyway. "I just knew," Danielle told me, "that if he were here, he would want a cake, so I just decided to make it with my mom." In their living room, I sat with Danielle, her fourteen-year-old brother, Chris, and big sister, eighteen-year-old Nicole. Frames on tabletops enclosed memories of ski trips, beach trips; a handsome family, rejoicing in its youth. Danielle was unassailably sweet, buoyant and precocious. I sensed an innocent wisdom so I asked: "People all over the world are trying to make sense of this. Kids and grown-ups alike don't really understand why this would happen. What do you think when you try to understand it?" I'd been right about the wisdom. "I think that these people just took my dad away from us for no good reason," Danielle said. "I don't know why. If they *met* him—" her eyes lit up at the thought "—I *know* they'd change their mind."

The number killed at the World Trade Center was 2,753.[116] That is 254 more than the number of Americans killed on

D-Day.[117] The catastrophe could have been far greater. September 11, 2001, was the first day of school for many children and a primary election day. Fewer than half of the usual occupants of the towers had arrived for work by the time the first plane hit at 8:46 a.m.

The remains of more than one thousand victims have yet to be identified. Among those still missing are Battalion 7 Chief Orio Palmer and Leon "Express" Smith. The Ladder 118 chauffeur with the reputation as the first to arrive, will be among the last to leave. The New York City Office of the Chief Medical Examiner has never stopped working to extract DNA from bone fragments that were discovered in the days, months and even years after 9/11. In 2017, the ME announced that new DNA technology allowed it to identify the 1,641st victim. It had been two years since the previous identification. In 2018, the ME reported that the remains of 59 percent of the victims had been identified.[118] Among them was Melissa Doi, who was identified three years after her call to 9-1-1.

In 2019, the remaining 7,930 fragmentary remains were stored seventy feet underground in a section of the National September 11 Museum. The 2,500 square foot repository is between the foundations of the towers. It is not open to the public but family members have access to an adjacent private room to explore their memories. This hallowed section of the museum has become a Tomb of the Unknowns.[119] On its exterior wall, the public sees an artist's impression of that day's sapphire sky. The words of the Roman poet, Virgil, are written across the blue field: "No day shall erase you from the memory of time."

In the span of an hour and a half, twenty-three New York City police officers were killed, alongside thirty-seven officers from the Port Authority of New York and New Jersey and three hundred forty-three members of the FDNY. Three hundred forty-three, the largest loss of life of any emergency service in history. I look at that number on this page and it's impossible for me to measure. They volunteered when they could have been home. They rushed to the cataclysm before the radio called. They climbed twenty-five, fifty, seventy-nine floors and with every step, they sacrificed themselves to clear a path for others. Their rescue work was a spectacular success. The authoritative study by the National Institute of Standards and Technology estimates there were 17,400 people in the two towers combined. Of the total, 87 percent evacuated. Of those who were below the points of impact, 99 percent survived.[120]

None of those who came to the rescue knew why the buildings had been attacked or by whom. But for them, it didn't matter what 9/11 was about, they knew what *they* were about. Each firefighter, paramedic and EMT had raised his or her right hand and sworn to faithfully execute their duties on behalf of the citizens of the City of New York. Even more, they had committed to acting with courage in defense of one another. In 1099 AD, the Knights of St. John became the first to forge this bond despite, or perhaps because of, the horror of fire. They dowsed burning men with their capes as Muslim occupiers of Jerusalem hurled naphtha from towering walls. Nine hundred years later, the bond held, as Islamist heretics rained fire on men and women still wearing the Maltese Cross.

CHAPTER TWO

Resolve

President Bush on 9/11

Tense, but always cool, in the familiar left seat in the cockpit of Air Force One, Colonel Mark Tillman pulled the jumbo jet into an ascent unlike anything the president or the White House staff had ever experienced. "Like a rocket," Communications Director Dan Bartlett told me. The morning of 9/11, the president's pilot was flying in a theater of combat. With his right hand, Tillman forced four throttles to full military thrust. The highly modified Boeing 747-200 leaped off the runway, blasting smoke and dust as it rose from Sarasota-Bradenton International Airport in Florida. President George W. Bush steadied himself against the extreme pitch and G-forces as the engines screamed for altitude. The assault on the World Trade Center had begun an hour before. The Pentagon was attacked as the presidential motorcade was en route to Air Force One. Before the missile-like ascent, Mr. Bush told his lead Secret Service agent, "Make sure my wife and girls are protected."

Only eight months before, Mr. Bush ascended to the presidency after a disputed election. He had been narrowly defeated in the popular vote but was handed a victory in the Electoral College by the Supreme Court of the United States. Florida gave the new president his unprecedented victory. But his return to the state in early September was as ordinary as they come. In a speech the night before 9/11, he urged Americans to unplug their idle phone chargers to save energy. Early the next morning he was reading *My Pet Goat* to students at Emma Booker Elementary School in Sarasota. In a nearby classroom, the White House staff was watching coverage of the fire in the World Trade Center. When the second plane hit, White House Chief of Staff Andrew Card stepped into the reading session and whispered in Mr. Bush's ear, "A second plane hit the second tower. America is under attack." No president since Madison had faced a successful foreign assault on the homeland. No president since Lincoln had seen an act of war spill so much blood on American soil.

President Bush would be criticized for spending most of 9/11 flying across the country from Florida to Louisiana, to a secret bunker in Nebraska and then to Washington. But I believe this was his single best day as president of the United States. His deeply rooted sense of resolve guided him through a series of decisions rarely faced by a commander in chief. Frequently he overruled the instincts and advice of those around him.

The public knew little of what happened to the president on 9/11 until the White House agreed to my proposal for an hour-long prime-time documentary for *60 Minutes II*. It would air on CBS the night of the 9/11 anniversary in 2002. The White House gave my team, led by producer Bill Owens, access to everyone who played a part in the first twenty-four hours after the attack. This was Air Force One's greatest role in American history since Lyndon Johnson was sworn into office with Jackie Kennedy by his side on November 22, 1963.

Colonel Tillman's plan was to get President Bush safely in the sky then streak to Andrews Air Force Base in Maryland. But as the ground fell rapidly away, Tillman was warned that Air Force One was the target of another airliner on a collision course. Air traffic control at Jacksonville Center sent a message that Tillman remembered to me this way: "Air Force One, you have traffic behind you and basically above you that is descending into you, we are not in contact with them. They have shut their transponder off." The transponder is a radio that tells air traffic control the identity, altitude, speed and direction of an aircraft. The terrorists made the hijacked planes difficult to track by turning the transponders off. This was their signature. The suspicious plane was still far enough away for Air Force One to evade. But Tillman told me, "It was serious before that, but now it's no longer a time to get the president home. We actually have to consider that everything we say, everything we do, could be intercepted [on the radio] and we have to make sure that no one knows what our position is." Tillman posted an armed guard at his cockpit door. The Secret Service swept the plane, rechecking the identity of everyone. The flight crew rehearsed the evacuation plan in case Tillman was forced into a crash landing. Using the classified codename for the aircraft, President Bush told his staff: "Angel is next."

"Women! Drop your heels and run! Women! Drop your heels and run!" Secret Service officers sprinted through the White House evacuating the 201-year-old mansion. One of the four hijacked airliners was aimed at Washington and appeared to be ten minutes out. Vice President Dick Cheney was in his West Wing office watching the burning towers on television when a Secret Service agent bolted through the door. "He said, 'Sir, we have to leave immediately,'" Cheney told me. "He put a hand on the back of my belt, another hand on my shoulder and propelled me out the door of my office."

"He picked you up?" I asked.

"I'm not sure," the vice president said in genuine wonder. "They must train for it. I'm not sure how they do it, but they sort of levitate you down the hallway. You move very fast. You don't have any choice but to go."

"There wasn't a lot of time for chit-chat with the vice president," Brian Stafford told me. The director of the US Secret Service spoke in a baritone drawl you'd expect from a lawman in a Western. As the attack unfolded, Stafford was in his command center near Capitol Hill executing, for the first time, the emergency continuity of government plan under the authority of The Presidential Succession Act of 1947. His officers were rounding up fifteen key officials including the Speaker of the House, Dennis Hastert of Illinois; the President Pro Tempore of the Senate, Robert Byrd of West Virginia; and nearly every member of the cabinet, in case one of them had to become president of the United States.

"You felt like you had minutes to work with?" I asked Stafford.

"Correct," he said. "We knew that there were unidentified planes tracking in our direction." The Secret Service agent who "levitated" the vice president took Cheney down a tunnel that burrows below the White House and leads to a bunker called the PEOC, the Presidential Emergency Operations Center. The PEOC offers a higher level of security than the more familiar White House Situation Room. The bunker was dug during the FDR administration. Its specifications are classified but it is said the PEOC can withstand a nuclear blast.

National Security Advisor Condoleezza Rice was being urged to get down to the PEOC, but she wouldn't get off the phone. She told me, "They were hurrying me off the phone with the president. He said, 'I'm coming back,' and we said, 'Mr. President, that may not be wise.' I remember stopping briefly to call my family, my aunt and uncle in Alabama and say, 'I'm fine. You have to tell everybody that I'm fine,' but then, settling into trying to deal with the enormity of that moment. In the first few hours, I think the thing that was on everybody's mind was, how many more planes are coming?"

Transportation Secretary Norman Mineta rushed through the PEOC door and settled at the conference table beside Cheney and the vice president's wife. Mineta told me he remembers someone counting down the progress of suspect airliners headed to the capital. "Mr. Vice President, there's a plane fifty miles out," Mineta recalled hearing. "Then," Mineta told me, "the man came in and said, 'It's now ten miles out. We don't know where it is exactly, but it's coming in low and fast.'" This was probably American Flight 77. Inside the PEOC, they could only guess at its target. At 9:32 a.m. air traffic controllers at Dulles International Airport in Virginia spotted an aircraft flying too fast, too low, with its transponder off. Dulles alerted the Air Force Northeast Air Defense Sector (NEADS) to an "aircraft six miles southeast of the White House." Two fighter jets from Langley Air Force Base in Virginia were already in the air. But they had taken off with no specific orders, so the fighters followed standard procedure and flew east over the Atlantic. They were more than 150 miles at sea when the order came to turn them toward Washington. The NEADS commander took over the communications network. "Okay, we're going to crank it up...run them [the fighters] to the White House. I don't care how many windows you break...damn it!" he said, authorizing the fighters to push to supersonic speed which would leave a chain of sonic booms in their wake.[1] Before the fighters arrived, at 9:37 a.m., American Flight 77 exploded into the Pentagon at more than five hundred miles an hour. It was the first successful attack on Washington since 1814 when the British burned the Capitol and White House.

Over the Gulf of Mexico, Colonel Tillman ordered fighter support. Two F-16s from the Texas Air National Guard, President Bush's old outfit, scrambled into the air. Their mission was so secret, the pilots were told *where* they were going but not *why*. The Texas Air National Guard commander told pilot Shane Brotherton, "You'll know it when you see it." Brotherton told me, "I didn't have any idea what we were doing."

"You knew it when you saw it?" I asked.

"Yes, sir," Brotherton replied.

Brotherton's agile F-16 Fighting Falcon was not much more than a seat bolted onto a galloping engine. I once flew in a two-seat version. The cockpit is so tight you have the sense of wearing the fighter. I found the slightest hint of a twitch on the control stick got an instant, muscular response. Brotherton and a second F-16 piloted by his wingman, Randy Roberts, soared over the Gulf. Looming into their acrylic canopies was the sleek symmetry known in the Air Force as a VC-25. There are only two in the world—identical except their tail numbers—28000 and 29000. Their call sign is SAM, for Special Air Mission, unless the president is onboard. Then the VC-25 is addressed as Air Force One. The Gulf Coast sun glinted off the 747's chrome belly. Above its wings ran a thin gold line and dark blue stripe that underscored UNITED STATES OF AMERICA. The typeface, called Caslon, was chosen because of its resemblance to the font in the title of *The Declaration of Independence*. The Seal of the President circled the space below the forward boarding door. The vertical stabilizer lofted the Stars and Stripes. The aircraft livery has remained the same since 1962, when President Kennedy commissioned the work from industrial designer Raymond Loewy—the man who sculpted the modern Coke bottle.[2] The plush leather and thickly carpeted interior of the 747 was fitted in beige, brown and tan—the palette of Nancy Reagan.[3] But the planes never served the Reagan White House. In 1989, I broke the story on the *CBS Evening News* that the new Air Force One was, in effect, too heavy to fly. The aircraft wiring had been shielded to protect against the electromagnetic pulse of a nuclear blast. But the miles of cables weighed too much. A solution delayed delivery until 1990—in the term of President George H. W. Bush.

My first flight on Air Force One was aboard the old Boeing 707 during the first half of George H. W. Bush's term. The late president held court with staff and reporters in the middle of the cabin. I admired the man enormously for his heroism in war, his life of service to the country and his unfailing good humor. In my view, he was a model president of the United States. As I left the plane, I swiped a powder blue book of matches emblazoned with the Seal of the President. I still have the matches in the top drawer of my desk. I suspect smoking onboard Air Force One retired with the 707s.

Boeing built the latter Bush's 747-200 jumbo jet to serve as a nuclear war "lifeboat" for the president. The plane was subtly studded with electronic countermeasures in case of attack. A missile approach warning sensor stood guard on the tail. Behind and above each engine, glass-covered pods projected infrared signatures to confuse heat-seeking missiles. Just in front of Colonel Tillman's windscreen, a hump above the nose of the 747 was a connection for midair refueling. The four GE turbofan engines were fitted with extra-large oil tanks to keep them running indefinitely. Air Force One could remain aloft for days. Its principal limitation was food.

Tillman's headset sparked to life. "Air Force One, got two F-16s at about your, say, your ten o'clock position," radioed an air controller. Riding shotgun to Tillman's left, the F-16s looked like small asphalt-gray darts. Each was armed with long-range radar and air-to-air missiles. F-16 pilot Randy Roberts told me, "We were trying to keep an eighty-mile bubble around Air Force One and we'd investigate anything that was within eighty miles."

The single aisle of Air Force One runs nearly the length of the plane along the left-side windows. This leaves maximum space to the right for the president's office, conference rooms and seating. When the F-16s arrived, Mr. Bush crouched in the aisle to peer out the left side. Above the pale blue cowlings of the 747's engines, he could see one of the fighters locked in formation. In an interview in his flying office a year later, I asked the president, "Were you worried about the safety of the people on this aircraft? Your own safety?" Mr. Bush wore a powder blue shirt and solid scarlet tie under his dark blue waist-length cotton flying jacket. The Seal of the President was embroidered over his right breast. "Noooo," Mr. Bush said, drawing out the word to match the rhythm of his shaking head, "I wasn't worried about it. I looked out the airplane and saw an F-16 on each wing. It was going to have to be a pretty good pilot to get us."

In the White House bunker, the confusion was maddening. How many hijacked planes were in the air? The estimate was eleven. "I discussed it with the president," Vice President Cheney recalled. "Are we prepared to order our aircraft to shoot down these airliners that have been hijacked?"

"That was your advice to the president?" I asked.

"It was my advice. It was his decision."

Mr. Bush told me giving that order was such a difficult moment for him, he left his staff in his office and stepped into his stateroom to make the phone call in private. "That's a sobering moment, to order your own combat aircraft to shoot down your own civilian aircraft," he told me. "But it was an easy decision to make, given the fact that we had learned commercial aircraft were being used as a weapon. Now, I say 'easy' decision." Mr. Bush raised his voice slightly to underscore his self-correction.

"I didn't *hesitate*, let me put it to you that way. I knew what had to be done."

Twenty-six minutes after the Pentagon attack, a passenger revolt brought down United Flight 93 near Shanksville, Pennsylvania. The vice president and National Security Advisor Rice told me that those in the PEOC believed the airliner had been shot down by an American pilot executing the orders of the commander in chief.

In the president's flying office, horrifying pictures of New York City and the Pentagon flickered in and out on the four by three glass tube television mounted in a maple cabinet. The signal was breaking up. The bubble top on the 747 is packed tight with classified communications gear and three Air Force operators manning consoles. And yet, Mr. Bush's calls to the vice president were being dropped. "This is inexcusable!" the president shouted. *"Get me the vice president!"* Mr. Bush told me, "I was trying to clear the fog of war and there *is* a fog of war. Information was just flying from all directions."

"I remember hearing that the state department might have been hit," Chief of Staff Andy Card told me. "Or that the White House had a fire in it."

"You feared all of that was true?" I asked.

"At the time, I did," Card nodded, eyes widening, still in disbelief nearly a year later. In a photograph of the president's airborne office the morning of 9/11, Mr. Bush is behind his desk, facing aft, with his Air Force One jacket draped over the back of his beige leather chair. Card is standing before the president, palms flat on the desk, leaning into Mr. Bush's full attention. Floor-length drapes are pulled fully back admitting a stratospheric glare. Mr. Bush strokes his thoughts in black felt-tip Sharpie on a yellow legal pad. Along with Card, other senior staff members—Deputy Chief of Staff Karl Rove and Counselor to the President Dan Bartlett among them—crowd a couch across from the president, some spilling off its edge to take a knee on the beige carpet.

A few steps forward from the president's office, up a flight of stairs and past the communications operators, Colonel Tillman was in his cockpit trying to turn the most visible plane in the world into a stealth aircraft. The 747 is longer than the White House mansion.[4] There wasn't much Tillman could do about that. To conceal his intentions from eavesdroppers, Tillman abandoned Air Force One's sophisticated communications system and picked up his personal cell phone. He dialed the numbers of air traffic control centers along his route. "We actually didn't tell them our destination or what direction we were heading," Tillman told me. "We basically just talked to them and said, 'We have no clearance at this time; we are just going to fly across the United States.'" Air traffic controllers warned each other to keep the plane's route secret as they passed Air Force One from one sector to another. One receiving controller asked, "Okay, where's he going?"

"Just watch him," came the reply from another controller. "Don't question him, where he's going. Just work him and watch him. There's no flight plan in and, right now, we're not going to put anything in. Okay, sir?"

"Copy that."[5]

In his airborne office, Mr. Bush told me, "I can remember sitting right here thinking about the consequences of what had taken place and realizing it was a defining moment in the history of the United States. I didn't need any legal briefs; I didn't need any consultations. I knew we were at war."

We now know the reported threat to Air Force One was part of the "fog of war," another phantom threat in the aerial chaos. But it had a powerful effect at the time. Mr. Bush hadn't been seen by the public since he made brief remarks before leaving Florida when very little was known. Mr. Bush improvised then, calling the fires at the World Trade Center "a difficult moment for America." After this statement, the Pentagon was attacked. But the American people would not hear from the commander in chief again for more than three hours. "The American people want to know where their dang president is!" Mr. Bush grumbled to his staff.[6] A telephone address to the nation from Air Force One was debated. Mr. Bush hated the idea. Instead, he ordered Tillman to land somewhere, anywhere, within thirty minutes. At 11:45 a.m., Air Force One settled heavily onto a runway at Barksdale Air Force Base southeast of Shreveport, Louisiana. Mr. Bush hurried off his plane to a gaggle of news cameras summoned for his statement. "The resolve of our great nation is being tested," Mr. Bush said. "But make no mistake, we will show the world that we will pass this test. God bless." There was that word, *resolve*. On this morning of horror, with fractured communications and wild rumors, Mr. Bush fell back on an inner compass. He might not have known the plans of the enemy but he knew his own mind. His senior staff would be reminded of that fact at the next stop.

After the Barksdale statement, the president was on a heading almost due north to a secret national command center at Offutt Air Force Base, Nebraska. The underground bunker there had been built with all the communications gear necessary for the president to fight a nuclear war.

Mr. Bush had asked his press secretary, Ari Fleischer, to take careful notes of what he said through the day. No one else was keeping a record for history. Fleischer shared his notes with me. They capture Mr. Bush's language, plain and unguarded. To the vice president, Mr. Bush said, "We're at war, Dick. We're going to find out who did this and kick their ass." Later, Mr. Bush said, "We're not going to have any slap-on-the-wrist crap this time." In our interview, Mr. Bush told me, "I can remember telling the secretary of defense 'We're going to find out who did this and then, Mr. Secretary, you and Dick Myers—who we had just named as the chairman of the Joint Chiefs—are going to go get them.'"

Finding out "who did this" didn't take long. Amy Sweeney, a flight attendant on the first plane to crash, American Flight 11, used an onboard phone to report the seat numbers of the hijackers. FBI Director Robert Mueller told me, "That was the first piece of hard evidence. We could then go to the manifest, find out who was sitting in those seats and immediately conduct an investigation of those individuals, as opposed to taking all of the passengers on the plane and going through a process of elimination." Some of the seats Sweeney identified had been occupied by known al-Qaida operatives traveling under their real names.

By 3:00 p.m. Eastern time, Air Force One rolled to a stop at Nebraska's Offutt Air Force Base. Mr. Bush and his team were herded across the tarmac to a small unmarked cinderblock hut that resembled an outhouse. It was the entrance to a stairwell leading to the US Strategic Command's Underground Command Center, built to provide the president with a military headquarters for months if necessary. As the president crossed the bottom step, the battle staff snapped to attention. Mr. Bush was escorted to a small conference room with a video camera. His encrypted image appeared simultaneously at the White House Presidential Emergency Operations Center, the Pentagon, FBI headquarters and the CIA. The intelligence agency was just settling back into its Langley, Virginia, headquarters after an evacuation. National Security Advisor Condoleezza Rice told me the president started with a question to his director of Central Intelligence, George Tenet. "Who do you think did this to us?"

Rice remembers Tenet's reply this way: "Sir, I believe it's al-Qaida. We're doing the assessment, but it looks like, it feels like, it smells like, al-Qaida."

Tenet's appraisal did not come as a surprise to the president or his national security team. Two months before, Tenet was sweating a summer of intelligence reports warning of an al-Qaida attack on American interests somewhere in the world. Often the reports lacked specifics. Some came from dubious sources. But the sheer number—another nearly every day—led Tenet to say at the time, "The system is blinking red." More than a year before 9/11, near the end of the Clinton administration, Tenet's team put together a CIA paramilitary plan to attack al-Qaida with air and ground forces in Afghanistan. President Clinton, who had once tried to kill Osama bin Laden with cruise missiles, declined Tenet's more ambitious plan. With the beginning of the Bush administration, Tenet saw another chance. In July 2001, about two months before 9/11, he asked for a meeting to brief National Security Advisor Rice. In an interview, Tenet told me, "Essentially, the briefing says, there are gonna be multiple spectacular attacks against the United States. We believe these attacks are imminent. Mass casualties are a likelihood."

I asked Tenet, "You're telling Condoleezza Rice, in that meeting in the White House in July, that we should take offensive action in Afghanistan, now?"

"We need to consider immediate action inside Afghanistan now. We need to move to the offensive," Tenet told me.

Rice put Tenet's warning on her agenda. But I wondered why Tenet didn't press for faster action. I asked, "You're meeting with the president every morning? Why aren't you telling the president, 'Mr. President, this is terrifying. We have to do this now. Forget about the bureaucracy. I need this authority this afternoon.'"

"Right," Tenet replied. "Because the United States government doesn't work that way. The president is not the action officer. You bring the action to the national security advisor and people who set the table for the president to decide on policies they're going to implement."

"You thought you had some time?"

"Well, you didn't know but yeah, you thought you might

have time. You can second-guess me till the cows come home. That's the way I did my job."

On September 4, 2001, one week before 9/11, Rice chaired a "Principals Committee" meeting on al-Qaida. The "principals" were the top members of the president's national security team. One of them, National Counterterrorism Coordinator Richard Clarke, sent Rice a personal note before the meeting. Clarke, like Tenet, was a holdover from the Clinton administration. He was beyond frustrated that he could not convince President Clinton to destroy al-Qaida in Afghanistan. His note to Rice painted a dire picture. He warned: "Decision makers should imagine themselves on a future day when the Counterterrorism Security Group has not succeeded in stopping al Qida [sic] attacks, and hundreds of Americans lay dead in several countries, including the US. What would those decision makers wish that they had done earlier? That future day could happen at any time."[7] That future day would be the next Tuesday.

While reviewing the records of the White House and the FBI, I discovered an astounding coincidence. On September 4th, at the same time the principals were debating whether to attack al-Qaida, the hijackers were buying their plane tickets. An FBI timeline shows Ahmed al-Haznawi was paying $1,721.50 for a ticket on United Flight 93, which would crash in Pennsylvania. Also, on September 4th, five other hijackers were buying tickets to travel from their base in Fort Lauderdale to Boston to prepare for the hijacking of United Flight 175, bound for the World Trade Center. That same day, terrorist pilot Marwan al-Shehhi purchased his first-class ticket on Flight 175. Three others, who would crash American Flight 77 into the Pentagon, found time on September 4th to use a temporary pass to Gold's Gym in Laurel, Maryland. The FBI discovered the pass in the wallet of al-Qaida's Nawaf al-Hazmi. Al-Hazmi's wallet was found in the wreckage of the Pentagon.[8]

As the hijackers made their final preparations on September

4th, the national security principals approved a draft presidential directive authorizing the CIA paramilitary campaign in Afghanistan.[9] But first, lawyers would have to write the legal justifications and money would have to be appropriated. Rice told President Bush it would take probably three years for al-Qaida to be crushed in its homeland. On Monday, September 10, the day before 9/11, Deputy National Security Advisor Stephen Hadley assembled the deputies of the principals to put the final touches on a multiyear strategy to disrupt al-Qaida and overthrow the Taliban government of Afghanistan.[10]

The next evening, the president of the United States was in his Nebraska bunker questioning decision makers who, in the prophecy of Richard Clarke, were now imagining those things "they wished they had done earlier."

Plans were made for a presidential address to be broadcast from the Omaha command center. No one believed it was safe for the president to return to Washington. But the thought of that image on television, the president confined to a bunker, pushed President Bush to his limit. He had more than enough of broken communications and flights that took him farther from the capital. Against advice, he ordered Colonel Tillman to take him home. The American people, he insisted, needed to see their president in the White House, not a jailhouse. Press Secretary Ari Fleischer's notes record the president saying, "I don't want any tinhorn terrorist keeping me out of Washington."

"Bullshit," I said, prosecuting Fleischer. "He didn't say 'tinhorn' terrorist."

"That's verbatim." Fleischer shrugged.

Mr. Bush put it more starkly to me in our interview. "Anybody who would attack America the way they did, anybody who would take innocent life the way they did, anybody who is so devious, is evil."

I asked, "In those early hours on Air Force One, you were

looking out on a world that was suddenly pretty black-and-white to you?"

"That's right. I felt that way."

Air Force One departed Offutt and flew toward the darkening east. Before Mr. Bush arrived at Andrews Air Force Base, 7 World Trade Center collapsed—the last casualty of 9/11. Mr. Bush arrived at Andrews nine hours after the attacks. The shadows were long and the evening was warm, eighty-two degrees, thick with humidity. The president stepped, grimly, down the red-carpet stairs that had been wheeled to the plane. At the bottom step, he returned the salute of an air force officer who, instead of the customary dress uniform, was already clothed in battle fatigues.

Marine One, a deep green Sikorsky VH-3D Sea King helicopter, received Mr. Bush for the ten-minute flight to the South Lawn of the White House. In the sky, the president's aircraft was joined by two identical helicopters, which traded places in a shell game meant to disguise which one carried the president. Mr. Bush's helicopter flew north, along the Potomac River. A tower of smoke from the Pentagon rose into Mr. Bush's left-side window. The marine pilots slipped the helicopter just to the left of the Washington Monument—a close approach the president normally found exhilarating. Over the lawn, the helicopter settled with the sun. The pilot pressed the foot pedals to swing the Sea King's tail clockwise ninety degrees. The president's view panned past the Oval Office before settling on the mansion. In a show of precision, the pilot lowered the machine inch by inch until it pressed its wheels stiffly onto three small metal pads sunk into the tall fescue grass. Mr. Bush stepped off, reflexively returning the salute of the Marine who had lowered the helicopter's door. He walked alone in gathering darkness toward the Oval. His communications strategist, Karen Hughes, stepped out to meet him. The sight of Karen was a relief to the president. He valued her judgment above all his advisors. Hughes was affable but unshakable. She always seemed to know what to do—and what to say—in a crisis. Her considerable talents may have been rooted in her "military brat" upbringing. Her father was a general in the US Army Corps of Engineers and was the last American governor of the Panama Canal Zone. I had known Karen even longer than the Bush family had. She was a friend from the late 1970s when she; my wife, Jane; and I were reporters in the same Texas newsroom. Karen covered the presidential campaigns of George H. W. Bush, the president's father. Later, she turned in her press credentials to become chair of the Republican Party of Texas. Two years before the attacks, Karen came to dinner in our home and told Jane and me that Governor Bush would soon announce he was running for president. Throughout the campaign she was in charge of communications and messaging. Now, on 9/11, she was drafting the most important speech of Mr. Bush's life. His address from the Oval was scheduled for 8:30 p.m. The president consulted with Hughes about edits to the draft speech, then he changed clothes and returned to the Oval and settled behind what is known as the "Resolute Desk."

The public does not know what happened in the Oval Office in the moments before the address. But I have seen an unreleased videotape. About three minutes before air, the president is resting his forearms against the desk, appraising the speech. But his attention is being pulled away by an argument he's having with a male aide standing off camera. Mr. Bush is angry, absolutely determined not to budge on a decision he made at the last minute against the advice of his senior staff. On the tape, Mr. Bush's voice rises like that of a man who refuses to be cornered. "You're trying to get me to make a promise we might not be able to keep!" he shouted at the aide. The president's palm crashes down on the desktop with a sharp slap.

This was not the first time the old desk had suffered a blow from a president in crisis. It was a gift from Queen Victoria to Rutherford B. Hayes in 1880—hewn from the timbers of the British Arctic exploration ship, *HMS Resolute*. In 1854, the barque-rigged sailing ship was entrapped in ice and abandoned. An American whaler found *Resolute* and returned her to Britain. In gratitude, Victoria ordered a desk built from the ship's oak timbers. The original specifications, written in longhand on yellowed drafting paper, envisioned "a library table with two fronts, one for the president's use the other for his secretary."[11] Today we would call that a partners desk. But, in practice, there is no lonelier helm in the world. Not all presidents choose to work behind the antique, but FDR was at the Resolute Desk in his private study when he heard about Pearl Harbor and it supported the weight of the world when JFK confronted the Cuban Missile Crisis.[12]

Now the desk was at the center of history again, less than a minute from President Bush's 9/11 address. Mr. Bush listened impatiently as his senior advisor pressed the argument to include the only line in Karen Hughes's speech that the president had specifically taken out. Mr. Bush dug in his heels. He argued and shouted nearly up to the second that the TV crew's cue would lift the curtain on a nation in anguish. Mr. Bush had made his edits with his preferred Sharpie felt-tip pen. The document was labeled Presidential Statement—Draft 2. Next to the title, a rubber stamp certified "President has seen" in red ink. A handwritten notation near the top reads "9/11/01." The president's edits were minor until he reached the line: "We will not relent until they are brought to justice." Mr. Bush swiped a swift single black streak through the sentence, then he went back over it, making a point of nearly obliterating the words. It is the only line the public never heard.[13]

As the seconds ticked toward 8:30 p.m. Eastern time, the senior advisor tried to convince the commander in chief to put the line back in. The TV crew counted: ten seconds, nine, eight, seven... The anger in the president's face was reflected on the shining leather desktop. Mr. Bush ended the argument. "I won't do it!" Five seconds, four, three, two, one. Turning to the camera, Mr. Bush passed instantly from anger to carefully calculated serenity. He read the words in the teleprompter which glowed on a one-way mirror in front of the camera lens. A year earlier, as the Republican nominee, Mr. Bush had scorned foreign entanglements and warned against nation building. But in all the years I've covered the White House, this much I've learned: presidents come into office to change history, but it's history that always changes them.

"Good evening," the president began. "Today, our fellow citizens, our way of life, our very freedom came under attack in a series of deliberate and deadly terrorist attacks."

The days that followed 9/11 marked the zenith of the Bush presidency. His resolve rallied a nation in grief. Bravely and without compromise he guided American fury away from religious bigotry and hate. His refusal to "make a promise we can't keep" was a moment of prescience as Osama bin Laden would outlast his presidency. As the speech scrolled up the screen, matching his pace, the president looked past the words into a dark, unpredictable future. Mr. Bush was about to begin two wars: one in Afghanistan and the Global War on Terror. In short order, the stubborn resolve that had served him well, would betray him in the invasion of Iraq. The conclusion of his address rose on the glass of the prompter: "We go forward to defend freedom and all that is good and just in the world."

On the paper draft, in the course of the entire speech, Mr. Bush had underlined only two words: *good* and *just*.

FIELD NOTE

Meeting the Late Don Hewitt in Botswana

"Do you know Don Hewitt?"

The question came from a shadowed figure on the windward side of a campfire. In 2008, my wife, Jane; our son, Reece; daughter, Blair; and I were on safari in Botswana's Okavango Delta. The stars of the southern sky had sparkled into view hours before. The question about the late, legendary creator of *60 Minutes* was about the last thing I could have imagined because it came from our safari guide, a delightful young Motswana, who had never followed his compass beyond Africa.[1]

"You work for *60 Minutes*, no?" he continued.

"Yes, I do."

"Then you *must* know Mr. Hewitt."

"Well, yes. Of course, I do."

"Yeesss, Mr. Hewitt," our guide remembered with fondness. "He is the only guest who has ever apologized to me."

There is something about a story, roasting over a campfire, that is unforgettably delicious. I loved this one because it revealed the main ingredient of my quirky, driven, infuriating hero.

It seems Don and his wife, Marilyn Berger, were on safari with our guide years before. Bouncing through the Okavango in an open Land Rover, they chanced upon a leopard napping in a tree. Two things to know about leopards: they are rarely seen and they are extremely dangerous. Leopards are known to leap from their lofts and disembowel humans at a stroke. Our guide told us he hesitated to bring the Hewitts close to the cat, but decided it could be possible on one, vital, condition. *"You must be absolutely still, absolutely quiet, silence, silence,"* he warned the Hewitts. Our guide admitted he had butterflies in his stomach but decided to take his chances on an experience many guests never have. Marilyn drew the family video camera. The Rover crept to a stop beneath the canopy of the tree. The leopard did not move. Marilyn pushed Record. The guide held his breath. The leopard did not move. A nearly imperceptible whir escaped from the videotape drive. And the leopard did not move. The breeze was slight. Twisting leaves exposed and shadowed the cat's glorious spots. And the leopard did not move.

Then, Don called out to Marilyn, "No! No! No! Zoom in! You're too wide! Zoom in! Tighter! *Tighter!*" he demanded, in his full-throated Studio 33 control room roar. "You're not getting it! Too wide! Closer! Zoom *IN!*"

The leopard moved.

The guide jammed the four-speed into first gear and crushed the accelerator. It would be a minute or so before he dared to see whether the leopard had shrunk sufficiently in the rearview mirror. Later that night, around a similar campfire (and probably after a mauling from Marilyn), Don apologized.

This was, in fact, the Don Hewitt I knew—a maniac in pursuit of perfection. I came to *"60"* near the end of Don's career. When he screened my stories, he found faults I had never seen.

He found better ways to relate to the audience—better ways to zoom in on the meaning of a story. Turn on a camera, any camera, and Don became myopically focused on making us the best we could be.

Rare.

Rare as a leopard in a tree.

CHAPTER THREE

Selflessness
Paulette Schank

The US Army Black Hawk helicopter seemed to be descending much too fast. It looked like it would fly through the concrete landing pad that was its target. Just short of the pad, the nose pitched up, the engines screamed and the helicopter hammered the ground with rotor wash. The maneuver was akin to stopping your car with the emergency brake. The helicopter's side door, marked with a red cross inside a white square, slammed open. Inside, Kenny Lyon was dying.

Lyon touched down, in the fall of 2006, next to thirty-two sand-colored tents that housed the US Air Force Theater Hospital in Balad, Iraq. From the outside, there was nothing notable about the dust-stained collection of canvas. But inside, a money's-no-object advanced trauma hospital stirred to action.

Every machine and every drug doctors could dream of was there, including some lifesaving devices that were still experimental and not available back home. The emergency room double doors seemed to explode off their hinges when Lyon's stretcher rushed through. I could see he was unresponsive. His right arm slipped limply off the stretcher. His left foot was cadaver white with no sign of circulation. "128 over 35!" a nurse called out.[1] The lower blood pressure number was about half of what was needed to sustain life. "Hemoglobin, 6.4," called another. "Damn!" he shouted. The measure of the oxygen-carrying protein was also less than half of what it needed to be.[2] The trauma team swarming around the marine corporal from Maryland didn't need the numbers to know that Lyon had nearly bled to death. So many doctors and nurses were placing IVs and taking tests that each had to shoulder through the crowd to reach Lyon's body. His last moments were slipping away through three lacerated arteries and too many cuts to count. He had been shredded by an enemy mortar while he was turning a wrench on a broken-down armored vehicle.

"It's a battle. You know? Sometimes people are fighting to die," Paulette Schank told me. She was a nurse anesthetist from a hospital outside Philadelphia. But in Iraq, she was Lieutenant Colonel Schank, US Air Force Reserve, in charge of the operating rooms at the air force hospital on an Iraqi air base.

"Fighting to die?" I asked her.

"Meaning their body is going further and further down the wrong direction. And you have to be able to resuscitate them so that we can stop that negative spiral downward, so we go back to the spiral of life." Schank stood over Kenny Lyon in her pastel scrubs, an abstract watercolor ensemble in pinks, blues and greens. A blue hairnet capped her close-cropped hair which was brown tending toward red. Her face was free of makeup that might have covered the scattering of freckles that bridged her nose. In her late forties, Schank worked with a quiet, gentle

confidence that told everyone in the room she had done this—
ten thousand times. If Lyon spent another minute in the emergency room, he would reach the end of his spiral. I followed as
he was rushed to the next tent, an operating room, where five
surgeons went to work—two at Lyon's head, one at his torso
and two at his legs. IVs of blood and fluids would buy time, but
if they couldn't stop the bleeding soon, they would lose him.

The 332nd Expeditionary Group had four hundred staff car-
ing for more than three hundred trauma patients a month. To
shorten the flight time for medevac helicopters, the hospital
was close to the battle. Doctors wore firearms in the operating
room. The sound of incoming wounded beat the canvas like
an alarm. I asked Lieutenant Colonel Schank, "When you hear
the helicopters coming in, is there a sense of dread about what's
going to come through the door next?"

"No," she said, "it's the next *challenge* that's coming through
the door. It's a chance to ward off that ugly death man who
wants to take away your patient. It's your job to make sure he's
not successful today."

The helicopters belonged to the army's 57th Medical Evacuation Company based at Balad. The 57th had been legendary
since Vietnam.[3] "*No one* dies in the back of my helicopter," a
reassuringly cocky Staff Sergeant Danny Stevenson told me.
"I'll do CPR all the way until the end. If they die, they die in
the hospital."

"You keep them alive," I said.

"That's right. I breathe for them, I beat for them, I do everything I can for them."

Stevenson was handsome enough to play himself in the movie.
On his shoulder was a patch with an eagle's head above the word
Airborne. Below that, an American flag. On the inside of his
right arm, peeking above his fireproof Nomex glove, there was
a tattoo of a female nurse, the 1940s-pinup kind—impressively

endowed—in an army uniform a couple of sizes too tight. Stevenson created the impression that he took nothing too seriously. But that would be misjudging him. He had been a staff medic at the Pentagon on September 11, 2001. And so he was among the first to see action in the Global War on Terror. After 9/11, Stevenson asked for a combat assignment.

The 57th's Black Hawks were sometimes fired on despite the red crosses which marked them as noncombatants.[4] One pilot suffered a bullet wound through her foot. "It's a lot of pressure," Stevenson told me with a smile. "And I can handle that kind of pressure." I thought, "Hey, Danny, Tom Cruise wants his smirk back." But on the other hand, how much confidence is too much in a combat medic? I flew with Stevenson on a mission to rescue two soldiers wounded in a firefight. In flight, I asked, "You ever scared?"

"I don't get scared."

I knew better. "Come on now. Everybody gets scared."

"I mean, some stuff freaks me out sometimes, but if you freak out on the scene, you're just going to lose control of it. And if you lose control of it, you're going to die."

In World War II, the average time for a wounded soldier to reach a field hospital was between twelve and fifteen hours. In Vietnam it was less than two hours. In Iraq and Afghanistan, the time was cut to between thirty and ninety minutes.[5] This made all the difference to Kenny Lyon.

Just as Stevenson boasted, Lyon had come off the medevac helicopter alive. But in the operating theater, his bleeding would not stop. The transfusions were endless, ten pints, twenty pints. There was no repairing his left leg. Paulette Schank watched over the amputation. "It's ugly," she told me. "This is the ugly side of war. But if they can control the bleeding, he has a chance of survival." I watched his battle for more than two hours when a nurse informed the surgeons that the bank had no more blood to give. The whole supply of fresh blood had run through Lyon's heart and out onto the white linoleum floor. "I'll get you more!" Schank called to the surgeons. She bolted out of the operating room. *More?* I said to myself. *There isn't any more.* I ran after Schank through the plywood corridor that led to the next tent. When I entered the blood bank, she had already opened her arm. Lying on a gurney, under the glare of bare fluorescent tubes, her blood was draining into plastic bags. She gambled that these pints might stall the "death man" while loudspeakers announced the shortage to every available airman.

Walt Whitman captured the sense of this. The American poet was a nurse in the Civil War. In *The Wound Dresser*, he writes of a fallen soldier:

One turns to me his appealing eyes—poor boy! I never knew you,
Yet I think I could not refuse this moment to die for you, if that would save you.[6]

Paulette Schank told me, "Our job is to resuscitate, to allow the surgeons time to stop the bleeding. *And you try.*" Her voice cracked under the weight of memories. "You try *so hard* and sometimes you're not successful." She paused, looked away to a distant time, then closed her eyes. Her voice dropped to a whisper. "*And it hurts.* You feel like you let the soldier down, you know? The wicked death spiral won and you fought...*so hard. We fight so hard* against him winning, you know? And sometimes the death man wins."

Outside the blood bank, more than two dozen volunteers, many out of breath, formed a lengthening line. Blood bought time. After several hours of surgery, the leg amputation was complete, arteries were repaired, and Lyon stabilized. The next day, he was loaded onto a US Air Force C-17 flying intensive care unit and flown to the air force hospital in Landstuhl, Germany.

The C-17 Critical Care Transport routinely evacuates patients who are much too sick to have been moved from a field hospital before. Each of the spacious four-engine jets can carry thirty-six litters and provide all the life support of any ICU.[7] The night I flew to Landstuhl, the bright white interior of the C-17 was filled with walking wounded and the critically ill. I noticed a badly hurt CIA officer shielding his face against any chance that our camera would stray too close. I couldn't bear to add to his troubles. I kneeled next to him and promised I would personally make sure no image of him would ever appear. He relaxed and so could I.

At Landstuhl, Lyon underwent several more surgeries. Then, he flew to Walter Reed National Military Medical Center in Washington, DC. That's where I met the conscious Kenny Lyon for the first time. He was learning to walk with his artificial leg. He had nerve damage in both arms, part of his tongue was gone and a wire was holding his jaw together. "I'm just happy," he told me. "I love coming here every day and doing my therapy and pushing myself. And every day I get stronger and better and faster and I can use my hands more and I'm having fun."

"You're having fun?" I asked.

"Why not? What else am I going to do? I might as well make the best of my situation. I mean, I'm better. I'm alive. It's all easy from here. It's all gravy."

Had Kenny Lyon been wounded in Vietnam, his name might be on the memorial wall. Back then, 24 percent of wounded troops who made it to a hospital died in treatment. In Iraq, that death rate improved to 19 percent.[8] Technology has a lot to do with the advancement. But technology isn't much good without the courage of selfless men and women who put themselves at risk to save people they have never met. The doctors and nurses of the US Air Force Theater Hospital rarely know how their patients fare once the wounded start the journey home. Patients they remember most are those they could not save. Paulette

Schank told me how she keeps their memories alive. "I still talk to them, up there." Her eyes reached beyond the canvas ceiling. "And I say, 'I need your strength with me today sergeant so-and-so. I really need your strength with me.' And I'll say his name."

"You remember the names?" I asked.

"Yep."

As she spoke, the percussion of rotor blades pummeled the canvas.

"I hear a helicopter," I said.

"Yes," Schank replied, turning for the emergency room. "And I'll think of my sergeant."

CHAPTER FOUR

Authenticity
Bruce Springsteen

Bruce Springsteen was shocked by my question. The idea had clearly never crossed his mind.

"You have got to be," I said, "wild guess, worth somewhere north of one hundred million dollars. Why are you still touring? You don't have to do this."

"What else would I do!" Springsteen laughed. "You got any clues? Got any suggestions? I mean, am I going to garden? Why *would* you stop? I mean, you play the music and grown men cry and women dance. That's why you do it."

"It's good to be a rock star," I observed.

"I would say that *yes, it is!*" Springsteen answered, still laughing. "But the 'star' thing I can live without. The music, I *can't* live without. And that's how it lays out for me. I got as big an

ego [as anyone] and enjoy the attention. My son has a phrase—
he calls it 'Attention Whore.' But you have to be one of those or
else why would you be up in front of thousands of people shaking your butt? But at the same time, when it comes down to it,
it's the way it makes you *feel*. I do it because of the way it makes
me feel when I do it. It gives me meaning. It gives me purpose."

The "star thing" was by no means a sure thing. His first two
albums, *Greetings from Asbury Park, N.J.* and *The Wild, the Innocent & the E Street Shuffle* were both released in 1973 and failed
to climb the charts. Springsteen spent more than a year working on his third album, which was likely to be his last attempt.
Born to Run screamed off the starting line in August 1975. It
propelled the title track, plus "Thunder Road," "Tenth Avenue
Freeze-Out" and "Jungleland" into millions of yearning hearts.
His voice was not beautiful but it was real. His notes were not
elegant but they were true. Like Dylan and Guthrie, he wrote
not lyrics but stories. From sound alone, you could picture axle
grease under his nails as he fingered the frets of a Fender. Every
young American who had lusted, loved and lost heard their story
and cranked the volume.

Authenticity is born to run on a road of its own creation.
The music industry was tone-deaf to the revolution roaring up
behind it. In 1976, after the release of *Born to Run*, the 19th annual Grammy Awards ceremony was hosted by crooner Andy
Williams. The winner of Best New Artist of the Year was Star-
land Vocal Band. There was no mention of Bruce Springsteen.[1]

In 2007, thirty-one years and fifteen Grammys after *Born to
Run*,[2] I was meeting "The Boss" in a bar in Springsteen's hometown, Asbury Park, New Jersey. *60 Minutes* producer John Ham-
lin, the mastermind of many of our most prominent stories in
the world of music, convinced Springsteen to let us tag along
as he began a tour to introduce his new album, *Magic*. Springsteen was hoping to recapture the magic of the E Street Band.
In recent years, he had ventured down musical paths without the

band that backed *Born to Run* and *Born in the U.S.A.* (1984). The day we met, E Street was back together and planning to debut his new music in the historic Asbury Park Convention Hall.

Springsteen sat down in a black V-neck T-shirt, silver chain orbiting his neck, a sharply pointed soul patch under his lip and three small silver loops piercing his left lobe. The day before had been his fifty-eighth birthday. No man, outside the world of rock 'n' roll, could pull off this look. And no fan could imagine Springsteen any other way. He was frozen in the moment his audience longed for.

"You're the shaman, you know?" Springsteen told me. "You're the storyteller. You're the magician. The idea is, whatever the ticket price, we're supposed to be there to deliver something that can't be paid for. That's our job."

That night, I was attending my first Springsteen concert wondering how this *could be* my first Springsteen concert. The Asbury Park crowd was rowdy, eager for the hometown hero. Soon I began hearing "Boooooo! *Booooo!*"

Are they booing? I said to myself. How could that be? Angry because the curtain is late, maybe? I turned to a fan standing at the foot of the stage. "Are they *booing?*" I shouted. "Naw, man!" the veteran scowled. "They're yellin' Brrr-ooooooooce." This wasn't an audience. This was a tribe; a tribe with its own language, culture, mores and rituals. "Brrr-ooooooooce," the shaman, was their spiritual leader. When he sprinted onto that small stage, two-thousand people sounded like two hundred thousand. The eighty-two-year-old building shook in the way that makes you reflexively check the quality of the ceiling. When he sang, *they* sang. If there was someone in the auditorium who didn't know the words, I never saw them. Springsteen fell to his knees and slid to the edge of the stage where he offered his guitar, straddling his lap, to a rapturous woman who (strummed? stroked?) the strings as Springsteen threw his head back in ecstasy. He gripped a wireless mic above him and bellowed the way a wolf warns the moon. The concert spectacle lasted nearly two hours, not because the ticket price demanded it, but because—covered in sweat and drenched in joy—Bruce Springsteen could not stop himself.

"Pretty good for fifty-eight," I told him in his dressing room as he mopped his face with a towel.

"Oh! That's nothing," he said, just a little out of breath. "I'm still a chiseled hunk of muscle so, I guess I'll keep going for a while."

Springsteen's route to authenticity began over four decades earlier in Freehold, New Jersey. "I was probably one of the smartest kids in my class at the time. Except you would've never known it," he told me. "Where my intelligence lay was not tapped within that particular system. And I didn't know how to do it myself until music came along and opened me up not just to the world of music but to the world period, to the events of the day, to the connection between culture and society. Those were things that riveted me, engaged me in life, gave me a sense of purpose. It's what I wanted to do, who I wanted to be, the way that I wanted to do it and what I thought I could accomplish through singing songs."

Listening to his voice, it struck me that Springsteen's natural cadence, his unconscious manner of speaking, arranged words as though they were lyrics. His brain, unappreciated in grammar school, decoded language in chained phrases like the ones I just heard.

"Those were the things that riveted me..."
"engaged me in life..."
"gave me a sense of purpose."
"It's what I wanted to do..."
"who I wanted to be..."

"It's not the singing," I suggested. "It's the writing, isn't it?"

"Of course," he agreed. "Every good writer or filmmaker has something eating at them, something they can't quite get off their back. And so, your job is to make your audience care about your obsessions."

It seemed to me that his recurring obsession was with his life as a boy, especially the harsh relationship with his "hard knocks" dad who didn't think much of a rock 'n' roll son. "It was a tough, struggling household," Springsteen confided. "People struggled emotionally. People struggled financially to get through the day. It's a small-town world which I continue to return to. When I write, I put my father's clothes on. The immersion in that world, through my parents and my own experience as a child, and the need to tell a story that was maybe partially his—or maybe a lot his—I just felt drawn to do it."

"Your dad wasn't all that proud of you as a young man," I said.

"Oh, he was *later*. When I came home with the Oscar [for "Streets of Philadelphia"] and I put it on the kitchen table, he just looked at it and said, 'Bruce, I'll never tell anybody what to do ever again.' I told him, 'Yeah, it's okay.'"

Before the Asbury Park *Magic* concert, I was backstage in Springsteen's dressing room watching him write out that night's playlist. One of his notes was shorthanded, "B2R." No matter how many songs he has written (about three hundred), no matter the passage of decades (four), Springsteen would not provoke the wrath of the tribe by failing to play "Born to Run" exactly the way they remember it. That was sacred text. I discovered this when I committed sacrilege by asking two thirty-year members of the E Street Band whether they ever tired of playing "B2R." "I wonder, is it like, 'Okay, boys, "B2R," play it like we've never played it before,'" I deadpanned. The eyes of keyboardist Roy Bittan and guitarist Steve Van Zandt widened in disbelief. "It's funny you said that," Bittan began. "Because I was watching something on TV and it was Tony Bennett. And they asked Tony Bennett, 'Aren't you tired of singing "I Left My Heart in San Francisco"?' And his answer was, 'It gave me the *keys to the world*!' Well, there it is," Bittan said. "That's it." Van Zandt laughed. "I figure if we do a few more tours I might actually learn it! I mean, we live in hope, right?"

Toward the end of the 1980s, Springsteen left the E Street Band. The split was wrenching. Bittan told me he felt abandoned. I asked Springsteen why he would leave the people who helped propel his success. "I wasn't going to be any good to them at that moment. You know? And I think what happens is sometimes you got to break your own narrative. We all have stories we're living and telling ourselves. And there's a time when that narrative has to be broken because you've run out of freedom in it. You've run out of places to go." Springsteen and the E Street Band had a proven formula with *Born to Run* and 1984's *Born in the U.S.A.* But Springsteen was compelled to be faithful, not to the record companies nor to success, but to himself—the essence of authenticity. I asked, "Why are you still writing?"

"It's how I find out who you are and who I am and then who *we* are. I'm interested in that. I'm interested in what it means to be an American. I'm interested in what it means to live in America. I'm interested in the kind of country that we live in and leave our kids. I'm interested in trying to define what that country is. I got the chutzpah, or whatever you want to say, to believe that if I write a really good song about it, it's going to make a difference. It's going to matter to somebody."

In 2007, the Iraq war was escalating. The mistakes that drew the country into Iraq were being laid bare. One of the tracks from *Magic* was titled "Last to Die." The chorus Springsteen wrote asked, "Who'll be the last to die for a mistake? Whose blood will spill, whose heart will break?" He explained his purpose to me this way: "What I do is try to chart the distance between American ideals and American reality. That's how my music is laid out. It's like we've reached a point where it seems that we're so intent on protecting ourselves that we're willing to destroy the best parts of ourselves to do so."

"What do you mean?" I asked.

"Well, I think that we've seen things happen over the past six years that I don't think anybody ever thought they'd ever see in the United States. When people think of the American identity, they don't think of torture. They don't think of illegal wiretapping. They don't think of voter suppression. They don't think of no habeas corpus, no right to a lawyer, you know. Those are things that are anti-American," he concluded.

"Well," I challenged, "this record [*Magic*] is going to be seen as antiwar. And you know there are people watching this interview who are going to say, 'Bruce Springsteen is no patriot.'"

His answer shot back instantly. "It's unpatriotic to sit back and let things pass that are damaging to the place that you love so dearly, the place that has given me so much, and that I believe in. I still feel and see us as a beacon of hope and possibility. There's a part of the singer, going way back in American history, that is the canary in the coal mine. When it gets dark, you're supposed to be singing. It's dark right now. And so, I went back to Woody Guthrie and Dylan and Pete Seeger. Seeger didn't want to know how a song *sounds*, he wanted to know, 'what's the song *for*?'"

Bruce Springsteen had a lot to prove at fifty-eight years old, but only to himself. He was writing because he could not do otherwise. Songs welled up and forced their way into being through strings and ink and sweat. And because this need arises from a source inside him, a source he may not fully understand himself, it has the honesty of authenticity—too rare in a world made dull by emulation. That's as good a definition of *artist* as any I know.

At the end of our interview, I asked, "In your opinion, at this moment in this country, what needs to be said?" When you read Springsteen's answer, remember this was 2007, not 2019.

"I think we live in a time when what is true can be made to seem a lie and what is a lie can be made to seem true. And I think that the successful manipulation of those things has characterized several of our past elections. That level of hubris and arrogance has got us in the mess that we're in right now. And we're in a mess. But if we subvert the best things that we're about, in the name of protecting our freedoms, if we remove them, then, who are we becoming? The American idea is a beautiful idea. It needs to be preserved, served, protected and sung out. *Sung out!* That's what I'm going to do."

CHAPTER FIVE

Devotion
David Hall

"Lance Corporal Hall!"

First Sergeant Robert Pullen's shout demanded the presence of one of his marines. Pullen's skin had darkened under the Afghan sun and so had his demeanor. The only answer to his call was a desiccated breeze that hurried the dust across Helmand Province. Pullen faced the marines of Company G, known as Golf Company, of the 2nd Battalion, 8th Marine Regiment, 2nd Marine Division. All were at attention, in rigid rank and file, inside their mud-walled compound under a transparent September sky.

"Lance Corporal *David Hall!*"

Pullen bellowed with frustration and anger. If you had met Pullen back in the States in civilian clothes, you would have picked him out as a Marine First Sergeant. His jaw had been designed with a T-square. Tall, broad-shouldered, Pullen was armed with a glance that could burn a hole through a young marine. The men feared his anger and knew, with certainty, he would never let them down in a fight.

"Lance Corporal *David... R.... Hall!*"

Pullen howled, stretching Hall's name and raising the decibels in search of the thirty-one-year-old. But as much as Pullen demanded to hear the voice of the marine from Lorain, Ohio, he did not expect it. Hall was dead. Seven of Golf Company's marines were dead. The calling of the roll, shouting each name three times, was a ritual nearly as old as the Marine Corps itself. The marines attending the battlefield memorial faced both Pullen and, to Pullen's left, seven battlefield crosses, a tradition dating from the Civil War. The "crosses" were assembled from each fallen marine's possessions. Their sand-colored boots stood on the hard-packed desert floor. Rising vertically, above the boots, muzzles down, were their M-16 A4 rifles. At the top, on the butt of each rifle stock, rested their Kevlar helmet. Dog tags dangled from each rifle grip.

"Lance Corporal Stroud!"

The veins in Pullen's neck swelled as he worked through the roll, pausing between each demand to let the echo fade. The assembled marines were expressionless statues except for eyes that glistened with memory. "Lance Corporal *Jonathan Stroud!*" If the power of Pullen's roar could have brought them back from the dead, it would have.

"Lance Corporal *Jonathan... F.... Stroud!*"

Chris Everson, a bull of a man, was having trouble focusing his camera. A tough, no-nonsense South African, Chris is a legendary cameraman who has worked with CBS News for three decades. His pictures of the struggle in South Africa helped bring down apartheid. Chris had been my eyes and my conscience in war zones since we met in the Gulf War in 1990.

Many years earlier, as a young cavalry soldier, Chris had been gravely wounded and nearly lost his life. He admired military men and swelled with pride at what they stood for. As Pullen called marines who would not answer, Chris's viewfinder blurred with tears.

Golf Company's battlefield memorial in 2009 was among the most moving events I witnessed in more than a decade covering the war in Afghanistan. Years after Pullen's roll call, David Hall's name continued to echo in my mind. Why had he sacrificed himself so freely? I discovered the answer many years later.

America's longest war was fought in a land of abiding antiquity. One marine described the sense of it, as we watched a boy herding sheep through an irrigation canal in the southern desert near Kandahar. The city, more than 2,300 years old, was the site of a settlement founded by Alexander the Great.[1] "Afghanistan," the marine told me, "is like fighting in the Bible."

On another trip, I was driving up the Shomali Plain northeast of Kabul. I came upon nomads in a caravan of twenty-two camels. Reds, blues and greens were woven into handmade clothes and saddle blankets. Tassels swirled in the wind. Small brass bells sang *tink, thunk, tink, thunk*, with each lurch of the camel's stride. The men carried rifles in saddle holsters. A ruckus of children walked with the women. The expression of the riders, looking back at me, was severe but without hostility. They did not use the road—they crossed it, from one wild land to another. The pavement was a twenty-first century intruder which, only momentarily, interrupted their seventh-century world. These were tough people of profound dignity whose character reminded me of farmers and ranchers I knew as a boy. My travels through Afghanistan have taken me from the deserts of the Southern Plateau to the soaring Hindu Kush where India's tectonic collision with Asia lifts the roof of the world.[2] Afghanistan is about the size of my native Texas. It is beautiful and brutal, filled with willful tribes prone to the past. Among its nearly 35 million people, 65 percent are illiterate, 54 percent live on less than one dollar a day.[3] Life expectancy is 64 years.[4]

To understand a people, I look to the games they play. I drew some insight into the Afghan psyche by attending ferocious battles of the national sport called Buzkashi, which, translated from the Persian means "goat dragging." It's an ancient contest that galloped into Afghanistan from China and Mongolia sometime after the tenth century. Buzkashi is played on horseback. It makes NFL football look like badminton. People are sometimes killed in Buzkashi, both players *and* fans. The field of play is a rectangle, larger than a football field, but about the same proportions. The object is to carry a headless goat, or headless calf, around a flag on one end of the field (inbounding) then charge 430 yards to the other end to drop the carcass in a chalk circle (the goal). Five men ride on each team. A calf is preferred to a goat because it is less likely to disintegrate during the match, which can last for hours. Here's the catch. All riders are armed with rawhide whips about six feet long. When a rider manages to hoist the calf from the ground and onto his horse, the five riders playing defense for the other team whip the "ball carrier" and ram his horse to force him to fumble the calf. The rider with the calf relies on his four teammates to run interference, but with his hands full, he is largely defenseless. Typically, the calf carrier holds his whip in his mouth. The rare, great players, the Tom Bradys and Whitey Fords, have the strength to hold the calf against the horse with their leg and thereby free their whip for self-defense. When the calf is jarred loose somewhere midfield, the horsemen collide in a violent scrum to pummel for the prize. Matches I attended in Kabul were played at a full thunderous charge, hooves pulverizing the earth, whips flailing the wind. Crowds of hundreds or thousands press to the edge of the open field and attempt to stampede away when play runs out of bounds. Slower or inattentive fans sometimes do not live to see another game. They have a saying in Buzkashi: "Few men win. And no man wins for long."

Buzkashi arrived on the ancient Silk Road which crossed Afghanistan and drew from both ends a Babel of cultures and religions. A century after Alexander's invasion, about 250 BC, the Buddhist king, Ashoka, declared enduring peace. His edict was carved in Greek and Aramaic on a limestone pillar in Kandahar.[5] The translation from the Greek reads:

> ...he has made men more pious and all things prosper throughout the world. And the king refrains from [killing] all living beings while other men and all the king's hunters and fishers have ceased failing to exercise self-control.[6]

The declaration of peace is durably carved but the reality never was. Through antiquity, the region of Afghanistan was conquered and reconquered by invaders from nearly all points of the compass including Greece, India and Persia. In the mid-nineteenth century, the British occupied Afghanistan twice—to protect their interests in India and keep the Russian Empire at bay.[7] These disastrous misadventures compelled Rudyard Kipling to write:

> When you're wounded and left on Afghanistan's plains,
> And the women come out to cut up what remains,
> Jest roll to your rifle an' blow out your brains
> An' go to your Gawd like a soldier.[8]

Russian soldiers faced a similar fate in the twentieth century when the Soviets invaded, in part, to create a buffer against the Muslim world. After Afghans cut up what remained of the Soviet's nine-year occupation, the tortured nation tipped backward into the dark ages. In 1996, the Taliban—whose name derives from the word *student*—rose from the south to impose totalitarian rule.[9] Girls were forbidden education, adulterers were publicly stoned to death, women were barred from work and men were whipped for smoking.

America's vital interest in Afghanistan began fifteen days after 9/11 when a covert CIA team linked up with the Northern Alliance—a force of Afghan insurgents opposed to Taliban rule. By October 2001, the Northern Alliance, US Army Special Forces, US Special Operations Forces and US Air Force bombers, broke the Taliban grip on the capital, Kabul, and scattered the enemy. It looked like victory. Instead, America found itself marching behind Alexander the Great, King Ashoka, the British and the Soviets on the eternal campaign for domination of Afghanistan. Great powers rise and fall. Afghanistan endures.

In 2009, President Barack Obama decided to double down on Afghanistan in the hope that more troops and more economic aid would end the war. Lance Corporal David Hall's Golf Company was part of an additional battalion of reinforcements from the 2nd Marine Expeditionary Force out of Camp Lejeune, North Carolina. The company's leisurely name was imposed by the NATO Phonetic Alphabet. *Alpha Company, Bravo Company, Charlie Company* and so on—down to Company G, *Golf.* Golf fought its way into Helmand Province in July that year. Helmand is the heartland of the Taliban, who were from Afghanistan's largest ethnic group, the Pashtun. The Pashtun are an ancient people who range from southern Afghanistan through neighboring Pakistan.[10] They speak a unique language, Pashto, and see the Afghan–Pakistan border as an imaginary line they can't imagine honoring. No US force had occupied Golf's AO (Area of Operations) before. By the time I arrived, the marines were taking the highest casualties in Afghanistan. For that reason, my producer Henry Schuster and I embedded with Golf for *60 Minutes.* Since joining *60 Minutes* a decade before, Henry had become one of the broadcast's finest producers. He would go anywhere, suffer any hardship, risk any danger to tell an important story. Wrapped in his impervious exterior was a first-rate analytical mind. At fifty-something, Henry had been everywhere and had seen everything which invested him with nonchalance that lent confidence to everyone around him. We handpicked our team from the best in the world. Chris Everson was my principal cameraman in Afghanistan, in Iraq, throughout Africa, the Middle East and as far away as Antarctica. Along with Chris, we brought cameraman Ray Bribiesca and soundman Anton van der Merwe. Ray, from Oklahoma, learned combat photography as a Marine Corps gunnery sergeant in Vietnam. He tended toward fearlessness and was tough as an old combat boot. The young marines of Golf called him "Gunny," slang for gunnery sergeant. Anton, another South African, had once suffered a leg wound from a grenade while covering a riot against apartheid. He kept working without mentioning the inconvenience. Anton was meticulous in the worst environments—disinclined to look away from the bouncing needles on the VU meters of his audio equipment even when the "bounces" were propelled by gunfire. These were deeply experienced men, artists in our world, with an easy manner and an eighteen-hour work ethic. For decades, in deadly terrain, we always looked out for one another.

My team of five was issued olive drab cots on folding aluminum frames in the mud-walled open yard of Combat Outpost Burrow. Marines name new outposts after their fallen. Lance Corporal Dennis Burrow from Naples, Florida, had been killed two weeks earlier. A three-foot cross fashioned from scrap plywood was nailed to one wall with "LCPL [Lance Corporal] Burrow" lettered in red, horizontally, across the intersection of planks. Above his name were the words "Rest in Peace." Combat Outpost Burrow was a jumble of about two dozen marines in a farmhouse loaded with body armor, sleeping bags and M240 machine guns. When we arrived, the marines were struggling with a difficult but not insurmountable problem. Someone back home had sent a pound of Starbucks coffee beans. Whole beans. Thoughtful, but not thought through. Lacking anything like an armored combat coffee grinder, the marines were using the flat side of an ax head to smash the beans. I've heard marines say, "If it doesn't fit, get a bigger hammer." There *would* be French Roast at Combat Outpost Burrow.

Ironically, Afghans know the territory Golf Company occupied as "Little America." Back in 1946, the Afghan government hired the American engineering company Morrison Knudsen to build roads, dams and a system of irrigation canals in Helmand Province.[11] Morrison Knudsen set up a headquarters in Kandahar and spent decades on the project, which was modeled on the dams of the Tennessee Valley Authority. Holding back the waters of the Helmand River was only part of the motivation. The Truman and Eisenhower administrations hoped the dams would also contain the tide of Soviet influence.

Helmand has to beg for three inches of rain a year. The miserly land is latticed with verdant strips, but only on narrow acres along the canals sated by the Helmand River. In 2009, America's project from sixty years before was nourishing fields of marijuana. Golf's marines marched through fields of "weed" five and six feet tall. On patrol, the marines chose to walk in furrows flooded with a mix of river and sewage. The enemy couldn't hide an improvised explosive device underwater because the electronic trigger would short. Chris, Ray, Anton, Henry and I followed, waist-deep in the canals, holding our cameras and equipment over our heads. The marines slogged in ninety-five-degree heat, under body armor and fifty pounds of gear. The man carrying the SAW gun, the Squad Automatic Weapon, labored under an extra forty pounds. Each step yanked stubborn boots from the sucking, fetid mud. The exhausting terrain was safest, but on the way back, near the end of a six-hour patrol, there was always severe temptation to step on solid ground.

Golf's headquarters was surrounded by an enemy they could rarely see—of that, the marines were constantly reminded. One marine had been killed in his bunk by a single round fired from outside the compound's mud walls. One evening, I watched a huge, lumbering CH 53 helicopter coming in. It was light gray, sooted black behind the engine exhausts and marked MARINES. The copter settled just outside the compound. It was delivering barbecue, a special occasion for men digesting their second month of field rations. The pilot kept the Super Stallion's rotors spinning for a quick escape. With the last of the pulled pork pulled, it heaved heavily back into the sky. I jumped at the sound of a sharp *WHOOOP! BANG!* An insurgent had fired a rocket-propelled grenade which just missed the CH 53. The five crewmen escaped as the rotors clawed for altitude. *Barbecue!* I thought. *Christ!*

Golf Company's mission was counterinsurgency—cut down the bad guys, build up goodwill for the US-backed government. "No greater friend, no worse enemy," the marines would say. The trouble was, the enemy was nearly impossible to identify. Camouflaged among the people were hardcore Taliban fighters, drug gangs, freelance warlords and mercenaries who would fight anyone for five dollars a day. "How do you know the enemy from the citizens?" I asked Dan O'Hara, a young lieutenant from Chicago who was leading one of Golf's platoons. O'Hara was composed of sharp angles, tall and lanky. He was earnest and eager to use his GI Bill benefits to go back to college. He joined the marines because he feared he would regret not serving his country after 9/11. "You *don't* know the enemy until they start shooting at you," he said. "They'll shoot and before you get the chance to close on them, they'll run away and kind of just blend back into the population."

By 2009, eight years into the war, civilian casualties had become the enemy of counterinsurgency. In a change in tactics, the marines were ordered to show restraint to avoid alienating the people. In the early weeks of its deployment, Golf reported zero civilian deaths but at the cost of seven marines. "Killing a thousand Taliban is great, but if I kill two civilians in the process, it's a loss." Battalion Commander Lieutenant Colonel Christian Cabaniss explained the trigonometry that connected his marines, the enemy and the people.

"How many of the enemy have you killed so far?" I asked.

"I have no idea and it's really irrelevant," Cabaniss shot back with an air of total confidence in the wisdom of the strategy. We were sitting in his plywood headquarters, with its entrance flanked by the Stars and Stripes on one side and the Afghan flag on the other. The plywood was shielded on all sides by corpulent, gray HESCO bastions. HESCOs (named for the British manufacturer) are giant cloth sandbags in a wire mesh that unfold to stand about five feet tall, three feet wide. Once propped open, they are filled with earth and stacked two deep and three high. Citadels of HESCOs became the architecture of the American occupation. Cabaniss was built of equally sturdy material: tall, athletic, blond, forty-something, Hollywood handsome. His diction was lightly shaded by Georgia palmetto. His father was a preacher. Apparently, adherence to the gospel, both divine and marine, ran in the family.

"Body count is not something that you track?" I asked.

"It doesn't tell me that I'm being successful. The number of tips that I receive from the local population about IEDs in the area or Taliban in the area—*that* is a measure of effectiveness."

"You talk about restraint," I asked Cabaniss. "What do you mean?"

"As I told the marines before we deployed, it's a three-second decision, especially with his personal weapon. The first second is 'Can I?' The next two are '*Should* I? What is going to be the effect of my action? Is it going to move the Afghan closer to the government or further away?'"

Solving the counterinsurgency equation so that it equaled the same number of marines he arrived with was up to the calculations of platoon leaders including Dan O'Hara. On a blistering summer day in August 2009, O'Hara was ordered to investigate one of those civilian tips about an IED that Cabaniss liked to count. O'Hara dispatched a squad led by Lance Corporal Jonathan Quiceno from Orlando, Florida. "Q," as the men liked to call him, carried a cocky, calming presence. He had a habit of repeating "easy day," like a mantra, as his squad threaded through small collections of mud-walled houses. He greeted farmers and swarms of curious children while expecting a gunfight at any moment. "Easy day" was a warning and a prayer.

At the head of "Q's" squad, taking point, was Lance Corporal David Hall. Hall was thirty-one, an old man for a lance corporal. He'd been a marine three years. Hall fought in Iraq for seven months followed by a year back home. Now, he could almost see the end of his deployment in Afghanistan. Hall was on a search for meaning in his life so there was something poetic about his job, preceding the squad, swinging a mine detector, *left, right, left, right, tick, tock,* searching for a fleeting electronic squeal that might betray peril in his next step.

Before he joined the Marines, Hall had followed his father, Del, to the assembly lines at the sprawling Ford Motor plants in Lorain and Avon, Ohio. Hall installed dashboards or clutch fans that cooled radiators as the chassis of embryonic Econoline vans clanked by. He worked a good deal of overtime. In his last year he made more than $100,000. But, as his sister put it, "He hated every minute of it." The Lorain plant's beige metal facade slouches on acres of asphalt—looking like an institution, a prison perhaps. These confines weren't for Hall. He'd caught a glimpse of the world at a young age when his mother, Lulu, welcomed exchange students to their home at 3863 Palm Street in South Lorain. The visitors came from Italy, Yugoslavia and Hungary. When the students returned home, Hall's imagination traveled with them.

David Hall dropped his wrench and joined the Marines because "he wanted to *do* something, something positive," his father told me. Hall considered nursing, but a friend encouraged
him to join the Corps. He had no trouble filling out his combat fatigues at six-four and two hundred pounds. A remarkable
achievement when you consider Hall came into this life weeks
too soon. At birth, he weighed three pounds. His parents fed
him with an eyedropper.

Now, in Afghanistan, Hall towered over his fellow marines.
They could see his name, lettered in black, on the back of his
Kevlar helmet as his head bobbed with each swing of the mine
detector. *Tick, tock, left, right.* The warning Hall listened for could
be faint, uncertain. There wasn't much metal to detect. Homemade land mines, IEDs, were buried on trails or in courtyards,
under a plywood pressure plate. The plywood was partially cut
down the middle so it would break under the weight of a boot
and close the circuit on a forty-pound bomb made of ammonium nitrate fertilizer. The enemy, whoever they might be on
that day, paid villagers to plant the mines at ten dollars each.

On the last day of August 2009, "Q" led his squad to check
out the tip about an IED. Maybe the tip was meant to be a trap,
maybe it wasn't, but the marines were soon pinned down by
snipers. The temperature was rising past 110 degrees. The men
needed cover from the rifle rounds and the lethal sun. David
Hall volunteered to sweep a nearby mud-walled compound with
his metal detector. "Q's" squad had been in the compound before and knew it well. Two marines went along to watch Hall's
back. Hall cleared one section, then another. Easy day. Then
came the rough, splintering sound of cracking plywood.

At Golf Company's headquarters, on a piece of scrap cardboard, a marine had carefully lined in black felt-tip squares the
days of their six-month deployment. The hand-lettered calen-
dar hung from a green cord on the HESCO bastion at the entrance to the sleeping quarters. A line was drawn, upper right

to lower left, through each passing day. At the top were lettered
the words "You Can't Stop Time…" The time that drew David
Hall's imagination was December 17. On August 31, he lacked
only 108 lines drawn through finished days. Hall told Lulu and
Del, back in Lorain, he would be home by Christmas. His parents planned to drive to Camp Lejeune, North Carolina, to
meet him as they did every time their son deployed or returned.

In the compound, a deafening eruption blasted a geyser of dirt
into the sky. Earth and a spray of blood fell with David Hall.
His fellow marines rushed to their first aid training. There was
a crackle of radios and within minutes a UH-60 Black Hawk
helicopter, decorated with large red crosses on white squares,
thundered onto a field near the compound. Dust scattered like
shrapnel. The marines rushed Hall onto the medevac. Twin jet
engines spun into a scream. The pilot pulled the control lever
called a "collective," forcing the four rotor blades to gouge their
pitch into the air. The Black Hawk leaped, tilting its nose down
and forward like a sprinter lunging off the blocks. As it rose,
enemy gunmen opened up with machine gun fire. The Black
Hawk was too nimble. The medevac made good its escape, but
Hall would not. He had been mortally wounded in the explosion of the buried IED.

The next day, I watched Lieutenant O'Hara gather Hall's
squad. When a marine is killed, the void he leaves is filled
by worry and doubt—which a platoon leader must cast away
quickly. O'Hara spoke quietly. This wasn't the first time the
young lieutenant had to have this talk. No one was in the mood
for bullshit. "His death is not the fault of anyone who is sitting
here," O'Hara began, granting absolution. "If it belongs to anybody it would belong to me because I was the one out there
who was in charge, making the decisions. So just understand,
we're doing the right things, we're doing good work, we're
making a difference here. We're here fighting for the people of
Afghanistan." O'Hara said what was expected of him. But no

one in the squad and not Lieutenant O'Hara himself, truly believed they were making *much* of a difference and no one gave a damn about fighting for Afghanistan. What compelled marines to their feet each day was devotion—devotion to one another. In Shakespeare's *The Life of King Henry V*, the king's force is badly outnumbered as he prepares to lead his men into the Battle of Agincourt in the Hundred Years War. Yet he shouts that he wants "not one man more" because that would only dilute the honor among the men he famously calls "we few, we happy few, we band of brothers."[12]

Only the bond of family is equal to the devotion that I have witnessed in combat. I saw it among the firefighters of the FDNY as they joined the battle of 9/11. Placing your life in the hands of another—and accepting responsibility for his or hers in return—is a singular combination of empathy, compassion and self-sacrifice—the universal constituents of love.

Lieutenant O'Hara ended his talk. "We're here, ultimately, fighting for our country, which is what we all signed up to do." None of the men had a problem following orders or "fighting for our country," but if they were ordered to fight they wanted to *fight*. The rules of engagement for counterinsurgency were costing American lives. "It sucks," Lance Corporal Quiceno told me on another foot patrol. Cameraman Ray Bribiesca and I dropped into tall grass with "Q" to watch a house where an enemy sniper was thought to be holed up. "Q" repeated, "It sucks. I don't know another word to say it. It sucks because all you want to do is get them, you know, for revenge."

"Because of the marines who've been lost?" I asked.

"Sure. I mean, how many times have we been shot at? How many times do we know a direction, a distance, a compound, a vicinity, where these guys are coming from and then, in a conventional war, that's *it*. That whole compound would go. But we can't drop ordnance on them because of civilian casualties. It's frustrating. I don't know if anybody really understands the amount of stress that the guys are already starting to feel, simply having their hands tied behind their backs."

On September 2, 2009, a sleek white Evergreen International 747-400 cargo plane broke through a partly cloudy sky and touched down at Dover Air Force Base, Delaware. Strapped inside was a silver aluminum transfer case with labels indicating TOP and HEAD. By regulation, the case was packed with about sixty pounds of ice along with a Department of Defense form DD 2064.[13] "Hall," the DoD Certificate of Death read, "David R." The case was tightly bound in the Stars and Stripes and borne off the plane by six fellow marines in battle fatigues and white gloves. Del and Lulu were there to welcome their son as they always did. Hall's transfer case was lifted into a hearse. White gloves snapped a farewell salute.

Seven years later, David Hall's sacrifice was still on my mind. In July 2016, I pulled into the driveway of a white clapboard house which presided handsomely over a manicured lawn. David's dad, "Del," short for Delmar, bought the house after his son's death. Del welcomed me with a swing of the glass storm door and introduced me to David's mother, Lulu, plus someone I wasn't expecting—a man with mahogany skin and ivory teeth. Jean Fenelus smiled broadly. He was a thirty-year-old Haitian American from Brooklyn, New York, who the Halls called, "our 'adopted' son." Fenelus had been a member of Hall's platoon. "If anything happens to me," Hall had told his parents, "take care of Jean." That's what they were doing, putting him up as their own while Fenelus studied for a degree in criminal justice.

Each piece of living room furniture matched as though it was still on the showroom floor. The word *Believe* was rendered in chrome over a doorway that led to the kitchen. In the adjoining dining room, a wooden cross threw a morning shadow on the wall. There was a pencil sketch of David mounted high in the living room, rendered from his official Marine Corps photograph. I settled into a couch next to the actual photo, mounted in a frame on a glass-topped end table. The Marine Corps seal, the Eagle, Globe and Anchor, was mounted inside the frame below Hall's image. The eagle clutched a banner in its beak reading Semper Fidelis, "always faithful." In the picture, David looks handsome with intense blue eyes and a long straight nose. He's wearing his "dress blues"—a white hat and dark blue tunic outlined in the red piping of an enlisted man. His hair, which judging from Del would have grown thick with salt and pepper, was light and shaved "high and tight." In the custom of all official Marine Corps portraits, David concealed his illuminating smile.

"David was always the one to volunteer," Del said. "He was spirited." Del and Jean, David's platoon mate, told me David insisted on being at the front of each patrol, waving the rod of the mine sweeper, divining the fate of the others. When he was promoted to another job, David raised hell until they handed him his minesweeper back. "He wanted to do the most for the other marines," Del told me. His father traced David's sense of duty to an incident in middle school when David was bullied so mercilessly he had to change schools. After David had grown from a barely viable infant to a man only a fool would cross, he became the protective big brother for those he loved.

Del told me his son became disillusioned with the mission in Afghanistan because of a local practice that horrified American troops. Afghans call it "Bacha Bazi" which translates, "boy play." It is the tolerated rape of young boys, most often by men of power including some Afghan military officers.[14] Americans were ordered to look the other way. They were told Bacha Bazi was a problem for Afghanistan to work out and imposing American values would threaten cooperation. Hall could not square this order with his conscience. Del told me David planned to leave the Corps and use his GI Bill benefits to return to his dream of nursing school. I asked Del for his last memory of his son. He recalled an image of David on his final departure from

Camp Lejeune. Framed in the window of the departing bus, David smiled back at his mother and father and raised two fingers in the gesture for peace.

Why did David Hall insist on "taking point"? Why did he demand his mine detector back after he was promoted to a safer job? I have a guess. Sweeping ahead of the squad carried with it unimaginable risk and unambiguous virtue. His mission, his *personal* mission, was not the dubious prospect of nation building or following orders that did violence to conscience. Skimming the soil with his divining rod was about only one thing, devotion to his brothers. Hall's entire life had been a restless interrogation of the path ahead, searching for meaning beyond the reliable conveyor of Econoline vans with their regular delivery of paychecks.

The bomb was meant for the squad. David Hall suffered it alone.

Just as he always intended.

"Lance Corporal Schimmel!"

The same week David Hall returned home, First Sergeant Robert Pullen called the last of the names in Golf Company's roll of the dead.

"Lance Corporal *Patrick* Schimmel!"

"Lance Corporal *Patrick... W....* *Schimmel!*"

Just as no answer was expected in the battlefield memorial, there were no ready answers to the questions Lance Corporal David Hall might ask or the questions of his family. The United States had no choice in entering Afghanistan, but *leaving* a war is always plagued with complexities not imagined at the start. As of this writing, in 2019, our forces are still fighting America's longest war. We have not won. Soon, young men and women who were not born to see 9/11 will be deployed in a cause they only read about in school. For every great power, through all eras of time, there should be a warning at Afghanistan's door: "Few men win. And no man wins for long."

FIELD NOTE

Kremlin Rules

L ying on my aching back, on the cobbles of Moscow's Red
  Square, I was amazed at the beauty of my prone perspective. My vertebrae throbbed where they collided with the granite paving stones, but with Lenin's purple-and-red step pyramid mausoleum to my right and the nine towers of the jewel box Saint Basil's Cathedral to my left, I realized I had never been thrown out of a more beautiful place.

On September 1, 1998, I had been compressed into a bus with about thirty other White House correspondents pulling up to the 630-year-old walls of the Kremlin.[1] President Bill Clinton was meeting Boris Yeltsin for a ceremonial greeting at the start of a two-day summit. For me, that trip was another in a lifelong attempt to decipher the country that Winston Churchill described as "a riddle wrapped in a mystery inside an enigma…"[2]

My first visit to Russia was seven years before to witness the fall of the Soviet Union. CBS News declined to assign me to this epic story so I took vacation, collected my wife and went anyway.[3] "Wanna go to Moscow?" I asked Jane.

"Sure, when?" she said.

"Tomorrow," I replied.

"Okay, let's go."

This was no small thing, she was four months pregnant with our first child and we were heading to Russia in December. But neither of us wanted to miss this titanic pivot in history. To get a sense of what it was like to be a Soviet Muscovite, Jane and I joined a long line outside a cheese shop on a cruel, cold day. After more than an hour we reached the clerk, who was handing out meager rations. We were amazed to see she was totaling purchases on an *abacus*. Later, we took the Red Arrow Express, the overnight train to St. Petersburg. Only six weeks before, the former imperial capital had returned to its historic name after sixty-seven years as Leningrad. I suspected the olive drab Red Arrow had once hauled Lenin's Bolsheviks into battle. It seemed January's subzero frost also had a ticket and was assigned to our compartment. The great green hulk pulled from the Moscow station more out of habit than dedication. Reluctant cars resisted and complained through the night. Days later, Jane wanted to return to Moscow by Aeroflot, the Soviet national airline. When I mentioned Aeroflot's dismal safety record in those days, Jane concluded that dying on Aeroflot was preferable to returning on the Arrow.[4] As we were departing the St. Petersburg airport we were led through a snowstorm to our plane on the tarmac. The ground crew was deicing our airliner with a novel machine apparently of their own design. A jet engine had been placed on a stand and bolted into the bed of a pickup truck. The truck drove around the taxiway training hot jet exhaust on frosty wings. Like so many things in the Soviet era it was blunt but effective.

Now, seven years later, looking out from the windows of the

press bus, I could see Moscow improvising freedom, opportunity and hope. Red Square was returning to the original meaning of its name. It's "Red" not because of the Bolsheviks, but because the word *krasnaia,* in seventeenth-century Old Russian, meant *beautiful* as well as *red.*[5]

The press corps bus was on roughly the same course through the square that Soviet intercontinental ballistic missiles had taken in each May Day parade. A White House deputy press secretary braced herself in the pitching aisle to relay a request from the Kremlin press office. "They're making a point of asking that none of you interrupt the ceremony with questions," she told us. I was mildly offended. We're reporters, not the Mongolian barbarians who compelled the construction of the Kremlin walls.[6] We do not, would not, interrupt a ceremony involving heads of state. But that never means we will hold off *after* the ceremony. The cacophony of shouted questions following a presidential event is tradition in Washington.

Yeltsin was planning to present President Clinton with a tray of bread and salt, a Russian tradition representing prosperity (bread) and good luck (salt). Mr. Clinton, at that very moment, would welcome a loaf of prosperity. The day before, the Dow Jones Industrial Average had fallen 512 points or 6.4 percent.[7] At the time, it was the second largest single-day point loss in the history of the index.[8] Mr. Clinton hadn't spoken publicly about the market swoon. The question was pressing even if it had to wait until after the diplomatic nosh. In the Russian president's office, bread was presented, broken, dipped in salt and ground behind formal smiles. Also served up were a few ambiguous words of friendship. None of the reporters said a word. Then we received the familiar twin signals of the curtain dropping on the performance: the deputy press secretary deadpanned, "Thank you, press," languid, insincere words of dismissal, and the lights for the cameras (controlled by the White House Communications Agency) were switched off. *Snap!* With the event irretrievably concluded, I raised the question on behalf of a jittery American public.

"President Clinton, yesterday the Dow…"

That's as far as I got. Two plainclothes security men grabbed me, one under each arm, lifted me off my feet and pulled me, backward, out of the room. I assumed that was that, but my journey was only beginning. We flew through a corridor, down a stairwell (my heels banging each step) and came out to a courtyard. A door opened in the Kremlin wall. The security men hauled me out the door, through the shadow of the Spasskaya (Savior) clock tower and heaved like Olympic shot putters on steroids. Upon my landing, one of the security men reached down, grabbed my White House press credentials and snapped them off my bead-chain necklace. Back through the walls of the citadel the security men went, having dispensed with another barbarian. So, there we were, the two of us, laid out in Red Square—me and Vladimir Lenin.

Yeltsin had once planned to throw out Lenin's waxy, seventy-four-years-past-its-prime corpse. The leader of the Bolsheviks was to be buried in St. Petersburg. But the next Russian president, Vladimir Putin, interred the idea. In later years, after Putin transformed the workers' paradise into the oligarchs' playground, I wondered whether the overseers of Lenin's mausoleum had to strap his body down to keep him from spinning.

Muscovites stubbornly embrace their fabled Russian depression. Younger residents are heartbroken that the new Russia didn't bring the democracy they expected. Older Muscovites miss the Soviet Empire. One January morning, in 1992, when even the air seemed frozen, I walked past the honored dead in the Kremlin Wall Necropolis. One memorial had by far the largest mound of fresh flowers. I was surprised to see it was Joseph Stalin, who is remembered by some not as a murdering tyrant, but as the man who won World War II and built the Soviet Union into a modern industrial power.

A few years later, I met a nostalgic Leonid Shebarshin, the last director of the feared KGB intelligence service. To him, the Cold War was something to be savored. Our interview was tough to get through because Shebarshin was also savoring chain smoking. When I mentioned the cigarette pack on his desk, Marlboros, he drew the burning end of the cigarette to his eyes for close inspection and said, "Yes, the Americans will kill me yet."[9]

More recently, I met the up-in-smoke dreams of the next generation of Russians at a dinner. I was seated by the wife of a government official. I told her about the visit Jane and I made during the democratic revolution in 1991. As I spoke, tears welled up in her eyes. She was upset, fighting to maintain dinner-party diplomacy. It occurred to me that she must have been nostalgic for the Soviet Union and resented my American enthusiasm for the change. How could I have been so insensitive to her feelings for a system she had been taught to respect? Then, she surprised me. I had misread the tears. "We had so much hope [for the end of communism]," she said. She searched her reflection in the bone china before her. "It could have been so much *better*."

Vladimir Putin became a new czar. Even the Romanovs would marvel at today's excess. Political opponents of the regime find themselves in prison or dead under "mysterious circumstances." Russians remain, as they always have been, a people ruled not by law but by power. Eighteen years after my Kremlin ejection, I returned to Moscow. In 2016, I was driving by the 1907 Hotel Metropol where Lenin had once rattled the atrium panes with revolutionary hectoring of the masses. On an exterior wall of the hotel, along Teatralnaya Street, there is a bas-relief of Lenin to commemorate the Bolshevik era. Next door resides the Bentley dealership selling $250,000 automobiles to Russians with cash.

No questions asked.

CHAPTER SIX

Audacity

Ben Bernanke

The American dream is durable. And there was something about living in a delivery van that made Arielle Metzger and her brother, Austin, believe in the dream all the more. "It's an adventure," fifteen-year-old Arielle told me. "Yup, that's how we see it," her thirteen-year-old brother added. In 2011, the Metzger kids were on an adventure of homelessness. Many Americans were on the same, unfamiliar ride. The years after the Great Recession set a record. Never before had unemployment been so high for so long.[1] Families who lost their homes to foreclosure moved into twenty-dollar-a-night motels. There were so many of these families in Orange County, Florida, that school bus routes had to be redrawn to stop at motel parking lots where kids lined up before dawn. As those families slipped to

the end of their savings, they lost their grip on the cheap motels and resorted to their last refuge—keeping up appearances
by day, sleeping in their cars by night.

My extraordinarily gifted *60 Minutes* producer, Nicole Young,
traveled to central Florida to spend long days and nights speaking to families in homeless shelters and knocking on windows
of lonely cars in Walmart parking lots. Nicole is a courageous
producer—among the best to grace the pages of *60 Minutes*. She's
been by my side in the war zones of Afghanistan, Congo and
South Sudan, but it is her compassion that makes all of her stories unforgettable. Nicole is tireless when she hears the voice of
the suffering. That's how she found the Metzger kids and their
widower dad, Tom. Arielle and Austin had been living in the
1970s model GMC truck for five months. Tom bought the truck
on Craigslist, with his last $1,000. The GMC was weary after
a long career. It was a faded lemon yellow "box truck" with a
roll-up rear door, the kind that might have been captained by
a milkman in a previous life. Jobs for carpenters like Tom were
obliterated by the mortgage meltdown. But his skills came in
handy. In the cargo box, he built fold-down bunks for the kids
and shelves for storage.

When I met the family, Austin sat on the front bumper, a
slender boy with noncompliant brown hair. Arielle stood next
to him with her blond hair pulled tightly back revealing shining blue eyes. Five months on the road made them wise beyond
their years. I asked, "When kids at school ask you where you live,
what do you tell them?" Austin spoke up: "When they see the
truck they ask me if I live in it and when I hesitate they kind of
realize. And they say they won't tell anybody..." Arielle finished
the thought: "Yeah, it's not really that much of an embarrassment. I mean, it's only life. You do what you need to do, right?"

With the help of Beth Davalos, an advocate for homeless
children in the Seminole County school system, Nicole Young
found dozens of families living in cars. These families had dis-

covered that homeless shelters had waiting lists and shelters are typically segregated—one for women and children, another for men. Living in the car kept the family together. The Metzgers had a well-worn routine common to many of the families I met. In the morning, they drove to a gas station so the children could use the restroom to wash their hair, brush their teeth and change clothes. Veterans of homelessness know it's best to rotate among gas stations so the managers don't get sore. Next, the family joined the drop-off line at school. Appearances are essential. If the school or the cops figure out the kids are living in the car, there's a chance the state will take them away. After school, the parent behind the wheel looked for a well-lit parking lot where the car wouldn't draw anyone's notice. One dad told me he liked to park outside hospital emergency rooms; they were busy, an overnight car wouldn't attract attention and they were reasonably secure. Another father told me, each night, he sat on a cooler next to his car watching over his wife and children, longing for the glow of another day. Before the Great Recession, fourteen million children lived in poverty nationwide. By 2011, there were sixteen million.[2] The counties around Disney World and Orlando, otherwise known as "The Happiest Place on Earth," were among those suffering the most. Just on Highway 192, the road to Disney World, sixty-seven motels housed about five hundred homeless kids. The government counts them as homeless if they have only temporary shelter. In Seminole County schools, one thousand students lost their homes.

"Who can tell me what it feels like to be hungry?" I asked middle schoolers at Castleberry School. "It's hard," one boy told me. "You can't sleep. You just…wait. You go to sleep for like five minutes and you wake up again. And your stomach hurts and you're thinking, 'I can't sleep. I'm going to try and sleep. I'm going to try and sleep,' but you can't because your stomach's hurting." Another boy described his stomach this way: "It's like a black hole. And sometimes when I don't eat, you can hear my stomach like it's growling. You can hear it." Another classmate, with tears rising, told me, "We have to sometimes take food from a church. It's hard because my grandmother's also out of work and we usually get some food from her."

"It's kind of embarrassing," another girl said. "Because the next day, you go to school asking kids if they want this food, or if they want that. If they have cereal and they haven't opened it yet, you go ask them if they want their cereal."

After classes at Castleberry, Arielle and Austin Metzger jumped into their truck headed for the town library where they take advantage of the lights, computers and air conditioning. Arielle told me, "Before the truck, I always saw all these homeless people and I would feel so bad for them. And then as soon as we started living in the truck ourselves, I've seen even more. And I just feel so bad. And even though I'm homeless myself, I want to do as much as I can to help them get up, back on their feet."

"You sound very adult to me," I said. Her little brother interrupted, "She is. She likes to take over." Not a bad thing, I thought, with such a brave outlook on hardship. Arielle continued, "Every time I see, like, a teenager or any other kid fighting with their parents or arguing with them, it really hurts me because they could be in my shoes. And, of course, I don't *want* them to be in my shoes. But they need to learn to appreciate what they have and *who* they have in their life. Because it may be the last day they might have it."

Families, approaching their last normal day, haunted Ben Bernanke. He was far from homeless himself but in the early days of the financial crisis, he did occasionally spend the night on a couch. In 2008, Bernanke was, arguably, the most powerful man in the world. In fact, the man who would have to *save* the world, if anyone could. So, it seemed like a hell of a thing for the chairman of the board of governors of the Federal Reserve System to have to sleep on the instrument of torture that passed for his office couch. As the nation's top banking regulator, Bernanke could ill afford to go home. Banks were imploding around the clock.

People tended to appraise the fifty-four-year-old Fed chairman as courtly, nebbishy and shy. Every inch spoke of an academic in an ivory tower. Bernanke was bald with a stole of dark hair wrapped from temple to temple. His full beard had surrendered almost wholly to gray. He was a little shorter and a little rounder than he might admit to the mirror. But to assay Bernanke by appearances was a mistake. In 2008, when America had been clubbed in a dark alley by Wall Street, and Washington stood paralyzed in fear—action was essential. This perilous moment demanded audacity—the audacity to invent, to improvise, to gamble, the audacity to seize the moment before it was too late.

"The *chairman* does *NOT* do interviews!" The public affairs man at the Federal Reserve in Washington, DC, was laughing, *laughing*, at the absurdity of my call. He was right; chairmen of the Federal Reserve didn't sit for interviews nor hold news conferences. A few words from the chairman could send markets on a terrifying Tilt-A-Whirl. Chairmen of the Fed inhabited a fortress of solitude on Constitution Avenue. They labored over compulsory congressional testimony precisely crafted to say nothing at all. The fact that the "chairman does not do interviews" was precisely why I wanted Bernanke on *60 Minutes*. "The Fed is doing *a lot of things* it has never done," I told the public affairs man as the world was plunging, eyes shut tight, into the Great Recession.

Few, including Bernanke's Fed, foresaw the nightmare lurking in the American dream of homeownership. Trusted American financial institutions sold mortgages to people who could never repay them, just to generate banking fees. The more subprime homeowners they could scam, the greater the fees. The mortgage originators then moved the risky loans off their books with the help of Wall Street which packaged hundreds of thousands of subprime mortgages into massive, doomed-to-fail securities. To cover up the true nature of these bundled securities, the banks demanded the highest quality grade from investment rating agencies, AAA. The rating agencies obliged because their fees were paid by the banks that were demanding the ratings. With AAA ratings, these time bombs could be purchased by the most conservative investors—pension funds for example. Moody's Investor Service, one of the major rating agencies, stamped AAA on forty-five thousand mortgage-related securities. At the time, only six private sector companies in the US enjoyed the same coveted rating. In 2006, Moody's put its AAA stamp on thirty mortgage-related securities every working day. In the end, 73 percent of Moody's AAA securities were downgraded to junk.[3]

These financial time bombs detonated in a chain reaction, maiming the giants of finance that helped create them: Bear Stearns, Lehman Brothers, Merrill Lynch, Citigroup, Wachovia, Washington Mutual, plus insurance giant American International Group.[4] Confidence snapped. Banks stopped taking each other's calls. Funding markets which keep America in motion by lending to businesses for a day or a decade seized like a hot engine drained of oil. Fear was so great that the interest rate on treasury bonds, backed by the "full faith and credit of the United States," fell to *zero*. In other words, investors sought refuge in the safety of treasury bills knowing they would receive nothing in return.[5] "That's the equivalent of sticking money in your mattress," Treasury Secretary Henry Paulson told me at the height of the crisis. Paulson was among those who understood that the seizure of financial markets in 2008 was a greater threat than the events that led to the Great Depression.

Everyone knows the Depression was set off by the market crash of October 1929, but everyone is wrong. It's not that simple. The many causes of the Great Depression have vexed dissertation writers for generations. A radical new view came into focus in 1963 when economists Milton Friedman and Anna Schwartz indicted the Federal Reserve itself in their classic, *A Monetary History of the United States, 1867-1960*. To reduce their 860-page analysis to bullet points would do violence to one of the most significant achievements in the history of economics, so with that in mind, here we go:

1) In 1928, the Federal Reserve was worried about wild speculation on Wall Street. The Fed decided to mop up the oversupply of credit by selling government bonds to banks—thereby reducing the cash banks had on hand. Then, the Fed raised interest rates to the highest level in seven years. The Fed's 1928 annual report noted with satisfaction, "There was no evidence of unfavorable effects of higher money rates on trade and industry."[6] But there would be. Tightening credit eventually triggered the collapse of a stock market that was inflated on borrowed money.

2) Panic! With no deposit insurance in those days, folks took their savings out of banks and stuffed cash into coffee cans. These "bank runs" effectively looted the banks and choked the supply of cash even more. Lending dried up. The Fed did nothing while 20 percent of all American banks failed.

3) Speculators took dollars to their banks and demanded gold. The Fed supported the value of the dollar by tightening the money supply even more.

4) The world went to hell in a handbasket.[7]

The Friedman/Schwartz theory that the Fed turned a garden-variety recession into a cataclysm caught the imagination of Ben Bernanke, a graduate student in economics at the Massachusetts Institute of Technology. Later in 1983, as a professor at Stanford, he expanded on the Friedman/Schwartz work with "Nonmonetary Effects of the Financial Crisis in the Propagation of the Great Depression." Titles like that led me to hand in my pencil as a freshman economics major.

Bernanke's early education in markets began at his grandfather's drugstore on Main Street in Dillon, South Carolina. In high school, Bernanke was quick with numbers. Because calculus wasn't offered in his school, Bernanke taught himself. When it came time for college, a friend recommended Harvard and Harvard obliged. The acceptance letter would thrill most parents, but not Bernanke's mother. Cambridge was too far from Dillon and besides, she insisted, he didn't have the clothes for Harvard. Somehow these obstacles were overcome. Bernanke dutifully returned to Dillon each summer to work up tuition payments as a waiter at a South Carolina roadside classic called South of the Border. The future chairman of the Federal Reserve wore a poncho while collecting salsa-stained tips to help pay for school. This eventually led to a PhD at MIT, an associate professorship at Stanford and the chair of the economics department at Princeton. I once asked Bernanke what he learned as a waiter. He told me, "I learned work is *hard*."

By 2006, Bernanke was sworn in as the Chairman of the Board of Governors of the Federal Reserve. He was recognized as one of the world's leading authorities on the causes of the Great Depression. This did not make Bernanke clairvoyant however. Just like the Fed in 1928 which saw "no evidence of unfavorable effects" from higher interest rates, Bernanke said in a speech in May 2007 that he saw "no broader spillover" emanating from the weakness in the subprime mortgage industry.[8] He told Congress on July 20, 2007, "The downturn in the housing market, so far, appears to be orderly."[9] Eleven days later, the markets suffered the first shock. Two Wall Street investment funds containing subprime mortgages imploded.[10]

Through the Great Recession and its aftermath, I traveled the country listening to people in the struggle of their lives:

the Metzger kids living in their van, sweatshop workers forging names on fraudulent mortgage documents and a few who thought suicide might be a way to cope with the end of ninety-nine weeks of unemployment benefits. I didn't know Ben Bernanke, but I had a hunch that a man from Dillon, South Carolina, who trafficked in tacos to put himself through college, would welcome a chance to answer the questions I was hearing.

"Are we going to lose our home? What are we going to do for *food*? These are questions that you'd never think that you'd ask yourself and now they're discussions in our home." Mike O'Machearley was waiting for the layoff notice that would leave him unable to support four children and a grandson. He was a broad-shouldered, bearded, Mack Truck of a man who drove an employee bus at the sprawling DHL distribution center in Wilmington, Ohio. Every week, more employees were stepping off his bus with pink slips in their hands. You didn't need an MIT PhD to figure, soon, DHL wouldn't need an employee bus or bus driver. "They always say that when God closes a door, he opens another one," O'Machearley told me as we sat in his kitchen. "We have faith he will." Faith was about all that sustained O'Machearley and the town of Wilmington when I first pulled onto Main Street in December 2009. Christmas garlands were draped on neat little brick shops—small-town "mom & pops" with one picture window display case on each side of the door. The early twentieth-century lane was spotless. Rows of cars were parked diagonally along each curb. The movie theater, coffee shop and bookstore formed a classic scene of middle America. Wilmington's Main Street would have caught Steven Spielberg's eye.

Wilmington had long depended on its Clinton County Air Force Base for its livelihood. In the 1940s, the navy conducted secret balloon tests there, setting off panicked reports of UFOs. In the '60s, the base was a launching point for nuclear bombers with navigation charts pointing to the Soviet Union.[11] In 1972, the base was decommissioned and the town lost its economic engine. Rather than giving in, Wilmington and its twelve thousand residents promoted the vacant installation as an airpark. The overnight delivery company Airborne Express set up its national distribution center on the lattice of abandoned runways. Once again, the sky was the limit. One-third of all households in Wilmington were getting a check from Airborne and later from DHL, which acquired Airborne Express. After the Great Recession crash-landed, businesses around the nation made overnight delivery the first notch in their belt-tightening. When I arrived, DHL was laying off Mike O'Machearley and eight thousand of his co-workers. Wilmington was like every town I visited in the Great Recession: laid-off workers were worried about money but what they *longed for* was dignity. They found honor in an honest eight- or twelve-hour day. They missed the compassion of lending a hand to the men and women struggling next to them. "We could tell you what we did on a daily basis, but you wouldn't believe it," DHL cargo handler Keith Rider told me. We met in a classroom where he and two dozen other employees were learning about unemployment benefits. Rider reminisced, "You load boxes in a big container and it'll weigh eight hundred pounds. You push it out the door through eight inches of snow and push it up on a barge. And we were idiots enough that we did it by ourselves! We worked as a team. You had a good friend right alongside you. You'll never understand it, but we loved it." Morris Deufemia cut in, "I remember people with scarves breathing through ice and just, unreal, their eyelashes frozen. I started in '81 and when you worked, you *worked*."

Mike O'Machearley had no problem with the "American Pact"—work hard, raise a family, start the kids on the rung above you. But, given his layoff notice, O'Machearley wanted to know where he could redeem his claim. After all, he figured, he had paid in full. "On November 2 of 2003," he told me, "my son was killed over the skies of Fallujah [Iraq] in a Chinook helicopter that was shot down. He died with sixteen other soldiers." O'Machearley was eager for work, not charity. He asked for opportunity, not entitlement. "I'm an old-school kind of guy," he said. "Maybe like on Tuesday nights, we're going to have 'no electricity Tuesday nights.' We're going to light the oil lamps and play checkers and read books by candlelight and just *talk* to each other. Maybe we'll become a tighter family through it."

On another Main Street in another down-on-its-luck town, I sat down on the wooden slats of a metal-framed bench. The railroad severed the asphalt just to my left and the storefront behind me had once been the Jay Bee Pharmacy. The scene was warmly familiar to the man sitting next to me. His grandfather had emigrated from Eastern Europe, passed through Ellis Island and settled on this corner to open his drugstore. Ben Bernanke had come home to Dillon to show me his roots. In this time of crisis, the Federal Reserve chairman had granted my request to break the long-standing tradition of refusing interviews. "Mr. Chairman," I asked. "I see we're on Main Street, but many people feel that guys like you are tuned into what happens on Wall Street and you forget places like this."

"I come from Main Street," Bernanke protested, urging me to glance up at the sign by the traffic light that bore witness to that truth. "I've never been on Wall Street. I care about Wall Street for one reason and *one reason only*, because what happens on Wall Street matters to Main Street." My hunch about the chairman had been right. During the months after I was laughed off the phone, Bernanke and his communications director, Michelle Smith, were developing a new theory. The Federal Reserve was a mystery to most Americans. But in March 2009, after the Dow collapsed 54 percent, after American homes lost 30 percent of their value and as unemployment and underemployment were rising to a combined 15.6 percent, maybe this was the time to throw open the shutters of the Fed's marble palace.[12]

It is one of Washington's ironies that the grand headquarters of the Federal Reserve was, itself, a Depression-era project aimed at creating jobs. The construction was undertaken by the Public Works Administration which was spending the equivalent of $110 billion (in 2017 dollars) on 34,508 schools, bridges, town halls, hospitals, airports and dams in all but three of the nation's 3,071 counties.[13] The PWA built New Deal icons including the Grand Coulee Dam in Washington State, New York's Triborough Bridge and LaGuardia Airport, and Los Angeles International. For the Federal Reserve headquarters, the US Commission of Fine Arts, which reviews such things, approved a four-story white marble structure of "impressive dignity" directly across the National Mall from the Lincoln Memorial.[14] Given lean times, it was felt that federal architecture should be classical but spare. In terms of the Fed's facade, PWA might as well have stood for Purchased Without Adornments. Only an American eagle, motionless in marble, is perched atop the Federal Reserve's austere entrance on Constitution Avenue. Inside, a two-story sunlit atrium is lined by two marble staircases which lead up to the governors' boardroom. If you had been in the crowd October 20, 1937, you would have seen Franklin Roosevelt standing on the second-floor landing with a forty-eight-star flag suspended above. His leg braces were masked from those below by a blue Seal of the President flag draped over the banister before him. Roosevelt opened the headquarters that day as a monument to his revolutionary vision of the national banking system. The original Federal Reserve was inspired by the bank panic of 1907. After much debate, it was created by Congress to stabilize markets by managing the supply of money.[15] You may notice that on every bill in your wallet "Federal Reserve Note" is engraved *above* the words "The United States of America." The Fed was created as a system of regional banks with little central authority. But with the Great Depression, Roosevelt signed the Banking Act of 1935, which concentrated control in Washington. The new board of governors was appointed by the president. The Fed became centralized, nimble and muscular. The day he opened the headquarters, the sound of the president's words reflected off the lobby's travertine. He defined the mission of his new Federal Reserve as providing "the greatest attainable measure of economic well-being, the largest degree of economic security and stability."[16] It would be seventy-three years before the extraordinary powers granted to the Fed would be needed to fend off catastrophe.

In the spring of 2008, nothing was well, secure or stable. Bernanke and his Federal Open Market Committee (FOMC) of Federal Reserve bankers had been slowly reducing interest rates as unemployment rose. But the time for traditional, measured action was about to end. One of Wall Street's storied investment banks, Bear Stearns, was hours from failure after suffering losses on its mortgage-backed securities. The firm was pushed to the brink when rumors caused Bear's trading partners to cut its sources of funds. Bernanke worried panic would trigger a cascade of collapsing financial giants so he invoked an obscure emergency clause in Roosevelt's Federal Reserve Act. The clause known as 13(3) had never been activated since the 1930s. It allowed the Fed, in times of emergency, to loan not just to customary commercial banks but to "any participant in any program or facility with broad-based eligibility."[17] In other words, just about anyone. During the Bear crisis, Bernanke announced the Fed would add investment banks to the usual commercial banks that were eligible for Fed loans. In a historic departure from normal practice, Bernanke agreed to accept mortgage-backed securities as collateral. This put the mortgage investments that no one wanted on the Fed's balance sheet. In exchange, the Fed put solid US Treasury securities into the banks. In a sense, it was a perfectly legal and altruistic form of money laundering.

Mortgages with a soiled reputation swapped for squeaky clean Treasury securities. Bernanke reasoned that the Fed could hold the mortgage-backed securities for years if need be and sell them at a profit when the market recovered.

Adding teetering investment banks to those eligible for Federal Reserve loans required Bernanke to trigger 13(3). But he kept that quiet. He told his board he feared that publicly invoking the emergency rule would result in "self-feeding liquidity dynamics"—which was Bernanke-speak for panic. The expanded lending was unprecedented but it was also too little, too late. In effect, Bernanke was waving a fire extinguisher in the middle of a panicked stampede for the exits. The theater was not yet engulfed in flames, but as Bernanke feared, "self-feeding liquidity dynamics" were like gasoline.

On September 7, 2008, the Bush administration was forced to seize control of the Federal National Mortgage Association (Fannie Mae) and the Federal Home Loan Mortgage Corporation (Freddie Mac).[18][19] The two failing finance companies held nearly 44 percent of all residential mortgages, which added up to $5.3 *trillion*.[20] That emergency takeover, on Sunday, was the start of a harrowing two weeks when pillars of finance crumbled one after another. On September 14, America's largest retail brokerage, Merrill Lynch & Co., was rescued in a fire sale to Bank of America. The next day, 164-year-old Lehman Brothers, Wall Street's fourth-largest investment bank, collapsed. Its demise was the largest bankruptcy in US history at $639 billion.[21] The day after, September 16, Bernanke faced a threat he believed was greater than all the others. The world's largest insurance company, American International Group, was insolvent.[22] AIG held $1 trillion in policies in 130 countries.[23] It was one of the few companies in America granted the highest credit rating, AAA, by both Moody's and Standard and Poor's.[24] But unknown to Wall Street, the global colossus had done the unforgivable. It recklessly insured billions of dollars in those worthless mortgage bundles, then it failed to increase its reserves to cover the potential losses.[25] The insurer which was supposed to make investors whole in case of default was effectively broke.[26] Because AIG was an insurance company, not a federal bank, it shouldn't have been Bernanke's problem. But the Fed chairman understood that every major financial firm could be devastated by billions of dollars in losses that were now uninsured. Bernanke could not hold his temper as he cut AIG a check for $85 billion. This would turn out to be just a down payment. "Of all the events and all of the things we've done in the last eighteen months, the single one that makes me the angriest, that gives me the most angst, is the intervention with AIG," he told me. "Here was a company that made all kinds of unconscionable bets. Then, when those bets went wrong, we had a situation where the failure of that company would have brought down the financial system."

"It makes you angry?" I asked.

"I slammed the phone down more than a few times on discussing AIG. I understand why the American people are angry. It's absolutely unfair that taxpayer dollars are going to prop up a company that made these terrible bets, that was operating out of the sight of regulators, but which we have no choice but to stabilize, or else risk enormous impact, not just in the financial system, but on the whole US economy." Bernanke may have had no choice but in the bargain, he made the bailout as painful as possible for AIG, its board and its shareholders. In return for the taxpayer rescue, 79.9 percent of AIG would be owned by the people of the United States.[27]

The day after the AIG rescue, the Dow dropped 449 points. Over the months, the index had lost 23 percent of its value compared to the year before. Bernanke told me, "In that period, I thought we were pretty close to a global financial meltdown." Bernanke had said publicly at the time that the debacle was the worst financial crisis since the Great Depression. But that was not what he believed. Privately, he thought the crisis was "almost certainly the worst in human history."[28]

Separately from Bernanke's action, the Bush administration quickly cobbled together a $700 billion plan to purchase toxic assets of financial firms. I was in the office of Treasury Secretary Henry Paulson as his team drafted the legislation. I noticed Paulson had Al Capone's revolver in a frame on his office wall. The Chicago mobster was disarmed by Treasury agents who arrested him on tax evasion charges. On Capitol Hill and among the public, the idea of a taxpayer bailout of Wall Street was about as popular as a raid at a speakeasy. I wondered whether the treasury secretary would need the six-shooter to get his bill passed. Paulson was the former chairman of Wall Street's Goldman Sachs.[29] Goldman was one of the firms dealing in rotten mortgages.[30] "We've got to get this up to [Capitol] Hill quickly," Paulson told me. The legislation would put Paulson in charge of the largest bailout in American history. He kept the draft to three pages. "We've got to keep it simple, very simple," Paulson told me. "So this is *only* about recapitalizing our banks and financial institutions." Paulson continued, "Scott, the last thing in the world I wanted to do is go up to Congress asking for these kinds of things. It is a terrible position to be in. The only thing worse is the alternative." Paulson and Bernanke were shouting "Mayday!" But members of Congress who did not represent Lower Manhattan could not see what this had to do with them. "I was addressing a caucus of congressmen," Bernanke told me. "And one congressman said, 'Mr. Chairman, I'm talking to bankers in my town. I'm talking to shopkeepers in my town. And they say things are normal. Nothing's going on. We don't see any problem.'" Bernanke paused for effect. "I turned to him and I said, *'You will!'*" In a meeting with Speaker of the House Nancy Pelosi, Secretary Paulson emphasized the emergency with a gesture some thought was a joke and others believed was a sign of desperation. In an interview, I said to

Speaker Pelosi, "I understand Secretary Paulson kneeled down and begged you to move this bill forward."

"Well, Secretary Paulson injected a moment of levity into the conversation," Pelosi told me.

"Levity on one knee?" I replied.

"He said, 'Please, please, I beg you, don't blow this up.'"

I asked Paulson about *his* view from the waistline of the speaker of the house. "There was a lot of tension and frustration," he said. "I wanted to break the tension. There was some shouting going on." A taxpayer bailout had the whole country shouting. I said to Bernanke, "You know, Mr. Chairman, there are many people who say, 'To hell with them. They made bad bets. The wages of failure on Wall Street should be failure.'"

"Let me give you an analogy," he said. "If you have a neighbor who smokes in bed, he's a risk to everybody. Suppose he sets fire to his house. You might say to yourself, 'I'm not going to call the fire department. Let his house burn down. It's fine with me.' But what if your house is made of wood? What if the whole town is made of wood? The right thing to do is put out the fire first and then ask, 'What punishment is appropriate? How should we change the fire code? What needs to be done to make sure this doesn't happen in the future?' That's where we are now. We have a fire going on."

On September 29, 2008, the House of Representatives debated Paulson's bailout. In offices across the country, investors turned from the southerly red arrows on their Bloomberg Terminals to watch C-SPAN. It was a foregone conclusion that the bill would pass. There was no choice. But the tone from the House chamber began to sour and so did the stomachs of those watching. The rescue of America's crooked banks was defeated by a slim bipartisan majority. Investors stampeded. The Dow Industrials dove 777 points. Seven percent of its value—1.2 trillion dollars—was vaporized in a day. At the time, it was the largest point loss in history.[31] As bad as it was, the Dow was just a barometer measuring the storm battering American families.

The economy began losing jobs at a rate of 741,000 *a month*. The unemployment/underemployment rate was headed to 17 percent.[32] Household net worth fell 20 percent, about $13 trillion nationwide. For comparison, household net worth declined only 3 percent in the Great Depression.[33] At that moment, one man in Washington had the authority *and* the audacity to act. Ben Bernanke did not need to debate or dither. He did not need the approval of Congress. The Federal Reserve is as independent of the deliberations and vanities of Washington as a government institution can be.

Like pouring water on a melting nuclear core, Bernanke flooded the banking system with cash and credit. He lowered the interest rate the Federal Reserve charges banks to *zero*. His team used the Fed's emergency authority to dream up thirteen massive lending programs that had never existed before.[34] He loaned troubled banks $1.6 trillion.[35] Then, over a period of years, he directed the Fed to purchase more than $2.5 trillion in mortgage-backed securities.[36] The Fed became the lender of last resort not only to America's financial system but to the world's. Because the dollar is the international currency of trade, Bernanke made sure central banks in fourteen foreign countries had plenty of greenbacks to lubricate commerce. Where did the money for these programs come from? Much of it he simply created. Bernanke directed the Fed to go online and add digital money to the accounts of the failing banks. He explained it to me this way: "The banks have accounts with the Fed, much the same way that you have an account in a commercial bank. So, to lend to a bank, we simply use the computer to mark up the size of the account that they have with the Fed. So, it's much more akin, although not exactly the same, but it's much more akin to printing money than it is to borrowing."[37]

"You've been printing money?" I asked.

"Well, effectively. And we need to do that, because our economy is very weak."

Critics warned against his aggressive interest rate cuts. Members of his own board complained he was moving too fast to hear their advice. Others believed he'd made a colossal mistake bailing out AIG. That criticism grew louder as AIG's abyss grew deeper. The US Treasury was forced to kick in another $49 billion to the AIG bailout. By the time it was over, taxpayers lent AIG more than $160 billion.[38] But Bernanke continued to expand the money supply in every way he could imagine— precisely the opposite of what the Federal Reserve Board of Governors had done in 1928. He was also dead set on avoiding the Depression-era Fed's other blunder. To that end, he made a pledge on *60 Minutes*. Bernanke explained the Fed was examining the books of all major banks, so I asked, "Are you committing in this interview that you are not going to let any of these banks fail? That no matter what their balance sheet looks like, they are not going to fail?"

"They are *not* going to fail," he declared flatly.

Not one more major bank would be allowed to collapse, but Bernanke emphasized, if a destitute bank had to be dismantled, the Fed would prop it up until it could be "unwound" in a safe and orderly way.

In those easy days before the crisis, the Federal Reserve maintained a steady, boring balance sheet with a fairly constant $800 billion on loan to banks at any given time. After Bernanke's host of emergency actions, the Fed's loans outstanding were $4.5 trillion.[39] Bernanke was certain he had learned the lessons of the Great Depression. But there was a risk that his unprecedented aggressiveness would set off runaway inflation. There were harsh lessons of history in that too.

Nearly three hundred years before, the French monarchy was devastated by one of the first stock market bubbles. Shares in what was known as the Mississippi Company became wildly inflated by fraudulent tales of riches in the French colony of Louisiana. It didn't help that the man behind the Mississippi Company, John Law, was also managing the French economy for the Regency under Louis XV.[40] In 1718, Law invented the first paper money in an experiment to revive the French economy. When his Mississippi Company began to collapse, he tried to support the plummeting shares by printing money—a lot of it. Unfortunately, the pit had no bottom. Panic ensued. There were bank runs—literally "runs"—in which people were trampled to death.[41] The collapse and lasting economic damage were among the events that laid the path to the French Revolution, seventy years later. Bernanke was playing with fire to extinguish the fire consuming the economy.

In October 2008, Congress returned to Hank Paulson's $700 billion emergency bailout and passed it on a second try. This gave Paulson, Bernanke and Sheila Bair, the Chair of the Federal Deposit Insurance Corporation, vital tools to restore confidence in the financial system and restart the heart of the economy. But investors remained unconvinced. Days after the bailout passed, the Dow Jones Industrial Average dropped into freefall. On October 9, the index fell 678 points. On October 15, it lost 733 points. That second week of October, the Dow lost 18 percent of its value—its worst week in its 112 years.[42] The history of the Great Recession records that the Dow peaked at 14,000 in October 2007. By March 2009, it stood at 6,600. This was one of those extraordinary times, not unlike 9/11, when it seemed the future unfolding was not the future we planned.

From his office, Bernanke looked across American elms on the National Mall toward the marble memorial of the sixteenth president. "Let us, to the end, dare to do our duty as we understand it," Abraham Lincoln had said.[43] Ben Bernanke was daring to take the Federal Reserve in directions no one, perhaps not even Franklin Roosevelt, had imagined. Bernanke would not repeat the old mistakes. If he was wrong, at least his mistakes would be original.

Late in 2008, George W. Bush had four months left in the White House. He summoned Bernanke and Hank Paulson to the Roosevelt Room across the hall from the Oval Office. In his book, *The Courage to Act*, Bernanke recalled the grim president's first question. "How did we get to this point?"[44] A large part of the answer was fraud, on a vast scale, which *60 Minutes* helped expose.

After the meltdown, banks were pursuing foreclosure on more than one million homes a year.[45] One foreclosure notice was addressed to Lynn Szymoniak in Florida. It had been several months since Szymoniak received notice of an interest rate increase from her mortgage holder, Deutsche Bank. She disputed the rate hike and refused to pay. Now, Deutsche Bank was suing to take the house. Her case would turn out to be, well, one in a million. The quibble over a percentage on a white stucco bungalow in Palm Beach would ultimately lead to an FBI investigation, a *60 Minutes* investigation and the exposure of mortgage fraud by the banks that gave us the Great Recession.

Lynn Szymoniak did not look like a slayer of Wall Street dragons. When I met her at her threatened home, she was pleasantly graying, middle-aged and might have been mistaken for a retired grandmother. But Szymoniak was a lawyer, trained as a white-collar fraud investigator. More than that, she was angry. She had been in court for months. The lawyers seeking to throw Szymoniak out of her home were forced to admit that the mortgage documents that established the bank's ownership were lost. Foreclosure was held up nearly a year until Deutsche Bank returned to court claiming the missing documents had been discovered. Szymoniak was suspicious. She had only to glance at the resurrected documents to see they were not just a forgery, but a forgery attempted by a moron. According to the miraculously recovered documents, Deutsche Bank filed for foreclosure three months *before* it had acquired ownership of the mortgage.

Oops.

These documents, "proving" the bank's ownership, were signed, as required by law, by a bank vice president. Her name was Linda Green. Her signature meant that an officer of the bank had examined the documents and found them whole and sound. Szymoniak went online where the State of Florida posts public mortgage records. She discovered Linda Green was an extraordinary banker. Green's signature validated tens of thousands of mortgage documents. And while the name was always the same, the signature varied widely. You might understand how Green's hand might be shaky, however. According to the documents she signed, Linda Green was executive vice president of twenty individual banks, *simultaneously*. After meeting Szymoniak, I decided I had to find Linda Green.

In our *60 Minutes* investigation, I worked with producer Robert Anderson who had built an enviable career with the legendary correspondent Mike Wallace. Our associate producer was Dan Ruetenik, a gifted and tenacious journalist. Dan burns a lot of shoe leather while reporting. He wore out a couple of soles tracking down Linda Green in rural Georgia.

Her modest home was in the woods with a couple of aging autos parked outside. Green and I stood beside her fence. She was camera shy, but otherwise more than happy to talk about her career as a prominent figure in the national mortgage industry. Green explained she was not and never had been a bank vice president. She told me she had been working as a shipping clerk for an auto parts supplier when her grandson told her about a job at a company called DocX. DocX occupied several rooms in an anonymous strip mall in Alpharetta, Georgia. Green's supervisor at DocX explained that all Green had to do was apply her signature to endless reams of paper that crossed under her pen. What DocX liked most about Linda Green was her name. It was short, didn't take too much time to write and it was easy to spell. So, her name was adopted by her many co-workers in what was a sweatshop assembly line for mortgage fraud on behalf of the most respected banks in America.

DocX had been invented by necessity. Wall Street cut a lot of corners when it created those mortgage-backed investments that triggered the financial collapse. Now, as the banks tried to foreclose, they discovered the legal documents behind the mortgages simply didn't exist. In court, banks demanded that home-owners have all *their* paperwork in order. But when the banks could not prove they actually owned the properties, many re-sorted to forged paperwork to throw people out of their homes.

Chris Pendley was one of Linda Green's co-workers. I asked him, "When you came into DocX on your first day, what did they tell you your job was going to be?"

"That I was going to be signing documents using someone else's name," he said.

I asked, "Did you think there was something strange about that in the beginning?"

"Yeah, it seemed a little strange. But they told us, and they repeatedly told us, that everything was aboveboard and it was legal."

"And your previous experience in banking?" I asked.

"None."

"In legal documents?"

"None."

"You just had to be able to hold a pen?"

"Yes, hold a pen."

"How many banks were you vice president of in a given day?"

"I would guess somewhere around five to six."

"What were you getting paid for this?"

"I'm embarrassed to say ten dollars an hour."

"That's not much for a guy who's vice president of five banks," I observed.

"Yeah," Pendley said with irony. "I was very underpaid for my status in the companies."

Pendley told me each employee was required to sign three hundred fifty mortgage documents an hour. He estimated he inked four thousand a day. After Pendley signed "Linda Green" to each legal document, it was left to co-worker Shawanna Crite to notarize the paperwork. I was a little confused by this step, so I asked Crite, "What was the role of the notary?"

"We were to make sure that everyone on the document was who they said they were and notarize the documents."

"But the people who were signing the documents *weren't* who they said they were," I said.

"Right."

"So, if Chris Pendley was signing for Linda Green, you'd notarize that document."

"Yes."

"And you were told that was okay?"

"Yes."

"What do you know now?"

"That it wasn't right," Crite confessed, stifling a laugh.

The actual Linda Green told me many of the bank "vice presidents," whose signatures were required by law, were high school kids who needed gas money. We will never know how many thousands of American families were evicted from their homes by banks whose ownership claim was not worth the paper it was forged on.

When DocX was exposed, the banks claimed to be shocked. They had farmed out their foreclosure processing to a subcontractor called Lender Processing Services. Lender Processing Services owned DocX. LPS claimed it was unaware of the fraud until 2010 when it closed DocX. The only person to go to jail was LPS executive and DocX founder, fifty-six-year-old Lorraine Brown. Brown pleaded guilty and confessed to overseeing at least one million forgeries. A federal judge sentenced her to five years.[46] After our *60 Minutes* report, several states and counties started investigations and discovered many thousands of "Linda Green" forgeries lurking in the shadows far beyond the Sunshine State. The banks and LPS claimed to be victims of Lorraine Brown, but the Federal Reserve and other federal regulators didn't buy it. The government declared ten firms had engaged in an unsafe and unsound mortgage processing scheme, including Bank of America, Citigroup, Ally Financial, HSBC, J.P. Morgan Chase & Co., MetLife, The PNC Financial Services Group, SunTrust Banks,

U.S. Bancorp, Wells Fargo & Company and Lender Processing Services. Together, the firms represented 65 percent of the mortgage servicing industry and nearly $7 trillion in mortgage balances.[47] In a settlement with the US Department of Justice, five lenders—Bank of America, Wells Fargo, J.P. Morgan Chase, Citigroup and Ally Financial—paid $5 billion in fines and committed to about $20 billion in refinancing and mortgage modifications for troubled borrowers. The judgment was the result of a suit filed by Lynn Szymoniak under the Federal False Claims Act. The Act allows private citizens to sue when they have evidence the federal government is being defrauded. It was created during the Civil War to stop profiteers who sold sick mules and faulty rifles to the Union Army. Szymoniak's cut of the settlement was $18 million.

She kept the house.

Our stories on the Great Recession for *60 Minutes* helped motivate a generous nation. When we introduced the families living in cars in Florida, donations of more than $5 million came in checks, large and small, to organizations for the homeless. One couple bought a home for Arielle and Austin Metzger to get them out of their truck. You know the names of this couple, but they would rather I not say. We reported that the collapse in home values meant the state of Nevada didn't have enough tax revenue to sustain its only chemotherapy center for the poor. After our story, a philanthropist wrote a check to keep the clinic open. We profiled Remote Area Medical, which was founded to air-drop doctors into inaccessible parts of Africa. But in the Great Recession, RAM was setting up free clinics in America. The day after the story, a wealthy New Yorker bought RAM a new aircraft to replace its geriatric WWII cargo plane. Our stories about the struggle of Wilmington, Ohio, inspired Jon Bon Jovi to write his anthem of the Great Recession, "Work for the Working Man." I have found, over decades, in disasters natural and manmade, all journalism has to do is investigate and report. Armed with reliable information, Americans always do their best.

★ ★ ★

We can never know what would have happened had Ben Bernanke not possessed the audacity to use his authority—some would say more than his authority—as chairman of the Federal Reserve. Another Fed Chair might not have recognized the similarities with the Great Depression. Another Fed Chair might have hesitated, waiting for political cover. Consider Bernanke's results. After September 1929, the Dow fell for thirty-four months and lost 89 percent of its value.[48] The 2007 market crash was arrested in seventeen months with a loss of 54 percent. The Great Depression lasted ten years. The Great Recession lasted one and a half.[49] Even so, the recovery was the slowest, flattest on record. My favorite measure of unemployment is what the US Bureau of Labor Statistics calls the U6 rate. U6 counts every unemployed person looking for work, plus everyone who is working part-time because they can't find a full-time job. The U6 rate peaked at 17.1 percent in April 2010. It took eight years to fall to 7.5 percent in September 2018.[50] Despite the slow recovery, Bernanke's investments turned out to be shrewd. All of the Federal Reserve's loans were repaid. The mortgage-backed securities recovered. As of 2018, the Fed was still holding trillions of dollars of these securities which produced billions of dollars in profit which the Fed returned to the US Treasury.

On his office balcony at the Federal Reserve headquarters, I stood with Ben Bernanke admiring the view of the Lincoln Memorial. I was intrigued by the storylines of two modest, small-town boys, self-taught, self-conscious of their clothes, who acted with audacity to rescue the nation, each in his way. It would be a mistake to overdraw the comparison. Lincoln's achievement, saving the Union and abolishing hideous slavery, can never be matched. But to the Metzger family living in an old yellow truck, or to Mike O'Machearley, who asked how he would feed his family, both men may be remembered as heroes who "dared to do their duty."

CHAPTER SEVEN

Invincibility
Nadia Murad

Her eyes were deep brown—beautifully clear—with an intensity enhanced by the swirl of a scarf that concealed her face. It struck me those eyes were much too young to have seen such cruelty. The scarf, in a pattern of taupe and black, swept across her forehead just above her dark eyebrows. It dropped clockwise around her cheek and flowed over the bridge of her nose. Nadia did not want to be seen, but she demanded to be heard. Her people, the Yazidis of northern Iraq, had been targeted for extermination. At the age of twenty-one, she was enslaved and tortured by the terrorist army that called itself Islamic State or ISIS. When Nadia told me her harrowing story for the first time, I could not have imagined the words she spoke and the torment expressed in her eyes would lead her to the highest honor the world has to give.

In the spring of 2014, the Sunni extremists of ISIS charged out of Syria and overran much of northern Iraq. The city of Mosul, Iraq's second-largest metropolis, fell to the terrorists. In the path of ISIS were the Yazidis, an ancient culture of less than five hundred thousand people farming the slopes of Mount Sinjar. The earth's tectonic forces had lifted the brief, sixty-mile-long Sinjar range in the far north of Iraq, near Turkey and just east of Syria. This was the watershed that the Yazidis came to venerate as their holy mountain. Their unique religion is thousands of years old, grown from the roots of Persian theology and Zoroastrianism. Because the Yazidi faith had no written text and was passed down orally, over the centuries it assimilated aspects of Islam, Judaism and Christianity. Yazidis believe a supreme god created the universe but left the running of the world to a deity called the Peacock Angel or Tawusi Melek, who personifies both good and evil.[1] [2] The faith has been misunderstood and misinterpreted as long as the Yazidis have clung to the Sinjar range. They are sometimes ridiculed as "devil worshippers" and apostates.[3] Their culture has been persecuted by every power to hold sway over the region: Kurds, Ottoman Turks and Saddam Hussein's Ba'ath Party. In 1978, Saddam's Revolutionary Command Council Decree 358 attempted to assimilate Yazidis out of existence through forced relocation to various Arab towns.[4] The Yazidis began to recover during the period of the American occupation of Iraq, but in 2014, the American-trained Iraqi army melted before the assault of ISIS. The fanatics of ISIS, enforcing their own malevolent interpretation of Islamic law, branded the Yazidis *kafirs* or nonbelievers—something less than human.

In late August 2014, I traveled to northern Iraq for a *60 Minutes* story about the depravity of the ISIS occupation. My producer, Henry Schuster, and associate producer, Rachael Morehouse, searched for witnesses in refugee camps near the city of Irbil.

This was territory in the hands of Kurdish Peshmerga fighters opposed to ISIS. Rachael reached a young Yazidi woman by phone. She was from the village of Kocho and had escaped ISIS captivity. Rachael convinced her to meet. A *60 Minutes* team, including Rachael, cameraman Thorsten Hoefle, CBS News security officer Karl Taylor and translator Aran Ibrahim, traveled to Lake Dahuk, where the Tigris River pools behind the immense Mosul dam. Near a camp, a child met the convoy to guide them to Nadia. Rachael found the young woman among twenty refugees huddled in two rooms of a mud-brick house. Nadia had escaped ISIS only a week before. She was still visibly shaken and nervous about meeting reporters from America.

Rachael Morehouse is among our most gifted associate producers. Her analytical mind and courage in the pursuit of justice are wrapped in a personality of great empathy. Only a woman of Rachael's compassion could have convinced Nadia to step out of the obscurity of the refugee camp.

Anyone would hesitate to talk about the horrors she endured, but Nadia had even greater concerns. The Yazidi culture is puritan by Western standards. Young people are not permitted to marry outside the religion. Women typically do not have sex before marriage. Rape is stigmatized. Nadia worried about how her fellow refugees would react to her story—especially surviving members of her extended family. She agreed to talk to Rachael only if all the men and all her relatives left the room. Over ninety minutes, Nadia told Rachael of her torment. Her mother and sisters were missing. Six of her brothers had been killed in a mass execution. Two brothers survived but were wounded. Nadia explained that the wounded brothers were still in a dirty makeshift hospital only because they had nowhere else to go. Rachael offered to pick up the brothers, reunite them with Nadia and bring all three to Irbil to speak to me, on camera, for *60 Minutes*.

The next day, Rachael led Nadia to a room that our team had

converted into a temporary studio. Nadia was hesitant. We were strangers. Our equipment, lights and cameras were intimidating. I told Nadia there was no obligation and that we should not do the interview if she wasn't sure. Everything in Nadia's culture counseled against speaking, yet she could not remain silent. She asked us to agree to her terms: the men on our team would stand behind curtains, out of her sight; the scarf would conceal her face; we would not reveal her identity and Rachael would sit beside her and hold her hand. I was reminded of another survivor of sexual assault I had interviewed a few years before in a refugee camp in the Democratic Republic of the Congo. She had been gang raped by soldiers. I asked her whether she wanted us to conceal her identity. "You show my face!" she shouted. *"You show my face! I want them to see me!"* But Nadia had a compelling reason to obscure herself. Her mother and two sisters were still in the hands of ISIS.

I find people often remember with precision the moment their lives changed forever. So it was with Nadia. "On Friday, August 15, at 11:30 a.m.," she began, "ISIS entered our village and told us all to come to the school. They told us, 'The ones who will convert [to Islam] may stay at their homes. The ones who will not can meet us at the school.'" The ISIS soldiers were well equipped with American weapons and vehicles that Iraqi soldiers had abandoned as they fled. When ISIS came to Kocho, they told the community that those who would not convert to Islam would be driven into Kurdistan and exiled.

"As we were entering the school," Nadia continued, "I was with one of my brothers. We saw a bulldozer and I asked my brother, 'Why is there a bulldozer here?' He replied, 'To throw dirt on the bodies when the killing is done.'"

The men were loaded onto trucks while young women and children were herded up to the second floor of the school. Nadia's brothers, Saeed and Khaled, were among more than three hundred men in the trucks. Khaled told me, "After taking us about three hundred yards away from the school they stopped by an open field and told us to get out and lay flat on our stomachs, and we did. Then about ten ISIS fighters stood behind us and started firing all types of guns."

"We heard shots fired," Nadia told me. "A lot of gunshots. We all thought it might be the military coming to save us and get us out."

"But the gunfire was not from troops coming to rescue you," I said.

"No, it was not the military. A little boy told us he saw them taking the men to the side of the village and killing them, but we didn't believe him. We kept hope. An older woman said, 'The boy is lying. [ISIS] promised to take us to Kurdistan.'"

Khaled and his brother Saeed hid beneath the bodies of dead friends and neighbors. Khaled was hit twice in the left elbow and once in the thigh. Saeed suffered five gunshots: two in the knee, one in the thigh, one in the back and a graze to the neck. The ISIS executioners searched for survivors and shot them dead. But before they discovered Nadia's brothers, the militants were frightened away by a fighter jet overhead. Khaled and Saeed waited, then crawled away. When we met them, two weeks had passed since they had been shot. Their bandages had not been changed in days and their wounds were infected and putrid. We arranged for a combat medic to clean and dress their wounds. The medic put them on powerful antibiotics. The brothers began to recover almost immediately.

In our interview, Nadia told me young women were loaded into buses, bound for a house in a nearby village. "And when you got there, what happened?" I asked.

"There was someone at the front door. He would take off our head scarves and rip open the fronts of our dresses. And he would touch us, sexually abuse us. They kept us until they brought the rest of the women in our village there."

In time, the women and girls of Kocho were driven to a

house in Mosul. It was there that they realized they were for sale. The house was a marketplace for sex slaves. "There were about seventy girls who were there already," Nadia said. "They were Yazidi girls from another village. They said, 'There were three hundred girls here before. Now we're the only ones left.'"

"What happened to the women in your group?" I asked.

"The next morning a sheik [religious leader] came and picked up three girls for himself. Two of them were my friends. He had the right to take three. An ISIS officer had the right to take one. A friend of mine, who was taken by an officer and later returned, told us, 'They're doing everything they please with us, raping us.' The ISIS men would tell them, 'If you do not convert, we will sell you to ISIS militants in Syria, where a young girl could be bought for about eight hundred dollars.'"

Nadia was selected by an ISIS officer who took her home and raped her at will. After several days she was traded to another ISIS soldier. She tried to escape through a window but was caught by a guard standing outside. As punishment, her captor lashed her with a whip and then allowed three guards to gang rape her. Nadia would later write of her torture, "The rape was the worst part. It stripped us of our humanity and made thinking about the future—returning to Yazidi society, marrying, having children, being happy—impossible. We wished they would kill us instead."[5]

Nadia was traded a second time and found herself in a home on a quiet street. Left alone, she discovered the door was unlocked. She ventured out. Panic rose inside her at the thought of being caught escaping again but she saw no one and made a break for it. A family she met while running away arranged for her to reach the refugee camp outside ISIS territory. She had been enslaved for nine days.

The only time in our interview that Nadia was overwhelmed with grief was in talking about her mother, Shami. Older women were often executed along with the men. Nadia had no word of her mother's fate. "Tell them," she shouted through tears, "tell them I just want my mother!" Nadia threw her head back, slapped her knees with both hands, rocked forward and sobbed.

At the beginning of our interview Nadia was shaking with apprehension. Her voice was high and tentative. But as she spoke, her words gathered velocity and power. I had the sense of a woman who had been speaking for herself until she realized she was speaking for her people. A change swept over her. Rachael drove her back and noticed Nadia seemed confident, empowered. She had discovered her voice and she liked the sound.

After months in the refugee camp, a German relief organization resettled Nadia in Stuttgart. There, she became active in a Yazidi human rights organization. In 2015, about a year after our interview, she accepted an invitation to speak at a United Nations symposium on human trafficking. The next year, the U.N. appointed Nadia Goodwill Ambassador for the Dignity of Survivors of Human Trafficking. She traveled the world demanding an end to rape and slavery as weapons of war. Nadia published a memoir of her captivity titled *The Last Girl: My Story of Captivity, and My Fight Against the Islamic State.* The title was inspired by her hope of being the last girl in history with a story like hers.

In the fall of 2018, I was preparing for an interview in Washington, DC, when I received the news that Nadia Murad had won the Nobel Peace Prize. She shared the prize with Congolese gynecological surgeon Dr. Denis Mukwege, who had established a hospital to heal thousands of rape survivors from Congo's vicious civil war. The chairwoman of the Norwegian Nobel Committee said, "We want to send out a message of awareness that women, who constitute half of the population in most communities, actually are used as a weapon of war, and that they need protection and the perpetrators have to be prosecuted and held responsible for their actions."

Tears came to my eyes as I thought of this frightened young

woman in a refugee camp who refused to be broken, refused to be silent, refused to accept anything but justice. Not unlike Viktor Frankl's epiphany in a Nazi death camp, Nadia Murad discovered she was not helpless. The power over her captors was always inside her—the invincibility of her soul.

FIELD NOTE

No Moss Gathers

My heart began to fall with the sink rate of the small private jet closing in on the dirt airstrip. It was April 1996. We were in the middle of nowhere on a desolate stretch of the Texas border with Mexico. There could be only one reason I was watching a chartered plane on final approach to this remote runway—the same reason I had landed here a couple of hours before. As the little Lear touched down and rolled toward us, I was climbing aboard my own plane, carrying what I thought was a major exclusive that would lead the *CBS Evening News* that night. The unwelcome visitor was surely one of my competitors out to spoil my day. The engines on my plane had already started. We were in a hurry to get to the CBS station in El Paso, Texas, where we could feed our story to New York. But I waited on the steps of my jet to see which of my adversaries was taxiing to a stop. The Lear door dropped down and my heart began to fly again. I recognized the passenger instantly. I mean, who wouldn't? He was the most famous man in the world.

This bizarre encounter came near the end of a high-speed day. The *New York Times* had broken the story that morning that Ted Kaczynski, the American terrorist known as the Unabomber, had a pen pal relationship with a Mexican man near the town of Piedras Negras. I decided to try to find Kaczynski's correspondent, Juan Sanchez Arreola. About noon, I landed on the dusty strip that was so lonely it never saw a need for the company of a terminal building. I drove across the border and began asking around. A man at a convenience store showed me where I could find Sanchez's home. Sanchez wasn't there, but his wife was more than happy to show me a twelve-inch stack of handwritten letters from the Unabomber. The correspondence had gone on for a decade. It turned out Kaczynski's brother had once lived in the region and made the introduction. Included in the mail was a tube, intricately carved with a cap that fit on the end. Sanchez's wife described it as a pencil case. It looked to me like the case for a pipe bomb.

The Unabomber, a Harvard-educated former math professor, had terrorized the nation with pipe bombs for over seventeen years. He killed three people and injured twenty-four. It was only after he demanded that the *New York Times* and *Washington Post* publish his thirty-five-thousand-word manifesto that his brother recognized the ranting and turned him in to the FBI.

Now, in 1996, I had this remarkable coda to a story that had spellbound the nation. I was thrilled that I hadn't run across any of my competitors all day. That was why I was crushed to see the second plane on the remote airfield. But when the aircraft door opened and the man bounded down the steps, I called out to my colleagues, already on my plane, "It's okay, guys. It's just Mick Jagger."

I did wonder why the lead singer of the Rolling Stones was stepping off a plane in a barren, sparsely populated part of Texas.

But I was more relieved that my exclusive was secure. I learned later that an expensive, luxury dude ranch nearby quietly welcomed high-rolling guests from around the world.

Despite Mick's 1965 lament, seeing that he wasn't working for ABC or NBC was all the satisfaction I needed.

CHAPTER EIGHT

Gratitude
Early Lessons

In 2011, when I became anchor and managing editor of the *CBS Evening News*, I adopted a new valediction for my emails and letters. Rather than "Thanks" or "Yours Truly" I end with "Grateful." The adjective captures how deeply I feel about the men and women who work too hard and risk too much to cover the news for us each day. I've tried to maintain that attitude of gratitude throughout my life. I believe no one is "self-made." We are fashioned from the generosity of others.

I did not imagine the adventures, the education, the privileges of experience I would enjoy. I was raised in Lubbock, Texas, the center of an orbiting system of farm communities on the great American plateau known as the Llano Estacado. The name was coined by Spanish conquistador Francisco Vazquez de Coronado during his exploration from 1540-1542.[1] Llano Estacado means "staked" or "palisaded" plain. There are two theories for Coronado's inspiration. If Coronado was riding below the plateau, the top would appear high and forbidding as if palisaded behind a high fence. If he was riding on top of the mesa, he was confronted by a horizon bereft of landmarks. Stakes were hammered into the ground to mark routes across the plains. Coronado may have been among the first to use these stakes as a road map home. In many nineteenth-century texts, the plains—black with buffalo and reaching into New Mexico—were terrifying in a way that is hard to appreciate today. To become lost was to die fairly quickly from exposure and thirst. In 1846, George Wilkins Kendall—America's first war correspondent, founder of the New Orleans *Picayune* newspaper and Texas pioneer—was separated from his party while on horseback on the Llano. He writes in his *Narrative of the Texan Santa Fé Expedition*:

There, as on the wide ocean, you find no trees, no friendly landmarks to guide you. All is a wide waste of eternal sameness.

Frederick Law Olmsted, the father of American landscape architecture, toured Texas on horseback in 1854. Olmsted designed Manhattan's Central Park and the grounds of the US Capitol. In his *A Journey Through Texas* he describes the Llano Estacado as:

An immense, desolate, barren table-land...destitute of water, bearing no tree, and, during a great part of the year, only dried grass, supporting no permanent animal life, and probably destined to be of little service to man.

Yup, that's my home.

The names of the settlements that grew in the wake of the wagon trains give you the lay of the land: Brownfield, Level-land, Littlefield, Muleshoe. As noted above, contour lines on the Llano Estacado are unknown. But "destitute of water" it is not. Olmsted didn't know, but below his dusty boots there was a vast underground lake which extends from South Dakota to south of Lubbock. Today, the Ogallala Aquifer is lifted by center-pivot irrigation systems and rains on some of the most productive land on earth. Tractors pulling disk harrows set their course for the horizon with nothing to turn them but the wire fence picketing the next farmer's field. In the middle of May, mechanical planters with a twelve-row span drop seed two inches below the furrow and press the earth behind them. In a little over thirty days, white flowers bloom. If the year is benevolent and there are no weevils or root rot then two months after the flowers, dark green stalks will strain under the weight of cotton bolls that eventually split along four seams like a kernel exploding from a corn popper. As a boy, my fall seasons clamored with great green John Deere strippers racing time to get the harvest to the gins. The fiber, and its value, were graded by color and length into categories including "good middling" or "strict middling." This is where we get the phrase "fair to middling," indicating the cotton is only so-so. Cotton was native to Arabia and North Africa. The Islamic Conquest brought cotton to Spain in the ninth century. The Spanish brought the fiber to the New World in the sixteenth. More than anything else, cotton created Texas. But, as elsewhere in the first half of the nineteenth century, cotton was a source of wealth that impoverished the soul. Land developer Stephen F. Austin enticed thousands of cotton farmers to emigrate from America's southern states. He offered vast, inexpensive lands and he worked tirelessly to protect and extend hideous slavery.[2] An important spark igniting the Texas Revolution was the defense of slavery against Mexican demands for emancipation. After independence, the Republic of Texas became the only nation in history to specifically enshrine slavery in its constitution.[3] Texans would not enjoy freedom until the Civil War broke the chains.

Today, the area around my hometown is the largest cotton producing region in the world with more than three million acres planted in some years.[4] My journalism career split from its boll at a TV station planted in the middle of a cotton field.

The other major feature of growing up in Lubbock was the annual swarm of tornadoes. Twister spotting was a spectator sport in the spring and summer, something like the running of the bulls in Pamplona, Spain. I remember climbing on the roof of our house with my friends and watching funnels parade in the distance—slender daggers in the sky.

We were not a farm family. My father was a serial entrepreneur: used cars, nightclubs, housewares. My mother sold homes and worked night jobs including "keypunch," an ancient form of computer data entry, and cotton classification. It was her income that usually brought the ends close to meeting.

Mom and Dad had grown up in Oklahoma Dust Bowl country. My father, John E. Pelley, volunteered for World War II right out of high school. He chose the US Army Air Forces because he liked the cut of the uniform. That was hazardous vanity. Lieutenant Pelley was a twenty-one-year-old bombardier in the 8th Air Force, flying combat missions over Germany from Mendlesham, England. For a time, the 8th Air Force suffered the highest casualty rate in the European Theater of Operations. Dad rode the glass nose of a B-24 and, later, a B-17-G which the crew named "Smokey Joe." His first sortie was on D-Day. He flew thirty-five missions, focusing a Norden bombsight on the Nazi war machine. On my desk, I have Dad's small leather notebook in which he kept a log of his combat missions. In blue ink and crisp cursive, his entries include:

Saturday, October 7, 1944

Up at 2:30 [a.m.]. Briefed for Merseburg [Southwestern Germany]. After an oil plant. The most horrible mission

I've flown. The flak was terrific. Our ship [B-17] looks like a sieve. A piece came right through the nose and hit me in the chest, but my flak suit stopped it. One ship of the lead squadron went down. I saw him, a direct hit. The boy had 34 missions. I don't see how they can expect men to fly 35 of these missions in 17s; it's next to impossible. We have four ships missing today. Well, I'll get to bed, we fly tomorrow.

Dad once told me that, on occasion, the squadron would return to find there weren't enough meals in the mess hall. The cooks hadn't expected so many men to survive.

Just before he shipped out for the war, Dad married his childhood sweetheart, my mother, the former Wanda Jean Graves. The *Daily Oklahoman* noted they were married in Hollywood, California (near my dad's training base), amid "baskets of Gladioli, Easter lilies and snapdragons."[5] Mom did her part in the war assembling "recognition models" for the US Navy Bureau of Aeronautics. These were scale model aircraft used to teach our troops how to identify enemy planes and not shoot down our own.[6] My big brother, John, was born shortly after the war. He was the smart one. John got in on the early days of information technology long before anyone called it "IT."

We always had a roof over our heads, cars in the driveway and plenty of food on the table. But much more than that was a reach. I learned something early in life that appeared to be magic. I could buy things simply by having a job. By the age of ten, I was selling garden seeds door-to-door in the spring, and Christmas cards in the fall. I lugged flyers to miles and miles of mailboxes announcing L & H Pharmacy's weekly specials. In middle school, I swept and mopped the local 7-Eleven store after closing. This was back when they were actually open from 7 a.m. to 11 p.m. The manager paid me twenty-five cents a night. When I told my mother about my recently acquired custodial position, she pretended to be proud. In truth, she was furious. She marched down to the convenience store and excoriated the manager. The next day, I got fifty cents. I ran through the door of our home yelling, "Mother! I got a *raise!*" I was thirty years old before she confessed to exactly *how* I got that raise. I learned that a kid could add up a pretty good income if he could just string together enough jobs. Magic.

As a boy in the 1960s, almost by definition, I dreamed of being an astronaut. I studied every spacecraft and every orbiting hero. We were going to the moon. *We* were going to the moon! I wrote NASA monthly and the space agency obliged with 8x10 color pictures of my heroes, who flew immediately to my bedroom wall. Then, about the age of thirteen, an insidious thing happened. My uncle, a wedding photographer in Dallas, gave me one of his used 35mm single lens reflex cameras. "That one's yours," he said. The Japanese Minolta was the most complex, elegant and expensive wonder I'd ever held in my hands. I set up a darkroom in a closet and fished for black-and-white images swimming in a tray of acrid Kodak Dektol developer. My orbiting heroes were replaced by a constellation of stars whose medium was light: Ansel Adams, Alfred Stieglitz, Margaret Bourke-White, Henri Cartier-Bresson and Gordon Parks. I peddled to the library, camera around my shoulder, to marvel at their work. Then, I'd shoot—anything and everything—searching for composition I could call my own.

The only place for a photographer at Coronado High School was in journalism class. In the "publications" classroom I found the captain who set my course. Marjorie Wilson was *on fire* to teach. In her journalism class there was no higher purpose, no greater thrill, than to gather the news and report to the public. Tall, slender, with bright eyes and raven hair, Mrs. Wilson was one of those teachers who reveals the world. Her enthusiasm was intoxicating, her patience, inexhaustible.

It was through Mrs. Wilson that I heard about a night job paying well in excess of fifty cents. The *Lubbock Avalanche-Journal*, the city's 90,000 daily newspaper, hired sixteen-year-olds to work as copyboys (gender insensitive, I know, but that was the title). The shift was perfect for a high schooler—3:00 p.m. to midnight. This would get me within a newsroom's length of the paper's photo lab, which could be my step to a career in photography. The only obstacle was temporal. I was fifteen years old. A career in search of truth began with a lie. I fibbed about my age. Each day, my co-conspirator, Mom, dropped me off a couple of blocks from the newsroom so no one could see I wasn't old enough for a driver's license.

The newsroom was the most exciting place I'd ever seen: an open floor of demanding phones, clattering typewriters and reporters whose cigarettes were as short as their deadlines. Overseeing it all, like the wheelhouse on a ship, was an elevated horseshoe desk called the "Rim." Five editors manned the wheelhouse and reporters supplicated to the Rim for the evisceration of their work. All the news in the world came into the *Avalanche-Journal* to be written, edited, cast in molten lead, printed in the furious blur of a high-speed web press and disseminated as far away as Muleshoe. Breathtaking.

Behind the Rim was a smoking, clanging wonder called the composing room. Rows of Linotype machines hulked on the composing room floor—each looking something like a pipe organ—and played by an operator wearing a paper hat he had folded out of newsprint. The Linotype, a massive contraption of spinning wheels, rotating belts and robotic arms, was designed in 1884. From the looks of the machines at the *A-J*, not a great deal had changed. To walk into the composing room was to be nearly struck down by heat and acrid fumes of molten lead. Old men's hands flew among ninety destinations on the Linotype keyboard. The clatter was like one hundred roller coasters clanking up the incline before the precipice. The Linotype assembled molds for letterforms, poured hot lead into the mold and kicked out an entire line of type. Hence the name. These lines of copy were stacked and bound in a frame called a galley. When complete, the galley held a single page of the newspaper, cast in metal. When ink came between galley and newsprint in the press, the day's news was unveiled. By the time I went to work for the *Avalanche-Journal* in 1972, many big city newspapers were switching to "cold type," a soulless digital process as frigid and devoid of passion as its name implied. In the Linotype, there was romance.

The newspaper's name seemed odd in a city on a tabletop mesa where there was no risk of anything rolling downhill. But the *A-J* was supposed to be "an avalanche of news" on your doorstep. The news began in the copyboy's wireroom, a glass-walled compartment inhabited by black, oily, complaining teletype machines. Like a player piano, the teletype keys flew as if struck by a ghost, crashing into a black ink ribbon and printing stories on a continuous roll of yellow paper. With fifteen teletypes running at once, the wireroom was hot, reeked of oil and assaulted the ear like a jackhammer. The machines were connected to the worldwide organizations of the Associated Press and United Press International. Each teletype told a different story. There was a weather machine, a Texas sports machine, a national sports machine, a machine for politics in Austin, another for politics in Washington, DC, and so on. My job was to keep the beasts fueled with ribbons and paper like shoveling coal into a furnace. From time to time, the roar was interrupted by a bell that defined the importance of the news flowing through the wire. A single "ding" would hardly register my notice. That was an "urgent," moderately important. Three dings would interrupt my high school homework. That was a "bulletin," a truly significant event. But ten dings would send me bolting to the teletype. After the tenth ring faded, the machine stopped, then five keys ominously slapped the letters *F-L-A-S-H*. A "flash" was extremely rare, once or twice a year. They announced the greatest events with such urgency that time for only two words could be spared. I have kept a few paper scraps from the days of the teletype. My collection of flashes includes "NIXON RE-SIGNS" and "SAIGON FALLS."

I was plotting a career path from the wireroom to the dark-room when, about a year into the job, my scheme was thwarted. One night, I was poring over homework in the wireroom when executive editor Dave Knapp shoved open the door. Knapp was a white-shirted, barrel-chested man under a silver crew cut. If he had not in fact been a marine, he could have been cast as one. "Do you want to be a reporter?" he demanded. The real answer was no; I wanted to be a photographer.

I said, "Well, I don't know. I haven't given it any thought."

"Well, *DO* you, or *DON'T* you?" Knapp demanded, his impatience surging to drill sergeant pique.

"Well, sure, I *guess*," I said, indifferently.

Knapp led me out of the wireroom and sat me down in front of a typewriter which I had no idea how to operate. I was six-teen years old. I have been a reporter ever since. I believe Dave Knapp saw my promotion as "giving a kid a chance." Some of my colleagues, as I would discover later, glanced at me peck-ing at an IBM Selectric typewriter and saw a menacing effort to hold down wages.

Like many green reporters, I was assigned to obituaries—"obits" we call them. This was phone work, ringing the fu-neral home and checking facts with the family. The format was standard and each was only 250 words or so. After interring dozens of denizens of Lubbock, I began picking up a few field assignments. I was dispatched to Dimmitt, Texas, to write about the fire truck that had defended the town since 1943. The ar-ticle, on page A-13, was headlined "Old Truck Poses Problem." Above the dateline were the words "By Scott C. Pelley *Lub-bock Avalanche-Journal* Staff." That was my first byline, Monday, December 17, 1973. The closing paragraph noted that the fire chief told me, "A new truck has been urgently 'neded' for the past three years." Apparently, I urgently "neded" copyediting skills. In another feature, I wrote about a farmer who was injured during the cotton harvest. His neighbors came with their strippers and picked his fields before the weather made his fiber "fair to middling." On my way off the farm, I drove the *A-J* staff car into an irrigation ditch. (I hadn't been driving as long as they thought.) One of the farmers piloting a stripper pulled me out. I judged this was something my editors didn't really need to know.

In time, I was entrusted to walk each night to police headquarters, a couple of blocks away, to make the last check of the police blotter. The crime beat in Lubbock was pretty mundane: holdups, car burglaries, usually a bar fight in there somewhere. But one night, shortly before the paper's deadline, a shooting was called into headquarters. A murder! This was the biggest story of my nascent career. I ran back to the newsroom with my notes and shouted the "flash" to the Rim as I settled in behind my typewriter. An editor called out, "Hold 'P-EYE' open!" P-I was newsroom slang for "Page 1." His order was analogous to "stop the presses!" I pounded out the narrative while another editor stood over my typewriter. As I typed the address of the scene of the crime, the editor said with surprise, "Wait! Is the victim *a black*?" He recognized the address in a neighborhood that was largely African American. "Yes," I answered, confused about the intent of the question. "Close P-I!" he bellowed. With disgust, he shot me a look that scolded me for not knowing any better. A dead white man was front-page news but a dead "black" would be cast by the Linotype somewhere in the back galleys. I was furious. The editor had spent his formative years in the South in the 1930s. He remained chained to the bigotry of his geography and time. Today, I can still hear the order "Close P-I!" and I feel the shock. Dr. Martin Luther King Jr. was fond of paraphrasing a quote that originated with a nineteenth-century minister, Theodore Parker. King would say, "The arc of the moral universe is long, but it bends toward justice." Journalism, I discovered, was no farther along the arc than the rest of society. I promised myself to do what I could to move the profession toward justice. I had learned journalism was capable of perpetuating the poison of prejudice. Never again for me. Never. Good lesson at seventeen.

Despite the occasional run-in with editors, I had found my career. I loved the work. I spent the next year making the rounds of police headquarters, obit duty and county commission meetings. One evening, executive editor Dave Knapp called me into his office. As kindly as he could, he fired me. It seemed an obituary I had written was shot full of errors: age, the spelling of the name, address, the most basic facts. The family called to complain and well, that's that. I was crushed and bewildered. How could I make so many mistakes in one obit? Maybe one, maybe, but this many? I went back to the composing room where a closet held all the copy from previous days. When I found my obit (*my* obit in *both* senses), I was perplexed. The page had been cut horizontally into thirds. The top third was the copy I had written. The bottom third was mine too. Scotch Taped in the middle was the section with the errors. No other story, in a pile of hundreds, had been sliced and pasted back together. I had not yet grown into my skepticism. I didn't recognize what I was seeing. Later, it dawned on me. Both the copy and I had been sabotaged. Someone wanted the teenage cub reporter out of the newsroom.

The vast majority of people I knew at the *Avalanche-Journal* were admirable, hardworking professionals consumed with the enormous task of putting out a daily paper. They were more helpful to me than they had time for and kinder than I could expect. The lessons I learned early, lessons in writing and reporting, and, yes, lessons in gratitude, I used every day as managing editor of the *CBS Evening News* and as a correspondent at *60*

Minutes. When we have someone in our newsroom today who can use a mentor, I keep my lucky experience in mind. There were hard lessons at the paper, but those are the most valuable. Dave Knapp launched my career and in firing me, set me on the long course that brought me to CBS.

Because the *A-J* was the only paper in town, a jobless journalist and recent college freshman had no options except the three television network affiliate stations. Too naive to know any better, I decided to have a go. I tormented the news directors at all three stations relentlessly, until one of them relented. Rusty Jones, news director of KSEL-TV Channel 28, the ABC affiliate, hired me in 1975 to shoot and edit film, report stories, produce the ten o'clock news and anchor radio newscasts on the weekend. I was thrown into the deep end of every skill a broadcast journalist needs. There was invaluable informal training as well. I broadcast live hourly news on KSEL radio. From time to time, while I was on the air, the newsroom practical joker would sneak up with a cigarette lighter and set my copy on fire. I had to continue reading, rescue as many words as possible with cold coffee from a Styrofoam cup, reconstruct the newscast with approximately one-fourth of the copy in ashes and still get off the air at the precise, last, second. It was not the joker's intention to sharpen my skills, but if you can read burning copy without changing your inflection and still get off the air on time, you've got a future in this business.

In the mornings, I attended Texas Tech University's journalism school. In the afternoons, I grabbed one of KSEL's Canon 16mm film cameras, shot a story, wrote the story while I processed the film, cut the scenes with a razor blade and stuck the film strips together with tape. Then I wrote the ten o'clock broadcast for the anchorman.

KSEL was the kind of place where professional disasters were grudgingly tolerated as part of the unavoidable learning process. One night, I reserved the entire first section of the broadcast for a single report, which regrettably, was not ready in time. After our big musical intro, I had left the anchor with nothing to say except "We'll be back in a moment." Another night, the weather service warned of a tornado. It was up to me to make the emergency announcement. I ran from the newsroom, down the hallway leading to the control room and charged up the stairs to an open microphone. When I arrived, my breath was still trying to catch up to my body. What followed sounded like hysteria. "Tor—(gasp), tor—(gasp), tor—(gasp)—nado!" For half a minute, I couldn't tell the good people of Lubbock County where the tornado was or where it was headed. Forty years later, when we reacted to a breaking news event, I always ambled slowly to the set of the *CBS Evening News*. Some mistook my gait for lack of urgency. But I know anchors have to *breathe*.

Each night, as I bungled away on copy, the network evening news broadcasts presented themselves on three monitors in the newsroom. John Chancellor (NBC), Harry Reasoner (ABC) and Walter Cronkite, anchoring the *CBS Evening News*, sailed on the air like capital ships of the fleet. Walter's broadcast was, by far, the most watched. Dan Rather, Lesley Stahl and Bob Schieffer were covering Watergate. Bob Simon, Ed Bradley and Richard Threlkeld reported from Vietnam. Bill Plante was dodging attack dogs and tear gas in the Civil Rights Movement. Charles Kuralt's feature writing was the top of the art. Urbane Eric Sevareid, among the original "Murrow Boys" of World War II, weighed in with commentary that made sense of it all. In a little newsroom in a cotton field, I believed I could join them. I simply did not know it was too wild a dream.

In 1976, I was fascinated by a fairly new program on CBS called *60 Minutes*. *"60"* went on the air in 1968, twice a month, as an experiment, featuring correspondents Mike Wallace and Harry Reasoner. What Reasoner described on the first broadcast as "kind of a magazine for television" was little noticed. The CBS News Division president, Dick Salant, had turned down the idea repeatedly before he relented under the badgering of *60 Minutes* creator Don Hewitt.

Hewitt was an irresistible creative force who invented a great deal of what we take for granted today as electronic journalism. He came to CBS News in 1948 and produced the first evening news broadcasts. He was director of *See it Now*, the legendary documentary series anchored by Edward R. Murrow and produced by Fred Friendly. In 1960, Hewitt staged the first televised presidential debate with John Kennedy and Richard Nixon. By the 1970s, Hewitt was looking for something new. He noticed the success of the photo-rich news magazines of the day, including *Life* and *Look*. Why couldn't television produce a magazine that combined serious news with features and celebrity interviews? Virtually no one at CBS News thought this idea had legs. The success of Hewitt's *60 Minutes* was not apparent for its first few years. The broadcast wandered the network schedule like a homeless orphan until it moved to Sunday night in an accident of bureaucratic meddling. To create more diversity in programming, the Federal Communications Commission ordered the networks to turn over the early Sunday evening time slot to their affiliates. The trouble was, the affiliates didn't want to go to the expense of programming the hour themselves.[7] Backtracking, the FCC allowed the networks to take the time back *if* they filled it with family-oriented or public affairs programming. CBS had *60 Minutes* lying around, so, in 1972, they dropped it into the breach. Thus began an American tradition. In 2018, *60 Minutes* celebrated its fiftieth season—the most successful prime-time television program in history.

Back in Lubbock, I noticed in the credits at the end of the broadcast that Hewitt was listed as executive producer. While thoughtfully chewing a slice at a Pizza Hut, I wrote Hewitt a letter. I don't remember my words, I was nineteen years old, but they were to the effect of, "Gee, Mr. Hewitt, how do you do it?" Each afternoon, I looked into the mouth of the mailbox searching for Hewitt's reply. One day, sure enough, the letters *CBS* were prominent on a buff-colored envelope. I tore it open to reveal a card which read, "Dear viewer, your letter has been received. A reply will be forthcoming." More than thirty years later, when I presented my first piece in the *60 Minutes* screening room I said, "Don, where the hell's my letter? You never wrote me back!" Apparently, my letter was more memorable to me than it was to Mr. Hewitt. The story I screened that day with Don and his deputy, Phil Scheffler, was about the discovery of mass graves in Iraq and a project to use DNA to identify the victims of Saddam Hussein's atrocities. The story appeared the next Sunday night. After the broadcast, our home phone rang. My then eight-year-old daughter grabbed the receiver. She slowly wandered in from another room saying to no one in particular, "Someone named Don Hewitt is on the phone?" Don's message was brief but he said it all: "Kid, it doesn't get any better than that." No sir, Mr. Hewitt, for a kid from West Texas, it certainly does not.

It wasn't long before an international tornado appeared on Lubbock's remote horizon. The Crown Prince of Iran, Reza Pahlavi, was living in Lubbock of all places, while learning to fly fighter jets at Reese Air Force Base. Reese was the school where US Air Force pilots grabbed the stick of a supersonic trainer, the T-38. My childhood was accustomed to sonic booms that swayed the doors in our home. In 1978, the son of the Shah of Iran was eighteen years old. His home in Lubbock attracted Iranian immigrant protesters from around the United States. "Stop training another fascist! *Down* with the Shah!" they chanted as they marched a circle in front of his house. The prince would learn to get comfortable in a T-38 ejection seat, but never in Iran's Peacock Throne. His father was ejected in 1979 by the Shiite Muslim theocracy of Ayatollah Ruhollah Khomeini.

My local brush with world events added a gloss to my limited experience, which was noticed by KXAS-TV, the NBC station in Dallas/Fort Worth. In my junior year at Texas Tech, KXAS offered me a job as a reporter. Leaving college without a degree was never in my plan, but this offer was akin to a college player being recruited by the pros. Lubbock was the 137th television market—Dallas/Fort Worth was number 10. I knew plenty of graduates who were going door-to-door, degree in hand, looking for work. At the age of twenty-one, I took the job. This turned out to be the best decision I ever made, not because of my career, but because I met the love of my life. Jane Boone, of Mooreland, Oklahoma, was an intern at KXAS while studying journalism at Southern Methodist University. I was producing a series of reports on arson investigations when I was told to "see the girl in the graphics department" about an animation I was thinking about. I remember the moment like it was twenty minutes ago. Her beauty triggered a pause in the rhythm of my heart. But her intellect and sexy self-confidence made "love at first sight" real. No one has been blessed with a stronger, more loving partner. In 1983, Jane and I were married in Dallas. By then, Jane was a successful news correspondent. With our busy careers, it was nine years before we started a family. Our son, Reece, was born in 1992. Nearly three years later, Jane called to tell me a prenatal test revealed she was carrying a girl. I was thrilled. I'd been secretly hoping for a girl but the odds seemed long given that my only sibling was my brother and Jane was the lone girl among five brothers. Our daughter, Blair, was born in 1995. Eventually our family followed the stages of my career: ten years in Northern Virginia after I became chief White House correspondent, eleven years in Connecticut as I transitioned to *60 Minutes* and the *CBS Evening News*. Now, Reece and Blair have embarked on their own careers. Jane and I are traveling the world from our ranch in Texas.

A reporter's life comes with too many nights away from family. When Reece was about five years old, we were out for a walk in our neighborhood. An airliner rumbled overhead. "Dad," my son advised, "next time you go on a trip, take a rope."

"A rope, buddy? Now, what would I want with a rope?" I asked.

"That way, when the plane flies over our house, you can throw out the rope and climb down."

Our family has enjoyed the great privilege of exploring the world together. I am the luckiest man you will ever meet. But all of us who travel for a living know the enduring ache of missed moments—the ones we know were there but did not see.

After several years at KXAS, I badgered my way into one of the nation's best local news operations, WFAA-TV, the ABC affiliate in Dallas/Fort Worth. I met with WFAA's legendary news director, Marty Haag. After that meeting, he was convinced that he didn't want me but I never let up. I called his office and sent him letters for more than a year. It almost seemed that his secretary's principal job was to make sure I never got through to Mr. Haag. One day, the secretary, Sydney Benton, stepped away from her desk. "Marty Haag's office," Marty Haag said. "Hello, Mr. Haag, it's Scott Pelley again." Haag was steamed. After I asked about openings, he said gruffly, "Yeah. I got a job open, eight hours *a week* on Saturday. You want *that*?"

"I'll take it, Mr. Haag," I replied. One day a week wouldn't pay the bills, but I had a plan. Most reporters at WFAA were writing one or two stories a day. I came to work each Monday and had all week to work on my Saturday piece. Assignments Editor Bert Shipp helped me find an empty desk and slipped me a spare cameraman when they weren't too busy. I wasn't getting paid for the other five days but given the lavish amount of time I spent producing them, my stories were terrific. After a few weeks of this, Haag put me on full-time. So began eight years at WFAA where I had the privilege of covering major events including the Space Shuttle *Challenger* disaster. I produced documentaries including an early broadcast in 1987 that sorted fact from fiction in the HIV/AIDS epidemic. My time under Marty Haag was a master's degree in journalism, but my ultimate goal was to work at CBS News, the shop of my heroes.

As excellent as WFAA was, attempting the leap to CBS was like moving from Division 1 college ball to the NFL. It was a wholly different competitive level. CBS News noticed stories I had done with Guatemalan refugees in the jungles of Southern Mexico. The network's director of recruitment invited me to New York. I bought a fresh tie and borrowed money from Jane—my fiancée at the time—to buy a new briefcase. I was headed to Manhattan to collect my reward.

The CBS Broadcast Center sprawls down one side of Midtown's 57th Street from 10th to 11th Avenue. The monotonous red-brick low-rise building was the Sheffield Farms Dairy in the 1940s and '50s. I spent two days in the Broadcast Center meeting the president of the division, the vice presidents, the national editor, the executive producer of the *CBS Evening News with Dan Rather*, and Dan Rather himself. During an *Evening News* editorial meeting, Executive Producer Lane Vernardos snapped up a ringing phone. He listened for a moment and looked at the senior producers and editors. "Someone says there's a bomb in the newsroom, anyone want to leave?" I was considering raising my hand when I noticed everyone else was stone-faced, silently communicating they weren't going anywhere. "Good," Vernardos said, dropping the phone in its cradle. *Tough crowd*, I thought. But I didn't know the half of it.

I went back to Dallas after what I considered to be two days of very successful meetings and I never heard a word. Nothing. They decided I wasn't ready and did not bother to let me know. My heroes at CBS didn't want me, so, by God, I was going to *make them* want me. A year later, I wrangled another invitation to the Broadcast Center and ran the same gauntlet of meetings. The director of recruitment said, "Damn it, Scott! If you were black or Hispanic, I'd have a job for you right now!"

I was surprised he said that out loud, but I didn't mind. CBS is a leader in diversity and I believe in affirmative action. If I had to sit out a round or two to bend the arc toward justice, I was fine with that. In fact, it reassured me that CBS enforced values I believed in. Another year passed. In 1988, I heard CBS was looking for three new correspondents. I called the new director of recruitment. "Scott," he said, "we know your work and there's no need for you to apply." I didn't give the sting a chance to settle in.

"Have you filled those jobs?" I asked.

"No," he said, "why?"

"I'm coming to see you," I replied. "I'll come on my own dime. I'm just asking for ten minutes of your time."

I drove straight to the Dallas/Fort Worth airport and flew to LaGuardia. The recruitment director was kind enough to see me for a half hour. In the Tom Hanks, Hollywood version of this movie, I get the job. But it didn't happen this time either. Another year later, 1989, Jane and I were returning to Dallas from a second honeymoon in Acapulco. This was before cell phones, when answering machines recorded messages on reel-to-reel magnetic tape. We heaved our bags through the door, late on a Sunday night, lightly sunburned and deeply exhausted. I noticed that the tape in the answering machine had run out. I rewound the messages and moved the clunky mechanical lever to Play. *Beeeeep*, "CBS calling for Scott Pelley, we have a reporter's job open and wonder whether you're still interested. Please call us as soon as you can." Then the next message, *Beeeeep*, "CBS calling for Scott Pelley. Please call us back, it's urgent." And the next, *Beeeeep*, "CBS calling, if you're not interested in the job, give us a call—we need to fill it this week." My hopes ran out with the diminishing tape. The next morning, I called New York. "Can you see us today?" the recruitment director asked. I dropped everything and drove straight to the airport. CBS hired me that same day. I was an overnight success, after five years of trying.

I wanted to take my career as far as it would go, but I never imagined I could be a correspondent for *60 Minutes* or the anchor and managing editor of the *CBS Evening News*.

In my first twenty-two years at CBS News, I was always a field correspondent. My home bureau was Dallas, but I covered every hurricane on the East Coast, every earthquake on the West Coast and most major stories in between. I became chief White House correspondent in 1997. Two years later, I joined *60 Minutes II* and, later, *60 Minutes*. In 2009, I was asked whether I was interested in becoming the anchor of the *CBS Evening News*. The thought of leaving the field didn't appeal to me. The next year, I was asked again. Finally, in 2011, I was asked a third time and I agreed. The broadcast had fallen on hard times. Viewership had dropped to historic lows. It seemed an interesting opportunity to steer the *Evening News* toward serious coverage of the day's most important stories and quality investigative journalism.

The single best decision I made at the *Evening News* was bringing in the first woman executive producer in the storied history of the broadcast. Patricia Shevlin was a CBS News "lifer" who had been a producer and executive producer for more than thirty years. In the crowning achievement of her career, she turned our broadcast into America's fastest-growing evening news—setting records that hadn't been seen in decades.

In my early days at the *Evening News*, I made one addition to the set. Discreetly beside the desk, I added small, black-and-white photographs representing the seventeen men and women who had given their lives in the line of duty for CBS News. The first was correspondent George Polk, who was killed covering the Greek Civil War in 1948. Among the most recent were my long-time friend, cameraman Paul Douglas, and soundman James Brolan, who died in a bombing in Baghdad in 2006. These men and women died defending the people's right to know. I wanted to be sure they were honored and remembered by everyone in our newsroom. You'll find their names at the end of this book.

Not long after I started anchoring the *Evening News*, I sat down with Vice President Joe Biden for an interview. Biden had been watching our broadcast. "I see what you guys are trying to do!" Biden said with a broad grin.

"What's that, Mr. Vice President?"

"You're trying to put real news back on television. Well," he said with a cackle, "we'll see if there's a market for *that!*" As it turned out, Mr. Vice President, there was.

A few months before Pat and I began, the *CBS Evening News* audience had fallen to an all-time low of 4.89 million viewers.[8] Pat stopped the decline and grew our viewership to more than 7.5 million.[9][10] Pat's achievement represented the largest audience for the *CBS Evening News* in ten years and the longest period of growth at the broadcast in thirty years. Her astonishing ratings success was matched by the quality of her journalism. Under Pat, the broadcast won all of the industry's most prestigious awards, including the Peabody, the duPont-Columbia and numerous Emmy Awards. With Pat at the helm we covered the news aggressively, originating the broadcast across America and around the world. Pat dispatched me to the Middle East, Europe, Africa and Afghanistan plus nearly every primary and caucus in the 2012 presidential election.

The *CBS Evening News with Scott Pelley* entered its sixth consecutive season of growth when Steve Capus succeeded Pat as executive producer.[11][12][13] By that time, the audience had grown 23 percent, which was more than double our two major competitors combined. Capus, who had previously been president of NBC News, charged headlong into every story. When we got word that Barack Obama was about to make a surprise announcement—normalizing relations with Cuba—Steve put me on a private jet to Havana *without obtaining permission to land.* He figured, by the time I got there, he would have worked out that small detail. He did. The day of the president's historic announcement, we were the only evening news broadcast to originate from the Cuban capital.

When I took the managing editor's job, CBS installed signage around our studio that read CBS Evening News with Scott Pelley. I had the signs removed and rewritten to reflect a larger truth. The signs in Studio 47 were revised to CBS Evening News with All of Us. Likewise, I never closed the broadcast with my name. I signed off with, "For all of us at CBS News, all around the world, good night."

I receive too much credit for the work of others. I have never won an award nor broadcast any story for that matter without photographers, sound engineers, editors and producers. Hundreds of men and women of CBS News have supported me with physical courage, astounding talent and exhausting hard work. Their sacrifice is humbling. I am also indebted to those who taught me harsh but valuable lessons: the prankster in the radio studio, the racist editor, the saboteur of my obit.

The people in my life have been stakes guiding my progress on the plains of my career. They marked the path that I was seeking and led me home when I was lost. When each of us looks over his or her shoulder we see our trails diverge, but they are all marked in the same way—by those who taught, counseled and opened opportunity.

To all of you at CBS News, all around the world, please know I am forever...

Grateful.

FIELD NOTE

Do You Believe in Signs?

Waiting for the introduction of the new pope left me bored *and* excited. Bored because the wait in the Eternal City seemed to be taking an eternity, and excited because he might be revealed any second. There was no way to tell when the moment would come. At least, I didn't believe there was until the seagull landed.

It was chilly and damp on the roof of the convent overlooking St. Peter's Square in Rome. In March 2013, we built a set among the nuns for the *CBS Evening News*. I was anchoring our coverage of the election of a new pope after the astonishing resignation of Pope Benedict XVI, the first pope to retire in nine hundred years. I was supposed to be on a family vacation to Easter Island. As often, the family went without me. "Nine hundred years and they pick *this* week," I muttered to myself. Our set had a high, commanding view of St. Peter's Square, St.

Peter's Basilica, the Sistine Chapel—the entire Holy See (which derives from the Latin *Sancta Sedes* or "Holy Seat").

The College of Cardinals flew in from around the world to roost in the Sistine Chapel where they would ask God's guidance in their vote. The Catholic world was waiting for the traditional white smoke from the chapel's metal stovepipe that would signal success. The first day, March 12, was filled mostly with ceremony, prayer and oaths sworn by the 115 cardinal electors in attendance. Late in the day, inside the chapel, the Papal Master of Ceremonies called, *"Extra omnes!"* or "Everybody out!" The electors were sealed in, watched over by God himself at the center of Michelangelo's masterpiece ceiling. There was time that first day for only one ballot. Black smoke rose from the chimney indicating that no cardinal received the required two-thirds vote to become pope. The second day, two rounds of votes in the morning were inconclusive. All I could do, sitting in the drizzle, was prepare. I read over my notes on the three dozen most-likely candidates. An associate producer handed me a sheaf of legal-sized papers. Each page listed five candidates and a short biography so I would have something to say immediately when the pope's name was pronounced in Latin, from the balcony of St. Peter's Basilica. "I'm really sorry," the young man apologized, handing me the notes. "We couldn't get these in alphabetical order. They're completely random." I looked at the pages, numbered one through seven with five cardinals per page. I thanked the associate producer, praised his effort and thought, "I'll never find the right guy listed randomly in all these pages while we're on the air."

Early that evening, I noticed one of Rome's recently ubiquitous seagulls gliding in from the low, gray sky. He (or she?) came to perch on top of the Sistine Chapel chimney, which had been so stingy with history. I asked one of our cameramen to tape a close-up of the roosting gull. This passed for amusement at the time. It was after 6:00 p.m. The sun had long crossed the Tiber

River and was settling into the Seven Hills. The rotund bird, white with dove gray wings, gripped the edge of the pipe with yellow talons and remained for the longest time. As the shadows climbed up Bramante's basilica dome, the damp chill fell to forty-three degrees. After dark, just on the far side of seven o'clock, the bird heaved its wings and jumped off the chimney. Seconds later, I saw why the bird bailed. It must have gotten hot up there. At 7:06 p.m. local time, the pipe exhaled white smoke. We flashed onto the CBS network with a Special Report. In short order it was announced the new pope was Jorge Bergoglio, formerly Archbishop of Buenos Aires, Argentina. He became the first pontiff from the Americas. He selected the pontifical name of Francis, after St. Francis of Assisi.

It didn't hit me at the moment, but about four hours later, when I was working with Chief Editor Jerry Cipriano on the copy for the *CBS Evening News*, I blurted out, "The bird!" Jerry looked up in surprise. "What bird?" he asked.

St. Francis is the patron saint of animals and the environment. He is nearly always depicted in paintings and sculpture with a bird in his hand. I was amused and metaphysically intrigued, so I wrote an essay for the end of the broadcast featuring the images of the gull on the stovepipe:

> Finally, tonight, if you believe in signs, you might have guessed the name of the new pope before the smoke rose from the Sistine Chapel. When this bird landed, we joked that it was a gull from the Holy See, "Holy See-gull," but if we'd only been more thoughtful, we might have imagined Saint Francis. Saint Francis—nearly always pictured with a bird in hand—is the twelfth-century founder of the Friars, known as the Franciscans, who celebrated poverty and nature. His name was the answer to the first question asked of Cardinal Bergoglio the instant he became pope, 'By what name will you be called?' When Pope Francis ap-

peared to the world, he was wearing not the gold, jeweled, papal cross but a simple wooden cross of his own. It will be lighter as he bears the heavy cross of a church struggling to find its way into a third millennium, a new pope, from the New World, for a new age.

After the *Evening News*, the TV lights went out and cold cups of coffee vaulted into trash cans. Our set on the roof was a muddle of soggy old notes and research papers. As I started cleaning up, I noticed the hopeless jumble of papal candidates that the well-meaning associate producer had handed me hours earlier. Among the three dozen cardinals, scrambled in nonalphabetical order across seven pages, I noticed Jorge Bergoglio of Argentina listed first—at the top of page one. Quite a coincidence. Unless you believe in signs.

CHAPTER NINE

Duty

Lessons in War

"Enjoy your stay. Don't stay too long."
    I glanced over my shoulder at the parting words of Sir Harold Walker, expecting to see an ironic smile. He looked back coldly, inviting me to read between his lines. It was mid-January 1991. War was imminent. CBS News producer Peter Bluff and I had been visiting with the British ambassador to Iraq in his colonial-era Baghdad embassy. Over tea and an immense bowl of dates, the ambassador served not one morsel of information on when the allied bombing of Baghdad would begin. After our goodbyes, he delivered his warning. That's when I knew we were counting hours, not days. Saddam Hussein had invaded neighboring Kuwait the previous August. The United States spent five months assembling a five-hundred-thousand-

man coalition army in Saudi Arabia. In the phrase of the ambassador's kinsman, Shakespeare: "The bow was bent and drawn."[1]

Over the next few weeks I would learn the meaning of duty. The American people send their sons, daughters as well as treasure into combat. The only independent source of information, the check on a government that is advocating war, is the reporter and photographer on the front line. During what came to be known as Operation Desert Storm, I would learn about the physical risks. But more important, I would come to understand the risk to democracy when the government stands in the way of honest reporting.

In 1991, as a young correspondent, I was guided through Baghdad by "Bluffie" as Peter Bluff was universally known. He was a proper Englishman, fifty-something, and among the best journalists CBS News had ever had the pleasure to base in its storied London bureau. Bluff had gray in his hair and mischief in his eyes. When he called me "dear boy" or "old bean," somehow it didn't sound as archaic as it reads on this page. On his British passport under "profession," it read "Gentleman." Bluff was as experienced in the region and in human fallibility as they come. He taught me the best way to disarm a gunman is to extend your hand, smile broadly and bellow a loud *"Helloooo, my friend!"* Believe it or not, that salutation has gotten me out of more than a few tight spots in the years since. On a mission to purchase a rug in Baghdad's nine-hundred-year-old souk, I watched Bluff reject a dozen beautiful new carpets until the merchant pulled out an old runner that was worn, tattered and fading. "Yes!" Bluff shouted. I looked at his choice with a harsh critique. He explained, "This rug has history! Imagine all the children who have run on it, the family who lived with it!" Bluff taught a young reporter the difference between looking and *seeing*—seeing the richness of humanity. He also taught me how to survive the tensions of working for CBS News. "Never ask New York what to do," Bluff said about our masters at headquarters. "You tell *them* what they are going to get. *We* know the story, not them." One night, I was sweating blood on a frightening deadline and couldn't move my mind beyond a blinking cursor. Bluff said, "You know what we should do?" I glanced up hopefully. "What?"

"Have tea!"

We did. And after the short break, the script flowed like Darjeeling.

We were joined in Baghdad by our crew—cameramen Massimo Mariani and Nick della Casa, and video editor Joyce Michaels. Our "bureau" was room 505 in the al-Rasheed Hotel near the Tigris River. The previous CBS News team had planted a plastic Christmas tree with a CBS logo on top. A pathetic single strand of colored lights was reflected in too many whiskey bottles. Bluff and I toned down the drinking in the bureau, a bit. The earlier producer and correspondent were pros. They had filled an entire bathtub with ice and beer. Impressive. The provisions had to be admired in a city where both malt beverages and the means to chill them were in short supply. Our meals in prewar Baghdad were the same every evening—scrawny whole roasted chickens in greasy paper bags. We bought them from a vendor on the street. As war drew closer, the birds grew thinner.

Saddam Hussein controlled our movements with escorts assigned to show us where we could and could not go. The dictatorship also held the keys to the only satellite uplink in Baghdad. This was nearly two decades before iPhones and apps like Periscope. Each evening, Bluff and I would bring our videotaped stories to the uplink where an Iraqi woman who looked like a 1950s high school librarian would feed our story to New York. She did not speak any discernable English but she was the government's ultimate censor. She edited by gut rather than comprehension. The control panel of her transmitter looked like an old-fashioned switchboard with fabric-covered cables plugged into innumerable slots. She swayed in her ankle-length cotton dress as the story rolled, never taking her eyes off the small monitor that framed the video. Anytime she was suspicious of what she saw, often when Saddam's picture popped up, she pulled the cable on the fly and cut off the transmission. The story would continue to roll in the tape machine and when she became more comfortable with the pictures, she plugged back in. So it went on every story—plug in, plug out, plug in, plug out. Our pieces arrived in New York in—pieces. Once we figured out which parts were "unplugged," we drove to the US Embassy, which was not under Saddam's control, and used the phone to call in the missing narrations to the *Evening News*. These were the closing days of the telegram and telex. One night, Bluff and I received this: "Telex from CBS News, New York. To CBS News, US Embassy Baghdad. Nice going. You led the show. Happy New Year."

With the start of 1991, there were only days before the allied bombardment began. Cameraman Nick della Casa and I sat in the parking lot of the US Embassy staking out its eventual evacuation. Della Casa was another Englishman. He was thirty-one, a former soldier, "Lawrence of Arabia" dashing and armed with a lethal smile. Nick and I had dropped by a local shop and bought a bag of two dozen meat pies. Each plump lump of dough was about the size of a golf ball, filled with the ground remains of an unidentified but acceptable mammal. An embassy guard, an Iraqi Kurd, watched intently as Nick and I finished off the bag. The guard ambled over to us. "You know," he said in fluent English, "you really *must* cook those first."

After a couple of days, the embassy staff walked out to a motorcade. I noticed the American diplomat in charge seemed to be lurching. He just caught himself from falling by leaning into the side of his car. I learned that the diplomat had sacrificed his own body to prevent the embassy's wine collection from falling into enemy hands. Patriotism knows many forms.

Nick was one of those cameramen who was in it for adventure. He had once been captured by RENAMO rebels in Mozambique and held as a prisoner for more than a year. After his release, Nick *returned* to the rebel group to shoot a documentary about them. Courage was packed with his gear. He met hardships and danger with unshakable good humor. Nick was the first colleague and friend that I lost in a war. After the US invasion to liberate Kuwait, he was shot to death in Northern Iraq while covering the Kurdish refugee crisis. Nick was a good colleague and a good man. His photograph was among those I later placed on the set of the *CBS Evening News*.

Shortly after the embassy evacuation, CBS News sent Bluff and me back to Dhahran, Saudi Arabia, where I had spent the previous four months in our main Gulf War bureau. "Sorry CBS go," Hoashoba, one of our drivers, told me. I was sorry too. The Iraqis were among the friendliest, most hospitable people I had met. When I introduced myself they would shout, "Welcome America! Welcome!" As I was leaving the embassy for the last time, an older Iraqi man who manned the reception desk asked me, "There is no hope?" I told him war was coming and soon. His already fragile faith in a better future snapped. "They are the biggest liars in the world!" he said with sudden rage. "They [Saddam and his Ba'ath Party] kill many people. I am Kurdish and they kill many Kurds. I *hope* the war comes so we can be rid of Saddam, we hate him!"

Dhahran, Saudi Arabia, lies along the Persian Gulf, a city of four million people with one reason to exist. In 1936, an American swaddled in Arab robes and a generous beard carried a hammer into this wasteland. Max Steineke broke rocks for a living, as he'd been trained to do at Stanford University.[2] He saw the world not as it is, but as it was, fifty million years before, when the escarpments of the Arabian Peninsula lay under a prehistoric sea.[3] For two years, Steineke weathered under the Saudi sun, drilling holes that ended in cave-ins and breakdowns. His bosses at Standard Oil of California insisted he stop wasting the company's time and money. But Steineke begged for one last chance. In 1938, Steineke was cajoling a crew of roughnecks to spin a rock bit deeper and deeper into a geologic formation called the Damman Dome.[4] Steineke's Damman Well No. 7 chewed down 4,742 feet into Eocene time which suddenly erupted into the present.[5] Lucky No. 7 filled the modern world with wealth, envy and treachery. Fifty-two years later, the stakes were not lost on Texas oilman George H. W. Bush nor on Saddam Hussein.

Dhahran was the Saudi kingdom's "Houston," three hundred miles down the coast from Iraqi-held Kuwait. In August 1990, we set up the bureau in a ballroom of the Dhahran International Hotel. Above double doors, a black bumper sticker staked our claim with CBS NEWS in white letters. Maps of the Gulf were taped to the walls' wood veneer. Long rows of tables were littered with hardline phones, portable computers, printers and moldy cups of coffee. Our Saudi bureau represented a passing of the pen to a new generation of CBS News war correspondents. About half the bureau staff were reporters and cameramen who had covered Vietnam. The rest of us, including myself, were young journalists who would have 9/11, Afghanistan and a second invasion of Iraq in our futures.

Totalitarian Saudi Arabia was anathema to a reporter, but useful to the US Department of Defense. In those days, the US Army in particular shunned reporters and censored our work by requiring us to travel with escorts—just like Saddam. We spent our days in a cat and mouse game—slipping out without escorts. Eventually, a hand-lettered warning went up on the butcher paper notice board, which stood on an easel in the hotel's Pentagon public affairs office.

It has been noted that some media members have been traveling to al-Khafji without any escorts. In order to avoid cancellation of press privileges, you are strongly advised not to travel to al-Khafji, or any other site, without securing an Information Ministry escort. If you have any problem with this directive, please confer with the Saudi Information Bureau.

We did have a problem. Reporters work for their readers and viewers, not for the Pentagon nor the Kingdom of Saudi Arabia. Journalism, with all its virtues and flaws, is a constitutionally mandated part of our American system of checks and balances. The only way to fulfill our duty to the Constitution and the American people was to break the rules and take some risks.

After five months covering the preparation for war in Saudi Arabia and Baghdad, I managed to hitch a ride on a US Navy helicopter to the USS *Missouri*. I was thrilled to be visiting the famous battleship where, on September 2, 1945, the Japanese signed the instruments of surrender in Tokyo Harbor. General Douglas MacArthur closed those proceedings with, "Let us pray that peace be now restored to the world and that God will preserve it always."[6] But for *Missouri* and the world, that prayer went unanswered. She was an old-school, Iowa-class battleship launched in January 1944 to confront the Japanese imperial armada. The enemy could not have been happy to see her. *Missouri* was 888 feet long; her armored hull was thirteen-inches thick. Four screws propelled her to a top speed of thirty-eight miles an hour.[7] On deck swiveled three turrets housing a total of nine 16-inch guns that fired shells the weight of Volkswagens.[8][9] She retired after combat in Korea, but Ronald Reagan recommissioned and modernized "The Mighty Mo" in his buildup of the navy.

As the helicopter approached, the gray dreadnought was steaming in the northern Persian Gulf. I landed on her aft deck at the end of what I thought was another routine day. But before I left her, the morning of January 17, 1991, would become a history-making entry in her logbook. My camera crew and I were shooting routine preparations for war when the PA system crackled to life with the shrill alert of the bosun's whistle. "Now hear this! This is the captain. We should consider that hostilities are imminent. Gentlemen, the bottom line is, the bell is about ready to ring and we need to make sure we are ready to answer it." With those words, we knew Operation Desert Storm was underway. *Missouri* and other warships blasted advanced cruise missiles into the darkness. A few days later, *Missouri*'s gun crews would fire 2,700-pound shells from her 16-inch guns—the first time the guns were heard in battle since 1953.[10] America was at war. I took the helicopter off *Missouri*'s deck and hurried back to Dhahran with the news.

As we went on the air with the *CBS Evening News*, navy and air force jets were swarming Iraq's air defenses. More than one thousand sorties were flown that night.[11] Over the next weeks, Saddam Hussein responded with eighty ballistic missiles trained on Dhahran; the Saudi capital, Riyadh; and Tel Aviv. These were short-range missiles the Iraqi's called the Al-Hussein but were better known by their NATO reporting name, "Scud." Each Iraqi Scud-B lofted a one-thousand-pound high explosive warhead about six hundred fifty miles. The Scuds could also be loaded with chemical weapons.[12] In 1991, the threat of chemical weapons was not academic. Three years before, Saddam's poison arsenal saved him from a much larger force in the Iran/Iraq war. He turned back tens of thousands of Iranian troops by raining mustard gas and nerve gas from jets, helicopters, artillery pieces and mortars.[13] Against this threat, we were issued protective suits called "NBCs," which stood for Nuclear, Biological, Chemical. The whiteboard in the bureau once noted, "Saturday. 0945. Chem Suit Fitting. Be there or be dead." In the event of a confirmed nerve gas attack, the protocol was for the hotel air raid warden to yell "GAS! GAS! GAS!" so we could quickly don our suits. One of the Filipino hotel workers was apparently confused on this point. With *every* air raid siren, he ran through the halls yelling "GAS! GAS! GAS!" After several nights of this, he was silenced. Someone either explained the difference or, perhaps, strangled him.

It was early in Saddam's missile campaign that I learned what duty meant to a war correspondent. During the first attack, the lights went out and the hotel air raid warden came into our office to hurry everyone down to a bomb shelter. In the shelter, I noticed that veteran CBS News correspondent Bob Simon was missing. Concerned for Bob's safety, I left the bomb shelter and went looking for him. I discovered Bob, on the roof of the hotel, with cameraman Tom Rapier. They were live on the network describing the careening, exploding warheads plunging into the city. Bob stood in a wedge of light explaining how it felt to be a resident of Dhahran: watching Patriot antiaircraft missiles bolting into the darkness and enemy warheads shedding sparks as they spiraled aimlessly into neighborhoods. This is what Edward R. Murrow had done on a London rooftop during the Blitz in World War II. Murrow, the legendary founder of CBS News, invented electronic journalism in those harrowing hours under Nazi bombardment. Bob followed the example with the same calm disregard for his own life that Murrow displayed fifty years earlier. *So, that's what it means to be a war correspondent*, I said to myself.

I had seen my first and my last bomb shelter.

Only a few days later, I stepped into Bob's place, reporting missile strikes from the rooftop. It was a terrible injustice to Bob. After waiting for months in Saudi Arabia, our best war correspondent would not be covering the war. This turn of events began January 20, 1991. I knew there was a good deal going on that our Saudi minders did not want the American public to see. I took a camera crew, slipped our escorts, and drove six hours northwest into the desert along the Iraqi border. We hit several military roadblocks and managed to talk ourselves through every one. On the Saudi–Iraqi border, we stumbled onto an exodus of thousands of villagers carrying most of what they owned. The Saudi military was evacuating border communities. Enormous columns of American armor were churning west. These were the final preparations for the invasion. We got out of the car to shoot video of the refugees but for the first time in my career, the cameraman refused to shoulder his camera. He reasoned we would have only one chance at this. Once the Saudi military discovered us, we'd be marched back to Dhahran. He didn't want to waste the opportunity on the rookie correspondent. The cameraman was an old hand who formed a special bond with Bob Simon during their years in Vietnam. The evacuation, the cameraman insisted, should be Bob's story. For context, I was an unknown, "the kid," and nobody owed me anything. Bob Simon, on the other hand, had become CBS's top foreign correspondent after covering Southeast Asia, South Africa and nearly every gunfight in the Middle East. The bonds made among colleagues in wartime are indelible and transcend rationality. My cameraman's refusal was understandable but irresponsible. In my view, our obligation was to the viewers of that night's *Evening News*. We drove back, another six hours. That night, the *CBS Evening News with Dan Rather* planned to lead with my report. I was going to describe what I had seen even though I had no pictures. At 2:30 a.m., local time, I was standing by live to New York listening to the opening theme of the broadcast. Dan Rather began reading the intro to my story when I heard chaos in the studio and shouting in my earpiece. Someone began yelling, "Fight AIDS, not Arabs! Fight AIDS, not Arabs!" Then, there was silence. The HIV/AIDS activist group "Act Up" had rushed into the CBS News Broadcast Center and burst into the studio to protest what they considered to be a lack of coverage of the AIDS crisis. The studio was cleared. The broadcast went back on the air. I had been prepared for an invasion of Iraq, but not an invasion of New York.

From my notes, I painted the picture of what I'd seen. I omitted the types of military units, their location and direction of travel. If a reporter takes on the responsibility of slipping the bonds of military censors he or she must understand when self-censorship is in the interest of national security. I think of myself as an American reporter, emphasis on *American*. The self-censorship was out of an abundance of caution. Certainly, the Iraqis could see for themselves what was happening on their border.

My loyal-to-a-fault cameraman eagerly described the scene to Bob Simon. Bob, sensibly, responsibly, assembled a team to go back to the same place the next day. Who knows? If we had come back with a complete piece that night, maybe there would have been no need for Bob's fateful trip.

I had tea with Bluffie on January 21. On parting, he offered up a "Cheerio" and set out with Bob, cameraman Roberto Alvarez (not my cameraman from the previous day) and soundman Juan Caldera. The day grew long and so did their absence. When Bob missed the 2:30 a.m. deadline for the *CBS Evening News*, we knew there was serious trouble. Bob didn't miss deadlines. We would learn, much later, that Bob's team had run into an Iraqi patrol on the border. He, Bluff, Roberto and Juan were captured and imprisoned for the duration of the war. Bob masterfully recounted more than five weeks of abuse and threats of death in his book, *Forty Days*.[14]

I learned more from Bob Simon than any other colleague. Not because Bob was a patient teacher, he wasn't the type. I learned from Bob by studying his example of courage and artistry. Bob was a hard-shell romantic who loved opera because it captured life's drama, tragedy and irony. He was an extraordinary writer whose precision, wit and use of metaphor brought more truth to a story than mere facts alone. Bob joined *60 Minutes* after his release and became one of its most memorable correspondents in a long career which ended too soon.

Twenty-four years after the Gulf War, I was admiring a story of love and loss on Broadway when a text message silently lit my phone. Can you call? a CBS News executive wrote. Emergency? I replied. There was a long hesitation then the screen lit again, Bob Simon is dead. I left my wife's side and made my way to our nearby studio to make the announcement on the network. After a life of high adventure, Bob was killed on the West Side Highway in Manhattan, riding in the back of a limousine that clipped another car and smashed into a concrete barrier. Bob was seventy-three. It was a hell of a thing for such a courageous, intrepid man to die in such a common way. No one would have appreciated the irony more than Bob.

After Bob's capture, salvos of Al-Hussein missiles increased with Saddam's desperation. We were on the roof of the Dhahran International Hotel every night. First, came the air raid sirens. Then the lights went out all over town. Next, we heard the sharp roar of Patriot antiaircraft missiles groping for their ballistic targets. At my side were my courageous producer John Paxson and cameraman Tom Rapier. "Pax," as we called John, was richly experienced and cool under fire. Rapier was a gifted artist with the camera and, as it happened, we had known each other since we were about twenty years old in Lubbock, Texas. We started at the same television station. Tom eventually worked with me at *60 Minutes*. On the roof, it would have been nice to know about our future longevity.

During one Scud attack, a US Army sergeant came through the rooftop door. "You gotta come in right now! We're expecting nerve gas!" I waved him off and put on my mask. "When this door closes," he shouted, "it's not going to open again!" I told him I understood. The door slammed. The deadbolt struck home. Patriots roared skyward. I watched one make a direct hit on the booster of a Scud, splitting off the warhead. The warhead spiraled down crazily and exploded in a neighborhood nearby.

From time to time the sergeant would reappear in the small square window of the door to see whether we were still alive. We were his canaries in a coal mine. I waved to let him know I was still chirping. My report that night interrupted an NFL play-off game. My wife, Jane, was watching. She spent the remaining quarters taking condolence calls from friends and family.

The imprecise Iraqi warheads fell randomly. The worst descended on February 25, 1991. The warhead found a US military barracks. Twenty-eight soldiers were killed, one hundred were wounded.[15] Thirteen of the dead were national guardsmen from the 14th Quartermaster Detachment from Greensburg, Pennsylvania.[16] They were water purification technicians, killed in their bunks.

That tragedy happened just as the liberation of Kuwait was beginning. February 24 was "G-Day." G for ground campaign. A few days earlier my crew and I had boarded a US Air Force C-130 transport headed west to link up with the Pentagon's "pool" system for combat reporters. We landed on hard-packed sand at an outpost called "Log Base Charlie." "Log," short for logistics. A Colonel Longsworth informed us of the rules for reporters. Stories I wrote would be reviewed by a military censor. We were prohibited from filming any injured American troops. In other words, no filming combat that wasn't going well. Finally, we would not be allowed to use our own equipment to feed stories by satellite from the battlefield. Instead, our work would be driven by military courier to the nearest air base, flown back to Dhahran, delivered to the Pentagon's Joint Information Bureau at the hotel and handed over to our bureaus. The American people would have to wait for independent reporting while the Pentagon told the story it liked to tell at its daily news conference, 450 miles from the battle, in a luxury hotel in Riyadh. In World War II, Korea and Vietnam, reporters had nearly independent access. The Gulf War was a break with American tradition and a breach of the public's right to know. I began to miss Saddam's persnickety matron of the Baghdad satellite up-link. Before a shot was fired, truth took a bullet.

Before I left our Dhahran bureau to join Combat Correspondent Pool #1, I asked our bureau chief, Susan Zirinsky, to hold a letter for my wife, Jane, in case I didn't make it back.

In the western desert, I joined up with the XVIII Airborne Corps. Jim Helling was my cameraman, Warren Arenstein, my soundman. Our military escort was Major Patrick Hermanson, an affable, part-time US Army National Guard officer who, in civilian life, was a hospital administrator back home in Montana. The night before the invasion, an army intelligence officer stopped by the reporters' tent to tell us that an analysis predicted we would be hit with nerve gas two or three times before the invasion force took out Saddam's chemical weapons. "You're going out with the battalions?" a headquarters captain asked me. "I take my hat off to you, I really do." Captain Ted Anderson told me of steaks being sent to his artillery crews. "Maybe it's like the last supper, who knows?" A chemical warfare specialist, who could not have been older than nineteen, helped us make sure our masks were sealing properly. He decided the straps on my mask needed replacement. He told me, "Like, so, like, if this doesn't fit, right? You'll be doing the Funky Chicken, okay?" We were issued one nuclear/biological/chemical suit each. Our specialist told us two was the minimum needed for decontamination and many soldiers had three. About midnight, we struggled into our heavy suits and pulled our gas masks over our faces. The army gave us a reel of two-inch adhesive tape, like duct tape, called M9 Detector Paper. M9 was chemically treated to change color in the presence of agents such as Sarin nerve gas. The intelligence officer explained that a single drop or whiff of Sarin would be lethal. Among the first signs of exposure would be what he memorably described as "explosive diarrhea." We laid a long strip of M9 across the hood of our SUV where we could watch it.

XVIII Airborne Corps was composed of the 101st Airborne Division, the 82nd Airborne Division, Corps Artillery, the 24th Infantry Division and the 3rd Armored Cavalry Regiment. The French 6th Light Armor Division and French Foreign Legion would screen our left flank to the west. This massive force was one of three lines of attack. The XVIII Airborne Corps was the farthest west. It would invade Iraq and turn east to cutoff Kuwait from the north. This prevented enemy reinforcement and retreat. Two more allied forces planned to invade Kuwait from the south. Those forces were the hammer. The XVIII Airborne Corps was the anvil.[17]

Surveying the vista, I thought the southern desert of Iraq was ideal for war. There was no chance of damaging anything other than enemy forces. The sand churning under the invasion was composed primarily of microscopic crystals of quartz—the last mineral that remains after all others have been worn to oblivion by weather and time.[18] Exhausted of life, color and form, the fetch of a desiccated sea receded beyond the horizon.

On G-Day, the desert was cool, forty-three degrees. For once the charcoal-lined confines of our nuclear/biological/chemical suits felt comforting. These were called MOPP suits for Mission Oriented Protection Posture. The orders were for "MOPP Level 4," the peak of incarceration with all protective gear—gas mask, suit, gloves. We were also armed with auto-injecting syringes. When jammed into the thigh, they fired a spring-loaded needle with a dose of Atropine, a nerve gas antidote. The ancient Greeks first refined Atropine from the deadly nightshade plant. The name is derived from the goddess Atropos who, with her shears, severs the cord of life and chooses each mortal's manner of death. The origin of the name did not inspire confidence in the auto-injectors.

The liberation of Kuwait began at 1:00 a.m. when XVIII Airborne Corps artillery opened up with 155mm guns and Multiple Launch Rocket Systems. Darkness was total. Young men fired artillery by memory and touch. A helicopter assault followed the shells and then, at 4:00 a.m., the lead ground elements were released at the Line of Departure.[19] Our path into Iraq was marked on the map as "Main Supply Route Texas," which, as a Texan, I decided to take as a good omen. Just as first light broke across the plain, tired, hungry, demoralized Iraqi troops came at us en masse, waving any white cloth they could find. Survivors were eager to surrender to the comforts of the Geneva Conventions after being mauled by thirty-eight days of air force and navy bombardment plus the terrifying onslaught of the morning's rockets and shells. These men were beyond military age. They had been discarded by Saddam on the frontline to adhere to the US advance. I was reminded of a military parade I had seen in Baghdad. Soldiers on the perimeter were sharp and well equipped. But when I looked through the legs on the flanks of the march, I noticed the men in the center did not have boots. Now on the battlefield, these men in ragtag uniforms were slowing down the invasion force which hadn't anticipated so many prisoners. To corral them efficiently, the POWs were herded into pens made of nothing but razor wire uncoiled in the open desert. I wrote my first story of the invasion about the huge numbers of prisoners. Major Hermanson looked over the script, saw nothing that concerned him and sent the story and our videotape to the rear.

Overhead, the 101st Airborne was executing one of the largest helicopter assaults in history. Sixty Black Hawks and forty Chinook helicopters from the Corps' 18th Aviation Brigade carried the troops of 1st Brigade 110 miles into Iraq. After establishing a Forward Operating Base, the 1st Brigade severed Highway 8, which would be a route for Iraqi reinforcement or retreat.[20] Not a bad day's work.

I joined elements of the 82nd Airborne in support of the French who were tasked with seizing a town marked on the battle map as "Objective WHITE."[21] It turned out to be the village of As Salman, which supported a military airstrip. My camera crew and I were making our way through deserted streets shooting a story about the capture of the airfield. Hermanson, our military escort, wandered several yards away. The next thing I heard was a hysterical US Army major running toward me with his pistol drawn. *"Where's your escort!"* he screamed. The major grabbed my shoulder and shoved me facedown onto the street. He aimed his pistol at my head and flipped his brain to fully automatic. Without hesitating for an answer, he shouted, *"Where's your escort! Where's your escort! Where's your escort!"* Had I been an enemy soldier, I might have been given the courtesy of surrender, but because I was an American armed with a notebook, I had a 9mm bullet anticipating my skull and a face full of asphalt. Hermanson came running and was excoriated by the major for allowing a reporter out of his sight for a second. I don't know what was going through the maniacal major's mind, but he may have been one of several soldiers I met in the Gulf War who'd fallen for the myth that "The Media" lost the war in Vietnam. It is thoroughly documented today that public support for Vietnam fell as American casualties rose.[22][23][24][25] The scholar John Mueller found the loss of support was much the same in Korea, with little TV coverage, as in Vietnam, which became known as "the living room war." In both, Mueller discovered, public opinion dropped about 15 percent for every tenfold increase in casualties. Three factors erode support for war and Vietnam was a combination of all three: lack of threat to the homeland, rising casualties and lengthening duration.[26] Vietnam stretched beyond ten years. The loss of American life climbed to 58,220.[27] Opposition grew not because of what the public saw on the *CBS Evening News with Walter Cronkite*, but because of the graveside services they saw with their own eyes. "The Media" did not con the American people into opposing a war that was going well.

After the major's weapon found its holster again, I quickly wrote a piece on the fall of As Salman. I hoped I'd beaten the deadline for that night's *Evening News*. Hermanson sent the videotapes by military courier. I dug a foxhole to spend the night.

From time to time, we were shelled by enemy 155mm artillery. But the shells were high explosive, not gas. Enemy fire was brief. US Army artillery radar tracked Iraqi incoming shells, calculated their origin and fired retaliatory rockets along the same arc almost before the first enemy rounds landed at our position. Iraqi gunners learned to "shoot and scoot," firing once, then towing their howitzer out from under the American rebuttal. US Air Force A-10 "Warthog" attack jets wheeled and dropped like cormorants on the scattering artillery.

On February 26, the XVIII Airborne Corps had blocked the Euphrates River Valley. The escape route for Saddam's best troops was sealed and so was their fate. A massive jam of enemy trucks and armor was stuck (pardon the phrase) between Iraq and a hard place. In one hundred hours, XVIII Corps covered more than one hundred miles north and seventy-five miles east.

By the time of the ceasefire on February 28, I had sent a half-dozen stories through the military system. I was in a hurry to get to liberated Kuwait City. There were few cell phones or satellite phones in those days so I was completely cut off from the world. But I imagined CBS News must have a satellite uplink in Kuwait City by now. It was nighttime. My team and I decided to try our luck driving over the desert to Kuwait. At the start, we ran into an army officer who told us he was headed to Kuwait as well. The officer boasted, "Land navigation is my hobby." His Humvee led our two SUVs south. After an hour or two speeding through the darkness, we were lost. A short time later, the Humvee crashed into coils of razor wire. This appeared to be Kuwait's northern border, which was intricately pebbled with land mines. Too bad land navigation was the officer's hobby—we needed a pro. After pulling razor wire from the front wheels of his vehicle, we decided to part company and get to Kuwait on our own. In another hour or so, we abandoned one of our SUVs after a rear wheel sheared off its lug bolts. We put all our gear in the "dead" SUV and compressed all our people into the other. Days later, the military declined our request to retrieve our truck telling CBS the area was too heavily mined. We groped in the dark until we intersected the main highway to Kuwait City. Across all four lanes, we found a grotesque military traffic jam. Iraqi vehicles, armor and artillery, were bumper-to-bumper for miles. They had been incinerated. Some were abandoned. Some were manned by the dead. The Iraqi retreat had been bombed and strafed. Our headlights panned cremated drivers and passengers, shoulder to shoulder, sitting upright in burned-out wrecks. Some must have counted themselves lucky to have squeezed into the last seats headed for home. I ran into a US Army medic walking among the wreckage. "Most of the enemy are dead," he told me. "A few are wounded. I don't mind helping them out."

To the east, it appeared the sun was rising but it was much too early. The light came into focus as rapacious spirals of fire, spectacular and horrific. More than six hundred oil wells had erupted into vertical flamethrowers. Each blasted a high-pressure inferno hundreds of feet above the desert. Orange brilliance—as bright and warm as the sun—forced my eyes away but I could not escape the sound—the howl of a conflagration devouring the atmosphere. The physical vibration reminded me of standing too close to fighter jets catapulting from the deck of an aircraft carrier. Saddam couldn't keep Kuwait, so he ordered the destruction of its wealth.[28] His troops dynamited wells and storage tanks across four major oil fields. Five million barrels a day were burning. I was among the first to witness the greatest intentional environmental catastrophe in history.[29]

We arrived in Kuwait City just as the actual sun was rising. A liberation Grand Prix was careening through the streets. Horns, flags and small arms fire filled the air. It was almost dangerous to be an American. We were hunted in the streets and pummeled with bear hugs and kisses. *"Tank you Amerikin! Tank you Amerikin!"* It was August 1944 and this was Paris. There was no electricity or water. The hotels were charred shells. But in one of them I found producer Susan Zirinsky setting up a make-shift CBS News Kuwait bureau. Susan is a legend at CBS News. She is one size too small for petite, but she is the largest presence in any room. Susan has been the producer behind many of our triumphs. She is such a larger than life character that Hollywood made a movie based on her—*Broadcast News*, starring Holly Hunter in the Zirinsky role. "Thank God you're okay," Susan said, returning the sealed envelope containing the letter to my wife. "We haven't heard from you for so long. What happened to you?"

"Haven't heard from me? I've been filing pieces one after another," I replied.

"We didn't get 'em," Zirinsky said.

As more embedded correspondents arrived in the dark hallways of the CBS News bureau, one by one they learned that few of our stories had made it from the hands of the military to the Broadcast Center in New York. Some vanished, some were delayed by days, making them useless to Americans back home. After prohibiting us from transmitting our reports ourselves, the military slow-walked our stories so that there was no possibility that firsthand reporting would conflict with the Pentagon's news conferences from the five-star hotel in Riyadh. The losers were the American people, our troops and the Pentagon itself. For example, I'll bet you've never heard of the Battle of 73 Easting. It may be the largest tank battle ever fought by American troops. In an epic feat of combat arms, The US 2nd Armored Cavalry Regiment wiped out Saddam's best-armored battalions.[30] But because reporters and photographers were not there, the battle named for its map coordinates is little known. (A reporter would have thought of a better name too.) How different Desert Storm was to the eyewitness reporting on D-Day by CBS News correspondents Bill Downs, Larry LeSueur and Charles Collingwood.[31] The Iraq campaign was well designed and deftly executed. It deserved to be seen. The American people had the *right* to see it.

When America goes to war, all of America must go. Wartime is when we need our collective judgment. The way "we all" go to war is through independent reporting. This chapter is entitled "Duty" because, in a democracy, war demands each of us to do his or her part. Reporters have the duty to go to war. The government and military have the duty to support them. The public has a duty to watch the reporting, understand the facts and debate the policy.

The word *democracy* is a mashup of the Greek *demos* and *kratia*, meaning "the people rule." Citizens cannot rule what they cannot see. When reporting is barred from the battlefield, the people no longer rule.

FIELD NOTE

The Last Shuttle

As an American kid in the 1960s, I wanted to be an astronaut. Who didn't? It was an age of heroes and wonder. I remember lying on the hood of my parent's car, gazing at the Texas stars for hours. The night in 1969 that Neil Armstrong carried humanity to the moon, I took pictures of black-and-white history on our TV screen. In my thirties, I made the first cut in NASA's Journalist-in-Space project.[1] And I was at the Kennedy Space Center that January day in 1986, when the manned space program reached its sobering maturity with the loss of *Challenger*, her six astronauts and Teacher-in-Space Christa McAuliffe. Until that morning, no American had ever been killed in spaceflight.[2] Over the next years, I covered the men and women of the space program as they grieved, recovered and returned Americans to orbit.

The *Challenger* tragedy ended the Journalist-in-Space competition and any pretense that the space shuttle was routine. There was nothing ordinary about the most advanced machine ever built. The shuttle was nearly the size of an airliner—its cargo bay as big as a boxcar. It could loft seven astronauts and it flew ten times faster than a rifle bullet.[34] Astounding.

I spent several years covering the space program for CBS News. Usually television makes events look grander than they are. A shuttle launch was the only event in my experience that was diminished by TV. Our equipment automatically limited the peaks of sound and brightness. As I stood in the wetlands of the KSC, the shuttle's main engines howled like a hurricane. The ignition of the twin solid rocket boosters set off a roar you felt in your bones more than your ears—crackling and popping as though the sky itself was fracturing. The flames from the boosters were brighter than the sun. After witnessing more than a dozen slow, majestic launches, I still marveled to myself, "There are *people* in there."

CBS television news and the space program grew up together. In the 1950s and '60s, Walter Cronkite brought the complexities of space down to earth and into our living rooms. Walter's first reports from Cape Canaveral were broadcast from the back of a station wagon. As the manned space program grew, so did our presence at what became the Kennedy Space Center. CBS News built the "Don McGraw" building, a two-story studio with a panoramic view of Launch Complex 39. Don had been our chief engineer for CBS coverage of John Glenn's orbital trip, Apollo 11's landing on the moon and many other moments of history.[5] The McGraw studio was three miles from the pads because engineers had calculated that three miles would be just beyond the range of flying debris from a hypothetical exploding Saturn V moon rocket.

In 2011, it became my sad duty to bring an end to the beginning of manned spaceflight at CBS News. On July 8, 2011, I had decided to anchor the *CBS Evening News* from the KSC studio. That day, the *Atlantis* orbiter was counting down to the last flight of the space shuttle program. The flight was known in NASA parlance as mission STS-135. It was the Space Transportation System's 135th shuttle mission. Beginning with the first flight in 1981, there had been 133 successes and two heartbreaking failures.[6] This last flight would leave America, for the first time in its history, with no successor vehicle waiting in the wings. For the foreseeable future, Americans would reach space only by paying a fortune for seats on Russian *Soyuz* capsules designed in the 1960s. I had become managing editor of the *CBS Evening News* only the month before. I had not imagined writing essays, but I was moved by this moment in history. At the end of the broadcast, I saluted America's achievements in engineering and courage with these few words:

> The shuttle had its critics. It was expensive. There were accidents. But there was nothing like it in the world and *Americans* conceived it. When tragedy struck, we pressed ahead without fear.
>
> To a generation, man-in-space seemed as American as the constellation in our flag. But today marked the end of the heroic age of spaceflight when we all claimed ownership. The last shuttle left the Earth, drawing a bright, burning line in the sky—the signature of people who dare to dream.

After the broadcast, a black thunderstorm gathered over the fifty-two story Vehicle Assembly Building where shuttles and Apollo missions were made ready. The men and women who repaired and launched America's spacecraft posed for final photos in front of the world's largest American flag, two-hundred-nine feet tall, painted on the VAB in 1976 for the bicentennial celebration. Looking through the downpour toward the launch pad I wondered when in history had a nation abandoned the most advanced technology on Earth without advancing to the next step? How do we challenge young Americans to dare to dream? The next chapter offers an answer.

CHAPTER TEN

Vision

Elon Musk

An ampere is the basic unit of electric current intensity. A single amp will kill a person. My hand was about to come to rest on an exposed battery pack loaded with 1,450 amps. "Oh," Elon Musk said with no emotion nor great concern, "you don't want to touch that."

Musk was showing me around the plant assembling his Tesla Model S all-electric four-door sedan. The battery was composed of seven thousand cells not unlike laptop batteries. The entire floor of the vehicle, from front axle to rear, was inhabited by this powerhouse that propelled a Model S from zero to sixty in 2.28 seconds.[1] That's beyond Lamborghini quick.[2] With no engine or transmission, the car was mute in motion except for the sound of rubber on pavement. Inside, most functions were controlled by a seventeen-inch touch screen large enough to inspire wonder. In 2013, the Model S had the highest crash-test safety ratings in *all* categories.[3] It appeared the car of the future had only one defect—it cost about $100,000. No one, not even the visionary Elon Musk, could build a successful car company with a product that none of its blue-collar employees could even dream of buying. But to worry about the viability of Tesla was to misunderstand Musk. He wasn't trying to build a car company. To him, Tesla was a vehicle designed to speed human evolution. "Mankind is running this very, very dangerous chemical experiment," he told me. "We're putting trillions of tons of CO_2 into the oceans and atmosphere to see what happens. *That* will be catastrophic. The only question is, when?"

Visionaries are risk takers and rule breakers. And like electricity itself, this trait can be enormously beneficial or nearly fatal. Elon Musk has seen both sides. In 2018, after a few wild and irresponsible tweets about taking the publicly traded Tesla private, the US Securities and Exchange Commission sued Musk for fraud. In September that year, Musk was forced to settle with the SEC by stepping down as Tesla's chairman and agreeing to pay forty million dollars in fines.[4] Musk's sometimes erratic behavior is not unlike the life and career of his car company's namesake. In the nineteenth century, the Serbian-American Nikola Tesla invented many of the devices that sparked our modern world, including the electric motor and the technology behind wireless communications. He also sank the fortunes of investors into dreams of transmitting electricity wirelessly; communicating with a civilization on Mars; and a "death ray" that would end all war. Often the flip side of genius is "wacky." For the purposes of this chapter, I'll concentrate on the side of Musk's vision that may yet change civilization on Earth for the better.

Nikola Tesla would have been impressed with the auto plant bearing his name sprawled outside South Fremont, California, just across San Francisco Bay from Palo Alto, the capital of Silicon Valley. In 2014, as I watched *Musk's* dreams parade down the assembly line, Musk was forty-two years old, a multibillionaire, whose vision defined the future long before the rest of us arrived. I said to Musk, "The last successful American car company was Chrysler, which started in 1929. How did you figure you were gonna start a car company and be successful at it?" I asked.

"Well, I didn't really think Tesla would be successful," Musk confessed. "I thought we would, most likely, fail."

"Then why try?" My question tilted Musk's head slightly to the right, his eyes narrowed with curiosity as though he was trying to figure out what was wrong with me. The query, which would be at home in most any boardroom, struck him as odd.

"If something's important enough you should try. Even if the probable outcome is failure," he said.

Failure is not something with which Elon Musk had a great deal of experience though he does come perilously close. To me, he seemed unnaturally oblivious to risk and unjustifiably optimistic about the future—two reality-repudiating traits shared by most explorers. I have learned, in Musk's case, this could be a genetic trait.

Elon Musk's maternal grandfather, Joshua N. Haldeman, was born in 1902. He arrived in a log cabin in Pequot, Minnesota. When he was just a boy, Joshua's family moved to the wild west of Canada. In a picture from about 1926, Joshua, in his mid-twenties, is smiling broadly, dressed in studded leather chaps, spinning a lariat so fast that both hand and rope have blurred into an arc. He was a handsome youth with rough-hewn features that would give him, later in life, a passing resemblance to Ernest Hemingway. Haldeman became a prominent chiropractor and national political activist. Like Hemingway, he didn't care much for the status quo. I found evidence of this in a tiny article on page nine of the *Ottawa Journal*, dated October 14, 1940. Wedged in a column next to a vitamin cure for gray hair and a cupcake recipe, the article tells us Dr. Haldeman was arrested by the Royal Canadian Mounted Police for being the head of Technocracy Incorporated for the town of Regina.[5] Technocracy was a Depression-era social movement that advocated replacing politicians with scholars, engineers and scientists who might know more about running the economy. These people would be known as "Technocrats." The group was outlawed in Canada during World War II but Haldeman refused to disband. It doesn't appear the authorities pursued his case with vigor. After the war, he expanded his ambitions in national politics and medical societies. By this time, he and his wife, Winnifred, had four children. The youngest were twin girls. One of the twins, Maye, would become Elon Musk's mother. Given the remoteness of Saskatchewan, Haldeman got a pilot's license in 1948. Apparently, he understood the first rule of every boat owner; he named his plane after his wife. The letters *Winnie* were painted in white block letters across the red engine cowling. Newspapers dubbed the family "The flying Haldemans." In 1950, still chafing under the Canadian political establishment, Haldeman loaded his Bellanca airplane and his family onto a freighter and sailed to South Africa. He had never been there—didn't know a soul—but he hoped he was destined for the rugged independence of his youth.[6]

Africa turned out to be the kind of place where he could throw his lariat in any direction and lasso adventure. Joshua and Winnifred mounted several desert expeditions in search of the rumored Lost City of the Kalahari. They didn't find it. But they did tie for first place in the Cape to Algiers road rally after enduring twelve thousand miles in a pale yellow station wagon with a V8 under the hood and water bags lashed to the grill.[7] In 1954, with Winnifred as navigator, Joshua piloted *Winnie* thirty thousand miles from South Africa to Australia—a feat that summoned the Australian prime minister to the runway.[8] Joshua was South Africa's national champion in pistol shooting. Winnifred was the women's pistol champion.

Their daughter, Maye, grew up to marry an electromechanical engineer and settle down in Pretoria to have three children: Elon; his younger brother, Kimbal; and a daughter, Tosca. The marriage short-circuited in less than ten years. Elon remembers an unhappy childhood, living for a time with his disagreeable father and suffering under the fists of bullies at school. Dissatisfied with the world as it was, he set about designing a new one to his own specifications. His mother told me Elon was brilliant in classes that he found interesting and poor in anything that bored him. His self-assigned homework included flying model planes, launching model rockets and divining the software inside his cherished 8-bit Commodore VIC-20 microcomputer brimming with 5KB of RAM. Musk told me the VIC-20 was "magic." He taught himself code writing at about age twelve and proceeded to write video games which he sold to raise money for hardware upgrades. Like his grandfather, he longed for a land where dreams run wild.

"Why your interest in America?" I asked Musk. We were sitting for a *60 Minutes* interview in his Bel Air, California, home in the foothills of the Santa Monica Mountains.

"Well, I'm interested in things that change the world," he told me. "I was interested in wondrous, new technology, where you're like, 'Wow, how does that even happen?' It seemed like the vast majority of such things came from the United States. I do have some American background. A lot of people think my name must be from some exotic location, but I was named after my great-grandfather, who was from Saint Paul, Minnesota. He was a school superintendent and part-time sheriff in 1900."

Musk got to America as quick as he could. He went to Canada for college, then transferred to the University of Pennsylvania where he earned a degree in physics. He followed up with a degree in economics from the university's prestigious Wharton School. After graduation, he and his brother, Kimbal, made for Silicon Valley. Elon was twenty-three, Kimbal, twenty-two.

"When we moved to Silicon Valley we had nothing," Kimbal told me. "We literally had a small amount of money and a goal to start a company." That company became known as Zip2. In 1995, it was among the first to harness the internet and big data to offer door-to-door driving directions. "We actually lived in the office," Kimbal said. "And we would sleep on the floor in the evening and go shower at the YMCA the next morning. We would be ready to go before our employees arrived, so they wouldn't think we were actually sleeping in the office, which, of course, we were." In 1997, the brothers sold Zip2 to Compaq Computer Corporation for $307 million. That would be more than half a billion in 2018 dollars.

"So, you and your brother went from $7,000 between you to a $300-million deal, in what period of time?" I asked Elon.

"In four years," he said.

"Only in America," I observed.

Musk's eyes ignited. "Right! Only in America, I agree. *Absolutely* only in America!" He said this not in greed, but in gratitude.

At the turn of the twenty-first century Musk saw the internet was a vast frontier of unfulfilled desires. He noticed that the financial services industry was slow to catch on, so he co-created PayPal, which he sold to eBay in 2002.

"And you sold PayPal to eBay for how much?" I asked.

"It was about $1.5 billion. So that was a good outcome."

I had to chuckle. Good outcome? Well, yes. I suppose it was. This was the moment I noticed that Musk tends to talk about money in a dispassionate deadpan. To him spectacular wealth is a data point that fails to fire his imagination. But when you talk about ideas, he sparks to life. The more far-fetched, the better.

Musk's share of the eBay deal was somewhere north of $200 million. In 2001, he imagined his next project would be an attempt to inspire the whole human race by landing a small greenhouse on Mars. "The furthest life has ever traveled," he said at the time. What he needed was a spacecraft. He found American and French booster rockets much too expensive so Musk went to Russia to shop for a surplus intercontinental ballistic missile. But, again, the booster that could do the job came with an astronomical price. Musk, a fan of the science fiction novelist Isaac Asimov, imagined that humankind would never colonize space without a cheaper way to get there. Unlike most of us, he decided this was his problem to solve.

"I think it's important that humanity become a multi-planet species," he told me. "I think most people would agree that a future where we are a space-faring civilization is inspiring and exciting compared with one where we are forever confined to Earth until some eventual extinction event. That's really why I started SpaceX."

In 2012, Musk and I walked the polished gray floors of his rocket plant in Hawthorne, California, near Los Angeles. Space Exploration Technologies Corporation, aka SpaceX, covered many acres under a ceiling that reached about five stories high. The plant was an example of what I thought of as Musk's Hermit Crab Theory of industrial development. Years before, another aerospace company built the factory to produce fuselages for 747 jumbo jets. The plant eventually fell into disuse. Likewise, his Teslas were rolling out of a factory that had been abandoned by a defunct joint venture of General Motors and Toyota. Both buildings were perfect shells for his creatures. He didn't have to build them or wait for them.

About seven thousand employees inhabit SpaceX. Some of those I met were newly minted engineers right out of college, others were rocket scientists with decades of experience at NASA. Hard hats swarmed over sections of booster rockets that looked like giant aluminum soda cans laid on their side. "That's the second stage of a Falcon 9 rocket," Musk said. All of the major components—engines, fuselages, electronics—are designed and built here. Metal comes in one end of the factory, rocket ships come out the other. The screech of power saws chewing aluminum and bolts spinning under pneumatic wrenches forced the volume of Musk's voice. "The odds of me coming into the rocket business, not knowing anything about rockets, not having ever built anything, I mean, I would have to be insane if I thought the odds were in my favor," he confided. *Or,* I thought, *insane to try.*

As we navigated the floor of the future he was building, Musk was just completing his own fortieth annual orbit around the sun. He's about six foot two, slender but not athletic. He looked every bit of his youth, except, I noticed, bags under his eyes suggested more than a few sleepless nights. He was dressed in the spectrum of Silicon Valley, which is to say, black jeans, black T-shirt, black bomber jacket. Musk is given to self-deprecating humor. His eyes rarely break contact. He tends to emphasize words with sharp forward jabs of the head. Musk is analytical to the point of awkwardness. Even when engaged in conversation, you have the sense he is elsewhere—pursuing a vision the rest of us will see only in the fullness of time.

"When I was in college, I was thinking, what are the things that would most affect the future of humanity?" he told me. "There were essentially five things: the internet, sustainable energy, making life multiplanetary, reading and writing genetic code, and artificial intelligence. So, the last two are in a questionable category, where it's a thorny issue of right and wrong. But the first three I thought for sure would have a positive impact on the future. So, I wanted to be involved in at least one of those three things. Space seemed like the one that would be least likely to attract other entrepreneurs."

"Well, there's a reason for that," I pointed out. "You'd have to be crazy to start a rocket company."

"Ha! That's what my friends said. I had so many people try to talk me out of starting a rocket company." Most of us write "Ha!" in text messages to indicate laughter. Musk is perhaps the only person I've met who actually *says* "Ha!" explosively, as a single syllable.

"What did your friends tell you?" I asked.

"One good friend of mine collected a whole series of videos of rockets blowing up and made me watch those," he laughed.

Rocketry, as it turned out, is a humbling profession. In the beginning, SpaceX would only add to the video canon of catastrophe. In 2006, Musk's first rocket, a single engine Falcon One, erupted from a launch pad in the Marshall Islands in the mid-Pacific. It flew thirty-three seconds before exploding. "Shook the coconuts off the trees," Musk told me. Musk had anticipated a learning curve, so SpaceX was budgeted for two more launches. Both were failures. He had to beg and borrow money. It wasn't easy to find investors who had watched three failures and were willing to pony up for a fourth attempt. Musk said, "When we'd call people and say, 'Hey, would you like to invest?' they'd be angry that we even *called*. Ha! It was not just 'no' it was 'no' with various expletives."

In our interview in Musk's Bel Air home, I took him back to those days of not so long ago. "In 2008, the rocket company is not going well, you've had three failures. The car company is hemorrhaging money and the American economy has tanked in the worst recession since the Great Depression."

"And," he interjected, "I'm getting divorced, by the way. Ha! Yeah, that was the worst year of my life. I remember waking up the Sunday before Christmas in 2008 and thinking to myself, 'Man, I never thought I was someone who could ever be capable of a nervous breakdown.'"

At the end of 2008, both SpaceX and Tesla were two days away from bankruptcy. Kimbal Musk told me his brother was "worse than broke." Elon told me he put his last dime in the two companies.

"Your *personal* money? Everything you had?" I asked.

"Everything," he said. "I had to borrow money from friends just to pay the rent."

"Anybody else would've said, 'I'm gonna protect what I've got left. The car business didn't work. I'm gonna let it go.'"

"If we had failed at that point," Musk insisted, "we would've been used as a counterexample to say, 'Oh, that silly company tried to make an electric car and they failed.' We might've set back the cause of electric cars more than if we hadn't started at all. For me, that was a no-brainer. The *hard* decision was that I had Tesla and SpaceX and they both needed money. I could either divide the money between SpaceX and Tesla and try to make them both survive, or I could pick one that's gonna die for sure."

"But you couldn't choose between your children?"

"That's right. It did feel like that."

SpaceX had entered a competition with major aerospace companies for a launch contract with NASA. With its multiple failures it didn't seem SpaceX was a likely choice. His funds were exhausted, investors were inventing new, colorful ways to say no. Musk went to bed, two days before Christmas, on the verge, as he said, of a nervous breakdown.

"The next morning," Musk told me, "NASA called and told us that we'd won a $1.5 billion contract. I wasn't expecting a call, especially just before Christmas. It came out of the blue. The head of NASA space flight operations said 'Congratulations, you won.' I just blurted out, 'I love you guys!'"

"They saved you?" I asked.

"Yeah, they did."

The next day, Christmas Eve, at 6:00 p.m., Musk arranged enough financing from weary investors to keep Tesla alive about nine months. The deal closed, as he put it to me, "at the last hour of the last day it was possible."

"Merry Christmas," I observed.

"Yeah. Ha! Merry Christmas indeed."

Two years after the Christmas miracle, SpaceX became the fourth entity in history to orbit a spacecraft and return it safely to the Earth. The others were the United States, Russia and China.[9] Two years later, in 2012, a SpaceX Dragon capsule was the first private spaceship to dock with the International Space Station.[10] In 2015, SpaceX became the first to return its spent boosters to their launch sites, landing them vertically on a column of fire. SpaceX wasn't carrying astronauts, but I couldn't help but notice in our walk around the plant, the Dragon capsules under construction all had windows. Musk told me it would be a relatively simple matter to install seats instead of supplies. In 2018, SpaceX introduced the Falcon Heavy booster which is essentially three Falcon 9s lashed together. Falcon Heavy became the most powerful operational rocket in the world on February 6, 2018. It thundered into orbit carrying a Tesla roadster as experimental cargo. Cameras beamed back pictures of the car, top down, with a space-suited mannequin at the wheel. As Elon would say, Ha!

Musk's second 2008 Christmas miracle allowed him to keep Tesla funded while he attracted more investors. One of them was Daimler AG, the maker of Mercedes-Benz vehicles, which wanted in on Tesla technology. Musk introduced his SUV, the Model X and then the car he needs to make the company viable for the long haul—the Model 3. At $35,000 the Model 3 is designed to be the mass production electric for everyman. Unless you drive a Tesla, you may not have noticed that Musk has built thousands of high-speed charging stations on major roads from coast-to-coast. He planned to convert many of the stations into giant batteries to store solar power. For Model S and Model X owners there's no charge for the charging. He told me, "So, the basic premise is you can drive for free, forever, on pure sunlight.

"The solar panels will charge the stationary battery pack which will charge the car. So, these will be off-grid. Even if there's a zombie apocalypse and the grid breaks down you'll still be able to charge your car."

"So," I asked, "there's a zombie apocalypse warranty?"

"Ha! Yes, you never know."

The key to managing the cost of an electric vehicle is controlling your own battery production. Musk built a sprawling plant in Nevada he called Gigafactory 1 to make all of Tesla's power packs. Then, he announced the development of a Tesla tractor for eighteen-wheelers and a new two-seat roadster. Critics said Musk had left reality in his rearview mirror. Production of the Model 3 was more troublesome than Musk had imagined. He overpromised and underperformed on the delivery date and production rate. Of course, Wall Street, nearsighted to the next quarter, punished the stock. Even worse, short sellers, who profit if the stock falls, organized media attacks on Musk and Tesla to undermine the company. (I understand investors should be allowed to make money on the upside or the downside in a free market, but for America's sake, shouldn't we be trying to create companies and jobs rather than destroy them?)

In late 2018, Tesla was still trying to outrun shortages of cash. For all the video he'd watched of exploding rocket ships it turned out the challenges of the car business were out of this world. Musk was showing signs of the nervous breakdown he had feared back in 2008. Still, no matter what the future holds for Tesla, Musk accomplished what he set out to do. He revolutionized transportation. By 2018 nearly all major automakers had announced development of electric models. For those interested in the mundane data points of wealth, 2018 was also the year that Tesla reached a market capitalization of $52 billion, which was greater than the Ford Motor Company.[11] Somehow, space-faring turned out to be a smoother ride. SpaceX became one of the world's most valuable privately held companies at $21 billion.

Vision, ironically, is a word we use for that which cannot be seen by most of us—the future yet to come. A twentieth-century visionary, the original American car guy, Henry Ford, is often quoted as having said, "If I asked people what they wanted, they would have said faster horses." For the record, I cannot find any indication that Ford actually said that, but the quote does capture his belief. No one had imagined flying from South Africa to Australia until *Winnie* touched down, Down Under.

If you see SpaceX as a rocket company and Tesla as a car company, you've missed Elon Musk's vision entirely. He created them to build vehicles to carry humankind to a future free of the hydrocarbons that cloud the thin wisp of blue we call an atmosphere—and to a future when Earth is known as "the home planet." Musk once told National Geographic, "I want to die on Mars, just not on impact."

In a now-revived manufacturing plant, where thousands of Americans could not build rockets fast enough to meet demand, Musk told me, "I think we're at the dawn of a new era. And it's going to be very exciting. What we're hoping to do is provide more reasons to be inspired to be human. America is the very distillation of the spirit of exploration."

CHAPTER ELEVEN

Objectivity

Learning from Unpleasant Truth

Our caravan followed the course of the Panjshir River toward its headwaters in the Hindu Kush. This was the Afghanistan of otherworldly beauty. Peaks, glazed white, had been forced to impassable heights 250 million years ago in violent tectonic convulsions.[1] The earth cooked emeralds, silver and iron into the folds.[2] Miners have burrowed here for thousands of years. The Hari-Rod geologic fault runs the width of Afghanistan and splits the country in two, north and south, tracking the cultural split that divides its people.[3] Pashtuns, who dominate the south, are rare here in the north. More than 70 percent of the inhabitants of the north are Tajik and speak Dari, a language unrelated to Pashto. Northern rains are far more generous than in the desert south. Farms grow prosperous on

Witnessing the collapse of World Trade Center tower one was the most wrenching experience of my life. CBS News was on the air for more than three days without a break. This was our finest hour.

In September 2002, President George W. Bush and I spoke in the Oval Office for a *60 Minutes II* documentary to air on the anniversary of 9/11. The president didn't like my questions about Iraq. We would learn later he was already far down the road to starting another war.

President Bush gave us full access to Air Force One for our *60 Minutes II* hour on the commander in chief's response on 9/11. This was the biggest role in American history for Air Force One since Lyndon B. Johnson was sworn into office after the assassination of John F. Kennedy.

My 2007 interview with George Tenet, the former director of the CIA, was among the most contentious of my career. Tenet had never been interviewed about the CIA's failure to detect the 9/11 plot nor the flawed intelligence that led to the war with Iraq.

Austin and Arielle Metzger lived in this GMC van after their father lost his construction job in the Great Recession. I was so impressed with their spirit. They told me other kids were worse off in central Florida. "It's just life, right?" Arielle said. A university president who saw the story gave them full scholarships.

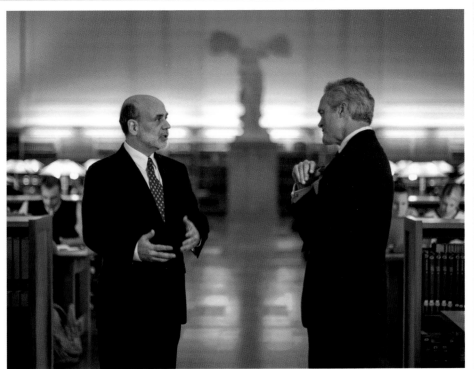

Federal Reserve chairman Ben Bernanke broke a long-standing tradition and agreed to speak to me for *60 Minutes*. In the grip of the Great Recession, Bernanke realized the Federal Reserve had a duty to be transparent to the people it served.

Photo credit: CBS

On the eve of the Democratic National Convention, I asked Hillary Clinton and running mate Tim Kaine the first questions about the Democratic National Committee documents stolen by Russian military intelligence. Secretary Clinton would be so offended by my questions about her honesty that she refused to appear on *60 Minutes* with me a few weeks before Election Day.

Photo credit: CBS

In my first interview with Donald Trump I was amazed by the false picture of America he painted. His Manhattan apartment reminded me of the over-the-top gilded palaces of Saddam Hussein.

Photo credit: CBS

We originated the *CBS Evening News* from both of the 2016 national party conventions. In his acceptance speech, Donald Trump claimed he understood America's challenges so well that "Only I can fix it." Russia's well-timed dump of stolen Democratic emails alienated the legion of Bernie Sanders supporters that Hillary Clinton would need in the run-up to Election Day.

Photo credit: CBS

Anchoring CBS News coverage of Election Night 2016 was a challenge. The vote totals in swing states were running too close to call well past midnight. You can see on the map behind me that Wisconsin, Michigan and Pennsylvania had not been decided. By razor-thin margins, those states would give Donald Trump his victory in the Electoral College.

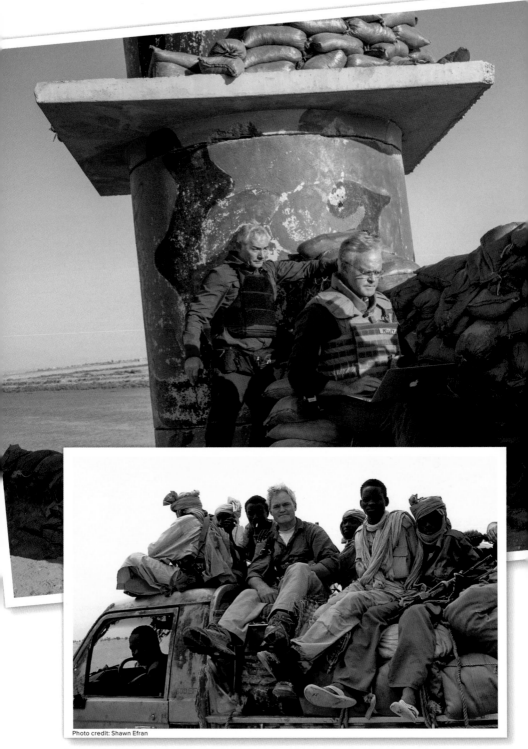

Photo credit: Shawn Efran

For our *60 Minutes* story "Searching for Jacob," cameraman Ian Robbie and I rode into Sudan with rebels fighting the government. We discovered evidence of the government-sponsored genocide that was killing thousands in the Darfur region. In gratitude, the rebels treated us to a meal of roast camel.

Sandbags mark the line where the Kurdish Peshmerga stopped the advance of ISIS or Islamic State into Northern Iraq. I'm writing copy that I'm planning to read to the camera in a "stand-up" for *60 Minutes*. It was on this trip that we discovered refugee Nadia Murad, who would go on to win the Nobel Peace Prize. CBS News security officer Geoff Mabberley is watching my back.

Photo credit: CBS

I've had the wonderful privilege of flying with the US Navy, Marine Corps, Army, Air Force and Coast Guard. This is the backseat of a navy F-14 shortly after we catapulted off the deck of the USS *Eisenhower* in the Atlantic. From the front seat, Lieutenant Commander Tony Ludovici was eager to show me what his fighter could do. We flew supersonic. We flew upside down. But I couldn't imagine how Ludovici was going to land on what looked like a postage stamp moving across the sea.

Photo credit: Eric Kerchner

In December 2003, Bill Owens and I rushed back to Iraq to cover the capture of Saddam Hussein. Soldiers of the 4th Infantry Division found him hiding in this hole near the former dictator's hometown, Tikrit. I took a camera into the horizontal hiding space, which had the dimensions of a coffin and a single battery-powered light.

Photo credit: CBS

Aboard Marine One, the presidential helicopter, President George W. Bush and I discussed his decision to send more troops to Iraq. The president wanted to explain his reasoning on *60 Minutes*. The weight of the war was showing.

Photo credit: George Christian/CBS

I anchored the *CBS Evening News* from Afghanistan on the tenth anniversary of the war. The extraordinary producer, Mike Solmsen, could get the broadcast on the air from any point on the earth. The vehicle behind us is an MRAP armored personnel carrier pushing a device designed to detonate land mines.

Photo credit: Vatican

This mother told me she had buried some of her children on the long march from her village in Somalia. Refugees were walking for weeks to flee the Somali civil war for the safety of Kenyan refugee camps. With the help of a rebel group, I entered Somalia and reached this United Nations emergency feeding station on the refugee route.

I met Pope Francis in St. Peter's Square on the eve of his visit to the United States. Associate producer Sabina Castelfranco, left, arranged the introduction and handled the translation to Spanish. As a gift, I gave the pope a leather-bound copy of Steinbeck's *The Grapes of Wrath*.

Bruce Springsteen and I walked the main street of Asbury Park, New Jersey. Somehow the sunglasses didn't keep us from being mobbed by fans within minutes. I expected to meet a rock star, but what impressed me more was the philosopher and poet who simply could not stop writing.

Photo credit: CBS

Photo credit: CBS

Fitness has always been my hobby, but Hugh Jackman wore me out with the routine he used to get into shape for his Wolverine movie role. Working out with Jackman in a Sydney gym sounded like a good idea for our *60 Minutes* profile until I tried to match bicep curls with a man who plays a superhero. When my daughter saw this picture she said, "Oh, great. It's Wolverine and Wolverine's dad."

Photo credit: CBS

My interviews with President Obama were frequent, especially in his second term. Here, we are speaking in the colonnade by the Rose Garden. Reasonable people will disagree about his policies, but I always found him thoroughly informed on the issues and deeply thoughtful about his proposed solutions. He graced the nation with a virtually scandal-free White House and a role-model family.

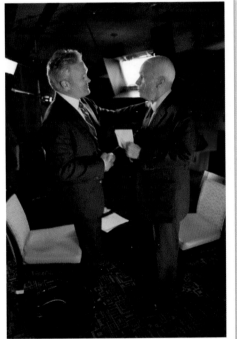

I got to know Senator John McCain while covering his 2008 presidential campaign for *60 Minutes*. Rarely in politics these days do you find the combination of heroism, principle and zeal that comprised the senator from Arizona. He actively sought compromise with Democrats everywhere he could. His bill banning torture put America back on the side of its ideals. The 2008 election gave us the first African American president. That was a momentous achievement. But, in my view, John McCain would have also made a very fine president.

I joined CBS News in 1989. The Oklahoma City bombing in 1995 was, at the time, the deadliest terrorist assault on America. I would spend the next two years attempting to understand the motives of the bomber, Tim McVeigh. The month after his attack, I broadcast a special report on the controlled demolition of what remained of the Murrah Federal Building.

Photo credit: Carol Powers

Soundman John Daily prepares for the *Evening News* broadcast on the north lawn of the White House. The West Wing is in the distance. In 1998, so many reporters from around the world came to cover the Lewinsky scandal that the National Park Service gave up tending the lawn and poured gravel over our "stand-up" location. We dubbed it Pebble Beach.

Photo credit: Rob Fortunato

In 2011, I became the anchor and managing editor of the *CBS Evening News*. The "fishbowl" is the *Evening News* wheelhouse. To my left is Patricia Shevlin, arguably the most successful executive producer in the broadcast's history. Her deputy, senior broadcast producer Jim McGlinchy, is standing. At the three o'clock position is senior producer Kim Godwin, the best newsroom manager and story producer I've had the pleasure to know. Back to my right, at the nine o'clock position, is senior producer Guy Campanile, who infused every script with clarity and accuracy.

Photo credit: CBS

Shortly after I began the managing editor job, David Letterman invited me on *The Late Show* on CBS. He asked if I was nervous about my new responsibility. "Dave," I said, "my daughter just turned sixteen and I'm teaching her how to drive. So, no, anchoring the *CBS Evening News* doesn't make me nervous."

In 2010, we visited children orphaned by the cataclysmic earthquake in Haiti. The orphans named me "Papa soft hair." They were eager to leave with me, wherever that might be. It seemed so unfair that such a catastrophe would strike a country already among the poorest on earth.

Photo credit: Nicole Young

In 2010, I trekked to the top of the erupting Eyjafjallajökull volcano in Iceland. My guide was world-renowned volcanologist Haraldur Sigurðsson. He taught me much about geology but was never able to teach me how to pronounce Eyjafjallajökull.

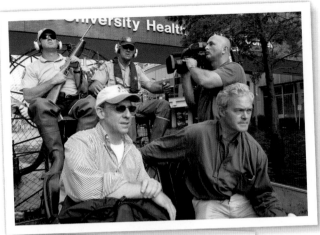

Producer Bill Owens and I hitched a ride on an airboat in downtown New Orleans after Hurricane Katrina. A few yards ahead of us, we came across a poor soul who had drowned in the flooded street. Cameraman Dennis Dillon has been our indispensable companion on many of the toughest assignments.

I've taken every kind of vehicle to reach our stories, from submarines to elephants. In India, this is the best vehicle to hunt for tigers. Somehow, the elephants don't mind the tigers and the tigers pay no attention to the elephants. Chris Everson and Anton van de Merwe are on the "camera elephant" shooting me and renowned photographer and naturalist Belinda Wright.

Outside of my work, I spent many years on the board of the International Rescue Committee. The IRC was founded at the suggestion of Albert Einstein to rescue Jews from Nazi-occupied Europe. In the decades since, the IRC has sheltered refugees in war zones and helped many become successful citizens of the United States. I witnessed these courageous and selfless humanitarians protect refugees from harm in Afghanistan, Thailand, Kenya, Haiti and Iraq. Here, I conferred with the IRC team in a Democratic Republic of Congo refugee camp.

Photo credit: Jane Pelley

Not as often as I would like, I leave the demands of journalism onshore and sail our little family sloop, *Boundless Blue*. Her name derives from Walt Whitman's "In Cabin'd Ships at Sea."

pomegranates, nuts and grapes. In 2007, six years into the war, I was riding through this cultural and geologic history in the bed of a Japanese pickup truck. A mercenary with an AK-47 assault rifle lifted a mass of green grapes toward my face. "This is going to give me dysentery," I mumbled to myself. But the generous gesture had to be met with appropriate gratitude. We depended on the young man and his well-armed team to keep my *60 Minutes* crew alive in case our trip ended in a gunfight. They were mercenaries we hired in Kabul because the US military declined to help us with this journey. I was also aware that this would be a story no one in America particularly wanted to see. But clear-eyed objectivity is the soul of journalism. Blind allegiance never ends in sound policy.

For months I'd been troubled by the deaths of Afghan civilians in US airstrikes. Among Afghans, support for the American occupation was already fragile. Civilian deaths were undermining the war. Some casualty reports were coming from the enemy and were wildly exaggerated. On the other hand, the people who ran the war at US Central Command (CENTCOM) in Tampa, Florida, were issuing reports of bombing runs that killed dozens of enemy fighters but rarely, it seemed, any civilians. I find the truth is usually somewhere in the middle and, in Afghanistan, the truth had profound implications for American success. I asked my intrepid *60 Minutes* producer Solly Granatstein to see what he could find. He researched recent airstrikes and found several that CENTCOM declined to talk about. One of them had targeted a small farming village on a tributary of the Panjshir River in Kapisa Province.

We were admitted to the village by a sturdy concrete bridge spanning a rapid stream. I was surprised to see such a well-engineered bridge out here. I noticed it had once been a source of pride. There was something like a commemorative plaque on one of the abutments. The plaque seemed to be in English, but most of the letters had been chipped away. *A _ _ft f _ _m t_e _ _ _ _ _ _ _ n Pe _ _ _e* were the only characters I could make out. The bridge led us to a short market street. This was the kind of village where word of strangers gets around. Children were curious. Everyone else was suspicious. We made a left into a collection of typical Afghan houses—two stories of mud and straw. One looked like an ancient ruin. Its broken walls filled a crater as big as a tennis court. In a cornfield behind the rubble, nine cloth banners snapped in the wind. Each was about twelve inches square, sewn in blue, gold and crimson. Slender reeds about six feet tall lofted the colors into the breeze. An Afghan would recognize the meaning. This was a graveyard. The earth was freshly turned. Four generations of one family had been laid to rest: an eighty-five-year-old man, four women and four children who ranged in age from seven months to five years. "Some of the bodies were missing a hand or a leg or half a head. We recognized one of them only by the clothes she was wearing," Gulam Nabi told me. We were sitting in the shade of an ancient tree directly across from the ruin. Gulam Nabi was a middle-aged Afghan with a graying beard who had spread an intricate rug to welcome his visitors. He was the brother of the man who owned the demolished house. "Who was the person you recognized?" I asked.

"It was Mujib's mother," he said. Mujib was the homeowner's son and Gulam Nabi's nephew. The twelve-year-old had a tousle of black hair and a face dominated by deep brown eyes. "I saw my mom, my sisters, my brother and my grandfather were dead. Our house was destroyed," he told me. Mujib survived because he had spent that night with his aunt and uncle.

Granatstein and I pieced together the events of that night from eyewitnesses and US military reports. We found that an enemy mortar team had fired a round at a nearby American combat outpost. They missed. No one was hurt.[4] But a pilot reported seeing two men with rifles run into Mujib's house. A US Air Force B-1B bomber was loitering in the area, on standby, in case it was needed to support troops in a firefight. These were the basic facts and, as always in war, they were ambiguous— open to what a former Pentagon official told me was "a macabre kind of calculus." Mark Garlasco said, "On every airstrike they try to figure out how many dead civilians is a dead bad guy worth?" Garlasco was chief of high-value targeting at the Pentagon at the start of the 2003 war in Iraq. When I spoke to him in October 2007, Garlasco was a consultant for Human Rights Watch. At the Pentagon, Garlasco had been part of a team trying to kill Saddam Hussein *before* the US invasion. The idea was to end the war before it began. Garlasco explained that, with a target of such high importance, a certain number of civilian deaths was permitted. "Our number was thirty," he said. "So, for example, Saddam Hussein, if you were going to kill up to twenty-nine people in the strike against Saddam Hussein, that's not a problem. But once you hit that number thirty, we had to go to either President Bush or Secretary of Defense Rumsfeld." Garlasco told me there were fifty airstrikes targeting Saddam and his senior leadership before the invasion. "How many high-value targets were taken out in those strikes?" I asked.

"None of the targets on our target list was actually killed," Garlasco told me.

"How many civilians were killed in those strikes?" I wondered.

"We're looking at a couple of hundred civilians at least."

In its campaign to assassinate Saddam Hussein, the Pentagon was "zero for fifty." But before you judge, consider, if Saddam had been killed, there might not have been an invasion. We now know that *not* invading Iraq would have saved more than 288,000 lives.[5] As Garlasco said, a macabre kind of calculus.

In previous wars, innocent civilians died when bombs missed their targets. Today that is rare for the US military. Precision weapons usually find their bull's-eye, guided by GPS or a laser to within twenty feet of the aim point. The failures these days are in *identifying* targets. It's a question of intelligence. Is it the right building? Who is in the building and who is not? When I was covering the Clinton White House in 1999, a US airstrike in Belgrade destroyed its intended target with great precision. Unfortunately, in a failure of intelligence, the building had been misidentified. It turned out to be the Chinese Embassy.[6] Another factor in the calculus is the ordnance at hand. A 250-pound bomb may be more than enough to destroy the target, but ground commanders are stuck with whatever happens to be on the plane. The sleek dark gray B-1B, invisible over Mujib's neighborhood, was loaded with "blockbusters," bombs weighing in at two thousand pounds each. Do you drop one on a neighborhood? Do you drop two? As Marine Corps Lieutenant Colonel Christian Cabaniss told his riflemen in Afghanistan, "The first question is 'Can I'? The second question is '*Should* I?'"

The night of the bombing, the ground commander, having suffered no casualties among his troops, decided to drop 2,000-pound bombs on a report of two men with rifles.[7] The B-1B swung open its bomb bay and let slip two Mark 84 bombs fitted with Guided Bomb Unit wings and seekers that would follow the mark of a laser to the target. The Mk-84 is among the largest bombs in common use by the US military. Depending on fusing and angle of attack, each Mark 84 can dig a crater approximately 50 feet deep and 34 feet wide. The radius of damage and injury is up to 250 yards.[8]

We discovered in our reporting that Mujib's father *had* been fighting for the Taliban. It was likely that he and a fellow fighter ran into his home. But their bodies were not in the wreckage. Somehow, they escaped. Only the family was killed. One of the neighbors, seething, told me, "We used to hate the Russians much more than Americans, but now when we see all this happening, I am telling you, Russians behaved much better than the Americans!" He was angry and dead wrong. No one knows how many Afghans were killed by the Soviets over ten years but the best estimates are one million and more.[9] Still, in the critical area of "winning hearts and minds" for the US-supported government, the context didn't matter. On street corners and in teashops, Afghans were vilifying America. The enemy was killing more civilians but not by much. In 2008, 26 percent of all civilian deaths were the result of US and allied airstrikes—slightly under the 34 percent who were killed by enemy suicide bombings and improvised mines.[10] Garlasco told me, "You have to ask yourself, is a midlevel thug worth nine dead civilians? But it goes beyond that. You're not talking about just losing nine dead civilians. You're also talking about violent protests throughout the country demanding a democratically elected government be taken down. You then take people who maybe were in a pro-government area and all of a sudden, you're turning them against you and turning them toward the Taliban."

CENTCOM and the Pentagon declined multiple requests for interviews. A *60 Minutes* Freedom of Information Act request about the strike on Mujib's house, filed in 2007, was still in process with CENTCOM five years later.[11] [12] In my view, this is always bad policy. First, there is another side to a story. The military could only benefit from being heard. Second, the Pentagon is obligated to explain itself. The war is prosecuted in the name of the American people with the sons, daughters and fortunes of the American people. When the Pentagon conceals information, it's not hiding from "The Media," it's hiding from the people, including its own soldiers, sailors, airmen and marines. We could not do justice to objectivity without hearing from the military, so we kept pressing the Pentagon.

After weeks of "no," the air force broke through the clouds and saw the light. They realized they *did* have a story to tell. But to hear that story, we had to fly 1,200 miles from Kabul to a secret air base in Qatar on the Persian Gulf. We packed up our thirty-seven cases of camera gear and headed southwest. There was trouble the moment we landed. The Qataris were happy enough to let us in. But a free press was odious to the emir so all of our camera equipment was impounded. As far as shooting for *60 Minutes* was concerned, we'd been shot out of the sky.

The Qatari Peninsula must be an air base architect's idea of paradise. It is dry, hard desert, completely relieved of relief. The spreading of concrete for runways must seem like a formality. The Qatari Air Force's al-Udeid base, southwest of the capital of Doha, took full advantage. Its strips stretched to invisibility. We were asked not to say so at the time, but this was also the forward headquarters of the United States Air Force Central Command. Hundreds of Americans worked inside a massive, unmarked building with air-conditioning that seemed to be pumped in from a Minnesota Christmas. In subdued light, air force personnel in sharply pressed, immaculate combat fatigues shuttled about waging war with clipboards. Giant flat screens suspended from the ceiling were alive with brightly colored triangles and circles hopping across maps like water striders on a river. Rows of consoles brought to mind NASA's mission control. Afghanistan was on the left screen, Iraq on the right. The airmen with the clipboards helped calculate who would live today and who would not. "What are all those points on the map?" I asked Air Force Colonel Gary Crowder, who was deputy director of the Combined Air Operations Center.

"Those points." Crowder pointed at the blinking triangles. "Each one of those is an individual aircraft."

"How often is an airstrike prepared that's called off at the last minute?" I wondered.

"Thousands and thousands of times a month. Very often, we track some insurgent leaders for days and days and we are prepared to strike them at any moment, but we can never get all of the criteria necessary to meet our rules of engagement." The Rules of Engagement (ROE) was a classified checklist that balanced the value of a target against the loss of innocent lives.

Crowder had been authorized to explain the painstaking procedure the air force used to minimize civilian deaths. He was as frustrated as we were that the Qataris had impounded our camera gear. Crowder was determined to find a way to complete his mission. "What do you need?" he asked our crew. Cameramen Chris Everson and Ian Robbie and soundman Anton van de Merwe gave Crowder a long list of cameras, lights, microphones, videotapes, etc. Crowder arranged to have the gear gathered from air force public affairs stocks in Germany, placed on an air force transport and flown directly to the US-controlled portion of al-Udeid. What our Qatari allies didn't know wouldn't hurt them—at least not until *60 Minutes* was on the air. The next day, we sat down for an interview with Crowder in the Air Operations Center. He explained that, with each proposed strike, civilian casualties are estimated. Then, the estimate is reported to the marine or army commander on the ground. "We rely on those commanders to make the assessment of what the requirement is," Crowder said. "The ground commander assesses proportionality. He assesses the validity of the military target."

"What do you mean by proportionality?" I asked.

"If we know that there's a sniper on a roof and the roof is in the middle of a mosque, which is a protected site, or in the middle of a very populated area, then dropping a 2,000-pound weapon on that would not be proportional to going after the sniper."

"Two men with AK-47s run into a house. Do you bomb the house?" I asked.

"In some circumstances, we will bomb the house. It is entirely dependent upon the circumstances on the ground and the ground commander's assessment of that particular situation."

Marc Garlasco, the former head of high-value targeting at the Pentagon told me, "I don't think people really appreciate the gymnastics that the US military goes through in order to make sure that they're not killing civilians."

"If so much care is being taken," I asked, "why are so many civilians getting killed?"

"Because the Taliban are violating international law and because the US just doesn't have enough troops on the ground. You have the Taliban shielding in people's homes and you have a small number of troops on the ground. Sometimes the only thing they can do is drop bombs." That said, no one we spoke to in the US military thought the strike on Mujib's home was proportional. We learned that American soldiers had been in the house the day before the strike and met the women, children and grandparents. We don't know what, if anything, from that reconnaissance was reported up the chain of command. The facts of that night were these: no US troops were engaged in a firefight; a single mortar round had missed the combat outpost; no American or allied casualties were suffered. In those circumstances, dropping a 2,000-pound bomb on a neighborhood to hit two men with rifles seemed reckless. Two 2,000-pound bombs seemed senseless.

We spent the better part of a day in Mujib's village speaking to witnesses, family and neighbors. Toward evening, we crossed back over the bridge outside the village and took a break on the riverbank to eat some sandwiches. I noticed that the abutment I had seen earlier was a white marble column. It looked to have been carved decades before as a dedication. I studied the remaining letters in an internal game of *Wheel of Fortune*. A _ _ft f _ _m t_e _ _ _ _ _ _ _n Pe _ _ _e. The bridge was a US foreign aid project, probably from the 1960s. I wondered how many years farmers with laden trailers drove to market over the river that had previously stood between them and prosperity. Someone had furiously brought hammer and chisel together to obliterate any memory that the bridge was "A Gift from the American People." On the marble column, there were chips of blue and red where the Stars and Stripes used to be. Mujib's home and a generation of goodwill had been destroyed in an instant. Nothing in warfare is as difficult as counterinsurgency—the competing duality of "no better friend, no worse enemy." This was the tension I saw every time I returned. This is how Afghanistan became America's longest war.

In 2011, on the tenth anniversary of the invasion, I decided to broadcast the *CBS Evening News* from Afghanistan. The army's 10th Mountain Division took us in at its Forward Operating Base Pasab west of Kandahar. *Evening News* Senior Producer Mike Solmsen had an uncanny talent for getting our broadcast on the air from any point on Earth. In Afghanistan, he orchestrated the generators, lights and satellite uplink that put us on the air live, at 2:30 a.m. Afghan time—6:30 p.m. in New York. Mike was an unflappable expert in the *Evening News* control room and matched his expertise with courage in the field.

The 10th Mountain Division's 3rd Brigade was responsible for 228 villages inhabited by about 90,000 Afghans. You couldn't get closer to the heart of the enemy heartland. The territory included the hometown of Mullah Omar, the fugitive leader of the Taliban. Colonel Patrick Frank led 4,000 soldiers in the 3rd Brigade Combat Team. I asked about his losses in the last few months.

"We have lost, in 3rd Brigade Combat Team, twenty-eight soldiers," he told me.

"And how many wounded?" I asked.

"We've had over three hundred soldiers wounded."

"How often do you have contact with the enemy?"

"On a given day, twenty to twenty-five contacts with the enemy."

With these sacrifices, Frank's troops had purchased just enough security to lay the foundation for counterinsurgency—a foundation for schools, hospitals and roads. But creating secure space was like blowing up an air mattress. There was progress only with constant pressure. If Frank's men stopped to take a breath, security began to deflate. The enemy was always sticking pins into Frank's plans. Colonel Frank took us into the nearby village to show us a couple of civic projects his soldiers had built. But to go where Frank was establishing civil society, we and his troops had to ride in massive, lumbering vehicles called Maxx-Pros. They were MRAPs, the new generation of Mine Resistant Ambush Protected trucks developed to deflect the blast of an IED. Each sand-colored four-by-four weighed thirteen tons and rose ten feet tall. Fully equipped, with automatic flame suppression and radio jamming equipment, each MaxxPro cost a little under $1 million and averaged about three miles per gallon.[13] Inside, eight armor-wearing soldiers breathed filtered air. On top, a gunner manned a turret. At the time of our visit, no soldier had ever been killed inside an MRAP. They were marvels of American ingenuity. But the steel hulks ran counter to counterinsurgency. Nothing said "We're not welcome here" like rumbling into a village sealed inside a latter-day Trojan horse. The thick walls and blast-resistant, steel-shaded windows gave those inside the feeling of being sealed in a diving bell, plunging into a hostile sea. To villagers, a worn, oily Chinese motorcycle was a symbol of nearly unapproachable wealth. The MRAPs were chariots of aliens.

Our first stop was a playground Frank's troops repaired. We were outside the MaxxPro for only a couple of minutes when a sniper opened fired on us. No one was injured. The shooter slipped away. Next, Frank took us to a new school that his soldiers set up on the edge of the village. More and bigger schools were needed because girls were retaking their seats after the fall of the fundamentalist Taliban. Our MaxxPro convoy bellowed a blue smoke roar as it climbed the hill where four long tents were set up around a swept-dirt courtyard. There were plenty of desks and books and students. But I noticed that each class was being led by a child. The teachers were gone. The Taliban had threatened to kill them. Frank's troops came back to guard the school in the hope of persuading the teachers to return. That is why America was in Afghanistan for more than a decade with no end in sight. It takes a squad of troops to secure the school but only the whisper of a threat to shut it down. America had taken on an impossible mission in the noblest of causes. On the *CBS Evening News* that week, I wrote this to close one broadcast:

> Ten years ago, US forces answered the worst foreign attack on the American homeland. American GIs are fighting here tonight, not to seize territory or wealth, but to build a better country for the people who harbored our enemies—a principle that is uniquely American.

On our last day, my *Evening News* team and I helicoptered back to Regional Command South headquarters near Kandahar. A clerk told us our flight to Europe was leaving from a civilian terminal just off the base. That was a first in my experience; all my previous flights had left from the base terminal, "inside the wire" as the troops called it. We loaded up two SUVs, one military, one civilian, and drove with a first sergeant and a specialist from army public affairs to the off-base terminal. After an hour there, we were told, sure enough, our flight was leaving from the base terminal and we had to go back. This is how World War II troops came up with the acronym SNAFU, "Situation Normal, All Fucked Up." As we drove out of the civilian terminal parking lot, I noticed a white sedan parked directly across the street. A young man was sitting behind the wheel. We turned right and drove past him. I remember glancing his way; he was looking straight ahead, not at us. In seconds, I felt a hot sting across the left side of my face. The sensation of heat was followed by a roar like a volcanic fissure opening the earth. The first sergeant screamed. My eyes snapped left. I saw a column of earth and car parts shooting into the sky. At the top of the column, maybe two hundred feet up, there was a long runner of white cloth, perhaps thirty feet in length. I have no idea what it was. Maybe ripped from a tent or an awning? The white cloth twisted in a ballet with the sky. The streamer seemed beautiful, somehow spiritual. We were unharmed. But I wonder, even now, who was that man with the car bomb? Who did he think we were? What was it about life that made death a cherished wish? Why did his bomb detonate ten seconds late, after we had passed? Short circuit? Weak battery? Weak conviction?

I've returned to Afghanistan many times over the years that the United States and NATO have struggled to build a coherent nation. The end seems as far away as ever. On October 18, 2018, seventeen years and 10 days after the US invasion, Taliban assassins tried to murder the top US general in charge of Afghanistan. They missed army General Scott Miller but managed to wound the governor of Kandahar province and kill his two top security officials. The parliamentary election scheduled for that week was postponed.

Peace is always more intractable and distant than war planners imagine. I find reporting to the American people with objectivity—facing facts—is the surest route to reach the end. Any objective appraisal of the American experience in Afghanistan must start with the unambiguous virtue of the cause. Under the Taliban, Afghans were submerged in vicious, totalitarian theology. The moral vacuum drew in al-Qaida, which became a threat to every nation. In 2019, Afghans had democracy—if they could keep it.

Call it a gift from the American people.

FIELD NOTE

Eyes of the Beholders

In journalism, when we hit the balance just right, we get double the outrage. Emails that pour into CBS after *60 Minutes* tend to reflect not bias in the reporting, but sincerely felt bias in the viewing. On October 1, 2003, I broadcast a report from Iraq which we titled "War and Peace." My producer Shawn Efran and I set out to get the views of everyone. We spoke to American troops, Iraqi citizens and an enemy soldier who was a member of the Fedayeen Saddam, a guerrilla force loyal to the deposed government. In my view, it's vital to know what the enemy is thinking. What motivates him? Why is he fighting? This is the kind of information US military intelligence spends all day and all night trying to gather. These are some of my favorite emails from October 2, 2003.

SHAME ON SCOTT PELAY [sic] WHAT A BIASED REPORT

HE DID ON IRAQ!! Abnoxious [sic], condensending [sic], arrogant reporter.—Glenn (last name not given)

My nephew is part of the Army National Guard Unit 1/124 Charlie Company serving in Al Ramadi. Your 60 Minutes segment was appreciated. I hope your segment will open not only the eyes but the hearts of Americans again, not to forget these men.—Theresa Roaf

Fire Scott Pelley. Revoke his citizenship. He should be tried for treason.—Chris Jessen

Correspondent Scott Pelley's story on the two Iraqs was a great piece of journalism. Pelley showed us that it's not all bad in Iraq, but it's also not all good. Great job!—David Anderson

Fuck you bastards. Scott Pelly [sic] is a bastard of the first order which means his Mother doesn't know who his Father is.—Robert Evans Smith

I hope one of the Fedayeen shoots you.—Jon Jacques

As the mother of an Army soldier assigned to Zone 17, Baghdad, Iraq it was refreshing to see some good news. This is a real morale booster for the 3rd of the 124th of the Florida National Guard. Thanks again for the good story.—Perry Benton

In December 2000, the Supreme Court of the United States was deliberating whether and how it would decide who would become president. At the Texas governor's mansion, I sat down with the Republican nominee, George W. Bush, for his first interview since the election. The interview was lively and conversational in the *60 Minutes* style. I must have hit the balance, judging from the next day's mail.

> The contempt by the interviewer, Scott Pelley, was oblious [sic] from the start. His body language and inflection of speech could not hold back his true feeling of hatred for Mr. Bush.—Tom Sparks Jr.

> What a great interview that was! Scott Pelley did a great job and president-elect Bush was at his finest yet. I will be looking at him with a renewed sense of respect.—Elaine Perna

> I am sorely disappointed in the way your journalist interviewed Gov. Bush. He was so disrespectful in his words and his demeanor.—Debra Thompson

> Perhaps Mr. Pelley took such a softball approach to curry favor with the man who might become president.—Roger Wilner

> I was disappointed that your reporter (Scott someone) was argumentative with Gov. Bush. He was deliberately trying to anger him and trip him up.—Donna Robinson

> I enjoyed the interview and hope we will have a chance to visit again. Laura joins me in sending our best wishes to you and your family.—George W. Bush

In the introduction of this book I mentioned that journalism strives to open minds, not close them. Some require a little more prying than others.

CHAPTER TWELVE

Hubris
Trump v. Clinton

This is one of the chapters of my career that lacks a hero. But the Greeks discovered in the sixth century BC that cautionary tales are the most enlightening. The playwrights of Athens gave us "hubris," defined as excessive pride or self-confidence—a fault that preened into the center spotlight in the election of 2016.

On Election Day, November 8, I was preparing to anchor CBS News coverage beginning with the *CBS Evening News.* An hour before the broadcast, I began to suspect the night was not going the way most everyone expected. We had reporters in precincts across the country asking voters how they voted and why. These "exit polls" were the subject of a confidential briefing by our director of elections and surveys, Anthony Salvanto,

PhD. As I started scanning his early exit poll report, my finger stopped cold in the middle of one column. I thought I was reading it wrong or the poll contained an error. "Anthony, does this show Trump winning among women?" Trump, after all, was running against a woman and, a month before, he was caught on videotape bragging about sexual assault. "That's right," Salvanto confirmed. "He's ahead with women." Ten hours later, I would be explaining to our audience how Hillary Clinton won the election but lost the presidency.

Weeks before, all the polls had the former secretary of state a full lap ahead of Donald Trump. I believed them. But I began to question my confidence as I listened to voters for a *60 Minutes* story we called "Ask Ohio." I'm not saying *60 Minutes* predicted the election upset, but I will tell you everything you needed to know to foresee the finale was in our story. Producer Henry Schuster, Associate Producer Dina Zingaro and I went to the "Buckeye State" because Ohio almost always gets the winner right. Since 1944, Ohioans have endorsed the loser only once—Nixon over Kennedy—and that 1960 election was one of the narrowest squeakers in presidential history.[1] Ohio is the ultimate swing state because of its demographics and because it splits roughly half and half, north and south, between factory cities and farm towns. The city of Lorain is one of those industrial cities—following the course of the Black River as it empties into Lake Erie—about thirty miles west of Cleveland. In 1895, the spark of the American Century ignited a blast furnace.[2] And for 121 years, a job at the Lorain steel mill was a birthright. The plant, two miles long, forged the rails, drill pipe, weapons and wonders of the twentieth century. "Oh my, it was wonderful. We were making *steel*. We were making *money*," Carlos Hernandez told me as we walked along the chain-link fence that bounded the mill. Making steel was all Hernandez knew for twenty-eight years. But, seven months before we met, he and 542 steelworkers punched the clock for the last time. Cheap

Chinese steel helped silence the furnace in a new century that the fifty-six-year-old Hernandez feared would not be America's. He told me, "It was just a funeral procession coming out the gate, knowing that you never was coming back. You know, we sacrificed time with our families to try to make this company succeed. And this is what it's come to. Just a ghost town. Just a rusted, empty, meaningless place." Across from the plant entrance I could see a shopping street of low red-brick buildings and beckoning plate glass. Windows that once hawked housewares, clothes and jewelry, now displayed only a reflection of the silent plant. Near the corner, a café appeared to be the sole survivor. Unemployment checks kept the coffee boiling. The counter seats were inhabited by the kind of misery that truly does love company. High on a shelf, in the direction of Heaven and just above the Coco Puffs, a figure of the Virgin Mary blessed the scene. Behind the counter, a warning reminded patrons that a certain dignity must be maintained. Pull Up Your Pants, it read. I stepped back outside onto the vacant sidewalk and noticed a black plastic trash bag covered the stoplight. Apparently, traffic had thinned to a point that the probability of a collision had fallen to zero.

Not all of Lorain was a ghost town. Hard times had not yet pulled in at George's Family Restaurant, something of a landmark. George's is the kind of place where pancakes are as wide as the plate and industrial grade coffee steams in white ceramic mugs with Made in China stamped on the bottom. The mansard roof of George's displayed the word *RESTAURANT*, but the painter had to hyphenate the noun to round a corner. This left "*-URANT*" across the front. "You rant," I thought. And inside, did they ever.

"Trump? I don't trust him. Can you imagine if he's the president of the United States, what he's gonna do behind closed doors with women, with his secretaries?" This was the view of Aury Hernandez, Carlos's wife who joined us for coffee. Aury was stubbornly for Clinton. Carlos was voting Trump. Given the family's Hispanic heritage, Aury was repelled by Trump's immigration proposals. Carlos, on the other hand, was a single-issue voter—jobs, specifically, his job. They had been married thirty-six years. I was hoping they'd get to thirty-seven. I said, "I'm sorry I wasn't there when you two sat down together to watch the first debate."

"Oh! We couldn't sit together," Aury said. "No, he sits in the bedroom, I sit in front of the living room TV." Carlos jumped in, "And then we come back and forth and argue." The Hernandezes were raising two grandchildren whom their daughter was unable to support. Carlos drew unemployment benefits. They also relied on a government child support program but were unaware the program had been created with the support of Senator Hillary Clinton. Aury was working, but fast-food wages left them going broke fast. Carlos told me, "It just shows how we're losing our jobs. How things are moving away. Everybody's saying how illegal aliens are coming in and takin' our jobs. Well, the jobs are *moving*. Immigrants don't need to come here anymore; jobs are going to them." It seemed to me Carlos had to be an outlier. I would expect a lifelong union man to be campaigning for the Democrat. So I went to the union hall of United Steel Workers Local 1104 and, as I expected, the front door featured a bright blue Hillary Clinton poster. But inside, the poster couldn't paper over the outrage of laid-off men. "So, show of hands," I said to a group of former mill workers. "How many Trump voters do we have?" All hands but one reached for the ceiling. The one was undecided. Greg Sedar told me, "We need jobs and we're desperate enough we'll take 'em from whoever is gonna give 'em." Wayne Townsend chimed in, "The idea of getting a good job like we had and working it for thirty years and getting the American dream of a house, a car, a child and a family and then retiring at a decent age before you're too old and too crippled to enjoy it—that's gone because of trade deals." I noticed in Local 1104 there were only two portraits on the wall: Philip Murray, who oversaw the bloody founding of the United Steel Workers in Cleveland in 1942, and Franklin Delano Roosevelt, the president who defined what it meant to be a Democrat in the twentieth century. It was the union leadership that Scotch Taped the Hillary Clinton poster to the door. The rank and file were lining up for Trump. For the first time in my career, I was in a Republican union hall.

For many years in America, blue collars have been turning red hot. The middle class has suffered with zero growth in inflation-adjusted income for the last five decades. To be exact, less than zero. The US Department of Commerce—using inflation-adjusted, 2016 dollars—reports that median income of men in 1973 was $38,921. In 2016, it was $52 *less*—$38,869.[3] Middle-class families were worse off than their parents. There are many reasons: the creative destruction of twentieth-century industries by twenty-first-century technologies, tax policy, federal and state regulations on businesses, the decline of labor unions, Wall Street's myopic obsession with quarterly growth and competition from overseas. Carlos Hernandez was right. China's pool of workers without a college degree is nearly four times larger than the same workforce in the United States.[4][5] When innovations in transportation bridged the Pacific, Chinese workers didn't have to leave home to dominate American craft industries such as textiles, furniture and steel. Everyone knows high technology is the engine of the new American economy—but our schools haven't caught up. The former CEO of Caterpillar, Doug Oberhelman, once told me that he *wanted* to open new American manufacturing plants for his mining and construction equipment. Many of his customers were in the US and, Oberhelman explained, Caterpillar would save a fortune in shipping its enormous machines. But he said he could not find enough young Americans with the education to operate high-technology machine tools. Oberhelman also lamented that when he did find an educated candidate, they often failed the drug test.

The most fundamental fact driving American society is this: the upper half of Americans takes home about 90 percent of all income, while the lower half takes home about 10 percent.[6] In 2016, few in Middle America could cite these numbers, but everyone could feel them.

On the day a Washington political website announced "Trump Loses Grip on Ohio," I was sitting on the white wooden steps of Lisa Tolbert's porch in a largely African American neighborhood in inner-city Cleveland.[7] The porch was sturdy, durable, but heavily worn. To her family, it had become familiar to the point of invisibility. Two doors down, we could hear wood splintering under the force of a backhoe. The former neighbor's house was being demolished. Cleveland was still culling homes that were abandoned in the 2008 financial crisis.

Tolbert told me she would vote Clinton, but her lack of excitement was expressed in downcast eyes. She preferred to reminisce about the election of Barack Obama in 2008. "*That* was a historic election," she told me. "You finally had a good candidate and he happened to be black. So that gave it an extra excitement. *This* election is a necessity." She meant "necessity" as in an unpleasant chore. I asked her, "Are you enthusiastic about Hillary Clinton or are you just voting against Donald Trump?"

"I don't know if I'm very enthusiastic about her," Tolbert replied. "I do think she's qualified. Looking at her résumé, she is qualified."

"But you'd really like to have another option?" I asked.

"If there *was* another option," she said wistfully. "But I believe she could do the job."

There was a loud crash. Up the street, another wall buckled behind a hydraulic left hook. I asked Tolbert, "When African Americans vote in large numbers in Ohio, Ohio votes Democratic. And when they don't come to the polls, Ohio votes Republican. What's gonna happen?"

"I'm gonna pray that they come to the polls."

"But you're not feeling that groundswell?" I asked.

"I'm not hearing it," Tolbert admitted.

Many dependable Democrats I spoke to were ambivalent about Hillary Clinton. She was durable but worn—familiar to the point of invisibility. Other Americans were looking for something new—the demolition of the status quo—shrieking, splintering destruction. That was the choice of 2016; repaint the porch or tear it down.

The struggles of unemployed steelworkers seemed far removed from Donald Trump's 5th Avenue apartment in Manhattan. In September 2015, I was waiting for the candidate in his living room admiring the high-rise view of Central Park but not so much his taste in decorating. The ceiling was frescoed. Most everything was gilded. The living room reminded me of the absurdly pretentious palaces occupied by our troops in Iraq. Mentally, I labeled the style of the Trump apartment, "Late Saddam." This was my first interview with Donald Trump for *60 Minutes*. The gold on the furniture would pale in comparison to the candidate's gilding of the facts. Trump swept into the room in an affable mood. He introduced his wife, Melania, who had declined an interview but still wanted to welcome her visitors. Trump and I sat down in an arena of light set up by our cameramen. *60 Minutes* Executive Editor Bill Owens and Producer Robert Anderson watched, a few feet away, on a bank of monitors connected to four cameras. Once we began, I was immediately surprised by Trump's lack of information. His blundering through the issues was unlike any presidential candidate I had ever met. That's not a partisan rebuke. At *60 Minutes*, I've interviewed Republican nominees George W. Bush, John McCain and Mitt Romney. I've done multiple interviews with Repub-

lican congressional leaders including John Boehner, Mitch Mc-
Connell and Paul Ryan. Each of them knew the issues cold.
You could agree or disagree with their policies but their proposed solutions to America's challenges were at least thoughtful
and plausible. Trump, on the other hand, had no idea what he
was talking about. He seemed confident his audience wouldn't
know the difference.

I asked Trump how a tycoon could understand the frustrations
of the unemployed. He said, "You look at the real unemployment rate is [sic] through the roof because all of these people,
ninety-three million, they can't get jobs, people can't get jobs. And
I will change that around very quickly."

Ninety-three million? His figure was absurd. The US Bureau
of Labor Statistics (bear with me here) reports that in October
2016, the number of people in the entire US labor force was
159,712,000.[8] Those were people who were working or recently seeking a job. So, if ninety-three million of them "can't
get jobs," that would mean the unemployment rate was 58 percent. For perspective, the estimated unemployment rate in the
1930s during the Great Depression, peaked at just under 25
percent.[9] As Trump and I spoke, the unemployment rate was
actually 5 percent—not 58 percent. And 5 percent was half of
what President Obama faced in his first year. The number of
jobless Americans looking for work was fewer than eight million, not ninety-three million. In a twisted way, Trump's figure was accurate, but it wasn't true. There *were* ninety-three
million Americans who were not working, but they were retired, in school, disabled or dealing with childcare—in other
words—Americans who had no intention of looking for a job.
Trump's version of what he called "the real unemployment rate"
left me with an image of my ninety-five-year-old mother-in-
law marching into a factory with a lunch pail and a time card. If
the unemployment rate *were* 58 percent, there would be a mob
waving pitchforks and torches, pushing down the fence at 1600
Pennsylvania Avenue. Perhaps this is what Trump understood.

He needed outrage to get his voters to the polls, so he trumped up an outrageous America.

About Obamacare, he said in our interview, "Unless you die, you get nothing." When we turned to the nation's infrastructure, Trump said, "You know, we have to do something. We have to fix our country. Sixty percent of the bridges are unsafe." Fortunately for our country, that was another crazy exaggeration. In 2017, the American Society of Civil Engineers' Infrastructure Report Card said the number of "structurally deficient" bridges amounted to 9.1 percent—not 60 percent.[10] The ASCE report noted that the number of deficient bridges was *decreasing* in 2016. Finally, on foreign policy, Trump offered me this appraisal: "Let me tell you, we don't get along with anybody, our country. We have bad relationships with *everybody.*"

In our interview and in his campaign, Trump created a wholly imaginary dystopian horror where unemployment is more than double what it was in the Great Depression, health insurance pays nothing until you die, *most* bridges are near collapse and, overseas, America has not one friend in the world. Then he offered miraculous solutions. On drug smuggling, Trump told me simply, "It's not going to happen anymore." He explained he would deport all of the estimated eleven million illegal immigrants, but he said, "We're rounding 'em up in a very humane way, in a very nice way. And they're gonna be happy because they wanna be legalized."

I got the impression Trump had little understanding of the challenges facing the country and not a clue about how government worked. It seemed to me he was a real estate huckster who believed his own advertising. In real estate "real" is what you say it is—all kitchens are "gourmet," all living rooms are "flooded with light" and all neighborhood schools are "superior." This is why he embraced the phrase "fake news." He had to come up with an alternative explanation because if what America heard on the news was real, then Donald Trump was a liar.

"You know," I said to Trump, "the problem with a lot of

these ideas is that the president of the United States is not the CEO of America."

"That's right," he acknowledged.

"The Constitution is gonna tell you, 'no,'" I said.

"We'll see," he replied.

"The Congress is gonna tell you 'no.'"

"We'll see."

"The Supreme Court is gonna tell you 'no.'"

"Well, we'll see."

As we wrapped up the interview, I concluded Trump wasn't serious about being president and the Republicans would never nominate him anyway. I believe I was right about Trump, but I was dead wrong about the Republican Party, which was willing to mortgage its conservative credentials to the flamboyant, womanizing, flimflam man. On July 21, 2016, I was in Cleveland's Quicken Loans Arena anchoring CBS News coverage of the Republican National Convention. Among those who were not there was the host governor, Republican John Kasich, who refused to support the nominee. During his acceptance speech, Trump laid out his proprietary litany of America's woes and then delivered words that sent me lunging for my notebook. "Nobody knows the system better than me, which is why I alone can fix it."

That's as good a definition of hubris as you are likely to find. The Greeks had a solution for excessive pride. The goddess Nemesis took revenge in many creative ways. She famously lured the young man Narcissus to a pool where he fell in love with his reflection and obsessed until he died.

In our interview I said to Trump, "You *love* hearing about yourself." His answer was, for once, insightful, informed and concise. "I do," he told me.

My reporting on Hillary Clinton went back twenty-four years to her husband's 1992 campaign when she was first lady of Arkansas. Mrs. Clinton debuted on the national stage as a character in a tragedy. Her husband's sexual predation damaged his candidacy before it began. When the arrows flew, she stood before him as a human shield. The Clintons were infamous before they were famous and so she was typecast the rest of her career. I always marveled at how indomitable she was: the punishing 1992 campaign; the humiliating 1998 impeachment; the blindsiding 2008 loss to Barack Obama, all made me wonder why she never gave in. In the summer of 2016, with confidence that the presidency was hers, she whispered to me in a single sentence why she never surrendered to those who were out to destroy her.

That moment came during a critical weekend for both the Clinton campaign and, as it turned out, for American democracy. The weekend of July 23, 2016, was the campaign's big launch in the final push to November. That Saturday, before a crowd of thousands at Florida International University in Miami, Clinton unveiled her running mate, Senator Tim Kaine of Virginia. The next day, Sunday, would be dominated by a *60 Minutes* interview with Clinton and Kaine that would raise the curtain on the Democratic National Convention set to begin the next morning. The carefully planned weekend was vital to Clinton and, so, it was the very moment chosen by Russia to launch an assault on the election. On Friday, July 22, the day before the Democrats' big push, the Russian military intelligence directorate known by its Russian initials "GRU," orchestrated the release of thousands of emails it had stolen from the Clinton campaign, the Democratic National Committee and the Democratic Congressional Campaign Committee.[11] The Democrats were blindsided. In the early hours, all questions were met with "no comment" or vague suggestions the emails were not authentic. Our *60 Minutes* interview, about twenty-four hours after the release, would be the first time Clinton was confronted with the pilfered memos.

In Miami, my team transformed a large meeting room at the Four Seasons Hotel into a temporary studio. The floor was a tangle of cables connecting cameras to monitors and leading to lights that towered over three pale gold chairs and white marble side tables. Seated at a long desk of monitors were the superb *60 Minutes* producers Henry Schuster and Ruth Streeter.

As we waited for the candidates, there was comical concern among the Clinton staff about the pillow on which the candidate would sit. "The key word was firm," one of the aides said to the others, relaying an instruction from some campaign authority one rank above them. By my count, six pillows were attempted, each squashed and massaged by the underside of the traveling staff. At last, one was selected as having superior attributes that were not apparent to me. To most, the effort would seem obsessive, but I could not blame the candidate for one creature comfort amid the genuinely inhumane grind of a presidential campaign.

Clinton and Kaine breezed into the room in an ebullient mood. Campaign Chairman John Podesta looked grim, as often. I had known him as White House chief of staff under Bill Clinton. His demeanor was a deeper shade of gray today because his emails were among those stolen by Russian military intelligence. The introduction of Kaine at the university had gone well that morning. The election wasn't in the bag, but all polls had Clinton well ahead of Donald Trump. Even so, I was surprised by how relaxed Secretary Clinton seemed at the end of a punishing primary season. Her Democratic Party had been nearly overthrown by the insurgent Senator Bernie Sanders of Vermont. Maybe Clinton was sitting on a firm cushion of relief.

It was Kaine's first day on the job and he was wearing that fact not on his sleeve but on his lapel. When he took his seat, I noticed he was branded with the campaign logo, a capital *H* with an arrow cutting through the middle, pointing toward the viewer's right. I suggested that he rotate the lapel pin before the interview because it was upside down with the arrow pointing left, not a direction the campaign wanted to go now that it was moving toward the general election. Clinton was wearing a bright lightweight pantsuit that looked like it had been color-matched to a robin's egg. The aides who had been on pillow detail were now troubling over the former secretary of state's necklace. They convinced her to button her jacket nearly up to her chin. This left her with a politically unfortunate image. "Madam Secretary?" I asked. "Do you think that looks a little Maoist?"

"You're right!" she said, tossing an incriminating glance over my shoulder at her hand-wringing staff. She unbuttoned the collar.

Earlier, I had debated with my producers whether to ask about the stolen emails. On the one hand, no one knew where they came from or whether they were genuine. But on the other, they were dominating the news of the day and the campaign needed to address them. In Miami, it became clear in a hurry that the campaign had not had time to assess the damage. The candidates were not prepared. I asked about an internal Democratic National Committee email that raised the idea of exploiting a rumor that Sanders was an atheist. "Did you know anything about that?" I asked Clinton. Her eyes widened. She didn't know where this was coming from nor where it was going. She looked vulnerable.

"No," she said. "And I didn't know anything about it. And I haven't read any of those [emails]. But I am adamantly opposed to anyone bringing religion into our political process."

"But the point is," I said, "you have people in the Democratic National Committee working against Bernie Sanders, their fellow Democrat."

"Again, I don't know anything. I don't know anything about these emails. I haven't followed it. But I'm very proud of the campaign that I ran. And I'm very proud of the campaign that Senator Sanders ran."

This was the interview equivalent of leaning back against

the ropes with your gloves protecting your face. There were no devastating bombshells in the emails but there was plenty of evidence that officials in the Democratic National Committee didn't want Sanders and had their thumb on the scale for Clinton.

This revelation is what was so shrewd about the Russian GRU's timing. Hillary Clinton was going to be the nominee—this much we knew—but she needed Sanders' legions of supporters to help her with the general election, especially with get-out-the-vote organization. The GRU dropped the emails like a cluster bomb on the Democratic convention in Philadelphia's Wells Fargo Center. Sanders supporters were angry and disgusted. Many wore protest T-shirts. The night Clinton won the nomination, I watched some of them walk out on the convention in tears.

I have no idea whether Russian President Vladimir Putin watched *60 Minutes* the night before the opening of the Democratic National Convention but this—Hillary Clinton, on America's preeminent news program, pummeled with embarrassing questions for which she was unprepared—was exactly what Putin had in mind. Two days later, in a news conference, Donald Trump invited the Russians to dig deeper. "Russia, if you're listening, I hope you're able to find the thirty thousand emails that are missing," Mr. Trump said. Apparently, Russia was listening. According to the FBI's investigation, that same day, the GRU launched its first hack attack on Hillary Clinton's personal email accounts.[12]

No blood was shed by the Russian attack on our democracy, but was it truly less harmful to the American *way of life* than the attacks on 9/11? I don't want to overdraw the comparison to the mayhem unleashed by al-Qaida. But if an adversary wants to destroy America, is it more effective with a violent frontal assault that unifies the USA, or with a clandestine attack that sets us at each other's political throats? Leave party politics out of this.

Maybe next time, the Russians, the Chinese or North Koreans will decide they don't like the Republican nominee. The important point is this: the Constitution of the United States rests in the National Archives in a bombproof vault, but the Russians got to it anyway.

The email debacle was damaging, but the greatest obstacle to Hillary Clinton's election was not the GRU nor Donald Trump, it was Hillary Clinton. Our CBS News poll revealed that 67 percent of Americans believed she was untrustworthy. No presidential candidate with negative ratings like hers had ever been elected. In every interview I did with Clinton in 2016, I x-rayed her Achilles' heel. In Miami, I asked, "Jimmy Carter said in 1976, 'I'll never tell a lie.' What can you tell the American people in this interview about your own honesty and the honesty of a Clinton White House?"

"I think if you look at my public service, I have been as straightforward and honest as I could be. I haven't always been perfect, but I don't know anyone who is. And we're going to have a campaign and a White House that the American people will be able to look at and believe that Tim [Kaine] and I are working every day for them, that they can count on us, that they can trust us." I followed up, "Your critics are going to say, 'See? She didn't say, I will never tell a lie.'" Clinton sharpened her tone, "Well, you've done this to me before, Scott. And I remember that very well." An interesting choice of phrase, I thought. Not, "You've asked me this before," but rather, "You've *done* this to me before." She was remembering our interview for the *CBS Evening News*, five months before, in Las Vegas, before the Nevada primary. When writing the questions for that interview, I included what I considered to be a "softball," a reference to Mr. Carter's quote from 1976. I thought of it as a softball because there was only one way to answer that question. But I included it because I knew it would make news—"Clinton Promises to Always Tell the Truth," was the way I imagined the headlines.

In her spartan Las Vegas campaign headquarters, I wound up and lofted the slow pitch right over the plate and watched with astonishment—a swing and a miss.

"You talk about leveling with the American people. Have you always told the truth?" I asked.

"I've always tried to. Always. Always."

"Some people are gonna call that wiggle room that you just gave yourself. Jimmy Carter said, 'I will never lie to you.'"

"Well, but that's, but, you know, you're asking me to say, 'Have I ever?' I don't believe I ever have. I don't believe I ever have. I don't believe I ever will. I'm gonna do the best I can to level with the American people, starting in this campaign where I and people supporting my analysis have said repeatedly that what I'm saying is supported by the facts."

The answer featuring four equivocations was seized savagely by the late-night comedy shows. *The Late Show* on CBS ran the clip and cut to a tight shot of Stephen Colbert shouting *"Noooooooooo!"* The Clinton campaign called my bosses to complain. Somehow, to the campaign, the question didn't seem "fair." I had thought questions about her trustworthiness would be *exactly* the questions she would welcome. Her perceived lack of honesty was a threat she needed to meet head-on. This was what Robert Kennedy liked to call, "Hanging a lantern on your problem." In my view, if reporters didn't ask, *she* should bring it up. But Hillary Clinton, after suffering through her husband's serial lying, was hypersensitive to the question of dishonesty. As I pressed ahead in our Miami interview, in July 2016, she explained why.

"Well, you've done this to me before, Scott. And I remember that very well."

"And it was a question you didn't like," I acknowledged.

"Well, no. But I guess my answer would be the same. I certainly never intend to. And I certainly don't believe I have. And so, yes, I can say I never will."

There it was, finally. Why did it feel like I was pulling a molar with pliers? Would it have changed history if she had come to this formulation a year before? Clinton continued, "And I wish you'd ask that question of everybody running. Because I think every one of us should be held to the same standard. I often feel like there's the 'Hillary standard' and then there's the standard for everybody else."

"What's the 'Hillary standard'?" I asked.

"Well, it is, as you heard at the Republican convention, unfounded, inaccurate, mean-spirited attacks with no basis in truth, reality, which take on a life of their own. I see it. I understand it. People are very willing to say things about me, to make accusations about me that are... I don't get upset about them anymore, but, they are very regrettable." She was right, of course, about the double standard. The appearance of dishonesty was gum on her shoe while the outright lies of her opponent never seemed to stick to Teflon Don.

On July 26, two days after the Miami interview, I was on the floor of the Philadelphia Democratic National Convention. No one would deny her this night—not her husband, not the Democrats, not the Republicans, not the Russians. For a quarter of a century, we had witnessed the pillorying of Hillary and yet, she never gave in. In our Nevada interview, I asked where her perseverance came from. She reached back to her childhood, remembering a turning point when she was bullied by kids in her neighborhood. "And so, the kids knocked me down, pushed me around. I ran back in crying. And my mother met me at the door. She said, 'There is no room for cowards in this house. You go right back out there and stand up for yourself.' I thought I was gonna die, Scott. I mean, I have never been more afraid. And I begged her, begged her. She said, 'Out! Right now!' So, I came back out. And I said, 'I'm not going inside the house. I'm here. I wanna play.' And literally, they formed a circle. And this one girl who had been so mean to me came over and she pushed me. And then I just pushed her right back. And she was so surprised. So, I played that day and every day after that. But if my mother had not given me that tough love that I think every kid needs at some point in his or her life, my life mighta been very different."

At the *Evening News* set on the floor of the convention, I was thinking back on her "tough love" story. I turned to my laptop and Googled her mother, Dorothy Rodham. Mrs. Rodham's birth date jumped off the screen. "Born 1919," it read. "I'll be damned," I whispered to myself. Dorothy Rodham had been born before women could vote. Now her daughter, on this night, would be the first woman nominated by a major party for president of the United States.

Her mother's lesson to "push back" only grew stronger with years. When our Miami interview ended, after the microphones went cold and the lights went dark, I leaned forward, took her hand and said, "Madam Secretary, reasonable people will disagree about you and your policies, but I've always been inspired by the fight in you." Her shield slipped for an instant. She leaned into me and whispered, "If they had left me alone, I probably would have quit by now."

About six weeks later, in September 2016, we were preparing for what had become a tradition at *60 Minutes*. The season's first broadcast in a presidential election year centers on interviews with the two major party nominees. *60 Minutes* established this in its first season in 1968 with Richard Nixon and Hubert Humphrey. In 2012, I did the profile of Republican nominee Mitt Romney. In 2008, I profiled GOP nominee John McCain. About a week before my scheduled interview with Secretary Clinton, her campaign advisors called *60 Minutes* to say they *would* do the interview but they *would not* do the interview with Scott Pelley. The advisors explained they didn't like my questions about trustworthiness and didn't want to get them again, as they said, "five weeks before Election Day." This demand from the campaign violated the ethics of journalism. An independent news organization cannot allow a campaign to dictate the terms of an interview. This is precisely why the National Commission on Presidential Debates does not allow campaigns to have any say in picking the debate moderators. Secretary Clinton was free to decline the interview, but she could not choose her interviewer nor decide which questions she wanted asked. In my view, the campaign was selling its candidate short. I thought Clinton had done a fine job with the "honesty" question in Miami and I was sure she would do so again. I'd known Clinton as long or longer than many of her senior staff members. There was one thing of which I was sure—ninety-nine times out of a hundred, she could handle herself in an interview. The irony in their demand, of course, was that a campaign battling ethics allegations was now insisting we do something unethical. *60 Minutes* told the campaign managers they could not choose their correspondent. They declined the interview. We cancelled an interview with Donald Trump, as it wouldn't be fair to do one without the other. The Clinton campaign's demand was fateful. Something on the order of thirteen million Americans would have watched *60 Minutes*. Secretary Clinton was a month away from losing the presidency by 77,000 votes.[13]

On election night, I walked under the lights of Studio 57 at the CBS News Broadcast Center in Manhattan. I sat down on my set to work on last-minute rewrites for the *CBS Evening News*. Our excellent head writer and chief editor, Jerry Cipriano, and I lobbed ideas at each other throughout each day and typically narrowed the script to a consensus a few seconds before air. Trump's lead among women in our exit poll was the most important development of the hour. But I could not reveal that to the audience. We never want our exit polls to influence voting, so we wait until the voting ends in a state before we tell the audience why that state voted the way it did. At the beginning of our night, voting was still underway everywhere. Deep in the back of the studio were the "brains" of our coverage. CBS News Director of Elections and Surveys, Anthony Salvanto, led a team of a dozen political scientists, statisticians and producers, who pored over a powerful computer program that pulled in data from official vote tallies and from our exit polls. After my reporting in Ohio, I *was* expecting a closer race than forecast but not one of us expected a Trump victory. An upset wasn't in our CBS News polling, nor was it in any other scientific poll.

After many predictable states voted predictably, I stood beside Salvanto and announced the first big swing state, Ohio, was leaning to Donald Trump. Salvanto explained that counties around Cleveland were contributing mightily to Trump's lead. Those were the counties I had visited. I thought back fondly to Aury and Carlos Hernandez—the married couple who couldn't watch the presidential debates together—and to the steelworkers pledging allegiance to Trump under the sorrowful gaze of Franklin Roosevelt. Salvanto pointed out that blue-collar workers in Pennsylvania, Michigan and Wisconsin who had been reliably Democratic were also voting Trump. At 10:24 p.m. I announced, "CBS News is projecting that, once all the votes are counted, Donald Trump will win Ohio. This keeps his hopes alive." Based on CBS News forecasts I was seeing, I sent a private text message to my wife: Trump real possibility. As the digital clock under my teleprompter flashed 11:29 p.m., we projected Trump would take Florida. We cut to our camera at the Clinton victory party. Thousands had gathered in an exuberant mood in the Jacob Javits Convention Center on the West Side of Manhattan. Now the crowd looked crestfallen, bewildered. The clock rounded midnight but the decisive states were too close to call. Salvanto surrendered his suit coat, his sleeves were rolled to the elbows and his wire-rimmed glasses were plotting their escape from the end of his nose. He gave us the "all clear" to project Iowa and Georgia for Trump.

Clinton didn't wait for us to declare the winner. At 2:50 a.m., Trump walked into Manhattan's Hilton Hotel ballroom. To my eye, he looked mildly surprised. In recent days, he had talked openly about returning to his real estate company. "I've received a call from Secretary Clinton," he began, interrupted by cheers. Trump pantomimed an embrace of the crowd. "She congratulated us, it is about *us*, for our victory. And I congratulated her and her family on a very, very hard-fought campaign. She fought very hard." He added, "We owe her a major debt of gratitude for service to our country." It was an unexpectedly magnanimous sentiment from a man who, days before, had been leading chants of "Lock her up! Lock her up!"

According to the final, official, tally of the United States Federal Election Commission, Hillary Clinton won the election by 2,868,691 votes.[14] But the president is not elected by the people. You may have voted in many elections, but you have never cast a ballot for president of the United States. Your vote has always gone to an elector who is pledged to your choice.

The architects of the Constitution had a difference of opinion over whether the president should be elected by Congress, state governors, state legislatures or the people. Some warned that a president elected by a legislature would be beholden to that legislature or would be tempted to bribe its members. Others insisted the people writ large couldn't be trusted with such a decision. This debate was so intractable that the vote was postponed to near the end of the Constitutional Convention of 1787. By then, the delegates had been sweating out the Philadelphia summer for nearly four months. On September 4 the convention's Committee of Eleven, also known as the Committee on Postponed Matters, presented its plan for electing the president.[15] The people would vote for electors who would be appointed by politicians in each state. After each election, this electoral "college" would be disbanded so they couldn't be bribed in the next election. The number of electors would equal the number of each state's senators and representatives. The convention's delegates debated the proposal the rest of the day. They were getting nowhere. The next day, delegate James McHenry noted, "The greatest part of the day was in desultory conversation on the part of the report respecting the mode of chusing [sic] the President—adjourned without coming to a conclusion."[16] It wasn't until September 6 that the plan to put electors between the people and their president passed on a vote of nine to two.

Today, forty-eight states and the District of Columbia are "winner take all." So, if a candidate wins a state by only 50.1 percent of the popular vote, he or she takes all of that state's electoral votes. (Maine and Nebraska are the two which award electoral votes proportionally.) This is how Donald Trump got buried in the popular vote and is now president of the United States. Trump clinched the Electoral College 304 to 227. He did it with slender margins in Wisconsin where he won by 22,748 votes, Pennsylvania with a margin of 44,292 votes and Michigan where he squeaked by with 10,704 votes. That was the closest presidential election in Michigan history. Added together, Trump won the presidency by 77,744 votes out of more than 137,000,000 votes nationwide.[17] [18] This represents a margin of 0.056 percent. Mr. Trump would later describe this as a "landslide," but in reality, it was about half a teaspoon of luck. Consider this: the number of votes for *write-in* candidates in Wisconsin and Pennsylvania were about the same as Mr. Trump's margins in those states.[19]

The Ghost of Elections Past warns President Trump to beware of his "landslide." Only four presidents before him have lost the popular vote, and three of them were voted out in the next election.[20] George W. Bush is the only president to lose the popular vote (2000) and serve two terms.

How did national polls fail to predict Trump? To a degree,

they didn't fail. Many polls accurately predicted Clinton's win by almost three million votes. What the polling failed to capture was the late, almost imperceptible shift in states that Clinton, through hubris or overconfidence, took for granted. The rising heat under those blue collars turned the collars Republican red. The Three Furies of Clinton's Greek tragedy went by the names Michigan, Wisconsin and Pennsylvania.

At 3:30 a.m., the morning after Election Day, I signed off with this, "We sure are grateful you stayed with us all this time. The raucous, rancorous election of 2016 now comes to a peaceful if improbable end. Seventy-year-old Donald J. Trump will be sworn in as the forty-fifth president of the United States on January 20th." As I spoke, I noticed tears streaming down the cheeks of my floor director standing next to Camera 3. She kept silent and professional but could not contain her anguish.

Most everyone I spoke with across the country felt strongly about the election. Either way it went, about half the voters were going to be—not just disappointed—but anxious. Before Election Day, a good friend of mine asked a question that caught me off guard. Her question led me to write an essay which I saved for the *CBS Evening News* broadcast the day after election night. At the time I wrote it, I didn't know who would win. But the words worked either way. I ended that broadcast with this:

In the days before Election Day, someone asked me a question I had never considered before, 'Are we going to be okay?' I didn't know who they wanted for president; it didn't matter. This was the 'anxiety election' on both sides of the divide.

Do *these* words sum up your fears of the election result: 'partisanship, absurd judgment and ambitious, self-serving behavior?' If so, consider, those are the words John Adams used to advocate for a constitution with three branches of government: separate, equal and hopelessly encumbered by hobbles known as checks and balances. James Madison called the separation of powers, 'The essential precaution in favor of liberty.'

The American government is inefficient. These days we call it gridlock. But that is what the founders were striving for: a system that would slow down—even stop—when politics became too partisan, absurd and self-serving. The Constitution is a circuit breaker that prevents real damage.

If you are among those who believe this was the election no one saw coming—you're mistaken. The founders could not have imagined the horizons of our modern world, but the range of human nature is ever the same. From the second-floor windows of a building in Philadelphia, they could see a distance of 229 years.

Are you going to get what you want from the next government? No telling. Are we going to be okay? No question. That's the *CBS Evening News*, for all of us at CBS News, all around the world, good night.

I'm sticking with that analysis because I take the long view. To paraphrase Walt Whitman, "He that sees the farthest has the most faith."[21] In the first half of the Trump administration the circuit breaker functioned as designed. When President Trump attempted end runs around the federal courts and the Congress, he was frustrated. When he fired his FBI Director, his own Justice Department appointed a special counsel to investigate. In 2018, when Mr. Trump stood next to Vladimir Putin and defended the Russian president against US government evidence of Russian election tampering, the public outcry, Republican and Democrat, forced him to read a retraction written for him by the White House staff. As of this writing, he has been unable to fulfil major campaign promises including prosecuting Hillary Clinton, the repeal and replacement of Obamacare and the deportation of eleven million illegal immigrants. Nor has he received congressional support for a two-thousand-mile border wall.

I'm reminded of what Mr. Trump said in our interview when I suggested that the president of the United States is not the CEO of America. "We'll see," he said then. Now, we have seen.

The 2016 split-decision election was the result of a nation struggling to decide between the two most unpopular candidates ever to run.[22] In my opinion, as of this writing in 2019, both political parties are failing the nation. They have exhausted their strength in endless battle to discredit one another. I am hopeful it will not take a cataclysm to shake Democrats and Republicans from their winner-take-all narcissism. As the Russian GRU understands, these times will not favor a deeply divided people.

Ohio's voters, as often, were prescient. Hillary Clinton lost because African American voters were no longer compelled by the excitement of making history, and blue-collar workers feared their best days *were* history. Craig Cooper, an unemployed steelworker, summed it up to me this way: "There's millions of people in the United States and *these* are the two best people that we can get to lead us? I just find that hard to believe. I really do."

CHAPTER THIRTEEN

Skepticism
A Failure of Government and Journalism

"So," I said aloud. "*That's* the last mistake I'll ever make."
People who know me understand I can occasionally be
forgetful of the necessities that crowd our lives: phones, keys,
flash drives, items that slip my mind when my body and brain
are not in the same place. This time, I was almost amused that
my absentmindedness would be the end of me after all, as my
wife had often predicted.

March 21, 2003, was the first day of the invasion of Iraq. I
crossed from Kuwait into Iraq with a CBS News team including producers Bill Owens and Mark Hooper, cameraman Sean
Keene, soundman Paul Hardy and satellite uplink engineer Perry
Jones. We were working independently, outside the official military embed system. A short distance into Iraq we came across US

marines fighting to hold Umm Qasr, Saddam's only deep-water port on the Persian Gulf. Iraqi Republican Guard troops were sheltered behind a building about two-hundred yards outside the port perimeter. They were lobbing mortar shells onto the marines' position. Fox Company seized a sandy embankment and opened a counterattack. When machine gun fire didn't stop the mortars, the marines brought up shoulder-fired anti-tank missiles. Two Javelin missiles rocked the Iraqi redoubt, but the enemy kept shooting.

An incoming Iraqi shell, unlike the ones before, rose directly above the marines and exploded in midair. Fox Company instantly recognized this as a classic dispersion profile for a nerve gas weapon. "GAS! GAS! GAS!" the marines shouted. Each man reflexively pulled his gas mask over his face in one swift motion and resumed fire. I looked to see that Sean and Paul had their masks on. Then I discovered, in my hurry to get to Fox Company's position, I'd left my mask in our SUV about one hundred yards away. Bill Owens, who had been my producer at the White House during the Clinton administration, was watching the battle and phoning in a report to CBS News radio. When I turned to measure the distance back to my mask I realized I was doomed. I braced myself. Then I noticed Owens running *into* the firefight. I thought, *What are you doing? Get down!* Owens had my mask in his fist. His legs were digging into the sand so hard he must have quickened the rotation of the Earth. With machine gun fire all around, shells rising and the belief that poison gas was descending, Bill shoved the mask into my hands. It was an act of extraordinary courage that can never be repaid, only admired.

We did not know the detonation over our heads was not poison gas. That first morning, we did not imagine that the sole justification for the war, like the shell, would go up in smoke. Saddam Hussein was a despot, a tyrant and a murderer, but he was not a liar when he denied concealing an arsenal of weapons of mass destruction. Fox Company was firing the opening rounds in a war that would rage for more than fifteen years and kill well over 280,000 people.[1] Included in this toll were 4,832 American and allied troops and 468 American and allied contractors.[2] I covered our forces in Iraq for more than a decade. I watched them sacrifice, fight and die to salvage something useful from one of the great foreign policy blunders in American history. Iraq was another failure to heed Winston Churchill's warning, "War now is nothing but toil, blood, death, squalor, and lying propaganda."[3]

Six months before that gunfight, Bill Owens and I were in the Oval Office to ask President Bush whether he intended to commit the nation to another war—one year after the invasion of Afghanistan. In early September 2002, Washington was ninety degrees and muggy. Morning sun glazed the eleven-foot windows that frame the Rose Garden. A team of CBS News photographers, sound engineers, producers and associate producers was busy with final adjustments in the president's 816-square-foot office. Nine television lights impaled on aluminum stands painted a circle around two upholstered, cane-back armchairs. The chairs were added by President Herbert Hoover during his restoration of the Oval after the West Wing was destroyed by fire in 1929.[4] The chairs, facing each other, were leaving an impression near the middle of the oval rug that covered all but the edges of the polished floor fashioned from walnut and quarter sawn white oak.[5] At the center of the rug, the Seal of the President was rendered in blue and gold which reflected the same seal, eighteen feet above, embossed in plaster on the ceiling. Franklin Roosevelt had another Seal of the President carved into a kneehole panel at the front of the president's desk. On the seal, an eagle holds the national motto in its beak reading *E Pluribus Unum*, Latin for "Out of Many, One." But when it comes to presidential seals in the Oval Office, you could flip that to read *Unum de Multis*. (Out of One, Many.)

Despite the heat oppressing the Rose Garden, Press Secretary Ari Fleischer came in with a revised forecast. "You're going to feel the chill," Fleischer warned me.

"Ari, I have to ask the president about Iraq, people need to know whether it's next," I protested.

"I'm just telling you, if you ask about Iraq, you're going to feel the chill," the press secretary insisted.

Our interview that morning was meant to be centered on the anniversary of 9/11, which was days away. Owens and I were finishing a documentary on how the president and the White House grappled with the day America was attacked. But "anonymous sources" and "senior officials" in the administration were leaking stories about an intolerable threat posed by Saddam Hussein. It looked to me like the beginning of an influence campaign to convince the public to support another war. Fleischer's warning was matter-of-fact. The sense of it was: "You want to wreck your interview with the president? Be my guest." Mr. Bush may not have wanted to hear questions about Iraq, but the American people wanted them asked. The earlier skepticism is brought to bear on issues of war, the more effective it can be in balancing the debate.

Mr. Bush walked into the Oval, a black mood in a blue suit. Someone had just told him something he didn't want to hear. I don't know what it was, but in this timeframe, the president was getting conflicting advice. Vice President Dick Cheney and Defense Secretary Donald Rumsfeld were arguing for war. They assured the commander in chief that Iraq would be quick and easy. Secretary of State Colin Powell—a retired army four-star general, the former chairman of the Joint Chiefs of Staff and the only member of the war cabinet with combat experience—counseled patience. Powell warned that the president could end up owning Iraq and the demands of its twenty-five million people.[6]

Mr. Bush and I sat down in the pool of light. Privately, before the cameras rolled, I tried to impress him with the importance of being candid on Iraq. I reached back to our shared West Texas heritage. "Mr. President," I said, leaning forward, my elbows pressing my knees. "We're hearing a lot of talk about Iraq all of a sudden. You're going to have to explain this to the folks at the feed store in Floydada, so they understand what their sons and daughters might be asked to do." Fleischer's forecast was off. It wasn't a chill; it was a hard freeze. The president set his jaw, narrowed his eyes and said not a word. The cameras rolled. I got to the point.

"Are you committed to ending the rule of Saddam Hussein?"

"I'm committed to regime change," the president said tersely. That was his full answer. "Don't ask again" was written all over his face. I tried another angle. "There are those who have been vocal in their advice against war in Iraq, some of our allies in the [1991] Gulf War—Saudi Arabia, Turkey, for example. Even your father's former national security advisor. What is it that they don't understand about the Iraq question that you *do*?"

"The policy of the government is regime change, Scott. Hasn't changed. I get all kinds of advice. I'm listening to the advice. I appreciate the consultations. And we'll consult with a lot of people. But our policy hasn't changed."

Nor would it. At the time that Mr. Bush and I were knee to knee in the Oval, the president was already far down the road to war.

The early discussions of Iraq came even before 9/11. In June 2001, Douglas Feith, Mr. Bush's nominee for undersecretary of defense, told the Senate Armed Services Committee that the US "has a strong interest...in facilitating as best we can the liberation of Iraq."[7] Mr. Bush's nominee for deputy secretary of defense, Paul Wolfowitz, told the committee, "We...are exploring whether more can be done to hasten the replacement of the present regime... Clearly our armed forces will have a prominent part to play in our national strategy toward Iraq."[8] Wolfowitz was among several of the president's top advisors who had been with the elder Mr. Bush through the Gulf War in 1990/91.[9] Back then, Vice President Cheney was George H. W. Bush's secretary of defense. Others who served the father and joined the son's administration included: Vice President Cheney's chief of staff, Lewis "Scooter" Libby;[10] National Security Advisor Condoleezza Rice;[11] her deputy, Stephen Hadley;[12] and National Security Council staff member, Zalmay Khalilzad.[13] In 1991, the president's father liberated Kuwait. But, wary of a quagmire, he refused to march on Baghdad to overthrow Saddam. Instead, the elder Mr. Bush went on the radio to encourage the Iraqi people to rise against the dictator. Many did. But with no combat support from the United States, they were massacred. From that moment, Iraq was unfinished business for the president's advisors. 9/11 presented a fresh chance to settle an old score.

Only seventy-six days after al-Qaida attacked America, a document stamped TOP SECRET CLOSE HOLD listed the issues to be discussed in preparation for war with Iraq. The talking points were prepared for a November 27, 2001, meeting between Secretary of Defense Rumsfeld and General Tommy Franks, the commander of US Central Command. In this document, war was the goal—the justifications for war were listed as options. One of the memo's bullet points is labeled "How start?" Below that heading the document reads:

Saddam moves against Kurds in the north?

US discovers Saddam connection to Sept. 11 attack or to

anthrax attacks? [Anthrax had been mailed to the US Capitol after 9/11.]

Dispute over WMD inspections? Start thinking now about inspection demands.

In a news conference after their meeting, Rumsfeld was questioned about operations in Afghanistan which had started fifty-one days before. He told reporters that General Franks was "Doggedly fixed on the objective."[14] But the truth was, Rumsfeld had just ordered Franks to turn his attention to Iraq. The talking points were declassified in 2010 and released in a Freedom of Information Act request made by the National Security Archive, a nonprofit research organization. At the end of the notes, on the bottom of page three, someone has written in cursive, "Influence Campaign... When begin?"[15]

There were several reasons for the early interest in Iraq. During the Clinton administration, US warplanes enforced two no-fly zones to protect communities opposed to Saddam. Once in a while Saddam fired a missile at the American jets. Saddam also did all he could to obstruct the United Nations' effort to ensure that Iraq's chemical, biological and nuclear programs had been dismantled. Another possible reason was personal. After the 1990/91 Gulf War, an allied intelligence agency uncovered an Iraqi attempt to assassinate George H. W. Bush. The former president was on a victory tour of Kuwait with his wife, Barbara and son, Neil, among others. A bomb was concealed in a Toyota Land Cruiser that was to be parked on Mr. Bush's route. A security source, intimately involved in the case, told me the explosives were so well hidden that the only thing out of place was an extra wire behind the lens of the glove compartment light. The plot was discovered before the Land Cruiser was in position. But I've often wondered whether Saddam's attempt to kill his family played a role in George W. Bush's decision to go to war.

Before beginning the campaign to influence the American people, the administration needed to select from among its three potential pretexts for war. For that, the administration turned to George Tenet, the longtime director of the CIA. Tenet had been appointed by President Clinton in 1997. In an unusual move, George W. Bush decided to keep him. One way to stay in an intelligence job is to stay out of the press. I once ran into Tenet at a Washington social event. I raised the possibility of going on *60 Minutes*. He pulled his thumb and forefinger across a wry smile. "My lips are sealed," he said.

It took a few years, but in 2007, shortly after his retirement, Tenet sat down with me for his first interview. Tenet never supported the second pretext for war listed in the Rumsfeld-Franks memo—"US discovers Saddam connection to Sept. 11 attack." Instead, he told me he was mystified by the Bush administration's post 9/11 haste to invade Iraq. Tenet described walking into the White House a day or so after 9/11 and running into Richard Perle, the chairman of the Defense Policy Board, a civilian advisory committee. Tenet remembered Perle saying, "Iraq has to pay a price for what happened yesterday, they bear responsibility." Tenet told me he was incredulous. "It's September the *12th*. I've got the [airline] manifests with me that tell me al-Qaida did this. Nothing in my head says there is any Iraqi involvement in this in any way, shape, or form and I remember thinking to myself, as I'm about to go brief the president, 'What the hell is he talking about?'" Tenet may have the day of the conversation wrong. He acknowledged later that it could have been a few days after 9/11, but he remains certain about Perle's remark. I asked Tenet in 2007, "You said Iraq made no sense to you at that moment. Does it make any sense to you today?"

"In terms of complicity with 9/11? Absolutely none," he told me. "It never made any sense. We could never verify that there was any Iraqi authority, direction and control, or complicity with al-Qaida for 9/11 or any operational act against America. Period." This left weapons of mass destruction as the most appealing pretext for war remaining from the Rumsfeld-Franks talking points memo.

In our 2002 Oval Office interview, Mr. Bush was batting away my questions on Iraq because the White House had carefully timed its "influence campaign" to sell the American people. The plan called for months of leaks to the press *before* the president began his argument to close the deal. The administration, principally the office of Vice President Cheney, began passing unreliably sourced information about Iraqi weapons of mass destruction to the *New York Times* and others. One of the first leaks was timed three days before the anniversary of 9/11 when emotions would be running high. The *Times* front page announced, "U.S. Says Hussein Intensifies Quest for A-Bomb Parts." Two months later, the *Times* followed up with "Threats and Responses: Chemical Weapons; Iraq Said to Try to Buy Antidote to Nerve Gas." The next month the paper announced, "CIA Hunts Iraq Tie to Soviet Small Pox." Two months after that, another *Times* story ran under the headline "Defectors Bolster U.S. Case Against Iraq, Officials Say." In March 2003, seven months after the propaganda campaign began, the *Times* headlined, "Iraq's Weapons of Fear."

The night of January 28, 2003, in his State of the Union address, the president made his case. There were fifty days left in the Pentagon's secret countdown. One of the president's key indictments centered on an alleged Iraqi nuclear program. Mr. Bush slowed his cadence and looked deeply into the House Chamber to underscore his point. "The British government has learned that Saddam Hussein recently sought significant quantities of uranium from Africa."[16] At the time that he said it, the president's statement was known to the administration to be false. George Tenet's CIA had found the documents that backed up the allegation were forgeries. Tenet asked that the claim be struck from an earlier October 7 speech Mr. Bush delivered in Cincinnati.[17] Yet, it slipped back into the president's most important, most widely viewed annual address. Tenet had been given a draft of the speech in advance for fact-checking. "I didn't read the speech," Tenet told me. "I was involved in a bunch of other things."

"Wait a minute," I said. "The president's *State of the Union*? You didn't read *that*?"

"Right, I didn't. I farmed it out. I got it at a principals meeting, brought it down the hall, handed it to my executive assistant. I said, 'You guys go review this and come back to me if I need to do anything,'" Tenet recalled.

"Nobody came back to you?" I asked.

"And therein lies why I ultimately have to take my share of responsibility," Tenet confessed.

The White House acknowledged the falsehood—four months after the invasion.[18] I asked Tenet how other claims of the president and vice president squared with what he knew at the time. I began, "The president, in October 2002, said, quote, 'We need to think about Saddam Hussein using al-Qaida to do his dirty work.'[19] Is that what you're telling the president?"

"Well, we didn't believe al-Qaida was gonna do Saddam Hussein's dirty work," Tenet said.

I followed up. "January '03, the president again, quote, 'Imagine those nineteen hijackers this time armed by Saddam Hussein.'[20] Is that what you're telling the president?"

"No," Tenet said.

Uranium ore cannot be concentrated to bomb-grade purity until it is spun in a centrifuge. Eleven days after the president's false assertion, Secretary of State Colin Powell presented this missing piece to the U.N. Security Council. He told the council that aluminum tubes, intercepted on their way to Iraq, were centrifuge parts. Powell's presentation on February 5, 2003, was the administration's closing argument. The war would begin in forty-three days. The secretary of state played audio tapes of Iraqi communications that he said revealed a nerve gas arsenal. It seemed, not only was Saddam pursuing an illicit weapon, he was developing *every kind* of weapon of mass destruction, simultaneously, while under more than a decade of crippling U.N. economic sanctions. The propaganda campaign brimmed with confidence, untroubled by doubt.

Producer Bill Owens and I had been looking for independent sources of information with inside knowledge of Saddam's weapons programs. That was difficult. For the most part, they were either inside Iraq or dead. But in February 2003, shortly after Secretary Powell's presentation, we aired an interview with General Nizar al-Khazraji, the former chief of staff of the Iraqi army. During Iraq's war with Iran from 1980 through 1989, al-Khazraji was a hero credited with saving Iraq. But al-Khazraji told us he was fired after he warned Saddam that Iraq would lose the war for Kuwait. In 1996, al-Khazraji slipped out of Iraq to a small town outside of Copenhagen. He bore a resemblance to Saddam: late fifties, receding black hair and a trim mustache obscured by smoke rising from a permanent cigarette. He seemed weary, weary of all he'd seen in life and weary of waiting for a bullet. In the living room of his small cottage, I asked him about Saddam's weapons program. Al-Khazraji offered this analysis: "If you mean the weapons of mass destruction, in my estimation Iraq does not have nuclear capabilities. And if we come to chemical weapons, I also believe that no chemical weapons currently exist. If they do exist, he has no means to use them. There remains the matter of biological weapons. It is probable that Saddam has biological weapons and it is probable that he will use them." Here was a man who had every reason to encourage an American invasion. He was exiled, waiting for Saddam's assassin. An Iraq without Saddam would welcome al-Khazraji as a national hero. Yet, he knocked out two pillars of the Bush administration's argument. No nuclear. No chemical. This also had to be assessed with skepticism, but I find when people speak against their self-interest, that's a strong indication they're telling the truth. General al-Khazraji's truth was nothing like what America was hearing from President Bush.

Journalism students sometimes ask me to name my biggest mistake. This is it. On *60 Minutes II*, we reported what General al-Khazraji told us. But in retrospect, I failed to grasp the importance of the interview. After al-Khazraji, I should have heard an internal alarm and aggressively investigated whether it was possible the administration was blundering into war. A reporter's most important tool is skepticism, what Ernest Hemingway called a "built-in, shock-proof, shit-detector."[21] There was some good reporting questioning the rationale for war but I believe our profession, writ large, let the nation down. What skeptical reporting there was, was shouted down by selective leaks and bellicose speeches. This is a cautionary lesson every generation must learn. It is precisely when the nation's temper turns to war that journalism must pursue the countervailing questions. Those stories and their authors will be excoriated as unpatriotic. But the reverse is true. Providing reporting that might keep America out of a misguided war is the zenith of patriotism. War, above all things, is not an administration's business—it is the *people's* business. When journalism fails to question an administration, the administration fails to question itself.

In the summer of 1971, the Supreme Court of the United States decided *New York Times Co. v. United States*. The Nixon administration sued to stop the *Times* and the *Washington Post* from publishing the Pentagon Papers that revealed how administrations, both Democratic and Republican, cooked the books on Vietnam to deceive the American people. The court found for the newspapers, which is to say, it sided with all citizens who have the right and obligation to inspect their government. Justice Hugo Black, a former US senator from Alabama, wrote a concurrence to the majority opinion which read in part:

> In the First Amendment, the Founding Fathers gave the free press the protection it must have to fulfill its essential role in our democracy. The press was to serve the governed, not the governors. The government's power to censor the press was abolished so that the press would remain forever free to censure the government. The press was protected so that it could bare the secrets of government and inform the people.
>
> Only a free and unrestrained press can effectively expose deception in government. And paramount among the responsibilities of a free press is the duty to prevent any part of the government from deceiving the people and sending them off to distant lands to die of foreign fevers and foreign shot and shell.
>
> In my view, far from deserving condemnation for their courageous reporting, the *New York Times*, the *Washington Post*, and other newspapers should be commended for serving the purpose that the Founding Fathers saw so clearly. In revealing the workings of government that led to the Vietnam War, the newspapers nobly did precisely that which the Founders hoped and trusted they would do.[22]

In 2003, the hidden "workings of government" provoked fear of Iraq in the public, while attempting to lower anxiety in Congress. Defense Secretary Rumsfeld decided in advance that the war would be quick and Iraq would be handed back to Iraqis in short order. Rumsfeld was contemptuous of the Gulf War in 1990/91. The force of about five hundred thousand US and allied troops was far too large in Rumsfeld's view. Rumsfeld was fond of noting that 80 percent of the ammunition sent to the Gulf War was returned.[23] Following his instincts, Rumsfeld cut the Pentagon's troop estimate by two-thirds. There was arrogance on the civilian side of the planning, a sense that the uniformed Pentagon just didn't understand the administration's concept of short, lightning-strike wars. One day in the Oval Office, I was surprised when President Bush confided to me before the invasion, "Yeah, we have a lot of nervous Nellies over at the Pentagon."

The president might have been referring to his army chief of staff, General Eric Shinseki. Shinseki didn't seem nervous, but after a lifetime in the army, he had a clear-eyed view of what the occupation of Iraq would look like. Twenty days after Powell's presentation to the Security Council, Shinseki was asked by the Senate Armed Services Committee how many troops would be required. He replied, "Something on the order of several hundred thousand soldiers is probably a figure that would be required. We're talking about post-hostilities control over a piece of geography that's fairly significant with the kinds of ethnic tensions that could lead to other problems."[24] Shinseki's prescient, honest appraisal blindsided the White House. Two days later, Rumsfeld's deputy, Paul Wolfowitz, was dispatched to the House Budget Committee with this rebuttal: "Some of the higher-end predictions that we have been hearing recently, such as the notion that it will take several hundred thousand US troops to provide stability in post-Saddam Iraq, are wildly off the mark."[25] His appearance before the committee came twenty days before the invasion. Wolfowitz calculated the total cost of the war at $10 billion with a worst case of $100 billion. The actual cost was more than $1 billion *a month*. By 2017 Congress had appropriated $807 billion. However, a study by the Cost of War Project at Brown University estimates the total is well over $2 trillion after you add costs including projected veterans' medical and disability benefits.[26] Wolfowitz's cost estimate was wildly off the mark because he naively ignored the fatal fault line in Iraqi society—the schism between the two main branches of Islam—the Sunnis and the Shiites. Wolfowitz testified that American troops would be "greeted as liberators." He assured the committee that post conflict peacekeeping demands would be low because there was no "record in Iraq of ethnic militias fighting one another." In truth, the record of ethnic militias fighting one another was nearly 1,400 years long.

The split in Islam began with the death of the prophet Muhammad in 632 AD. The divide is more about politics than theology. Shiites believe Muhammad appointed his son-in-law, Ali, as his successor. Shiites hold that only blood relatives of Muhammad can lead the faith. Sunnis, on the other hand, believe Muhammad died without appointing a successor so any learned and righteous member can be appointed leader. A decisive battle was fought in 680 AD near the town of Karbala in present-day Iraq. The Shiite forces were massacred and the Shiite leader was killed.[27] Despite their defeat, today in Iraq, about 65 percent of Muslims are Shiites, only 30 percent belong to the victorious Sunni sect.[28] And therein lies the animosity. From the creation of modern-day Iraq, the minority Sunnis have held power. A rough analogy is South African apartheid—a minority using brutality to repress the majority. It doesn't take a great deal of imagination to predict a Shiite lust for revenge if Saddam was suddenly removed. The Shiites stood to take power for the first time in the democratic system the US intended to impose.[29] [30] General Shinseki foresaw civil war when he warned Congress about "ethnic tensions that could lead to other problems." There *was* a weapon of mass destruction in Iraq. But it was President Bush, not Saddam, who was about to set it off.

Certain of swift, low-cost victory, the civilian leadership of the Pentagon organized an elaborate embed system that assigned journalists to dozens of military units. For the American people, it was an enormous improvement over the censorship and obstruction imposed in the 1990/91 Gulf War. In 2003, as excellent as the embed system was for the public, I felt there should be a role for independent reporting. Bill Owens and I prepared to cover the invasion on our own, unattached to any unit. The risk was high but the principle was vital. The public had a right to independent reporting unaffiliated with the self-interested Pentagon, as Justice Black wrote in his Pentagon Papers opinion, "just as the Founders hoped and trusted we would do."

Our jumping off point was a farmhouse that we rented in the demilitarized zone on Kuwait's border with Iraq. We chose the house because a gap, thirty yards wide, had been bulldozed through the eight-foot-high sand bastion the Kuwaitis erected after their 1990 experience with Iraq. We didn't have to be von Clausewitz to figure out the freshly dug breach was a likely invasion route. But we did not know when the war would begin. We assembled a satellite uplink in the bed of a pickup truck and provisioned the house for a long stay. Our first night was March 20, 2003. Producer Mark Hooper and I were on the flat roof of the house where a camera was tethered to the satellite dish. Winds were light and cool—fifty-nine degrees. In the darkened distance, we heard rumbling. "Sounds like helicopters," Hooper said. "No," I replied. "That's the sound of tank treads on blacktop." We stretched our ears toward the approaching clatter.

"Helicopters," Hooper repeated.

"Tanks," I insisted.

The next moment, two US Marine Corps AH-1 Super Cobra helicopters skimmed the roof of our house. They bolted over the border into Iraq and launched Hellfire missiles into a communications station. *Whoop, Boom! Whoop, Boom!* An image of the desert froze in the flash of each exploding missile. Hooper didn't take time to say "I told you so." He called up the camera crew, Sean Keene and Paul Hardy, and asked our engineer, Perry Jones, to fire up the uplink to bounce our pictures off a satellite twenty-five thousand miles above us. I grabbed a microphone and spoke to the CBS News control room in New York. "The war has started, put us on the air!" I said to the senior producer in charge of our prime-time coverage. Another sortie of attack helicopters thundered over our heads and into Iraq. *Whoop! Boom!* "Stand by," the control room producer said. There was a long, unexplained wait as another nest of Super Cobras released its burden of missiles. "Scott," the New York producer said into my earpiece, "we've checked with our Pentagon correspondent. He cannot confirm that the war has started." One had to admire the usual CBS News caution, but *seriously*? I asked Sean to turn the camera 180 degrees, away from me and onto the explosions illuminating the landscape. *Whoop, Boom! Whoop, Boom! Whoop, Boom!*

"*Jeez!*" the control room producer yelled. "We're coming to you *now!*" That is how America first learned the war was on. Not from the Pentagon, but from independent reporting. There was no danger of giving away any secrets. I took care not to report exactly where I was along the border, and the Iraqis, by this point, were well aware they were under attack. We broke the story from our outpost and remained on the air continually until the sun was up in the DMZ. Our coverage was notable for another reason. Because we were on a farm, there was a chicken coop next to the house. With every explosion, the roosters sounded off. *Boom! Cock-a-doodle-doo! Whump! Cock-a-doodle-doo! Bang! Cock-a-doodle-doo!* They had a lot to crow about, but it was a ridiculous soundtrack. It crossed my mind that I could wring the necks of the roosters. I didn't. We had to live with our comical rendition of "Ol' McDonald had a war."

Shortly after daylight, with the combed cacophony full-throated, a curious US Marine Corps Super Cobra helicopter dropped toward our rooftop and stopped to maul the air forty feet or so above us. The glass Cyclops eyes of Hellfire missiles stared blankly from the hard points on the gunship's stubby "wings." A 20mm Gatling gun was pointing at me, mounted just below the masked pilot in the front seat. I hoped he was a devoted viewer of CBS News and might recognize me, but instead, he seemed to be trying to figure out what we were doing there with something large on a tripod, overlooking a choke-point for the invasion force. *He's either going to shoot us, or he's not,* I said to myself. Then, I remembered a cloth I had in the front left pocket of my pants. It was a cheap facsimile of the original, made in China. With the Super Cobra coiled and motionless in front of me, I pulled out the cloth and unfurled thirteen stripes and fifty stars. Without acknowledgment, the great machine tilted left and peeled away.

American and British armor were flowing through the gap like a torrent through a breach in a levee. They spread across the alluvial plain onto what was, very likely, humanity's first battlefield. Mesopotamia—Greek for, "The land between two rivers"—was the birthplace of civilization. Before recorded time, floods on the Euphrates and the especially unruly Tigris laid layer upon layer of rich, dark earth. Everything that was touched by water sprang aggressively to life. About 10,000 BC, Neolithic nomads, in what is now Iraq, invented agriculture and cattle breeding.[31] With mere survival checked off its "to do" list, humanity had a moment to think. Mesopotamia gave us the wheel and the first written accounts of astronomy, mathematics, law, politics, organized religion and organized murder.[32] History's first record of war was immortalized in about 2700 BC on the Sumerian King List, a four-sided clay column, eight inches tall. The column is in a museum at the University of Oxford.[33] The clay testifies that the Sumerian king, Enmebaragesi, defeated the city-state of Elam.[34] The cuneiform symbols note that the king "carried away as spoil, the weapons of the land of Elam."[35] Forty-seven centuries later, the rationale for *this* war in Meso-potamia was precisely the same—to carry away the weapons of mass destruction of the land of Saddam.

At the farmhouse, we had two SUVs and a Chevy pickup with our nine-foot-wide satellite dish resting in the bed. Bill and I got the team together and asked who wanted to join the invasion. Each man raised his hand. We compressed more food, water and jerry cans of gasoline into the vehicles than their springs should shoulder. Water and gas could be lethal limitations. We'd have to beg and borrow more of both or our coverage would be limited to three days or so. We twisted ourselves into body armor, slid into the heavy, complaining vehicles and lumbered through the severed embankment, joining the invasion flood. We planned to navigate the open desert to intersect Iraqi Freeway 1, which linked the Persian Gulf port of Umm Qasr to the city of Basra, an ancient inland port from which the mythical Sinbad sailed. Within half an hour we ran across another team of reporters with the same idea. We stopped for a familiar face peering through the other windshield. Fifty-year-old Terry Lloyd was a longtime foreign correspondent for the British television network ITN. Lloyd had reported from the Middle East for more than two decades. It was Lloyd, in 1988, who revealed to the world that Saddam Hussein had massacred five thousand Iraqi Kurdish civilians with nerve gas. Anytime I covered a story in the region it seemed Terry Lloyd was several steps ahead of me. I was an admirer and a fan. We spoke to Lloyd through the open driver's side windows for a few minutes, comparing notes. My team drove on to Umm Qasr. Lloyd and his team headed in the opposite direction to Basra. About an hour later, Lloyd's SUV ran across an Iraqi army unit. His truck turned around and headed toward a platoon of US marines. Inside Lloyd's vehicle, that must have seemed prudent. But, from the marines' point of view, Lloyd's SUV was coming at them from the Iraqi line. The marines opened fire. The Iraqis responded. Lloyd, his cameraman, Fred Nérac, and a Lebanese interpreter, Hussein Osman, were killed. Cameraman Daniel Demoustier, the lone survivor, was wounded. Later, a British government inquest would judge the deaths "unlawful."[36] I agree that more care should have been taken before opening fire on a civilian SUV, but I can also see how the situation must have looked from the marines' perspective.

The few teams of reporters that were independent of the military embed system assumed all responsibility for the risk. We stood to be killed by either side. Mistaken identity was a danger we could mitigate only with four long strips of duct tape on the hood and doors of our vehicles that intersected in the lines "TV." Many days into our journey, the Pentagon called CBS News headquarters to insist that my team be ordered off the battlefield because the military said it "couldn't guarantee our safety." Our New York headquarters dutifully and clearly passed on the message by satellite phone but we all agreed the order was "garbled" and impossible to understand. In a second attempt, an army public affairs major back in Kuwait warned us by satellite phone that "no unilateral reporters would be allowed north of Tallil," a large Iraqi air base. I had to explain to the major, in all honesty, we were already one hundred miles north of Tallil and headed to Baghdad. No one was asking the Pentagon to guarantee our safety. Most every day, someone at CBS News risks his or her life to provide the American people with independent reporting from the most dangerous points on Earth. There are many professions in which dedicated people put their lives on the line to serve the public: police officers, firefighters, the military—and journalism is another. Since 1948, seventeen CBS News journalists have given their lives in the line of duty. Many more have been wounded or endured captivity. ITN's Terry Lloyd was likely the first casualty among reporters in the Iraq war, but over the decade to follow, there would be many more. Some of them dear friends.

My team rolled into Umm Qasr. The heavy steel gates that barred the road to the port were mangled. A US Marine Corps tank had defeated the padlock and everything it was attached to. Umm Qasr connected to the Persian Gulf via the man-made Khawr az-Zubayr Waterway canal. If allied reinforcements or humanitarian aid were to be delivered en masse they would have to come by sea. Umm Qasr was the only way.

Our three-vehicle convoy entered a vast expanse of concrete, warehouses and railcars on the shore of the steel gray Gulf. The new owners, as of that morning, were the marines of Fox Company, part of the 15th Marine Expeditionary Unit out of Camp Pendleton, California. It was with Fox Company that I had forgotten my gas mask during the ensuing firefight. For Fox, seizing the port had been tougher than expected. Iraqi forces were dug in, armed with anti-tank rockets and mortars. The marines won the battle without casualties. But the enemy declined the defeat. They weren't playing by the rules. "I certainly thought the laws of war would be understood," Fox Company's commanding officer, Captain Rick Crevier told me. "I didn't think that we were going to be encountering enemy carrying white flags and dressed in civilian gear. We've learned they don't respect the white flags. We've learned that they wave white flags at us and go on back to their defensive positions, so it requires us to have our head on a swivel."

"Puts you in a hell of a spot," I said.

"You're right. It has put us in an awful spot."

Corporal Mike Breslin from Maryland told me, "The Iraqi infantry is just too cowardly to wear their uniforms and stand up and fight us. They're just using, basically, terrorist techniques to inflict 'onesies' and 'twosies' of casualties instead of fighting us like men." Breslin didn't know it, but he had just described the next fifteen years of the American experience in Iraq.

Along Highway 1, a few miles from the port, was the village of Safwan. There, I caught an early sign that even civilians who benefitted from the end of Saddam were furious with America. A long line of people carrying buckets cued up behind a tanker truck filled with fresh water. A tall, older gentleman walked straight up to me. "Where have you been!" he demanded in an angry voice just below a shout. *"Where have you been?"* The man's English was perfect. His suit was dirty and wrinkled but was of a cut that suggested better times. "Our families have been hanging from lampposts for twelve years!" he shouted at me. "Where have you been?" His gray hair and beard gave him the bearing of a college professor. It turned out he was an English instructor, although unemployed. He was bitter—the kind of bitterness that is wrung from a broken heart. "You *asked* us to rise up! You *encouraged* us. Why did you forsake us?" he howled. He was referring to George H. W. Bush's call to the Iraqi people in 1991 to overthrow their despot. The downtrodden Shiites rose up and were massacred by Saddam's Sunni minority dictatorship. The idea that American troops would be "greeted as liberators" betrayed the ignorance of the war advocates in the Bush administration. Iraqis I spoke to did not believe the US invaded to seize weapons of mass destruction. The only rationale that made sense to them was that an ally of Israel invaded to seize Iraqi oil. I heard that from Safwan to Baghdad to Mosul and beyond. It occurred to me that people always come up with a nickname for foreign troops. I asked one Iraqi if they had a nickname for us. "Yes," he said without hesitation. "We call you, 'the Jews.'"

This was the first morning of America's first decade in the occupation of Iraq. The marines on the firing line did not yet know loss, nor anger, nor revenge. All of that would come. America's head would be continually "on a swivel" as the "nervous Nellies" at the Pentagon were proven prescient and the Bush administration's hubris was fed, page by page, into shredders.

After two weeks sending stories to *60 Minutes II*, we received terrible news by satellite phone. Bill Owens's mother, who had been ill, was in the last days of her life. We drove through the battlefield back to Kuwait. Bill made it to her bedside in New York in time. I picked up a fresh crew including producer Shawn Efran, who would become a distinguished combat journalist and

gifted filmmaker; cameraman David Gladstone; and soundman
Matt McGratten. This time, the toughest part of the journey
was getting back into Iraq. An iron curtain had descended on
the border. The military ordered it sealed. I was desperate to get
to Basra where the British were planning an assault to take the
city. I stopped by the Pentagon public affairs operation to see if
I could find a way in. Public affairs was based in Kuwait City
at a luxurious seaside Hilton Hotel with a Starbucks attached.
These troops in the rear were dining on an endless buffet of
seafood and lamb courtesy of the emir of Kuwait. The soldiers
and marines I had just left in the field were searching through
dusty cardboard boxes in hope of their preferred MRE (Meals
Ready to Eat) menu. Cajun Chicken, in a brown plastic pouch,
heated on a Humvee engine block was a favorite. The real pros
memorized which MRE menus contained M&M candies.

While stuck in Kuwait, I checked with one well-fed public
affairs major about getting a lift to Basra. He had an idea. The
major had boxes filled with thousands of four-inch American
flags on little black sticks. He hoped to organize a helicopter to
get the flags into the hands of the grateful people of Basra as the
city fell to allied forces. Imagining the blizzard of red, white and
blue, he told me, "It'll be awesome on TV." He said he would
try to find me a seat on the helicopter. The major was in a hurry.
He worried the flags wouldn't reach Basra before the cameras.
The "Hilton heroes" were dining on the same rich optimism
that fattened the imagination of Washington. As it happened,
the major needn't rush. It would be weeks before Basra fell, after
some of the hardest fighting in the invasion.

As I searched for the breakthrough that would get my team
across the border, I wondered why we had not heard anything
about Saddam's weapons of mass destruction. More than two
weeks had gone by. I knew the Pentagon sent teams of scientists and engineers directly to the dictator's suspected arsenals.
The 75th Exploitation Task Force (XTF) included the Chemi-

cal Biological Intelligence Support Team—twenty-one specialists, towing trailers packed with sophisticated laboratories. One
trailer manned by the army's Edgewood Chemical Biological
Center was engineered to handle nerve gas and blister agents.
Another, operated by the Naval Medical Research Center, was
equipped to classify virulent germs down to their unique genetic codes. The team was supported by the 75th Field Artillery
Brigade from Fort Sill, Oklahoma. One reporter was embedded with the 75th XTF—it was the *New York Times* correspondent to whom the vice president's office had fed its misleading,
menacing tales in the months before the war. She had been re-
warded with the coveted, exclusive embed. The army expected
such momentous results from the 75th XTF that it attached an
official military historian to the team to chronicle its achievements.[37] About three weeks into the war, I happened to run into
the 75th XTF. We were both checking out the discovery of a
warehouse full of bodies. The army took me to the warehouse
because they suspected the two hundred or so corpses were
evidence of a Saddam war crime. I asked one of the chemical
biological unit's senior officers whether his commander would
talk to me. "No way!" the officer said, nearly laughing at the
thought.

"Why not?" I asked.

"Because we're not finding *anything*!" He italicized his last
word with frustration, dismay and a hint of panic. He continued,
"We kind of thought we'd have [Iraqi] generals saying, 'Here it
is,' but, no. We haven't found a thing." Every report of a chemical or biological weapon was a goose chase. Even the warehouse
of the dead was a dead end. The bodies were those of Iraqi soldiers stored for identification and return to their families.

In the days after my brush with the XTF, I took my team to
a US base on the border. It was an act of desperation. I had no
plan. But being closer to Iraq had to be better. Producer Shawn
Efran and I spent a day at the front gate with our thumbs up as

military vehicles rolled north. Once in a while, curiosity would get the best of a driver who would stop at our sand-covered figures. When he found out what we wanted he'd leave us in another layer of dust. At the base, we were sleeping in our vehicles. But eventually we were taken in by an army reserve unit which had a little space in its barracks. Each day, the reservists watched Shawn and me come back to their plywood sleeping quarters with faces of dejection from rejection. One evening, one of the unit's sergeants stood up, walked to a blackboard and began an impromptu briefing. "Men, this is a Black Op," the sergeant announced. "I'll be taking only volunteers. We're going to get the CBS News crew to Basra." I could not believe what I was hearing. I was pretty sure we were serving as the butt of a joke. But the sergeant explained the route and the number of Humvees he would need, which was three. Just then, the lieutenant colonel in command of the unit walked in unexpectedly. My heart sank. He hesitated suspiciously in the doorway.

"Sergeant!" he demanded. "Is this something I should know about?"

"No, sir! It is not!" the sergeant replied.

"Thank you, sergeant!" the lieutenant colonel barked. He wheeled on his heel and walked out. It was like a scene from *M*A*S*H*. The Black Op briefing continued.

Before dawn, the reservists led my vehicles over the border and twenty-eight miles to Basra. They needed to hurry back before they were missed, so they left us with 3 Commando Brigade of the British Royal Marines. I would like to take this moment to name these soldiers who understood the vital role of journalists in war, but I won't. Some of them might still be serving in the military. I fear they'd be reprimanded even after all these years. You know who you are. And I am deeply grateful.

In Basra, the British had taken ownership of Saddam's palace the day before. Saddam had confiscated waterfront real estate for his sprawling complex on the wide Shatt al-Arab waterway, which drains the Tigris and Euphrates into the Gulf. There were acres of palms shading a dozen buildings wrought in marble and mosaics. We rolled over bridges spanning man-made canals that flowed into pools. Nothing was more precious than water. The brimming palace grounds were meant to project careless excess. I ventured outside the gates where the liberated people of Basra gathered in numbers the American major of public affairs had imagined. But if his flags had arrived, I didn't see them. Nor were the people of Basra particularly enthusiastic about liberation. A man with contorted countenance thrust his face into mine and screamed in fractured English, "You tell Bush, Water! Water! Water! You tell Bush, *Water! Water! Water!* You tell Bush, *Water! Water! Water!*" Rather than liberators, we were greeted as plumbers late for an appointment. After thirteen years of United Nations economic sanctions, liberation was far down the list of Iraqi expectations, somewhere below water, sanitation, electricity, schools and health care. The crowd fired salvos of grievances at the only American in range. My translator, who was listening to the mob in Arabic, said, "We have to get out of here."

"Okay," I said. "I'll just get a couple more interviews."

"No!" he yelled. "We have to leave *now!*"

We dove into our cars and headed back to the protection of the British at the palace. My translator explained that he had overheard a man tell someone in the crowd he would be right back, he was going home to get his gun. Nothing in the early weeks of the war filled me with dread like the Basra mob. Iraqis expected the United States to rebuild their country and fast. *They think they're the fifty-first state,* I said to myself. That night, in our small CBS encampment inside the palace grounds, I switched on my shortwave radio. Voice of America bounced off the ionosphere and ricocheted the voice of President Bush reading his Saturday radio address from the White House. The president said, in part, "As people throughout Iraq celebrate the arrival of freedom, America celebrates with them. We know that freedom is a gift from God to all mankind and we rejoice when others can share it."[38] "Whooo-boy," I whispered to myself. "I wish the president could see this—there's not a whole lot of celebratin' goin' on." Presidents, I thought, should be required to tour their battlefields. The Bush administration imagined a fully functioning modern society waving flags in gratitude and saying, "Thanks, we'll take it from here." In truth, Iraq was a failed nation inhabited by a destitute, bitterly divided society. Without the crushing gravity of a police state, freedom was a centrifugal force pulling Iraqis apart along the seam of Islam's great divide. By the time I entered Baghdad on April 9, the specter of civil war was spreading like a shadow. I ran into Peter Bluff, the legendary CBS News producer. Peter had spent a lifetime covering the region. His first words to me after, "Hellooooo, dear boy," were these: "The Shiites have taken over the hospital." I understood. Nothing more needed to be said. The Shiites, the majority oppressed for generations, were rising.

I watched Baghdad tip into chaos. Looting, arson and old scores settled with a bullet went unchecked by an American force much too small to impose its will on the city of seven million. US reinforcements had been on their way as part of the original invasion plan, but they were *turned around en route and sent home* by the oblivious civilian leadership at the Pentagon.[39] Given the mayhem, most citizens were not infused with confidence in America. "If this is the best you can do, then *go out!*" one man shouted at me. Many Iraqis refused to talk to me at all. They believed Saddam might return.

Over the next weeks, the 75th XTF pulled its trailers to more than six hundred suspected sites of weapons of mass destruction. They found nothing.[40] In my interview with former CIA director George Tenet, I read aloud the first key judgment his agency wrote in its prewar National Intelligence Estimate, "Baghdad has chemical and biological weapons."

"Period," I added.

"High confidence judgment," Tenet confirmed.

"How could you make such a bold statement?"

"We believed he had chemical and biological weapons."

"But there was no hard evidence," I said.

"No, no. There was lots of data," Tenet countered. "There's lots of technical data. So, you put all of this together. It's not evidence in the court of law. Remember, when you write an estimate, when you *estimate*, you're writing what you *don't* know. You might win a civil case. You're not gonna win a criminal case, in terms of evidence."

"We are going to war," I said. "Tens of thousands of people are going to be killed. And you're telling me you had evidence to prove a civil case, not a criminal case?"

"Well, as you know, hindsight is perfect. For professionals who pride themselves on being right, this is a very painful experience for us."

Tenet's National Intelligence Estimate also claimed that Saddam possessed, conservatively, between one hundred and five hundred tons of chemical weapons.

"Where did these numbers come from?" I asked.

"From our National Intelligence Estimate. You don't make this kind of stuff up," Tenet said.

"Wait a minute!" I said incredulously. "You *did* make this stuff up."

"Scott, you're doing it again. You're impugning the integrity of people who make analytical judgments and make their best judgments about what they believe the Iraqis possessed. Intelligence, you know, my business, is not always about the truth. It's about people's best judgments about what the truth may be. We believed it. We wrote it."

None of the equivocation so abundant in our interview had been revealed to the American public before the war. I wondered whether any senior officials had tapped the brakes on the road to Iraq. I asked Tenet, "Did anyone at the White House, did anyone in the defense department, ever ask you whether we *should* go to war in Iraq?"

Tenet confessed, "The discussions that are ongoing in 2002 in the spring and summer of 2002 are *how* you might do this. Not *whether* you should do this."

"Nobody asks?" I said.

"Well, I don't remember sitting down in a principals committee meeting and everybody saying, 'Okay, there's a deep concern about Iraq. Is this the right thing to do? What are the implications?' I don't ever remember that galvanizing moment when people sit around and honestly say, 'Is this the right thing to do?'"

Having chosen war, it suited the Bush administration to promote vague conspiracy theories that suggested a link between Saddam Hussein and 9/11. That was item number two under the heading "How Start?" in the talking points drafted for the meeting between Secretary Rumsfeld and General Franks. There was no evidence for that either, but it worked—too well. On a former Iraqi air base, in the shadow of an ancient step pyramid, a US Army sergeant told me, "They [Iraqis] want to stop us from going to Disney World!" I scanned his face for satire. It wasn't there. "Those bastards come over here [on 9/11] and impose their way of life on us? There's gotta be more to life than banging your head on the ground five times a day!" he said, referring to Islamic prayer. He continued, "We have to defend our right to listen to rap. We have to defend guys going to Disney World on their once-every-five-years trip. You have the right to enjoy seeing your children have a good time!" His rant misunderstood most everything about 9/11, Iraq and Islam. His take was extreme, but some variation of the theme was not uncommon among our troops. Years later, I was standing in the kitchen of an Iowa National Guardsman who was leaving for his first tour in Iraq. His son was also going as part of the same unit. I asked the guardsman why he felt it was important for him and his son to fight. "Well," he said. "They attacked *us*, so we have to go over there and set things right." I didn't argue. If that was what he believed, or needed to believe about Iraq, it wasn't for me to raise doubts on the eve of his deployment.

By January 2007, American troops were being cut down in the crossfire of an Iraqi civil war. President Bush decided to double down and commit about thirty thousand reinforcements in what was called "the surge." It was a turning point and the president wanted to explain it on *60 Minutes*. Mr. Bush announced the surge in an address from the Oval Office. The next day I was escorted across the South Lawn to Marine One. Mr. Bush had invited me on a trip to Georgia.

"Scott, how ya' doin'?" Mr. Bush said, standing up from his seat in the helicopter and extending his hand.

"Good morning, Mr. President. Thanks for the lift. How are you?"

"Doin' fine, welcome."

We settled, face-to-face, into cream-colored leather seats. His was the only one onboard embroidered with the Seal of the President. Two marine pilots would speed us the ten minutes to Andrews Air Force Base, Maryland. We would travel the rest of the distance to Georgia on Air Force One. "This [the surge] was a hard decision," the president told me. Raising his voice above the chop of the Sikorsky's rotor blades, he said: "But once I make up my mind, I know it's important for me to explain it as clearly as I can. And I'm going to go down to Fort Benning today to continue explaining the decision I made to men and women who wear the uniform. I owe it to the troops to explain my decision and to thank them and to thank their families. It's an extraordinary country to have men and women volunteer in the face of danger." The overnight polling showed his Oval Office address had not convinced many Americans of the wisdom of the surge. A CBS News/*New York Times* poll showed 61 percent of Americans said the US should have stayed out of Iraq and 63 percent disapproved of the job Mr. Bush was doing.[41]

On Air Force One, Mr. Bush and I settled on a couch that ran parallel along the windows on the left side. The president complained that the new Iraqi government was a large part of his problem. He leaned forward and began poking me in the chest when talking about Iraqi Prime Minister Nouri al-Maliki. "Scott, that Maliki is a son of a bitch! But I have to deal with him." Each word landed on the point of a presidential index finger.

The war that was expected to be so quick that reinforcements were turned around, was now demanding that individual troops make two, three, four, five even six deployments. The all-volunteer military was too small for a prolonged occupation of Afghanistan *and* Iraq which former army chief of staff General Eric Shinseki had understated as "a piece of geography that is fairly significant."

"When is enough, enough for these families?" I asked the president.

"You know, Scott, we're fortunate that people are willing to continue to serve. I've talked to some wives, and their husband's been over there for their second time. I said, 'How you doing?' They said, 'Doing fine. My husband understands what we're doing.' The military is motivated."

I followed up, "In Vietnam, you served 365 [days] and you were done."

"This is a different situation," the president said. "This is a volunteer army. In Vietnam, it was, 'We're going to draft you and you go for a year.' This is a military where people understand there may be additional deployments."

At Fort Benning, Mr. Bush spoke to several hundred soldiers in an aircraft hangar. After his speech, he slipped through a nondescript door for a meeting. Few people were aware that he had done this often, always out of sight. The room was filled with families who had lost sons and daughters on his orders. You could not accuse the man of dodging the heartbreaking reality of his decisions. Most often, the families were respectful and appreciative. Sometimes he was excoriated by a tearful parent. Mr. Bush understood what the American people wanted to see in a wartime president: confidence held high with self-deprecating, relaxed authority. But after the family meeting, I found him careworn—just on this side of tears. "It's, you know, it's hard for the family members to recount or relive their love in front of the president," he told me. I was struck by his use of the word "love" rather than "son" or "daughter." Mr. Bush continued, "And yet, you know, once we get beyond the initial, kind of, meeting, it's amazing how strong these folks are. And they want to let me know a lot of things. They want to let me know what their son or husband was like."

"What are the stories you heard today?" I asked.

"Oh, you know, one mom said, 'My son was six foot five, good-looking guy.' She showed me the picture. He was in a Humvee. IED hit. He was so big that his body shielded four other troops from death. I asked her, 'Well, did you get to meet the other four?' And she said, 'They're like my family now.' You know, a lot of them say, 'Mr. President, don't let my son die in vain.'"

In moments of personal pain, I noticed Mr. Bush had a way of ending a conversation with a click of his tongue. I'd seen it before, through tears, when he was telling me about meeting the young son of an FDNY firefighter who was missing at Ground Zero. Mr. Bush had told the boy he was sure his daddy would be fine, when, of course, the president knew the man certainly must have been killed. He hated everything about that moment: the death of the firefighter, the sadness of the boy, the comforting falsehood that a president must tell a child. *Click,* he signaled with his tongue to end my questioning. It meant, 'That's it, I can't say any more.' With that same palatal *click* at Fort Benning, Mr. Bush ambled back to Air Force One.

The next day, I met the president at Camp David, Maryland, for our main interview. I was surprised that Mr. Bush wanted to do an interview at Camp David. He considered the cabins folded into the Catoctin Mountains a sanctuary from all he did not like about Washington. After six years in office, he had spent 365 days at Camp David—precisely one year. Winter had stripped the dense woods. It was fifteen degrees the night before. But by the time the president and I were walking along a narrow, winding road, it was fifty degrees and breezy. He dressed for the location with Topsider shoes, a blue, open-collar, pinpoint Oxford shirt and a fleece-lined bomber jacket in green, with the Seal of the President stitched in yellow on his right breast. "President Bush" was threaded underneath the seal. In the shade of an immense spruce, I gave the president a pre-interview pep talk. "The folks at home need to understand why sending more troops is a good idea in your view. You need to be as forthcoming as you can," I said. In my effort to persuade, I found myself tapping the president on the chest with my fist, much as he had with me on Air Force One. It didn't seem inappropriate. Over the years I had found Mr. Bush was physically casual. Once, after an interview on Air Force One, Mr. Bush walked to his stateroom to change clothes. Apparently, he forgot to tell me something. He walked back into his office, stripped of his dress shirt. It never occurred to him that a partially clad president of the United States would be remarkable to my crew and me.

Now, with the surge, the commander in chief was gambling that he could make a success of Iraq in his last two years. Republicans had been badly beaten two months earlier in the 2006 midterm elections. "A thumpin'," he called it. As a concession to defeat, Defense Secretary Donald Rumsfeld resigned immediately. In our walk at Camp David, I leveled with the president from the start.

"You're not very popular in the country right now, to be frank," I said.

"I'm afraid you're right," the president acknowledged, half chuckling.

"Does that get to you?" I asked.

"Not really." Mr. Bush shrugged.

"You know that there's a perception in some quarters of the country that you're stubborn. What do you think?"

"I think I'm a flexible, open-minded person. I really do. Take this policy. I spent a lot of time listening to a lot of people because, Scott, I fully understand the decisions I make could affect the life of some kid who wears the uniform or could affect the life of some child growing up in America twenty years from now."

As we walked in the woods, the extraordinary *60 Minutes* producer Harry Radliffe II and our camera crews were setting up Laurel Lodge for the "sit down" interview. Laurel is Camp David's mess hall and meeting space serving a dozen or so guest cabins. In my experience, President Bush didn't like interviews. He seemed to consider them a necessary chore. He once said to me, "You just want to get me 'on the couch,'" as though I was a psychiatrist pulling his inner thoughts by their roots. Mr. Bush left me to change clothes and then returned to Laurel Lodge in a motorcade of golf carts. We settled into a pair of chairs with Radliffe and his team seated at a long table of monitors nearby.

Before we began, the former owner of the Texas Rangers Baseball Club threw a brushback pitch. "Those your questions?" Mr. Bush asked, glancing at the notes on my lap.

"Yes, sir, Mr. President," I replied.

"Well, you'd better start cuttin' them back."

Harry Radliffe and I had started the night before with a list of about sixty questions which we culled down to a dozen. That may not seem like many, but I always make room for follow-up questions that spring to mind during the interview. Those "unscripted" moments usually provide the unexpected insight that illuminates the issues better than anything I write beforehand.

It had been in Laurel Lodge that President Bush made the decision to go to war in Afghanistan. The fall of the Taliban and the scattering of al-Qaida were, he judged, among his greatest achievements. I said to the president, "Back then, the whole country was with you. Now you seem to have lost them." Mr. Bush reflected, "The Iraq war hasn't gone as well as I had hoped at this point in time. And people are discouraged. They don't appreciate, they don't approve of where we are. And so, I think that's where the country is."

The White House communications office knew this was going to be a tough interview. They couldn't tell me what to ask, of course, but they did control how much time I had. The interview was scheduled for twenty minutes and they came up with a new tactic apparently designed to get inside my head. A White House staffer, in my line of sight, but off camera, held up time cues behind the president's head. On white cards, in black marker, I was reminded of the countdown, "Ten minutes...five minutes...two minutes." I've never seen that in a presidential interview before or since.

I moved to the heart of what disturbed many Americans about the war.

"Sir, you know better than I do that many Americans feel that your administration has not been straight with the country, has not been honest. To those people, you say what?"

"On what issue?" he asked.

"No weapons of mass destruction. No credible connection between 9/11 and Iraq. The Office of Management and Budget said this war would cost somewhere between $50 and $60 billion and now we're over $400 billion..."

Mr. Bush jumped in to stop my litany. "I got you. I got you. I got you," he said.

"The perception, sir, more than any one of those points, is the administration has not been straight with us."

"Well, I strongly disagree with that. I strongly reject that this administration hasn't been straight with the American people. The minute we found out they didn't have weapons of mass destruction, I was the first to say so."

"You may have been wrong, but you weren't dishonest?"

"Oh, absolutely. Everybody was wrong on weapons of mass destruction and there was an intelligence failure which we're trying to address. But I was as surprised as anybody he didn't have them."

I reminded the president of the polls. "Most Americans don't believe in this war in Iraq," I said. "They want you to get us out of there."

"I would hope they'd want us to succeed before we get out of there. That's the decision I had to make. Scott, I thought a lot about different options. One was doing nothing, just kind of the status quo. And I didn't think that was acceptable and I think most Americans don't think it's acceptable. Secondly, was get out."

"You thought about that?" I asked.

"Of course I have. I think about it a lot, about different options, and my attitude is if we were to start withdrawing now, we'd have a crisis on our hands in Iraq. And not only in Iraq, but failure in Iraq will embolden the enemy. And the enemy is al-Qaida and extremists. Failure in Iraq would empower Iran, which poses a significant threat to world peace. So, then I began to think, 'Well if failure's not an option and we've got to succeed, how best to do so?' And that's why I came up with the plan I did."

In his address to the nation that week, Mr. Bush acknowledged "mistakes," but hadn't mentioned what any of them might have been. My job was to get specifics.

"What mistakes are you talking about?"

"Abu Ghraib was a mistake," the president said, referring to the depraved abuse of Iraqi prisoners by US Army jailers in the Abu Ghraib prison. Mr. Bush continued, "Using bad language, like, you know, 'Bring them on' was a mistake." Mr. Bush was recalling his public taunting of the enemy. "I think history is going to look back and see a lot of ways we could have done things better. No question about it."

"The [low] troop levels, sir?"

"Could have been a mistake," he conceded. "And the reason I brought up the mistakes, I don't want people blaming our military. We got a bunch of good military people out there doing what we've asked them to do. The temptation is going to be to find scapegoats. Well, if the people want a scapegoat, they got one right here in me because it's my decisions."

"Mr. President, do you think you owe the Iraqi people an apology for not doing a better job?" Mr. Bush wasn't sure he heard me right. He asked, "That *we* didn't do a better job or *they* didn't do a better job?"

"That the United States did not do a better job providing security after the invasion."

"Not at all. I am proud of the efforts we did. We liberated that country from a tyrant. I think the Iraqi people owe the American people a huge debt of gratitude. That's the problem. Here in America [Americans] wonder whether there is a gratitude level that's significant enough in Iraq."

After the fall of Saddam, Iraq split three ways with Kurds fighting for independence in the north, the Shiites fighting to take over from the south and the minority Sunnis fighting to carve out the center. Mr. Bush told me, "Some of my buddies in Texas say, you know, 'Let them fight it out. What business is it of ours? You got rid of Saddam. Just let them slug it out.' And that's a temptation that I know a lot of people feel. But if we do not succeed in Iraq, we will leave behind a Middle East which will endanger America in the future."

"But wasn't it your administration that created the instability in Iraq?"

"Well, our administration took care of a source of instability in Iraq. Envision a world in which Saddam Hussein was rushing for a nuclear weapon to compete against Iran."

There it was again. I was surprised to see the president reach back, reflexively, for his discredited prewar talking points.

"My decision to remove Saddam Hussein was the correct decision in my judgment. He was a significant source of instability."

"It's much more unstable now, Mr. President," I said.

"Well, no question, decisions have made things unstable. But the question is can we succeed? And I believe we can. I, listen, I'd like to see stability and a unified Iraq. A young democracy will provide the stability we look for."

The surge resulted in the bloodiest single year for the US military in Iraq with 904 Americans killed. But in the short run, it worked. Casualties plummeted afterward. And, in a masterstroke of counterinsurgency, American troops convinced alienated Sunni communities to join the fight against extremists. The progress, however, was doomed by an unstable government in Baghdad. In 2014, the Sunni fanatics of Islamic State or ISIS defeated the American trained and equipped Iraqi Army and seized one-third of Iraq.

Mr. Bush's warning in our interview that "if we do not succeed in Iraq, we will leave behind a Middle East which will endanger America in the future" was prescient. The US did not succeed and Islamic State inspired mass murder in San Bernardino, California; Orlando, Florida; plus, Paris, London, Manchester, Brussels and Istanbul. By 2018, Islamic State had lost its stronghold in Mosul and was withering under the counterattack of the Iraqi army backed by about five thousand US troops. Americans continued to fight and die in Iraq, but after fifteen years of war, the American public largely lost track of our troops and their mission. In 2019, the government in Baghdad remained at war with itself. And Iran, not the United States, became the greatest influence on Iraqi policy.

In the last two years of his presidency, Mr. Bush continued to read casualty reports every morning and put his preferred black Sharpie to every condolence letter—about 4,222 letters by the time he handed the unhappy duty to Barack Obama who, in turn, handed an unstable Iraq to Donald Trump. Estimates of Iraqi dead exceed 288,000.[42] In one of the most insightful studies of the war, Richard D. Hooker Jr. and Joseph J. Collins, editors of National Defense University's 2015 *Lessons Encountered*, wrote:

> Neither national-level figures nor Field Commanders fully understood the operational environment, including the human aspects of military operations. To fight, in Rupert Smith's term, 'war among the people,' one must first understand them. We were not intellectually prepared for the unique aspects of war in Iraq and Afghanistan. In both conflicts, ethnic, religious, and cultural differences drove much of the fighting. Efforts to solve this problem…came too little and too late.
>
> Our lack of understanding of the wars seriously retarded our efforts to fight them and to deal with our indigenous allies, who were often more interested in score-settling or political risk aversion than they were in winning the war.[43]

The best-trained, most professional military force in the world cannot make a success of bad policy though, my God, how they tried. I returned to Iraq twenty-three times over the next ten years. For the most part, I witnessed Americans fighting with distinction, winning every battle, upholding our ideals. They were professionals who did, honorably, what they were ordered to do. Reasonable people will disagree, but in my view, the failure in Iraq lies with uninformed civilian leadership that created an existential threat where none existed. The administration accepted only evidence that supported its plans. Then, rejecting expert military advice, it stubbornly stuck to an implausible ending—a quick, easy war celebrated by cheering faces behind a blur of tiny American flags, a war that would be "awesome on TV."

Nearly five thousand years after mankind's first recorded war in Mesopotamia, it turned out there were no "weapons of Elam" to carry away.[44] But the descendants of Sumer did possess one weapon of mass destruction never imagined by the White House nor alleged by George Tenet. The weapon was patience. Iraq claimed as many Americans as possible, not in a battle, but in a decade. Thirty-two years after the Pentagon Papers, the American people and most reporters were persuaded by the false "influence campaign" of an administration bent on war. There will be another time.

Skepticism is patriotism.

FIELD NOTE

Stranger than Fiction

Mark Twain observed, "Truth is stranger than fiction, but it is because Fiction is obliged to stick to possibilities; Truth isn't."[1] In my line of work, I am often reminded of this, but never more so than one day in the White House in 1998. I was opening a stack of mail in the CBS News office in the West Wing when I ripped off the end of a large manila envelope. Out slipped an 8x10 color photo. Photographer Dennis Brack, of the Black Star photo agency, sent the image of a younger me, interviewing a soldier in the 1990 run-up to the Gulf War. There was nothing special about the scene. I wondered why, in that 1/500th of a second, Brack even bothered to pressure his shutter release. My seated profile is on the left side of the photo, facing the center. The soldier is on the right, facing me. He has turned his back on a game of checkers and is sitting backward in his chair. The soldier is dressed in Desert Storm camouflage pants and a white T-shirt. His profile is prominent. A heavy, ridged brow presides over his long nose that sharpens its downward angle just below the bridge, leaving a ridgeline as if the nose had run into a fist. His light brown hair, in military parlance, is "high and tight." The background is filled in by my cameraman, Mike Marriott, bent over his tripod, eye to the viewfinder. My soundwoman, Mary Beth Toole, is holding a microphone on a long boom that resembles a fishing rod. Gray sandbags are stacked about six feet high behind the camera crew. Brack had been editing his old 1990/91 files when the image stopped him cold. What caught Brack's eye eventually hit me like an electric shock. The soldier I am interviewing is Timothy McVeigh. Five years after the picture was taken, McVeigh would dominate my career when he lit the fuses on a five-thousand-pound homemade bomb. The enormity of the coincidence seized the breath in my throat. I had met, interviewed and forgotten Tim McVeigh long before he became the Oklahoma City Bomber.

In the Gulf War, Sergeant Tim McVeigh had been assigned to a Bradley Armored Fighting Vehicle. He liked soldiering and he was good at it. His fitness reports were exemplary. After the liberation of Kuwait, McVeigh was selected for evaluation for Special Forces. But what looked like another step in his advancement became a mysterious break in his life. McVeigh washed out of the Special Forces program after only a couple of days.[2] He would later tell me that he was in poor physical shape after months in the desert. I suspect it was much more than that. Whatever it was seemed to be personal. McVeigh became severely disillusioned and immediately quit the army. He drifted through the Midwest and Southwest attracted to anti-government groups and their inane conspiracy theories. That is what led him to Waco, Texas, during an FBI standoff in 1993. I was there too, covering the negotiations with a religious sect that called itself the Branch Davidians.

★ ★ ★

The Davidians formed a community in 1934 to await Jesus Christ. The day of the second coming was specified as April 22, 1959. When that day passed uneventfully, a group of followers split from the original sect and set itself up on a seventy-seven-acre ranch outside Waco. Eventually, they came under the charismatic spell of a self-styled preacher named Vernon Howell. Howell traveled the world to recruit members to his commune. He brought families from Great Britain, Australia and Israel to live with several American families in a sprawling, two-story ranch house. In 1989, Howell declared himself "The Lamb of God," changed his name to David Koresh and reserved the right to have sex with any of the women and girls in the commune.[3] The Davidians remained obsessed with the end of days. Apparently, they expected the end to be violent. Koresh amassed an arsenal. The local sheriff became concerned the Davidians were purchasing parts to make grenades and to convert legal semi-automatic rifles into illicit fully automatic machine guns. The suspicion was the basis of a federal search warrant and an arrest warrant naming Koresh.[4] The Federal Bureau of Alcohol, Tobacco and Firearms (as it was known then) planned an elaborate surprise for the morning of February 28, 1993. Seventy-six heavily armed agents planned to assault the ranch house. Many of them were to be towed to the front door hidden inside a long cattle trailer. They had rehearsed entering through multiple doors and windows, using ladders to assault the second floor. The hope was to get the drop on the estimated one hundred Branch Davidians before they had a chance to arm themselves.[5]

It might have worked but for a TV news crew that had been tipped off to the raid. In its preparations, the ATF had placed an ambulance on standby. The ambulance dispatcher told a friend at the TV station. In the hours before the ATF raid, the news crew was looking for a vantage point from which to film. The reporters spotted a mailman. They explained they were there in preparation for a federal raid and asked for directions to the Koresh compound. Unfortunately, the mailman was David Koresh's brother-in-law.[6] When the ATF arrived, the Davidians were armed and ready. A gun battle erupted. Four ATF agents were killed and twenty were wounded. Six followers of Koresh were killed. Koresh and several others were shot. The Davidians barricaded themselves in the compound. So began a fifty-one-day standoff, with more than 650 law enforcement officers surrounding the ranch. FBI hostage negotiators spoke to Koresh on the phone and succeeded in convincing fourteen adults and twenty-one children to surrender.[7] Over nearly two months, the FBI spoke to fifty-four individuals inside the compound for approximately 215 hours.[8] I covered the siege for the CBS News magazine *48 Hours*. My son, eight-month-old Reece, took his first steps in a Waco motel room.

Tim McVeigh was one of those attracted to Waco by the notion that the federal government was oppressing a religious group. Zealots argued the Davidians had a right to defend themselves and should be left alone—never mind the illegal arsenal and the murdered federal agents. McVeigh parked his battered Chevy under a live oak tree on the perimeter of the siege. He sold anti-government bumper stickers displayed across the hood. "Fear the Government that Fears Your Gun," one read. Another warned, "Ban Guns. Make the Streets Safe for a Government Takeover."[9] On a piece of cardboard, held in place by his right windshield wiper, McVeigh noted the bumper stickers were $1 each or five for $4.

On April 19, 1993, the end of days dawned for the Davidians. The FBI lost patience with a seven-week negotiation that was now heading nowhere. An armored vehicle pushed in a wall of the ranch house. Tear gas was fired inside. Smoke began to curl from the breach. The house suddenly erupted into an inferno. Nine Davidians ran for their lives. But seventy-six bodies, including that of David Koresh, were found in the wreckage. The

US Department of Justice investigation concluded that the Davidians placed containers of gasoline around the house to ignite in the event of an all-out assault. During the fire, at least seventeen of those inside, including several children, were shot to death by other cult members.[10] Tim McVeigh drove away from the ruins and wandered until he settled on a destination.

Two years later, April 19, 1995, I was trying to shoulder my car into the usual morning traffic between my home and the CBS News Bureau in Irving, Texas, a suburb of Dallas/Fort Worth. On the seat next to me, a beige, brick-sized Motorola cell phone shuddered to life. My boss, bureau chief Wayne Nelson, said, "Hoss, there's been some explosion in Oklahoma City. They think it's a gas main or something. There's a Learjet waiting. You need to be on it." I turned to Dallas's Love Field airport. It didn't cross my mind that this was the second anniversary of the Branch Davidian fire.

The flight took barely thirty minutes. From the jet, I could see smoke and ash rising thousands of feet. The front half of the nine-story Murrah Federal Building had collapsed. The little jet rumbled as it forced its landing gear into the slipstream. I realized this wasn't just an explosion, it was a national disaster. When I reached NW Fifth Street, downtown, first responders and civilians were climbing a mountain of debris in search of survivors. The office tower housed about five hundred fifty federal employees from a variety of agencies and—a day care center. One hundred sixty-eight people were dead, including nineteen children.

The bomb had been built by McVeigh and an old army buddy named Terry Nichols. They had spent weeks buying and stealing the ingredients: five thousand pounds of ammonium nitrate fertilizer mixed with nitro methane racing fuel and an industrial explosive called Tovex.[11] They packed the explosives in several fifty-five-gallon drums and placed the drums in the back of a panel truck that McVeigh had rented in Kansas. Nichols stayed behind as McVeigh drove the truck into Oklahoma City a little before 9:00 a.m. As he approached the Murrah Building, he lit two fuses: a two-minute fuse and a backup five-minute fuse. He parked in front of the Murrah's immense glass facade, locked the truck and walked to a getaway car he had stashed in an alley nearby. The stupendous blast broke a column that shouldered an architectural feature called a "transfer beam." The beam, which ran horizontally across the front of the building, "transferred" the load of the structure to its supporting columns and foundation. When the transfer beam buckled, the front half of the building roared to earth.[12]

Several miles north of Oklahoma City, ninety minutes after the blast, state trooper Charlie Hanger noticed the derelict 1977 Mercury Marquis ahead of him was missing a rear license plate. He stopped the car. Tim McVeigh stepped out. Hanger noticed a bulge under McVeigh's jacket. He ordered McVeigh to raise his hands and turn away. As a point of information—not as a threat—McVeigh confessed, "I have a gun. And it's loaded." By this time Hanger's pistol was near the back of McVeigh's head. "So's mine," Hanger replied. Without incident, Hanger arrested McVeigh and took him to the Noble County jail on a weapons charge.[13] McVeigh was wearing a T-shirt printed with the Latin phrase *"sic semper tyrannis"* which translates, "Thus always to tyrants"—the words allegedly called out by John Wilkes Booth as he assassinated Abraham Lincoln. McVeigh was not a suspect in the bombing. He had been arrested only for the gun, so he was processed in the jail and scheduled for release in a few hours.

In a triumph of police work, the FBI found an axle from the bomb truck. A vehicle identification number engraved on it led to Elliot's Body Shop, an agent of Ryder truck rentals in Junction City, Kansas. Employees at the body shop remembered the young man who rented the truck under a false name and gave a description. An FBI artist drew a likeness, which the agents showed around Junction City. Lea McGown, the owner of the

Dreamland Motel, told me she recognized the sketch immediately when the FBI brought it through her door. McVeigh was memorable, she said. He was neat, polite and asked for a discount. In a later interview, McGown showed me what she showed the FBI. In the motel registration book, McVeigh had used his own name. When the name was typed into a national crime database, it led to Charlie Hanger, who told the FBI he left McVeigh in jail. McVeigh was due to be released in an hour. The FBI asked the sheriff if he would be kind enough to hold McVeigh until they arrived.[14] Then, on April 21, Terry Nichols learned he was wanted by the FBI and turned himself in. Ultimately, Nichols would be sentenced to life with no possibility of parole.

I spent two weeks at the Murrah building and in hospitals, interviewing survivors and piecing together the investigation. Then, I hurried home to Dallas in the nick of time to see the birth of my daughter, Blair. My overwhelming feeling of joy that day was strangely entangled with the loss of the nineteen children in Oklahoma.

The Oklahoma City investigation and the trial of Tim McVeigh were the assignments that got me promoted to the White House. Now, sitting in the West Wing holding the photograph, I had no memory of the wartime interview. I asked the archivists at CBS News in New York to search for the videotape. A vast storehouse is filled with CBS News images and interviews from the late 1940s to the present. It is an irreplaceable treasure of world history. The archivists are famous for finding the obscure, but not this time. Tapes of what had been an unremarkable prewar interview with an unknown soldier went MIA in the chaos of the combat to come. I sent the photo to McVeigh's attorney, Stephen Jones. On February 16, 1999, Jones wrote, "What a remarkable coincidence. Seriously, no doubt that is Tim McVeigh and a younger Scott Pelley." I also sent the picture to McVeigh, who was biding his time before his execution at the United States Penitentiary Administrative Maximum (ADX) better known as "Supermax" on the plains of Eastern Colorado. On March 6, 1999, I received an envelope with a Stars and Stripes stamp. In vanishingly small letters in the upper left-hand corner, tight by the edges of the envelope, was written "T. McVeigh 12076-064 P.O. Box 8500 Florence, CO." He had two years and two months before his life would end by lethal injection. The Oklahoma City Bomber wrote on lined paper in blue ink. He printed tiny letters as though he was squinting through a jeweler's loupe. "Hey Scott," McVeigh wrote, "I don't know what to tell you about that (alleged) photo—it's got me stumped too! I figure it can be one of three things: me, a look-alike (*really* alike), or a computer-assisted composite fake." McVeigh's mind, so susceptible to conspiracy theories, devoted considerable thought to his analysis. "If it's a fake, it's a good one as the sun appears to be striking us all from the same angle and direction," he observed. McVeigh discounted his look-alike hypothesis by noting the soldier "apparently shares my habit of sitting backward in chairs in casual environments." His letter is neat, every word spelled correctly, the grammar and punctuation precise. What it lacked was clarity. McVeigh wanted to be an enigma. He left his analysis without a conclusion. "Anyway, the photo provides me with mental exercise—thanks!"[15]

For me, the most disturbing thing about Tim McVeigh was his sanity. He was not mentally ill. I met him in jail twice and found him to be thoughtful, composed and rational—although he would say nothing about the bombing. I have read dozens of reports by prison psychologists who came to the same conclusion. In evaluations over years, the psychologists described him as cheerful, polite, conversational—possessing a "sharp wit" and "not in need of psychological services." One of these reports noted that he expressed "no remorse for what he did."[16]

We tend to dismiss people like McVeigh as "crazy" or "evil." Sometimes they are, but labeling terrorists in this way can rob us of thoughtful analysis that would serve us well. I believe

McVeigh was an early example of how far wrong a hapless man can go when he immerses himself in conspiracy theories without bothering to investigate the facts. McVeigh wasn't insane, he was gullible. He came by his virulent obsessions the old-fashioned way, not on the internet, but with obscure fliers and publications including the venomous, racist novel, *The Turner Diaries*. He expected the bombing would ignite a revolt against the federal government. On June 2, 1997, McVeigh was convicted in a Denver federal court. That night, I wrote an essay for the *CBS Evening News with Dan Rather*. The essay ended with this:

> Timothy McVeigh fancied himself the leader of a people hungry for revolution. Instead, he finds himself alone, among those who love justice.

McVeigh isolated himself in a society of extremists. He drove thousands of miles all over the West and Midwest to meet them. Today, the world's drifters find like-minded fanatics online. Connections that took McVeigh weeks and months to make are now accomplished in minutes. The alienated, looking for something to believe in, find encouragement from a world wide web of outrage, entitlement and hate.

In 1995, the catastrophe unleashed on Oklahoma City was the worst terrorist attack in US history. We did not know Tim McVeigh was just a snapshot of the horror to come.

CHAPTER FOURTEEN

Perseverance

The Mothers and Fathers of Sandy Hook

We had finally made it into the twelve days of Christmas. By December 14, 2012, the news had slowed as usual and we were looking for Christmas themes for the *CBS Evening News*. Executive Producer Patricia Shevlin suggested a series of interviews on the subject of peace. That idea led my senior producer, Nicole Young, to the 5th Avenue office of Elie Wiesel. Wiesel, a Romanian American, had won the Nobel Peace Prize. He was the author of the classic Holocaust memoir *Night*. Wiesel had been imprisoned as a child and orphaned. But to describe Wiesel only as a Holocaust survivor shortchanged his contribution to humanity. Wiesel was an irreplaceable Holocaust *witness*. And he continued to proclaim his witness on this winter day, at the age of eighty-four.

"Would you say that your humanity was broken, destroyed, as you came out of Buchenwald?" I asked.

"Probably, yes," Wiesel told me. "Everything was broken. But the mystery in life is not only to begin but to begin *again*. What to do with what remains of broken faith, of broken principles, of broken ideals? There must be desire to rebuild and start again."

Within minutes, I too would feel that "everything was broken." And I would spend the next several years witnessing the heroic "desire to rebuild and start again." My conversation with Wiesel moved into the next several questions until Nicole stepped in discreetly and whispered in my ear. "There's been a shooting at a school in Connecticut. We may have to go."

Wiesel continued, "In those times, the principles that we had about goodness, about faith, about hope, they were all reduced to ashes. What do we do? What did we do then? What *could* we do then except build on the ruins, hoping to teach a lesson? And that hope, in itself, was an act of faith."

I ended the interview sooner than I wanted. Nicole briefed me on what she knew so far. The school was in Newtown, seventy-five miles from Manhattan. Several people had been shot. Their conditions were unknown. Pat Shevlin thought we should anchor the *Evening News* that night from Newtown. On the way to Connecticut, I stopped at the CBS News Broadcast Center to get the latest. I trotted into the glass-enclosed *Evening News* office called "The Fishbowl." Pat looked shaken. I glanced at her deputy, senior broadcast producer Jim McGlinchy. "Jimmy, how many?" I asked.

"Twenty-six," he said.

I wasn't prepared. I could feel my heart break.

"Children?" I asked.

"Twenty," McGlinchy said.

"Hospital?"

"They're all dead."

9/11 had been the largest loss of life I had ever witnessed—a cataclysm. But somehow this, this intimate horror, the targeted deaths of innocent children, triggered a grief in me that was just as deep. I made my way to Newtown with a sense of dread and the words of Elie Wiesel fresh in my thoughts. "For me," he said, "the greatest sadness was, and remains, when I saw what was the fate of Jewish children during the war. I could forgive many things, but not what they have done to children."

Newtown and its enclave village, Sandy Hook, were founded by the English at the turn of the eighteenth century. Three hundred years later, the inhabitants of this colonial postcard still numbered fewer than twenty-nine thousand. Sandy Hook Elementary had 489 students.[1] On bright, cold mornings like this, school buses would turn at the Sandy Hook firehouse where the white wooden sign on Dickinson Drive greeted, "Sandy Hook School 1956 Visitors Welcome."

Christmas decorations gilded the squat red–brick fire station, which was dominated by seven garage doors. Police cars and ambulances were jumbled in the parking lot, in neighbors' yards, in the street, wherever they had been yanked into Park. Throughout town, stuttering thumbs fired text messages in every direction. Go to the firehouse. The children are in the firehouse. The fire company's trucks had been pulled outside leaving the sprawling garage for parents who sprinted forward with palms pressed in prayer. Some mothers and fathers bolted out with their children bound in a greedy embrace. "There were just people everywhere," Nicole Hockley told me. Hockley arrived at the firehouse in search of her six-year-old son, Dylan. "There were several rooms," she said. "And you really had to push to get through. And we're all just jostling. We're trying to find our kids. And a woman asked me, 'What classroom was your child in?' And I said, 'Miss Soto.' And she said, 'I heard she got shot.' And I got really angry at her. And I remember very clearly saying, 'Don't you dare say that to me if you don't know it's true!' And I just pushed by her, but I couldn't find Dylan's class or anyone from his class anywhere."

Jimmy Greene scanned the firehouse for his son and daughter. "I saw my son's teacher in a living room area of the firehouse and all of the kids in her class, seated on the floor. And I ran in the room and Isaiah popped up and I just went and grabbed him and held him and he was just crying, 'Daddy, there were so many gunshots.' So, I just took my son in my arms. He's a big kid. I took him like he was two years old again and held him on my shoulder and just was running from room to room trying to locate Ana's class." Greene's wife, Nelba Marquez-Greene read a text from her husband that said Isaiah was safe, but Ana was missing. "So, I was driving with my friend back to Sandy Hook," she told me. "And I just kept texting Jimmy every ten or fifteen seconds: Ana? Question mark. And then, Ana! exclamation point, because we had Isaiah. I didn't understand why we didn't have Ana."

With joyful reunions all around her, Nicole Hockley noticed how the firehouse was changing. "It just started to be fewer and fewer parents and kids in the room. And then they asked everyone who was left to come to one of the back rooms."

Nelba Marquez-Greene told me, "I remember looking at Jimmy and saying I don't want to go in that back room. I don't want to go in that back room. Because I know what the back room meant. In my heart, as a mother, I know what the back room meant."

"Eventually," Hockley said, "they announced that there had been a shooting. And they told us that people had died. And the room just erupted with anguish. But even then, you still think, 'Dylan's okay, he's got to be okay because this wouldn't happen to Dylan.' And then, it was several hours later that I believe it was Governor [Dannel] Malloy who had the duty to stand in front of a room and tell us that if we were in that room our child or adult wasn't coming back to us."

★ ★ ★

Three months after their unimaginable loss, several parents felt strong enough to sit down with us on *60 Minutes*. Seven families responded to an invitation from producer Henry Schuster. They joined us at the old white clapboard town hall where Henry set up semicircles of chairs on risers. Mothers and fathers sat side by side holding 8x10 color portraits of their sons and daughters—forever six years old. They were joined by families of some of the six adult educators who were killed. I didn't know how to face them. I've spoken to thousands of grieving people over these many years. But on this morning, as old window panes spilled early sun on more than twenty people who lost loved ones, the gravity of grief overwhelmed me. I did not feel worthy of being with them.

To start, I asked each parent to tell us about their murdered child. Jimmy Greene, a Grammy-nominated jazz saxophonist, introduced the portrait in his hands. "Our daughter, Ana, was six years old. And in those six years, I can look back and say it was an honor to know her. She taught me about how to love, how to give. She was beautiful and every day I cry." Francine Wheeler spoke up, "This is Benjamin Andrew Wheeler. Ben was six years old. He has a brother named Nate. And Nate was hiding when he heard Ben and his classmates and educators get shot." Our camera panned to Mark Barden. "We lost our sweet little Daniel Barden. He was known as the kid that would talk to somebody who was sitting alone. He was genuinely an old soul." Nicole Hockley's voice wrapped cold grief in a blanket of memory. "This is Dylan. I think the picture kind of sums him up perfectly. He was always smiling and always laughing. And he was very pure. Possibly because of his age—he was six—and possibly because he was autistic." Bill Sherlach's wife, Mary Sherlach, was fifty-six and had plans to retire. "Mary was the school psychologist at Sandy Hook for eighteen years," Bill told us. "And truly believed that was the place she was meant to be, doing what she would call 'God's work.'" Thirty-year-old Lauren Rousseau had a fresh master's degree in elementary education. She'd worked at Sandy Hook for a month. Her mother, Terri, told me, "Lauren grew up with this idea that she wanted to be a teacher and work with other children. She had a sort of innocence about her, a kind of denial of all the ugly things in the world. We had no idea that some ugly thing would come and take her from us."

This chapter of the book is about what Elie Wiesel called "building on the ruins," and so, I don't want to dwell on the shooting. But to understand the path of the Sandy Hook parents, a few facts from the State of Connecticut investigation are essential. The "ugly thing" was profound mental illness.[2] The twenty-year-old gunman had attended grade school at Sandy Hook.[3] He lived nearby with his divorced mother. Friends I spoke to say she devoted every hour to him. He had been diagnosed with Asperger's syndrome and obsessive-compulsive disorder. But Asperger's and OCD are not predictors of violence. He suffered with afflictions that were much more troubling. His mother described him to others as intensely sensitive to light, noise and touch. His bedroom was blacked out with trash bags over the windows. Recently, he'd been communicating with his mother only by email. His computer stored tales of mass murder, a spreadsheet of mass killings and photos of himself holding guns to his head. His mother prepared the only foods he would eat—arranging them on the plate precisely to his preference. Most of his life she sought treatment for him. But he refused medications and therapy. Firearms were her hobby, which she passed to her son. The weapons used in the killings had been purchased legally in her name. In the few months before the shooting, she told her son of her plan to move them from his boyhood home. This was a home he refused to leave even when the power was knocked out for days by a storm. On December 10, 2012, she went to New Hampshire, a rare, perhaps un-precedented trip without him. She returned late on December 13.[4] Perhaps he felt his tightly wrapped world unraveling. The next morning, he shot his mother to death in her bed and left for Sandy Hook School.

Dressed in black, from his sneakers to his polo shirt, he car-ried a Bushmaster XM15-E2S semiautomatic assault rifle and two semiautomatic pistols. As part of its routine, the school locked its doors at 9:30 a.m. The gunman fired eight rounds through a plate glass window to get in.[5] The school princi-pal, Dawn Hochsprung, and school psychologist Mary Sherlach went to investigate the noise. They were apparently the first to die. The Bushmaster was fed by six PMAG 30 magazines, each loaded with thirty rounds. At least two of the magazines were taped together inversely, so the pair could be flipped for near instantaneous reloading. In Classroom 8, investigators found eighty spent shell casings among the bodies of fifteen students and two teachers. In Classroom 10, forty-nine spent shell cas-ings lay among the bodies of five students and two teachers. The shooter shot himself to death as police closed in. He had been inside the school only ten minutes.[6] On his body, investigators found another 253 rounds of ammunition.[7] The coroner noted he was six feet tall and weighed 112 pounds.

The parents who sat with me in April 2013 were lobbying for restrictions on weapons. Nelba Marquez-Greene told us they had come a long way in their education. "At first, my heart was, 'Let's have a big bonfire and burn everything. Let's burn all these damn guns.' I have since learned that it's a more complex issue than just saying, 'Let's ban assault weapons.' We're look-ing for real change and commonsense solutions, not things that just sound good." The week before our interview, they con-vinced the Connecticut legislature to limit the capacity of am-munition magazines to ten rounds, require background checks for all private firearm sales—including previously exempt gun shows—and expand the state's assault weapon ban to include one hundred specific guns. The legislation was bipartisan and not an easy reach in Connecticut, which is home to some of the best-known firearm manufacturers. Fresh from their victory in Hartford, these parents were now walking the polished stone corridors of the US Congress. What Bill Sherlach wanted most was a restriction on the thirty-round ammunition magazines that allowed the shooter to fire 130 shots in the few minutes it took police to arrive. "It's just simple arithmetic," he said. "If you have to change magazines fifteen times instead of five times, you have three times as many incidents where something could jam. Something could be bobbled. You just increase the time for intervention. You increase the time frame where kids can get out."

President Barack Obama was with them. Polls showed most Americans were too. But the personal lobbying by the parents, which had tightened gun laws in Connecticut, New York and Maryland, failed in Washington, DC. An assault weapons ban that included a magazine capacity limit and a bill to expand background checks failed in the Senate. Nicole Hockley told me, "It was like all the air went out of your body in one quick swoosh. That was a gut-wrenching defeat. How could this have happened?"

I asked her, "Was there a sense of, 'Okay, we tried. I'm going home'?"

"Never," she said. "Why would we do that? That's not honoring our children. There is a saying, 'Fall nine times, get up ten.' We'll just keep getting up."

Five years after our interview in 2013, producer Henry Schuster, associate producer Rachael Morehouse, and I went back to Newtown to follow up with the families. It occurred to me that there is no word in the English language for a parent who has lost a child. We have *orphans*, *widows* and *widowers*, but no noun for a bereaved parent. Maybe it's an abyss so deep that we don't dare make it real by giving it a name.

I asked Nelba Marquez-Greene and Jimmy Greene about the passage of time. "Have you found people, after all these years, expecting you to get over what happened?"

Nelba's eyes widened. "You just took my breath away because that happens a lot and it is so incredibly painful. It's like losing her all over again." Jimmy added, "There have been those that have said things like, 'So you guys are good now?' or, 'I hope you've had some closure to your daughter's murder.' In my heart, and I know in Nelba's as well, our family will never be intact again." There was no moving on for any of the families, but they had found ways to move forward. Nicole Hockley and Mark Barden founded Sandy Hook Promise to train teachers and students to recognize those who are on a pathway to violence. Hockley got the idea after an FBI official explained to the families that the Sandy Hook gunman was showing signs that are common to many mass murderers. Hockley told me she said to the agent, "Well if *you* know these things about shooters, if *you* know that these signs and signals are given off, how come *we* don't know?" She remembered his explanation this way, "We just don't have the resources to train everyone in the country. We train law enforcement. But we can't do it for the mass public." Hockley continued, "For me, that was the moment I said, 'Well if *you* can't, we can.'" Now, Hockley spends six months a year on the road, in classrooms, teaching the warning signs of social isolation, sudden changes in dress, talk of suicide and violent posts on social media. One Sandy Hook Promise program called "Start with Hello" teaches students to reach out to peers who are ignored or bullied. Another, titled "Say Something," trains teachers and students to speak up when they see warning signs. In 2015, Mark Barden trained students in Cincinnati. A short time later, a middle school student started writing in social media about building a bomb. Barden told me an eighth grader who attended their training saw the post and spoke up. Hockley told me, "Sandy Hook was preventable. Had someone been able to see those signs and signals that our shooter gave off throughout his life and connect those dots and make an intervention, I wouldn't be sitting here talking to you today."

A parent who has lost their child has one fear remaining—the end of memory. Many Sandy Hook parents started charities to keep their child alive in the thoughts of others. Five years after his death, Ben Wheeler was still being introduced to new people by his parents, Francine and David Wheeler. Their foundation, Ben's Lighthouse, creates service projects for Newtown kids. Francine surprised me. "What a wonderful way to honor him and continue to be his parents," she said.

"*Continue* to be his parents?" I asked.

"Yeah. I can't live the rest of my life *not* talking about him. I mean, imagine you having a six-year-old and then you don't anymore. Are you going to stop talking about them? The worst thing you can do to a grieving parent is not to mention the child. Then you're not acknowledging his existence. And so, when people *do* acknowledge it, I'm so appreciative. I say, 'Oh, thank you.' And if I'm crying, they're like, 'I'm sorry I made you cry.' I say, 'No, you didn't make me cry. You brought him back.'" David added, "It's like having him back for a minute."

Two years after Ben was killed, the Wheelers brought another boy into this world, Matthew Bennett Wheeler, a little brother for their surviving son. "You try to make the world into the place you want it to be," David told me. "And many times, the only area you have control over is the square footage of your own house. And so, you do what you can." David Wheeler, a former actor and a graphic artist, was often among the most eloquent of the parents. In our first interview, five years before, he threw down a challenge that I believe should be hand delivered to every home in America. Wheeler said:

I would like every parent in this country—that's a 150 million people—I would like them to look in the mirror. And that's not a figure of speech, Scott. I mean, literally, *find a mirror in your house,* and look in it, and look in your eyes and say, '*This will never happen to me.* This will never happen in my school. This will never happen in my community.' And see if you actually *believe* that. And if there is a shadow, the slightest shadow, of doubt about what you've said, think about what you can do to change that in your house, in your community, in your school, in your country, because we have an obligation to our children to do this for them. It's going to happen again. *It is going to happen again.* And every time, it's somebody else's school, it's somebody else's town. It's somebody else's community, until one day, you wake up and *it's not.*

"I'm still trying to figure out who I am now," Nicole Hockley told me. In the years since the murders, she had divorced and given herself completely to the work of Sandy Hook Promise. She explained, "I couldn't be any more different from the confident, optimistic, happy-go-lucky type person I was beforehand."

"Have you given yourself time to grieve?" I wondered.

"No. No. I'm working on that right now. This is kind of my year that I'm feeling it's time to start finding myself again but also to accept that no matter what I do, I can't get Dylan back."

Jazz musician Jimmy Greene summoned his daughter with his saxophone. He recorded *Beautiful Life,* an album inspired by Ana Grace. The recording was nominated for two Grammy Awards. Ana's mother, Nelba Marquez-Greene, is a behavioral therapist. She started The Ana Grace Project to educate teachers about mental health. In our conversations, she often spoke of her faith. I asked her, "I wonder how your faith may have changed in all of this?"

"One of the most compelling sermons I've ever heard was

given at my daughter's funeral," she said. "It was just a beautiful sermon. It talks about Jesus being with us in every season of our lives, including the winter. And that Ana's death would signify the beginning of a long and hard winter season and that winter would be made better with faith and family and friends. And I still feel that way. I really do."

"Is it springtime yet?" I asked.

"I can't imagine a day that it will be spring. The moment I'm reunited with her, I want to hear two things. I want to hear, 'Well done, my good and faithful servant.' And I want to hear, 'Hi, Mom.'"

Without legislation from Congress, President Obama signed several orders to restrict gun sales to ineligible buyers. One of his presidential memorandums built on a law signed by President George W. Bush in 2008. That law required federal agencies to report ineligible persons to the National Instant Criminal Background Check System.[8] After Sandy Hook, President Obama ordered the Justice Department to make sure all agencies were following the Republican-passed law.[9] In response, the Social Security Administration adopted a rule to report to the background check system certain people who were receiving disability benefits because of mental disorders. That covered an estimated seventy-five thousand mental patients. But in February 2017, the House and Senate passed bills to reverse the Social Security Administration's rule.[10] President Trump signed into law the restoration of firearm eligibility to those who are so mentally ill that they are considered by the government to be disabled.

For the record, my wife and I enjoy shooting sporting clays as a hobby. My father taught me how to handle firearms. But in my view, removing the names of thousands of mentally disabled persons from the background check system is the definition of insanity. Mass murders since Sandy Hook have become more frequent and deadlier. In October 2018, eleven worshippers were murdered in a Pittsburgh synagogue by a deranged gunman who told police he wanted to kill Jews. In 2017 and 2016, the FBI reported 50 active shooter incidents in 21 states. The worst of them were: Las Vegas, 58 killed, 489 wounded; Orlando, 49 killed, 53 wounded; and the First Baptist Church in Sutherland Springs, Texas, 26 killed, 20 wounded.[11] FBI data show that the number of casualties in active shooter incidents varies year to year, but the trend line is only rising. In 2000, the FBI recorded 7 casualties, in 2017 there were 729.[12]

Perseverance changes the world. It is the only thing that ever has. The families of Sandy Hook rose from devastation, fought back to win early victories, suffered defeat in Congress and still pressed on with new ideas to save lives.

The day of Sandy Hook, my morning began with a man who had fully explored the path that was only beginning for Newtown. Sixty-eight years before, at the age of fifteen, Elie Wiesel was brought into the death camps. He concluded that God was dead. But with perseverance, he returned to his dialogue with God—armed with many pointed questions. That December day in 2012, as the inexplicable murders were underway, I asked Wiesel how peace could be possible given the faults of man. It is astounding how closely his answer mirrors David Wheeler's challenge to take personal responsibility:

Oh, we speak so much about peace and aspirations for peace. I think it should begin with the individual. Nations can make peace by signing a peace accord, that's not enough—it starts with the human entity, the single individual. Just as we teach mathematics, we should teach children the honor and happiness and the joy and the humanity of creating peace around us. Start at home, at the table, parents and friends. Peace is something that cannot remain an abstraction. It must be practiced, created and recreated.

Only peace can be noble. We speak about heroism. Heroism usually is a result of war. *No!* I believe in simple heroism. If you go into the street and you see a woman who needs help, you help, a child who needs a smile, you smile, a beggar who opens his palm, you put something in that hand. Look, that's already a gesture [of peace]. Start in your circle. No one person can make world peace. Even God cannot, otherwise there would be peace all the time. This is *our* endeavor; it's our duty, it's our obligation, it's our fight.

CHAPTER FIFTEEN

Deceit

The Fabulist Mr. Clinton

Deceit is the fault that enables all vices.

In my experience, stories of deceit are often anchored to the same dateline. I am not one to damn Washington. Contrary to legend, I know many patriots, hardworking professionals, who toil away in thankless jobs in the capital because they believe in the American ideal. Politicians I have come to know, too often, are another matter.

In January 1992, as a young CBS News correspondent coming off the Gulf War, I was assigned to one of the candidates running for president. Because I was relatively new, I was attached to a largely unknown candidate, the governor of Arkansas, who appeared to have little prospect of winning the Democratic nomination. The Democrats didn't stand a chance in the general election anyway. After the war, George H. W. Bush was cresting on an insurmountable 89 percent approval rating.[1] Top Democrats who might have run, including Governor Mario Cuomo of New York and Senator Al Gore of Tennessee, didn't want to get flattened by the Bush juggernaut, so they opted out. Only dark horses were at the starting gate: former California Governor Jerry Brown; former Massachusetts Senator Paul Tsongas; Senator Tom Harkin of Iowa; Senator Bob Kerry of Nebraska; and my candidate, forty-five-year-old Governor Bill Clinton, the youngest of the lot. I suspected Clinton was running in 1992 to develop a national organization and the name recognition he would need for a serious run in 1996. Still, I was glad for the assignment—my first presidential campaign. I planned to join the campaign a few days before the New Hampshire primary. But before I had a chance, I got an urgent call from the CBS News National Desk. "You've got to get to Little Rock right now. Your guy is dropping out of the race," the national editor told me.

"What? What's happened?" I asked. The editor said, "There's a woman who claims she had a twelve-year affair with Governor Clinton, so he's done. We'll need a story tomorrow about him dropping out." I was steamed. The other candidates were assigned and my guy was toast before the first primary. That night, the Clinton campaign arranged for me to fly with Bill Clinton from Little Rock to Manchester, New Hampshire. Rain was running in rivulets down the sides of a Westwind ten-passenger jet parked alone on the tarmac. I was escorted onboard and to a seat facing aft at the rear of the plane. I hoped the governor would sit near me so I could introduce myself, but under the circumstances, I seriously doubted he wanted to meet a reporter.

Governor Clinton stepped onboard, silent, glistening with rain. His eyes seemed to be searching for something beyond the floor. He sat in the rear, facing forward, directly in front of me. We were knee to knee. The whine of the aft-mounted engines enveloped us as we taxied through the rain and pulled into the sky. Minutes passed. Governor Clinton did not speak, did not look up from his shoes. It was going to be a long fifteen hundred miles to New Hampshire. As we leveled off, I leaned toward the governor's ear. "Governor?" I tried. No response. "Governor? My name is Scott Pelley. I'm with CBS News and I'll be covering your campaign." For a moment there was no movement. Then, without straightening, he lifted a remorseful face. "Well," he told me, "let's hope it lasts a long time."

"Lasting" would turn out to be the special talent of Bill and Hillary Clinton. They would be savaged by critics from that night to this day. Some of it was unfair—partisan vendettas and loony imaginings of conspiracy theorists. But Mr. Clinton brought much of the torment upon himself. Deceit creates a vacuum which draws in the storm.

Hillary Clinton possessed a strength her husband did not. She would teach him a few things about lasting. But on that dismal night, neither appeared to have a future beyond Little Rock. For me, the flight to Manchester was the first leg of a twenty-five-year odyssey. Along the way, I covered Mr. Clinton's improbable victory, his second term in the White House, his impeachment and the rise and fall of Hillary Clinton.

The late Don Hewitt was fond of saying that Bill Clinton would never have been president had it not been for Hewitt's *60 Minutes* broadcast of January 26, 1992. The revelation of the affair with a woman named Gennifer Flowers was being delivered to every grocery store checkout aisle. The *Star*, a disreputable tabloid, paid Flowers for her story and for tapes of her phone conversations with the governor. "My twelve-year affair with Bill Clinton" moved down black conveyor belts among dozens of eggs and gallons of milk. In Arkansas, I was meeting people who told me the governor had committed serial sexual assault and used state troopers to procure women. The Iowa caucuses were little more than two weeks away. The New Hampshire primary was three weeks off. America was losing any appetite it may have had for the governor of Arkansas.

An interview was arranged with *60 Minutes* correspondent Steve Kroft. In a suite at a luxury hotel in Boston, a dozen TV lights hung from above and picketed the perimeter of a couch where Governor and Mrs. Clinton would be seated. To their right, a fireplace warmed the scene. Across a coffee table, Kroft was shuffling a multitude of papers with a single line of questioning. As the CBS News correspondent on the campaign, I was admitted to the suite. I took the opportunity to meet Mrs. Clinton for the first time. While the governor was having his makeup done, Mrs. Clinton and I sat alone in an adjacent room. I broke the ice, telling the first lady of Arkansas about what I'd been learning about her husband's impressive record on economic development in the state. She nodded as though she were listening but her mind was on the interview. She dreaded it. When had the spouse of a presidential candidate appeared on prime-time television to defend her husband's infidelities? She seemed vulnerable, without the heavy armor she would acquire in the vicious political battles to come. The futures of both candidate and spouse were riding on the next few minutes. The distracted, nervous woman glancing at the floor that day was Hillary Clinton in training.

Don Hewitt rushed around the room, exceedingly impatient as always. He often seemed nearly out of breath, demanding that everything around him accelerate toward his vision. Hewitt didn't often attend interviews but this was big news on the biggest night in television. The Clintons would appear immediately after Super Bowl XXVI on CBS. Hewitt knew the stakes and relished them. He was equal parts newsman and showman. The *60 Minutes* broadcast was to be prerecorded and truncated— only nine minutes long. But the championship audience would add up to eighty million viewers. Hewitt leaned over the governor to deliver a piece of slightly disingenuous advice designed to make the broadcast as news making as possible. Don advised Mr. Clinton, "I think at some point you are going to have to be as candid as you know how and from there on you say, 'I said it on *60 Minutes*. If you want to know what I think or say on the subject, go get the tape, I've said it all.'"

Kroft was a hard-nosed interviewer who never let the profound discomfort of his interviewee throw him off his pursuit. He opened with Gennifer Flowers. "She's alleging, and described in some detail in a supermarket tabloid, a twelve-year affair with you." Mr. Clinton leaned in with an answer as brief as a gunshot. "That allegation is false." Mrs. Clinton nodded intently. Kroft followed with, "I assume from your answer that you are categorically denying having an affair with Gennifer Flowers?" Clinton, evading a direct answer, said something that was undeniably accurate. "I've said that before. And so has she." Kroft came back, again and again, in *60 Minutes* style, trying to extract a straight answer. The governor declined to be specific other than to say he had caused "pain in our marriage." I noticed Mrs. Clinton had a habit of leaning back on the couch with her arm stretched across her husband's shoulders when he was speaking, but when she spoke, she leaned deeply forward in Kroft's direction. In those days, she spoke with a pronounced Southern twang which is jarring to hear today. "I'm sittin' here because I love him and I respect him and I honor what he's been through," she said. "And what *we've* been through together. And if that's not enough for people then, heck, don't vote for him!" As the sparring moved into the next round, no one noticed that one of the heavy television lights hanging above Mrs. Clinton's head was gradually slipping on the bolt that secured it to the ceiling. Hillary Clinton was leaning in to an answer when a thundering crash launched her off the couch. *"JESUS, MARY AND JOSEPH!"* she screamed reflexively. I jumped from my seat too. The Clintons were now standing, gripped in each other's arms. The light slammed into the back of the couch and the bulb exploded precisely where Mrs. Clinton's head would have been had she been listening rather than speaking. The realization of what would have happened but for a couple of inches was almost nauseating. Mrs. Clinton blew out a breath to slow her gasping. "*Whooo!* I'm okay! *Whooo!* I'm okay. *Whooo!*" After a moment, Hewitt approached the shaking couple and urged them back onto the couch. Hewitt didn't *say* anything like this, but his *demeanor* in the moment carried the sense of, okay, sure, that nearly killed you, but this is *60 Minutes*, we have to go on. He *did* tell them that what Mrs. Clinton had been saying at the moment of the light's meteoric fall "was the high point of the whole thing." So, Hewitt argued, they *had to* sit down and continue. Which they did. The near calamity was edited out of the interview. Putting the crash into the story would have overwhelmed everything the Clintons had to say. As it turned out, it wasn't the words that mattered, it was the image. Hillary Clinton sitting by her man, arm intertwined with his, nodding resolutely whenever he spoke. She saved him. She saved herself. Maybe it was an omen that the Washington Redskins beat the Buffalo Bills that night. After the interview, some campaign staff members were in tears. Mrs. Clinton told me, "I think people have a lot of good common sense and I think they have good instincts and I'm going to trust that." One senior member of the campaign staff told me, "New Hampshire will decide this issue."

Hewitt may have been right about the interview making Bill Clinton president. But that wasn't obvious in the weeks that followed. Clinton was crushed in Iowa by favorite son Tom Harkin. In New Hampshire, he lost to Paul Tsongas of neighboring Massachusetts. History told us Clinton was done. No candidate in modern times had lost the first two contests—Iowa *and* New Hampshire—and recovered to win the presidency.[2] On primary night in New Hampshire, I attended the Clinton rally. The grim results were in. I expected the usual concession and a vow to go on, instead, Governor Clinton came on stage and anointed himself "The Comeback Kid." Standing in the celebration, I said to myself, "Did you say comeback? What comeback? You lost, by nine points!" Along with the rest of America, I watched the performance of an illusionist for whom facts were frangible—an early version of Donald Trump. Why be limited to the truth when so many other words were available? Only "lasting" mattered. The man who denied being a sexual predator was denying the verdict of Iowa and New Hampshire. As he advised Gennifer Flowers, in one of their recorded phone calls, "Just say no and go on."

Six years later, in July 1997, Bill Clinton invited me to the Oval Office for a private chat. I had just been appointed CBS News's chief White House correspondent and Mr. Clinton wanted to welcome me. The president offered me a seat on a couch near the fireplace. He sat on the opposite couch, not unlike the first time I met him on the campaign plane in 1992. I decided to recall for the president that lonely night when he said of his campaign, "Well, let's hope it lasts a long time." I thought starting the conversation there would give him a chance to reminisce about his eventual triumph. Now secure in his second term, I was certain the president would find the memory amusing. He didn't. Mr. Clinton's eyes narrowed. His smile fell with a nearly audible crash. I had expected him to laugh and say, "Boy, I sure showed 'em, didn't I?" Instead, the silence in the Oval suggested the flaws in character that threatened his campaign were not so distant a memory. *Why so touchy?* I thought. After the awkward silence, I pivoted to policy and the president recovered his equanimity. After half an hour or so, I walked the thirty yards to the CBS News office in the West Wing. I took my seat, looked around the room and mused aloud, "I sure hope something interesting happens while I'm here."

The public knows well the James Brady Briefing Room,

where the president's spokesperson parries the press. The briefing room was built by the Nixon administration over the now abandoned swimming pool dug in 1933 for FDR.[3] I suspect some press secretaries have fantasized about installing a retractable floor under the rows of reporters. My job came with the best seat in the house. In the center of the front row, a small brass sign on the chair read CBS. What you haven't seen, beyond the briefing room, is the maze of closet-sized spaces that serve as offices for White House correspondents and photographers. Our office was about five feet wide and twelve feet long with a microphone and audio booth at one end. I shared the confines with two other CBS News correspondents, a stack of years-old newspapers and an occasional mouse. I am certain the DC fire marshal would have condemned the briefing room and its warrens, but I'm not aware there had ever been a fire inspection. In the "booth," as we called our office, a continuous countertop ran the length of one wall providing a desk for the three of us who sat shoulder to shoulder. Our computer screens and telephones were mounted on the wall. With no windows, the booth had the claustrophobic feel of a submarine. My crewmates included Bill Plante, the legendary, urbane, CBS News correspondent who had covered the civil rights movement, Vietnam, the Cold War and every White House since Jimmy Carter. Bill was the dean of White House television correspondents and the patient mentor I needed. Also wedged in the booth was correspondent Mark Knoller, who saw to the needs of millions of CBS News radio listeners. It was rumored that Knoller had been born in the briefing room but I knew this to be untrue. Knoller was acknowledged by the White House and by our competitors as the leading in-house expert on the history of modern presidents. "Mark, how many times has the president played golf this year?" "Mark, what day was the president's last statement on Libya?" "Mark, how many executive orders does this make on immigration policy?" When the president's press secretary didn't have the answers, the White House itself would ask Knoller. Presidents come and presidents go. Knoller was always there to show them in and see them off.

When I took the job, I was asked who I wanted as a producer. I said, "Give me the guy who's been doing it for years." That was Bill Owens. Bill was nearly ten years younger than me. He descended from Scottish stock and was raised with five sisters on Long Island in Oyster Bay, New York. Bill's father had been a US marine who was wounded storming the beachhead at Iwo Jima. A considerable amount of his father's grit had been passed down to the son. Bill was sometimes kidded about his reddish hair. His nose proudly testified that he had never stood down from a fight.

A news producer is the correspondent's partner. We're a reporting team. You won't often see the producer on the screen, but his or her work is in the reporting, fact-checking, writing, graphics and video. At the White House and later, Bill and I became inseparable. In late 1999, Bill joined me at *60 Minutes II*. Together we've covered difficult and dangerous stories around the world. Eventually, Bill rose to executive editor at *60 Minutes*, overseeing all the correspondents. Then, in 2019, Bill was made executive producer of *60 Minutes*, the top job, and only the third boss in the broadcast's fifty-one year history. Bill used to work for me, now I work for him. Our partnership never ended. I doubt there would have been a "Scott Pelley" without Bill Owens.

Many White House correspondents spend decades questioning the daily press briefing, attending speeches and zooming along in the presidential motorcade. I wanted to change the way CBS News covered the president. I was interested in the way the White House affected people's lives. When President Clinton held a daylong conference on single mothers, I started the day with a single mom in Maryland who was getting her children dressed for school and riding multiple bus routes that led to her job. When the president embarked on his state tour of China, Owens and I visited the place Mr. Clinton could *not* go, Taiwan, the greatest irritant in Sino-American relations. For about a year I was able to examine the White House by searching beyond it. Then, in 1998, the story dragged me all the way back to where I had started with the Clintons. My wish for "something interesting" was answered in abundance.

In January, President Clinton was forced to testify before Federal District Judge Susan Webber Wright in a closed deposition. The case was a civil suit titled *Jones v. Clinton*. Paula Jones, an Arkansas state employee, accused then Governor Clinton of sexual harassment. Under oath, she testified that Clinton ordered a state trooper to bring her to a hotel room in Little Rock. She claimed Clinton exposed himself and asked for sex. Jones testified that the incident caused her "severe embarrassment, humiliation, grief, shame, anxiety and fear." She said she refused the governor and worried she could lose her job. The president fought his summons to testify all the way to the Supreme Court of the United States. In a countersuit, *Clinton v. Jones*, Mr. Clinton's lawyers argued that responding to the suit would be an unreasonable burden on the president's time. The president lost. The justices were unanimous. In the months to follow, the "unreasonable burden" would not be on the president, it would weigh on the people of the United States.

On Saturday, January 17, I followed the president's motorcade from the White House to the office of his attorney. In a private conference room, Mr. Clinton was sworn to tell the truth and nothing but the truth. In addition to questions about Paula Jones, Mr. Clinton was asked about someone the public had never heard of. Monica Lewinsky had been an intern at the White House when she was twenty-four years old, nearly thirty years younger than the president. Paula Jones's attorney asked, "Did you have an extramarital sexual affair with Monica Lewinsky?"

In that millisecond after the question mark, President Clinton might have asked for a private discussion with his attorneys. He might have decided settling the Jones case with no further questions would be best for himself, his family and the nation. Instead, Mr. Clinton did what had always worked for him. He lied. "No," he said. The attorney for Paula Jones pounced, "If she [Lewinsky] told someone that she had a sexual affair with you beginning in November of 1995, would that be a lie?"

"It's certainly not the truth. It would not be the truth," the president replied. Mr. Clinton added, "I have never had sexual relations with Monica Lewinsky. I've never had an affair with her."[4] Some legal scholars would describe that as perjury in an attempt to obstruct justice. It seems unlikely that the president, a former law school professor, was unaware of the consequences. Mr. Clinton bet his presidency on an apparent belief that Monica Lewinsky's testimony would match his own and the Jones attorneys could not prove their allegation. He had not yet heard of Linda Tripp.

The woman with the Dickensian name was a friend in whom Monica Lewinsky unwisely invested her trust. Lewinsky confided in Tripp, over the phone, about her conflicted feelings for Mr. Clinton and their trysts in the Oval Office. One of these sexual encounters, Lewinsky said, occurred while the president was on the phone with a member of Congress. Tripp listened patiently as her tape recorder immortalized the conversations.

Across town, a bookish, former federal appeals court judge, Kenneth Starr, was pursuing a long-running and wide-ranging investigation of Bill Clinton. He had been appointed to the Office of Independent Counsel by the DC Court of Appeals to investigate a number of allegations, including a soured Arkansas real estate deal called Whitewater; the replacement of the White House travel office staff with Clinton associates; and the suicide of Deputy White House Counsel, Vince Foster. None of the OIC's many investigations was going anywhere until Linda Tripp delivered her tapes to Ken Starr.

The day after the president's deposition in *Jones v. Clinton*, the *Washington Post* broke the Lewinsky story on its Sunday front page. The *Post* reported that the president was under investigation for encouraging Lewinsky to lie when she testified under oath. So began one of the most professionally hazardous stories of my career. When investigating the president, you can never be wrong.

On January 21, the president told the same lie to the public that he told in the deposition four days before. He was asked about Lewinsky on PBS's *The NewsHour with Jim Lehrer*. "That is not true," Mr. Clinton said. "That is not true. I did not ask anyone to tell anything other than the truth. There is no improper relationship."

"No improper relationship. Define what you mean by that," Lehrer asked.

"Well, I think you know what it means. It means that there is not a sexual relationship, an improper sexual relationship or any other kind of improper relationship."

"You had no sexual relationship with this young woman?"

"There is not a sexual relationship—that is accurate."

This disingenuous phrasing, the use of the present tense verb, would later lead Mr. Clinton to tell a grand jury with a sly grin, "It depends on what the meaning of '*is*' is."

The day after, the president met in the Oval Office with Palestinian leader Yasser Arafat. The press pool asked about Lewinsky. Mr. Clinton denied all and concluded with a nonsensical statement that suggested that getting to the truth was a complicated matter. "I'd like for you to have more rather than less, sooner rather than later. So, we'll work through it as quickly as we can and get all those questions [sic] out there to you."

Toward the end of January, I joined my colleagues in the Roosevelt Room for a presidential statement. The conference room was once Theodore Roosevelt's office. Roosevelt built the famed West Wing in 1902 after the White House staff had grown to *thirty* people and Mr. Roosevelt's six children filled up the White House residence.[5] Mr. Clinton came into the room and stood beneath *Rough Rider,* the equestrian portrait of Roosevelt. The president jabbed his finger at the television camera, "I want to say one thing to the American people. I want you to *listen* to me. I'm going to say this again. I did not have sexual relations with that woman, Miss Lewinsky. I never told anybody to lie, not a single time—never. These allegations are false. And I need to go back to work for the American people." My eyes were drawn to the oil painting of the hero of San Juan Hill charging forward as President Clinton beat a hasty retreat.

For nearly a year, the White House and Washington were paralyzed as the president stonewalled. Bill Owens and I worked to develop confidential sources among the president's confidants and those familiar with the investigation of the Office of Independent Counsel. No one was supposed to be talking about any of this, but Bill and I established relationships of trust with sources who felt it was vital that the public had accurate information. Presidents tend to use the words *leak* and *leaker* as pejoratives. But I believe any person telling the truth to the public when politicians are lying is doing a brave thing for the country. Imagine how our experiences with Watergate and Vietnam could have been different if there had been no "leaks" of the truth.

Bill and I met our sources, clandestinely, sometimes on a particular bench in Lafayette Park across from the White House, sometimes in an out-of-the-way booth at the historic Willard Hotel. We avoided the phones in the CBS News booth even though they were not connected to the White House switchboard. I preferred a pay phone on the corner of Pennsylvania Avenue and 17th Street. I assigned code names to our sources to avoid revealing their identities. Only Bill and I knew the code. Given my well-documented dependence on coffee, the code names included *Starbuck* and *Seattle.* And, no, Starbuck was not Ken Starr. We never burned our sources. They gave us straight information in a time of hysterical rumors. Often, they helped us keep information off our broadcast that they knew was false.

On April 30, a presidential news conference was scheduled in the White House East Room. This is the largest room in the White House, where Abigail Adams used to hang laundry. On the east wall you will find Gilbert Stuart's 1796 life-size portrait of George Washington which Dolley Madison saved from the flames of the British invasion in 1814. On this day in 1998, the laundry hung out to dry in the East Room would not have met Mrs. Adams's approval. As I waited for the president to call on me, I noticed a new tactic in Clintonian obfuscation. By tradition, Helen Thomas, the longest serving White House correspondent, got the first question. "Mr. President, in view of a new court ruling, Monica Lewinsky may have to appear before a grand jury. Under the circumstances, do you stand by your previous denials of any relationship with her or that anyone encouraged her to lie?"

The president replied, "I have answered repeatedly and have nothing to add to my former answer. I have repeatedly said what the answer to that question is." The president was turning Don Hewitt's 1992 advice on its head. Instead of telling all and declining to answer more questions, Mr. Clinton had told nothing but claimed he'd said it all.

Sam Donaldson of ABC News followed up. "Does it matter, what you do in private moments as alleged? And, particularly, does it matter if you have committed perjury or in another sense broken the law?"

"Well, since I have answered the underlying questions, I really believe it's important for me not to say any more about this," the president concluded.

"Answers?" I whispered to myself. "What answers?" It had been fourteen weeks since his "sooner rather than later" declaration. Mr. Clinton looked up from his predetermined list of correspondents. "Scott?" he said.

"Thank you, Mr. President," I began. "It was suggested at the beginning of this news conference, sir, that you've answered the questions about Monica Lewinsky. But, respectfully, there has been no explanation for her dozens of visits to the White House after her employment here ended. No explanation for the Secret Service concern about her behavior in the West Wing. No explanation about the extraordinary effort by your secretary and your closest friends to find her a job. Sir, could you now give us some better sense of what appears to be an extraordinary relationship that you had with this woman and fulfill your promise to the American people of 'more rather than less, sooner rather than later'?"

"Well, first of all, you have more information than you did when I said that." (We didn't.) "And secondly, I have nothing else to say. I have been advised, and I think it's good advice under the circumstances, but I just don't have anything else to say about that." This was a rare case in which the question revealed more than the answer.

The Office of Independent Counsel invited Mr. Clinton to testify to the grand jury. The president's lawyers stonewalled. The OIC hesitated to force the president to testify by issuing a subpoena. No president had ever been summoned to a grand jury. After weeks of silence on this issue, I called my source we codenamed Starbuck. "I think the president has been subpoenaed," I told him. I was guessing, but it was an educated guess.

"I can't talk about that," Starbuck replied.

"How about this?" I suggested. "If the president *has* been subpoenaed to testify before the grand jury, don't say a word, just hang up the phone. If he hasn't been subpoenaed, let's keep talking."

Click. Dial tone.

A few seconds later, the phone rang. It was Starbuck. "Do you understand what I just did?" he asked.

"Yeah, I told you, if the president has been subpoenaed by

the grand jury, you should hang up the phone. Otherwise, we'll keep talking."

Click. Dial tone.

That night, on the *CBS Evening News* we broke the story that William Jefferson Clinton had become the first president of the United States to be subpoenaed by a federal grand jury. Three days later, almost by accident, we broke the most important story in the Lewinsky investigation. The paparazzi found Monica Lewinsky traveling in Manhattan. The pictures were all over morning TV. I called her attorney. His assistant answered. "I'm sorry, Mr. Pelley," she said. "He's in meetings in New York today. I'll let him know you called." I continued making my daily rounds with a call to one of Ken Starr's top deputies. He never gave me information, but I lived in hope. His assistant apologized as well. "I'm sorry, Mr. Pelley, he left this morning for a meeting out of town, but I expect him back in the afternoon." *Quick trip,* I thought, so I ventured, "Oh, he must be in New York?"

"Yes, that's right," she confirmed. "I'll let him know you called."

Now I had Lewinsky, her attorney and Starr's right-hand man in "meetings" in New York on the same morning. I put two and two together and started calling some of our more knowledgeable sources. "Is a deal happening with Lewinsky?" I asked. "Everybody seems to be in New York for a meeting."

"They have a deal," one of my sources told me. "She's cooperating." I took that to another source who confirmed it. That night I reported that Monica Lewinsky had become a cooperating witness for the Office of Independent Counsel. She too had lied in her sworn testimony in *Jones v. Clinton.* Under the terms of the New York deal, she would testify against the president in return for immunity for her perjured testimony. Lewinsky gave the FBI a blue dress that was allegedly stained with the president's semen. DNA tests matched the president.

On August 17, 1998, Mr. Clinton testified before the grand

jury by video link. Ken Starr had withdrawn the subpoena in exchange for the president's voluntary appearance. That same night, Mr. Clinton appeared from the White House Map Room in a national address unlike anything since the resignation of Richard Nixon.[6] "As you know," the president began, "in a deposition in January, I was asked questions about my relationship with Monica Lewinsky. While my answers were legally accurate, I did not volunteer information. Indeed, I did have a relationship with Ms. Lewinsky that was not appropriate. In fact, it was wrong. It constituted a critical lapse in judgment and a personal failure on my part for which I am solely and completely responsible. But I told the grand jury today and I say to you now, that at no time did I ask anyone to lie, to hide or destroy evidence or to take any other unlawful action. I know that my public comments and my silence about this matter gave a false impression. I misled people, including even my wife. I deeply regret that."

Legally accurate? False *impression*? The public confession itself was deceitful and would lead to more trouble. In the speech, the president complained that "our country has been distracted by this matter for too long," as if it wasn't he who had lied in the first place and stonewalled for as long as he could get away with. On camera, the president was tight as piano wire, striking a note of unmistakable anger. The lack of humility made matters worse. And there was a significant omission—no apology to Monica Lewinsky.

The first family escaped to Martha's Vineyard, Massachusetts, for a private vacation. I remember watching them walk to the helicopter on the South Lawn, Mrs. Clinton and Chelsea arm in arm, the president walking apart and alone. At what must have been the nadir of his life, Mr. Clinton received a lifeline of compassion from the legendary CBS News anchorman, Walter Cronkite. Walter and his wife, Betsy, had retired to a home on the Vineyard. They invited the first family to go sailing. The image of the exiled president standing next to the former anchorman known as "the most trusted man in America"[7] spoke to Cronkite's selflessness and his understanding that, for the good of the country, confidence had to be restored in the American presidency—if not the president himself.

On September 11, 1998, Mr. Clinton attempted contrition. He spoke to religious leaders at a White House prayer breakfast. "It is important to me that everybody who has been hurt know that the sorrow I feel is genuine. First and most important, my family, also my friends, my staff, my cabinet, Monica Lewinsky and her family and the American people. I have asked all for their forgiveness." As the president spoke, I noticed a significant mark above his left eye. At the afternoon press briefing, I asked press secretary Mike McCurry how the president cut himself. "Oh, that's a little bit of his rosacea," McCurry said. "Which comes out from time to time." I didn't think any more about the mark on the president's forehead until a few days later when I was in the makeup room in the CBS News Washington Bureau. I was preparing for a roundtable discussion on impeachment as a guest on *60 Minutes*.

"Nasty cut on the president's forehead," the freelance makeup artist said.

"No, no," I told her. "That's rosacea, it breaks out on the president's skin from time to time."

"It's a *cut* and a bad one," she countered. "I know because they called me in to make him up."

Well, now I'm intrigued. We checked our sources who told us the first lady had landed a blow on the president of the United States. One source believed the projectile was a cell phone. "Yeah," the source said. "She smacked him pretty good."

Cell phone justice is swift, but impeachment is from an era when parchment was delivered on horseback. Congress, the White House, and the nation were tied up four more months. Impeachment is a political act, not a legal one. It is the job of the House of Representatives to decide whether a president should be "impeached," which is the equivalent of an indictment. If so, then the Senate puts the president on trial to determine whether he should be removed from office. There was no surprise that the Republican-controlled House voted to impeach Mr. Clinton on December 19, 1998. Two articles of impeachment were approved: one for lying under oath and the other for obstruction of justice. Article I of the impeachment resolution written by the House Judiciary Committee claimed the president had "willfully corrupted and manipulated the judicial process of the United States for his personal gain and exoneration, impeding the administration of justice…" Mr. Clinton became the second president impeached after Andrew Johnson, who ascended to the presidency after the assassination of Abraham Lincoln. Johnson was a poor substitute for "Honest Abe." He was often drunk and, after supporting Lincoln's position on black suffrage, he joined those who sought to deny civil rights to emancipated slaves.[8] In 1868, Johnson angered Congress further by firing the secretary of war, Edwin Stanton. Johnson was accused of violating the Tenure of Office Act. When he went on trial in the Senate, Johnson was acquitted by a single vote.

Mr. Clinton did slightly better. On February 12, 1999, the Senate, controlled by the Democrats, acquitted President Clinton, 55-45, on the perjury charge. Then the senators voted 50–50 on the obstruction of justice article. A two-thirds majority is required to remove the president, so even 50–50 was far short of the 67 votes needed to convict. Mr. Clinton did not do as well in federal court where the judge in the *Jones v. Clinton* sexual harassment case found Mr. Clinton guilty of essentially the same charges. District Judge Susan Webber Wright ruled that Mr. Clinton was in contempt of court for what she called "false, misleading and evasive answers that were designed to obstruct the judicial process." Judge Wright addressed the tortured logic of the president's denials. In her Opinion and Order she wrote, "he [Clinton] did state that oral sex performed by Ms. Lewinsky would not constitute 'sexual relations'…" And "it appears the president is asserting that Ms. Lewinsky could be having sex with him while, at the same time, he was not having sex with her." The president's lies, the judge wrote, "undermined the integrity of the judicial system."[9] She fined the president $90,000. In a deal to avoid disbarment in Arkansas, the president accepted a five-year suspension of his law license.[10] In order D-2270 "In the Matter of Discipline of Bill Clinton," the Justices of the Supreme Court of the United States disbarred Mr. Clinton from practicing before their bench.[11] As for Paula Jones, Mr. Clinton paid $850,000 to settle the case, which he might have settled thirteen months earlier, privately, without committing perjury and without being impeached. In the context of the 2017 #MeToo movement, it is hard to imagine President Clinton surviving the judgment of popular opinion. But 1998 was still a time when bosses could get away with sexually abusing young women in the workplace.

President Clinton was in office during, what was then, the longest peacetime economic expansion in US history.[12] That expansion and his tax increases on upper-income Americans helped balance the federal budget, something no president has managed since.[13] Mr. Clinton worked with Republicans to pass sweeping reform of welfare benefits. In my view, he was gifted in the one-on-one of retail politics and gifted in his ability to memorize and master intricate details of policy. I have never met his like. But these abilities only magnify the tragedy of failed character. Could there have been other achievements had it not been for his serial sexual abuse of women?

A quarter of Mr. Clinton's second term was spent in daily battle to escape the scandal. Hillary Clinton would never escape. She became one of the most experienced candidates ever to run for president. But defending her husband against charges of sexual assault left the public with indelible doubt. The excoriating media firestorm created in her an obsession with privacy that gave the public more reason to doubt. By 2016, Americans responding to our CBS News poll voted Hillary Clinton the second most distrusted candidate ever to run for president. The only candidate more distrusted was Donald J. Trump.

CHAPTER SIXTEEN

Courage
Bao Tong

Presidents have one priority in their first term: a second term. So, in early years, most of their travel remains within arm's reach of the voters. But in year five, presidents begin to explore the range of Air Force One. On June 25, 1998, President Clinton embarked on a ten-day state tour of China. Bill Owens and I were along on an itinerary that included Xi'an, Beijing, Shanghai, Guilin and Hong Kong. For Mr. Clinton, the trip had the added benefit of being almost precisely on the opposite side of the world from the grand jury in Washington.

In terms of foreign policy, the journey was meant to be a new beginning. Mr. Clinton would be the first American president to visit China since the Tiananmen Square massacre. Nine years before, hundreds of pro-democracy demonstrators were killed by the People's Liberation Army in the square that lies before the Great Hall of the People. To get an idea of what a cataclysmic event this was, imagine hundreds of unarmed citizens being gunned down by the US Army on the lawn in front of the US Capitol. Unimaginable, of course, but that's the horror that befell Beijing. Before the president's trip, the Chinese Communist Party had been highly successful in covering up the killings. Because the party controls all media, the vast majority of Chinese never knew Tiananmen happened. Mr. Clinton had a secret plan to bring it up in a news conference that was to be televised live throughout China. Mr. Clinton planned to say, "The use of force and tragic loss of life was wrong."[1] He would be standing alongside Jiang Zemin, the general secretary of the Communist Party and Chinese president who had been installed twenty days after the Tiananmen murders. (It is telling that Chinese heads of state place their party title ahead of "president.")

There was one political dissident who the Communist Party was determined to muzzle during President Clinton's visit. In 1989, as fifty-thousand protesters swept into Tiananmen Square, Bao Tong was watching from his office. He was political secretary to the Politburo's Standing Committee and a member of the party's Central Committee. Most important, he was a close advisor and personal secretary to the politically progressive general secretary of the Communist Party, Zhao Ziyang. Communist Party hardliners saw the democracy demonstration as a threat. Protests spread to four hundred towns and cities. Among leaders in the Central Committee, a debate raged between those who wanted to crush dissent and those, like Bao and Zhao, who saw opportunity for political and economic freedom. Bao could not accept ordering Chinese troops to murder Chinese citizens. On May 28, 1989, Bao discovered the side of the angels was the wrong side of history. He was called to a meeting and arrested.[2] One week later, over his objections and the objections of President Zhao, the order for the massacre was given. The night of

June 4, troops swarmed the square, killing hundreds, perhaps more than one thousand unarmed fellow citizens.[3] For his opposition, Bao was sentenced to seven years in prison, most of which was solitary confinement.[4] When I arrived in Beijing in 1998, Bao had been out of prison a little over a year, but he was under constant surveillance.

No one could speak to the Tiananmen tragedy like Bao. An interview with him, when the world was watching President Clinton's visit, would demand courage on his part and ingenuity on ours. Our Beijing producer, Natalie Liu, contacted Bao. He was willing to risk his freedom to speak for freedom. Our challenge was how to pull it off. Chinese police stood twenty-four-hour guard at his home. They would never allow us to visit.

Bill Owens designed a plan that would unfold in Purple Bamboo Park, a 115-acre oasis of lakes and lawns in northwest Beijing, an affluent part of the capital where universities are clustered. When we arrived in the park, summer was blossoming. The sky was gauzed by high cirrus. Families in canopied boats drifted through groves of lotus, propelled by gondoliers sculling red oars in a lazy rhythm. One boy, pleased with his cleverness, plucked a broad lotus flower and raised it against the sun like a parasol. Along the edges of the park's concrete trails, bamboo pickets were set to keep visitors off the carefully tended greens. The gardens that later became Purple Bamboo Park were originally ordered in the year 1577 by Wan-li, the 13th emperor of the Ming Dynasty.[5]

On June 27, 1998, Bao Tong ambled down one of the pathways in the park and settled onto a green wooden bench. Across the path, directly opposite Bao, our cameraman, Rollie Malicsi, sat with a camera hidden in a shoulder bag. I came from the opposite direction and sat with Bao. A nearly invisible wireless microphone, pinned inside my shirt, transmitted our conversation across the path to Rollie's recorder. There was no telling what would happen next as this soft-spoken man risked everything to test his people's right to be heard. Bao was fifty-nine when he went to prison for "revealing state secrets and counterrevolutionary propagandizing."[6] That's the same ambiguous charge China uses to jail journalists today. Despite prison, Bao looked younger than his sixty-six years. He was as slender as the reeds nodding in the lake. He wore a teal polo shirt, untucked, hanging loosely over black trousers. His smooth face was dominated by outsized silver wire-rimmed glasses. I had noticed Bao tended to walk holding his arms behind his back as if handcuffed. He surprised me with a complete lack of bitterness about his years in solitary. He said isolation had liberated his mind from Communist Party dogma. Bao began, "According to our constitution I have the freedom of speech. However, whether I do indeed have the freedom of speech, I do not know. I think CBS can conduct a test. Let's see whether I get into trouble after your interview with me. If so, it will demonstrate that our government does not respect our own constitution."

"What should Americans understand about the struggle in China?" I asked.

"If people can check and balance the power of the government, then the government can become a force that safeguards world peace. Otherwise, it is a dangerous force."

Bao told me China could not progress politically until the party publicly admitted the Tiananmen massacre was wrong. "I feel sad, ashamed and proud at the same time," he told me. "Proud of those students, the citizens of Beijing, the people."

After a few minutes, we parted. Bao ambled away. I walked in the opposite direction. That's when I noticed, out of the corner of my eye, another cameraman with a shoulder bag. From the zippered opening protruded an absurdly large lens. He was a member of a Chinese secret police surveillance team. Bill, Natalie and I quickened our pace slightly but deliberately. A moment later, I saw a furious man sprinting toward us. He was red with rage and closing fast. We began an undignified trot, but the man kept accelerating and screaming, now waving a fist. I began wondering about Chinese jails as we broke into a full run. The man matched our pace. Natalie and I were falling short of breath when I shouted, "What's he saying? *Huff, huff,* what's he saying!"

"He's saying, 'Keep'...*huff, huff*...

"'off'...*huff*...

"'the *grass!*'"

Apparently, the Chinese secret police had nothing on a manic gardener charged with keeping ten million Beijingers off the tender shoots of Purple Bamboo Park. We escaped the gardener and put Bao's first television interview on that night's *CBS Evening News with Dan Rather.* The highest-ranking Communist Party official to be jailed for opposing the massacre had his say the day the American president landed in China.

In the days that followed, I learned something about the deft hand of the Communist Party of China. Nothing happened to Bill nor me. Nothing happened to Bao. There was no blowback that would have turned a leaf in the well-guarded park. Instead, the police state waited two months to send fourteen cops into Natalie Liu's apartment as she was getting her young children ready for school. They seized her notebooks and videotapes, handcuffed her and took her away without explanation. By this time, I was traveling with the president in Ireland. When word of her arrest reached me, I asked the White House to intervene. I have no idea whether the request was helpful, but two days later, Natalie was deported to the United States. She and her family settled in the Washington, DC, area where Natalie continued a distinguished career in journalism at Voice of America. The courage of Bao wouldn't have mattered were it not for the courage of Natalie to arrange for his voice to be heard. In the years since, the danger to those who report outside the bounds of the Communist Party's Central Propaganda Department has grown much more acute. China is one of the largest jailers of reporters in the world. In 2018, Reporters without Borders counted fifty jailed journalists in China, including ten considered in danger of losing their lives because of intentionally deplorable conditions of confinement. The 2018 World Press Freedom Index ranked China 176 out of 180 countries.[7]

The Communist Party propaganda headquarters tells China's newscasts, websites and newspapers what they can say and what they must hide. It is the stated purpose of the Chinese media to serve the interests of the party. I'm often amused when an American politician rails against "The Media" as though American reporters and editors get together each morning to decide on a single message. In America, "The Media" is a cacophony of thousands of broadcasts, websites and publications, large and small, in a competitive frenzy to clobber each other with better coverage. But in China, the Central Propaganda Department actually *does* get up each morning to plan what 1.4 billion people are allowed to see and hear.

Despite President Clinton's mention of Tiananmen on Chinese television in 1998, the Communist Party has done a remarkable job continuing to hide the truth. Not long ago (I won't say where or when for reasons that may be obvious by now), I met a young Chinese woman. She was very well educated and pursuing a sophisticated career. One evening, a group of Americans began discussing the significance of Tiananmen. The Chinese woman was curious because she had little idea of what they were talking about. The Americans showed her the famous picture of a lone, unarmed Tiananmen protester who stopped a battle tank by refusing to move out of its way. She began to weep. The image was startling to her because, in that moment, she realized she had been deceived her entire life. For anyone who is persuaded by President Trump's "fake news" campaign, have a look at China. The news becomes "fake" not when there is competitive reporting, but when the *government* decides what is true and what is not.

★ ★ ★

It seems nearly every time I conspire to commit journalism in China I end up in a physical confrontation. In 2008, my team at *60 Minutes* was investigating illegal trafficking of hazardous waste from the United States to China. The revolution in electronic devices has led to a little-known environmental crisis. All those batteries, dead cell phones and old cathode ray televisions have to go somewhere. There are American companies that claim to recycle them according to EPA standards, but in reality, we found hundreds of tons of devices dumped in China where women and children break them down. Their medieval working conditions poison them and the land. The town of Guiyu, in South Central China, was developing a reputation as a rapacious consumer of this toxic trade. Usually we could not get Chinese visas as journalists, but as it happened, Beijing was hosting the Summer Olympics that year. The International Olympic Committee insisted on unfettered access for journalists in the months before the games.

I rolled into Guiyu with my producer, Solly Granatstein; associate producer, Nicole Young; our camera team and Jim Puckett, an environmental researcher whose work exposed these poisoned wastelands. We were in town less than ten minutes before we were pulled over by plainclothes police officers. They took us to city hall where we were greeted by the jovial mayor. The mayor was tall and slender; he looked to be about forty-something. He sat us down to cups of tea and asked how he could help. We were completely honest about our interest in Guiyu's fast-growing industry. The mayor said he was proud of their electronics recycling and he would be happy to show us the operation himself. My cameraman and I slipped into the back of the mayor's car. We were driven to a tidy storefront where computers and monitors were stacked along one wall with circuit boards scattered along another. No one was working there. We shot the Potemkin still life before being hustled back in the mayor's car. In the back seat, my cameraman pushed Record and I described our visit this way, "The mayor told us that we would be welcome to see the rest of the town, but Guiyu wouldn't be prepared for our visit for another year. So, we were allowed to shoot at that location [the storefront] for about five minutes. Now, we're back in the mayor's car headed to city hall, where I suspect, we'll be given another cup of tea and sent on our way out of town with a police escort." Sure enough, the tea hadn't gone cold before we were run out of town by the cops. We were told in polite but certain terms that we should never come back.

The next day, we ditched our rented cars, hailed local taxis and headed into Guiyu by a different route. In a destitute neighborhood clinging to the edge of town, we found women and children dripping sweat into open fires. Circuit board melting was a cottage industry. Bare hands held boards from last year's American Christmas presents over the flames. Eyes, stung by acrid smoke, watched metal connections among the chips blur, then roll in tiny rivulets into buckets. For eight dollars a day they plucked microchips, transistors and resistors from the green boards to be resold for next year's marvel under the tree. The dirt paths of the neighborhood were walled five feet high with discarded monitors, TVs, computers and hard drives. Cadmium, mercury, chromium and polyvinyl chlorides gathered in a stream that relieved itself into a pond. There was no way to know how much lead and mercury was flowing in the veins of the children inhaling the fumes.

After shooting for a half hour, Puckett and I began taking soil and water samples to be analyzed later. That's when a dozen young men, looking very much like the plainclothes cops from the day before, jumped us. They struggled for our cameras and the samples. Puckett and I put up such a show over our dirt-filled plastic bags that, for a moment, our attackers were distracted from our cameramen. Saving the videotapes was critical. Nicole Young grabbed a heavy tripod and began swinging it like a Louisville Slugger. Behind her defense, cameraman Brad Simpson seized the moment to bolt, carrying his tapes into a passing taxi. While the men struggled to take a small camera I had, cameraman David Lom slipped his tape to Nicole who, with a little prestidigitation, caused it to vanish inside her waistband. Our soil and water samples were yanked away. Lom made a drama of reluctantly surrendering some of his blank video cassettes. I quickly texted Bill Owens, back in New York, "attacked in Guiyu" so that if we disappeared, *60 Minutes* would know where to start looking. Our assailants chased us on foot into a busy market street, where, much to my surprise, we were met by the mayor and his two-car motorcade. We had no place to go but into unmarked police cars and, I presumed, jail. After a short silent ride, we pulled up in front of a restaurant. Inside, an elaborate banquet was laid on a round table set for ten. For two hours, the mayor hosted us to lunch and drinks, lamenting the unfortunate misunderstanding and explaining that Beijing had ordered all local party officials to avoid any conceivable embarrassment leading up to the Olympics. With handshakes all around, we were thrown out of town again and told, "Seriously, *don't* come back." Nicole managed to smile all the way through lunch with that videotape compressed in her pants. With her tripod defense and sleight of hand, and Simpson's prudent escape, we managed to save all the tapes. Our *60 Minutes* story, entitled "The Wasteland," resulted in the federal prosecution of an American recycling company. The CEO, who lied to us and his customers about how he disposed of electronics, went to prison. In China however, no hint of this illegal waste disposal was reported.

The throttling of free speech and a free press is growing more severe as the Communist Party struggles with the proliferation of media. In 2016, Communist Party General Secretary and President Xi Jinping chaired a conference for China's reporters and editors. He required of them *biao tai*, a loyalty pledge. Xi told the journalists, "All news media must work to speak for the party's will and its propositions. And protect the party's authority and unity." He reminded them to "strictly adhere to the news viewpoint of Marxism."[8][9] Xi has grown only more autocratic since then. In 2018, he had himself enshrined, by name, in the national constitution.

A few years ago, a liberal-minded Chinese newspaper called *Southern Weekly* prepared a front-page editorial entitled "China's Dream, the Dream of Constitutionalism." In the same way that Bao Tong tested the constitution in our interview, the newspaper's opinion piece looked forward to the day that China actually practiced the freedoms its constitution proclaims. But before *Southern Weekly* went to press, a propaganda official rewrote the editorial under the headline "We Are Now Closer to Our Dream than Ever." The new version praised the leadership of the Communist Party. In a fierce reaction, Chinese reporters and editors stormed the internet to protest.[10] But their posts were instantly deleted and their accounts were closed by another hand of the party. The State Internet Information Office moves over the World Wide Web with the agility of a spider. A law passed in 1997 makes it a crime to use the internet to "injure the reputation of state organizations."[11] This presumably outlaws uncovering corruption or exposing hazards to public health and safety. The same law prohibits internet posts that "harm national unification." The State Internet Information Office blocks sites it finds controversial. It deploys URL filtering to stop searches of keywords that the office deems suspect. This has been called the "Great Firewall of China."

Today, in the virtual world and in the real world, China is the leading surveillance state. The clunky secret police camera I confronted in Purple Bamboo Park has been transformed into millions of tiny lenses focused on the people. Recently I visited Chinese companies that have developed advanced facial recognition systems and artificial intelligence software that are rapidly becoming capable of automatically keeping an eye on anyone the Communist Party wants to tail. George Orwell's "telescreen" of *1984* watched the people of Oceania when they were home or at work.[12] Now, Big Brother is watching from every lamppost, in every elevator and every hallway. Some Chinese police officers are testing eyeglasses that incorporate facial recognition technology. True, video surveillance is also ubiquitous in much of the United States, but in China, the Communist Party receives the data it wants with no need for warrants, probable cause or court orders. What Bao Tong did to speak to me in 1998 demanded great courage. But imagine the bravery required today to speak for freedom.

The Communist Party is attempting to exploit the economic benefits of the digital age while walling off free-flowing information. If the party wants to see how this tension ends, there is a handy analogue that is thirteen-thousand miles long. Emperor Wan-li, who created the gardens that became Purple Bamboo Park, was among the last of the Ming leaders because he mismanaged his administration and opened his people to the conquest of the Manchus who breached The Great Wall in 1644.[13] Walls fail when they collapse from within. In my view, modern China cannot be considered a fully developed nation until it emerges from its single-party infancy. (There, I just got my book banned in China.)

As of this writing, Bao Tong is in his mideighties, living in Beijing with his family, under surveillance. His son, Bao Pu, lives in nominally independent Hong Kong where he publishes works banned in the rest of the country.

Bao Tong saw hope crushed in Tiananmen Square in 1989 but managed to hope again during President Clinton's visit. As he and I parted amid the lawns and watchful gardeners of Purple Bamboo Park, neither of us could foresee the relentless trampling of the tender shoots of freedom.

FIELD NOTE

Hello, Mom?

The American invasion of Iraq set the townspeople of Numaniyah one against the other in a bitter dispute over the
time of day. Saddam Hussein had imposed daylight saving time
on Iraq. When *his* time ran out in 2003, Numaniyah split between those loyal to "Saddam Time" and those who were suddenly free to "fall back." This temporal tempest in a teapot vexed
Marine Lieutenant Colonel Brent Dunahoe. He'd become the
accidental mayor of Numaniyah, a town of forty thousand with
no power, no trash collection, no drugs in the hospital and no
children in the school. Dunahoe called meetings of town elders,
but stubbornly, many insisted on appearing in their own time,
whichever time that might be.

In truth, Dunahoe had time only for Numaniyah's bridge.
The concrete arc over the Tigris connected Route 27 to Highway 6 and the last 225 miles to Baghdad. It was the job of his

3rd Battalion of the 2nd Marines to hold the bridge for invasion traffic. My *60 Minutes II* team stopped short of the bridge and camped in a grove of date palms. We decided to stay a couple of days to shoot a story about Dunahoe and the demands of America's new Iraqi wards.

One evening, several enlisted marines told me they had been out of touch with home for weeks. The men were desperate to let their families know they were alright. The marines had no way to communicate with the States, but my team had a phone that patched into the satellite uplink that we used to transmit our stories. I told Lieutenant Colonel Dunahoe, privately, that he could tell the marines they were free to use my phone. He thanked me. In a few minutes, his answer was apparent. Weary marines, in dusty camo, pulled themselves up from their camp and formed a disciplined line beside my truck. As word got around, the line grew, until its length vanished in darkness. I counted one hundred men before I stopped counting. I had to come up with a system or the marines in the last half of the line would never get to the phone. I asked all of them to make one call each and to keep it to two minutes. One marine volunteered to stand by the phone and act as the MP of the stopwatch. I stood far enough away to ensure the callers had some privacy. As each said goodbye he handed the receiver to the next homesick caller. Imagine the families, after weeks of hearing nothing, picking up this unexpected voice. A sister of one of the marines refused to hang up until she had a chance to thank my producer, Shawn Efran. I was watching the progress with a steel mug of instant coffee in my hand when a young marine walked up with a request. He was shy, couldn't have been much more than nineteen years old and he really didn't want to ask. "Sir?" he said. "Can I make two calls?"

"I'm sorry," I told him. "If we don't keep this line moving your buddies in the back of the line will be here at dawn. I gotta make sure everyone has a chance."

"Yes, sir," he replied. "It's just, if I can make two calls, sir, I can tell Mama to call my dad and my brothers in from the fields. Then I can call back and talk to them all. I won't take my full two minutes, sir, I promise." Suddenly, two calls seemed very reasonable to me.

In the darkness, I looked toward the bridge, four lanes confined by abutments on each side. It seemed to me the war was just like the bridge itself. Once you started, there was no way off until the end. We did not imagine how long the journey would be. Marines waited in the phone-home line for four hours and more. The satellite time must have cost CBS a fortune, but I never heard from the accounting department. In Iraq, in Afghanistan, and in the Gulf War, my life had been saved many times by these troops.

At last, I had a chance to do something for them.

CHAPTER SEVENTEEN

Valor

Patrick Marc Rapicault

Each sunrise, on a peninsula in the Euphrates that the marines called Hurricane Point, the Stars and Stripes rose silently, save for the jangling of dog tags. *Tink, tink, tink.* The pewter-hued IDs were linked to the brass grommet that secured the flag's lower corner to the halyard that raised it. By the time I arrived at Hurricane Point in the fall of 2004, there were fourteen names embossed in steel hanging on the flag, one for each marine killed in this deployment of the 2nd Battalion of the 5th Marine Regiment. "2/5 Marines" was attempting to pacify the city of Ramadi, Iraq, or at least secure it enough so elections could be held under the new American-sponsored constitution. But Ramadi was the capital of Anbar Province and therefore, the capital of the anti-American insurgency. The people of Anbar were Sunnis. In Iraq, they were the minority denomination of Islam who had been deposed from power and dispossessed after the American invasion. Anbar saw no percentage in American success.

This was 2/5's second deployment to Iraq. In a little over a year between those deployments, the war had undergone a vicious evolution. During the initial invasion, 2/5 lost one marine killed in action over a seven-month stay. By 2004, with the explosion of the insurgency, 2/5 lost fourteen marines and had one hundred seventy wounded in four months. Their camp was a foothold, not a stronghold. Lieutenant Colonel Randall Newman told me, "We've been in a fight since the day we arrived." Newman led the eight hundred marines in 2nd Battalion. He was tall and lanky, soft-spoken and, like a lot of marine commanders I've met, a thinker. His priority was taking care of his marines. Second to that, he was wrestling with one of the most complex missions any American battalion commander has faced in a generation.

Ramadi was a little smaller than Kansas City, with a population of about 375,000. Newman explained his marines were fighting a "three-block war." Three blocks was the reach from the fortified gates of Hurricane Point to Anbar's provincial capitol building. If he did not control this stretch, neither the new Iraqi government nor the Americans had any credibility. The straight, dusty, two-lane road to the capitol building was known to Iraqis as Highway 10. Marine Corps tactical maps labeled it "Route Michigan."

Over breakfast, a lance corporal told me traveling those three blocks was like "a cross between the *Sopranos* and *Mad Max*." "We're getting a lot less cooperation than we used to," he said. "The townspeople are afraid the 'Muj' [Mujahedeen insurgents] are going to kill them if they talk to us."

A few hours after I arrived, enemy mortars exploded near my tent. I stepped out to find Lieutenant Colonel Newman surveying the damage to the roof of his headquarters and assessing a geyser shooting from an underground pipe that had been laid bare in smashed pavement. None of the marines was hurt, nor particularly concerned. Mortars were background noise. Enemy mortar teams were rarely caught because of a trick they'd perfected. The insurgents froze a ring of ice around the mortar shell so it was a little too wide to slide down the firing tube. The shell was stuck, wedged by the ice, at the top of the tube. The enemy walked away from the firing position. It would be several minutes, maybe an hour, before the ice melted, freeing the shell to slide down the tube which caused it to launch. Sending a Quick Reaction Force of marine infantry to catch the mortar team had become a useless exercise and often, an invitation to an ambush.

Hurricane Point was a plywood village. The construction was hasty and, it was hoped, temporary. The mess hall interior, overexposed in fluorescent glare, was regimented into rows of long tables and gray metal folding chairs that screeched across a concrete floor. Beyoncé Knowles presided over the mess hall as a full-sized cardboard cutout. She was selling Pepsi and was doing a pretty good job of it too. Reenlistment posters stapled to the walls urged, "Stay Marine." Tabasco bottles from New Iberia, Louisiana, blurred in short stabbing arcs over scrambled eggs, biscuits and cream gravy. Well-intentioned care packages from churches and schools back home were spilling their guts across the floor—toilet paper, Gatorade powder, the kind of stuff you'd send to a kid at camp. One marine wearily rolled his eyes. He asked me, "Please tell the folks at home to stop sending this stuff." A sign, within Beyoncé's line of sight, reminded the diners, "Place your weapon on the deck." After chow, if they weren't headed up Route Michigan, the marines passed the time in a plywood computer room. The front door conspired to escape in the wind and so, because they were marines, there was a warning which read Maintain Positive Control of the Hatch.

Closing the hatch behind him, a marine would find this warning inside, "Do not open any porn. Virus will infect the LAN." Another caution over the monitors read, "Do not send pix of dead or detained enemy—violation of Geneva Conventions. You can be charged."

But the threat of software transgressions was nothing compared to the hardware Ramadi stored in abundance. A marine major told me, "The enemy has an endless supply of munitions. The whole country is an ammo dump." Somehow, the early planning for the invasion didn't foresee securing Saddam's arsenal. Ammo dumps were looted and the weapons were passed out among the insurgents. The insurgents knew very well how to use them. Early in the occupation, the US Coalition Provisional Authority in Baghdad disbanded the Iraqi military, leaving tens of thousands of military men with nothing to do.

On Ramadi's Route Michigan, roadside bombs were often composed of 155mm artillery shells remotely detonated by the signal of a cell phone or the key fob of a car. One crossroads on Michigan concealed Improvised Explosive Devices so often the marines called the intersection "The Axis of Evil" after George W. Bush's memorable phrase from his 2002 State of the Union address. Against these threats, 2nd Battalion was forced to send marines into Ramadi in a mix of armored and unarmored Humvees. The US wasn't prepared for the advent of the IED. After it became the most devastating weapon in the enemy arsenal, it would take a year to deliver do-it-yourself armor kits to retrofit Humvees and give our troops a fighting chance. The military calls unarmored vehicles "soft skinned." But for 2/5 marines it was worse than that. Their Humvee version of a pickup truck had no skin at all. The truck was called a "10-man" because two marines rode in the cab and eight sat on benches in the *wide-open bed*. You could argue this arrangement was hazardous back at Camp Pendleton, California, but in Ramadi, I could not believe this was the best the Pentagon could do for men headed into battle. Still, I heard no complaints. Marines are trained to make do. They have a certain vanity about it. "Adapt, improvise, overcome" is an unofficial motto. To improvise and overcome the liabilities of the 10-man, the marines of Hurricane Point scavenged scrap metal and welded quarter-inch steel onto the back of the trucks. They were "Franken-trucks" with welded junk rising about four feet high around the bed. This improvisation couldn't withstand a 155mm shell, but there was a chance it might slow a 7.62mm rifle round from Ramadi's ubiquitous AK-47s. I traveled to the capitol building in the back of a 10-man and had to be reminded more than once to keep my head below the edge of the improvised armor. Mentally, I renamed the rickety jalopy a Tin Man.

On this second tour, the marines of 2/5 were neither fresh nor victorious. The men were quick to follow orders and passionate about watching each other's backs, but cynical about whether the road to the capitol building would lead to something that looked like success. A young lance corporal, who had not yet grown into his wisdom, told me, "We tried winning their hearts and minds. Now it's time to tear them out."

The capitol building, a four-story hulk the color of the desert, cowered behind sandbag ramparts. American gun emplacements on the roof were makeshift redoubts shielded behind bullet-resistant windows salvaged from blasted Humvees. Lieutenant Colonel Newman and I climbed up to the roof. "Off in the distance, you see that tall building with the charred-out window?" Newman asked.

"Got it," I said.

"That's where a sniper worked on us about a month ago."

"It makes you wonder who owns Ramadi," I said.

"It's difficult, when you're fighting an insurgency, to say who owns anything on any given day. I think that's why the requirement to win this type of fight requires patience, presence and persistence," Newman said.

"You're going on your third governor," I noted.

"Yes, that's correct. Third governor in about fourteen months or so."

"First governor quit. Why?"

"Governor Bargas quit because they kidnapped his family and threatened to kill them."

"And the mayor of Ramadi, they blew up his office last week," I said.

"Mayor Awad's office was attacked, yes, with an IED that destroyed the building."

I asked Newman about another recent murder. "Do you think they killed the doctor because the doctor accepted medical supplies from you?"

"Absolutely. That's absolutely what they did."

"I understand that even the Iraqi man who collected the trash on your base was murdered."

"That's correct. *Anyone.* They will target anyone with fear and intimidation."

"Hard to run the city and Anbar Province with kidnappings, murders and the bombing of offices," I said.

"Sure. The fear and intimidation campaign is difficult for the Iraqis to accept and for us to work against. We're making headway, slow but sure," Newman told me.

One of the marines Newman depended on to make headway was a barrel-chested thirty-four-year-old named Patrick Rapicault. Captain Rapicault led the 180 men of 2/5's Whiskey Company. He was built like an inside linebacker. His face was drafted in handsome right angles. What remained after a Marine Corps haircut was black as tar and repeated in heavy eyebrows. In a US military composed entirely of volunteers, Rapicault was possibly unique. Born on the French Caribbean island of Martinique, Rapicault was raised in France and came to Mississippi as an exchange student. He joined the Marine Reserves in college. If there was anything Rapicault wanted in life other than to be a United States marine, he kept it to himself. Only US citizens can be commissioned officers, so he took the oath of a naturalized American at age twenty-five. He went to Officer Candidates School in Quantico, Virginia, and graduated first in his class from the US Army Ranger School. Despite all his training, the Marine Corps had been defeated in its assault on Rapicault's accent. Marines called him "Frenchy," which he didn't mind. Those new to Whiskey Company had to learn the cadence of a Mississippi Frenchman who pronounced "y'all" in the manner of the Cote d'Azur.

Rapicault approached the streets of Ramadi the way Edmund Hillary closed on Everest's summit: one step at a time, always forward, never flinching. By the time *60 Minutes* began riding with Rapicault in "Whiskey Six," his armored Humvee, he had survived more than two dozen IEDs but six of his marines had been killed. Most recently Sergeant Doug Bascom had died in the blast of an IED. At Bascom's battlefield memorial, Rapicault kneeled, cap in hand, and asked for God's mercy.

The election in Ramadi was a few weeks away. The insurgents were so pervasive the Iraqi government kept the location of polling places secret, to be revealed only on Election Day. "We're constantly under observation from those guys," Captain Rapicault told us. "They know where we go. They know where we like to set up and of course, like anything else, the key is to avoid any kind of repetition. Change your route, change the buildings you use. Otherwise, they come at you to booby-trap those buildings and try to blow them up."

Pat Rapicault's job had recently become much more dangerous. Five months before, US forces laid siege to another important Sunni city, Fallujah—just 30 miles from Ramadi. American wrath destroyed the city after insurgents there murdered several American contractors and hung their charred bodies from a bridge. The three-week Battle of Fallujah took the lives of twenty-seven Americans and more than six hundred Iraqis. After

losing Fallujah, Iraqi Sunnis intensified their resistance throughout Anbar Province.

Rapicault was attempting to apply one of the lessons of the
Battle of Fallujah. On a foot patrol, Rapicault took a knee
and inclined his head just beyond the corner of a building. He
searched his rifle scope for threats downrange. *60 Minutes* associate producer Kirk Spitzer rolled a camera and asked about the
mission. As Rapicault answered, he never looked away from his
scope. "I think the biggest difference between here and Fallujah
is, we could very well go ahead and do the same thing, bomb
every building we get contact [enemy fire] from. But then again,
that's not the purpose we are here for. We are trying to have this
country *rebuilt*. This is the capital of the province."

With 2/5 marines, it struck me how little had changed for
the infantry at war. True, the marine has night vision goggles
and his Humvee has a computer screen, but the hard work of
battle—clearing streets and holding them—was the same as ever.
In my notebook, I reduced Ramadi to its elements: "Truck, gun,
man—a very young man."

What *has* changed for Americans at war is not so much on
the battlefield as the home front. The Pew Research Center
found that less than one half of 1 percent of American families had someone in the military.[1] And only 1 percent of adults
were on active duty. Iraq and Afghanistan became our nation's
longest wars with the smallest participation of American families. I believe those two facts are related. Would 2/5 marines
have been under fire in Ramadi in *pickup trucks* if the marines
had been called to duty from among the 99.5 percent? Would
the public stand for men and women deployed to combat tours
three, four, five and six times? Would the wars in Iraq and Afghanistan have become the longest in our history if our troops
had been randomly drafted? Would Iraq have happened at all?

The draft was created in the Civil War. Young men were conscripted again in World War I, World War II, Korea and Vietnam. Today, America does not need a draft to fill the ranks of the armed forces. But without one, there remains a civic obligation for the 99.5 percent to commit to much more than "Thank you for your service." In my view, there is an obligation to understand the volunteer military class and understand what it is asked to do. We can repay their valor in battle with valor on the home front. This requires real effort to give our professional troops the same attention, care and scrutiny of policy as if they had left *our own* kitchen to go to war. It is noble to donate to wounded warrior charities, but it is patriotic to analyze and question the plans for war before our sons and daughters are sent to fight in the first place.

In Northern Virginia, Robert E. Lee's mansion looks down from the summit of 624 acres. In every direction, white monoliths recede to the horizon. By regulation, these stones are 42 inches tall, 13 inches wide, 4 inches thick and shaped from 230 pounds of marble or granite.[2] They are known as the "general" headstone of Arlington National Cemetery.[3] After 2001, these stones came to attention in ranks and files in a once undisturbed field now known as Section 60. Resting here are men and women whose lives were left in Iraq and Afghanistan. Section 60 lies on the southeast corner of Lee's front yard, reaching for the Potomac River. It is one of the sections nearest the Pentagon. On site 8077 a Christian cross is carved into the apex of the stone. Below, lettered in black, the visitor reads:

Patrick

Marc

Rapicault

US Marine Corps

Mar 27 1970

Nov 15 2004

Silver Star
Purple Heart
Operation
Iraqi Freedom

Pat Rapicault shunned repetition in Whiskey Company's ma-
neuvers. But in Ramadi, he was boxed in by the one route that
offered no detour. Route Michigan was the entrance to the front
gate of Hurricane Point. Insurgents could never tell when a patrol was leaving, but once the marines were "outside the wire,"
the enemy knew the Americans would be coming back. At the
gate's tower, young marines stood behind an M240 machine
gun and watched through binoculars to ensure no IEDs were
placed on the approach. But, as Lieutenant Colonel Newman
told me, the enemy was "adaptive." On November 15, 2004,
Rapicault's Whiskey Six was leading two other Humvees back to
the gate when an insurgent sped into the convoy and detonated
an enormous car bomb. Despite its armor, Whiskey Six was demolished. Rapicault and two of his marines were killed. The
Silver Star for valor was awarded posthumously. The Silver Star
citation noted Rapicault had survived fifty firefights, twenty-
seven IEDs and "gallantly gave his life in the cause of freedom."
Years beyond his death, Pat Rapicault was still teaching young
marines. The Marine Corps Officer Candidates School which
Rapicault attended has used our *60 Minutes* story about its graduate and Hurricane Point to acquaint the next generation with
the valor demanded by war.

On the day he was laid to rest in Section 60, after the chords
of the navy hymn "Eternal Father Strong to Save" began to
fade, those who knew Rapicault spoke of his "fearlessness." It
was meant, of course, as the highest compliment. But "fearlessness" inadvertently sells valor short. Valor isn't the absence of
fear. Valor is the acknowledgment of fear overcome by the will

to go on. As Edmund Hillary said, "It is not the mountain we conquer, but ourselves."[4]

In October 2004, with only three weeks left to live, Rapicault closed his eyes and kneeled in prayer. The twin silver bars of his captain's insignia flashed the glare of the sun as he reached out to lay his left hand on Sergeant Doug Bascom's combat boots. The tan leather boots formed the base of a battlefield memorial which was also composed of Bascom's rifle, helmet and dog tags. Rapicault spoke of Bascom's dedication to his marines and his leadership by example. But I suspect these were traits of valor Sergeant Bascom had admired in Rapicault himself. Rapicault led Whiskey Company from the front. He understood, if he exposed himself to fire and did not waver, his marines would follow. After Bascom's dog tags were raised in the sunrise ritual at Hurricane Point, Pat Rapicault inspired his marines to follow him on another patrol in Ramadi.

FIELD NOTE

The Madman of Obock

He was an architect. And even in madness, or perhaps because of it, he thought of morality as a sheet on a drafting table to be framed, limited or expanded with a T-square and pencil. His English was beautiful. Not merely accurate or comprehensive, but truly beautiful, slightly British, with a cadence that arranged the facts of his life into a tragic melody.

He'd been born in 1952 to a well-off family of professionals in Aden, the port city on the southern end of Yemen where the Arabian Peninsula almost touches Africa. At the time of his birth, Aden was the capital of the British colony. This accounted for his English. His name was Ali and in addition to his gift for language, Ali was handsome. Elder Omar Sharif handsome. At sixty-five years of age, his hair was thick and waved in white and black. His cheeks, nose and chin were angular, chiseled—an architect's romantic version of an architect's facade. He expressed more with his eyes than his words. That's where I first noticed Ali's psychosis. It seemed as though he had trained his body for composure and all his anxiety was forced through his eyes like nozzles compressing water. "How long have you been in this refugee camp?" I asked. "Twenty-six months," he said. His eyes widened as if to say, "Can you understand what that means?"

The desolate desert camp was animated by Yemeni families who had fled the Yemen Civil War. They had sailed across the Red Sea to Djibouti, the impoverished nation just above East Africa's horn and only twenty-five miles across the water. The camp was near the village of Obock on the northern shore of the Gulf of Tadjoura. The waters of the gulf were spectacular, dense with life. But the shore died millennia ago. Hard-packed desert was rubbled with rock. The miracle of photosynthesis seemed unknown. The temperature on this day was 110 degrees Fahrenheit. A member of the refugee camp staff told me, in all seriousness, it was a good thing I came in September because in the summertime, "It's hot." The United Nations refugee organization, the UNHCR, hammered tent stakes along imaginary straight-lined streets and avenues for seven thousand refugees. But few stayed in the tents. Unbearable heat and humidity were no more bearable when confined by canvas.

"They are *crazy* people!" said Ali, who was in a position to know. One side or another in Yemen's latest war had fired a missile into Ali's apartment in 2015. He lost everything he owned. Yemenis have been at each other's throats for hundreds of years. Shiite tribes in the north are in constant competition with Sunni Muslims who occupy the coasts. The American ambassador to Yemen explained the context to me this way, "The world shakes its head at the endless violence in the Middle East. But in the Middle East, they shake their heads at the perpetual bloodshed in Yemen."

I met Ali in the refugee camp while covering the famine and cholera epidemic that erupted in Yemen in 2017. Two years before, Ali decided to leave his homeland "forever." He managed to get onboard a small boat which took him to a tanker ship that would carry him and three hundred other refugees to Djibouti. The night of his escape, Ali's skiff pulled next to the towering tanker. The tanker crew lowered a basket to raise him more than forty feet onto the deck. During that hoist, rising vertically above the sea, the basket lifted Ali to an epiphany. "The crazy people do not have the *height* dimension!" he explained. "They have only *two* dimensions!" Ali presented his right palm, flat as a drafting table. "The crazy people have only length and width," he said. He drew the two dimensions in imaginary lines on his outstretched palm. Then, with his left hand, the one holding a phantom pencil, he drew a vertical line up from his palm, stopping at the level of his eyes. "You must have the *vertical* dimension to be truly human," he said. The imaginary vertical line stood balanced on his palm. Ali's eyes crossed slightly as he focused on the point of his invisible pencil. The line rose, like a cable lifting a basket, into a third dimension beyond humanity's binary divisions: beyond the choice of Sunni or Shiite, Muslim or Christian, political left or right.

Ali was mad. Maybe the war pushed him into insanity. Maybe it was the torturing heat. But within insanity, there can be a kind of clarity unavailable to those who consider themselves sane. In his escape from Yemen, swaying in a basket in the night, Ali saw something—something that looked to the rising draftsman like compassion, forgiveness and empathy—a third dimension, the dimension of peace.

CHAPTER EIGHTEEN

Arrogance
A Cautionary Tale

In the early weeks after 9/11, my colleague Mike Wallace led *60 Minutes* with a story that had me steamed. Mike's piece asked whether the United States would resort to torture in its war on al-Qaida. I was angry because I thought the idea was absurd, so off base that it tarnished the credibility of *60 Minutes* itself. I told Mike precisely what I felt that night, scolding his image on my TV. This prompted my young daughter to ask, "Daddy? Can the people on TV hear you?" No, sweetheart. And I'm awfully glad because, as often, I was dead wrong.

I spent the next several years investigating extrajudicial abductions and killings committed in the war on terror. Some of the victims were hard to shed a tear for; others were tragically innocent. The attack on America led some in the Bush administration to arrogance—a sense of entitlement. In their minds, the enemy's depravity justified payback in kind. Would al-Qaida's horrific act of war force America to abandon its values? The enemy certainly hoped so.

You wouldn't figure Willie Brand as the kind of man who would torture someone to death. Brand was from Cincinnati, in his early twenties, with a round face, soft eyes and a voice that barely stirred the air. He was a US Army specialist who volunteered to be a prison guard at America's sprawling air base at Bagram, Afghanistan. The Russians built Bagram when they occupied Afghanistan in the 1980s. Its runways, hangars and office buildings seemed to have waited patiently for America to take its turn. One of the conveniences of Bagram was a prison that the army used to hold and interrogate suspects. *60 Minutes* producer Shawn Efran, a superb investigator, had been looking into reports of abuse at Bagram. In 2006, Shawn and I were interviewing Willie Brand who was being court-martialed on charges of maiming, assault and involuntary manslaughter.

In the fall of 2002, a Bagram prisoner Brand was guarding was found beaten to death. His body was hanging by its wrists, which were shackled to the ceiling of his cell. Brand, who was nearly as low on the chain of command as a soldier can get, pointed up that chain. "I didn't understand how they [the army] could do this [court-martial] after they had trained you to do this stuff and they turn around and say you've been bad. Now they're going to charge you with maiming and unvoluntary [sic] manslaughter? How can this be when they trained you to do it and they condoned it while you were doing it?"

"The army says you're a violent man," I told Brand.

"They do say that," Brand acknowledged. "But I'm not a violent person."

The violence done to the prisoner was sadistic. He was a cab driver named Dilawar, who, like many Afghans, used only one name. Dilawar was picked up after a rocket was fired at an American base. A later investigation would find that he was just a cab driver who was passing by at the worst possible moment. The US military pathologist who conducted the autopsy on Dilawar's body said his legs had been, in her memorable word, "pulpified." It was concluded that if Dilawar had been found alive in his cell, doctors would have been forced to amputate his legs to save his life. On Dilawar's US military death certificate, under the heading Mode of Death, the pathologist checked the box next to "Homicide." But "homicide" was not what the American people were told. When the military public relations office at Bagram announced Dilawar's death, it explained the cause was a heart attack owing to Dilawar's coronary disease at the age of twenty-two. Someone, somewhere along the chain of command, had decided to cover up the murder. That might have been the end of it had it not been for a feat of classic shoe-leather reporting. Carlotta Gall, an intrepid correspondent for the *New York Times*, traveled through dangerous territory to visit Dilawar's family, including his wife and two-year-old daughter. The family didn't know much, but Dilawar's brother showed Gall a piece of paper the US government included when it returned his body. Because the document was in English, the brother didn't know what to make of it. Gall could see it was Dilawar's military death certificate with the X next to *Homicide*. Four years after Gall's reporting, army prosecutors recommended criminal charges against twenty-eight soldiers assigned to the Bagram jail.

The US Army's troubles with torture were first exposed in 2004 by correspondent Dan Rather on *60 Minutes II*. The report revealed stomach-turning images of torture inflicted by American soldiers in Iraq's Abu Ghraib prison. Among the outraged viewers was Secretary of State Colin Powell, who had spent his life in service to the army. Powell asked his chief of staff, retired army colonel Lawrence Wilkerson, to investigate how the army that liberated Nazi concentration camps could now be involved in torture. "I could smell that I was looking at a cover-up," Wilkerson told me. "That alarmed me as much as the abuse itself because it looked like authorization for this abuse went to the very top of the United States government."

In 2002, the very top of the United States government was divided over whether the Geneva Conventions applied to prisoners in Afghanistan. A presidential directive was written to nullify the international law that requires humane treatment of prisoners of war. The Bush directive says, "armed forces shall continue to treat detainees humanely." But it went on to say Geneva would apply only "to the extent appropriate and consistent with military necessity." Wilkerson told me, "That essentially says to the troops at the bottom rung that you have a new game. You can use methods that aren't in accordance with Geneva. You can use methods other than what you've been taught and told you could use. That is an invitation, a license, to go beyond—especially when you're also putting them under tremendous pressure to produce intelligence."

The head of the army lockup at Bagram told me the rules for prisoners were never understood. "Who are these people?" Captain Christopher Beiring asked in our interview. "Did they sign the Geneva Conventions? Who are they and what do we do with them?" Beiring was among the soldiers, along with Specialist Willie Brand, charged in the death of the Afghan cab driver Dilawar.

Among the methods not "in accordance with Geneva" was a technique for controlling prisoners called the Common Peroneal Strike. A guard would knee the prisoner in the thigh with so much force that the common peroneal nerve would be momentarily disabled causing the prisoner to buckle. It was supposed to be used rarely and in self-defense. But at Bagram, the Common Peroneal Strike became...common. An internal army investigation from October 2004 found some guards earned grotesque nicknames. "You've read the army investigation," I said to Captain Beiring. "Some of the witnesses say one of the soldiers was nicknamed the 'King of Torture,' another one possessed, quote, the 'Knee of Death.' You were there. Were you not seeing this?"

"No, I was not," Beiring replied. "Some nicknames, as a commander you are fairly removed from the junior soldiers, so nicknames could have occurred that I did not know about."

"It's not the nicknames," I said. "It's how they *got* the nicknames."

"I can't say for sure. I can only say I never witnessed any of my soldiers do anything that was out of line," Beiring said. Prosecutors said the Common Peroneal Strike was how Dilawar's legs became "pulpified," and how he and another prisoner at Bagram died within a week of each other. Of the twenty-eight soldiers against whom army prosecutors recommended action, fifteen were charged. Most charges were eventually dropped. Five soldiers pled guilty. The toughest sentence was five months in prison. Only Willie Brand was convicted at trial. After our interview, the military jury found Brand guilty of assault and maiming. But the jury decided to have it both ways. They convicted him and let him go. His rank was reduced from specialist to private. That was all. Brand received an honorable discharge and returned to his family. Lawrence Wilkerson, Colin Powell's chief of staff, spent thirty-one years in the army and drew his own conclusions: "It went wrong because we had a secretary of defense [Donald Rumsfeld] who had never served on the ground a day in his life, who was arrogant and thought that he could release those twin pressures on the backs of his armed forces. The twin pressures being a wink and a nod: you can do a lot of things that you know don't correspond to Geneva, don't correspond to your code of conduct, don't correspond to the army field manual—and, at the same time, 'I want intelligence, I want intelligence, I want it now.'"

The pressure for intelligence, and the trouble with torture, extended beyond the armed forces. Prisoners held by the CIA were dying too. But their homicides were concealed under the heading TOP SECRET.

Two months before Dilawar's death, a prisoner in Afghanistan was found dead in a secret CIA cell. Unlike Dilawar, Gul Rahman was not an innocent bystander. He was a senior member of a militant group with a relationship to al-Qaida. The CIA abducted him in Pakistan and brought him to the "Salt Pit," a secret CIA prison outside Kabul. The CIA hoped to get actionable intelligence from Rahman, perhaps prevent another attack on America. The Salt Pit was a so-called "black site," an off-the-books prison, fashioned from an abandoned brick factory. No one was supposed to know it existed, let alone anything about what went on inside. But our *60 Minutes* investigations of the CIA program turned up witnesses. And I found revealing details in CIA memos that were declassified in 2016. One of them, dated January 28, 2003, is marked "TOP SECRET" across the top and bottom of each page. After "Subject," it reads, "Death Investigation—Gul RAHMAN." The CIA investigator began his report with a description of the standard procedures for Salt Pit prisoners. "Blindfolds are placed over their eyes and a hood is placed over their heads," the investigator writes. "Earplugs are also placed in their ears. Prisoners are dressed in sweat suits and adult diapers. The diapers are used…as a means to humiliate the prisoner. When sleep deprivation is utilized, the prisoner is chained by one or both wrists to a bar running across the ceiling of the cell." The report adds, "No prisoner should undergo more than 72 hours of sleep deprivation."

Rahman was so combative, according to the investigation, that he was restrained in the "short-chain" method. "In the

'short-chain' method," the report reads, "the prisoner's hands
are shackled together, as are his feet. Then a short chain is used
to shackle the hands…within several inches of his feet. The
prisoner's feet are then shackled to the wall." Rahman's interrogators were frustrated. The report notes, "Despite 48 hours
of sleep deprivation, auditory overload, total darkness, isolation,
a cold shower and rough treatment, RAHMAN maintained a
high interrogation resistance…"

If Rahman had any secrets, he would keep them. On the
night of November 20, 2002, the temperature around Kabul fell
to twenty-six degrees. The CIA prison had no insulation and
no central heat. The investigator's report reads, "RAHMAN
was shackled in a sitting position on bare concrete while nude
from the waist down. The manner in which he was shackled
prevented him from standing upright." A guard, who checked
Rahman early in the morning, told the CIA investigator, "At
0400 (4:00 a.m.) RAHMAN was sitting in his cell, alive and
shaking." The guard said he wasn't concerned because "the
prisoners were always shaking." Over the next six hours Rahman froze to death. The CIA report explains that "chained in a
short-chain position prevented him from standing up and moving around to warm up his body." Finding that Rahman died
of hypothermia, the CIA investigation reached this conclusion:
"There is no evidence that suggests RAHMAN was tortured."

George Tenet was wary of the powers his CIA had been
granted in the heat of passion, six days after 9/11. He *wanted*
the authorities, but he didn't trust them. As director of Central
Intelligence, Tenet had mastered America's secrets, especially
the dark art of surviving the mercurial values of Washington.
He was going to make damn sure none of his people would be
prosecuted for acts of torture after passions inevitably cooled.

Only John Foster Dulles, the original head of the CIA, had
been director longer than Tenet. Tenet was the son of Greek im-

migrants, raised in the Flushing section of Queens, New York. Like many young men and women, he came to Washington by way of an entry-level job with a member of Congress. Tenet found his way to the staff of the Senate Select Committee on Intelligence. By the mid-1990s he was staff director. President Clinton appointed Tenet to lead intelligence analysis for the National Security Council. Then, Mr. Clinton sent Tenet to CIA headquarters in Langley, Virginia, as deputy director of central intelligence. In 1997, Tenet was elevated to director. When George W. Bush was elected in 2000, he kept Tenet on. This was extremely rare for a White House in metamorphosis from one party to another, but Tenet was Mr. Bush's kind of guy, a character—pugnacious, confident to a fault, a serial mauler of cold cigars. Tenet's qualities of leadership were not learned, they were coded in his DNA. He was passionate in defense of the people who did America's intelligence work. But he was hell on those under his command who screwed up. To some within the agency, being chewed like a stogie by the boss was known as receiving "The Full Tenet."

The morning of 9/11, Tenet and hundreds of CIA personnel were forced to evacuate their headquarters. Tenet seethed. He didn't need an analyst to tell him who did this. As we've seen earlier in this book, he struggled to convince two administrations of the imminent threat posed by Osama bin Laden. Tenet chafed when the Clinton administration shelved his audacious plan to use CIA paramilitary forces to attack al-Qaida in Afghanistan. Washington, in his view, had been too timid, too bureaucratically hamstrung. Now, Tenet wanted new powers, what government lawyers called "authorities." On 9/11, long before he was allowed back to the seventh floor of his headquarters, George Tenet had taken the gloves off.

Six days after 9/11, President Bush signed a secret Memorandum of Notification (MON) informing Tenet that his CIA was now authorized to apprehend terror suspects anywhere in the world and interrogate them, indefinitely, in off-the-books prisons. The memo was a triumph of arrogance over values. The administration empowered itself to violate any border, friend or foe, and ignore the rule of law. A top secret report described the Memorandum of Notification as "one of the most sensitive activities ever undertaken by the CIA..." The president's notification specified that suspects to be abducted "must pose a continuing, serious threat of violence or death to US persons and interests" or "must be planning terrorist activities."[1] No independent judge was making that determination. No suspect was allowed to ask a court to examine the facts and legality of his detention. Since "abduction" carried an unfortunate connotation, this procedure was named "rendition." People who might have information about terrorism were snatched off streets, shackled to the floor of a CIA plane and "rendered" to black site prisons. The Salt Pit in Afghanistan was one such prison. Another was set up in Poland, another in Thailand. It's likely there were others.

By 2002, Tenet established the Renditions and Detainees Group to run the program. Tenet had the written permission of the president, but that wasn't enough for him. Some of the interrogation methods envisioned were clearly criminal under the federal statute that banned torture. A draft memorandum to Attorney General John Ashcroft from the associate legal counsel of the CIA's Counterterrorism Center admitted as much. The draft memo was written early in the program when interrogators wanted to waterboard Abu Zubaydah, an al-Qaida operative captured in Pakistan. The draft memo, labeled "Eyes Only" was declassified in 2016. I noticed most of it is redacted, but under "Dear Mr. Attorney General," the memo reads in part, "the use of more aggressive methods is required to persuade Abu Zubaydah to provide the critical information we need to safeguard the lives of innumerable innocent men, women and children... These methods include certain activities that normally would appear to be prohibited under the provisions of

18 U.S.C. 2340-2340B." America's torture prohibition, passed in 1994, covered a wide range of abuse and it provided a legal definition of the word *torture*. "Torture," it said, "means an act committed by a person acting under the color of law specifically intended to inflict severe physical or mental pain or suffering…" The law goes on to define "severe mental pain or suffering" as "the prolonged mental harm caused by or resulting from the intentional infliction or threatened infliction of severe physical pain or suffering…or the threat of imminent death."[2] The CIA memorandum to the attorney general proposed this solution: "I respectfully request that you grant a formal declination of prosecution, in advance, for any employees of the United States, as well as any other personnel acting on behalf of the United States, who may employ methods in the interrogation of Abu Zubaydah that otherwise might subject those individuals to prosecution…"[3] In other words, the CIA acknowledged what it proposed was criminal, so it wanted the Justice Department to guarantee that prosecutors would look the other way. The reply came July 26, 2002, in a top secret message from the CIA's Office of General Counsel: "This afternoon I received a telephone call from Deputy Assistant Attorney General John Yoo… Yoo advised me that Attorney General John Ashcroft approved the use of the waterboard in the interrogation of Abu Zubaydah."[4]

That same month, the CIA presented the Justice Department with a list of interrogation techniques it wanted clearance to use. Justice Department lawyers authorized a list of "Enhanced Interrogation Techniques" that they would not prosecute. They included:

"Cramped Confinement"—folding the prisoner into a small box.

"Stress Positions"—difficult postures such as sitting on the floor with legs outstretched without supporting the back.

"Sleep Deprivation beyond 72 hours." (A CIA report help-fully noted that the Guinness Book of World Records sleep deprivation champion logged 205 hours with no significant psychological problems.[5])

"The Use of Diapers."

"Insects Placed in Confinement Box."

"Mock Burial" in which the prisoner is sealed in a cof-fin, lowered into the ground and made to think he's being buried alive.[6]

"Waterboarding."[7]

Waterboarding is described this way: "Individuals are bound securely to an inclined bench. Initially, a cloth is placed over the subject's forehead and eyes. As water is applied in a con-trolled manner, the cloth is slowly lowered until it also covers the mouth and nose. Once the cloth is saturated and completely covering the mouth and nose, the subject would be exposed to 20 to 40 seconds of restricted airflow. Water is applied to keep the cloth saturated. After the 20 to 40 seconds of restricted air-flow, the cloth is removed and the subject is allowed to breathe unimpeded. After 3 or 4 full breaths, the procedure may be re-peated."[8] The space in each prison where these Enhanced In-terrogation Techniques were to be applied was known as the "Conditioning Room."

Some within the CIA refused to abandon the values embod-ied in the Constitution that they had sworn to uphold. In Janu-ary 2003, a member of the Counterterrorism Center Rendition Group sent an internal email. The names of the writer and the recipient were redacted when the email was declassified in 2016. It reads, "This morning I informed the front office of CTC

[Counterterrorism Center] that I will no longer be associated in any way with the interrogation program due to serious reservation [sic] I have about the current state of affairs. Instead, I will be retiring shortly. This is a train wreak [sic] waiting to happen and I intend to get the hell off the train before it happens."[9]

That CIA officer wasn't the only one with concerns. Another CIA memo notes the aversion of President Bush. Again, the names of sender, recipient and most of the memo for that matter are redacted. The lone surviving paragraph reads, "The DCI [Director of Central Intelligence] conveyed that the President was concerned about the image of a detainee, chained to the ceiling, clothed in a diaper, and forced to go to the bathroom on themselves."[10] The president's concern was ignored and, as I would discover, so were his orders in the Memorandum of Notification.

Khalid al-Masri, a German citizen and car salesman, found himself bound, blindfolded and deafened by earmuffs. The diaper he was wearing suggested to him that the silent men who hustled him onto an unmarked Boeing 737 were not going to entertain a request to go to the lavatory. In January 2003, al-Masri was on a trip to Macedonia. He told his wife and children he would be home soon. When police in Macedonia stopped the bus he was riding in, al-Masri didn't imagine it had anything to do with him. But al-Masri told me the police examined his German passport, pulled him from the bus and delivered him to the masked men. I met al-Masri in 2005 in a hotel in Germany. The events that he claimed had happened more than a year before seemed vivid in his memory. "They took me to this room and they hit me all over and they slashed my clothes with sharp objects," al-Masri told me. The mystery men removed his clothes, "maybe with knives or scissors." Al-Masri continued, "I also heard photos being taken while this was going on. They took off the blindfold and I saw that there were a lot of men standing in the room. They were wearing black masks and black gloves." After he was loaded on the plane, al-Masri's journey consumed hours that he had no way to measure. By the time the blindfold was removed again, he found himself on the floor of a cell in a crude prison without insulation or heat. There was a little bedding and a bucket for his waste. The prisoner in the next cell welcomed him to Afghanistan. If al-Masri was telling me the truth, he would be the first person to describe a CIA abduction in the Rendition and Detention Program. Al-Masri had been discovered by *60 Minutes* producer Graham Messick, who breaks many of the program's stories involving the netherworld of intelligence. Our problem was finding a way to corroborate or refute al-Masri's remarkable and, at the time, hard to believe story.

Messick found that a witness to an earlier rendition in Pakistan had the presence of mind to take down the tail number of the otherwise unmarked Gulfstream jet that carried that suspect to oblivion. The number started with *N* which is the international designation reserved for aircraft registered in the US. Messick looked up the tail number in public records and found the plane was owned by Premier Executive Transport Services in Dedham, Massachusetts. But Dedham was a dead end. The address led to the second floor of a bank building. There were no offices for Premier Executive Transport Services.

The only remaining clue was a note in the FAA records that showed Premier Executive owned another plane. This one was a Boeing 737 and the tail number was listed. Because pilots file flight plans and because those plans are public records, it didn't take long for Messick to find that the 737's itineraries read like a tour of the Global War on Terror. It appeared the aircraft was based in North Carolina. Usually, its first stop was Dulles International Airport, not far from CIA headquarters in Virginia. In the records, we found thirty trips to Jordan, nineteen to Afghanistan, seventeen to Morocco, sixteen to Iraq. Other stops included Egypt, Libya and Guantanamo Bay, Cuba. But, of all these flights, the one that caught our eye occurred on the same date Khalid al-Masri claimed he was abducted. The flight began in Skopje, Macedonia, continued to Baghdad and carried on to Kabul, Afghanistan, near the Salt Pit. "When I opened my eyes in the cell," al-Masri told me, "the guards were Afghani. So, it was clear that it was Afghanistan."

Al-Masri had a round, boyish face that made him look younger than his forty-two years. He had fully recovered the fifty pounds he said he lost in prison. I asked him to draw a floor plan of the Salt Pit, which he did without hesitation. He said other prisoners he met there were from Pakistan, Tanzania, Yemen and Saudi Arabia. Al-Masri was raised in Lebanon. His English was only serviceable. He told me his American interrogator spoke to him in Arabic through an interpreter. "He yelled at me and he said, 'You're in a country without laws and no one knows where you are. Do you know what that means?' I said, 'Yes.'"

"What *did* that mean to you?" I asked.

"It was very clear to me that he meant I could stay in my cell for twenty years or be buried somewhere and nobody knows what happened to me."

What to do with Khalid al-Masri was a pressing problem in George Tenet's office at CIA headquarters. The agency had come to realize al-Masri was just a car salesman from Germany. The rendition team picked up the wrong Khalid al-Masri. But the Salt Pit continued to hold him because the CIA couldn't let it be known that it had kidnapped an innocent German citizen. The agency especially did not want the German government to know. The Salt Pit sent a top secret cable (they still call them cables) to headquarters asking for guidance, "because of [al-Masri's] awareness of US Government involvement in his detention." The message ends with, "Appreciate in advance Headquarters immediate attention to this important issue."[11]

Unfortunately for al-Masri, "immediate attention" was not what the CIA had in mind.

★ ★ ★

In 2006, George Tenet and I sat down for eight hours of conversations, over two days, in the opulent library at Georgetown University in Washington. Tenet had accepted a professorship there after his retirement from the agency.

Tenet had kept his mouth shut through 9/11, Iraq and the Global War on Terror. The pressure to come out swinging against his critics had been building a very long time. When I brought up torture, Tenet's voice rose in the direction of a shout. He told me, "The image that's been portrayed is, we sat around the campfire and said, 'Oh, boy! Now we get to go torture people!'" Tenet slapped his hands together and massaged his palms in mock delight. "Well, we *don't torture people.* Let me say that again to you. *We don't torture people!* Okay?" His claim brought me to Khalid Sheikh Mohammed, the depraved mind that conceived of the 9/11 airliner attacks. Mohammed received 183 applications of water in a total of fifteen waterboarding sessions.[12]

"Come on, George," I countered.

"We *don't* torture people!" he insisted.

"Khalid Sheikh Mohammed?"

"We don't torture people."

"Waterboarding?" I asked.

"I don't talk about techniques."

"It's torture," I said.

"We don't torture people. Now, listen to me. *Listen to me!*" Tenet rocked forward, raised his index finger and jabbed at his face, "I want you to listen to *me.* The context is, it's post-9/11. I've got reports of nuclear weapons in New York City, apartment buildings that are gonna be blown up, plot lines that I don't know. I don't know what's going on inside the United States. And I'm struggling to find out where the next disaster is going to occur. Everybody forgets one central context of what we lived through—the palpable fear that we felt on the basis of the fact that there was *so much we did not know.* I know that this program [Rendition and Detention] has saved lives. I know we've disrupted plots."

I followed up, "But what you're essentially saying is, some people need to be tortured."

"No! I did *not* say that. I *did not* say that!"

"You call it, 'Enhanced Interrogation,'" I said.

"Well, that's what we call it."

"And that's a euphemism," I told Tenet.

"I'm not having a semantic debate with you. I'm telling you what I believe."

"Have you ever seen any of these interrogations done?"

"No."

"Didn't you feel like it was your responsibility to know what you're signing off on?"

"I understood. I'm not a voyeur. I understand what I was signing off on."

"Lose any sleep over it?"

"Of course you do!" Now Tenet was shouting. "Of course you lose sleep over it! You're on dub...new territory." Tenet edited himself, midsentence. Was he about to say "dubious" territory? He leaned into my face, voice rising, releasing the pressure of the years. "But that's not the point!" he said. "What's this tension? The tension is, I've just lived through three thousand people dying. This is not a clinical exercise. Maybe for *you guys* [the media], it's a clinical exercise. Not for *me*! Three thousand people died. *Friends* died! And then everybody says, 'You *idiots* [the CIA] don't know how to connect the dots. You *don't* have imagination! You were *unwilling* to take risks to protect this country!'"

"Let me ask the question this way," I said. "Why were Enhanced Interrogation Techniques *necessary*?"

"Because these are people that will never, ever, ever tell you a thing. These are people who know who's responsible for the next terrorist attack. These are hardened people that would kill you and me thirty seconds after they got out of wherever they were being held and wouldn't blink an eyelash. You can sit there five years later and have this debate with me. All I'm asking you to do is, walk a mile in my shoes when I'm dealing with these realities."

There it was. George Tenet has never, will never, acknowledge that the CIA's program was torture. But in that answer was the explanation for why he pressed for the authority to violate the law.

From his perspective, the Clinton and Bush administrations failed to heed the urgency in his pre-9/11 warnings. Then, after 9/11, he watched the CIA take the blame. "People don't understand us," Tenet told me. "They think we're a bunch of faceless bureaucrats with no feelings, no families, no sense of what it's like to be passionate about *running these bastards down*. There was nobody else in government that felt what we felt before or after 9/11. Of course, after 9/11, everybody had that feeling. *Nobody* felt like we felt on that day. This was personal."

The conversation with George Tenet, which aired at twice the usual length of a *60 Minutes* story, is one of my favorite interviews of all time. After the broadcast, a friend of mine who had worked in the CIA's Clandestine Service told me, "Boy! You got 'The Full Tenet.'"

It is sometimes said in Washington that the staircase of security classification rises from "Confidential" to "Secret" to "Top Secret," but the highest classification of all is "Embarrassing." That was Khalid al-Masri's problem as he languished, month after month, in the Salt Pit. The more the CIA looked into his case, the more embarrassing it became. Unknown to the public, the CIA's Office of Inspector General completed a secret investigation in July 2007. "The Rendition and Detention of German Citizen Khalid al-Masri" is labeled "TOP SECRET// NOFORN." The latter means no foreign nationals, even allies, are allowed to see it. Fortunately for the American people, there are lawyers and law. The American Civil Liberties Union sued the CIA for access to the report under the Freedom of Information Act. There are many national security exemptions to the Act, which is why the inspector general's report is heavily censored. Many pages are blank. But what remains tells us much more than we knew back in 2005 when I was interviewing al-Masri and in 2006 when I spoke with Tenet.

Al-Masri's abduction was ordered by what was known as ALEC Station. ALEC Station opened in 1996 after Osama bin Laden declared jihad on the United States. ALEC was a collection of two dozen CIA officers operating from an office building not far from CIA headquarters in Northern Virginia. The officer in charge named the new station after his son. ALEC Station ordered the abduction of al-Masri because it was believed that al-Masri might know people who knew about plans for terrorist attacks. That, the CIA inspector general concluded, was a violation of the president's Memorandum of Notification which specified that the CIA could abduct only those who, *themselves*, posed an immediate threat of terrorism. Because ALEC Station believed al-Masri was traveling on forged documents, its officers didn't bother to examine his German passport. In March 2004, al-Masri's passport was found in an unopened box at headquarters. The officer who stumbled across it had the passport analyzed by agency experts who immediately found it to be genuine. Not surprisingly, interrogators at the Salt Pit were telling ALEC Station that al-Masri wasn't giving up any information. Still, as the CIA inspector general report says, "the two agency officers primarily involved in al-Masri's rendition justified their commitment to his continued detention, despite diminishing rationale, by insisting that they knew he was 'bad.'" As al-Masri's detention wore on, a medical officer from the CIA Office of Medical Services found al-Masri "agitated and frustrated—visibly trembling from the anger he is currently experiencing." The medical officer described him as "openly tearful and speechless." The medical officer concluded, "Subject's mental and emotional status is likely to continue to deteriorate."

It took only two weeks to determine that the al-Masri they had was not the al-Masri they wanted. But, now that they had him, the CIA could not figure out how to let him go. The agency could not let Germany find out that one of its citizens had been kidnapped by the United States. This is why they snatched al-Masri in Macedonia in the first place. While debating ways to unload al-Masri, one CIA officer came up with a novel idea. He reasoned, because al-Masri was displaying contempt and anger toward his captors, he could be declared a threat to US armed forces. That would allow the CIA to dump al-Masri on the US military as a prisoner of war. The CIA dropped the idea because, according to the inspector general report, "the US military would register al-Masri and notify the Red Cross of his detention. He could be a free man within hours..."

A lesser nation might have just put a bullet in this problem. But instead, the CIA finally came up with a humane, if absurd, solution. Al-Masri was told he would be released if he agreed not to tell anyone about his abduction. Specifically, not the media and not the German government. He was told the CIA would watch him constantly and "any breach of his pledge would have consequences." There was one more thing. The CIA informed him that the $3,000 in currency the agency confiscated from him when he was abducted had unfortunately gone missing.

Five months after his capture, al-Masri was shackled, blindfolded and, once again, a guest of Premier Executive Transport Services. The CIA gave him 14,450 Euros (about $17,000) for his trouble. The money was limited because German customs would start asking questions on any amount of cash above 15,000 Euros. This time, al-Masri was allowed to fly without a diaper. He told me the CIA jet landed in Albania where he was driven to a desolate road in the woods. This was where he expected the CIA to resolve the inconvenient fact of his existence. Al-Masri told me, "I was in a place where there were no people, in the dark, and they told me to take a path and not look back. I walked along the path and thought they would shoot me in the back."

In the conclusion of its report, the CIA inspector general's office cites "a series of breakdowns in tradecraft, process, management and oversight." The investigation blames "officers who exaggerated the nature of the limited data on al-Masri...who exaggerated the basis for al-Masri's alleged ties to al-Qa'ida; and who failed to act in a timely manner following prompt assessment that the Agency lacked sufficient justification to continue to detain al-Masri."

For me, the most chilling conclusion of the inspector general's investigation is contained in paragraph 204 which notes, "Interviews of some of the key personnel involved in the case of Khalid al-Masri, and review of some of the documentary evidence, indicate there were individuals in addition to al-Masri who were captured, detained, and rendered by the Agency based on the legally insufficient justification used in the al-Masri case...it is unknown if all cases have been identified and acted on."

The inspector general's investigators believed they had found plenty of reason in the al-Masri case to refer agency employees to the Department of Justice for prosecution. The US Attorney's Office for the Eastern District of Virginia declined to prosecute.

Al-Masri sued the US government in federal court. A district judge dismissed the case because there was a likelihood that state secrets would be exposed at trial. An appeals court concurred. The Supreme Court of the United States declined to hear al-Masri's claim.

In the Rendition and Detention Program, the executive branch approved illegal acts, CIA officers exceeded the limits on those acts, Congress was kept in the dark, and the judiciary looked the other way. Today, you know what happened to the innocent victims because journalists fulfilled their constitutional role. When all three branches of government fail, journalism remains to act in the interests of the people.

Albania, where al-Masri was dumped, is one thousand miles from his home in Germany. By the time he got home, his wife and children were long gone. They had moved to Lebanon to be with his wife's mother. After all, he had vanished five months before, without a word, without a trace.

Shortly after taking office in 2009, President Barack Obama signed an executive order closing the CIA's "black sites" and prohibiting the use of the Enhanced Interrogation Techniques. In 2015, Congress reaffirmed the anti-torture law and restricted interrogation techniques to those listed in the Army Field Manual. Waterboarding is now recognized, by law, as torture.

Any nation could have overreacted to 9/11. That is what our adversaries hoped and it would defy human nature to think it could have been otherwise. What I notice when I comb through the CIA's memos, cables and reports are the rules that attempt to constrain depravity. The specifications for torture are so exacting, they seem to have been written by America's corporate alter ego. An interrogator can stuff a person in a "confinement box" and introduce insects into the box, *but* the confinement can last only one hour. He can put a prisoner in a coffin, lower the coffin into the ground and begin to bury it, *but* the coffin must be built with a specified number of concealed ventilation holes to facilitate breathing.

The rules were not always followed, but as Americans, we aspire to *have* rules. Khalid Sheikh Mohammed didn't consult limits or morality when he planned 9/11 nor when he beheaded *Wall Street Journal* reporter Daniel Pearl before a video camera. In many countries, Khalid al-Masri wouldn't go home with $17,000 in his pocket. He would never go home.

There hasn't been another 9/11 in the United States. I believe that is because many thousands of Americans in the intelligence community, law enforcement and the military did hard, honorable work to protect the nation. But it is also true that some innocent people were detained, tortured and murdered by Americans after the administration decided to violate US and international law.

The day the US Senate passed the 2015 torture ban, its co-sponsor, John McCain, Republican of Arizona, walked onto the Senate floor, stiffly, still wearing the crippling injuries his North Vietnamese captors inflicted on him nearly fifty years before. McCain told his fellow senators, "I believe past interrogation policies compromised our values, stained our national honor and did little practical good. This amendment provides greater assurances that never again will the United States follow that dark path of sacrificing our values for our short-term security needs. I know that such practices don't work... Our enemies act without conscience. *We* must not."[13]

FIELD NOTE

Empathy

Kabul was a desolate ruin when I arrived during the US military campaign in October 2001. Once, the city's river was described in the *Rig Veda*, a Hindu text from 1,200 BC, as beautiful, fair to see.[1] But all I could see was a vision of Dante's Seventh Circle of Hell. The civil war that began in 1992 and ended with Taliban control in 1996 destroyed 80 percent of Kabul. Now, with the fall of the Taliban, three million people scavenged the remains of grotesque privation. The economy, security, even dignity had collapsed. The most destitute were widows, covered head to toe in sky blue burkas overcast with filth. Bound by the chains of Taliban piety, even their eyes were covered by gauzelike screens. Because the Taliban forbade women to work and because their husbands had been killed in war, the widows could only beg in the streets. After the US rid Kabul of its totalitarian masters, homeless women were no longer beaten by the roving goons of the Ministry for the Promotion of Virtue and Prevention of Vice, but hunger had starved them of their humanity. The moment I stepped from my car, I was swarmed by desperate souls. Four veiled figures pulled at my clothes and gripped my arms and legs as though I was a lone timber in a rolling sea. The Afghan capital had become a feral frenzy. Their shrieking, their despair, broke my heart.

I was on my way to Bagram Air Force Base to link up with US Army Special Forces. I fumbled for the few Afghani bills I had in my pocket, but these women were determined to go with me, wherever that may be. I peeled fingers back, one by one and escaped into the car. Starving, shrouded ghosts beat the roof and howled as we pulled away.

Empathy is the greatest gift a reporter can possess. But the gift is not free. Reporters are haunted by memories: the faces of, or in Kabul, the hands of souls he or she cannot make whole. With empathy we explore, we understand, but in the bargain, the grip of tragedy is never peeled away.

CHAPTER NINETEEN

To a Young Journalist

There is no democracy without journalism.

Our citizens depend on independent, reliable information to make decisions in their lives and in the life of the nation. The *quality* of our democracy is bound to the *quality* of our journalism. Like other freedoms, quality journalism must be defended, renewed and fought for by every generation, by *your* generation. What is the greatest threat to democracy? Is it war? Terrorism? Recession? I believe the fastest way to destroy democracy is to poison the information. In my view, there are four threats poisoning our democracy today:

Biased media on the Left and the Right that treat their work not as a responsibility but as a business model.

Aggregators who recycle stories without checking the facts.

Hostile nations and political operatives.

Charlatans who peddle outrage to compel clicks on advertising algorithms.

Let me take a moment to explain this threat and how journalism can be our national shield. Not long ago, the dividing line in media lay between New Media (Facebook/Twitter) and Legacy Media (CBS News/*New York Times*). That distinction is no longer meaningful. Today, all media are available on all platforms. The dividing line that matters now is the one between journalism and junk. The 2016 presidential campaign was the first in our history in which citizens were awash in false stories masquerading as news. Much of this was a disinformation campaign engineered by domestic political partisans and by Russia. Their weapons targeting democracy were fashioned from an internet idiosyncrasy—stories that provoke outrage are less likely to be true, but more likely to be clicked. Algorithms at Facebook, Google and others prioritize content based on the number of likes, shares and comments. So, the algorithms themselves are unconsciously biased in favor of outrage. You may be thinking lies have outpaced truth for hundreds of years. You're right. In 1710, Jonathan Swift wrote in the *Examiner*, "Falsehood flies, and truth comes limping after it..."[1] But what has never existed before is the internet. Today we live in an unprecedented age in which falsehoods fly at the speed of light and multiply exponentially to fill devices we carry 24/7.

After the election, I wanted to understand the hidden machinery of the information age. There was no one better to investigate this than *60 Minutes* producer Guy Campanile. Guy had been my "right hand" as a senior producer on the *CBS Evening News*. He is a careful, no-nonsense newsman. Guy's Italian surname translates "bell tower." His work always has the clarity and resonance his name implies. Somehow, Guy convinced several people to explain to us how they scammed the voters. Among them was Jestin Coler, who created two fake news sites, *National Report* and the *Denver Guardian*. Coler told me "outrage" is the key to all fake news. During the election, he used a keyboard to push people's buttons on issues including abortion, immigration and Obamacare. He told me, "We did a piece on Radio Frequency Identification chips being mandated through the Obamacare exchange."

"And what are those?" I asked.

"Essentially a tracking device. So, as part of signing up for Obamacare, you had to be implanted, essentially, with this tracking device."

That false story was read 1.6 million times. Another fake story he wrote was about an FBI agent investigating Hillary Clinton's email server, who was murdered in his own home. It was completely false, there had been no murder, no FBI agent. Another Coler creation involved a Texas town quarantined by the military because of an outbreak of Ebola. There was no Ebola, no military quarantine, but the story got eight million views. At the time, that was only slightly more viewers than one edition of the *CBS Evening News*. Coler told me that, for him, "It's kind of an addiction, right? You see something really take off and then you're kinda lookin' for that next high." His highs were profitable, with each click he made money on ads. He told me he was making $10,000 a month.

"Facebook was key to what we did," Coler said.

"How?" I asked.

"Well, we would basically join whatever group it is that you're trying to target on Facebook. Once they took the bait, so to speak, they would spread this stuff around."

"Some people watching this interview are thinking that you're an evil guy," I suggested.

"I get that a lot," Coler said. "And that's fair. You know, I can take criticism. There have been stories that we've published that I do regret. Overall, I think the larger body of work of *National Report* and the contributors that I have is something I'm still very proud of."

"What did you discover about the audience?" I wondered.

"You know, people, in general, are quick to believe anything—well, not anything—but, well, *yeah*, basically anything that's put in front of them in a format that is 'news-ish.'"

How can people be so gullible? In *The Knowledge Illusion*, scientists Steven Sloman and Philip Fernbach argue knowledge is collective, not individual. Here's what they mean. You know too much candy can lead to obesity and diabetes. How do you know that? Is it because you've spent a lifetime in diabetes research? Probably not. You know because someone told you. You are probably an expert in the thing that you do—nuclear engineering, welding, cotton farming—but for most everything else in a complex world, you rely on what you read and hear. You have to accept the responsibility to carefully choose an information diet that will nourish your mind.

False Russian content, intended to influence the election, was seen by an estimated 126 million Facebook users according to Facebook's testimony to Congress.[2] Google's YouTube told Congress that more than 1,000 Russian-produced videos were uploaded, masquerading as American political debate.[3] These are not significant numbers in the world of the World Wide Web, but they don't have to be. Remember, the presidency was won in 2016 by a total of about 77,000 votes in the states that put Donald Trump over the top in the Electoral College. The number of people reached on Facebook by the Russian disinformation campaign is equal to 92 percent of all those who voted in 2016.[4]

Twitter reported to Congress that it discovered 36,746 fake, automated users known as "bots" infesting the election.[5] These bots sent 1.4 million election-oriented tweets concocted by the Russians. Bots are a little terrifying when you understand how insidiously efficient they are. Guy Campanile and I decided to try spreading an innocuous message with bots to see how far we could go. We had help from Jim Vidmar, a Nevada based internet consultant who specializes in getting new products noticed online. Vidmar was a slender man, forty-something, with a close-trimmed beard that began just below the rim of his black baseball cap. Given the scorching Nevada sun, his pale skin suggested to me he was spending far too much time at the keyboard. Vidmar's home was short on furniture but packed with servers and flat screens. With Vidmar's help, we purchased five thousand bots from a vendor in Russia. Most anyone can do this. Our five thousand bots cost only a few hundred bucks. The bots were programmed to automatically create false user profiles for themselves. Ours stole head shot photos, randomly, from the internet and automatically wrote little autobiographies for themselves. Because of the way our bots were programmed, most of them were soccer moms. All of this took half an hour or so. Now we had five thousand Twitter accounts masquerading as real people. On my actual Twitter account, I tweeted, "What happens when *60 Minutes* investigates fake news?" Normally, I would expect a few dozen retweets from real people over a period of hours. But Vidmar set our bots loose with instructions to retweet anything I tweeted. He punched the Return key. "There you go," Vidmar said. "Now you've got 3,200 retweets right there. Now, it's 4,400." The numbers raced higher and, within one minute, the reach of my tweet was 9,000 percent higher than normal. I pushed our experiment one step further. This was March, so the NCAA basketball tournament was in full dribble. I wondered what would happen if I simply added the hashtag "#Marchmadness" to my tweet—a tweet that had nothing to do with basketball. It was a slam dunk. My bots instantly pushed my tweet to the *top ten* posts of the tournament. You can think of bots as the booster stage of a rocket. They get the message off the ground, the second and third stages are actual users. "Real people start seeing it," Vidmar explained. "They start retweeting it and responding."

Now, imagine what well-funded frauds, including nation-states, can do with *millions* of bots. The artificial intelligence (AI) algorithms of Facebook, Google and others prioritize content by the number of likes, regardless of whether they're human or automated. I believe this is more fairly described as "artificial stupidity" (AS). If Facebook and Google inserted reporters, editors and fact-checkers into this loop, the false stories would never take off. Internet search engines make billions of dollars in the information distribution business without taking adequate responsibility for what they distribute. After the election, Mark Zuckerberg, the founder of Facebook, defended his social media site by saying, "Determining the truth is complicated." Well, yes. Yes, it is. Determining the truth is so complicated that people go to universities to learn how to do it. Some get master's degrees in the subject or PhDs. These are called journalism degrees and the people who care deeply about seeking truth for democracy are called journalists.

What responsibility do search engines have to the public? Are they simply utilities, conduits for anything and everything, or do they have a responsibility to use human intelligence to stop the false reporting that poisons our democracy? Facebook calls part of its site its "Newsfeed." It is reckless to claim to be in the news business while disregarding the values and principles of journalism.

To their credit, Facebook and Google have begun experimenting with filters and human intervention to screen malicious content. Both companies have become more vigilant since 2016. But so much more can and must be done to protect our country. The titans of Silicon Valley are the great innovators of our age. Shouldn't they be able to handle something "complicated"?

Another problem with the notion of "new versus old media" is that it suggests the rules of content have changed. The turn of the twenty-first century brought us a revolution in *distribution*. But the rules of *content* never change. With every story, the journalist asks: "Is it right? Is it fair? Is it honest?" Have I double-checked the facts with a skeptical mind? Have I balanced the variety of views? Have I written impartially, without placing my thumb on the scale of opinion? Journalism has much in common with the scientific method. In reporting, we don't care what the results are as long as they are true. The principles of honest content have not changed in hundreds of years. Whether you are writing on a stone tablet or a glass tablet, the audience must have accurate, evenhanded reporting.

Hard to imagine, but there was a time when there were three commercial television channels in America. Back in 1972, a major poll found *CBS Evening News* managing editor, Walter Cronkite, was "The Most Trusted Man in America."[6] By the time I took over as managing editor of the *Evening News*, in 2011, the universe had changed. Vietnam, Watergate, the Clinton impeachment, the 2003 war in Iraq and the Great Recession made us a much more skeptical people. By and large, that's good. But in this evolution, journalism itself has become suspect and we journalists have to own up to our failures that contribute to the corrosive cynicism about the news media.

Our credibility is damaged when reporters reach for fame rather than public service. It has become common for reporters to appear in movies and fictional dramas. One night, the reporter is relaying election results on a news program, the next night, you encounter him in a movie reporting an invasion of aliens from space. This desire for personal fame is the same instinct that leads some reporters to embellish their reporting or embellish their role in their reporting. To them, it is more important to be celebrated than believed. Reporters who grasp for fame have forgotten that journalism has *nothing to do with being popular*. If you report the facts with courage and without bias, you're more likely to be unpopular. It has been argued to me that no viewer would misunderstand the role of the reporter on election night and his or her fictional account of an alien invasion. I agree. That is not the point. The problem comes when the audience becomes skeptical of the reporter's motives. Is he in this to inform, or is he in this to be famous? If the reporter is in this to be famous, what is he or she willing to compromise to become a celebrity?

A few years ago, my friend, the immensely talented comedian Stephen Colbert, asked me for permission to stage a gag for *The Colbert Report* on the set of the *CBS Evening News*. I had to decline because the *Evening News* must be, always, a place for reliable reality, not satire. I assumed Stephen thought I was being a pretentious snob. I was surprised months later, when he told the story to an audience and, in all seriousness, said, "Thank God *something* is sacred."

When reporters make every story, essentially, about *themselves*, we squander the public trust. We undermine the indispensable role of journalism in democracy. This is no small thing. Cynicism, as distinct from healthy skepticism, allowed President Trump to describe the media as "a great danger to our country." When I offered frank coverage of the president's demonstrable falsehoods on the *CBS Evening News*, Mr. Trump attacked CBS News as an "enemy of the American people." Days later, at the White House, I suggested to Mr. Trump that his "enemy of the American people" language could lead some deranged soul to commit violence at a newspaper, website or television station. I asked him to consider the consequences. He thought for a moment and said, "I don't worry about that."

Late in 2018, I couldn't help but wonder whether Mr. Trump's hostile rhetoric in some way encouraged Saudi Arabia to order the torture, murder and dismemberment of *Washington Post* columnist Jamal Khashoggi. Many world leaders look to the president of the United States to set the norms and the limits of behavior. At the least, Saudi Arabia could have calculated it wouldn't have to fear Mr. Trump's reaction to a government murder of a reporter. They turned out to be right about that.

Mr. Trump's irresponsible rhetoric continues to inspire. Two weeks after the butchering of Khashoggi was uncovered, a fanatic mailed pipe bombs to a dozen people he considered to be enemies of the president. I was on the bomber's target list. An FBI special agent called to tell me the bomber had a file on me in his computer, which included my home address. The FBI arrested the man before he could mail a bomb to my family.

During America's midterm elections in 2018, Mr. Trump endorsed a candidate for the US House of Representatives who had pleaded guilty to body-slamming and punching a journalist. Mr. Trump called the candidate, "My kind of guy."

Now, let me tell you about *my* kind of guy.

Hadi Abdullah was a resident of Aleppo when Syria's largest city was under siege by the dictatorship of Bashar al-Assad. Assad was committing every kind of war crime to retake the city from rebels who rose up against his family dynasty in 2011. The Syrian Air Force bombed hospitals and schools. Syrian artillery hammered apartment buildings into rubble. Civilians were dying by the thousands. Few news media could get past the dictatorship's cordon around Aleppo. Hadi had not been a reporter but he became one. With a small camera and a friend to shoot the pictures, he chronicled the catastrophe and posted his reports on YouTube. The dictatorship noticed. One night, when Hadi was returning to his apartment, a bomb connected to his front door detonated. His cameraman was killed. Hadi was rescued by a White Helmets civil defense team, but as they prepared to rush him to a makeshift hospital, they were forced to leave his legs behind. Both had been crushed. I met Hadi, twelve surgeries later, for a *60 Minutes* interview. What was most remarkable about Hadi's story was not his initial sacrifice. After months of recovery in Turkey, he went back to Aleppo, in a wheelchair, to continue his reporting. *That* is a reporter. With no regard for himself, Hadi Abdullah risked his life to give voice to the voiceless of Aleppo—a people suffering the most grotesque atrocities of the twenty-first century. Hadi isn't likely to be an actor in a movie nor push his wheelchair down a red carpet. He is the purest form of journalist and he is not alone. There are many like Hadi Abdullah who shine their light on the dispossessed, taking care to stay out of the light themselves.

Among the worst self-inflicted wounds in journalism is the headlong rush to be first with a story. Ironically, this has no value whatsoever to the audience. It is a narcissistic game we play in our control rooms as we keep score among the video monitors carrying the coverage of our competitors. Our audience would prefer we be right rather than first.

In 1993, I was reporting live from the site of the World Trade Center bombing in Lower Manhattan. Days had passed since the truck bomb attack. I was preparing for that night's broadcast when a producer in the control room crackled into my earpiece, "Stand by! We're going on the air with a Special Report! They've just found a survivor. Here we come!" One of our competitors was reporting a rescue. Now, finding a survivor in the wreckage days after the bombing would be big news. You would also expect a good deal of commotion at the scene. As I looked around, I saw cops milling about and firefighters passing the time. "Hold on," I told the control room. "Don't put me on the air, let me check this out." I walked over to the police command post. "You guys hear anything about a survivor rescue tonight?" I asked. The sergeant had his feet on his desk and a Styrofoam cup of thin, cold coffee. He said, "Nope," but his expression was, *Seriously*, buddy? Do youse think I'd be sittin' here drinkin' coffee? I went back to my microphone and told the control room what I learned. "No! No!" the producer yelled, watching our competitor. "They *found* him. Stand by, we're coming to you!"

"Wait!" I told her. "I'll check again." This time I found an FDNY officer under a white helmet. He confirmed no one had been found since the day of the bombing. Like the cop, his admonishing expression said, Look around, pal. Does it *look like* we just rescued a guy? I told the control room, "I've got this confirmed two ways. No rescue." But by this time, the story on the competing broadcast was only getting better. The control room producer said, "The victim is in an ambulance headed to Roosevelt Hospital right now. Stand by! Here we come."

"I'm not reporting this!" I told her in a chargeable act of insubordination. "Don't put me on the air because I will *NOT* report this." The producer had no choice but to watch additional channels pick up the breathtaking details of the miracle rescue. The competition was killing her. She was livid and I couldn't be sure I would have a job after I got back to the studio. If other reporters had better sources than mine, so be it. I may be getting my ass kicked, but I was not going to report other people's reporting that I could not confirm.

As it turned out, a man reported missing in the blast *had* been found that night. He had been found in a bar on the Lower East Side. The man had been *reported* missing after the bombing, but in fact, he hadn't been at the World Trade Center at all. He was unaware that he was "missing." Someone, somewhere, maybe a police radio dispatcher, maybe a green reporter, assumed that if a missing person had been found, he must have been found in the wreckage. The story of the ambulance was a misunderstanding based on a falsehood. The pressure to be first with the story took it from there.

In 2013, a similar emergency called the CBS newsroom to battle stations. The hunt was on for the Boston Marathon terrorists. It was midafternoon, my team and I were in the *Evening News* office going over the lineup for our broadcast. A major cable channel flashed on the air to report the bombers had been arrested. We fired up the lights illuminating the *Evening News* set in Studio 47. I climbed into my chair in anticipation of confirming the story. As my soundman pinned a microphone to my lapel, a major wire service ran a bulletin with the same story citing its own anonymous sources. I had imposed a rule at the *CBS Evening News* when I was managing editor: breaking news required two independent sources and extraordinary news absolutely demanded them. Other news media *were not* sources. We did not report the reporting of others without independent confirmation of our own. We stayed off the air. Within a minute or so, I got a call on the set from our veteran Justice Department correspondent. "Yes," he told me. "A highly placed federal source confirms the arrests."

"That's great!" I said. "Now, get us another source." Waiting on the set, I watched one news organization after another flash on with the story. Now cable channels were reporting the suspects were on the way to the Moakley Federal Courthouse in Boston. That reporting gave me more reason to pause. The courthouse would not be an early stop after an arrest. The suspects would be booked and processed at the jail and the FBI would try to interview them. I knew, by law, the government had up to seventy-two hours to present the suspects before a magistrate for a preliminary hearing. I figured in a case like this, the feds would take all the time they had coming. Mentally, I pressed the brakes harder. On monitors in my studio, I watched live shots from helicopters flash onto our competitor's broadcasts. A massive crowd was gathering outside the courthouse. The pressure was building in my newsroom to go on the air with a Special Report. I was beginning to look obstinate. I could hear the restrained frustration of the executive producer of special events as he spoke into my earpiece. Still, he did not suggest we go on the air; he knew my rule. Under the anchor desk, my heels were dug in.

The more we tried to confirm the story, the more we couldn't. Reliable contacts, one after another, told us that all they knew was what they were seeing on TV. We never reported the arrests that we could not confirm. We did not go on the air until the FBI arranged a hasty news conference. The FBI's special agent in charge, clearly agitated and angry, scolded reporters. There had been no arrests. He went on to say the false reporting of arrests had disrupted the biggest manhunt in Boston history. I don't know how that rumor got started or how it mutated into reportable "fact." But the immense pressure to *"be first!"* seriously damaged many reputations. I have a maxim that I often repeat around the newsroom: "If we're first, no one will remember. If we're *wrong*, no one will ever forget."

Now, a few words on writing.

There is no such thing as good writing; there is only good *re-writing*. Reflection is the greatest gift writers can give themselves. Write your first draft then put it away—for an hour, a day or overnight. I guarantee when you come back to it, you will see problems you didn't expect and opportunities you hadn't imagined. Of course, in journalism, all depends on the deadline. At *60 Minutes*, we rewrite our scripts until they're perfect. At the *CBS Evening News*, we rewrite them until 6:30 p.m. Even on a tight deadline, it is often possible to write, reflect and write again. Don't stop rewriting until your deadline makes you stop.

Reporting and writing are first and foremost about "seeing." You can't write about what you did not see and most of us are terrible at "seeing." Here are a couple of exercises to practice. In your home, find twenty things you've never seen before. I promise you there are two thousand. Also, a few times a day, stop and ask yourself, "If I had to write about this place, or this person, or this moment, what are the unnoticed details that would bring my story to life?" For example, imagine trying to get a sense of the voters before the 2016 election as we did in our story "Ask Ohio" for *60 Minutes*. When you're in the coffee shop interviewing out-of-work steelworkers, turn the coffee cup upside down. "Made in China," ironic. In the greasy spoon restaurant in Lorain, Ohio, notice the shops on either side of the café are boarded up. Notice the Virgin Mary standing on the shelf above the Coco Puffs. Notice the sign that reads Pull Up Your Pants! With just these observations, the reader gets a pretty good idea of what kind of place this is, who works there and who eats there. John Steinbeck called this "layering detail upon detail." The author and journalism professor John McPhee tells his students at Princeton, "A thousand details make one impression." In the minutia, you will find richness, texture and truth. Think about it this way: if you don't see more than I do, why do I need your journalism?

"Seeing" is also about working equally hard to see both sides (or the many sides) of a story. You will be surprised how often a story isn't what it seems. In my experience, stories are rarely what they seem. I'll give you a brief example. A snowstorm engulfed a major airport. Hundreds of flights were cancelled. A local TV station received a complaint from a family who said their elderly, wheelchair-bound mother languished many hours in the terminal after she was abandoned by the airline. This narrative of outrage—elderly woman stranded by profit-pinching airline—was repeated by news organizations across the country. The airline told the station that it would investigate. But the station ran the story without the benefit of hearing the results of that investigation. Two days later, the airline had security camera video that revealed the woman had been taken by an attendant to a wheelchair waiting area in the airport. Her family picked her up forty-five minutes later. Why did the family tell the story of abandonment? Believe me, people do strange, inexplicable things. Let that be the first thing you understand as a reporter. The only way to protect yourself, the only way to protect your viewers and readers, is to dig into every side. Don't publish until you know the whole story. Relying on one point of view is dangerous, unethical and foolish. Hold the story until you know what you're talking about.

Now, the Great Divide. In journalism, there is breaking news copy and there is feature copy. Respect the Great Divide. If you are covering the five-alarm fire or the summit meeting between heads of state, write the news straight and unembellished. *What happened?* "Who, What, When, Where, Why and How" remains the trite and true method of telling a complete news story. There is art in crisp copy composed of simple declarative sentences. And please, make them sentences. In recent years a bizarre fashion has arisen, even in network news, to drop verbs. You end up with nonsense such as "President Trump, surprised by the House vote, and angry at the outcome," or "Scientists, giddy over the result of their experiment." The deletion of the "to be" verb—*was* in the first example and *were* in the second—is not a new style. It is illiterate. If you do not respect language, you are not a writer. If you are not a writer, you are not a reporter. The word *verb* is Latin for *word*.[7] They important.

On the other side of the Great Divide lies feature writing, which is often what we do at *60 Minutes*. I turn to two bits of priceless advice from Don Hewitt, the creator of the most successful prime-time television program in history.

First, *"Find people who can tell the story better than we can."*

In journalism, insightful, poetic quotes are the spice in your copy. In *video* journalism, they are the difference between success and failure. Everyone has a story, but in my experience, only about 5 percent can *tell* his or her story well. Those are the people you want to interview. For our story "Hard Times Generation" about homeless children living in cars, *60 Minutes* producer Nicole Young made her way through shelter after shelter, soup kitchen after soup kitchen, talking to fifty people to find the five we would interview. There are natural poets in our world, gifted storytellers. They are rare, but you can find them.

Interviews are your oil paints. How much vibrancy and color do you want to work with? I, again, acknowledge the guillotine of the deadline. If you're covering the five-alarm fire and your story goes up in fifteen minutes, you're going to grab anyone who happens by. But if your deadline allows, remember: great characters can save a weak story, poor characters will kill a great story. *"Find people who can tell the story better than we can."*

Don's second piece of advice was simply, *"Tell me a story."*

For the journalist, this directive is a powerful concept camouflaged in simplicity. If you went into Don's corner office and said, "Don! We need to do a story on the war in Sudan," Don would look up from the copy he was editing and say, "That's an *issue*. Tell me a *story*." An example is our 2008 *60 Minutes* story on the genocide in the Darfur region of Sudan. We called it "Searching for Jacob." Jacob was a boy in a village that had been burned down by Sudanese military forces because Jacob's people were the "wrong" ethnic group. One of Jacob's charred notebooks from school was in a genocide exhibit in the United States Holocaust Memorial Museum in Washington, DC. We decided to try to find Jacob in the desert refugee camps bordering Darfur. We enlisted the help of an expert in the region, John Prendergast, a former National Security Council official and the founder of the "Enough Project." Prendergast, photographer Ian Robbie, and I slipped into Darfur with the help of a militia fighting the Sudanese government. After several hours driving overland, we found Jacob's village. Sudanese government forces and their allies left only ashes. The round thatched huts that once sheltered hundreds of families were leveled. Everyone in the village was either dead—or had fled. We camped in the desert overnight. The next morning, on the way back into neighboring Chad, the militia leader roasted a camel to celebrate our safe return. We chewed the gamey, charred dromedary with gratitude, but no one on my team felt much like celebrating after surveying the landscape of a people marked for annihilation. Ultimately, after searching the records of the

United Nations refugee relief agency, we found Jacob in Chad's Sahel Desert. He was amazed and delighted to see his notebook again. "Where did you get it?" he asked. We explained it had been part of an exhibit in a Washington museum. Jacob, who was about fifteen years old, asked if we would do him a favor. Would we take the notebook back to Washington so America could understand the atrocities devastating his people? We were glad to oblige.

Our story was about one boy, but through his struggle we were able to explain all the "issues" driving the conflict. The director Steven Spielberg makes cinematic art from this storytelling principle. He didn't shoot a movie called *D-Day*. He made a movie called *Saving Private Ryan*. He didn't make a film called *The Holocaust*. He made a film called *Schindler's List*. In telling "small" stories, we illuminate titanic events.

"Tell me a story" can lead to a dramatically unique approach to breaking news. In 1963, in the days after John F. Kennedy's assassination, every important journalist in the world had picked up his bags at National Airport and headed east, across Arlington Memorial Bridge, into Washington, DC. Jimmy Breslin, a thirty-three-year-old reporter for the *New York Herald Tribune*, turned west, against the prevailing traffic, to Arlington National Cemetery. There, he found Clifton Pollard, a man gnawing the earth with a backhoe. Breslin wrote:

Pollard is 42. He is a slim man with a mustache who was born in Pittsburgh and served as a private in the 352nd Engineers Battalion in Burma in World War II. He is an equipment operator, grade 10, which means he gets $3.01 an hour. One of the last to serve John Fitzgerald Kennedy, who was the 35th president of this country, was a working man who earns $3.01 an hour and said it was an honor to dig the grave.[8]

Find Breslin's article in its entirety. Infer the questions Breslin must have asked to tell the story of Pollard's day. Detail, layered upon detail. Seeing what others don't see.

To write well, study writers. I would guide you to Steinbeck's *The Grapes of Wrath* and to *Coming into the Country* by John McPhee. McPhee is among the best who craft nonfiction in literary style. Lucky for all of us, McPhee wrote his first book about writing in 2017. It's called *Draft No. 4*. I'd say he's lucky to get it in only four drafts, but McPhee is a vastly better writer than I am. Read for the rhythm in sentence structure in McPhee and Steinbeck. For example, in *The Grapes*, Steinbeck's line "And her joy was nearly like sorrow" describes Ma's reaction when her son, Tom, returns from prison.[9] Now, make an innocuous change in the line. Notice how "And her joy was like sorrow" falls flat. The loss of the two syllables supplied by "nearly" are indispensable to the cadence. This is what Mark Twain meant when he wrote, "The difference between almost the right word and the right word is really a large matter—'tis the difference between the lightning-bug and the lightning."[10] Steinbeck wrote *The Grapes* longhand, on a legal pad. His rhythm was timed to a washing machine he kept running in the background like a metronome. If you despair (and you will) that you were not cut out for writing, read the journal Steinbeck kept while he was writing *The Grapes*. This daily diary was published as *Working Days*. The journal exposes his self-doubt, the anxiety in his inability to realize the work he dreamed of. *The Grapes*, of course, won the Pulitzer Prize and helped Steinbeck win the Nobel Prize for Literature.

If you think you are writing well, you're not trying hard enough. If you think you are writing badly, you have probably found the right path. Never give up. Journalism shares at least one attribute of poetry. Both the journalist and the poet are working to convey maximum meaning with minimum words. It's helpful and a pleasure to read the poets. Hear their song. Feel the cadence. See how words convey meaning beyond their definitions. May I suggest Whitman, Sandburg and Yeats? That's a start.

If you are a young journalist or student of journalism, I want you to know *we need you*. Your country needs you. But we need you to be good. Journalism is hard work with tough hours and far too much time away from family. The hard work comes in digging for truth, verifying facts with original sources and writing clearly and concisely on deadline. It is not for the faint of heart and not for those who just want to be famous. But, if you have fire in the belly for it, I cannot imagine a more fascinating, rewarding career. Journalism is the world's greatest continuing education program. It is also one of those professions where values and ethics matter every day. Journalism is a vocation in which you can pursue justice *and* practice art.

If you are just coming out of college, or you are early in your career, I urge you to refuse to be defeated when looking for a job. The only people who don't find work in journalism are those who quit. It *is* hard to get started. The rejections are going to come at you thirty to one. But remember my experience. It took four years of intense work to get CBS to hire me. I kept coming after they told me to stop. If journalism is the song in your heart and others can't hear it, *they are wrong*, not you. You keep going, keep growing. Never give in. Sing the song in your heart.

Your country *needs* you.

I wrote earlier that there is no democracy without journalism. But there was a brief, dark moment in American history when Congress imposed government control over both Freedom of Speech and Freedom of the Press. The Sedition Act of 1798—promoted by Alexander Hamilton no less—was among the great blunders of the US Congress. The Act read in part:

If any person shall write, print, utter or publish…any false, scandalous and malicious writing or writings against the government of the United States, or either House of the Congress of the United States, or the President of the United States, with intent to defame the said government, or to bring them into contempt or disrepute; or to excite against them...the hatred of the good people of the United States...then such person, being thereof convicted before any court of the United States having jurisdiction thereof, shall be punished by a fine not exceeding two thousand dollars, and by imprisonment not exceeding two years.[11]

Congress made it a crime for *anyone* to "utter" criticism of the House, Senate or the president. Not to put too fine a point on this, but consider, adjusted for inflation, $2,000 in 1798 equals more than $38,000 in 2019 and would have bankrupted a newspaper of those days. This repudiation of the First Amendment was passed by Congress and signed into law by President John Adams. There were numerous prosecutions of citizens; many went to jail. The Sedition Act was exactly the tyranny James Madison was determined to prevent when he wrote the First Amendment in our Bill of Rights:

Congress shall make no law respecting an establishment of religion, or prohibiting the free exercise thereof; or abridging the freedom of speech, or of the press; or the right of the people peaceably to assemble, and to petition the Government for a redress of grievances.[12]

To see how Madison *really* felt about Freedom of the Press, look at how he described it in his original draft of the First Amendment:

The people shall not be deprived or abridged of their right to speak, to write, or to publish their sentiments; and the freedom of the press, as one of the great bulwarks of liberty, shall be inviolable.[13]

The Sedition Act outraged Madison and Thomas Jefferson. Have a look at Madison's rebuttal in his "Report on the Virginia Resolutions," from 1800. Madison writes that Congress has assumed a power over a free press that is...

...expressly and positively forbidden by one of the [constitutional] amendments thereto: a power, which more than any other, ought to produce universal alarm; because it is leveled against that right of freely examining public characters and measures, and of free communication among the people thereon, which has ever been justly deemed the only effectual guardian of every other right.[14]

The Sedition Act figured in Adams's defeat by Jefferson in the next election. It expired, in 1801, on the last day of the Adams administration.

What Madison meant by "press" was *every American* and his or her right to say what they want to say, write what they want to write, read what they want to read. Don't be misled. Any constraint on "the press" applies to every citizen's voice. "Enemy of the American people," in President Trump's phrase? We *are* the American people. Journalists bring vitality to the national conversation. We bridge differences, serve public safety, expose corruption, constrain power and give voice to the voiceless. As Madison might say today, Freedom of the Press is the right that guarantees all the others.

The stakes are high.

Become a journalist. We'd be proud to have you.

CONCLUSION

How Many Stars in Your Flag?

We began this journey, dear reader, because we share the anxiety of unfamiliar change. This era of the American Experiment is one in which terrorism seems ever present, elections are unpredictable, the economy is uncertain and much of our information is untrustworthy. In Washington, politics has become an autoimmune disease bent on the destruction of our body politic.

We began with the advice of Holocaust survivor Viktor Frankl who urged us to look within when we are overwhelmed by forces beyond our control. The journey took us through the lives of people who've discovered extraordinary gifts within themselves: the gallantry of New York City's firefighters, the audacity of Federal Reserve Chair Ben Bernanke, the courage of Chinese dissident Bao Tong, the selflessness of nurse Paulette Schank, the valor of Marine Captain Pat Rapicault, the perseverance of the Sandy Hook parents, the vision of Elon Musk.

When life asked, "What's the meaning of you?" each found in themselves the power to bend the arc of history toward the better. Now, I'd like to end with how virtues can help answer another urgent question—what's the meaning of "American"?

It is a paradox of the twenty-first century that, at the moment communication has become truly democratic and fluid, "We the People" are walling ourselves off from one another. Accelerating this trend is the business model of biased media on the Left and the Right. These channels and websites seduce their audiences with confirming information, "news" that assures you that what you already believe is right. Much of this is *designed* to provoke outrage. When you find yourself so furious that you want to punch your finger through the screen, there's a better than even chance you are being played. Most often, this is a fund-raising or advertising ploy. I once asked an educated and well-off friend why he didn't subscribe to a daily newspaper. He thought for a moment and said, "I *like* what I know." Yes, but in times of accelerating change, in times of accelerating diversity, we must like what we *learn*. Learning is knowing that we don't know enough. Until we take responsibility, instead of taking sides, I believe we risk a new Cold War—this time, a civil war.

I have no affinity for a political party. Maybe because I started in journalism at the age of fifteen, nonpartisan impartiality was in my upbringing. It defies human nature to attribute sound judgment to one party and incompetence to the other. Parties are people and therefore just as likely to go wrong as right. We should be profoundly skeptical when one party claims certainty and blames the other for our problems. That's a con. You know life isn't like that. That's why we invented democracies in the first place.

When people wrap their point of view in the flag, notice the number of stars in which they have clothed themselves. There are fifty. There are no versions of the Stars and Stripes that eliminate conservative states or liberal ones. There are *fifty* stars. The blue field on which those stars shine isn't called "the Union" for nothing. If you honor the flag, if you like to stand during the national anthem, you are adopting all the stars. Our flag is the very image of compromise. If you chose America, you chose *all* of America, "Indivisible with Liberty and Justice for all." No democracy has survived any other way. It *is* easier to listen to the drone of confirming information, to reject, out of hand, ideas that question what we believe. But democracy is not for the lazy.

Not many years ago, within my lifetime, both parties understood nothing lasting could be done without buy-in across the political spectrum. To these legislators, it would have been unthinkable to revolutionize national health care or tax policy, without *any* votes from the other party. But that is what the Democrats did with healthcare in the Obama administration. The result tied up Congress for eight years and more. Then, Republicans vigorously pursued precisely the same mistake. The 2018 tax reform law was pushed through without any votes from Democrats. What are the chances that the tax law will endure, like Obamacare, balanced precariously on a single party?

I trace much of this dysfunction to virulent political speech, biased media and the "closed loop" of social media groups. There was a time in Washington when the opposing legislator had a bad idea. Today, the opposing legislator is a *bad person*. When we vilify our opponents, there can be no compromise. In a conversation at the White House, President Obama once described Republicans to me as "those people." I mentioned to the president that his words were precisely how Robert E. Lee described his enemies in the North.[1] America cannot work when presidents and members of Congress refuse to listen and learn. I once asked a chairman of the Joint Chiefs of Staff what he had learned in a lifetime of military service. He said simply, "Don't declare enemies." He meant, don't rule out an entire people or nation as an "enemy." Better to reward them for the good they do and oppose the bad. The same is true when we choose to paint our politics in a palette of only red or a palette of only blue. Recently, a man I'd never met came up to me in a restaurant and said he didn't like my politics. Really? Was it my position on NATO? My view of abortion? Maybe it was healthcare or my thoughts on the national park system. He had chosen me as an "enemy." As I understood him, we could never begin to work together on anything. I am certain, if he bought me a couple of beers (I think he owed me at that point), we would discover both differences and a good deal on which we agree. Unfortunately, he already "liked" what he knew about me. As human beings, we are given to snap judgments in the absence of facts or in the presence of falsehoods. We have the free will and moral obligation to overcome that weakness. In *The Ethics of Belief* (1877), Cambridge philosopher William Clifford writes, "It is wrong always, everywhere, and for anyone, to believe anything upon insufficient evidence. If a man…keeps down and pushes away any doubts…the life of that man is one long sin against mankind."[2]

Just as "We the People" owed marines in Ramadi our best efforts to get them out of pickup trucks, we now owe each other the sweat-breaking effort to engage, listen, debate and reconcile. Have we become too lazy, too shallow, too deaf to nurture a democracy? I believe the heroes in this book suggest otherwise.

America can fail if *we* fail her—if we wall ourselves off from one other in digital citadels of confirming information.

"United We Stand" has never been the secret to America's success. We are an amalgam of all the peoples of the world. "Divided We Stand" is our strength. With all our diversity, in all our languages and cultures, we should agree on one big idea— each of us belongs, each of us contributes and each of us must be heard. We are *all* woven into the tapestry of stars. That is a fight worth winning. And a truth worth telling.

★ ★ ★ ★ ★

ACKNOWLEDGMENTS

It is said that every writer needs an editor. Naturally, I assumed an exception would be made in my case. Fortunately for both the reader and the author I met Peter Joseph, editorial director of Hanover Square Press. Peter saw potential in early drafts. He made innumerable suggestions that sharpened this book's message, style and clarity. He maximized my strengths and minimized my weaknesses. In short, Peter took a woeful stack of pages and created a book. I am deeply grateful for his talent and his wisdom.

I am also in the debt of the legendary book agent Esther Newburg at ICM Partners. Esther and her protégée, Zoe Sandler, guided this longtime journalist but first-time book author through the dense jungle of publishing. I owe them for leading this work into the light of day.

The reader owes more than they can imagine to my brilliant, relentless research assistant, Dina Zingaro. Her precise checking of the facts was infuriating and lifesaving.

This book, and most of my work for that matter, would not be possible without my longtime assistant, Jan Mann. Jan keeps me moving, keeps me sane and coordinates all the moving parts of my career. Colleagues have asked how I wrote this book while anchoring the *CBS Evening News* and contributing a full schedule to *60 Minutes*. The answer is Jan—imperturbable, unflappable, indispensable Jan.

As you have seen in the endnotes, this book is informed by many dozens of reference works but a few on which I relied require special thanks. "Gallantry," the story of the FDNY on 9/11, was richly informed by the oral histories collected by the FDNY World Trade Center Task Force. Technical analysis was based largely on the painstaking work of the National Institute of Standards and Technology, a service of the US Department of Commerce. For those who have seen the moronic conspiracy theories about 9/11, wade through the fifty-six NIST 9/11 studies and see the exacting work of the world's leading scientists and engineers.

The chapter entitled "Audacity" relied in part on the generous help of the researchers at the US Federal Reserve. The Federal Reserve "FRASER" Archive was enormously helpful in my research of the Fed during the Great Depression. I am also indebted to *The Financial Crisis Inquiry Report* by the US Financial Crisis Inquiry Commission.

The State of Connecticut investigation of the Sandy Hook murders helped separate fact from fiction in "Perseverance," the chapter on the Newtown parents. The National Defense University's "Lessons Encountered" added scholarly perspective to my experiences in Afghanistan and Iraq. The public archives of the Central Intelligence Agency gave invaluable insight into the agency's work after 9/11.

Finally, I am grateful to the first readers of the manuscript, my wife, Jane; my daughter, Blair; and son, Reece. Their edits and observations added precision and merciful brevity. Although, perhaps not enough of the latter.

IN MEMORIAM

The men and women of CBS News who gave their lives to bring truth into the world.

Greece, 1948

George Polk

Cambodia, 1970

Tomaharu Ishii
Remnik Leckhi
Sam Leng
Gerry Miller
Kojiro Sakai
Dana Stone
George Syvertsen

United States, 1972

Odell Vaughn Jr.

United States, 1972

Michelle Clark

Cambodia, 1975

Put Sophan

Lebanon, 1985

Tewfik Ghazawi
Bashir Metni

Iraq, 1991

Nick della Casa*

Iraq, 2006

James Brolan
Paul Douglas

Iraq, 2007

Anwar Abbas Lafta

*Employed by the British Broadcasting Corporation at the time of his death.

NOTES

What This Book Is About
A Search for Meaning

1   Henry St. John Bolingbroke, *Letters on the Study and Use of History* (London, 1735).

Chapter One
Gallantry: The FDNY

1   *The 9/11 Commission Report: Final Report of the National Commission on Terrorist Attacks Upon the United States*, The National Commission on Terrorist Attacks Upon the United States (W. W. Norton & Co, 2004), 4.

2   Transcript of conversation between Flight Attendant Betty Ong of American Airlines and the American Airlines Southeastern Reservation Center, Federal Bureau of Investigation, September 12, 2001.

3   Interview with AAL Flight Service Manager Michael Woodward, FBI, FD-302, September 12, 2001.

4   Interview with AAL employee Winston Sandler, FBI, FD-302, September 13, 2001.

5   FDNY Public Affairs, April 2018.

6   J. R. Lawson, Robert Vettori, "The Emergency Response Operations," Building and Fire Research Laboratory, National Institute of Standards and Technology (September 13, 2005): 193.

7   Federal Aviation Administration, Aircraft Registry, N334AA Boeing 767-223, Engines: 2 General Electric CF6-80A2.

8   "Final Report on the Collapse of the World Trade Center Towers," National Institute of Standards and Technology (September 2005): 20.

9   *9/11*, Jules and Gédéon Naudet, documentary (2002).

10   "Transcripts of Dispatch Records from 9/11/01," Fire Department of the City of New York. Manhattan master tape 442.

11   Ibid.

12   Firefighter Frank Sweeney interviewed by the FDNY World Trade Center Task Force, October 18, 2001.

13   Interview with Chris Ganci by Dina Zingaro, 2018.

14   National Fallen Firefighters Foundation, www.firehero.org/fallen-firefighter/peter-j-ganci-jr/.

15   Chief of Operations Daniel Nigro interviewed by the FDNY World Trade Center Task Force, October 24, 2001.

16   Fire Marshall Steven Mosiello interviewed by the FDNY World Trade Center Task Force, October 21, 2001.

17   Chief of Operations Daniel Nigro interviewed by the FDNY World Trade Center Task Force, October 24, 2001.

18   "Transcripts of Dispatch Records from 9/11/01," FDNY.

19   Ibid.

20   Spinelli family audio recording supplied to the author.

21   "The Children of September," CBS *60 Minutes II*, October 17, 2001.

22   Albert Turi, "Peter Ganci, A Firefighter's Firefighter," *The Farmingdale Observer* (September 13, 2016).

23   Deputy Assistant Chief Albert Turi interviewed by the FDNY World Trade Center Task Force, October 23, 2001.

24   Firefighter Scott Holowach interviewed by the FDNY World Trade Center Task Force, October 18, 2001.

25   "Final Report on the Collapse of the World Trade Center Towers," 38.

26   *The 9/11 Commission Report: Final Report of the National Commission on*

Terrorist Attacks Upon the United States (W. W. Norton & Co., 2004), 293.

27   "Final Report on the Collapse of the World Trade Center Towers," 39.

28   Ibid., 42.

29   "9/11 Commission Report," 293.

30   "Final Report on the Collapse of the World Trade Center Towers," 6.

31   David A. Fenella, Arnaldo Derecho, S.K. Ghosh, "Design and Construction of Structural Systems, Federal Building and Fire Safety Investigation of the World Trade Center Disaster," National Institute of Standards and Technology (2005).

32   "Final Report on the Collapse of the World Trade Center Towers," 10.

33   Leslie Robertson interview with Dina Zingaro, 2018.

34   Ibid.

35   "Final Report on the Collapse of the World Trade Center Towers," 6.

36   "The World Trade Center Bombing: Report and Analysis," Federal Emergency Management Agency (February 1993).

37   "World Trade Center Bombing," FBI Famous Cases, www.fbi.gov/history/famous-cases.

38   "Final Report on the Collapse of the World Trade Center Towers," 19.

39   "FDNY Vital Statistics," Fire Department of the City of New York.

40   Lieutenant Gary Gates interviewed by the FDNY World Trade Center Task Force, October 12, 2001.

41   "Final Report on the Collapse of the World Trade Center Towers," 136.

42   EMS Chief Zachery Goldfarb, interviewed by the FDNY World Trade Center Task Force, October 23, 2001.

43   Deputy Assistant Chief Albert Turi, interviewed by the FDNY World Trade Center Task Force, October 23, 2001.

44   Assistant Chief Joseph Callan, interviewed by the FDNY World Trade Center Task Force, November 2, 2001.

45   "Answers to Frequently Asked Questions," National Institute of Standards and Technology, accessed August 30, 2006, www.nist.gov.

46   Chief Joseph Pfeifer, interviewed by the FDNY World Trade Center Task Force, October 23, 2001.

47   Firefighter Edward Cachia, interviewed by the FDNY World Trade Center Task Force, December 6, 2001.

48   Deputy Assistant Chief Albert Turi, interviewed by the FDNY World Trade Center Task Force, October 23, 2001.

49   "Flight Path Study American Flight 77," National Transportation Safety Board (February 2002).

50   "9/11 Commission Report," 314.

51   Lawson and Vettori, "The Emergency Response Operations," 16.

52   "Final Report on the Collapse of the World Trade Center Towers," 31.

53   Ibid.

54   Lawson and Vettori, "The Emergency Response Operations."

55   "9/11 Commission Report," 299.

56   "Final Report on the Collapse of the World Trade Center Towers," xi.

57   Ibid., 155.

58   "9/11 Commission Report," 285.

59   "Final Report on the Collapse of the World Trade Center Towers," 24.

60   Lawson and Vettori, "The Emergency Response Operations," 214.

61   Ibid.

62   Fire Marshal Steven Mosiello interviewed by the FDNY World Trade Center Task Force, October 23, 2001.

63   Firefighter Richard Boeri interviewed by the FDNY World Trade Center Task Force, December 10, 2001.

64   "9/11 Commission Report," 309.

65   Firefighter Derek Brogan interviewed by the FDNY World Trade Center Task Force, December 28, 2001.

66   Rudy Giuliani interviewed by *Forbes* on the tenth anniversary of 9/11, 2011.

67   *FDNY 9/11 Response* (McKinsey and Company, 2002), 3.

68   Lawson and Vettori, "The Emergency Response Operations."

69   *FDNY 9/11 Response*, 6.

70   "Final Report on the Collapse of the World Trade Center Towers," xxxvii.

71   Ibid., xxxviii.

72   "Final Report on the Collapse of the World Trade Center Towers," 154.

73   Ibid.

74   *United States v. Zacarias Moussaoui, Criminal No. 01-455-A,* US District Court, Eastern District of Virginia, Prosecution Exhibit P200016.

75 "Final Report on the Collapse of the World Trade Center Towers," 38.

76 Lawson and Vettori, "The Emergency Response Operations," 209.

77 "Federal Building and Fire Safety Investigation of the World Trade Center Disaster," National Institute of Standards and Technology (September 2005).

78 "Final Report on the Collapse of the World Trade Center Towers," xxxviii.

79 Ibid., xxxix.

80 John Peruggia interviewed by the FDNY World Trade Center Task Force, October 25, 2001.

81 Richard Zarrillo interviewed by the FDNY World Trade Center Task Force, October 25, 2001.

82 Fire Marshal Steven Mosiello interviewed by the FDNY World Trade Center Task Force, October 23, 2001.

83 Richard Zarrillo interviewed by the FDNY World Trade Center Task Force, October 25, 2001.

84 Fire Marshal Steven Mosiello interviewed by the FDNY World Trade Center Task Force, October 23, 2001.

85 Deputy Assistant Chief Albert Turi interviewed by the FDNY World Trade Center Task Force, October 23, 2001.

86 "Final Report on the Collapse of the World Trade Center Towers," 44.

87 Lieutenant Gary Gates interviewed by the FDNY World Trade Center Task Force, October 12, 2001.

88 Richard Zarrillo interviewed by the FDNY World Trade Center Task Force, October 25, 2001.

89 Captain Michael Donovan interviewed by the FDNY World Trade Center Task Force, November 9, 2001.

90 Firefighter Christopher Murray interviewed by the FDNY World Trade Center Task Force, December 12, 2001.

91 Lieutenant Neil Brosnan interviewed by the FDNY World Trade Center Task Force, December 12, 2001.

92 Battalion Chief Brian O'Flaherty interviewed by the FDNY World Trade Center Task Force, January 9, 2002.

93 Chief Salvatore Cassano interviewed by the FDNY World Trade Center Task Force, October 4, 2001.

94 Fire Marshal Steven Mosiello interviewed by the FDNY World Trade Center Task Force, October 23, 2001.

95 Ibid.

96   "9/11 Commission Report," 307.

97   "Final Report on the Collapse of the World Trade Center Towers," 85.

98   "Patrick J. Brown," National Fallen Firefighters Foundation, www.firehero.org/fallen-firefighter/patrick-j-brown/.

99   "Final Report on the Collapse of the World Trade Center Towers," 33.

100 Paramedic Karen Lamanna interviewed by the FDNY World Trade Center Task Force, January 23, 2002.

101 Deputy Assistant Chief Albert Turi interviewed by the FDNY World Trade Center Task Force, October 23, 2001.

102 "9/11 Commission Report," 10.

103 Ibid., 11.

104 Ibid., 14.

105 Ibid.

106 Fire Marshal Steven Mosiello interviewed by the FDNY World Trade Center Task Force, October 23, 2001.

107 Lieutenant John Mendez interviewed by the FDNY World Trade Center Task Force, October 31, 2001.

108 Deputy Assistant Chief Albert Turi interviewed by the FDNY World Trade Center Task Force, October 23, 2001.

109 Captain Ray Goldbach interviewed by the FDNY World Trade Center Task Force, October 24, 2001.

110 Captain Michael Donovan interviewed by the FDNY World Trade Center Task Force, November 9, 2001.

111 Ibid.

112 Fire Marshal Steven Mosiello interviewed by the FDNY World Trade Center Task Force, October 23, 2001.

113 Lawson and Vettori, "The Emergency Response Operations," 86.

114 Chief Joseph Pfeifer interviewed by the FDNY World Trade Center Task Force, October 23, 2001.

115 "Brooklyn Bravest Found at WTC 3," *New York Daily News,* January 3, 2002.

116 "Fiscal 2018 Preliminary (NYC) Mayor's Management Report for the Office of the Chief Medical Examiner," City of New York (March 20, 2018), 8.

117 D-Day Plaque Project, National D-Day Memorial Foundation, www.dday.org/d-day-plaque-project. "2,499 fatalities were from the United States."

118   "Fiscal 2018 Preliminary (NYC) Mayor's Management Report for the Office of the Chief Medical Examiner," City of New York (March 20, 2018), 8.

119   Ibid.

120   "Final Report on the Collapse of the World Trade Center Towers."

Chapter Two
Resolve: President Bush on 9/11

1   "9/11 Commission Report," 27.

2   Raymond Lowey, *Industrial Design* (The Overlook Press, 1979).

3   Rudi Williams, "Reagan Makes First, Last Flight in Jet He Ordered," American Forces Press Service (June 10, 2013).

4   The White House Historical Society, "The White House Mansion is 168 feet long." Also, "Air Force One," Boeing, http://www.boeing.com/defense/air-force-one/index.page, "Aircraft length 231 feet."

5   Federal Aviation Administration transcript.

6   Ari Fleischer, White House Press Secretary. Contemporaneous notes shared with the author.

7   "9/11 Commission Report," 212.

8   "Hijackers Timeline," Federal Bureau of Investigation.

9   "9/11 Commission Report," 213.

10   Ibid., 206.

11   Drawing of Proposed Library Table to be made from timber of the late Arctic Ship *Resolute* for presentation to the President of the United States of America, September 1879, Collection of the Royal Museums Greenwich.

12   "Treasures of the Resolute Desk," White House Historical Association, Office of the Curator, The White House.

13   "Presidential Statement—Draft 2," The US National Archives.

Field Note
Meeting the Late Don Hewitt in Botswana

1   "Botswana," *The World Factbook*, US Central Intelligence Agency (2018). In the Setswana language, the plural demonym is Batswana. The singular is Motswana.

Chapter Three
Selflessness: Paulette Schank

1   "Low Blood Pressure (hypotension)," Mayo Clinic. A blood pressure reading lower than 60mm Hg for the bottom (diastolic) number is generally considered low.

2   "Hemoglobin test," Mayo Clinic (December 2017). Normal Range for hemoglobin in men is 13.5 to 17.5 grams per deciliter.

3   Peter Dorland and James Nanney, *Dust Off: Army Aeromedical Evacuation in Vietnam*, Center of Military History United States Army (2008). "Arriving in April 1962, the 57th [Medical Detachment (Helicopter Ambulance)] remained through the next eleven years of American military involvement in [Vietnam]."

4   The Geneva Conventions. Chapter IV, Article 24 (1949). "Medical personnel exclusively engaged in the search for, or the collection, transport or treatment of the wounded or sick…shall be respected and protected in all circumstances."

5   M. M. Manning, Alan Hawk, Jason Calhoun, Romney Andersen, "Treatment of War Wounds: A Historical Review," *Clinical Orthopaedics and Related Research* (February 2009).

6   Walt Whitman, *Leaves of Grass*, Book XXI Drum-Taps (1855).

7   David Rice, George Kotti, William Beninati, "Clinical Review: Critical care transport and austere critical care," *Critical Care* (March 2008).

8   Matthew S. Goldberg, PhD, "Death and Injury Rates of U.S. Military Personnel in Iraq," *Military Medicine*, vol. 175 (April 2010): 223.

Chapter Four
Authenticity: Bruce Springsteen

1   19th Annual GRAMMY Awards (1976), Recording Academy Grammy Awards, www.grammy.com/awards/19th-annual-grammy-awards.

2   Recording Academy Grammy Awards. Springsteen would continue to add to his Grammy collection. As of 2018, he had twenty gramophone statues. In addition, his albums *Born to Run* and *Born in the U.S.A.* were inducted into the GRAMMY Hall of Fame.

Chapter Five
Devotion: David Hall

1   AI. N. Oikonomides, *Alexander the Great at Alexandria in Arachosia (Old Kandahar)* (Zeitschrift fur Papyrologie und Epigraphik, 1984), 145-147.

2   Peter Molnar, "The Geologic History and Structure of the Himalaya," *American Scientist*, vol. 74, no. 2 (1986): 144–154.

3   World Bank. Country Profile, Afghanistan. World Development Indicators Database.

4   Ibid.

5   Paul Bernard, "Hellenistic Arachosia," *East and West*, vol. 55, no. 1/4, Istituto Italiano per l'Africa e l'Oriente (December 2005): 13–34.

6   Ibid.

7   Louis Dupree, *Afghanistan* (Oxford University Press, 1973).

8   Rudyard Kipling, "The Young British Soldier," *The Scots Observer* (June 28, 1890).

9   Amineh Ahmed, "Understanding The Taliban Case Through History and the Contest of Pukhtunwali," *The Cambridge Journal of Anthropology*, vol. 22, no. 3 (2001): 86–92.

10   Ibid., 87.

11   Nick Cullather, "Damming Afghanistan: Modernization in a Buffer State," *The Journal of American History* (September 2002): 512–537.

12   William Shakespeare, *The Life of King Henry V*, Act IV, Scene III, The English camp at Agincourt, c. 1599.

13   Joint Publication 4-06, *Mortuary Affairs*, Office of the Joint Chiefs of Staff (October 2011): IV-47.

14   2018 Trafficking in Persons Report, *Afghanistan*, Office to Monitor and Combat Trafficking in Persons, United States Department of State.

Field Note
Kremlin Rules

1   Arthur Voyce, *The Moscow Kremlin: Its History, Architecture and Art Treasures* (University of California Press, 1954), 12.

2   Winston Churchill, *The Russian Enigma*, BBC Broadcast, October 1, 1939.

3   The Soviet flag was lowered at the Kremlin for the last time on December 25, 1991.

4   Aviation Safety Network, Flight Safety Foundation, https://aviation-safety.net/database/operator/airline.php?var=6834. 144 accidents and incidents in database.

5   David Weber, *Changing Sacredness and Historical Memory of Moscow's Red Square,* Studies in Slavic Cultures (University of Pittsburg), 53.

6   Arthur Voyce. *The Moscow Kremlin.*

7   Securities and Exchange Commission, *Dow Jones Industrial Average*, August 28, 1998, 8051.68, August 31, 1998, 7539.04.

8   Dow Jones Incorporated, *All-Time Largest One Day Gains and Losses.*

9   Indirectly, Shebarshin may have been right. The former spy master suffered a stroke, perhaps a complication of chain smoking. The stroke left him blind. In 2012, Russian media reported he committed suicide with the ceremonial pistol he was given on retirement. Shebarshin was seventy-seven.

Chapter Six
Audacity: Ben Bernanke

1   "The Recession of 2007-2009," US Bureau of Labor Statistics (February 2012).

2   "Child Poverty in the United States," American Community Survey Briefs, US Census Bureau (November 2011).

3   "The Financial Crisis Inquiry Report," National Commission on the Causes of the Financial and Economic Crisis in the United States (January 2011).

4   Ibid.

5   Stephen Cecchetti, "Crisis and Responses: The Federal Reserve in the Early Stages of the Financial Crisis," *Journal of Economic Perspectives*, vol. 23, no. 1 (Winter 2009): 68.

6   Federal Reserve Annual Report, 1928. Federal Reserve FRASER archive.

7   For expert counsel on this shameless condensation of the scholarship of Friedman and Schwartz, the author received guidance from Michael Bordo, Board of Governors Professor of Economics at Rutgers University. Dr. Bordo was a student of Friedman who worked with Schwartz. He is the author of ten books on the history of monetary policy.

8   Ben S. Bernanke, "The Subprime Mortgage Market," Speech before the Federal Reserve Bank of Chicago 43rd Annual Conference, May 2007.

9   Ben S. Bernanke, Subprime Mortgage Lending and Mitigating Foreclosures, Testimony before the House Committee on Financial Services, July 20, 2007.

10   "Financial Crisis Timeline," Federal Reserve Bank of St. Louis.

11   "Clinton County AFB, OH," https://www.globalsecurity.org/wmd/facility/clinton_county.htm.

12   Statistical data from Stacey Standish and Gary Steinberg, US Bureau of Labor Statistics, and Howard Silverblatt, Sr. Industry Analyst for Standard & Poors Down Jones Indices. Interviews with Dina Zingaro, June 4, 2018.

13   *America Builds: The Record of PWA*, by Public Works Administration. Professor of American History Jason Smith, author of *Building New Deal Liberalism: The Political Economy of Public Works, 1933-1956*. Interview with Dina Zingaro, 2018.

14   Federal Reserve Bulletin (September 1937). Federal Reserve FRASER archive.

15   "Federal Reserve History," Board of Governors of the Federal Reserve (April 2017).

16   "The Public Papers and Addresses of Franklin D. Roosevelt," University of Michigan, 459.

17   "Powers of the Federal Reserve. (3) Discounts for individuals, partnerships, and corporations," Federal Reserve Act, Section 13.

18   Robert McDonald, Professor of Finance at Northwestern University and Research Associate at National Bureau of Economic Research. Interview with Dina Zingaro, 2018.

19   Mauro Guillen, "The Global Economic & Financial Crisis: A Timeline," The Lauder Institute, Wharton School, University of Pennsylvania, https://lauder.wharton.upenn.edu/wp-content/uploads/2015/06/Chronology_Economic_Financial_Crisis.pdf.

20   Standard & Poors. Fannie Mae and Freddie Mac mortgage share 43.8 percent.

21   Mauro Guillen, "The Global Economic & Financial Crisis."

22   "The Financial Crisis Inquiry Report," National Commission on the Causes of the Financial and Economic Crisis in the United States (January 2011).

23   Ibid., 139.

24   "The Financial Crisis Inquiry Report."

25   Ibid., 352. "The Commission concludes AIG failed and was rescued by the government primarily because its enormous sales of credit default swaps were made without putting up initial collateral, setting aside capital reserves, or hedging its exposure—a profound failure in corporate governance..."

26   Ibid., 344.

27   Federal Reserve, "American International Group, Maiden Lane II and III," Regulatory Reform, February 12, 2016.

28   Ben S. Bernanke, *The Courage to Act: A Memoir of Crisis and Its Aftermath* (W. W. Norton & Company).

29   Henry M. Paulson, Jr., *On the Brink: Inside the Race to Stop the Collapse of the Global Financial System* (2011). Before joining the Treasury Department, Paulson had a 32-year career at Goldman Sachs, serving as chairman and chief executive officer following the firm's initial public offering in 1999.

30   "Goldman Sachs Agrees to Pay more than $5 Billion in Connection with its Sale of Residential Mortgage Backed Securities," The United States Department of Justice, April 11, 2016, https://www.justice.gov/opa/pr/goldman-sachs-agrees-pay-more-5-billion-connection-its-sale-residential-mortgage-backed.

31   The crash of 777 points is now the second largest point drop. On February 5, 2018 the Dow Industrial Average fell 1,175.

32   "Labor Force Statistics from the Current Population Survey," Bureau of Labor Statistics. Rather than using the traditional unemployment rate, I prefer the Bureau of Labor Statistics "U-6" data. U-6 is the total unemployed plus those who are forced to work part-time while looking for full-time work. The U-6 total peaked in April, 2010 at 17.1 percent.

33   "Rescuing the Economy from the Great Recession," Government Publishing Office: 42–43.

34   "Federal Reserve Bank Credit," Annual Report, Federal Reserve Bank of San Francisco (2008).

35   John Weinberg, "Federal Reserve Credit Programs During the Meltdown," Federal Reserve History, Federal Reserve (November 22, 2015).

36   "Impact of the Federal Reserve's Quantitative Easing Programs on Fannie Mae and Freddie Mac," Federal Housing Finance Agency Office of Inspector General.

37   Ben S. Bernanke interview with the author. *60 Minutes* (CBS, 2009).

38   "The Financial Crisis Inquiry Report," 350.

39   "Federal Reserve's Assets," Federal Reserve Board (2017).

40   Larry Neal and Eric Schubert, "The First Rational Bubbles: A New Look at the Mississippi and South Sea Schemes" (University of Illinois Urbana-Champaign, September 1985).

41   Will Durant and Ariel Durant, *The Age of Voltaire: The Story of Civilization*, vol. 9 (Simon and Schuster, June 2011).

42   E. S. Browning, "Wild Day Caps Worst Week Ever for Stocks," *Wall Street Journal* (October 11, 2008).

43   Abraham Lincoln, "Cooper Union Address," New York (February 27, 1860).

44   Ben S. Bernanke, *The Courage to Act*.

45   "Mortgage Originations and Delinquency and Foreclosure Rates 1990 to 2009," US Census Bureau, Statistical Abstract of the United States 2011, 743.

46   United States Department of Justice press release (June 25, 2013).

47   Federal Reserve Consent Decree press release (April 13, 2011).

48   Statistical data from Stacey Standish and Gary Steinberg, US Bureau of Labor Statistics, and Howard Silverblatt, Sr. Industry Analyst for Standard & Poors Down Jones Indices. Interviews with Dina Zingaro (June 2018).

49   Howard Silverblatt, Sr. Industry Analyst for Standard & Poors Down Jones Indices. Interview with Dina Zingaro (June 2018).

50   "Labor Force Statistics from the Current Population Survey" Series ID LNS 13327709. Series Title: Total unemployed, plus all marginally attached workers, plus total employed part time for economic reasons, as a percent of all civilian labor force, plus all marginally attached workers. Seasonally Adjusted. Bureau of Labor Statistics (October 17, 2018).

Chapter Seven
Invincibility: Nadia Murad

1   Eszter Spat, "Religious Oral Tradition and Literacy among the Yezidis of Iraq," *Anthropos*, Bd. 103 (2008): 393-403.

2   Garnik Asatrian, Victoria Arakelova, "Malak-Tawus: The Peacock Angel of the Yezidis," *Iran and the Caucasus*, vol. 7 (2003): 1-36.

3   W. B. Heard, "Notes on the Yezidis," *The Journal of the Royal Anthropological Institute of Great Britain and Ireland*, vol. 41 (1911): 200-219.

4   Eva Savelsberg, Siamend Hajo and Irene Dulz, "Effectively Urbanized: Yezidis in the collective towns of Sheikhan and Sinjar," *Etudes Rurales*, no. 186 (2010): 101-116.

5   Nadia Murad with Jenna Krajeski, *The Last Girl: My Story of Cap-*

tivity, and My Fight Against the Islamic State (New York: Tim Duggan Books, 2017).

Chapter Eight
Gratitude: Early Lessons

1   Art Leatherwood, *Llano Estacado*, Texas State Historical Association.

2   Andrew J. Torget, *Seeds of Empire: Cotton, Slavery, and the Transformation of the Texas Borderlands 1800-1850*, The University of North Carolina Press, Chapel Hill (2015). "Texas must be a slave country," [Austin] declared, "circumstances and unavoidable necessity compels it."

3   Constitution of the Republic of Texas (1836) General Provisions. Section 9. "Congress shall pass no laws to prohibit emigrants from the United States of America from bringing their slaves into the Republic with them, and holding them by the same tenure by which such slaves were held in the United States; nor shall Congress have power to emancipate slaves; nor shall any slave-holder be allowed to emancipate his or her slave or slaves, without the consent of Congress, unless he or she shall send his or her slave or slaves without the limits of the Republic. No free person of African descent, either in whole or in part, shall be permitted to reside permanently in the Republic, without the consent of Congress, and the importation or admission of Africans or negroes into this Republic, excepting from the United States of America, is forever prohibited, and declared to be piracy."

4   *Cotton Producing Regions of Texas*, Texas A & M University.

5   "Maud Couple's Vows are Read in California," *The Daily Oklahoman* (May 9, 1943).

6   "Certificate in recognition of wartime service," Wanda Jean Graves. United States Navy Bureau of Aeronautics (May 16, 1942).

7   "Prime Time Access Rule," *Encyclopedia of Television*, Museum of Broadcast Communications. "With respect to the development of community-oriented local programming, the PTAR was a dismal failure, as most local television stations opted to purchase inexpensive syndicated entertainment programming, such as game shows to fill the access hour rather than developing their own public-affairs programs."

8   *Adweek*. "For 2nd Straight Week, *CBS Evening News* Ties Lowest Viewership Ever. Last week, the *CBS Evening News* averaged 4.89 million total viewers." (August 31, 2010).

9   CBS Press Express (June 6, 2016). "The 'CBS EVENING NEWS WITH SCOTT PELLEY' finished the season by delivering the largest audience in the time period for CBS in 10 years. The CBS broadcast

also added the most viewers among the network evening news broadcasts (7.35m, up +2% from 7.23m a year ago). The broadcast posted its sixth consecutive season of growth, a first for a network evening newscast since the 1987 advent of people meters. Since Scott Pelley became anchor in June 2011, the 'CBS EVENING NEWS' has added +1.4 million viewers, double the growth of ABC and NBC combined."

10   CBS Press Express (September 20, 2016). "The 'CBS EVENING NEWS WITH SCOTT PELLEY' finished with CBS's highest ratings in the time period in 10 years (since the 2005-06 broadcast year). This year marks the sixth consecutive broadcast year of viewer gains for the CBS EVENING NEWS, the first time any network evening news broadcast posted six consecutive broadcast years of viewer gains in the 28 years since the advent of Nielsen people meters in 1987. Additionally, the 'CBS EVENING NEWS WITH SCOTT PELLEY' closed the viewership gap with NBC by 113,000 viewers compared to last year—the closest CBS has been to NBC in viewers for a broadcast year in 15 years (since 2000-2001)."

11   CBS Press Express (November 10, 2015). "The 'CBS Evening News with Scott Pelley' Posts The Biggest Audience Gains Among The Network Evening News Broadcasts. The 'CBS EVENING NEWS WITH SCOTT PELLEY' posted the largest year-to-year increase in viewers (+4%, 7.57m from 7.25m) among the network evening news broadcasts for the week ending November 6, according to Nielsen live plus same day ratings."

12   CBS Press Express (August 2, 2016). "The 'CBS EVENING NEWS WITH SCOTT PELLEY' posted its best July Sweep delivery in adults 25-54 in three years (since July 2013). CBS is in its closest competitive position with ABC in adults 25-54 for a July Sweep in at least 22 years (since at least the July 1994 Sweep, which marks the start of CBS electronic sweep records). CBS was just 0.1 ratings point off ABC in adults 25-54 for the July 2016 Sweep."

13   CBS Press Express (June 1, 2016). "The 'CBS EVENING NEWS WITH SCOTT PELLEY,' America's fastest growing network evening news broadcast, finished the 2015-16 television season with CBS's highest ratings in the time period in 10 years (since the 2005-06 season), according to Nielsen most current ratings. The 'CBS EVENING NEWS' has grown its audience for six consecutive seasons, a first-time achievement for any network evening news broadcast since the advent of people meters (since at least 1987). Under Pelley, who assumed the anchor chair in June 2011, the 'CBS EVENING NEWS' has added +1.4 million viewers and an audience increase of +23%,

which is double NBC and ABC's growth combined over the same period (since the 2010-11 season)."

Chapter Nine
Duty: Lessons in War

1 William Shakespeare, *King Lear.*

2 Heather Woods, "Ancient rocks and modern collaborations in Saudi Arabia," School of Earth, Energy & Environmental Sciences, Stanford University (2013).

3 Mohamed Boukhary, Osman Abdelghany, et al., "Upper Eocene Larger Foraminifera from the Damman Formation," *Micropaleontology*, vol. 51, no. 6 (2005): 487-504.

4 Rasoul Sorkhabi, "Max Steineke (1898-1952): A Pioneer American Geologist in the Early History of Oil Exploration in Saudi Arabia," Petroleum History Institute, 2012.

5 Hamed A. El-Nakhal, "New observations on the geological age of the Dammam Formation in Arabia," *Micropaleontology*, vol. 34, no. 3 (1988): 284-285.

6 "Japanese Sign Final Surrender," US National Archive, Archival Research Catalog Identifier 39079.

7 "United States Battleship Missouri, The second decommissioning Program," US Navy (March 31, 1992).

8 Harry Butowsky, *Warships Associated with World War II in the Pacific*, National Park Service History Division (May 1995).

9 "16-inch" refers to the gun caliber, the approximate internal diameter of the barrel.

10 *Thunder and Lightning—The War with Iraq*, Naval History and Heritage Command.

11 *War Chronology: January 1991*, Naval History and Heritage Command.

12 "Theater Ballistic Missile Systems and Capabilities," *Arms Control Today*, The Arms Control Association (March 1996).

13 Javed Ali, *The Nonproliferation Review* (Spring 2001).

14 Bob Simon, *Forty Days* (G. P. Putnam's Sons, 1992).

15 J. C. Humphrey, "Casualty management: scud missile attack, Dhahran, Saudi Arabia," US National Library of Medicine, National Institutes of Health (May, 1999).

16 "Senate Concurrent Resolution 32 Recognizing the soldiers of the

14th Quartermaster Detachment," Congressional Record (February 25, 2016).

17   "War in the Persian Gulf: Operations Desert Shield and Desert Storm August 1990–March 1991," Center of Military History, US Army.

18   S. S. Goldich, "A Study in Rock Weathering," *Journal of Geology* 46 (1938), 17–58.

19   "War in the Persian Gulf."

20   Ibid., 38–40.

21   "War in the Persian Gulf."

22   Scott Althaus, Brittany Bramlett, James Gimpel, "When War Hits Home: The Geography of Military Losses and Support for War in Time and Space," University of Illinois Urbana-Champaign.

23   S. S. Gartner, G. Segura. "War, Casualties, and Public Opinion," *The Journal of Conflict Resolution* (June, 1998) 278–300.

24   Mark Lorell, Charles Kelley, Jr., "Casualties, Public Opinion and Presidential Policy During the Vietnam War," The Rand Corporation, Prepared for the US Air Force (March 1985).

25   John E. Mueller, *War, Presidents and Public Opinion* (John Wiley & Sons, 1973).

26   Craig Chamberlain, "Did news coverage turn Americans against the Vietnam War?" University of Illinois Urbana-Champaign.

27   Vietnam War Fatal Casualty Statistics, National Archive.

28   "Report to Congress United States Gulf Environmental Technical Assistance," US Environmental Protection Agency (January 1992).

29   "Report to Congress United States Gulf Environmental Technical Assistance."

30   W. M. Christenson and Robert Zirkle, "73 Easting Battle Replication," Institute for Defense Analyses (September 1992).

31   "Correspondent Charles Collingwood reports on D-Day," Library of Congress, LCCN 2004653885.

Field Note
The Last Shuttle

1   The Association of Schools of Journalism and Mass Communications, Journalist-in-Space Project, *Final Report*, July 31, 1986. Semifinalists. Scott C. Pelley of Dallas, Texas, reporter WFAA-TV.

2   Three Apollo astronauts, Gus Grissom, Ed White and Roger Chaffey

died previously in a fire during a countdown test on the launch pad on January 27, 1967.

3   "The Orbiter," National Aeronautics and Space Administration, www. nasa.gov/returntoflight/system.

4   Depending on the round, a rifle bullet flies at 1,700 miles per hour. To establish a sustainable orbit, any object, including the Space Shuttle, must reach 17,500 mph.

5   Alfred Hogan, "Televising the Space Age: A Descriptive Chronology of CBS News Special Coverage of Space Exploration from 1957 to 2003," University of Maryland, 2005.

6   "Space Shuttle Era Facts" (NASA, April 2012). The shuttle *Challenger* was destroyed on liftoff on January 28, 1986. The shuttle *Columbia* broke apart on reentry on February 1, 2003.

Chapter Ten
Vision: Elon Musk

1   Frank Markus, "2017 Tesla Model S P100D First Test," *Motor Trend* (February 7, 2017). "A new record zero to 60 in 2.28 seconds."

2   Johnny Lieberman, "Lamborghini Huracan LP 610-4 First Test," *Motor Trend* (March 9, 2015). "Zero to 60 mph in 2.8 seconds."

3   2013 Tesla Model S, National Highway Transportation Safety Administration, US Department of Transportation.

4   "Elon Musk Settles SEC Fraud Charges," US Securities and Exchange Commission, September 29, 2018.

5   "Technocracy Leader Charged at Regina," *Ottawa Journal* (October 14, 1940).

6   Joseph Keating, Jr. and Scott Haldeman, "Joshua N. Haldeman, DC: the Canadian Years, 1926-1950," *Journal of the Canadian Chiropractic Association* (1995).

7   Scott Haldeman, Photograph of Joshua and Winnifred Haldeman, Cape to Algiers motor rally.

8   Photograph of Haldeman with P.M. Menzies, *International Review of Chiropractic* (December 1954).

9   "Falcon 9 and Dragon demonstration flight," SpaceX Launch Manifest (December 8, 2010).

10   "NASA Resupply Mission to ISS," SpaceX Launch Manifest (November 8, 2012).

11   "NASDAQ Tesla Incorporated Market Summary," NYSE Market

Summary (July 2018). Market Capitalization $52.57 billion. Ford Market Capitalization $41.99 billion.

Chapter Eleven
Objectivity: Learning from Unpleasant Truth

1   Russell Wheeler, Charles Bufe, Margo Johnson, and Richard Dart, "Seismotectonic Map of Afghanistan," US Geological Survey (2005).

2   Stephen Peters, "Summary of the Panjsher Valley Emerald, Iron, and Silver Area of Interest," Summary of Important Areas for Mineral Investment and Production Opportunities of Nonfuel Minerals in Afghanistan, US Geological Survey (2011).

3   Wheeler, et al., "Seismotectonic Map of Afghanistan."

4   "Troops Capture Terrorists in Afghanistan; Rocket Misses Coalition Base," DoD News, US Department of Defense (March 6, 2007).

5   "Iraq Body Count, Conflict Casualties Monitor" (May 2018), Iraqbodycount.org. Total violent deaths including combatants, 288,000.

6   "DCI Statement on the Belgrade Chinese Embassy Bombing," CIA (July 22, 1999).

7   "Troops Capture Terrorists in Afghanistan; Rocket Misses Coalition Base," DoD News, US Department of Defense (March 6, 2007).

8   "J-FIRE Multiservice Procedures for the Joint Application of Firepower," Air Land Sea Application Center, November 1997. Table 12. Risk Estimate Distances for Aircraft Delivered Ordinance. Mk-84 10% Probability of incapacitation within 225 Meters.

9   Lasha Tchantouridze, "Counterinsurgency in Afghanistan: Comparing Canadian and Soviet Efforts," *International Journal*, vol. 68, no. 2 (June 2013): 334. "More than one million people died of inflicted wounds, exposure, starvation, deprivation and unsanitary conditions while hundreds of thousands were injured, maimed and sickened."

10   Ian Livingston, Heather Messera, Michael O'Hanlon, "Afghanistan Index: Tracking Variables of Reconstruction & Security in Post-9/11 Afghanistan," Brookings Institution (February 5, 2010).

11   FOIA Request ID FY07-0251, filed August 27, 2007.

12   US Special Operations Command, 2011 FOIA log, "CONSULT CENTCOM:" Request ID 2011-H-189.

13   Michael Bulkley and Gregory Davis, "The Study of Rapid Acquisition Mine Resistant Ambush Protected (MRAP) Vehicle Program and its Impact on the Warfighter," Naval Postgraduate School, June 2013. MaxxPro Per Vehicle Costs $774,639.

Chapter Twelve
Hubris: Trump v. Clinton

1   Historical Election Results, National Archives and Records Administration.

2   "History of Lorain, OH," Lorain Public Library.

3   US Census data tables, time-series, P-4 for male/female historic median income. https://www.census.gov/data/tables/time-series/demo/income-poverty/historical-income-people.html.

4   World Bank, "China's Modernizing Labor Market: Trends and Emerging Challenges," 78. Human Development United East Asia and Pacific Region (August 2007). In 2001, 95% of China's labor force had education below the college level.

5   "Percentage of labor force by educational attainment, 25 years and over, 2016 annual averages," Bureau of Labor Statistics, Profile of the Labor Force by Educational Attainment (August 2017). "No college = 27%."

6   "Selected Measures of Household Income Dispersion," US Census Bureau Current Population Survey. Also, Thomas Piketty, Emmanuel Saez and Gabriel Zucman, "Distributional National Accounts: Methods and Estimates for the United States," 2016, Cambridge, MA: National Bureau of Economic Research.

7   "Trump Loses Grip on Ohio," *Politico* (October 16, 2016).

8   US Bureau of Labor Statistics.

9   Stanley Lebergott, "Annual Estimates of Unemployment in the United States 1900-1954," Bureau of the Budget (1954): 215.

10   "2017 Infrastructure Report Card," American Society of Civil Engineers. "The US has 614,387 bridges, almost four in 10 of which are 50 years or older." "56,007 bridges or 9.1 percent were structurally deficient in 2016."

11   *United States of America v. Viktor Netyksho et al.* United States District Court for the District of Columbia (July 13, 2018).

12   Ibid., 7.

13   "2016 Official Presidential General Election Results," Federal Election Commission (January 2017).

14   Ibid.

15   Max Farrand, *The Records of the Federal Convention of 1787*, vol. 2.1 (Yale University Press, 1911). "Tuesday, September 4th. The honor-

able Mr. Brearley from the Committee of eleven informed the House that the Committee were prepared to report."

16 Max Farrand, *The Records of the Federal Convention of 1787*, vol. 2 (Yale University Press, 1911). "Septr [sic] 5."

17 "2016 Official Presidential General Election Results," Federal Election Commission (January 2017).

18 Ibid.

19 "2016 Official Presidential General Election Results." Wisconsin write-ins: 22,812. Pennsylvania write-ins: 43,601.

20 "Historical Election Results," US Electoral College, National Archives and Records Administration. Presidents who lost the popular vote. 1824, John Quincy Adams. 1840, William Henry Harrison. 1876, Rutherford B. Hayes. 2000, George W. Bush.

21 Walt Whitman, "By Blue Ontario's Shore," *Leaves of Grass*.

22 Anthony Salvanto, "Donald Trump and Hillary Clinton viewed unfavorably by majority," CBS News/*New York Times* Poll (March 21, 2016).

Chapter Thirteen
Skepticism: A Failure of Government and Journalism

1 "Iraq Body Count, Conflict Casualties Monitor" (May 2018), Iraqbodycount.org. Total violent deaths including combatants: 288,000.

2 Ibid.

3 Winston Churchill, Radio Interview, New York City (March 10, 1935).

4 Franklin D. Roosevelt at Work with his Personal Secretary, The White House Historical Association, photograph (1934). In the photograph, the chairs are in place on either side of the Hoover desk. FDR did not change the furnishings immediately after the Hoover administration. In reviewing the photographs of the White House Historical Association, I found the cane-back chairs have been silent witnesses to great moments in history. Oval Office furniture comes and goes but the chairs are seen, in varying upholstery, with presidents including FDR, Harry Truman, Dwight Eisenhower, JFK, LBJ, Richard Nixon, Gerald Ford, Jimmy Carter, Ronald Reagan, George H. W. Bush and Barack Obama in addition to George W. Bush.

5 The White House Museum.

6 World Bank. Iraq population 2002: 24,939,299.

7   Hearings before the Senate Armed Services Committee, June 5, 2001.

8   Ibid., February 27, 2001.

9   The American Presidency Project, UC Santa Barbara. Under President George H. W. Bush, Dr. Wolfowitz served as Undersecretary of Defense for Policy. President Bush Nominates Paul Wolfowitz Deputy Secretary of Defense (February 5, 2001).

10 "Department of Defense Key Officials." "Scooter" served as deputy undersecretary of defense for policy under George H. W. Bush.

11 State Department, Office of the Historian. In 1987 Rice served as an advisor to the Joint Chiefs of Staff, and in 1989 was appointed director of Soviet and East European Affairs on the National Security Council. In 2001 she was appointed National Security Advisor by President George W. Bush, and succeeded Colin Powell as Secretary of State in 2005.

12 United States Institute for Peace. From January 20, 2001 to January 20, 2005, Hadley was the assistant to the president and deputy national security advisor, serving under then National Security Advisor Condoleezza Rice. From 1989 to 1993, Hadley served as the assistant secretary of defense for international security policy under then Secretary of Defense Dick Cheney.

13 White House archives. Between 1991 and 1992, Dr. Khalilzad served as Assistant Deputy Under Secretary of Defense for Policy Planning.

14 "Secretary Rumsfeld and General Franks Speak to Reporters," C-Span (November 27, 2001).

15 "The Iraq War—Part I: The U.S. Prepares for Conflict, 2001," The National Security Archive (September 2010), https://nsarchive2.gwu.edu.

16 "The State of the Union Address by the President of the United States," Congressional Record, vol. 149, issue 15 (January 28, 2003).

17 Steven Hadley, Deputy National Security Advisor, Iraq Weapons of Mass Destruction and the State of the Union Speech, Press Briefing, The White House (July 22, 2003).

18 Dan Bartlett, White House Communications Director, Iraq Weapons of Mass Destruction and the State of the Union Speech, Press Briefing, The White House (July 22, 2003).

19 "Remarks by the President in Michigan Welcome," The White House, Waterford, Michigan (October 14, 2002).

20 "President Delivers the State of the Union," The White House (January 28, 2003).

21 Ernest Hemingway, "The Art of Fiction No. 21," interview by George Plimpton, *The Paris Review*, no. 18 (Spring 1958). "The most essential gift for a good writer is a built-in, shock-proof, shit detector. This is the writer's radar and all the great writers have had it."

22 *New York Times Co v. United States*, Supreme Court of the United States. 403 US 713 (1971) 714.

23 Donald Rumsfeld, *Known and Unknown: A Memoir* (Sentinel, 2011), 428.

24 Senate Armed Service Committee (February 25, 2003).

25 Committee on the Budget, House of Representatives (February 27, 2003).

26 Catherine Lutz and Neta Crawford, "Iraq War $2.2 Trillion," The Cost of War Project, Brown University. The estimate includes the anticipated cost of veterans' healthcare through 2053.

27 John Calvert, *Divisions within Islam* (Mason Crest, 2010).

28 CIA, *The World Factbook*. Iraq.

29 Andrew Terrill, "Strategic Implications of Intercommunal Warfare in Iraq," Strategic Studies Institute, US Army War College (February 2005). "Many Sunni Arabs worried that they would be forced to pay for their history of discrimination against the Shiites if the roles were ever reversed..."

30 Ibid., 8. "Republican Guard tanks crushing the rebellion were often painted with the slogan, 'No more Shiites after today.'"

31 "Ancient Mesopotamia: This History, Our History," Oriental Institute, University of Chicago (2007).

32 Ibid. "The Sumerians of ancient Mesopotamia are credited with inventing the earliest form of writing which appeared ca. 3500 BC." "The Mesopotamians were the first to give a number a place value and to recognize the concept of zero." "They revolutionized transportation around 3500 BC by inventing the wheel."

33 "The Sumerian King List," Ashmolean Museum of Art and Archaeology, University of Oxford.

34 Piotr Michalowski, *A Man Called Enmebaragesi*, 195.

35 Thorkild Jacobsen, "The Sumerian King List," The Oriental Institute of The University of Chicago (1939), 83.

36 "CPS decides no prosecution over death of ITN's Terry Lloyd in Iraq," Crown Prosecution Service, news release, July 28, 2008.

37 Col. Gregory Fontenot, LTC E.J. Degen, LTC David Tohn, *On Point:*

The United States Army in Operation Iraqi Freedom, 30th Military History Detachment (DS 75th XTF) Combat Studies Institute Press.

38   Public Papers of the Presidents of the United States: George W. Bush, The President's Radio Address, US Government Publishing Office (April 12, 2003).

39   Donald Wright, Colonel Timothy Reese. *On Point II: Transition to the New Campaign* (Combat Studies Institute Press, June 2008), 27. "Rumsfeld voiced concerns about deploying the 1st Cavalry Division, already loading its equipment in the United States for deployment to Iraq. This decision stemmed from the belief, at the national level, that 1st Cav's soldiers would not be needed to stabilize Iraq."

40   Ibid., 335. "By the end of major combat operations, the 75th had not discovered any weapons of mass destruction."

41   CBS News Elections and Polling Unit (May, 2007).

42   "Iraq Body Count, Conflict Casualties Monitor" (May 2018), Iraqbodycount.org. Total violent deaths including combatants: 288,000.

43   Richard D. Hooker, Jr. and Joseph J. Collins, *Lessons Encountered* (National Defense University Press, 2015), 11-12.

44   Fontenot, Degen, and Tohn. *On Point: The United States Army in Operation Iraqi Freedom,* 335. "By the end of major combat operations, the 75th had not discovered any weapons of mass destruction."

Field Note
Stranger than Fiction

1   Mark Twain, *Following the Equator: A Journey Around the World* (Doubleday & McClure Co., 1897).

2   Paul Gill, "Tracing the Motivations and Antecedent Behaviors of Lone-Actor Terrorism," International Center for the Study of Terrorism, Pennsylvania State University (August 2012).

3   "Report of the Department of the Treasury on the Bureau of Alcohol, Tobacco and Firearms Investigation of Vernon Wayne Howell also known as David Koresh" (September 30, 1993).

4   Ibid., 8.

5   "Report of the Department of the Treasury on the Bureau of Alcohol, Tobacco and Firearms Investigation of Vernon Wayne Howell also known as David Koresh" (September 30, 1993).

6   Ibid., 14.

7   "Report to the Deputy Attorney General on the Events at Waco,

Texas February 28 to April 19, 1993," United States Department of Justice (October 8, 1993).

8   Ibid.

9   CBS News video archive.

10   "Report to the Deputy Attorney General on the Events at Waco, Texas."

11   Paul Gill, "Tracing the Motivations and Antecedent Behaviors of Lone-Actor Terrorism."

12   "Oklahoma City Bombing 1995," National Institute of Standards and Technology, NIST Engineering Laboratory (January 2017).

13   *Jim Norman, Case Agent, Oklahoma Bombing Investigation*, FBI Oral History Project.

14   Ibid.

15   Timothy McVeigh, "Hey, Scott" letter of Feb 26, 1999. From the author's collection.

16   Timothy McVeigh Central File, United States Department of Justice Bureau of Prisons, released under FOIA.

Chapter Fourteen
Perseverance: The Mothers and Fathers of Sandy Hook

1   "Report of the State's Attorney for the Judicial District of Danbury on the Shootings at Sandy Hook Elementary School and 36 Yogananda Street, Newtown, Connecticut on December 14, 2012," Office of the State's Attorney Judicial District of Danbury (November 25, 2013).

2   FBI Electronic Communication Case ID # 4-NH-2619946 (December 14, 2012). "...was a functioning autistic with a personality disorder and was a recluse."

3   FBI Electronic Communication (December 18, 2012). "The shooter attended the school as a child..."

4   "Report of the State's Attorney for the Judicial District of Danbury on the Shootings at Sandy Hook Elementary School and 36 Yogananda Street, Newtown, Connecticut on December 14, 2012," Office of the State's Attorney Judicial District of Danbury, November 25, 2013.

5   Ibid.

6   Ibid.

7   Ibid.

8   *H.R. 2640—NICS Improvement Amendments Act of 2007*, US House

of Representatives. Passed into Public Law No. 110-180 on January 8, 2008.

9   "Presidential Memorandum—Improving Availability of Relevant Executive Branch Records to the National Instant Criminal Background Check System," The White House (January 16, 2013).

10   "H.J. Res. 40—Providing for congressional disapproval under chapter 8 of title 5, United States Code, of the rule submitted by the Social Security Administration related to Implementation of the NICS Improvement Amendments Act of 2007," Signed into Public Law 115-8 on February 28, 2017.

11   "Active Shooter Incidents in the United States in 2016 and 2017," FBI (April 2018).

12   "250 Active Shooter Incidents in the United States from 2000 to 2017," FBI, www.fbi.gov/about/partnerships/office-of-partner-engagement/active-shooter-incidents-graphics.

Chapter Fifteen
Deceit: The Fabulist Mr. Clinton

1   "Presidential Approval Ratings—Gallup Historical Statistics and Trends," Gallup.

2   "Past New Hampshire Primary Results," www.primarynewhampshire.com. "Caucus History," www.caucuses.desmoinesregister.com.

3   Jacobs, James, "The President, the Press, and Proximity," The White House Historical Association.

4   Videotaped Oral Deposition of William Jefferson Clinton, *Paula Corbin Jones vs. William Jefferson Clinton and Danny Ferguson*, Civil Action Number LR-C-94-290.

5   William Seale, "Theodore Roosevelt's White House," *White House History Journal*, number 11. The White House Historical Association.

6   The White House Map Room in the mansion is named for the World War II battle maps FDR used to follow progress in the war. The maps on display in the room today are from April 1945. The last maps FDR saw before his death depict the front line as the Allies pushed toward Germany.

7   Oliver Quayle Poll conducted in 1972 among 8,780 respondents. Among those "most trusted," Cronkite came in with 67 percent; "the average senator" 59 percent; Richard Nixon, 54 percent.

8   "On several occasions, it appeared that the President had had too much to drink..." University of Virginia, The Miller Center, Johnson: Chal-

lenging Congress and Impeachment, https://millercenter.org/president/johnson/life-in-brief. During the years immediately following the Civil War, Johnson clashed repeatedly with the Republican-controlled Congress over reconstruction of the defeated South. Johnson vetoed legislation that Congress passed to protect the rights of those who had been freed from slavery. This clash culminated in the House of Representatives voting, on February 24, 1868, to impeach the president. (September 26, 2018) https://www.google.com/search?q=US+Senate&ie=utf-8&oe=utf-8&client=firefox-b-1-ab).

9   *Jones v. Clinton*, Memorandum Opinion and Order, No. LR-94-290 (April 12, 1999).

10   Notice of Suspension of Attorney's privilege to Practice Law, Arkansas Supreme Court Committee on Professional Conduct (February 21, 2001).

11   Orders of the Supreme Court of the United States, D-2270 In the Matter of Discipline of Bill Clinton (October 1, 2001).

12   Martin S. Eichenbaum, Northwestern Professor of Economics and Center for International Macroeconomics, Longest economic expansion was 120 months between March 1991 and March 2001.

13   US Office of Management and Budget. Confirmed by Martin S. Eichenbaum, Northwestern Professor of Economics and Center for International Macroeconomics. The only time the federal government *not* in deficit was from 1997 to just after 2000.

Chapter Sixteen
Courage: Bao Tong

1   The President's News Conference with President Jiang Zemin of China in Beijing, official transcript, The White House (June 27, 1998).

2   Zhao Ziyang, *Prisoner of the State* (Simon and Schuster, 2009).

3   Cable From: Department of State, Wash DC, To: US Embassy Beijing, *China Task Force Situation Report No. 3*, Situation as of 1700 EDT, 6/4/89 (June 4, 1989). "Casualty estimates vary from 500 to 2600 deaths, with injuries up to 10,000."

4   Criminal Verdict returned by The Beijing Municipal Intermediate People's Court (1992) Intermediate/Criminal No. 1582. "It is hereby decided that he will serve a total fixed-term period of seven years imprisonment."

5   Denis Twitchett and Frederick Mote, *The Cambridge History of China: Volume 8* (Cambridge University Press).

6   "The Trial of Bao Tong," Asia Watch (August 3, 1992).

7   "2018 World Press Freedom Index," Reporters Without Borders for Freedom of Information. Ranking immediately below China are: Syria, Turkmenistan, Eritrea and, finally, North Korea.

8   *People's Daily* (February 2016).

9   "Media Censorship in China," Council on Foreign Relations (February 17, 2017).

10   Ibid.

11   "Freedom of Expression and the Internet in China," Human Rights Watch.

12   George Orwell, *1984* (Harcourt, Inc. 1949).

13   Herbert Gowen, *An Outline History of China: Part 1* (Sherman, French & Co., 1913).

Chapter Seventeen
Valor: Patrick Marc Rapicault

1   "The Military Civilian Gap: Fewer Family Connections," Pew Social Trends (November 2011). Pew's research discovered a fascinating breakdown in demographics. When Pew asked what percentage of Americans had an immediate family member in the military, the generational breakdown was: 18-29 years old, 33 percent; 30-49 years old, 57 percent; 50-64 years old, 79 percent.

2   US Department of Veterans Affairs, National Cemetery Administration.

3   Ibid., "History of Government Furnished Headstones and Markers" (April 17, 2015).

4   Bill Steigerwald. "Sir Edmund Hillary has held on to his lofty ideals," *Pittsburgh Post Gazette Magazine* (November 9, 1998).

Chapter Eighteen
Arrogance: A Cautionary Tale

1   "The Rendition and Detention of German Citizen Khalid Al Masri," CIA FOIA, Documents Related to the Former Detention and Interrogation Program, Document Number 6541725.

2   Cornell Law website, 18 U.S.C. 2340-2340B.

3   "Eyes Only Draft," CIA FOIA, Documents Related to the Former Detention and Interrogation Program, Document Number 6541505.

4   "Eyes Only, Where we stand re: Abu Zabaydah," CIA FOIA, Documents Related to the Former Detention and Interrogation Program, Document Number 6541711.

5   https://www.cia.gov/library/readingroom/docs/0006552083.pdf.

6   "Eyes Only, Where we stand re: Abu Zabaydah."

7   "Alleged Use of Unauthorized Interrogation Techniques," CIA FOIA, Documents Related to the Former Detention and Interrogation Program, Disposition Memorandum (December 2006).

8   "Description of Physical Pressures," CIA FOIA, Documents Related to the Former Detention and Interrogation Program, Document Number 6552083.

9   Email January 22, 2003, CIA FOIA, Documents Related to the Former Detention and Interrogation Program, Document Number 6541516.

10   "7 June meeting with DCI," (Sanitized), CIA FOIA. Documents Related to the Former Detention and Interrogation Program.

11   "The Rendition and Detention of German Citizen Khalid Al Masri," CIA FOIA. Documents Related to the Former Detention and Interrogation Program, Document Number 6541725.

12   "Study of the Central Intelligence Agency's Detention and Interrogation Program, 85," Report of the Senate Select Committee on Intelligence. "KSM is waterboarded 183 times."

13   "Senate Approves Amendment Sponsored by Senators John McCain & Dianne Feinstein Affirming Prohibition on Torture," John McCain Press Release (June 16, 2015).

Field Note
Empathy

1   R.T. Griffith English Translation of the *Rig Veda*, "The Rivers," Hymn LXXV.

Chapter Nineteen
To a Young Journalist

1   Jonathan Swift, *The Examiner*, No. 14 (November 11, 1710). "Falsehood flies, and truth comes limping after it, so that when men come to be undeceived it is too late."

2   "Testimony of Colin Stretch, General Counsel, Facebook," United

States Senate Committee on the Judiciary, Subcommittee on Crime and Terrorism (October 31, 2017), 6.

3 United States Senate Committee on the Judiciary, Subcommittee on Crime and Terrorism. Testimony of Richard Salgado, Senior Counsel, Law Enforcement and Information Security, Google (October 31, 2017), 3.

4 "Official 2016 Presidential General Election Results," Federal Election Commission, January 30, 2017. Total Votes, 136,669,237.

5 "Testimony of Sean J. Edgett, Acting General Counsel, Twitter Inc.," United States Senate Committee on the Judiciary, Subcommittee on Crime and Terrorism (October 31, 2017), 6.

6 Oliver Quayle Poll conducted in 1972 among 8,780 respondents. Among those "most trusted," Cronkite came in with 67 percent; "the average senator," 59 percent; Richard Nixon, 54 percent.

7 *Oxford Dictionary of English*.

8 Jimmy Breslin, "It's an Honor," *New York Herald Tribune* (November 26, 1963).

9 John Steinbeck, *The Grapes of Wrath* (Viking Press, 1939).

10 Mark Twain, Letter to George Bainton (October 15, 1888).

11 "An act for the punishment of certain crimes against the United States," Fifth Congress Session II, 1798, Chapter LXXI, Section 1, Library of Congress.

12 *The Constitution of the United States*, Amendment I, National Archives, presented in New York City 1789. "Congress shall make no law respecting an establishment of religion, or prohibiting the free exercise thereof; or abridging the freedom of speech, or of the press; or the right of the people peaceably to assemble, and to petition the Government for a redress of grievances."

13 Amendments to the Constitution, The Annals of Congress, House of Representatives, 1st Congress, 1st Session (June 8, 1789), 451.

14 "The Report of 1800," National Archives (January 7, 1800).

Conclusion
How Many Stars in Your Flag?

1 Douglas Southall Freeman, *R. E. Lee* (Scribner, 1978).

2 William K. Clifford, *The Ethics of Belief* (Contemporary Review, 1877).

INDEX

ALSO BY JOHN EDWARD

Books

CROSSING OVER: *The Stories Behind the Stories*

ONE LAST TIME: *A Psychic Medium Speaks to Those We've Loved and Lost*

WHAT IF GOD WERE THE SUN? (a novel)*

Audio Programs

CROSSING OVER: *The Stories Behind the Stories* (audio book)

*DEVELOPING YOUR OWN PSYCHIC POWERS**

*UNDERSTANDING YOUR ANGELS AND MEETING YOUR GUIDES**

*UNLEASHING YOUR PSYCHIC POTENTIAL**

WHAT IF GOD WERE THE SUN? (audio book)*

*Also in Spanish

All of the above are available at your local bookstore, or may be ordered through the Princess Books distributor, Hay House, Inc.:

(800) 654-5126 or (760) 431-7695
(800) 650-5115 (fax) or (760) 431-6948 (fax)
www.hayhouse.com

AFTER
Life

ANSWERS FROM

THE OTHER SIDE

John Edward

with Natasha Stoynoff

Princess Books
New York, NY

Published in the United States by: Princess Books, a Division of Get Psych'd, Inc., New York, NY

Distributed in the United States by: Hay House, Inc., P.O. Box 5100, Carlsbad, CA 92018-5100 • (760) 431-7695 or (800) 654-5126 • (760) 431-6948 (fax) or (800) 650-5115 (fax) • www.hayhouse.com • *Distributed in Australia by:* Hay House Australia Pty Ltd, 18/36 Ralph St., Alexandria NSW 2015 • *Phone:* 612-9669-4299 • *Fax:* 612-9669-4144 • www.hayhouse.com.au • *Distributed in the United Kingdom by:* Hay House UK, Ltd. • Unit 202, Canalot Studios • 222 Kensal Rd., London W10 5BN • *Phone:* 44-20-8962-1230 • *Fax:* 44-20-8962-1239 • www.hayhouse.co.uk • *Distributed in Canada by:* Raincoast • 9050 Shaughnessy St., Vancouver, B.C. V6P 6E5 • *Phone:* (604) 323-7100 • *Fax:* (604) 323-2600

Editorial supervision: Jill Kramer • *Design:* Summer McStravick

Library of Congress Cataloging-in-Publication Data

Edward, John (John J.)
  After life : answers from the other side / John Edward.
    p. cm.
  ISBN 1-932128-06-9 — ISBN 1-932128-07-7 (pbk.)
  1. Edward, John (John J.) 2. Mediums—United States—Biography. I. Title.
  BF1283.E34 A3 2003
  133.9'1'092—dc21

2003011255

Hardcover ISBN 1-932128-06-9
Tradepaper ISBN 1-932128-07-7

06 05 04 03   4 3 2 1
1st printing, September 2003

Printed in the United States of America

In memory of Charles . . .

This book has two distinctly different dedications:

For Carol Spadaro—thanks for being
the "whole army" to one 'warrior.'

And for all the skeptics/cynics:

May the White Light of the Other Side burn bright
enough to assist the spiritually blind to see. . . .

Contents

Foreword

JOHN EDWARD CERTAINLY IS ONE OF THE MOST EXTRAORDINARY PEOPLE I've ever known or interviewed. He has appeared on my show many, many times, and to say the least, provides fascinating TV. I'm a pure agnostic. That is, I don't know if there's a God or not, I don't know if there are other universes or not, and I certainly don't know if there's some sort of life after death.

I'll admit, John often provides insights into the departed that are not explainable. I don't know if he's seeing or hearing from the departed or if he's tuning in to the viewer's vision of the departed. I'm not even sure if there is such a thing as psychic phenomena. However, I cannot deny that John Edward often amazes.

In this, his third nonfiction book, he takes us into a further exploration of the Other Side, as he sees it. Using intimate stories from his own life, he explains how to continue relationships after this tour on Earth. Another fascinating aspect is his tour of Australia. And, naturally, the book is loaded with readings, including celebrities. We also learn of John's admitted errors, and I like the idea of a summation at the end of every chapter.

Believe him or not, you will find this book a treasure of exploration into what I call the unknown and what John calls the known. Dull, it isn't. Enjoy!

— **Larry King**, June 2003

*"The more I study the universe,
the more I believe in a Higher Power."*

— Albert Einstein

Acknowledgments

AS WITH ANYTHING IN MY LIFE, I'd be remiss if I didn't communicate my appreciation and validate my lovely wife, Sandra. Thanks for always being supportive of me and the work . . . I love you.

I also must acknowledge my three "kids": my two dogs, Jolie and Roxie, for providing me with constant unconditional love; and my beautiful li'l boy, Justin Michael, for opening up doors in my heart that I forgot were there.

To Grandma Lina and Grandpa Fernando—thanks for taking such good care of Justin.

"The Boys"—you lead, I follow . . . in this dance of spirituality.

Jon Campo, I don't have enough space here to thank you for your friendship, so always remember that there is "NO" spoon. . . .

Stacy Campo, first, we must find you an "e" for your first name. This way I stop misspelling it. ☺ First, we were all friends, and now . . . simply family.

Lydia Clar—you're still an inspiration.

Marc Chamlin, my attorney and friend, you are someone who has always been a constant in a world of variables. Thank you for your sage advice and energy.

Reid Tracy, publishing has been an evolving journey—with you as "the predicted man from the West" to be my guide. THANK YOU!

Gina Rugolo-Judd, you're the best at what you do, *and* you manage to make me laugh. Thank you for believing in me.

"Fritzarella"—a personal and private thank you. You did what only one other person in my life has ever done—and that was a college professor. She took the concept of statistics and made it easy and fun. You did that with publicity . . . thanks for becoming family.

Jack Rico—"what up, roo?" The trip to Australia would not have been the same without you acting as Barbara Walters after each seminar, dissecting each reading and questioning each moment. Thanks for your friendship. And for future reference, when a large kangaroo stands up and starts pounding its chest and flexes its muscles, it ain't bein' friendly! ☺

Natasha Stoynoff, when you approached me a few years ago and interviewed me for a few magazine stories, I knew at that time that we'd work together. Thank you for collaborating with me on this book. I hope you enjoyed the process, and becoming one of the "sitters" when you were least expecting it. I would also like to thank your other personality . . . *"Nay Tay Shay."*

Corinda Carford, you're still my publishing goddess!

Frank Sepe, your energy, sarcasm, and wit is never ending—and you're a great trainer. Thanks for your focus and time, and for pushing me to achieve my goals.

Rick Firstman, because of the time and energy you devoted to *One Last Time* and *Crossing Over,* this book now has parents. . . .

Patti Leoni—what a cook! What an energy! What a friend! Sandra and I are so happy to have met you.

Bonnie Hammer, you have been a constant supporter with honesty and friendship. Thank you!

Paul Shavelson, you drive me crazy—keep it up for many years to come.

To everyone who works so hard on *Crossing Over,* thank you for honoring the process and not succumbing to the pressures of television. You all help to share the experiences of what happens in our "gallery," and teach that life and love survive physical death. . . .

The "angels" at Media Savvy—look what you started. . . .

Isabel—if you could be cloned, we would eradicate unhappiness. And yes, they are okay!

Lucille, Joanne, Ruth, and Phil, your energy and words have helped so many of the people that I work with. Thanks for always being there.

Diane, thank you for allowing me to share your "angel" with the world.

To my Australian friends—my down-under family—I look forward to working with all of you again in the near future. Kristen, you rock! Leon . . .well, you really should be the ambassador for the country!

Steve Irwin, although I didn't get the chance to meet you personally, I really want to acknowledge the amazing work that you and your team at the Australian Zoo perform.

And while on the Aussie subject, a special thank you to the WIGGLES for managing to soothe Justin when he was cranky. All together now . . . "Hot potato, hot potato . . ."

Tricia Greenidge, thanks for taking such good care of Sandra and me when we are in "your" part of the world.

Liz Arias, a.k.a. "La Liz," thank you for always being there, here, and everywhere. . . .

Risa, no more fish photos, VIRGO! Thanks for your sense of style.

Stacey Leinson, a.k.a. "Shaloma"—your energy, enthusiasm, and professionalism are gifts. (I look forward to the first Jewish rap tour.)

Ace, Frank, John, Lance, and Marc, thanks for watching out for me.

Fran and Lowell—Mr. Leinson and Mrs. Leinson, or "Lois," as I affectionately refer to her—your escapades have kept me entertained through many of our 50 states.

Michael Logan, thanks for illuminating so many in darkness with the power of your pen.

Linda Eder, for having the voice of an angel. Your voice and music help me to relax after every event.

Whoopi . . . what can I say . . . but . . . you know!

"The 31 Club" . . . you make Wednesdays fun.

For all the energies on this side and on the Other that have helped in making this book come to life. . . .

And finally, I want to thank YOU—the person reading this—for supporting me in my quest to teach about life, love, death . . . and what comes *After Life*. . . .

Introduction

IS THERE SOMETHING AFTER DEATH? Is there eternal life, as promised by certain religions? Does love transcend physical death? Are the loved ones you miss terribly still with you? And if so, are you aware that there is something *after life?*

As I worked on this book, I reflected on my career of nearly two decades as a psychic medium. I called this book *AFTER LIFE: Answers from the Other Side,* to help explain some of the lessons I've personally learned from doing this work. I initially thought that I was going to simply answer the basic questions people always ask me about this process of spirit communication. But when I sat down at my computer, it was clear that I needed and wanted to dig deeper than that and pick up where my first book, *One Last Time,* left off.

In a way, this book is kind of *One Last Time: Part II.* Even though I've written two books since that first one, many readers have told me that they resonated most with the tone, message, and sharing of intimate personal stories in that work—for example, where I described my formative years as a teenage psychic in blue jeans. Twenty years later, I'm still a psychic in blue jeans, and I'm still learning and growing.

This might be a good time to explain to newcomers who've picked up this book who I am and what I do. I'm a psychic medium who connects with loved ones who have crossed over to the "Other Side"—a place many people like to call "heaven" or "the here-after." The first question everybody asks me about this process is: How does it work? Well, basically, as a medium, I have the ability to perceive the vibrations and frequencies of those who have crossed over. Through meditation and prayer—usually with the rosary because of my Catholic upbringing—I'm able to *raise* my vibration level while the energies on the Other Side *lower* their vibrations in an effort to communicate with me.

As I've described many times, if you can imagine a helicopter propeller that moves so fast that we can't see the propellers themselves—that's how fast or high the vibrations of these energies on the Other Side are. In comparison, we on this side have a vibration more like a slowpoke ceiling fan on a hot, lazy day.

For a little while, as I speed up and they slow down, across the great divide between our two worlds we meet somewhere in the middle and communicate. The energies send me thoughts, feelings, and images—which I then relate back to the living. I always like to state right off the bat that I'm not 100-percent accurate when I relay these messages, but I do believe that the Other Side is always *completely* accurate when they deliver them. Whatever I see, hear, and feel (also known as clairvoyance, clairaudience, and clairsentience, respectively), I interpret using my own frame of reference to the best of my human abilities and perceptions.

You'll hear me describe energies coming through as being "above" (a parent, aunt/uncle, or grandparent type figure); "below" (a child); or "beside" (a contemporary—a sibling, cousin, or friend) in reference to the *sitter* (the person I'm reading—I use the term *client* and *sitter* interchangeably in this book). The genesis of these descriptions comes courtesy of my mother, who had taken it upon herself one day to research our genealogy. She sent away for one of those poster-sized charts from a catalog with a big picture of a family tree and spots for everyone's names on the branches. But when she received it in the mail, she had to laugh. The poster only had five "branches" sprouting out from the parents, and my grandmother had *11* children.

"We don't need a family tree," my mom joked, as she tucked it away behind the hope chest at the top of the stairs. "We need a family forest!" A few years later, after my mother had passed away, I was doing a reading for a client at my home and I was getting frustrated as to how to explain a male energy coming through. I felt that it was someone around the same age as the client, but I didn't know how else I could describe it. Then I looked across the room and saw a branch of that old, unused family tree sticking out from behind the chest, and the whole concept jumped out at me. I quickly said to the sitter, "To the side . . . like a brother/cousin relationship," and the woman knew who it was immediately. After the reading, I pulled out that chart and chuckled. From that day on, I started to receive my information like the branches of a family tree that stretch out above, below, and to the side.

During a reading, I rarely ask questions of the living to elicit information, which is the common argument presented by skeptics trying to explain how psychics "pull off" their so-called tricks. Instead, I *give* the information I'm getting and ask for validation. If a medium is constantly asking questions during a session, I call that "lazy mediumship." There really is a big difference between the two ways a medium can deliver the same message, which go something like this:

1st way: "Has your father passed?" (lazy medium)
2nd way: "I'm getting that your father has passed. Is that true?" (non-lazy medium)

Both mediums are receiving the same information that Dad is on the Other Side, but one sounds like he's fishing for the info while the other is stating it more as fact. When a psychic uses the lazy approach, the cynics have a field day. It gives them ammunition to jump up and yell, "See! He's getting the information from the client!" and it makes a case for refuting the validity of this work. It drives me nuts when I see a psychic who has genuine ability take the lazy route. But even I'm guilty of getting "lazy" sometimes, although I strive not to. When I catch myself giving information in question form, I give myself a nudge. I try to state the information I'm shown exactly as I see it without questions or too much editing. If a client is unable to confirm the information, I ask him or her to write it down, because one of three things is happening: (1) I misinterpreted the information I was given; (2) the sitter doesn't remember or know the information; or (3) sometimes the information I was given hasn't happened yet.

One typical example of a misinterpretation occurred while I was reading for a group, and an older male came through showing me a gun, a New York City yellow taxicab, and a younger male. I stood in front of the group insisting that someone there knew an individual who had been murdered by gunshot in a cab—that was my interpretation of what I was seeing. No one acknowledged this, but the images were clear and unrelenting.

After much frustration on my part, I finally gave the message to the group minus my angle on it: "I'm seeing a gun, a young man, and a cab. Do all these things together mean anything to anyone?" It wasn't long before someone validated that their father-in-law was coming through about his son who was shot while in the front part of a large truck—the "cab" area of the truck. I had confused both the group and myself because, first, I assumed the younger male had died from the gunshot, which he hadn't. Second, I had no idea that the front part of a truck was called the "cab," and I just figured that the gun went off in a taxi. If I hadn't relayed the information exactly as delivered, it might never have been validated.

After honing my skills doing private readings and seminars for many years, my name became highly recognizable as the host of the show *Crossing Over with John Edward,* where I conduct random readings for a gallery group in a studio. I wrote extensively about my television experiences in *CROSSING OVER: The Stories Behind the Stories,* so I won't go into detail here reiterating the behind-the-scenes scoop. Instead, for this book, I want to respond to all the letters I've received over the last few years and give you more of what you've asked for: personal and professional stories related to my interactions with the Other Side.

I BEGAN MY CAREER AS A MEDIUM after a reading with another psychic, Lydia Clar, when I was 15 years old. She'd been invited to my grandmother's home for a "psychic party," and I decided that I was going to show my very gullible family that they were being bilked by this con artist. Well, the opposite happened: I found Lydia's abilities amazing, and she changed my perspective about the world of psychic phenomena in just one session. It was at that meeting when she told me I had psychic ability and would one day be internationally known for it. I'll be turning 34 soon, and I feel that I've fulfilled Lydia's premonition of my destiny.

People always ask me what I get out of doing this work. *What's in it for me?* Well, the answer to that has changed over the years. I started off as a general psychic and was "wowed" by the fact that I could predict a person's future. Then, after two close members of my family passed on, the focus of my work shifted to mediumship and talking to the Other Side.

Often, it's the death of someone close that motivates a person to explore this subject. I'd guess that many of you readers have suffered a personal loss that inspired you to pick up this book. It was the same for me regarding my own personal development as a psychic. After the death of my uncle and my mother within two years, I needed to know they were fine and still around me. By doing readings and connecting strangers with their own loved ones, I was indirectly healing and finding closure for myself. Each time I showed someone that their mother or child was still with them, it validated for me that my family was still a part of *my* life as well. In sharing the experiences with the people who have graciously allowed me to tell their stories in this book, I hope that you, too, will find healing and closure and apply what I've learned from the Other Side to your own lives.

EVERY TIME I START TO WRITE a new book, I feel that my readers and I are like characters in *The Wizard of Oz,* traveling down that yellow brick road in search of the Emerald City and the truths behind the curtain. And at the end of our journey, we discover that life and love are eternal. And they always were . . . we just couldn't see it before.

Now . . . come with me as we follow the
yellow brick road all the way to Vegas. . . .

CHAPTER ONE

Living on This Side

IN LAS VEGAS YOU DON'T HAVE to be a medium to see dead people. Just take an early-morning walk through any casino and you can't help but see them at every turn. You know the type—the ones with the zombie stares and hypnotic arm lifts, dropping coins all night hoping to hit "The Big One."

Now, you might be saying, wait a minute . . . casino? . . . psychic? . . . *kaaaa-chingggggg!* It's funny to watch those serious-looking men in suits, the ones casinos pay to keep an eye out for crooked gamblers, when they recognize me at the tables. As soon as they spot me, they're watching me like hawks, trailing me from table to table, making sure I'm not using my abilities—like they're expecting me to start communing with the Other Side to find out which number is going to come up on the roulette wheel.

Well, I'm sorry to report that, at least for this psychic, being in touch with the spirit world doesn't guarantee a jackpot. And God knows I've tried—in casinos from the Caribbean to California. A long time ago, "The Boys" (the nickname I've given to my own personal spirit guides) taught me an expensive lesson—trying to cash in on my abilities will cost me big time. I remember standing in front of a roulette table many years ago getting an unmistakable vision of the number 18 in my mind—a "sure thing." I bet ten bucks on lucky number 18 and . . . lost. I bet another ten and lost again. Then another. Ten minutes and 300 bucks later, still no 18. I pulled myself away from the table and gave myself a scolding: *You know this doesn't work for you! Give it up!* But as I wandered away, I noticed everyone surrounding the table pointing and staring at me. As soon as I'd stopped betting, the roulette wheel hit 18 . . . once, twice, three times . . . six times in a row! Well, at least someone made a few bucks. So do yourself a favor . . . if you're standing next to me at a craps table sometime, don't put your money where my chips are.

But on this particular Vegas trip, I wasn't in a betting mood. I was here to work and conduct a seminar, answering questions and conducting readings for a large audience. I didn't have any sleight-of-hand tricks or a crystal ball, and I certainly can't read minds—even though that's all the cynics seem to think I'm good at. They're convinced that there's a sucker born every minute and psychics carry a bag of parlor tricks just waiting to con them. The cynics have plenty of ways to describe the methods they claim we use to fool people. They use terms like "cold reading" and "painting a bulls-eye around a lucky guess." They think we read body language, picking up facial clues or listening for voice clues. They've accused me of hiding microphones in audiences and using private detectives. I'm surprised that none of them have claimed I bug people's bedrooms to get intimate information. I haven't been accused of that one yet, but just give those cynics time!

As a medium, I've always made it a point to never try to convert anyone to my beliefs or convince anyone of my abilities. In fact, the exact opposite is true. I encourage people to be skeptical and question this process, but with an open and objective mind.

I received a letter last year from one woman who embarked on a year-long mission to expose me as a fraud. Marcia Secaur, a vice president at a major securities firm in Cincinnati, Ohio, had attended one of my seminars with a bunch of her friends on a lark.

She didn't believe in mediums and came prepared to, at the very most, have a good laugh. Instead, she ended up being shocked.

She recalled, "In a roomful of 200 people, you walked right up to a woman at the back of the room and told her she had a family member coming through who was run over by a train. And you were right."

Marcia left the seminar determined to figure out how I was tricking everybody. As someone who worked with facts, it was in her meticulous, diligent nature to get to the root of the matter—to reach the bottom line.

So she began researching the topic of mediumship—reading articles and speaking with "professional" cynics who taught her the "tricks of the trade." Then, with notebook in hand, she dissected episode after episode of *Crossing Over* to spot my con.

"I tried to take the show apart," said Marcia. "I spent a week on my couch with all my information about cold readings in front of me, and I tried to make it stick." When it didn't, she decided she had to inspect me in person. Marcia attended four seminars in a span of a few months to catch me in the act of faking it. But once again, she couldn't. So her last resort was to decide I was using a staff of detectives to dig up information about people before I read them.

"The problem with that theory," said Marcia, "was that with all the people you've worked with over the years, I couldn't believe there'd be such a vast conspiracy of silence out there that not one person would have come forward to expose."

Defeated, but not disappointed, Marcia told me that by the end of her quest, she'd become more distrustful of the cynics than of me. "It's actually the Leon Jaroffs, James Randis, and Michael Shermers of the world that frighten me," she wrote. "These are people who want to take away the comfort and peace you have given to so many people and glibly treat what you do as though it were the punch line in a bad stand-up routine. That is not practicing skepticism, it's being cruel and close minded. Discrediting you and undermining the experiences you have brought people seems more a form of entertainment for them than any noble endeavor. To attack a person's fundamental beliefs about life and death is the kind of thing wars have been fought about for centuries. Perhaps that's why your guides say you will have the role of warrior in regard to your field."

Warrior or not, it's not my job to change people's minds, and it's not my business to prove that what I say is true. I'll never defend what I believe in or what I do. If I did, I'd be admitting that there's something to defend—and there simply isn't.

My role is to be a bridge between our world (the physical) and the spirit world (the nonphysical), and to deliver messages from the Other Side to the living. But often that's easier said than done. There are times when I receive, interpret, and pass on a message to the person I'm reading and the information is easily validated. But there are also times when I get something and the person I'm reading doesn't understand the information right away.

Or, in some cases, the message might not even be intended for the person I'm talking to—but for another relative, a friend, or acquaintance who isn't present during the session. This type of message might not get validated immediately, and in some cases it might take weeks or even months for the validation to occur. I call those validations "Aha!" moments, a phrase I coined many years ago because I saw this delayed validation scenario happen so often. I can't count how many times I've passed on information to a sitter that they didn't understand, only to get a phone call the next day saying something like, "I just checked with my mom, and I didn't know this, but she *did* have an Aunt Gertrude who died in a plane crash over the Amazon. . . ." Or even, "Oh, that 'Thomas' you kept mentioning? It didn't hit me that you could mean my *brother* Tom. . . . "

This is what is also known as "psychic amnesia," another phrase I coined that means the complete and sudden deterioration of your memory when a medium is talking to you. You forget how and when your relatives passed, you forget their names, your own name . . . I've seen it happen time and time again.

Sometimes the person the message is for just isn't paying attention—even if that person happens to be a seasoned psychic medium like yours truly. . . .

IT HAPPENED IN VEGAS on an unusually crisp January afternoon. More than 2,000 people had turned up at the banquet hall at the MGM Grand Hotel hoping to get messages from their loved ones who had crossed over. Many of them *did* get messages, but the one that came through strongest was the one I received myself—and it would change my life forever. It was an earth-shattering "Aha" moment of my own and, just like I've seen it happen to others, it took me weeks to figure out.

I walked onto that Vegas stage and, despite the huge crowd, felt right at home. There were a few familiar faces in this audience who had known me since I was a kid and had come to see "little Johnny" all grown up. One of them was my good friend and fellow psychic, Virginia, who came to cheer me on. Try to picture Judge Judy as a psychic and you've got Virginia: a real no-nonsense type. I also spotted my Uncle Carmine's sister, Loretta, and her family and friends. (For those of you who read *One Last Time,* you might remember that I talked about Uncle Carmine and the premonition I had about his very young passing from a heart attack.)

The air was charged with the usual electricity that often fills a room just before I do a group reading. Everyone is excited and nervous, wondering, *Will someone come through for me? Who will it be? What will they tell me?*

But whether it's Vegas or Vermont, readings are always a gamble, a crapshoot. Sometimes I feel as if those who attend an event are like players in a poker game, laying down those hard-earned chips and praying they'll get the right card. Hopefully, they walk away without being too disappointed if it wasn't their lucky night.

But I like to think that everyone comes away a winner.

I often explain that a group reading is like a birthday party. Imagine that you're a kid and it's your birthday—there's a cake in front of you loaded down with glowing candles and your name across the top in big, loopy letters. But just because it's *your* party and those are *your* candles marking *your* special day, it doesn't mean this is a private celebration. Every person at the party will get a slice of your cake and come away with a goodie bag. The same holds true with a reading for a large group of people. If the seminar is a party and the reading is the cake—even if the cake isn't specifically yours with your name on it, but is intended for another person or family, you still get a slice of it just by being at the party. Because you're listening and taking part, the reading is just as much for you (conceptually) as it is for the other person. So you go home with the goodie bag—the knowledge that life and love are eternal.

That night in Vegas, I was about to get an amusing lesson in birthday-party etiquette from the Other Side. I knew that I had a big cake to divvy up, but I had no clue that it had my name on it.

The trip had already started off on a strange note. You see, my wife, Sandra, decided to accompany me. Not that that's a bad thing, but she usually doesn't want to come on these tours. When I'm on the road, I'm usually booked to appear in several cities in a very short time period. It's always a hectic schedule, so there isn't much time to do anything except rush to the airport, hop on a plane, check in to a hotel, and then do the seminars. There might be time for a quick bite afterwards and maybe a fast workout if I'm lucky, then a few hours sleep and up early to do it all over again.

It can go on like that for days, so I usually discourage Sandra from coming along because, quite honestly, when she's there I can get a little distracted—worrying if she's bored and trying to make sure she's having a good time. But this time, she wanted to be there . . . and I don't believe anything is ever a coincidence. The Other Side had a message for both of us.

HOLLYWOOD AND WHINE

SANDRA AND I DECIDED TO SPEND A COUPLE OF DAYS IN L.A. to squeeze in a mini-vacation before my hectic work schedule kicked in. We planned to meet with a few friends and do a little sightseeing, shopping, and "stargazing." On one of the nights we were there, the Golden Globe Awards happened to be taking place, and we were invited to go to one of the after-parties. Now, I usually don't like to attend these "Hollywood" things because of all the fuss that goes along with it, but I must admit that I'm as excited as the next fan to meet the celebrities I admire.

I remember a few years ago when I caught sight of my favorite singer, Linda Eder, on 6th Avenue through the glass of the restaurant where I was having lunch. Next thing I knew, I was racing through the crowded street and pushing aside pedestrians like a quarterback running for the end zone. I caught up to her on the sidewalk and babbled something charming and intelligent like, "OhMy-GodAreYouLindaEder?" and told her that I'd been her biggest fan since my early days on *Star Search*. I handed her my card, which read "John Edward—Psychic Medium" and asked her if she could include my name on any mailing list she might have for upcoming concerts. She looked at my card, then back at me, perplexed.

"Um . . . or if you're ever interested in speaking with any of your dead loved ones," I added, "please give me a call!" (Note: She never did. Then two years later I attended her concert at the PNC Arts Center in New Jersey and had the chance to go backstage afterward. In a room crammed full of people, I was trying to hang back . . . hoping Linda wouldn't recognize me as the weirdo who'd chased her down 6th Avenue. But when Linda's publicist ushered me forward to introduce me, Linda said I looked familiar. "Oh, he's that *stalker fan* you met on the street a few years ago!" Sandra chimed in.)

So I'm not immune to the lure of stargazing once in a while, and this Golden Globes party would definitely be wall-to-wall stars. So what would keep me from a star-studded event like this? Three words: the press line. See, I don't consider myself a celebrity. Yeah, I'm on TV and people recognize me at the supermarket and at the mall. But the truth is, I don't do what I do to gain fame. I do it to help people. It's an ability I've been given, and I want to share it with as many people as I can. Being on television and touring the country doing seminars allows me to do that. But I'm just not a Hollywood type of guy, and photographers snapping my picture and reporters sticking microphones in my face just unnerves me.

No offense to any reporters reading this—you're just doing your job. It's not you, it's me. I have no problem getting up in front of thousands of strangers and bringing through loved ones from the

Other Side . . . energies who often send me very intimate and potentially embarrassing messages. I pass the juicy details along for all the world to hear without much wavering. If you want to talk to me about my work, I'm fine. But put me in front of a TV camera to talk about myself and I become a ball of nerves . . . because then it's about me the *person* and not me the medium.

When it comes right down to it, I'm really a shy guy who has purposely stayed in the background most of my life. Anyone who knew me growing up can attest to the fact that I never wanted to be "known" or "famous"—quite the contrary. I never liked being in the forefront of anything, whether it was in school or on the job. My biggest dream as an adolescent was to own my own deli. After that, it was to be behind the scenes in the health-care field. To this day, I'm just a few credits short of my master's degree in health-care administration. (As parents say, "It's something to fall back on.") So for me, to be thrust in front of the spotlight has had its uncomfortable moments.

Okay, okay . . . I know what you're thinking (and not because I'm psychic). *Poor John. He has his own TV show, chitty-chats with Larry King on CNN, and gets invited to stroll down the red carpet into star-studded parties . . . and all he can do is complain?!* Believe me, the person playing the air-violin the loudest is my lovely wife, Sandra, who enjoys attending these glittery affairs. So when we landed in L.A. with invites to the Golden Globes party in our suitcase, Sandra was raring to go, and she wasn't about to hear me whine about having to walk past a few eager shutterbugs to get there. That's why what happened next seemed all the more strange.

As I mentioned, Sandra was excited about the party, so she went out and bought a new outfit and could talk about nothing else during the entire trip out to L.A. The night of the party, she spent hours getting ready, but I have to admit, it was all worth it. She looked incredible—glowing, in fact. She was wearing a strapless evening gown and these sexy shoes that tied up around her ankles.

We headed off to the party with Sandra anticipating the celebrities we were likely to see. Now most people would have hired a limo—or at least a driver in a town car—to take them to the event.

But this would have attracted too much attention for my taste. Instead, I rented a car so we could pull up to the side and slip in to the party unnoticed. When I turned onto Santa Monica Boulevard and got close to the famous Trader Vic's restaurant, where the party was being held, it looked like a paparazzi convention. I looked at Sandra, said "No way," and kept driving.

Five long L.A. blocks later, I found a parking spot, which meant that Sandra had to walk a half mile in those new, skinny heels. She didn't say much—but I knew that she wasn't a happy camper. By the third block, she'd decided to break her silence and let me know exactly what she thought about my parking plan . . . let's just say she wasn't entirely pleased. She was feeling tired, her feet were killing her, and we had to stop half a dozen times so she could hike up her gown and retie those shoes.

When we got to Trader Vic's, I guided Sandra toward a side entrance, sneaking past the media mob, where we bumped into a tall, stone-faced security guard who asked to see our passes.

"Security passes?" I asked.

Right. I knew exactly where they were. They were sitting on the end table back at the hotel.

"Ah . . . go ahead, I know who you are," the security guard said, and waved us in with a smile of recognition. "What's the matter? Didn't anyone up there remind you to bring them?" Heh, heh. Phew . . . thanks to my "celebrity" status, we were quickly moving down an empty hallway headed straight to the party. If we were turned away from the door because I forgot those security passes, Sandra would have never let me hear the end of it. She was still miffed about our hike from the car, but once we got to the party she forgot all about it. There were stars from our favorite TV shows and movies everywhere we looked—Benjamin Bratt, Andie Mac-Dowell, Maggie Smith, Josh Hartnett. I was glad we'd come and was anxious to start mingling.

We'd been there just under an hour when Sandra—AKA Miss Party Animal—turned to me and said she was tired and wanted to leave.

"But . . . but . . . Will and Grace are over there, two feet from us . . . and you want to leave?" I protested.

"If we don't leave this minute," she said, "I'm gonna crawl over there, curl up on Will and Grace's laps, and go to sleep. . . . "

I'd never known Sandra to want to cut out of a good party— let alone one set in a galaxy of stars. But as soon as we were back in the room, she hit the sack and was out like a light. I figured that the traveling and the time difference had really knocked her out.

IS THERE A PSYCHIC IN THE HOUSE?

THE NEXT DAY WE WERE OFF TO VEGAS and back to work. Sandra kept busy at the seminar handling one of the microphones, running up and down the aisles and squeezing between the rows of people in the audience, making sure everyone could hear each other during the Q&A period and the readings. The validations were coming through nice and easy until one of the last readings of the day when I was pulled to the back of the hall. When I say "pulled," I don't mean someone—living or dead—was physically grabbing ahold of me and dragging me. It's not a physical pull; it's an *energy* pull. I feel like I'm being tethered by an invisible line of energy from my sternum leading directly to where the message must be delivered. Whether I'm reading a group of 12 or 12,000, it's the same feeling.

On the television show *Saturday Night Live,* comedian Will Ferrell does a really funny parody of me being "pulled" all over the place, kind of like a frenetic cross between Jim Carrey and Gumby. I'm the first one to laugh at it—and myself—folks. The other thing people like to kid me about is how during a reading I can turn into a pit bull. I'll sink my teeth into a bit of information coming through and not let it go until someone validates it. And if the person can't validate it after much persistence on my part, I make them write it down to check later, hopefully for an "Aha" moment to come.

So on this night, I was pulled toward the back of the room. I sensed a female energy coming through "from above," like a grandmother, and had a strong feeling there was a young woman in that section who had recently lost her grandma . . . or at least, there was someone sitting there who was *connected* to a young woman who just lost her grandmother. When no one put up their hand, I explained to the audience that this girl didn't have to be in the room, but could just be linked to a person who was present. I told them that if anyone had a relative, friend, or co-worker who was not with them today and their grandmother had passed within the last few weeks, they should please put up their hand. Sandra, who was standing in the back of the hall, looked around, ready to take the microphone to the person who could acknowledge this message.

Nada.

The next message came through loud and clear. Somehow connected to this girl with the deceased grandmother was another girl in the room who was pregnant.

A hush came over the room.

Now, one of my favorite things about this work is watching the similarities in people's reactions all over the country when I make certain statements. Whenever I announce that someone in the room is pregnant, no one wants to put her hand up. It's as if I'm handing out some sort of horrific diagnosis—no one seems to want it. This day was no different. Someone was pregnant, but she wasn't about to own up to it. After I spent about 15 minutes delivering this same message over and over . . . the grandmother . . . the pregnancy . . . I just thought, *Wow . . . some woman is soooooo pregnant and maybe she doesn't know it yet. Surprise, surprise!*

But I was starting to get frustrated, too. Okay, maybe you don't know you're pregnant, or you don't want to tell hundreds of strangers that you are, and that's fine. But why was no one acknowledging a grandmother who'd recently passed? The problem with a message not being validated in a big group is that during the long pauses in the session, other energies trying to connect with their own family will jump in and try to take over. They see an opening and grab it. And that's exactly what happened in this case. While waiting for the grandma and the pregnant woman to show themselves, I saw a flash of steel bars in front of me.

"I'm seeing bars," I told the audience. "To me, this means someone may have a relative in prison or was in prison, and this might be connected as well. Does someone back there understand that?"

Shake of heads. If this had been baseball, I'd be batting zero.

I now had the pregnancy, the grandmother, and someone else's family (I thought) coming in with some type of incarceration issue. And nobody was fessing up to any of it. I could see it was going to be a long night.

This back-and-forth went on for at least a half hour. This was really getting to me, but I assumed my pit-bull stance, planted my feet solidly and squarely apart, dug in my heels, and stood my ground. I wasn't going anywhere until we figured this out. Whoever was coming through wasn't giving up either, so I asked the grandmother figure for help—literally. When I say this, I mean I actually asked her for help. I silently urged her in my mind, *Ya gotta give me something more to work with here. Give me a detail someone will recognize.* Well, she did. She told me she was connected to the initial "J," as in Joanne or Josephine. (Again, just to explain the process, it's not that I'm *seeing* this granny in front of me. What I was actually seeing was my own grandmother in my mind's eye, which always signifies to me that it's a grandmother coming through. Then, I could hear the "JJJJJ" sound in my head.)

Still, of the 2,000 people in the room, no one claimed this grandma who was working really hard to come through. And here's where I laugh at what the cynics say about this process. According to them, all these gullible, stupid people are just hanging on to my every word, waiting and hoping with bated breath to pounce on whatever far-fetched information I'm giving so they can yell, "Yessss, it's meeeee!" because they're so desperate to believe anything. Well, the cynics would be hard-pressed to describe anyone in this audience as jumping on that message.

I began to get impatient with whoever in the audience could not, or rather, would not, validate this message. Again, you'd know if your grandmother just passed, right? And if you had a friend whose name began with a "J" like Joanne or Josephine who just lost her grandmother, you'd remember that. Maybe I was dealing with a severe case of psychic amnesia. By this point, I was positive that the woman who was pregnant was in the room, and was in the area I was being pulled toward. Then I got another detail . . . an image of my wife and singer Ricky Martin.

"The person this is connected to is a huuuuuugggge Ricky Martin fan," I told the group, "and I know this because they're showing me a picture of my wife, Sandra, and a picture of Ricky Martin!"

My friend Liz, who also has a teenybopper obsession with the magnetic Mr. Martin, was on microphone duty that day. She started to tease Sandra in the back of the room, saying, "Maybe it's you he's talking about . . . Ricky Martin fan, back of the room, and he saw your face. Maybe it's you!"

Sandra laughed. "Yeah, right . . . " and continued to look around to see if anyone would own up to this reading. After much frustration, I had to give up. I guess the pregnant woman with the dead grandmother and the hots for Ricky Martin just wasn't ready to come forward.

ESP vs. EPT

ON THE FLIGHT BACK TO NEW YORK, our friends continued to tease Sandra and me that the "unclaimed" message was for us, but we laughed it off. We were getting ready for the family-planning phase of our lives together, it's true, but we hadn't officially begun the *trying* phase yet so . . . no way. It wasn't us.

A week later, it was the anniversary of my grandfather's death—and also his wife's—my grandmother Josephine's—birthday. The day is always filled with a lot of emotion for the family, and every year we have a Catholic mass in their honor and a get-together afterward at my grandmother's old house in Glen Cove, Long Island. That was the house I grew up in, which is now my Aunt Roseann's home.

As the usual cast of lively characters of aunts, uncles, and cousins in my big Italian family sat around the table and reminisced about one thing or another, I started daydreaming, glancing up at the walls at the old family photos hanging there. Everywhere I looked, I saw reminders of my childhood and of the family parties gone by. It was such a feeling of "home" for me. As I continued to study the photos, I was drawn to the portrait of my mom hanging on the wall, and I felt a weird twinge. Time seemed to freeze. It was as if all my relatives on the Other Side suddenly wanted to make their presence known to me in a major way, like I was getting my own reading with my entire family. I glanced at the photos, then over to Sandra . . . and it hit me.

Aha!

The second we left the house, walking down the driveway, I blurted it out: "You're pregnant!" Sandra looked at me like I was crazy.

In any case, we drove right over to the local Glen Cove CVS pharmacy—directly across the street from the strip mall where I worked in my teens, and bought a pregnancy kit. When we got home, Sandra ran to the bathroom while I let our dogs, Jolie and Roxie, outside. By the time I brought the dogs back in, Sandra was standing in the hallway, holding up the little blue stick.

"It's positive." She smiled. "We're pregnant!"

Now Sandra's fatigue at the Golden Globes party made sense. And so did the messages in Vegas. The Ricky Martin fan, the picture of Sandra, the pull to the back of the room, the pregnancy . . . was all for *us*. Seems I'd hit the Vegas jackpot after all. But there was one thing that didn't make sense. Who was the grandmother who'd just passed connected to the "J" name? Who was our kindly messenger? The answer would reveal itself shortly.

JOANNE GETS CALLED TO THE OFFICE

BOTH SANDRA AND I HAD LOST OUR GRANDMOTHERS a few years earlier, so we knew that this grandma didn't belong to us. We were perplexed. But I knew that this older woman had to belong to someone Sandra or I was connected to. Here she was, good enough to bring us our news, and I had no clue how to let her family know that she'd come through. Then my friend Liz, who's also the supervising producer on *Crossing Over,* remembered something. Our post-production supervisor, Joanne, had recently lost her grandmother. Liz insisted that we call Joanne and quiz her about it. But I started to wonder . . . could I have misinterpreted the message? Could it have been *my* grandmother, Josephine, coming through?

Liz was insistent that the message was for Joanne. (Liz has great intuition, and I always tease her about it, saying she's not allowed to have her own show called *Crossing Over with La Liz.*)

"John, you're being a relative stealer," Liz accused me, referring to how I describe audience members who insist information is coming through for them when it's not. "You don't like it when people do it in the gallery, and now you're doing it yourself!" Liz had paid very close attention to the details of that session in Vegas and was determined to find the true recipient.

"The grandmother was connected to the 'J' name," she corrected me. "She herself wasn't the 'J' name. Remember?"

Of course I didn't remember. When I do readings, it's as if the images and impressions are downloaded into me from the Other Side like a computer downloads onto a disk. The thoughts don't originate in my own brain, so I rarely remember them afterwards.

"And," Liz added, "Joanne's grandmother just passed away."

Before I could protest anymore, Liz called Joanne and began interrogating her on speakerphone. Had her grandmother passed? *Yes, about a week before.* And . . . um . . . don't mean to pry . . . but did she happen to have a family member in jail? Joanne had no idea about that one. And, if we didn't mind, why were we asking?

"We can't explain just now," I spoke up, "but can you check it out?" Poor Joanne—we probably freaked her out. She made some frantic phone calls to her mother and her aunt and called back within 15 minutes to let us know, in a surprised and slightly trembling voice, that, yes, as a matter of fact, she did have a relative in jail. . . .

"Get over to John's office right away," Liz told her. *Click.*

The post-production facility for the show, where Joanne supervises the editing, was just around the corner from my office, but she must have sprinted anyway because when she arrived a minute and a half later, she was gasping for breath and looking queasy. Actually, she looked terrified. She expected me to give her some sort of tragic family news—and who could blame her?

"No, no . . . don't worry," I told her. "We actually might have good news for you." I sat her down in a chair so her knees would stop shaking, and started to relay the story slowly, step by step, so I wouldn't shock her or anything.

"Joanne, I understand your grandmother just passed. . . . "

"Yes . . . "

"Well, when we were in Vegas, we had a grandmother come through at the seminar . . . "

"Okay . . . "

"She came through with the news that Sandra was pregnant . . . "

"Wow . . . cool . . . "

"And she was connected to a 'J' name."

"Uh-huh."

"Maybe a 'Joanne.' We think it was your grandmother. "

A look of total relief washed over Joanne's face. "You're kidding!" she squealed. We described the rest of the reading, detail by detail, and Joanne agreed that it was her grandma. But strangely enough, of all the emotions Joanne was feeling at that moment, surprise wasn't one of them. With a triumphant smile on her face, she told us why her grandma Anne, who'd passed away at 91 from Lou Gehrig's disease, had made such a timely appearance.

"On the last night of my grandmother's wake, a week before, all of my cousins brought photos and different things to put in the casket with her . . . but I didn't have anything. I'd gone through all my photos of us together the night before, and I wanted to keep all of them, so I was very upset that I didn't have anything to put in. Then my mother said to me, 'Why don't you put in one of your *Crossing Over* business cards?' I took one out and, because my grandmother always used to kiss our birthday cards with a big lipstick kiss, I kissed the back of the card with a big lipstick kiss myself. And with a pen I wrote on the back: 'I love you, Grandma. Please go to John!' I tucked the card under her vest, over her heart, and I never told anybody about it."

Liz and I were floored by Joanne's story and were glad that the mystery grandma had finally been identified.

"We've spent days trying to figure this out," Liz told her. "John's been driving me crazy ever since Thursday."

Joanne got a funny look on her face.

"Thursday? Did this happen Thursday of last week?"

We nodded.

"What time?"

Now it was our turn to be curious. We told her it had happened around 7 P.M. Vegas time, and Joanne jumped up out of the chair and shrieked.

"Oh my God! That night, right around that time, I was looking at a picture of my grandmother on the fireplace mantel, and I was thinking that both my grandmothers were gone. I got very upset and cried, and I just looked up at the sky and said out loud, again, 'Grandma, please go to John!'"

Okay, now I was turning into mush, and all three of us were grinning from ear to ear.

"Well, that explains the timing of it all," I told her. "But I still wonder . . . of all the information your grandmother could have come through with, why would she choose to talk about Sandra's pregnancy?"

Joanne thought about this for a minute and remembered something.

"Maybe my grandmother was repaying a good deed," she explained. "My aunt was sitting in the gallery watching a taping of *Crossing Over* a few months ago, and John had told her that in January there was going to be a big event—a celebration—in her family, and that my uncle, who had passed six months earlier, was going to be there for it. And then John got a number five attached to it. As it turned out, in January, after many years of trying, my cousin was able to adopt a baby. They signed the papers and brought the baby home on January 5th. It was a really big to-do for the family. Maybe my grandmother was repaying John. He'd brought us news about my cousin's baby, and she was now bringing him news of his *own* baby."

That worked for us. I loved the whole circularity of it all.

And so, I found out I was going to be a dad from my co-worker's deceased grandmother, whom I'd never known in life. It was a validation that neither Joanne nor I will ever forget. And it's a good example of how the Other Side has its own reasoning and rationale about the way a message comes through. I would have expected a relative of mine to come through to deliver baby news like that rather than a complete stranger—that would have been the logical route for them to take. But the Other Side is not logical in human terms; they operate on their own agenda and are much wiser than we are. This way, I got my news, and at the same time, a co-worker received validation that her grandmother was alive and well on the Other Side. Someone else might have been disappointed that Grandma didn't have a specific message for her, but Joanne knew her big message was just that her grandmother came through as requested in spite of the fact that Joanne wasn't even in the room.

So often, energies come through when they know someone in the room can pass on the message to a loved one. I can't count how many times a person has come for a session, and on their way to my office a co-worker jokingly mentions, "Hey, say hi to my Aunt Susan who passed away last year!"

Well, wouldn't you know it, Aunt Susan shows up in the middle of the reading. Or, to your dismay, she takes up your *entire* reading. And then you have to go back and report all the details to your buddy because the reading ended up being for her.

We actually did an entire episode of *Crossing Over* (called "Being the Messenger") on this very phenomenon. It was full of very moving accounts of readings I did for people who weren't even in the studio. But their friend/relative/co-worker or acquaintance was there, and they had to scribble down every word I said so they could pass it on.

It's not such an easy task—being the "spiritual mail carrier"!

IT'S A GIRL—NOT!

THE OTHER SIDE WASN'T THROUGH WITH ME just yet.

Throughout her pregnancy, Sandra and I were toying with whether or not we should find out if the baby was a boy or girl. For all of you who are asking, why I, a psychic, would have to ask a doctor . . . well, predicting the sex of a child for me is like predicting the next card at the blackjack table—it's not my strong suit. This specialty was my mother-in-law, Lina's, domain, who's about 95-percent accurate in predicting the sex of a baby just by looking at the mother. Her prediction for us was that we were going to have a girl, and that was her final answer. So, we all planned on a girl. We were struggling to come up with female names we could agree upon, but only seemed to agree on a boy's name—Justin. We kept joking that it would be a lot easier if it was just a boy, since we already had the name.

The night before we were due to have the second-level sonogram, I had a dream that I was wrestling with Roxie, one of my two bichon frise pooches. During this dream, she morphed into a fat baby wearing a stinky diaper that needed to be changed, and in the dream, I changed the diaper. And lo and behold, the "she"-baby was most definitely a "he." At three o'clock in the morning, I leaned over and woke Sandra up to tell her that "Muffina," as I was affectionately calling the baby, was now going to have to be called "Muffin-o" because we were having a boy. I was sure that my psychic dream would override my mother-in-law's old-world maternal instincts. But even after this revelatory dream, Lina was still insistent that it was a girl. And so was everyone else, even though the psychic in the house begged to differ. Well, you should have seen the look on Sandra's face when the technician told her we were indeed having a boy. Lina was sure the doctors were all wrong until the day Justin Michael was born.

LABOR DAY

Justin, as we knew his name would be, didn't like the concept of being upside down and would not turn to make a natural delivery possible. The doctors decided that Sandra would have to have a cesarean section—something she was not at all opposed to after the last sonogram told us our baby would be a big, strapping eight-plus pounds.

"We're going to schedule the cesarean for next Tuesday," the doctor told us.

I shook my head. No way.

Now, imagine if you will, that you're an obstetrician and your patient's husband tells you he doesn't want to have the baby on a specific date because of the child's astrological chart. Actually, I should clarify here; Sandra was ready to have him pronto, right in the doctor's office—that's how ready she was. But I really wanted Justin to be a Libra, like Daddy. Since the baby and Sandra were in no danger and there was an opening in his schedule the following week, the doctor agreed to change the date by a couple of days to please me. But I'm sure he was thinking all the while: *These people are nutty!*

The delivery date was now going to be September 25th (the Libra sun sign begins on the 23rd). We checked into the hospital with quiet excitement, knowing that in a few short hours our lives would be changed forever. As the doctors prepared for surgery and Sandra was wheeled into the operating room for pre-surgical procedures, I was out in the hall in a surgical gown and mask, preparing for the big event.

I expected, of course, that all of my relatives from the Other Side were going to show up. I was positive that my mother, grandmother, uncle, aunt, and other family and friends would be right there with me when Justin came into the world so they could be the first to congratulate us. It was going to be standing room only in this delivery room!

Out in the hall, I prayed the rosary and meditated as if I were preparing for an uber-marathon reading session. I did my special breathing exercises with the visualization that all would go exactly as planned. And when they called me into the delivery suite, I was serene, prepared, and confident. I looked at my beautiful wife, knowing that something out of this world was about to happen.

And that's when it happened.

Nothing! At least, not from the Other Side.

In front of me, on this side, plenty was happening—my son was being born. But why wasn't I getting anything from the Other Side? I sharpened my psychic tuning fork and put my faculties on high alert. Nothing. I neither heard, felt, nor saw a thing.

Meanwhile, Sandra was busy becoming a mother and wondering where the heck I was. She looked over at me with such love that, in an instant, I was brought back to this world.

And what proceeded from there was truly wondrous. I became a dad and watched the miracle unfold right in front of me as my little boy arrived into the world.

But I won't lie and tell you that I wasn't disappointed that no vision, thought, flash, or feeling was downloaded to me from my family on the Other Side. Part of me was borderline devastated. At that moment, I fully understood how my clients feel when they don't get what they're looking for from a reading.

It was strange to feel such extreme emotions at once—total joy at holding my son for the first time, yet total sadness that my mother wasn't "with me" when my first child was born. I felt kind of deserted by her and let down by my guides. Was it too much to ask if just once I could get a validation of my own in the way I'd envisioned it? It took me a minute or two to shake off the self-pity as I gave myself an imaginary slap on the wrist for doing exactly what I tell my clients not to do: expect the Other Side to serve us like we're at a restaurant ordering a meal.

I looked up at my wife's smiling face and realized an important lesson: We can't get caught up with the spiritual world and forget to pay attention to the physical world—to what's right in front of us. We can't constantly look for validations from the Other Side every step we take or we'll miss all the little joys of life on this side. We're here for a reason—to live our lives as best we can and to be as fully present in our lives as possible. We have to appreciate the validations as they come . . . in their own way.

Once I got that, then the validation *did* happen. But not in the way I expected it. As the doctors, nurses, and technicians were finishing up all their individual tasks, they began discussing the rest of their day. It was informal banter among colleagues, but one by one, in their conversation, they began unknowingly naming all my family members who had passed that I hoped would be there.

"Oh, look at him," said one of the technicians, gazing at Justin. "You had a little boy! So you got a prince instead of a little princess!" "Princess" was my mother's nickname, and every time I hear it or see it written, it's a hello from mom.

"Hey, Rachel, can you pass me the . . ." Rachel was my aunt. Josephine, my grandmother, was then mentioned, and within two minutes, three other family members were named out loud in succession. Coincidence? I don't think so. The Other Side has their own agenda and their own way. I tell people that over and over all the time. The mere acknowledgment of my family's names in that passing conversation was validation enough for me that they were there in the delivery room, sharing my joy.

CHAPTER TWO

Shining Star Never Fades

EVERY NOW AND AGAIN, I meet up with people who think they're being funny—and original—by asking me if I've talked to Elvis lately. With the recent release of Elvis's number-one hits CD, I had a ton of radio stations calling me up, trying to book me on their shows so I could get them an exclusive "interview" with Elvis from the Other Side. And that request was one of the more *sincere* ones. Some of the others were way out there—even for a guy who talks to the dead.

But even if I *did* connect with Elvis, I wonder if his fans would be disappointed. Would he still be "The King" on the Other Side? I often advise people not to expect their loved ones to be *exactly* as they were when they were here in the physical world. There's a process we go through—a shedding of the Earthly world that we leave behind—that's part of the transition. When we shed our bodies, our worldly limitations disappear . . . our physical weaknesses are gone, and our emotional burdens dissolve. It's like the worm going into the cocoon, shedding skin, and becoming the butterfly. We *are* that worm as we move through life, and one day we become that butterfly when our physical body dies, allowing our soul to soar.

Don't get me wrong—your loved ones' personalities will be intact when they connect with you either through a medium or through your own experience. You'll definitely be able to recognize them and know that they're still connected to you. But there are also times when they'll come through to you and seem different from what you remember. I like to believe that the reason for the change is that transition, that shedding—and now they see life from a different perspective. For example, if someone was extremely prejudiced in life, I'm positive that upon their transition that type of mind-set *has* to change. I was shown by my guides many years ago that we're all wearing an invisible coat with many pockets. Pockets of love, fear, disappointment, and judgment line this coat, and when we cross over, part of our transition is to empty out those pockets and examine their contents—whether positive or negative—as part of our soul's progression. In time, once we fully understand our "pocket" issues, they become embedded in the fabric of our soul and we take off the coat.

As this progression occurs, our spirit changes. Our negative issues soften, and our positive issues are highlighted. So if you've had a psychic experience where a loved one came through and their personality seemed different to you, this might be why.

Shortly after my mom crossed over, she came to me in a dream, but not just a regular dream. It was a very vivid experience, and so real that I remembered every last detail when I awoke. The details stayed with me for years afterward. This is how I know it was more than a dream, more than a manifestation of my subconscious. This was a "visit." A visit is when someone who has crossed over connects with us in our dreams. It's the number-one way for an energy to come through to a human being. Why? Because in the dream state, we accept the experience more readily—it's "safer."

When most people are visited by a loved one in a dream, it doesn't scare or confuse them, as opposed to what would happen if all of a sudden their deceased mom appeared at the foot of their bed in broad daylight. In a dream, we have the luxury of rationalizing that "it was just a dream," while at the same time, actually experiencing a bona fide visit.

In the dream/visit I had with my mother, I kept asking her to tell me what to do about a certain frustrating situation I was going through at the time, but all she would do was smile, tell me that she loved me, and remind me that she was there for me. Being the relentless person I am, I wasn't satisfied with such a fluffy, angelic-type response, and I kept trying to pin her down to a more definite answer. She finally told me that those on the Other Side aren't allowed to tell us what to do because we're here to learn specific lessons for our own soul's growth, and they can't interfere with our learning or take on the responsibility for our actions. And then she told me again that she loved me, and blah, blah, *blah*. . . .

When I woke up, I was really ticked off. If my mother were alive, she wouldn't have wasted a second telling me exactly what she thought about the situation and what do to about it—and she would have more than likely kicked my ass for finding myself in that situation anyway. (For curious readers out there wondering about my predicament, it's nothing juicy enough for me to go into detail about. But for a 20-year-old who had just lost his mother, who was trying to take on the financial responsibilities she'd left behind, and who was taking care of his grandmother and aunt as well, my plight seemed disastrous at the time.) During my visit, it was as if my mother had undergone some type of Stepford-Mom personality transplant and a flower-power energy had taken over to scatter tulips for me to tiptoe through. I had to realize that with her new knowledge and experiences on the Other Side, there would also be a new side to my mother.

So, what about Elvis? JFK (Sr. and Jr.)? Princess Diana? Mother Teresa? Or even Hitler? All these larger-than-life individuals are no longer the exact same energy on the Other Side, but their experiences on this side help define who they are and how they may change after they cross over. What we go through here in the physical world helps shape the lessons of the soul, both here and on the Other Side.

For example, let's say that a white man was a bigot in his Earthly life and his daughter fell in love with and married an African-American man, causing a rift between father and child.

When this man dies and does his life review—that is, empties his pockets—I believe he'll find a pocket of judgment and prejudice and recognize that he allowed those beliefs in life to affect the relationship he had with his daughter. He'll then see the error in his old way of thinking.

People continue to learn and grow on the Other Side, and their growth may alter their energies. Hitler, for example, probably had to do a heavy-duty soul cleansing and life review as a result of the life he led here. Faced with his past, he might have seen his errors, understood them, and then tried to atone for them—perhaps by assisting others on Earth as a guide.

And there are no red-velvet ropes, VIP sections, or celebrities on the Other Side the way we define them here. Just because someone was famous in this life doesn't mean they're well known after they cross over. I believe that we only get "special treatment" once we cross over if we lived a truly good and spiritual life on the Earth plane—and if we truly absorbed the lessons we set out to learn. If we get far in our spiritual development here, we arrive there on more of an "advanced" level. Not that we're treated any differently, but we probably have less work to do and a lot more fun. But even though celebrities aren't signing autographs up *there*, they can still come through in readings and talk about signing autographs *here* . . . and explain who they were in this life.

In *CROSSING OVER: The Stories Behind the Stories*, I introduced you to Debbie Swift, the daughter of songwriter/singer Carl "Blue Suede Shoes" Perkins. Perkins's career was awe-inspiring, and he was truly a granddaddy of rock 'n' roll. However, when he came through to his family in a phone reading, he was just "Daddy," and not the famous person others perceive him to be.

The only clues I kept getting during the reading that made me think that the person coming through was famous in life were specific, celebrity-related items he was showing me. He showed me Elvis Presley's belt, and I saw images of celebrities such as Wynonna Judd, George Harrison, and Roy Orbison. At first, I thought I was just getting information in my usual, pop-culture way, until his daughter started acknowledging the celebrity names I was listing as the people who had been at her father's memorial or had worked with him in some way. That, I must say, was a wild experience.

I did another celebrity reading on *Crossing Over* the TV show where I read actress Tracy Nelson, the daughter of '50s teen heartthrob Rick Nelson. The reading was scheduled by the show's producers, who were careful to keep Tracy's identity a secret from me. To take the secrecy a step further, I arranged for her to sit down behind me after I was already sitting in the chair so that I couldn't see her face during the reading. I didn't do this to create any dramatic TV *oooohs* and *aaahhhhs*, but rather the opposite. I thought if I didn't see the person I was reading, whoever it was would relax during the session and pay closer attention to what I was saying without wondering if I'd recognized them and if I was giving them certain pieces of information because I recognized them.

I told Tracy to just respond with a yes or no, and the session began. Her dad came through almost immediately, and as soon as he did, he acknowledged that his sons were there in the studio as well, so the producers brought Ricky's twin boys, Gunnar and Matthew, to the stage to experience the session with Tracy. Now I had three celebrities sitting behind me, and one on the Other Side. But of the many validations that came through during that reading, there was only one detail I recall about him being famous— a reference to a performance he'd given at a theater like Carnegie Hall. That was it. From my perspective, the man coming through was basically a dad talking about his family and their personal, intimate connections with each other. The message that came through the strongest, which helped the family know that it was Dad, had nothing to do with his career accomplishments—rather, it was a reference to a special "coin" in the family. And one of the kids had brought the coin to the studio that day and had it in his pocket.

Another more recent example was one that will stick in my mind for years to come.

On a cold Thursday afternoon in February 2003, I was maneuvering through Manhattan traffic to get to a hotel on the west side for a reading I was asked to do. When working on my nonfiction books, I collaborate with another writer to make sure there's a journalistic objectivity to the readings we write about—whether they're transcribed directly or paraphrased from either my perspective or the perspective of the sitter. And in the case of any celebrity-related readings, I get the writer—in this instance, my friend and *People* magazine correspondent Natasha Stoynoff—to organize the session so I don't know whom I'm reading beforehand or any details about them.

This day, all I knew was that I'd be meeting with a client at 4 P.M. at a hotel in Manhattan's Columbus Circle area, at the foot of Central Park. I left early from my home in Long Island and drove into Manhattan, listening to my all-time favorite singer in the world, the amazing Linda Eder (I mentioned her earlier). Her latest CD, titled *Broadway, My Way* was in the CD changer, and I played it during the whole ride in. Linda's voice is so powerful that I listen to her music before most of my readings or events, and after them as well.

As she was belting out a ballad, Sandra called me on my cell phone. "Hey, where are you?" she asked. "Do you have a meeting today?"

"I'm on the Triboro Bridge on my way to do a reading Natasha scheduled for the book."

"Cooool . . . is it someone famous?"

"I have no idea. But I'll find out shortly. . . . "

AFTER I MADE IT INTO THE CITY, I had to maneuver through cars double-parked on both sides of 9th Avenue. An enormous snowstorm had hit the northeast three days earlier, and the piled-up snow made traffic even worse than usual in midtown Manhattan. I made it to my appointment right on time. Natasha, whom you'll read about throughout this book, met me in the lobby. She was there to tape-record and take notes on the session.

As we rode the elevator to the seventh floor, I looked over at Natasha, who was excited and nervous. Since she and I had begun working on this project, she had sat through more group readings and seminars than most people I know, and now this was to be her first, in-person private session to witness and document. We rang the bell of Suite 722, and a very attractive woman named Diane, whom I didn't recognize, answered the door and welcomed us in. She seemed very gentle, quiet, and sad.

We sat on the couch in front of a table laid out with a single red rose and a lit candle, and began what proceeded to be a very emotional, tear-filled session. Almost immediately, a strong energy took over and dominated the entire reading—which is rare. Usually three or four energies will come through in a private session, vying for attention.

Although you might be able to figure it out earlier than I did, it wasn't until we were finished over an hour later did I learn who the "celebrity" in question was. What follows is an abridged version of the reading, which is too long to include in its entirety. But I present most of it, in chronological order, so you can experience the process as it unfolded. And as you'll see, the information flowed with intensity—with messages from a strong energy who had a strong presence in life, too.

John: Okay, the first thing I'm going to tell you is that I have a male who's coming through, claiming to be above you, and he's making it like he's either your father or your stepfather, but he's an older male. He's making me feel that I need to acknowledge the letter "W," like he's connected to the letter "W."

I also have somebody younger who's passed. I feel like somebody lost their child. And the older man is letting me know that *the child is here.* But with this child, this isn't a health-care passing—this is something that happened.

So it's got to be an event or something that actually takes place that causes the person to pass. To me it feels impact related. So I feel like somebody passes with an impact, somebody passes with a vehicle accident, somebody passes with a gunshot, there's a BANG that takes place, and it's not a suicide. This is not a suicide, this is not somebody claiming responsibility—well, it's not that they're not claiming responsibility, they *are* kind of claiming responsibility.

They're making me feel like they put themselves in the wrong position, the wrong place at the wrong time.

And this event was extremely publicized. There are headlines and spotlights all around it. And they're showing me that there are three or four occurrences when people were reporting something that seems to be slightly off, like something was being reported and things were being left out of the report. And the way it was being reported made this individual look bad, and I feel as if I need to bring this up in some way. I don't know, it's like this weird—I don't want to call it controversy, but there's some controversial issue that comes up with this, okay?

Now, I'm going to go back and say that this male who's coming through again is claiming to be above you—that means the father, the uncle, the grandfather. He's telling me to let you know that he's here. He wants me to know that this younger male is coming through with him. I'm calling it a male energy because there's a very dominant energy attached to this. It may be female, but if this is a girl who's passed, I'm getting a very dominant energy. I have to let you know that he comes through with this child, but in particular, I know that you lost a child. You understand that? Is that true?

Diane: Yes.

John: Now there's an "A" name connection that comes up here. They want me to acknowledge the "A," okay? And they're making me feel like I also need to acknowledge the other son, the brother. They tell me to acknowledge the boy who's here.

They're showing me your son—living, then you have a daughter that passed. Right?

Diane: Yes.

John: Okay, here's the deal. She has a very dominant energy. The way it comes across, I would think you lost a son, because this energy is very masculine, very strong and tough. But her toughness is not exterior; it's not an external toughness. It's an internal, spiritual kind of toughness.

And she wants her brother to know that she came through. Her major concern is for you. She's making me feel like you two were more like sisters, or buddies. She wants me to tell you to talk about going to the church, going to the priest, going to the place, and you were there by yourself. I'm feeling a very spiritual-feeling place, whether it be a church, a temple, I don't know. I'm in this place, and while I'm here, I feel like nobody is physically there with you, it's like your quiet time, it's your place to be there. And she's making me feel like she was there with you.

I don't know if you're coming up on the second month of her passing, if you're coming up on the second anniversary of her passing, but I feel like we're coming up on two, and she's making me feel like I need to talk about you selling your property, or you selling the house, or you selling the stuff that's coming up, and she sees this. Okay? She doesn't talk about her father, though. The father is not around?

Diane: He is, he's around.

John: He's living?

Diane: Yes.

John: Where does the "L" come in for him? Like Len, or Leo or Lee or Leah . . . ?

Diane: That's her name.

John: She wants me to acknowledge the Len, Lee, Leo kind of version. I feel like—I want to take that and call her that . . . or Dad maybe called her that.

Diane: He called her LiLi most of the time!

John: She's telling me to tell you that what you wrote was published, that something you wrote was published, and she's acknowledging that. And she wants to know about the yellow tattoo or a yellow painting thing that comes up here that she wants me to bring up. Okay? She shows that.

I'm back to the fact that her passing was an event. There's an accident. But she's not driving this car; this is not something she was responsible for. But I feel like "I don't have to be here," like "I don't have to be in the vehicle," like "I didn't have to be here."

Diane: Mm-hmm.

John: But it's the right time because she was done with what she had to do here, as hard as that might be to say. But I feel like she's doing more now there. She wants me to go back again, because one of the major things you're having a hard time with is how she passes.

Diane: Yes.

John: And she's making me feel like she doesn't want to tell me. She doesn't want to tell me how she passed. She's making me feel like you understand what I'm saying and I don't have to describe to you exactly what happened, although I'd rather hear it from her. But she's saying she won't, she's not going to go there.

She's making me feel like . . . she's in the backseat, and I feel like she could have been taking a nap, she could have had her headphones on, she could have been reading a book, whatever. There's all this hustle and bustle happening. She's getting whooshed off, like I feel like I'm being whooshed, like I have to go to my next place.

Diane (nodding): Yes . . .

John: Now, she did not pass on September 11th, but she's telling me to tell you 9/11, she's showing me 9/11. There's something about 9/11 connected to her in some way or to your family or to her, but it's like some of the families that I dealt with that are 9/11 related, they didn't have the ability to physically memorialize the person. You were able to do that in some respects, but there are things of hers that were not reclaimed, were missing, were things that you didn't get back.

Diane: Yes.

John: She's telling me that April is a significant month. It might be a birthday or an anniversary.

Diane: Okay . . .

John: Now, I feel very, very clearly that you walk around acknowledging her, you know there's something else. Your belief, your faith, and your spirituality are very much intact. What you're not honoring, and I'm sorry to put you on the spot, because I don't really know you, but what you're not honoring is your own grief. And one of the things that I have to tell you is that I believe the only way to get back the love that you have, that unconditional love as a parent for this child, is to honor that grief.

Because grief is the other side of love. When you take away the physical person, the object you direct that love toward, you don't know where to put that love. You don't know where it goes. But she's still here. She's still connected here. You know, she's the one who arranged this. It's like she's taking the credit for doing this. And she's making me feel that there's so much stuff left that's not finished with her, like the stuff that she was working on, something wasn't finished.

Diane: Yes, yes.

John: Did she write? She must have been a writer, 'cause she had to do something that would be—they're making me feel that something important is coming out, like being published. There's a writing thing about her. I think they're making a movie of her, or on a smaller level maybe you're making a documentary of her? They're showing me Selena. You're not related to Selena, are you?

Diane: No.

John: Then she's got to be like Selena.

Diane: Uh-huh.

John: She wants me to acknowledge your mom—your biological mom. Your mom and she have overlapping similarities. There's a parallel between both, whether it be the same names, similar dates, there's like a similarity that comes up there . . . and a few people pass in a short period of time as well . . . that you don't finish grieving one person and then this happens, that's my feeling. You're still dealing with the loss of one person, and now this compounds that feeling.

Diane: Yes.

John: If they're going to do something writing-wise about her, you need to do it. You need to be the person to do it. Not somebody else. With her own stuff, whatever she did job-wise, was she trying to get more active in the control?

Diane: Yes!

John: She wants you to learn the same. So when you do something, it's going to be therapeutic and healing to you, and you're going to get it right. Your son shouldn't do it—*you* should do it. Even if you have to work with a writer who's going to capture your voice, your feelings, and your private moments that you want to share. And then, if there's a movie or whatever, it can be made from your book. Not on what somebody else's idea is, or what they think it should be.

You know, I feel like—I don't know if that gold chain is yours, if she gave that to you, but she wants me to acknowledge that . . .

Diane: [crying]

John: She was very happy to help you accomplish things, to take care of you in some way. She wanted to make sure that stuff you did was in style and classy. It's all about classy. Everything's gotta be classy.

Diane: [nodding]

John: She's talking about getting hair, getting a wig. Is somebody going for hair extensions? Did somebody get some type of . . . after she passed, did you find something or have something delivered that was hers, hair related?

Diane: Yes.

John: From when she was a child?

Diane: Yes.

John: She must have been out of my state when she passed. She wasn't here in New York?

Diane: No.

John: Where's Betty? Betsy or Beebee, or there's a "B" name she's trying to acknowledge. It might be her way of saying hello to somebody who's still here. She said it's weird that you got this room. Was there something in this room when you got here that struck you as a sign from her? Or the number? What room is this?

Diane: 722.

John: 722? Does 722 have a meaning for you? This is a big building, and there could have been a lot of rooms they could have given you. But we got this one. She's highlighting this.

Diane: She was 22 when she passed.

John: Okay.

Diane: And she loved this hotel . . . it was her favorite.

John: You have an unconditional type of connection to her, that whatever she did you encouraged and were excited about. She doesn't want to tell me how she passed? I'm *begging* her . . . sometimes they won't do that; sometimes they feel like it's more important—and she does in this case—to move away from the physical passing and focus more on the living, on herself, on those still here. Did you make your own DVD or CD of her stuff, that other people wouldn't have access to?

Diane: I have a CD that only I have.

John: Nobody else has it, right? She's acknowledging that.

Do you have an SUV? She's telling me there's a joke about the navigation thing in the car—either her making a joke with you about that or you were driving and it was telling you where to go and telling you what to do, and you said out loud to yourself, or to her, that if she was here she'd be making fun of this.

Diane: Yes, she joked a lot about that!

John: She says something about the pink blouse, the pink shirt . . . do you still have that?

Diane: I do.

John: You just need to know that the stuff she's coming through with—the older man we talked about in the beginning—that father figure, your mom, the great-aunt—these are the people who are with her on the Other Side. She's not alone; she's got family and friends there. She's very clear in the fact that she was a social person in life, and she's equally social on the Other Side.

Your spiritual beliefs—hold on to them. They're going to pull you and your family through this. But she's making me feel like you need to be the matriarch, that you need to be the person that . . . you know when you sit on the plane and the oxygen mask drops down and they say you need to put your mask on first before you can help the person next to you? That's what your life is like right now. If the mask drops down, you've got to make sure you take care of yourself first. You've got to take care of *you* so that you can be able to take care of the other people in your family.

Once you do that, then you can incorporate her still being part of your life, and in *knowing* . . . and that word is probably the one thing that I want you to leave here with today: "knowing." Because the only thing that got me through when I was 19 years old and just lost my mother was that I had that *knowing*.

I remember pulling up one night at 5 A.M. after being out all night and thinking, *Nobody cares right now that I'm out at 5 A.M.* Sure, my grandmother was downstairs, and yes she cared, but she was afraid to say anything to me.

My point in saying this right now is that I feel like everybody's in that spot I just described. They're all pulling up at 5 A.M. thinking that nobody else cares. Your son, you, your husband. But every time you talk about your daughter, you'll realize that you all care, you all care about the same thing, and by honoring that and by talking about her and what she's left . . . because according to her, she's left a lot—and I don't mean money, I mean like her persona, herself, her image . . . whatever. By honoring that, you can know she's still connected by the bonds of love that bound you all when she was here.

36

Diane: [crying softly now]

John: Okay, now she keeps showing me some sort of—I haven't said this yet because I don't know what it means, but she keeps showing me the parking garage on West 56th Street where I taped the show for the first two years. She's showing me standing at the entrance of that parking garage at West 56th. Do you have any ties to that parking garage on West 56th?

Diane: No.

John: I literally feel like I'm standing right there where there's the wall with the advertisements. I'm not sure if she's talking about the advertisements, could be, I don't know.

Diane: She used to go to the studio around there.

John: Maybe she parked there?

Diane: Could be . . .

John: But I need to make sure that you know that she's okay. And that she understands how painful of an experience today has been, and how painful dealing with all of this has been for you. And she's making me feel like it's really important that you know she appreciates everything you tried to do and that you continue to do. And she has let you know she's around. You do sense her, but at the same time you wish it away or you're kinda . . . "I'm making it up" or "I'm not really sure." Today's different, because it's like she's really unleashing herself on you in a way that you weren't ready for until very recently. And I feel like all of a sudden it became, "Okay, I can do this, I can do this."

Diane: Yes.

John: And then there's like an apprehension. I would have to say that within an hour before we even got here, you probably were saying, "I don't want to do this, I don't want to do this, I don't want to do this." Do you understand?

Diane: Yes, I do.

John: But she's okay. She's definitely, *definitely,* okay. Now when all this is said and done, I want you to have something tangible. And that little flower on the table, I don't think it's there by accident. So what I would like you to do is take that today, and that rose represents this experience. Because you need to have something tangible that we met, that she came through. This is very, very, important that she knows you have that. That's important for her.

Did she go by three names? Don't say the names, but did she go by three names?

Diane: Yes.

John: You know, just because somebody is physically not here, that doesn't mean we don't get the opportunity to work through some of the issues you didn't work through when they were here. So if you need to sit down and write a letter to your mom or write a letter to your aunt or write a letter to your daughter—any one of the people who have passed—to express and get out what you've been holding in for such a long time—it's not a bad thing.

One thing you need to realize is that if you were driving by yourself in a vehicle that maybe she never saw, and yet she can come here and talk about the fact that you have it and she sees you driving it and the fact that you were joking about the directions and what she would say if she was here, that's their way of continuing to let us know they're still connected to us. Those are the trivial, minute little details that validate the fact that they're still part of our lives. They do still see what's happening with us.

Let's say your daughter was still alive, and there was a different type of death—the death of the English language, and your daughter was only able to speak in ancient Aramaic, what would you do?

Diane: I'd learn the language.

John: Absolutely, you'd learn the language. That's how I want you to perceive this. Because she's still here, she's still connected to you. There's a different type of communication that's happening. It's the language of energy, and I do believe that she'll send you little signs, and she'll send you acknowledgments, and you might have a dream of her, you might have a feeling of her. But it's not something you should look for, because if you look for it, then you miss it. If it happens and you recognize it, that's a beautiful thing. If it happens and you're uncertain about it, acknowledge it in your mind: "Hey, I know you're here, I know you're trying, and thank you and keep up the good work. I appreciate it."

Diane: Does she know how much her friends love her? They miss her so much.

John: Absolutely. One of the major things people always say during a session is: "Tell her that I love her." My answer to that is: "You just did." You don't need to see a medium to connect with your daughter. Because the relationship is 365 days a year—and one day when the right time happens, you guys will connect again.

And when it's time for you to leave and you're done teaching and learning the lessons you need to learn here and you make that transition, I'm positive that the people we love will be there to meet you. Positive! I have no doubt! I know it from doing this work. People come through and say, "I was met by so-and-so," or "I was met by this one," or "I'm with these people."

I hope this has helped you. I can still feel the very emotionally charged situation in connection with her. Just know she's okay, and you and your son will be okay, too.

The energy pulled back, and I sat back in my chair, both tired and curious. Who was this celebrity? "I'm freaking out here," I said to Natasha and Diane. "You're going to tell me who this person is now . . . *right?!*

"John," said Natasha, "it's the young, beautiful, and talented *Aaliyah.*"

Singer/actress Aaliyah had died in a plane crash on August 27, 2001, along with a group of friends and co-workers, when taking off in a small plane in the Bahamas. She was en route to New York after shooting a music video in the islands. Now it made perfect sense why she refused to tell me *how* she had died—not only would it have given me a major clue as to who she was, which could have made my knowledge "shut down" (I would have been self-conscious throughout the reading and would have known too much information from the get-go), but also, I was getting on a plane early the next morning and I hate—I mean *hate*—to fly. Natasha most likely didn't tell me so I wouldn't freak out and get nervous.

Once I knew who Diane's daughter was, other pieces of the puzzle started to come together, and I realized that this reading was indirectly connected to my publicist, Jill. A year and a half earlier, when it came time for me to pick someone to handle publicity after *Crossing Over* gained recognition, I chose Jill for a number of reasons. First, she'd been to the studio several times with other celebrity clients who had come for a reading, and I was impressed with how she looked after their interests and how kind yet super professional she always was. But after we'd had an official meeting together to see if we wanted to work together, I knew that there was another reason why I'd chosen her.

I told our supervising producer, Liz Arias; and Carol, my assistant, that I felt Jill *needed* to be connected to this work at this point in time—that it would help her. I wasn't sure what the reason was, and I didn't understand why I felt that way, but now I thought I knew the answer.

Jill and I were leaving the *Crossing Over* studio to do our first satellite TV interview one day, and on the way out of the building she told me that one of her clients had just passed—Aaliyah. That must have been what I was feeling when I first met her—that she was going to be questioning life and death, her own mortality, and grieving the death of someone close to her. That person must have been her close friend Aaliyah.

When Jill first told me about Aaliyah, I offered to talk to the singer's family, but it wasn't until now, a year and a half later, that Diane felt she was finally ready. I've often said that it's usually best for people to get through the initial stages of grieving before they consult with any medium. Mediumship should never be a first option, because what if the person you want to connect with doesn't show up? The trauma could exacerbate your grief.

Up until Natasha and I had arrived at the hotel, Diane was questioning her decision to get a reading— a fact that came through in the session. As she explained to me afterward, "I was in the hotel, and I walked around by myself thinking, *Should I do this? Does LiLi want me to do this?* I knew she had a very strong belief in the afterlife. She had begun to talk about it quite a bit as she got older, and she had bought books on it. That's another reason why I wanted to do it, because she had the belief. And the reading really did help me. It really did. It was amazing . . . there were so many parts that were so right on point. Some of the things you said were things that were so Aaliyah." Or "LiLi," as she was often lovingly called by her family. "She really was called three names: 'Baby Girl,' 'LiLi,' and then 'Aaliyah,'" said Diane, as she pointed out the validations in the reading.

As soon as the "dominant" energy came through to me, even though I thought it might be male, Diane knew it was her LiLi. "That was so on point," she says, "because she was sweet, thoughtful, compassionate . . . but at the same time, she had this strength that I was in awe of. I used to tell her, 'I think you are a magnificent human being, and I am truly in awe of you.' And she'd say, 'Really, Mom?'

"When something went wrong, she exhibited a strength that was magnificent. And I truly looked up to her." The two of them were indeed good buddies. "There was nothing she couldn't say to me and nothing I couldn't say to her," Diane remarked. "We talked about everything. She was my best friend. I would call her for advice! Who would think that a 22-year-old could give me advice! But that's how she was."

What really hit home for Diane were the little, intimate details that came through that only people close to her knew about. Like Aaliyah's pink clothes.

"The color pink, that was a color she began to like when she was about 18 years old. It was my mother's favorite color, and they were very close. All of a sudden one day, I noticed she'd been wearing a lot of pink . . . and I said, 'LiLi, you're liking pink now?' And she said, 'I don't know what it is . . . maybe it's Grandma!' Nobody really knew about this . . . maybe a couple of her close friends. For you to mention pink, it just hit me."

Other private moments, such as Diane's lone visit to their favorite church, also hit home.

"Aaliyah and I used to go to St. Patrick's Cathedral when we'd go shopping in the city. We'd be holding hands and we'd stop in there. A month after this happened, I went back to St. Patrick's alone, and I saw the priest and sat in on a service. I was by myself, trying to get some inner peace. And I've been there several times since."

Diane also confirmed that she has a piece of music of Aaliyah's that no one else has. "She made an audition CD to get into the performing arts high school, and she sang 'Ave Maria' in Latin. I found that CD, and we played it at the memorial mass we did for her. That CD is mine. No record company or anybody has it . . . it's mine, and it's awesome. It's just her with a piano accompaniment."

A reference that the family had written something about Aaliyah that was recently published was also true— "That was correct, too," acknowledged Diane. "Rashad wrote an article on his sister for *Teen Vogue* called 'Little Sister Lost' for the June 2002 issue."

One word that came up a few times in the reading was *classy*, which Diane says describes her beautiful daughter to a T.

"She always wanted to do things in a 'classy' way," said Diane. "And that was always how we described her. And when you said she was the kind who lived without regrets, that was so true, too. She would always say, 'You know . . . you can't live your life like that . . . ya gotta do what you gotta do . . . what will be, will be.' So when you said that, it was almost like she was talking to me right there in the room. LiLi liked to live in the moment, and whatever that moment was, she cherished it, she embraced it, and she always said, 'We have no control. If something's going to happen, it's going to happen.'"

As Diane and I continued to talk after the reading, some other validations started to emerge. I realized that the parking-lot reference was a validation directed toward *me*—I had parked in that lot every day when I was working at the studio nearby and remembered that there was a gigantic billboard for the movie *Queen of the Damned*, with Aaliyah's face about 20 feet high next to the lot. I couldn't help but see that billboard each day for months as I entered the studio. Diane also made the connection for the male with the "W" name who appeared first in the reading, bringing through her daughter.

"My best friend, Keeth Wallace, he was on the plane with Aaliyah. I didn't get it at first. He was very close to us, and like an uncle to LiLi. That's why he went with her on this trip. Because I had surgery and couldn't go, he took days off from work to go with her. He said, 'Diane, since you can't go, I'll go.'"

As our session came to a close, Aaliyah's strong energy still lingered in the room. I saw a flash of an ethnic-looking bracelet in my mind's eye.

"Diane," I asked, "where's the bracelet? Do you know if she had a scarab—an Egyptian bracelet?"

Diane wasn't sure, although she did know that her daughter had a lot of Egyptian jewelry. Diane's homework was to check on the bracelet as well as other information she didn't understand—such as the "B" name that I'd gotten. [Diane now believes that this might be her niece, Blair, whose birthday is in April—this would refer back to April being significant, and the "B" name.]

Although Diane's spirits seemed a little lighter than when we'd first shaken hands an hour earlier, I could still feel the high emotion of the loss for her.

"Sometimes it's all so unbearable," she said, softly weeping. "Some days, I just want to . . . I'm in a daze. Yesterday I just walked in circles and cried my heart out. It's hard to go on. . . . "

"That's a very human feeling," I told her, "but you're still here because you've got stuff you need to do. You have to be the person to honor your daughter's memory. Because then people are really going to get a chance to understand who she is."

Before I departed the hotel—with Diane clutching the red rose as a memento—I left her with one last thought. "Diane, I want to be bold enough to tell you this: Your daughter is larger than a plane crash. That plane crash happened in a minute, but her life was a lot longer than that. You have to look at everything she accomplished. And even though she did leave us physically, she's still here; she's still connected to you. And the love you have for her and the love she has for you is still very much here and alive."

I reminded Diane that the most important thing for her to do now was to honor her grief—to feel the pain so she could get back to feeling some joy instead of pacing around her apartment and cutting herself off from life.

"Aaliyah is still connected to you, and she's counting on you," I told her. And all of us must remember this when we lose someone we love. Cry, then pick yourself up bravely, because they're watching over us and hoping we'll do well during the rest of our years here, fulfilling whatever destiny we have.

"And one day you will see her again," I told her. "I promise you . . . one day, when the time is right, you will see your daughter again."

CHAPTER THREE

Going Down Under

A ROO IN THE HEADLIGHTS

Until I stepped foot on rugged Aussie terrain, I always thought that a wombat was one of those mythical creatures, like a unicorn or a mermaid. I never thought I'd one day be holding one—never mind doing a *psychic reading* on one.

I'd arrived in Sydney, Australia, the day before to embark on a two-week seminar tour in January 2003—the first one I'd done outside of the United States since I began this work. In the last few years, I've had countless invitations to conduct seminars in other countries including England, Canada, and even Japan—where I was offered $100,000 (U.S.) to do two one-hour TV appearances—but I always turned them down. Why? First and foremost, I'm not motivated by money, and I know that the green stuff can never be the force behind spiritual work like this. If it is, then my work will inevitably suffer.

I know that a lot of people don't believe me when I say this, because they see me as a TV celebrity "cashing in" with books and seminars and such. But I stand by my words: I honor the work and the process first. The other reasons I turned down the invitations are that I'm naturally a homebody and don't like to travel too far from my family, and also—I'm quite patriotic. I always felt if I had the time and energy to do this work, I should do it for my own country. And, God knows, it wasn't as if I were running out of dead people here. But after *Crossing Over* went into syndication in Australia, the people "down under" really took to the subject matter, and the show took off like a rocket.

"Why don't you go down?" Reid Tracy, president of Hay House, Inc. (the distributor of this book), urged me over lunch one day last spring. "The show is a hit, and the people love you. It would be fun, like a vacation. Go somewhere new. Take the family. . . . "

Carol, my assistant, was lunching with us and began to launch into our standard excuse about how I don't like to leave the country . . . blah, blah, blah. So I don't know what came over me, but in a moment of inspiration, I interrupted Carol's speech with an *"Okay, let's do it!"* Carol and Reid were shocked—Reid *pleasantly* so, since he thought he'd have to do way more convincing than that. But I was probably more stunned than either of them. Reid was right—maybe it *was* time to spread my wings and have a bit of an adventure.

Before I could change my mind, he had arranged a two-week, three-city tour, and when tickets went on sale, they sold out in a record nine minutes for venues holding up to 10,000 people. So far the biggest group I'd ever worked with was an audience of 8,000 in Anaheim, California—but that time I was one of four speakers. This time it was going to be just me, *solamente*.

I had no worries about getting the job done—there could be 50,000 people in a room and someone might be sitting in the last row in a dark corner . . . but if I'm meant to read them, I'll feel the pull and find them. So I wasn't worried about the Other Side speaking up loud and clear. I was more worried about us *living* beings on *this* side understanding each other. Would the rugby player in Brisbane be able to comprehend my obscure American pop-culture references? Would I understand *their* lingo? And then there was the accent. When I was visiting the Dominican Republic with a friend over a decade ago, I tried to show off my limited understanding of Spanish by conversing with a waiter. The only thing was, I had to ask him to repeat what he was saying three times, and *slower*, please—until my buddy Lisa couldn't stand it anymore.

"He wants to know if you want a glass of water!" she blurted out.

"How do you know that?" I asked.

"John . . . he was speaking *English!*"

But in Australia, the communication gap started before I even got there. During a stopover in Los Angeles, I gave a satellite interview with the Australian version of the *Today* show. The reporter started out with the usual questions: "When did you know you were psychic? How does it work?" And then she hit me with a zinger. "John," she continued, leaning in,"what would you say to one cynic here in Australia who says you're just an elitist vulture circling the corpses?"

Ouch. I couldn't believe this woman had just asked me that. I'm all for somebody expressing their views and saying they don't believe in what I do . . . but have a little respect, please. (I don't even remember how I answered her, as I'd slept very little that night and felt groggy and edgy.)

Boarding the flight for Sydney, everything was in slow motion— my thoughts, my reactions, even the rapid-fire speech that I'm so infamous for (and often admonished for)—and I wondered if my guides were "slowing me down" to make sure that not only would I understand my foreign audience, but they'd understand *me*. By the time we reached the customs counter in Sydney 20 hours later, my reflexes were set on "sluggish."

"What's in the tins?" the customs guy asked as he ruffled through my luggage.

"Excuse me?" I had no idea what he was talking about.

"What's in the *tins*, mate? *The tins!*" My friend Jesse, who was behind me in line, pointed to my six-pack of protein drinks as I watched the customs guy shake them and read the tiny ingredients list on the back. Once he was confident I wasn't bringing in any strange American animal product into the country, he waved me on.

We arrived at our hotel in downtown Sydney for one night's rest before traveling to Brisbane, where the seminars were slated to start. As soon as I checked in, I took a much-needed walk around the edge of the harbor by the Sydney Opera House to stretch my legs after that long flight. To tell you the truth, my first glimpse of Sydney reminded me of downtown Manhattan. From where I stood, I imagined looking to my right and seeing the Statue of Liberty. I telephoned Sandra in New York and woke her up.

"What time is it over there?" she asked, half-asleep.

"I have a better question for you," I responded. "What *day* is it?" I had crossed the international dateline and was 16 hours ahead of home time. My body clock was in flux. I'd traveled into the future.

Sandra and Justin had stayed home on this trip since he was barely four months old and we thought it best he stay landlocked for a few more months. Accompanying me instead was a group of friends and co-workers: *Crossing Over* executive producer Paul Shavelson, producer/cameraman Duncan Cameron, and actor and camera dude Jesse Shafer (all there to shoot a documentary about the tour for the Travel Channel); my buddy and *TV Guide* reporter Michael Logan; my publicist, Jill, and her boyfriend, Jack Rico—a journalist for the Spanish TV station Univision; and Natasha (the *People* magazine correspondent I introduced you to earlier), my collaborator on this book.

After another sleepless night on my part, we all hopped into a water taxi the next morning and headed off to our first tourist attraction—The Taranga Zoo. And this is how it came to be that I "read" a wombat. As soon as we arrived at the zoo, a tour guide plopped little Digby, a baby wombat, into my arms. He was really cute and lovable, even if he did look kind of like a humongous rat. The guide filled me in on the wombat's tragic history and told me that his mother had been hit by a car months before and he had been found in the pouch, alive, and had been brought to the zoo to live. As she was talking, I started to pick up on Digby's energy.

"Did he have a problem with his skin or his fur when he first came in?" I asked. Yes, he did, she said. Before I knew it, I was spouting out all sorts of information, casually, as if I read wombats every day. Reid Tracy, who was also with us that day, was the first one to notice. "Oh my God," he exclaimed, "he's reading the wombat!"

Well, to be more specific, I was getting information from my guides *about* the wombat. It's not like I was getting Digby's mother coming through . . . or a wombat *to his side*. But I think anybody who has pets knows what it's like to connect with an animal psychically. I'm always able to sense when our dogs, Jolie and Roxie, are hungry before they come to me with their tongues hanging out of their mouths. Digby would be the first of many animals I would connect with on this trip . . . you might say he was my "warm-up" wombat.

At the zoo, I also got a taste of my apparent "celebrity status" in Australia. Probably ten times more people than usual recognized me with a nod or a smile, but it was much more relaxed than what happens in the States. They didn't come up to me and demand a reading on the spot like some New Yorkers do on Manhattan sidewalks. One little boy about seven years old approached me and asked if I would pose in a picture with him and his school chums, all big fans of the show. Well, that just about blew my mind. I was amazed that *Crossing Over* was reaching such a young audience here and could only assume that there must be more of an openness toward spirituality in general in this country. My theory would prove to be right.

Leaving the zoo that day, I had a moment of homesickness . . . and felt a warm, powerful sense of my mother around me, embracing me like a warm sweater. I was standing next to this big glass tank filled with sea lions, and I looked into the water. Two seconds later, a white feather started to slowly float upward in the tank.

"Duncan, *get that on tape!*" I said as I grabbed our camera guy. Duncan began to roll film, all the while asking me why he was shooting a boring tank of water. What did it mean? That's a job hazard (or perk, depending on how you look at it) when you work with me—most things usually mean *something*.

"It's a message from an old friend," was all I told him, and a second later the tape ran out.

As some of you might know, the feather was a message from my mom. In my second book, *CROSSING OVER: The Stories Behind the*

Stories, I revealed the three signs my mother and I decided upon together before she died that she'd send me from the Other Side (a reference to her nickname, "Princess"; a reference to Pooh Bear; and some mention of the town Springfield from her favorite soap, *Guiding Light*). But right after she passed, I also asked her to send me one additional sign to let me know she was making the transition okay—and that sign was a white bird. That white bird appeared on a floral arrangement at her funeral, giving me the validation I needed. Since then I've received the "abridged" version— a white feather—several times, and that, too, has come to mean a message from my mom. There I was, thousands of miles from home and already feeling homesick, and here was Mom to remind me: *You're not alone.*

By the time we reached Brisbane for the first two seminars, I was running on four days of no sleep and walked out onstage with my body and brain still on 4 A.M. Eastern Standard Time. But as soon as I keyed into the enthusiasm of the 4,000 people packed into the convention center that first night, their energy lit me up like a Christmas tree, and I was on. I was able to give dozens of mini-readings that night, which were simultaneously projected onto three giant screens in the venue for everyone to watch. In total, we did so many fantastic readings during the Australia tour that I could write a whole book on it. Here, I'll include just a few snippets.

In one of the early readings the second night, I was drawn to a woman in the front row as the sound of gunshots went off in my head.

> **John:** Somebody here was shot. Somebody passes from a gunshot in this area.
>
> **Woman:** My husband was shot.
>
> **John:** By somebody he knows? Because I have a familiar feeling attached to this—
>
> **Woman:** Yes. He was murdered by a friend of a friend.
>
> **John:** And the friend got away with it?
>
> **Woman:** He got away with it for a few hours.
>
> **John:** I have a feeling that . . . as far as being punished, it's like the person got off in some way.

Woman: Yes. The person who shot my husband was an escaped prisoner, and my husband's friend was harboring him. I don't think he meant for the prisoner to actually take the shot at my husband that killed him, but he was as much to blame as the other one, even though he wasn't the murderer.

John: He was your second husband. . . .

Woman: Yes.

John: Can I be really blunt?

Woman: I would expect that, actually.

John: Did you hit him?

Woman: Um, we hit each other. He was very frustrating . . . but I didn't hit him hard! [laughter in the room]

John: Let me tell you what he's showing me. He's making me feel like he provoked a level of emotion in you that would make you do that. Follow me?

Woman: Correct.

John: He asks if you're going to get your two back teeth pulled or fixed.

Woman (laughs): I haven't had time to do it yet!

John: But do you know what he means?

Woman: Yes!

The brief reading I did on this woman, whose name I later found out was Kerry Davies, shows how a loved one from the Other Side often picks out a small yet intimate detail to identify him- or herself to their relatives. In this case, Kerry's husband, Peter, brought up his wife's teeth that still needed to be fixed.

After the reading, Kerry, 44, a homemaker living outside of Brisbane, commented on her experience. "I couldn't believe that came through. Peter always used to say to me, 'You're a beautiful woman, but you have to get something done about your teeth!' because I'm losing them in the back. And that was quite funny to hear. No one else knew that."

But in his brief appearance, Peter also touched upon the serious issues of their volatile relationship and his murder. "Peter was quite violent because he had been a heroin addict for 20 years," Kerry explained. "But he had finally given it up. And it was sort of sad, because after he died, we got the medical report and it said he was clean. I couldn't believe it . . . because six months before he wasn't. Now he was, and he was dead."

His murder 15 months earlier had been big news in the local papers—an escaped convict harbored by a friend of Peter's killed him because he suspected Peter was going to turn him in to the police.

"I walked into the front yard and saw him shoot my husband with a 30-30, blowing his head off in front of me," Kerry described. "Peter was lying there . . . and I could feel the zapping of his energy. For three days afterwards, I knew he was in the house with me . . . I could feel it. It was a frantic energy, a frantic spirit. And then it just seemed to go. Although I still often feel Peter's energy in the house with me, I don't feel that frantic panic anymore."

As the evening progressed, I noticed that a lot of people, like Kerry, seemed to be in touch with their own psychic side or intuitive abilities. I asked Sydney-based Leon Nacson, managing director of Hay House Australia, about it. "It's cultural," he told me. "We're more apt to seek out self-empowerment, psychology, and self-help."

My own theory was also this: Since Australians are somewhat isolated from the rest of the world, and their country is less densely populated than many, they're more in touch with their primitive feelings and learn to rely on their instincts and intuition, so their spirituality has been fostered. That same night, I keyed into yet another high-profile murder case, this time involving a young girl, which was solved by one relative's psychic vision. It was a highly emotional reading for the two family members in attendance, but in the midst of all the seriousness, I also had a little laugh at myself as I stumbled across my first Australian-American pop-cultural gap. Did the Australians know who Howdy Doody was? I was about to find out.

John: I have a younger female coming through . . . a younger sister, a niece. I don't think it's a daughter. I'm with someone with a "Benny" sound . . . a Bonnie, Benny . . . a "B" name.

Woman: I have a step-granddaughter who was tragically killed.

John: She's not coming through as a daughter; she's coming through as a sister. . . .

Woman (pointing to young woman next to her): She was like a sister to my daughter.

John: She's coming through below you, so was she much younger than you?

Daughter: Yes.

John: I need to acknowledge she's here, and there's a unique "B" name connected to her.

Woman: Her last name was Beasley.

John: There's an unanswered feeling about this. There are question marks all over the place, as if you guys have not had the answers you would have liked. Do you understand this?

Woman: Yes.

John: I have an out-of-country feeling about this. The person who did this, was he not from here?

Woman: Right, he came from another country.

John: Now, I could be bringing in someone completely different here . . . but . . . was she strangled? She was either strangled or asphyxiated because I feel like I can't breathe.

Woman: Yes! She was asphyxiated. We have an idea how it happened, but we don't know all the details.

John: This is going to sound strange, but . . . it does feel like it was an accident to me.

Woman: He was saying that from the beginning . . . that he didn't really mean to do it . . . that it was an accident.

John: It was *not* intentional. I don't feel a brutal, intentional, premeditated feeling. This is a quirky, irresponsible event . . . but I'm not saying it was acceptable. She's show-ing me pink roses. She wants me to talk about the white bird connection you have. Did you have a special floral arrange-ment made for her?

Woman #2 (sitting next to her): Yes, my daughter did.

John: She wants me to acknowledge a special floral arrangement. *Special.* Not just flowers . . . there's also a thing about a white bird.

Woman #2: Yes, I had a special floral arrangement made.

John: She's got the cousin with her on the Other Side. The male figure to her side.

Woman: That would probably be her half-brother who passed as a baby.

John: Please let the family know she came through and that they need to let go of how she passed. They're too stuck on this. You're never going to forget it; it's never going to go away. But to find some type of closure and heal-ing, you need to move away from the event so you can move through your grief.

You have to go on that journey, because when you get through your grief, you get back to love. It's like grief is the other side of love.

Woman: Okay . . .

John: And she's making me feel like . . . do you know who Howdy Doody is? She's showing me Howdy Doody.

Woman: No . . .

John: Um . . . okay . . . uh . . . how do I describe this . . . he's a puppet . . . and . . . *red hair and freckles?!*

Woman: Oh, that's my other daughter, Harmony! She has red hair and freckles!

Young Sheree Beasley, only six years old, was riding her pink bike one sunny afternoon in 1991 when she was abducted and mur-dered. She was missing for three months before police found her dead in a drain under a country road, her clothing scattered at the scene, and her body so decomposed she had to be identified by her nails. Not only was the case big in the papers in Australia, but one of the detectives on the case wrote a book about the investigation called *The Murder of Sheree Beasley*. Sheree came through at the seminar for her step-grandmother, Denise Greenhill; and aunt, Adele, with details of her murder and the hopes that her family would move on from the horrible way she died.

"The guy who did it claimed the killing was accidental, that he never meant to do it, he never meant for it to go that far," Denise confirmed, "but that didn't lessen our anger toward him. We still feel the anger. How do you get over that?" After the police had found the body of a young girl, they had trouble identifying it, and the only item of clothing left on her was a T-shirt with a picture of a big cat on the front. Sheree's mother couldn't remember what her daughter had worn the day she was abducted because Sheree had dressed herself that morning—or if she even owned a T-shirt like that. But that night, Denise had a dream—of Sheree standing in front of her wearing her beloved roller skates . . . and a T-shirt with a cat on it. She got up and woke her husband, who then contacted Sheree's paternal grandparents. They rifled through the family photo albums and found a picture of Sheree wearing that same shirt.

Hearing Sheree come through at the seminar helped the family find some closure. Denise remarked, "Sheree must have known that we really needed to hear from her. We've all had such trouble dealing with her death and getting past how it happened. But she says we have to just get past it. I know we have to. I will take that message home with me—especially to my ex-husband—that we have to live on."

KARANGATUDE!

MY NEWFOUND KINSHIP WITH THE NATIVES—and I'm talking about the animal kingdom here—continued, to the point where Leon joked that he was going to nickname me "Dr. Doolittle." On yet another tourist adventure, our group packed into a bus like schoolkids and made our way to Steve Irwin's Australian Zoo—founded by Mr. Crocodile Hunter himself!

On the ride there, the landscape looked strangely like suburban Florida. The roads were lined with palm trees and strips malls, with Burger Kings and McDonald's—which was all very fine and good by me. I'm a lifelong picky eater, so by day five I was subsisting on the familiar: Mickey D's.

Jill, a fellow food purist, was living on chocolate and French fries but no burgers—after biting into one at the hotel, she became paranoid that they were made of kangaroo, or "roos," as we now called them, as per the local slang. As the landscape whizzed by, we passed a street named "Edward Street," and then a block later, a street named "Gallery on Edward." I took it as a sign that I was on the right road.

The first thing I noticed about the Australian Zoo was that, in a funny way, I felt as if the *humans* were the attraction. Usually when you go to a zoo, the animals are in cages and the people mill about staring at them. Here, you walk among the animals' natural habitats, and they come right up to you and check you out. We petted the dingos (and I had to hold myself back from doing my Meryl Streep impression: "A dingo stole my baby!"), fed the kangaroos, and took our turns doing "the koala cuddle," as they call it, balancing a little koala named Lawson on our chests. After lunch, I was feeling daring enough to let one of the guides wrap Rosie, a boa constrictor, around my neck. (She was named Rosie for her pink cheeks, I was told.) The whole place was very impressive, and I really feel that Steve Irwin is an amazing man doing incredible things to educate people about animals and to provide a good home for these wonderful creatures. If that doesn't come across in his TV shows, I'm telling you now—his dedication to their cause is admirable.

The energy of the animals at the zoo was so pure that I once again felt an easy and natural connection with them. But even I was a bit surprised when we met Harriet, a 178-year-old turtle who had at one time belonged to evolutionist Charles Darwin. As Harriet nibbled at the hibiscus flowers from my open palm, I started plugging into her energy. . . .

"Who's the blonde girl who used to look after Harriet?" I asked our guide.

"Oh, that's Joy! She used to take care of her."

"Did she talk differently than everyone else?"

"Yes, yes, she had a very strong English accent."

"Did you ever keep Harriet in a different part of the zoo? Because I'm getting that she likes it better here than where she used to be. She felt kind of isolated there."

"Yes! She used to be closer to the entrance; it was away from the people."

"Did someone knit her a special blanket? Did someone mark her on her back?"

The information kept coming, and the guide kept validating. And Reid, of course, was flipping out all over again. For the rest of the trip, I'd hear him on his cell phone time and again telling someone, "He read a freakin' wombat and a turtle!"

But Jill, a Manhattan publicist in the truest sense of the job description, was naturally pushing for more play here.

"John," she asked, as I was quietly communing with Harriet, "do you think you can get *Darwin* to come through . . . ?"

FROM BRISBANE, IT WAS BACK to Sydney for three seminars. I stepped onstage the first night in Sydney, and the applause was deafening. I actually got a standing ovation for just walking out there! It was staggering.

I'd been reading the local reviews of the seminars we'd done so far, and the critics were writing that I had "rock-star status" and that the people were "embracing" me. While I do appreciate acceptance like that, I don't want people to pay too much attention to the messenger and miss the message. It's not about me; I'm just the speaker . . . an amplification of the process. In the past, attention like that used to make me feel embarrassed and self-conscious, until I broke it down mentally in a way that made sense to me: The audiences aren't really clapping for me, but for their own relatives. The yells and cheers are for what I represent. They might think they're clapping for the guy on TV, but ultimately what they're applauding is the idea that their loved ones are still connected to them. And I would clap for that, too.

Oftentimes, I wish people at the seminars could see the bizarre pictures I'm shown when loved ones from the Other Side try to capture my attention. Let me just say this: The Other Side has one wacky sense of humor. I started off one night with an image in my mind of a woman biting her toenails with her teeth as she watched television. Was I seeing this correctly? Could this be right? You betcha. After much prodding on my part, the nail biter, a former contortionist, it turns out, eventually raised her hand and owned up to her nasty habit so she could get her messages from Mom on the Other Side.

There were no drinks and food allowed in the auditorium we were in, but that same night I got an image of a hunk of gooey cake someone was hiding in a purse. I could practically taste it.

"Who's got the cake?" I demanded. I got off the stage and walked through the aisle looking for this mystery dessert. Finally, one woman shyly raised her hand.

I pointed to her. "Show me the cake!" And voilà, she did—she produced a wedge of cake from her pocketbook. She had bought it on the way to the seminar because she'd missed dinner and had planned to secretly nibble on it throughout the evening. After she admitted to her "cake crime," then, and only then, could I give her the messages from her dad on the Other Side.

Sometimes the images I get start even before I arrive at an event, and at the most inopportune moments. It was our first workday in Sydney, about five hours before the seminar that night, and I was in the shower washing up after a gym workout. Just as I was rinsing the shampoo out of my eyes, I got a nudge from a boy on the Other Side.

"Hey," I urged him, "come back tonight when your relatives are in front of me!" I was eager to finish washing my hair . . . *alone*. He obliged. So when I got to the event later that evening, I started off the readings with David, the shower crasher.

John: At 1 P.M. this afternoon, someone's son came through to me while I was in the shower. He's coming through for his mom. He's been gone a long time, 20 to 30 years. He was there to meet Dad. Dad just passed. There's a February connection here. And the woman I'm looking for is white-haired or gray-haired or platinum blonde. The son needs to let the mom know not to worry about Dad. I'd like to know what you were doing at one o'clock this afternoon. And there's also a connection to the 16th.

Woman: My son died 20 years ago, but my husband died before him.

John: There's another male figure to the side there for you. February is important here. You must have the February connection.

Woman: I have a grandson who will be two years old in February.

John: This male figure showed up at 1 P.M. today, and he's the son, gone 20 years. He was there to connect to an older male figure after him, and he says you'd have another contemporary there as well, that you lost a male to the side as well. Is Richard connected to you? Or Robert? Who is the "R" name?

Woman: My husband is Robert.

John: And there is a train reference here.

Woman: My older brother worked with the railways for a long time.

John: Were there six of you? I'm getting you were a family of six kids.

Woman: I was one of five.

John: Do you know if your mom miscarried?

Woman: Oh, yes, she did . . . one time.

John: With your husband, Robert, was there a question of someone's paternity? Or that someone acted as a father to someone's child? Or maybe there's a joke about the paternity of a child. . . .

Woman: Yes, my husband's brother kind of took over for the kids as a father figure.

John: He helped with their schooling.

Woman: Yes.

John: There's a story about the man who acted as the father figure, a story about him being shot. But he did not die of this gunshot. He died the same way Robert and your son died, with an impact. They all died from something impact related.

Woman: Yes.

John: And someone is known for raising chickens or birds.

Woman: Yes, my brother raised birds!

Kay Dunn's son, David, had died in a car accident 20 years earlier, and Kay told us after the reading that she got the news of her son's death through a visit from her father in a dream.

"The day my son was killed, I woke up after having had a dream of my father sitting on a fence with all this green grass around him, and he was telling me, 'Don't worry, everything's going to be all right.' I remember looking at the clock when I woke up that morning, because I was a bit shook up, wondering, *Gee, what was that? Why did I have a dream like that?* A few hours later, [the authorities] came and told me that David had died, and it had happened just a little bit before the time I had the dream. I don't talk to people about this much because I think people will laugh at me!" Kay's son, her husband, and her brother-in-law all passed in vehicle accidents, she confirmed, which came through in the reading with the three "impact"-related deaths.

Kay's son also had a knack for unique timing like his grandfather when it came to coming through from the Other Side. At 1 P.M. that day, as David's energy ambushed me in the shower, Kay and her niece, Jan, were having lunch with friends and telling them about the seminar that night. "At about 1 P.M., I said, 'Look, we've got to go . . . we need to get ready because we're seeing John Edward tonight,'" Jan recalled.

The seminars in Sydney ended on a sentimental note when two brothers, separated by death, reunited using their love of a football (or soccer, to us Yanks) team as their means of connection. It was also one of many funny moments during the trip that made the audience chuckle at my self-confessed lack of macho sports knowledge.

> **John:** Someone has a dog on their shirt.
>
> **Man** (standing up): I do, it's the Bulldog.
>
> **John:** There's a bulldog on your shirt?
>
> **Man:** Right . . . from the football team. Best football team in the world!
>
> **John:** I'm sports-illiterate in the U.S., never mind Australia! Someone wants me to acknowledge your marriage, and they weren't able to be there physically, but they were at your wedding from the Other Side. And I need to acknowledge the two kids.
>
> **Man:** Yes, yes.
>
> **John:** They want me to talk about the man with the really strong, baritone-type voice.
>
> **Man:** We had an uncle who had a really loud voice like that.
>
> **John:** And they clearly want me to acknowledge the older male figure who was at the wedding.
>
> **Man:** I had an older brother
>
> **John:** He'd wear the same shirt as you?
>
> **Man:** Of course! We buried him in it.
>
> **John:** I was going to say . . . there's a joke about burying him in an opposing team's shirt! He says he would not be wearing that shirt. He says there was another team he liked a little bit more. . . . Who's Steven? He could be a player for all I know.
>
> **Man:** There was a player, Steven, who was a favorite when my brother was alive.
>
> **John:** Then I have to tell you, that team was a "different" team when he was alive.
>
> **Man:** No, it's not the same team now . . . all the players are different, and the shirt is different.
>
> **John:** Your brother sends a hug to Mom.
>
> **Man:** She's right here, next to me.

John: He says that when he passed, your mom said that he'd be illuminating heaven.

Mom: Yes, I say that all the time.

"As soon as you said there's a dog on a T-shirt," recalled Angelo Dimitrakas, "my wife was nudging me to get up, get up!" At the last minute before coming to the seminar, Angelo decided to put on his old football jersey belonging to the Canterbury Bulldogs, his favorite Sydney football team, when he and his older brother, who passed over in 1994, were growing up. They buried Angelo's brother in the jersey the team wore when he passed away.

"We joked a bit about swapping the shirt and putting him in another jersey," Angelo said. "If I'd done that, he would have really been ticked off. But it's true that when he was alive it was really a different team, a different generation, and a completely different jersey but with the same colors. Now the team has all new players. The other team was always on top, but this new team is way behind. So when he says it's a different team . . . it sure is."

Angelo's brother had died a few months before Angelo's wedding and before the birth of his two kids, which Angelo acknowledged in the reading, as well as noting the loud uncle with the booming voice: "That man, when he talked, not only did the whole room hear him, but the whole neighborhood heard him." And finally, "My brother was the life of the party, and he made an impression on everybody he met. When he died, we thought that he'd do the same there, in heaven. My mother says it all the time: 'He'll brighten the place up—up there.'"

BEFORE MOVING ONWARD TO MELBOURNE, there was one more journey to take. Everyone kept telling me I had to do "The Bridge Climb" in Sydney, but I had no idea what that was. Then, from the balcony of my hotel, I saw it: The long Sydney Bridge stretched out far and very high, with people who looked like tiny little ants making their way up it. *Hmm. I don't know about this.*

Because we were filming the *John Edward Goes to Australia* documentary, Paul had instructed Jesse and Duncan to film my every waking moment on this trip and get me doing something more interesting than ordering my daily Happy Meal at McDonald's. But if you know me, you know that I'm not exactly the easiest person to "capture." Even though I had agreed to do the documentary, I didn't want a camera stuck in my face all the time. In fact, I'm sure Duncan and Jesse have at least 50 censored bloopers from our two-week trek showing me holding my hand up to the lens, threatening their lives, or describing to them in detail just how painful a tripod up their . . . how do they say it in Australia?—their *backsides*—would be.

But Paul was excited to capture the whole climb on film and told me I had to do it for his art. He then informed me that he, of course, would *not* be accompanying me on the climb, as he was afraid of heights. Ah, this is where the fun began for me. If he wasn't coming, I told him, I wouldn't do it. So the whole gang—Paul, Jill, Jack, Mike, Duncan, Jesse, Natasha, and me—filed into the chamber where you register and go through "training" for the climb.

One wall was covered with photos of celebrities who had done the climb and lived to pose for a portrait, and I noticed that they were all wearing the same outfit—a sort of gray jumpsuit with a Batman-like utility belt. The belt, our trainer explained, would hook us onto a cable that lined the bridge the whole way up and down, so if a strong gust of wind knocked us over, we wouldn't plummet to our deaths. No. Instead, we'd just dangle there for a while until someone could hike over and rescue us. I glanced over at Paul, who had gone pale. He looked at me with an "Are you really going to make me do this?" look. Yep, I was.

Because our group was so big, Jack and Jill joined the group behind us (and please, no jokes about their names and the fact that they were about to go "up a hill" together—they've heard it all). What I didn't know was that Jill was also freaked out about making the climb. After we changed into our gear and watched the instructional video, it was time to march on.

Duncan and Jesse hooked me up for sound with a wireless microphone, and we followed our tour guide, a very pretty young woman named Amanda. We had a choice, she told us: We could either take the elevator to the top and then walk across the bridge only a short distance, *or* we could climb each of the rafters, level by level, over the Sydney harbor and across the fast-moving traffic below. Paul perked up at the first suggestion.

"Oh, no," I told Amanda, with a smile, "we want to do the whole climb, every step of it."

I have to share with you the pleasure I was getting in making Paul squirm. Paul and I have a great relationship, but because a good portion of it is spent on work-related stuff, it's usually about him making me do things I don't want to. For example, he'll make me record voice-overs for the show again and again until I get it just right because he heard a little something in the background. Or, when I introduce a segment—a "wraparound"—on *Crossing Over,* he'll make me redo it because there was a wrinkle in my shirt, or a few hairs on my head were out of alignment. At least once a week, he starts a sentence off with "Hey, wouldn't it be *great* if . . . " to which I usually shake my head no, but end up doing it anyway.

Now the tables were turned, and it felt pretty good. I only felt bad about it once during the climb . . . the time Paul was crying for his mommy. Um, okay, I made that last part up. But he did look like he was going to cry for his mom when he was taking his tiny, measured, delicate steps up, moving ever so slowly.

Natasha, a very strong Slavic girl, was behind Paul the whole way and promised to catch him if he fell. We paused at the bridge's highest point, and the views of the harbor were magnificent. Amanda told us stories about the builders who had died while constructing the bridge, and we all stood there high over Sydney, enjoying a panoramic, spiritual moment. For once, I was glad that we'd caught something like that on film. As we began to descend, I looked over at Jill in the group behind us and noticed she was in that same senior-citizen posture Paul had adopted.

"Having fun?" I yelled over to her. And her response was a pleading, "Get me off this thing!" All right, enough was enough. I pulled Amanda aside and asked if we could take a different downward route . . . say, in the elevator? She sweetly agreed to rescue us all, and I told Jill that she owed me big time. The next time she wanted me to walk the press line and I didn't want to do it, all I had to do was give her the magic word: *brrrrrridge!* As we descended (yes, in the elevator!), I thought of the bridge as a metaphor for all our souls' journeys. Regardless of where we are—in a physical body or not—we strive to put one step in front of the other, however tentative, as we travel on our spiritual path.

DO YOU VALIDATE?

I WOKE UP IN MELBOURNE, the last city on the tour, to hear myself being discussed on one of the early-morning talk shows. I was just sort of lazing about in bed flipping the channels when I heard a reporter and the guest astrologer, Athena Starwoman, gabbing about what they thought of me. *Amazing,* I thought. My level of public recognition down under was still difficult for me to grasp. Back home, an ocean away, the talk was all about the impending war. The night before I'd seen Saddam Hussein's son on CNN threatening the U.S. that if we attacked Iraq, the tears we cried over 9/11 would seem "like a picnic" compared to what *will* happen. His words shook me up.

Now I switched channels to CNN again and felt a wave of patriotism for America as I watched our troops hugging their wives, husbands, and kids good-bye and getting on ships going God knows where. It totally put me over the edge when I saw one news clip of a soldier telling a reporter, "You know, my baby son is going to be crawling when I see him next." I thought of Sandra and Justin back home and missed them terribly. I wondered if they were asleep and if it was it too late to call and send good-night kisses over the phone.

I was still feeling pretty emotional as we drove to the convention center that night. When we arrived, our driver couldn't find the proper entrance and turned into the wrong road in front of a locked gate. While we were waiting for him to figure out which way to go, a bunch of religious protesters approached the car holding up signs. Once they realized I was in the car, they began banging on my window for me to roll it down. I've had a few experiences with holy rollers who show up at these events claiming I'm a fraud and it's all entertainment. As I've said, I totally respect the fact that some people don't believe in what I do—it's their choice. But the last thing I felt like hearing that night was someone yelling in my face that I was doing "the devil's work."

Those words in particular make me want to tug off my spiritual gloves and knock the person on their ass. I don't need anyone questioning my faith. And anyway, to me, this work isn't religious, it's spiritual . . . it's painting an energy portrait. Whatever canvas or framework an individual uses to paint that portrait is their choice and based on their own belief system. One person might have a Catholic framework, and another might have a Muslim framework, and somebody might have a Jewish framework, and somebody might have no framework at all because they're atheistic. The atheists, interestingly enough, are usually the loudest energies who come through once they get to the Other Side because they have so much to say after they realize, *Yikes—I was wrong, there is an afterlife after all!*

So, needless to say, I didn't roll down my window. I just smiled and waved as we drove away to the proper gate, leaving the protesters muttering to themselves in the parking lot. For the duration of our trip in Australia, these were the only demonstrators I attracted. And before introducing me that night, Leon told the audience he was nicknaming our time down under as "The Silence of the Skeptics Tour" because we'd barely heard a peep from the diehard cynics.

One of the last readings in Australia turned out to be one of the funniest and most dramatic moments on tour. It was for two sisters, Jeannie-Marie and Victoria; and Jeannie's mother-in-law, Carmel. The sisters had come to the seminar together thanks to Victoria's 18-year-old daughter, Kerrina, who had given up her cherished ticket so that the two women could have a night out together. They didn't know that Carmel was in the audience until they saw her face on the giant video screen as I was giving a reading to someone sitting near her. And then, I felt a pull in two opposite directions. . . .

John: I have two families who are split. I have somebody on one side of the room who's connected to somebody
on the other side of the room. So if you know you have family here and you're not sitting next to each other, say, "I'm
over here!"

[A young woman stands up and waves wildly, dancing
around.]

Jeannie: Hi, Mom! I love you!

John: Can somebody claim this child? [Much laughter.
A woman stands up directly on the other side of the room.]

Carmel: That's my daughter-in-law!

What followed was a back-and-forth family reading worthy of
a tennis match at the Australian Open. Carmel's husband, who had
passed from cancer, came through and brought with him the family cat, a child connected to Victoria, and also shed light on a
naughty family romance. I was even able to use my TV pop-culture
reference to unearth more family mysteries.

John: Okay, do you guys know *I Dream of Jeannie?*

Jeannie: That's me! That's my name! [dancing around]

John: But there's more to it than that. In *I Dream of Jeannie,* the astronaut lands his spaceship on a deserted beach,
and *poof,* there's the bottle. There's got to be a story in your
family where your husband landed someplace he thought
might have been deserted, or there had to be some type of
unique landing and then he found out . . . there's a funny
story at the end of that somewhere . . . . where he might
have thought he landed in enemy territory and he landed
on his own Air Force base. Do you know what he means
when he's talking about the unique landing or the funny
story like that?

Carmel: Yes!

John: Can you explain that?

Carmel: No . . . it's private! [more laughter]

The audience had a good time and a lot of laughs with this family reading, but never knew of the dramatic scene that followed later that night. After the seminar, Natasha and Duncan walked Jeannie-Marie and Victoria back to their hotel where Kerrina was waiting. Kerrina was originally going to accompany her mother to the seminar because she was anxious to connect with a childhood friend, Ryan, who had died nine years earlier from leukemia. The women weren't sure how she was going to react when they told her the good news: that they had a reading . . . and the not-as-good news: that Ryan didn't show up.

When the gang reached the hotel, Kerrina, who had been curled up in front of the TV, answered the door in her pajamas.

"You had a reading?" she asked, hopeful, after one glance at their smiling faces. "Who? *Who was it?*" she demanded, excited.

When the women told her that Ryan didn't come through, Kerrina burst into tears.

"But why, Mom? *Where is he? Why didn't he come through?*"

The three women stood in the hallway of the hotel hugging and crying. Natasha and Duncan—pulled into the group hug—tried to console young Kerrina.

Kerrina's disappointment is something I face every time I do a reading. I try to prepare people for the possibility that you won't always hear from those you want to hear from—we don't have control over who comes through. Sometimes it's difficult to find the words to ease the pain.

"He'll be in heaven, darling," Victoria told her daughter, stroking her hair as she sobbed. "There wasn't a message for you this time. It's like John says, not everybody gets a reading, but everybody's in heaven."

What happened next, says Natasha, was a moment as heartfelt as they come—and it carries with it a message with a capital "M" for all of you reading this.

"Kerrina dried her tears with her sleeve, looked up, and smiled," recalled Natasha, "and she realized she'd helped get the reading for her mom, her aunt, and for Carmel, and she was so happy. Here was this teenage kid who suddenly realized how, in this universe, we are all wonderfully connected."

Through her broken heart, Kerrina saw the bigger picture. And in doing so, she was able to be happy for her aunt, who had a reading instead of her because of her selfless act.

"The three of them were meant to be there together," Kerrina said, still sniffling, "and it just wasn't my turn. Not yet."

BY THE END OF THE TRIP, I was tapped out energy-wise, but also exhilarated. I was pleased to find that no matter where we are in this world, the human experience of love and loss is universal. Despite my sporadic fumblings with the down-under dialect, I realized that Australia and America weren't all that different. The spirit world crossed barriers in culture and geography. So far from home, people here were just as anxious to connect with their loved ones, be assured they were okay, and know they weren't so far away after all.

CHAPTER FOUR

Houston

I'VE ONLY BEEN TO HOUSTON, TEXAS, a handful of times in my life, but each time, I've been wowed by the readings I've experienced there—two seminars in particular were especially memorable for me.

The first, in February 2002, was unforgettable because of the unusual way one energy from the Other Side grabbed my attention. I was preparing for the seminar in my usual manner—doing the rosary and meditating—when Ace, one of my security guys that day, knocked on my hotel-room door to check if I was ready. I popped my rosary beads into my pocket, grabbed my sunglasses, and we hopped into the elevator together . . . and that's when it started. I was suddenly distracted—not by the living people coming in and out of the elevator—but instead, by a young girl from the Other Side.

If an energy tries to get through to me when I'm "off duty," so to speak—that is, when I'm not specifically doing a reading or paying focused attention to the Other Side—I'll feel a buzzing at the base of my neck. This can happen before a seminar has begun or even when I'm on vacation, when I'm at the gym . . . it even happened on my honeymoon in the middle of the night (Sandra was a good sport about it). It's like I've turned off or tuned out from my phone line to the Other Side, but I'm on eternal "vibrate" just in case of an emergency.

That buzzing means *pay attention to me!* It started in the elevator, and it followed me through the lobby, out the front door, and into the car. As soon as I buckled my seatbelt, this young girl let the information fly. I saw a picture of a room that looked like a lecture hall. Was it tonight's venue? I had no idea, since I'd never been to this auditorium before. I saw a picture of a large American flag in the back, left-hand section of this room. The young girl told me that she belonged to someone who would soon be sitting in that flag section, and then she continued sending me messages—including one about an organ-donation issue. During the entire drive to the seminar location, this girl wouldn't stop. I was getting pictures and feelings . . . and that buzzing at my neck. So much was coming through so fast, I was afraid I wouldn't remember all the information for the seminar an hour later. So I started to repeat it out loud to Ace as he drove.

Ever since my popularity has escalated, I've had to travel with a security crew whose job it is to check the entrances and exits of venues where I'm appearing and make sure our routes are planned and I stay safe. Ace—a big, muscular, retired court officer—was not only acting as driver and bodyguard this day, he was also trying to help me remember the information bombarding me. I kept getting flashes of this room with the American flag, so I asked Ace if he'd noticed the Stars and Stripes on the back wall as he did the security walk-through of the venue earlier that day. He couldn't remember. I had a hard time believing that he'd forget seeing this humongous flag I was envisioning in my mind if it was there, but of course, Ace's focus is on security—not on the room's decor.

I kept repeating the information over and over to him so that between us, we'd remember it. When energies come through early like this before a seminar, it kind of feels like they're "jumping the line" or "cutting in"—as if they're afraid they won't be able to get through once I'm in front of a big group of people and their respective dead relatives, battling it out for stage time. My guides, who act as my Other Side "security," don't usually allow energies to come through at random times. They put up the Do Not Disturb sign to make sure I can go through my daily routine like everybody else and not be interrupted every morning when I shave or every night at the dinner table. So when energies *do* get through, it means that they've convinced The Boys it's something important enough to warrant special treatment. As far as I'm concerned, whoever gets through to me is *meant* to get through, so whenever this happens, I listen.

As we pulled up to the convention center, Ace noticed a row of flags on the building next door and pointed them out. But I was sure that the flag I was seeing in my mind was *inside* the room, not outside. The girl showed me the image again and then continued throwing information at me. I had to start this reading pronto; this girl wouldn't let me rest. We rushed inside, and when I got backstage, Carol, my assistant, noticed that I was restless.

"What's wrong?" she asked.

"Carol, I have to start the seminar *right away*," I told her. "I have a girl coming through, and she's insisting I start with her—*now*." I told her about the American flag message and asked if she'd seen one in the room. She shook her head no.

"Well . . . anyway, we *have* to start," I said. I was anxious to get this message out of the way and was worried that if I didn't, this energy might mess up the entire seminar. I usually like to lecture for at least an hour before I start doing readings, to familiarize the audience with how I work. If they aren't accustomed to the process and an energy from the Other Side is trying to relay a message and the relatives here don't know how to "receive" it, the whole thing gets very frustrating, and it feels like trying to talk on the phone with a child (in this case, the Other Side) tugging at my sleeve.

But we couldn't start the seminar yet, Carol informed me, because people were still arriving and finding their seats. I put the microphone in her hand and begged her to just introduce me, and do it fast . . . the floodgates were opening, the information was flowing, and I was about to burst.

Carol peeked her head through the black-velvet curtains to check again on the audience. Doing intros was not her usual duty.

She hated speaking in front of large groups of people, and usually we have a local radio personality introduce me. But today it was *her* job, so she was already nervous to begin with. Then, I'd doubled her panic because of the urgency I was feeling at the moment. And now, I was pushing her to start ahead of schedule. Carol walked out onstage, anxious and flustered, and cleared her throat.

Backstage, I did some last-minute meditating. I closed my eyes and silently told this female energy coming through that it was "showtime" for her and her family. I asked her to come through with information to help her family recognize her, and let them know how important it was to her to come through *first*.

"Ladies and gentlemen," I heard Carol say, voice quavering, "Um . . . John is ready to begin immediately . . . uh . . . if you all would please take your seats . . . and please . . . turn off all your cell phones and . . . um . . . vibrators. . . . "

My eyes popped open, and I looked at Ace. "Did Carol just say to turn off your *vibrators?!*" He didn't have to answer. A second later, the audience erupted into thunderous applause at Carol's blunder. Of course she'd intended to say, "Please turn off your cell phones and *put your pagers on vibrate. . . .*" The audience was in hysterics, and I was laughing so hard from backstage that tears were dripping down my face. When Carol returned to where I was waiting, she was a shade of red so bright I laughed even harder. It was a major icebreaker that day, and Carol's flubbed line became a classic story to tell at subsequent seminars.

But now, it was time to get serious and deliver this girl's message. I walked out onto the stage in front of the 2,500 people there and immediately scanned the back, left-hand side of the room, expecting to see the American flag. *No flag.* I paused, a bit surprised. Maybe I'd misinterpreted the message? I began telling the audience what had taken place on the car ride over, hoping that someone would connect with the information I'd been given.

As a medium, I knew I had to surrender my ego and keep going with the information as I saw it, even though I risked being "wrong." My job is to honor those on the Other Side and the information I'm given as it comes to me. I rattled off the details again, looking over at Ace to make sure I was getting it right, and I repeated everything twice as I paced up and down the stage. I looked out to the back section of the room where the flag *wasn't,* and searched the sea of faces in the crowd to see if anyone showed a hint of recognition.

The room was quiet, and everyone was still. Those minutes standing onstage felt like a lifetime, and all I could think was that I'd made a poor decision. As a teacher, which is ultimately how I see my work, maybe I shouldn't have deviated from my normal curriculum. Because I hadn't given my usual explanation of the process, this girl's family might not understand what I was saying, and this message wouldn't make it through. I was kicking myself for making a bad call when very, very slowly, a woman stood up in that section in the back. Everyone turned and gasped. This woman was cloaked in red, white, and blue. She was wearing a big leather bomber jacket in the same shape, design, and colors of the American flag. She then proceeded to validate each and every detail that had come through to me earlier, courtesy of her dear daughter who had crossed over.

HOUSTON, WE HAVE A PROBLEM

ALMOST ONE YEAR TO THE DAY, I was back in Houston. It was a chilly February morning in 2003, and I was fighting a cold but losing the battle. One funny thing about being a medium is that when I do readings while I'm sick, the Other Side suspends my symptoms and carries me through. But when I'm finished the reading, I feel sicker than ever. It's like I use up any reserve fuel I have and am left depleted. I began the seminar by telling the audience the story of the woman wearing the American flag jacket the year before, and many who were present—who were also in attendance the year before—remembered the moment.

This time, I started the seminar in my usual way—giving a talk about how the process works and taking questions from the audience. Some people asked the standard questions about my personal experiences, while others took the microphone to thank me for doing what I do. One woman in particular almost reduced me to tears when she shared that she'd recently lost a baby, and watching *Crossing Over* had become a form of therapy for her in dealing with her overwhelming grief.

When people tell me things like that, I feel an immediate and emotional reaction deep down inside my gut, inside my inner being . . . like I just won the spiritual lottery. But instead of money as the reward, it's joy. When someone appreciates my work, it's truly like they're handing me a gift. It's not easy for me to leave my family behind and travel from city to city as much as I do—so often that I sometimes forget what city I'm in. So when someone takes the time to communicate with, appreciate, and validate *me* . . . well, I just melt into a mushy puddle. So, thank you to all the people out there who have done that for me. It makes all the sweat and the B.S. that sometimes comes with this work worth it.

As soon as the lecture and Q&A period were over, I was pulled to the middle section of the room. I remember standing on the stage of the theater, extending my arm out in front of me and pointing— drawing a straight line from me to the center of the audience. As I did so, I had a powerful image in my mind's eye . . . it was the Columbia space shuttle. I just knew . . . I *knew* . . . this message coming through had something to do with the explosion that had occurred just three weeks earlier, and someone right in front of me was connected to it.

My own connection to this disaster began before it even happened. I'd watched the shuttle take off on television on January 16 from home with Sandra, and I remember getting a really bad feeling as it shot into the sky. It was just a general "not good" feeling— nothing specific. That's how I often feel these kinds of premonitions—my guides don't show me details. So when people ask why I don't do anything to prevent some tragedy, that's my answer: I don't know myself what's going to happen.

Five days later in Los Angeles, en route to Australia, I did a magazine interview, and the reporter asked me if I get premonitions, and could I give her my most recent one. I said sure, but it wasn't a very positive one. I told her that I'd watched the Columbia launch and felt concern for the astronauts. The reporter immediately jumped on it and asked, "Is it going to crash? Or explode?" and I freaked out a bit, realizing maybe I'd said too much. I tried to backpedal a bit to calm us both down, saying, "No, no . . . I just don't have a good feeling."

That was the last I thought about the shuttle until the final night in Australia, on January 29, 2003, when we had a huge dinner in Melbourne with all the people who had helped organize the tour, as well as the Hay House Australia team—my new Aussie family. Natasha and I were digging into our steaks and making idle chitchat about the local wine when I froze mid-sentence, fork in air.

"John . . . what's wrong?" Natasha asked. She recognized that *look* on my face.

"I feel like something is exploding," I told her, putting my fork down—"and there's some kind of . . . Israeli connection to it."

What? When? *Where?* She asked about a dozen reporter-like questions, whipping out her pen and notebook, but I couldn't answer any of them because I didn't know the answers myself. I told her not to worry about it for now, and I pushed the feeling out of my mind. I kind of thought, okay . . . Israel . . . they have explosions there all the time . . . this isn't so psychic of me. We both went to sleep that night a little uneasy.

The next day we boarded the plane for the long flight back home. As we waited for our connecting flight in Los Angeles, there it was on CNN. The shuttle had exploded that morning, killing its entire seven-member crew—including the first Israeli in history to ever make that expedition. Sitting in the airport that morning, I felt the deep sadness I always experience when a bad premonition comes true, and I said a silent prayer for the crew members and their families.

"I feel really awkward saying this," I told the audience in Houston, "but is there someone here connected with someone who perished in the recent shuttle disaster?"

There was an immediate hush over the room. I felt uncomfortable asking this question because the time frame was so close to the disaster, and I was sure that anyone connected would still be emotionally raw. I always tell people that mediumship is not a cure for grief, and can only be helpful at the right time during a person's journey *through* this grief—which is rarely right after their loved one has passed.

I discourage people from seeing a medium right after a loss. I used to think this was because a person/energy who recently left their body for the Other Side wouldn't be "ready" to come through yet—maybe they first need time to rest up and adjust to their new world. But now, I think the un-readiness has more to do with us here. Right after a person crosses, the loved ones left behind are usually devastated, and they feel a gaping hole in their hearts. It's important to "honor" this pain. And when I say "honor," I don't mean that you should be all happy about it or throw a party. I mean you must let the grief evolve through you naturally—that is, you should feel the pain, cry into a pillow, yell and scream and oversleep, and most important, work with a counselor, therapist, support group, priest, rabbi, minister—anyone who can help you get through this and get to the core of the hurt.

Once you get to the core of the pain, you can start finding your way back out again. And for each person, this journey through pain—then beyond it—is a unique, important, and healing experience. If someone seeks out a reading too early, it may interfere with their natural stages of grief—which can take months or years, depending on the person.

In my novel, *What If God Were the Sun?*, I explored this journey through the life of a fictional family. I stress the word *fictional,* because many people, even some of my family members, thought it was autobiographical. Yes, there were hints of my family in there, but it was more an amalgamation of the many families I've sat down with and read over the years.

In the novel, the family learns about "honoring their grief" and how grief is really the other side of love. Think about it: Your love for a person is like a flow of energy, and it's directed from you to them. But when the person dies—or when their *body* dies—many of us don't know where to put the love/energy anymore, and it gets backed up. This causes a blockage of energy within us, and this blockage locks our grief. Understanding their death, honoring it, accepting it, and walking that long road through grief helps us move through that blockage and then understand that our loved ones are still a *part* of our lives—not *apart* from our lives.

When we move through the blockage, we get back to the love. For those of you who have experienced severe loss, you're well aware that you never get over that loss entirely. You get *through* it, and it changes you. Those who haven't lost a loved one can't understand this feeling, and often say to those who are grieving: "Aren't you over it yet? He's in a better place now. It's better this way . . . she's out of pain." If you don't know what to say to a friend or loved one in pain, just say: "I'm here for you." Those four words are helpful.

Back to the reading in Houston. I was hesitant to bring up the shuttle disaster for fear that the loss was too recent, but my main rule in this work is: *If they show it, so do I.* A big part of the process is not editing what I get.

"Someone right in that section," I said, pointing out front, "is connected with one of the astronauts who crossed on the space shuttle Columbia three weeks ago." A woman directly in front of me, in the very back of the room, stood up.

"My husband is Rick Husband's cousin," she said.

I didn't know whom she was talking about, since I didn't know the names of the astronauts. The woman explained that Rick Husband was the commander of the Columbia, and a cousin by marriage. Once she validated this, the information started to flow. Rick said that there would be additional information about the disaster that the families of the astronauts would be receiving—perhaps a video, which may or may not become public knowledge. There were also "audible" messages of the shuttle crew on tape that the public didn't know about yet, but would soon. I was shown that the passing of the astronauts was fast and somewhat of a surprise, and they were unconscious before anything happened to their physical bodies.

"It's as if they were asleep," I told the audience, as I dropped my head to the side in a sleeping position to show what I was feeling and seeing. Everyone applauded at that, in relief for the astronauts and their families.

"Rick comes from a religious family . . . " was the next bit of information I got. The entire room nodded in unison. Everyone seemed to know this about their hometown son except me.

"There's an 'LN' name . . . like Lynne . . . connected to Rick. Is this you?"

She shook her head no. And then I felt a split pull—as if I were a sheet of paper torn in half and separated in two opposite directions.

"Is there someone else here in the room who also knows Rick? Or is there someone else here connected to *another* member of the shuttle crew?"

A petite woman about ten rows in front of me raised her hand. "Yes," she said, "I knew the Israeli astronaut on that flight, Ilan [pronounced *Ee-LAN*]."

Okay, so that explained the "Lynne" name. For me, when I hear names that start with a vowel, I will not hear that first vowel. I'll hear the consonant sounds following the vowel as strong and predominant. So in this case, "Ilan" became more of a "Lan" or "Lin" sound in my head, because I didn't hear the "E" sound. Information started coming through from this second astronaut.

"He wants me to acknowledge his kids . . . and something about the music. Was someone singing either to him from here, or was he singing to here from there?"

"He and his wife had a song about being far away," the woman answered in an emotional whisper, "and she sang it to him while he was there." At this point, I was getting emotional, too.

"And his daughter, his little girl," the woman continued, "watched her father take off in the shuttle. And at that moment, she said out loud, 'I just lost my daddy.'"

All right, now I was doing everything possible to keep myself from losing it right there onstage. Normally when I do readings, I can stay detached from the feeling part of it—that's how I'm able to relay such poignant details time after time without becoming a sobbing wreck. But this last image of the astronaut's little girl waving good-bye to her daddy just got me. Ever since my Justin had been born, readings that deal with parent-child relationships have an even deeper and more heartbreaking effect on me than before.

After the event, Carol told me that it was highly publicized and reported in the newspapers that the astronaut's daughter had said those words as the shuttle blasted off. So did the little girl sense what was going to happen? Well, I do believe our soul decides when it's completed its lessons here in the physical world. And when that time comes, we allow ourselves to exit. Some events, which we call "accidents," may not be accidents at all in terms of the Other Side.

I'd describe it more like this: Let's say you're on a business trip and you've finished your meetings early, but your flight home isn't until the next day. You might try to hop on an earlier flight to get home sooner. If you do, it was your decision to alter your path. I believe that the soul makes that same decision to change its journey, to go *home* home—to its spiritual home. Some people, often children, can be aware when it's time for a soul to leave this world. What that little girl experienced is nothing short of a gift, and to me, it's clear she was given a validation that it was her dad's *time*.

Think about the people you love who have crossed over. If it wasn't a long illness that brought them to the Other Side, and it was more of a sudden event, examine what they were doing or saying during the months leading up to the moment they physically left. You might discover clues that their soul was getting ready to "go home." Maybe the person recently gave away a treasured piece of jewelry or reconciled with an estranged friend. Maybe they got all their paperwork in order and wrote a will. The soul knows it's getting ready to leave, and that unconscious thought flows into our everyday lives. After reading dozens of September 11 families in the last year and a half, I can tell you that I've seen examples of this over and over. Both the energies coming through, and their loved ones here, often talk about signs—whether spoken or acted out— that signaled they were going to leave.

BY THE END OF THOSE TWO READINGS in Houston, the astronauts had also brought through the parents of the two women. I hope that they found comfort in that, and in knowing that the astronauts saw them as an opportunity to pass on messages to their loved ones here and let them know they're okay.

Two weeks after the seminar, on March 1, news reports validated the information that came through in the reading. The New York *Daily News* revealed that a video had been found in Texas showing the crew's last moments—laughing, talking, and not knowing anything was wrong. It was "a remarkable fragment of video that survived the terrible fires that consumed the space shuttle Columbia," the report said. "There is not even a hint of concern, anxiety—nothing . . . trauma specialists said the cheerful images would bring comfort to the families, who were shown the video and agreed it should be made public."

SPIRITUAL MAIL CARRIER

A MONTH AFTER MY STAY IN HOUSTON, I was contacted by Nancy Marlowe Sheppard, Rick Husband's relative whom I'd read at the seminar. Sheppard, a retired school teacher, was eager to tell me what had happened to her before she even got to the reading that day. Ever since the shuttle explosion, she'd been having strong feelings that she needed to attend a taping of *Crossing Over*—that if she did, something important might happen. When she learned about the seminar that was to happen nearby, she called the venue to get a ticket but was told it had been sold out for months.

Nancy recalled, "I said to the woman on the phone, 'Look, I *really* need to go. Can't you try again?'"

Often, I believe, the Other Side really does have a hand in getting people where they need to be. In many cases, people who have tried to get tickets for the *Crossing Over* gallery, or for a seminar or private reading, often get them as a fluke or seemingly by "coincidence"—and they end up having a dramatic reading.

But, once again, I don't believe anything is ever a coincidence—the ticket agent suddenly "found" two tickets for Nancy to the sold-out seminar. As she was preparing to leave her house for the event, she had hopes that her deceased parents might come through that day. But before she left home, Nancy had what can only be described as a premonition: Rick's energy came through to her. "I felt Rick's presence," she said, "and I knew he was going to come through at the reading." Her premonition included information that "he and the rest of the crew did not suffer and were grateful for the love America had shown to them."

The message surprised Nancy, but it wasn't a complete shock. "I've always been intuitive," she said, "ever since I was a child. But I always pushed away the hunches, the feelings, the visions, the knowing." It's not uncommon for many people to feel in touch with the spiritual world—whether they get a thought, hear a voice, or smell a whiff of perfume that Mom used to wear—most people at one time or another have had psychic experiences. We all have this ability within us to different degrees, but rather than pay attention to it, many ignore it. Nancy had tried to ignore her "hunches" her entire life, but on the day of the reading, she couldn't do it anymore.

"I was sitting in the second-to-last row, in the last seat. I know you couldn't even see me from up on the stage," recalled Nancy. "When you asked if there was anyone related to the Columbia crew and I stood up, I was the only one standing in the room, and my heart was beating so fast. I told you I was connected to Rick, and then you said, 'Rick Husband is *here*.' One of the messages you got was that Rick was a religious man—and it's true. He went to church, he spoke in Sunday school, and did all sorts of things like that. And then my parents came through in the reading. . . . "

Nancy was overjoyed that her mom and dad came through and made a "cameo appearance," giving accurate family birthdays, anniversaries, and illnesses so that she knew it was them. But what affected her most was something I said to the group at the end of the evening.

Nancy remembered, "You paused, and then you said, 'Did someone here know *before* the seminar that this was going to happen?' That's the part that was so awesome for me. I was still standing, and I said, 'I knew!'"

A month after the seminar, Nancy sent a letter to Rick's mother and wife to tell them about her experience, and as this book goes to print, Nancy hadn't heard back from them yet but is hoping that the words gave them peace. That day in Houston was Nancy's introduction to being a "spiritual mail carrier." It began with her premonition earlier in the day and continued with her delivering a message for the Other Side when she mailed that letter to Rick's family.

Being a spiritual mail carrier is a job many of us undertake although we may not be aware of it. The young girl watching her father leave on the shuttle was passing along a message, too. You don't need to be a medium to work with the Other Side; you just need to be open to the vibrations and be willing to listen.

"I really think I was supposed to be there," Nancy continued. "I think that's why I got the ticket at the last minute. I think Rick Husband knew I'd be there and chose me to get his message out."

CHAPTER FIVE

Telephone Tag

SOME READINGS FLOW EASILY, with information coming through from the Other Side clearly, and the sitter recognizing the details immediately. Other sessions can be more of a challenge, and there are a number of reasons why. First, I might be interpreting the information incorrectly, like in the instance I spoke of earlier when I got the gun-taxicab image and thought a young man had been murdered in a taxi, when he was actually shot in the front part—the "cab"—of a truck. That's an example of how I'm shown images by the Other Side that could take on a number of meanings, and my immediate interpretation is one meaning when it's actually another.

Second, a sitter might not be approaching a session with an open mind. Some people are determined to hear from certain people and assume that they'll say certain things, closing their brain off to other possibilities. Sure, you might want to hear from Uncle Harry and hope he'll tell you where the family treasure is stashed. But instead, the guy who had a crush on you in college comes through and jokes about how you cheated on that French exam. But you don't recognize this guy because you only want to hear from Uncle Harry. When this happens, it doesn't matter how hard the energies or I work to open your eyes—nothing will make you see. And then you go home disappointed, assuming that the process just "didn't work" for you.

Sometimes a reading is off because what's coming through isn't intended for you. Usually after a bit of confusion and a few minutes—if we're lucky—we discover that the information is actually for a friend, co-worker, or relative. If possible, we get that person on the phone, and when we do, the validations again flow like the Mississippi.

Other times, a reading gets jammed up and I can't pinpoint the problem. The information is coming through to me clearly, but the sitter doesn't understand it for herself or for anyone else she knows. This is what happened during a recent phone reading I did with a very nice woman named Deanna, a medical reporter in Chicago, who was hoping to connect with her young son who had passed away a few years earlier.

During the reading, the information struck me with the force and clarity of a hardball hitting me in the gut. I was sure of it. But for the most part, that ball dropped to the ground with a *thud*. Deanna couldn't connect with what I was telling her. In most readings, if a detail can't be validated, it's no big deal. I try to reinterpret the message or we call up a family member—and if those two things don't work, I insist that the sitter write it down to check later, and then we move onward.

Often, the sitter calls me weeks or months later to tell me— *Aha!*—they figured it out A string of non-validations during a reading do become a problem, however, when the energy is insistent and will not let it go. Because then I get persistent myself, which frustrates the sitter, and all three parties get caught up in a three-way wrestling match of spiritual proportions. For example:

John: Somebody's claiming that their actions brought about their passing, which for me would be like somebody taking responsibility for how they crossed. This doesn't encompass an actual suicide, but is like a weird passing where somebody is slightly responsible for it.

Deanna: No . . .

John: Uh, *yes*. You just might not be aware of it, or it might hit you later, but I assure you this is definitely connected to you.

[Then later in the reading, it comes up again.]

John: Okay . . . there's somebody who's claiming that their actions brought about their passing.

Deanna: No . . .

John: Well, I'm gonna disagree again.

[The issue comes up a third time later.]

John: Okay, are you positive there's nobody in that family who crossed themselves over, or something that they did caused how they passed?

Deanna: I'm positive.

John: Well, again I'm going to disagree.

John: Were your son and his dad at odds?

Deanna: No.

John: He's making me feel an issue about dealing with Dad and being at odds. Also, I'm supposed to be talking about Mark, or Marky.

Deanna: No . . .

John: Oh, *yes*.

Deanna: I can't think of anyone.

John: Would he have a male figure to his side, like a good friend who got married or celebrated something after he left?

Deanna: No.

John: Are you positive?

Deanna: Positive.

John: Really? He's harping on this. Was he an insistent energy? I mean, was he somebody who would not drop things?

Deanna: No.

John: Okay, they're telling me to go straight north. So, to me, I want to go to upstate New York . . . I want to go to Canada . . .

Deanna: No.

John: There must be some ties. They're trying to get me to get you someplace north to understand what's coming through.

Deanna: No, I don't understand that.

John: I know you don't. That's why I keep saying the same thing over again, because they're trying really hard to get me to get you where they want, and that's up north. And they're also claiming somebody just passed. Did you just lose a cousin or an aunt?

Deanna: No.

John: Are you sure?

Deanna: I'm positive.

John: Oh, I think you're wrong. This is the part of my job that I absolutely hate, like talking to a complete stranger and now arguing with her about her family! [laughs] This stuff is not changing . . . I went through like seven pages already on the same stuff. Let me start over.

The reading went on like this for a while, and both of us were sighing and trying to focus. I know it sounds illogical for me to be telling someone she's wrong about her own family, but when the same thing is shown to me repeatedly from the Other Side, I become that bulldog. Thankfully, sprinkled within the confusion in Deanna's reading, her son did come through, and we got some specific, intimate family details that rang true as a bell and ended the session on a very happy note for both of us.

IF YOU'RE THINKING THAT DEANNA'S READING was a challenge because it was over the phone, that's a common misconception. Most people imagine that if I'm going to communicate with someone who's "dead," I'd at least need their living, breathing relative to be sitting in front of me in the flesh. Not so. Ever since I started this work, I've done phone readings for clients who couldn't travel to my office. I also routinely do phone sessions when I'm a guest on radio or television shows where people call into the show to be read over the air.

Whether the session is face-to-face, on the phone, or even over the Internet—which I've also done—it all works the same way . . . with energy. And energy knows no distance.

To understand how it works, you first need to be aware that the energies that come through to me are connected to *you,* the person I'm reading—not to myself. Their home base isn't around me or my office or at the studio where I shoot *Crossing Over.* The energies surround and sort of "travel" with the person they "belong" to . . . whom they're connected to on this earth. (I don't say this to freak you out. Don't worry, they aren't lingering and leering in the bathroom every time you take a shower. They have other things to do.)

So the energies are linked to you, and then they try to get my attention because, first, they know I can hear them; and second, they know I'm talking to you and keying into you and the energies around you. Whether the reading is in person or on the phone, I get the messages in a similar fashion. If it's in person, the energies around you as you sit in front of me vie for my attention and say, "Hey, John . . . over here!" It's the same on the phone. Imagine that I'm chatting with you on the phone and you're at home, and one of your family members yells over your shoulder into the phone, "Yo, John . . . over here!" Same deal. I hear it in the same way. All of our energies connect whether I'm two feet or 200 miles away from you.

Just to show you that the phone line had nothing to do with the hurdles in Deanna's session, here's another reading I did over the phone just one hour before Deanna's. If we were to consider this a phone "experiment," we might say that I was the constant, and the sitters and the Other Side were the variables. I don't know how these variables differed from each other, but as you'll see, the two readings were poles apart.

The first reading, as I found out afterward, was with writer Norris Church Mailer, wife of two-time Pulitzer Prize–winning novelist Norman Mailer. Norris telephoned my office in Huntington, New York, from her home in Provincetown, Massachusetts, and I conferenced-in Natasha from her apartment in Manhattan.

Natasha had organized both Deanna's and Norris's sessions and was listening in on the other end of the three-way phone chats, taking notes and tape-recording the exchanges. (Of course, we'd checked in with Natasha during Deanna's reading to see if any of the unvalidated information was for her—it wasn't.) It was just as important to Natasha, a seasoned news reporter, as it was to me to know that the integrity of the readings remained intact and that I knew nothing about the person or whom they were trying to connect with.

As you'll see, the loved one Norris wanted to hear from the most came through right away, and with tremendous clarity—that is, until the reading took a surprising turn and the Other Side came through with an unexpected gift. You may have noticed during some of the episodes of *Crossing Over* that anyone in my energy area—either physically or on the phone—has the potential to be read. It happened during Norris's reading, and in this case, it was someone else on the phone line. From the get-go, an energy came through—a mother figure with a "MAR" name—who wasn't connected to Norris. For a moment, we were confused.

But in this case, the mix-up was sorted out right away.

Little did I know that Natasha had lost her mother, Maria, ten years earlier . . . and here was Mom showing up while her daughter was busy at work so she could say hello to her little girl.

I'd known Natasha professionally for four years (as a journalist, she'd interviewed me several times), and we'd become friends in the last year, yet she'd never told me that her mother had passed. Why? She hid this bit of information from her psychic buddy, she told me later, because she was secretly hoping to one day have a reading of her own and didn't want to divulge any of her pertinent Other-Side details. During the dozens of seminars she attended since we started writing this book together, she was always hopeful that her mother would come through at some point, but each time, Natasha left the sessions with notebooks full of readings for other people and not herself. When she finally came to terms with the fact that it would only happen when it was meant to—*it happened.*

John: The first thing I'm going to tell you is that I have an older male coming through, and to me, I would see that being the father figure, the uncle, the grandfather . . .

Norris: Okay.

John: And I don't know if this would be a father figure— like Dad for you, but I'm going to tell you I have a ten connection that comes up. Ten to me means October . . . or the tenth of a month . . . it's a birthday, anniversary. They're also telling me to talk about Mary or Marie. There's an "M-a-r" name that they want me to acknowledge that's connected to the family. I don't believe it's his name, but I believe he is either with "Mar" on the Other Side, or he's acknowledging her as being there. He's also making me feel like, I don't know how to put it, but . . . did you just have a cancer scare?

Norris: Yes.

John: Okay, because they're making me feel like you just went through something that would be like a cancer scare. I literally feel like I'm going into this tunnel, and you're saying to yourself there's no life in here. Okay, but this is a tunnel—I'm going to eventually get to the Other Side. And you kept venturing inside this tunnel, and there's still no life. And the darkness that I have all around this, to me feels like we're going through a very scary place. I have to tell you that they don't think you're out of that place yet, by the way.

Norris: Yes.

John: I feel like you're still there and you're still moving. I feel like you're 80 percent—85 percent through the tunnel, and you can now start to see a little light at the end, but what you need to hear from him is that as long as you keep your eyes closed, you can't tell that you're in the dark, so it's a matter of keeping your eyes closed and walking straight ahead, and allowing your faith to guide you . . . with what you're dealing with and what you're moving forward with. You follow what I'm saying?

Norris: Yes.

John: Now, I don't know if your birthday is in June, but I feel like I need to talk about the celebration or the congratulations that happened in the sixth month. So either this person is aware of what's happening in June, or what happened in June.

Norris: Okay.

John: I also have somebody else coming through. The first gentleman, I think, passes from a health-care-related illness. This other person I'm getting passes in an event, something massive. So whether this was a very bad car accident or they had some type of impact of some sort . . . I want to talk about an explosion. There's a Chris that I'm supposed to bring up around this. I don't know if the person I'm talking about is Chris, or they're connected to Chris or Chrissie or Christine, but there's like a Chris connection that comes up with it, and they're telling me to tell you 15. So the 15th has to be linked to this whole thing. To me it feels like this could be a contemporary of you. Or the first gentleman we talked about, it might be a contemporary to him. There is this Chrissie, Chris, Christine, "C" or "K" connection that comes up, but then there's a big boom. Is there a Robert connected to you? A Robert or Robbie or Roberta that might be connected to your side of the family?

Norris: I can't think of any Robert, but that doesn't mean there's not one.

John: Okay, hold on one second. I want to go back . . . no, no I don't. I want to stay here. Hold on. Your mom's passed?

Norris: No.

John: I have someone here who's claiming to be Mom. Wait, wait, wait. Hold on. She's claiming to be connected to Robert. She's connecting herself to what I just said—this whole impact, Chris, the number 15, the "R" name like Robert, and the mom energy is all linking itself together for me.

Norris: None of that is ringing bells for me. The other stuff definitely rang all the bells.

Natasha: Um . . . John? It makes sense to me. . . .

John: What makes sense to you?

Natasha: Mom passed, and a Robert.

John: Robert's connected to you?

Natasha: Yes.

John: Is Robert still here?

Natasha: Yes. My brother.

John: Okay, then, where does the Chris or Christine or Christopher come up?

Natasha: That part doesn't make sense to me.

John: Okay, there's a definite "C" or "K" connection, there's a 15 connection, which to me means date-wise of the 15th of the month, or that someone was 15 years old. There's a definite explosion of some sort, as if somebody passed in an impact. But if there was an impact, then something fiery had to happen at the same time. It's kinda like it's gruesome—but that's where they're going with this. It all seems connected. Natasha, the mom energy—your mom's passed?

Natasha: Yes . . . and, just a moment . . . my mother's last name has "Chris" in it.

John: In the beginning?

Natasha: Yep. Her last name was Christoff.

John: Okay, that would make sense. Your mom had cancer?

Natasha: Yes.

John: Okay, then I need to tell you that there had to be either three or four hospitalizations, or three or four different types of procedures or things that she had to deal with that would be in conjunction with her type of cancer.

Natasha: Correct.

John: And there had to be some type of false hope, I mean massive false hope, like one of the opportunities going into this, they thought, okay, they got it. And then

I feel like it just flips to the opposite end very, very quickly. I'm also gonna tell you that the 23rd is connected.

Natasha: That's her birthday—March 23rd.

John: Ok, um . . . I never knew your mom passed, Natasha!

Natasha: I don't tell you everything!

John: Do you keep a picture of her on your desk, to the left?

Natasha: Uh, no, I'm looking, I don't see one. . . .

John: How about reader #1. [laughs] Do you have anything near you?

Norris: I have a picture of my father. It's sorta to my right.

John: What's kinda funny is that your dad and Natasha's mother are battling for time here!

Natasha: We thought this might happen!

John: This is funny. Had they known each other in life?

Norris and Natasha: No . . .

John: I want to go back to Dad for a second. I don't know if your dad has the "J" or "G" connection—

Norris: J.

John: He wants to talk about the two boys.

Norris: Yes!

John: He's also making me feel like he has his brother with him, by the way

Norris: Oh, good!

John: He also wants to acknowledge your mom and a sister.

Norris: He has a sister who's alive, yes.

John: He's making me feel like he's got somewhat of a— I don't call it sarcastic, but he's got a quiet way of making a point.

Norris: Yes, exactly.

John: I don't know if you're his baby, but he's making me feel like you're the youngest, or you're the baby girl, or you're the only girl.

Norris: Yup, yup.

John: He tells me to remind you about the rotten eggs, the smelly eggs, making bad eggs, or doing something with eggs.

Norris (laughing): Is it eggs Benedict?

John: It's a bad egg thing for you, for him, whatever . . . like you made them for him, or he made them for you. He's saying to go back to 1992. So 1992 has got to be a turning point for your family. I also feel like your dad either had a military background or there has to be some type of military connection.

Norris: Yes, yes.

John: What he's showing me is some really cool military stuff. There's a trunk, and in the trunk there might be his flag, his pictures, his patches, his this, his that, but there's a coin collection. A few coins, a few medals, or medallions. Is this a recent passing?

Norris: Last July.

John: Okay, to me that's a recent passing. Natasha, your mom's gone for a while? Like just over ten years?

Natasha: Exactly ten years.

John: There was an issue, I believe, well, I'm attaching it to your mom, but if it's your dad, let me know. There's an issue about teeth, or an issue about problems with gums, teeth, the bleeding . . . teeth falling out . . .

Norris: My father had teeth problems.

John: Yep, we've got parents dueling this out now, guys! Um, I do feel that your dad either struggled to leave, or there was a difficulty in some capacity with him leaving.

Norris: Yes.

John: This might not have been an easy passing, just so you know. If you were there watching it, you would know what I'm talking about. Okay, this might be weird, but did you ever see the musical *Dreamgirls?* There's that song, "And I am telling you, I'm not going, I'm stayin' . . . "

Norris: Yeah, yeah, yeah.

John: When he left, he left without saying good-bye or without letting two people see him.

Norris: Yes!

John: And he knows that it was very difficult on the two of them, because they didn't get a chance to bring closure. He did that for their best interest.

Norris: We know he did . . .

John: Okay, because he does not feel that they would have been able to handle the passing, number one; and number two, I think it would have been very difficult for him to be able to leave with them being there or having them there.

Norris: Yeah, he sent us away so he could leave.

John: Yeah, it's not uncommon, it's not uncommon at all. A lot of times they just need that private time to be able to leave, to know that it's okay. Your dad is making me feel that his voice is very raspy. He's making me feel that he had a very difficult time communicating. Either he was on a respirator or there was some type of breathing apparatus that would have made it harder to hear him. And he's saying to tell you "Charlie." So I don't know if Charlie is his friend, but he's telling me to acknowledge Charlie. I almost want to go as far as saying that there's a financial connection—it might just be his way of saying that when you go back and you talk to your mom, and you talk to the family and say did Dad know a Charlie, they'll say yes, a guy he worked with.

Norris: He used to work for a man named Charles.

John: These are the little trivial details that to me are so significant. Now he's telling me that his sister is in a different state than either of us. He says she's a tough lady.

Norris: [laughs] Yes, she is!

John: She's a tough lady. He's telling me to tell you to pass this on, because she might be a little like, *You talked to who, who does what? Oh, I don't know if I believe in all that crap.* But she'll listen. Now the reason why she'll listen is I think she lost a son.

Norris: I don't think so . . . but it's possible.

John: Your dad is acknowledging a younger energy connected to the sister. So she might have miscarried a boy; she might have had a child that passed that the family doesn't know about. It needs to be acknowledged that the younger male is there as well. The only other way I can interpret this would be if Natasha's mom lost a son.

Natasha: Not that I know of.

John: Okay, if your mother has a nephew or a grandson who has passed, then that can be of significance because I need to acknowledge if the younger male is there.

Natasha: She has a brother who died as a child.

John: Younger than her?

Natasha: No, he was older.

John: Then that's not it. So I'm gonna leave it with her dad. Are they southwest of me?

Norris: Yes.

John: Okay, because they're making me feel like it's—geography's not my best—but they're taking me straight down and over to my left a little bit.

Norris: Yup, yup, yup—it's Arkansas.

John: Now, is Lynn connected to you? They're making me feel like I have to say it's an "L-N" name like Lynette, Lynnie, Lenore, Leon. It's like an "L-N" name . . .

Norris: I do know someone named Lynn who just passed.

John: Your dad is making me feel that I need to acknowledge the "L-N" name. I feel like I need to let you know that this person's there as well.

Norris: Okay.

John: Okay, now, I don't know—you definitely have had a two-year tumultuous period.

Norris: Right.

John: I mean we're talking like a *major* emotional, mental, spiritual roller coaster.

Norris: Yes.

John: Your dad wants me to tell you that you need to be happier, like you need to be . . . I mean, I don't want to sound all "foo-foo" here, but I really feel like you need to be a little more appreciative of the smaller things. I don't know if you're a control freak, but I feel that you were trying to dominate and control everything, and you won't be able to, you know. If you're so busy juggling everything, you're gonna drop the things that are right in front of you that need your attention.

Now I don't know if your husband's been traveling a lot for business—

Norris: That's where he is now.

John: Okay. But your dad is making me feel like there's immense, immense traveling that's going to be coming up real soon. So if he traveled twice a year last year, guess what? He's traveling like ten times this year.

Norris: Oh, yeah.

John: Now is Michael, Mikey, connected to you?

Norris: My stepson, Michael—I call him Mikey.

John: Okay, 'cause your dad has told me to acknowledge the Michael or the Mikey as part of his family, so it's important that you know that he sees that as being his family. You're having a hard time dealing with your dad's passing from what he's showing me, is that true?

Norris: Yes.

John: He's making me feel that . . . he's stepping forward . . . and when someone steps forward in a session, it's usually their way of letting me know *why* the session's happening. He's making me feel like people did what they had to do leading up to his passing. People said the things they needed to say . . .

Norris: Okay . . .

John: And some of the people who were there weren't as verbal. I don't think you were very verbal with your dad when he was passing. I don't think you said to him, "It's okay to go, we're gonna be okay, I love you." I don't think you did any of that, but you know what? You didn't have to, because it's not how your family dynamic is set up. The fact that you were there, that spoke volumes.

He does want you to highlight his sister. So I don't know if she's the older sister or if she's the—

Norris: Younger.

John: Well, he's making me feel like she's the matriarch.

Norris: Yeah, she's the youngest, but she *is* the matriarch.

John: She feels like she's the matriarch, you know. I see the mother from Dallas, and that's the matriarch.

Norris: Yes, yes, yes, the boss!

John: The buck stops there. And she knows it, by the way.

Norris: [laughing] Yes.

John: Now, does your mother live in the area?

Norris: She's near me.

John: She has something like a respiratory thing going on?

Norris: No, I don't think so . . .

John: But she has—like asthma or something or—

Norris: Yes.

John: Okay, you're going to have to watch something around her. This could be minor, this could be the beginning of a chest cold, it could be something that she's developing. I don't know exactly what this is, but they're showing me . . . like, *caution*—and I'm always saying I'm not a doctor, I can't diagnose, but they're showing me a yellow light flashing, and they're putting it over her chest.

Norris: Okay.

John: Your dad is telling me to tell you that where you are sitting . . . are you like holding the phone to your right ear?

Norris: Left ear.

John: All right, okay . . . but are you playing with your ear? Or with the hair on the right side . . . ?

Norris: [laughing] Yes!

John: Because he wants to make sure you know he's with you and he's not with me. So he's telling me to tell you he knows what it is you're doing.

Norris: [lots of laughing] Oh my God, I'm twisting my hair!

John: And he's saying to let you know that he's there, and he's still around. He's pulling his energy back.

Natasha, your mom's making me feel like she had to wait to do this. And she doesn't make me feel like anything was impeding her from being able to do this before. But you needed to be at a certain place in your spiritual development . . . whatever this means for you. She does say that her mother is there, so her mom's dead, too?

Natasha: Yep.

John: And she's telling me that you have . . . not disowned your roots, that's not my feeling . . . but I feel you have not taken something that you were supposed to take. Something is yours, but you have not taken it to your house. So if Grandma has a broach that was passed down to your mom, which is now supposed to be passed down to you—you haven't taken it. I don't care if it's a cup, a dish, a fork, a knife, I have no idea what it is, but it's tangible, and you don't have it. I don't know. . . .

You're mom's saying that she pre-deceased one of her own parents?

Natasha: A mother-in-law.

John: She's claiming that she met one of her parents. Like she passed, and then one of her parents passed, because she helped cross that parent over. So if you told me that your dad's mom passed after your mom, that would make sense.

Natasha: Yes, that's exactly right.

John: Okay, I'm also going to tell you that not your mom, but someone above her, one of your grandparents or one of your great-aunts, either suffered from Alzheimer's or had some type of dementia while they were here, because I'm seeing, "I've got my faculties back, I've got everything back." That's connected to the Betty, or the "B" name like Betty or Betsy or something "B"-related. I think that's on your dad's side.

Natasha: My dad's father was going through that. My dad is a "B" name—Basil.

John: And there are three or four important dates in December for your family, Natasha. Like around Christmas. So you could have three birthdays, three anniversaries, three things that take place in the month of December for the family.

Natasha: Yes! We have three birthdays.

John: What is today? Today is February what?

Natasha: 18th? 19th?

John: Now, I know it's not *your* birthday, Natasha.

Natasha: Right . . . that's very good . . . there is a birthday—

John: Yes, there is a birthday like *now*—

Natasha: There's a birthday today! I made a birthday call . . .

John: Okay, because they're telling me to acknowledge the white rose, because they showed that to me before you called me. I know it's not yours, but I want you to know that your mom is seeing the birthday around now.

Natasha: That's amazing! It's her sister's birthday.

John: She's telling me to tell you . . . and I want you to hear this very clearly—this is not the first and this will not be the last time you hear from her. I want to let you know that she's made connections to you previously, which either means you didn't acknowledge it or you just rationalized it away. . . .

Natasha: Right.

John: The group reading you did . . . she's not making me feel that she came through, is that true?

Natasha: Um . . . the person who did that group *said* she was there, but I didn't feel like she was. As a matter of fact, today I was speaking aloud to my mom, saying, "I didn't feel like you were there."

John: Okay, that makes sense with what the message is, then. You did have that previous experience, but you were rationalizing that she wasn't there. My message to you is that she *was* there. I will say that if she did come through, then you got about two seconds—

Natasha: Yeah, it's true.

John: I also feel that she recognized that that might not have been . . . and this is very key Natasha . . . she might not have been ready to come through at that time, either because of the "medium" or the facilities that were given to her to do this. She might have felt like . . . *that's not my style, I'm not gonna go there.* You follow what I'm saying?

Natasha: Exactly. I wasn't comfortable with the facilities or the medium either.

John: She's telling me to tease you about the candy, the chocolate. I don't know if there's a joke about the black-and-white cookie. But there's like a black-and-white cookie, black-and-white toffee, taffy, I don't know what this is.

Natasha: There's a chocolate connection that we have.

John: She's making me feel like you'll hear from her again. Did her cancer affect her stomach?

Natasha: Not really.

John: She's showing me a tube coming out of the stomach. Something coming out of her side. Either that or she had a feeding tube in. Is that back to your dad?

Norris: My father had a feeding tube.

John: He had two "J" names?

Norris: His name was James, but people called him Jay.

John: Okay, he had two "J" names . . . that's his way of jumping back in. I guess he got a second wind and had to pop back in. [laughing]

Norris: [laughing] Good!

John: I had a big pull-back. They're pulling back their energy. Just know that they saw this as their way of coming through . . . .

I always try to make it a point to tell a sitter *everything* that comes through to me during a session, no matter how serious, silly, or confusing I think it might be. So I was kicking myself after this reading when I found out who Norris was. I looked down at the notes I'd scribbled during the session and at the recurring doodle that covered the entire first page of my notebook: *a mailbox*. During the reading, I couldn't figure out why I kept getting an image of a mailbox in my mind, and why my guides weren't showing me my usual symbol for mail—a letter. Did Norris have a mailman in the family? I meant to ask. But obviously, there were several "Mailers" in the house!

Norris's reading was the culmination of many starts and stops in the setting-up phase. Natasha was initially trying to arrange for me to read a couple for this book to show an example of a family-type reading. She had contacted Norris—whom she'd interviewed years before—in the hopes that she and her husband, the renowned author Norman Mailer, would be interested in doing a reading together. Norris was already a big fan of *Crossing Over,* but unfortunately, as she recalled with a chuckle, "My beloved husband didn't share my enthusiasm. If I was watching the show and he came into the room to watch TV, I had to turn it off. I'm not sure why he reacted that way, but he did."

So it was no surprise that Norman wasn't eager to do a reading. Natasha informed me that she was chucking the "couple" idea and setting up a one-on-one, in-person session with just the wife she'd contacted. That was fine by me, but once again fate intervened. As she was arranging the solo reading for the following week, Norris got the news that her cancer had returned. She had to go into surgery immediately and couldn't make the trip to New York for the reading. Undeterred, and certain that Norris was "meant" to get this reading, Natasha set up a post-surgery phone reading for two weeks later, when Norris would be home convalescing and the skeptical hubby would be out of town on business.

As soon as we started the reading, Norris's dad came through and validated his daughter's physical and spiritual struggle with cancer, as well as the fact that she was still in the midst of this battle. But what impressed Norris most were the details that came through about her father's own illness and the very intimate moment when he sent Norris and her mother out of the room so he could cross over.

"He sent us both from the room in a big, clear voice after not being able to speak at all for weeks," Norris recalled. "He said, 'I want you to take your mother to the cafeteria and make her eat a good breakfast. She hasn't been eating right.' I naively thought, *Wow, he's able to speak! We'll go get breakfast and then come back and have a good conversation.* He died soon after we left. As we sat in the cafeteria, my mother started to shiver and said, 'It's so cold in here.' I knew later that he had to send us away in order to be able to cross over. But hearing it during the reading made it much easier."

Norris's dad, James, talked about other family members during the reading and gave very accurate details. Norris noted, "What you said about his sister was right on the money. She was younger, but always tried to boss the family around, and especially tried to boss *him,* which he hated, although he loved her. You got that there was some difficulty with someone not being able to tell him she loved him, and that was her. She thought if she told him she loved him he'd know he was dying . . . so she would say, 'We'll see you,' when she left. She told me more than once that she regretted she didn't say 'I love you.' When I called her right after the reading, she listened with interest, but you were right again when you said that she wouldn't really believe in it."

But Norris herself found much comfort in the details of the session, especially knowing that her dad was, literally, in the room with her during the reading—as well as being with her in spirit during her cancer battles.

She recalled, "During the reading you asked, 'Do you keep his picture on your desk to the left?' In the room where I sat during the reading, I had a picture of my father on my right, which I mentioned. But later, when I went to my computer at the desk, I saw the big picture of my father on my *left,* as it has been for years!"

Another bit of "trivial" information that wowed Norris was the mention of the "rotten eggs." That message may have seemed trivial to me as I gave it, or to you as you read the transcript—but it was of vital importance to Norris. The night before the reading, she'd had a little "chat" out loud with her father and asked him to come through with a secret sign to prove it was him . . . to mention the runny eggs Benedict he'd tried for the very first time when he'd had breakfast with Norris during the publicity tour for her novel, *Windchill Summer,* three years earlier. Dad indeed came through with the "rotten" eggs, and "it was such a clear message, it totally blew me away," said Norris. "I couldn't stop laughing. There is *no way* anybody but Daddy would have mentioned the eggs!"

Mention of her dad's friend, Charlie, hit home as well. Charlie had passed away just a few months before Norris's dad. And the Lynn who dropped by to say hello, said Norris, was her own friend Mara Lynn, a former Broadway dancer and showgirl, who had paid Norris a visit to say good-bye before she passed away last year. The last few validations during the reading—her father's two "J" names, the feeding tube, and a painful tooth "disaster"— were "totally" validating for Norris. "He just wanted to make good and sure I knew it was him, but in my mind there was no question at all."

But the biggest, most dramatic validation that Dad was with her was the mention of Norris twisting her hair as we spoke on the phone that night. "It's a habit of mine, and I was doing it! So Daddy was standing there watching me. It was so comforting." The hair-twisting, and the picture of Norris's father that I mentioned earlier, are good examples of how a phone reading can really work to the sitter's benefit—when I can come through with information about an object or an action going on in the room where the sitter is while I'm hundreds of miles away.

Norris got off the phone that night determined to heed her father's encouragement to open her eyes to every wonderful moment life had to offer, and close her eyes during the dark moments. "My father mentioned a tunnel, which might have several meanings, but a new one surfaced a few weeks after the reading," Norris told me. "I had to have an MRI, which is sort of like a scary tunnel, and he'd said, 'If you close your eyes, you won't know you're in the tunnel,' so while I was in the machine, I closed my eyes and pretended I was at a John Cage concert, and it worked pretty well."

Norris waited a day or so before calling up husband Norman on his business trip to tell him about the reading. She didn't know what kind of reaction to expect from him. As it turns out, he had a good laugh about it—"He figured I'd sneak around and do it when he was out of town." Norris laughed. But once her doubtful husband got home and read a transcript of the session, even *he* was somewhat swayed. "He said, 'Well, I may not believe in all this, but I believe the man has *something*.' I haven't given up on converting my husband, who is, by the way, also spiritual in much the same way I am. He'll just have to come to it in his own time."

Speaking of timing, when it was all over I wondered why Natasha's mother had chosen Norris's reading to finally come through even though the two parents didn't know each other. I asked both if they had any thoughts on that, and did they ever. When setting up the reading, Norris had casually asked Natasha if she'd ever had a reading herself, to which Natasha replied no, but she hoped one day to have one because she really wanted her mom to come through. The two women joked on the phone that maybe Norris's relatives would be ever-so-kind enough to bring Natasha's mom through for a cameo appearance during her reading—*ha, ha, ha*. Well, it's not so funny, lemme tell ya. If I had a dime for every time someone requested something like this aloud, in jest, and then it *happened*—I'd be richer than Rockefeller . . . or even Oprah. The two parents obviously heard this appeal, got together, and made good on it.

Some of the information that didn't make sense for Norris during the session made perfect sense for Natasha, including the reference to the number 10 (her mom passed 10 years ago), the name "Chris" (her mom's last name was Christoff), and perhaps the impact related to the number 15.

Natasha's mom, Maria, had left her hometown in Macedonia during WWII when she was 15 years old, and she used to tell stories about hearing bombs exploding near her home and seeing the war close-up. The mention of the three birthdays in December was correct (Natasha, her husband, and her twin brother); and the current birthday was also on target. Natasha had called her aunt, her mom's sister, in California just before the reading to wish her happy birthday. But the writing-in-the-sky validation for my friend was the reference to chocolate. The mother and daughter shared a passion for chocolate—and many a chocolate bar—together.

But that's not the end of it. The two also share chocolate in the *afterlife* together. Like Norris's dad, Natasha's mother couldn't speak for many weeks prior to her passing because her brain tumor had affected her speech. But there was one articulate moment during that time, for about five minutes, where she spoke perfectly.

"And of all things, she asked me if I had any chocolate," Natasha recalled, "and those were the last words I ever heard her speak." In honor of those words—and of their mutual love of the stuff—Natasha has kept up a chocolate ritual with her mom. Whenever she visits Mom's gravesite, she takes a chocolate bar or a cookie and "shares" it with her mother—eating half and breaking off the other half to leave on the tombstone. Like Norris, Natasha had given Mom specific instructions at their most recent chocolate party together. With a mouth filled with an Oreo cookie, Natasha said aloud: "Mom, if you ever come through to John, mention our chocolate. . . . " And she surely did.

The reading with Norris and Natasha, just one hour before Deanna's session, was a model of an extremely smooth reading. But let's go back to Deanna for a moment. Although her reading had some bumps in the road, it was still a positive journey. In fact, Deanna was very happy with the validations she did receive after we waded through the murky parts. First and foremost, she wanted to connect with her son, Nicholas, and she felt confident that we'd done that.

"The most amazing part for me was when you told me that someone I knew or myself had lost a child . . . and that it was a son, and that his death was sudden, which it was," Deanna told me. "Nicholas had epilepsy most of his life and suffered from seizures. But the last year and a half of his life, his health had improved through medication and diet, which is something that came through in the reading. In fact, the day before he died, he was outside playing. He went to sleep and didn't wake up in the morning."

One misinterpretation that was causing confusion in the reading, we later discovered, was that Nicholas was coming through to me as if he were at Deanna's "side," like a buddy. And that affected how I was seeing all the other relationships and "levels" he was talking about.

"It's true, I've always said to people that Nicholas was like my friend and he helps me," said Deanna. Once we cleared up that misunderstanding, we were able to move on with more ease. "You began connecting with family members who had passed, and were able to say the first names of my father and grandfather and grandmother . . . which blew me away. You figured out correct illnesses and locations where people lived.

"I was also floored when you mentioned that my son was at a recent family celebration. At first I couldn't think of anything, and we let it go. But later during the reading when you said my son was mentioning a recent celebration again, this time it clicked . . . the week before I had gotten engaged. During my engagement, I was thinking about my son, and at the same time my fiancé said, 'I feel like Nick is here.' Now there's no doubt for me that my son was present to join in our celebration. And another specific point was that Nicholas died on the 20th, and his father's birthday is the 24th. So we wanted to have the funeral before the 24th because his dad didn't want to have the funeral on his birthday."

The two readings for Deanna and Norris were two entirely different experiences, and that's why I always tell people to check their expectations at the door beforehand. You must be prepared for both disappointment and surprises during a session. The process doesn't always work perfectly, or work as we think it should or want it to. But in its imperfection, it's still a supreme gift from the Other Side.

Before Deanna and I hung up, she asked me about the concept of a "visit." She said that she often feels her son around her—especially in moments when she needs help—and she feels that he comes to her aid. I told her that I had no doubt at all that her son was looking out for her. Our children on the Other Side look out for us just as much as our parents do. And the intertwining of Norris's and Natasha's readings, with the small but important details that came through—the "eggs" for Norris and the "chocolate" for Natasha—is reason enough to believe that our loved ones hear our prayers . . . and answer them.

CHAPTER SIX

Circle of Love

As my co-workers at *Crossing Over* know all too well, no one within a 100-foot radius of me when I'm in reading mode is immune to Other Side radar. The episode of the show that viewers ask me most about is the one where I did a reading for a guy named Basil (not Natasha's dad), who was the manager of the parking garage adjacent to our first studio in Manhattan. This guy wasn't even in the room, but his relatives from beyond saw that he was close enough to be pulled into the studio from outside so they could say a few words. Dozens of crew members on *Crossing Over,* including the cameramen and producers of the show, have been surprised during the taping of the show when I've zeroed in on *them* instead of members of the gallery.

Another example of a "surprise" reading happened early in 2003 when I was a guest on *Larry King Live.* Live TV is a great arena to illustrate how this process works, moment by moment. Since *Crossing Over* is taped, TV audiences don't get a chance to see the instant electricity happening the way the members of the gallery do. On this night, after chatting with Larry, we opened up the phone lines so I could give quick readings to callers watching the show. When

I do this, the phone lines are usually jammed up within seconds, and the callers wait for a long time to finally get on the air and get their two-minute connection to me and the Other Side.

This day was no different, as people called in from all over the world and the lines lit up like a pinball machine. But wouldn't you know it . . . of all times to get stuck during a reading, it happens on live television. I was on the phone with an eager caller, and he wasn't validating a word I was saying. And yet, this information was coming through to me with such clarity. *Was anyone else in the room with him?* I asked. Nope. *Was this for a relative or friend?* Nope.

The lights on the phone were blinking with dozens of callers on hold, but this energy coming through wasn't going to let me move to the next person until I finished with him first. I was starting to worry that we were in for a major delay, when out of the blackness of the studio someone spoke up. "I think it might be for me," said the voice, coming from the shadows. It was a relative of the studio makeup artist, sitting way off to the side. I didn't even know she was there, but she heard the information and knew it was for her.

I started giving her a reading, and we continued on into the commercial break and after we came back on the air. When we were through, I was able to move on to the next caller. But it just goes to show you that the Other Side doesn't take note of doors or walls . . . and it doesn't care whether you've made an appointment or not. If you're nearby, you're fair game. I don't control who comes through or when, but I do know that timing is everything for all involved—both for the energy on the Other Side and the friend or relative here. The energy coming through has to be ready to come through, and the person here has to be ready to receive the messages.

ON FEBRUARY 11, 2003, I was scheduled to read Kristin Chenoweth, a well-known Broadway performer, on *Crossing Over.* I'm a big fan of Kristin's (I will admit it, I brought one of her CDs to the studio so she could autograph it), and she and the two pals she brought with her were avid fans of the show. It's always a pleasure do a reading for people who are familiar with the process and eager and open to see it in action . . . so I was looking forward to it.

That morning I was on my way to the gym when I felt that unmistakable tingling at the back of my neck . . . an energy was trying to get my attention, and I knew from past experience that this energy must "belong" to the reading I was to do later that day. I made a mental note to myself that it felt like a husband/brother/friend vibration coming through, and I asked him to wait and come back later at the beginning of the reading.

When I walked onto the set that afternoon, I was introduced to a very bubbly Kristin and her two best friends from grad school, Denny and Erin—and, surprise, surprise, take a guess who was also with Kristin acting as her publicist? None other than our Jill! I hadn't seen Jill since Australia, so we exchanged a few *G'day, mates* and *Good on ya's* before she scooted up to the control room. Then Kristin, her friends, and I got down to the serious business of the reading.

From the start, the reading seemed to jump around a lot . . . going from Kristin to Denny to Erin and back again. But there was that one male figure who came through first, and kept coming back, who didn't connect with either of the three people in front of me. *Here we go again,* I thought. *I wonder who he belongs to?* I really wanted Kristin to have a good session, and here was this male figure coming through with all this information that no one could validate. I struggled with it for a bit and continued to deliver his messages, hoping that something would ring a bell for one of them. When it didn't, I decided that the male coming through must be for a friend of theirs not present—which, I explained to them, does happen sometimes. Just when I thought we could move forward, the voice of our director, Dana, came over the public-address system.

"John . . . it's possible that what you were saying is for someone here in the control room. . . . "

Well, well . . . the staff does it again, I chuckled to myself. And in the middle of a celebrity reading! I wondered, *Who is it this time?*

John: I have to tell you that before I even got here today I was getting an energy coming through, and since you're the only people I'm reading today, it must be for you. It was a male energy to the side—like a husband, brother, or friend. When somebody jumps out first, it's for a reason. They either don't think they're going to get my attention or they want to make it clear that *I'm the first one here!*

It's a brother figure who passed . . . and he's connected to two "J's." There has to be a "JE" or a "JL" who's still here . . . a Jenny or a Jeffrey. And there's a celebration coming up . . . an engagement or a wedding in the family. I feel like I'm outside of my state here . . . like I'm right below New York in New Jersey or Pennsylvania. I feel like his passing is subtle. It's not a long, drawn-out feeling. It's like he's here, and then he leaves. The month of May also has a connection with the family.

Connected to you, Kristin, I feel a grandmother energy that has passed. The energy is connected to the father's side . . . connected to her is a symphony of music and prayer. It's like a blend of spirituality and music going out to the masses. And I feel like she wants me to compliment you on the blend. I need to acknowledge something that happened when you were nine or ten. I don't know if it's the first time you did something in front of her? But it was major.

Kristin: It makes sense.

John: Now, I'm also supposed to talk about this male, this first male I talked about. I don't think he's related by blood to any of you, so one of you has a friend who lost a brother or husband. He's the first person who got my attention before I even got here.

There's another male to the side coming through. He wants me to acknowledge that someone's going out to the West Coast, and it's going to be fun and sun and festive and gambling, so that makes me think Las Vegas.

And there's a father figure who's passed . . . it's not with Kristin. It's a father-in-law, a father, or an uncle who's connected to the "B" name. He's the "B" name or there's a "B" connection to him . . . like Benjamin or Benny. And October is connected here as well. It could be a birthday [looking at Erin]. I believe he passed from something cardiovascular or stroke related. The passing was quick, but I do think he was ill for a while. I just don't think it was detected. I think they almost detected something two to three months prior to his passing, but it was overlooked. There's a "Michael" connection to one of the people we're talking about . . . I think Michael is here . . . and they're making me feel like someone's birthday is in April. The first person who lost a brother . . . ?

Erin: Cousin.

John: A male cousin?

Erin: Yes.

John: Do you have the out-of-state connection? And there are two "J's." No . . . someone else has the brother who passed, or you guys are connected to the person whose brother has passed.

He's kind of a smart-ass. He's making me feel like, "I said I was gonna do this, and now I'm doing this—I'm back." I don't know if someone made a statement to him knowing that you were coming here . . . saying, "You better show up today" . . . but he's joking, like, "Well, I'm *here!*" And I'm being shown the month of April and white flowers, which to me is a birthday. And they're showing it to me twice. There's got to be something two times in April. . . .

The information I'm giving at this point just isn't ringing a bell with any of the sitters. I was about to repeat it all again, when Dana interrupts me from the control room to let me know that the "smart-ass" most likely belongs to someone in there. He asks if that person should come out and do the reading face-to-face, but I said no. I figured I could probably get their reading done and over with quicker if I didn't know who it was. And while I wanted to honor this person and their loved one on the Other Side, I was also anxious to continue with Kristin's reading.

We arranged for Doug, the stage manager, to give me yes/no answers given to him through his earpiece from the mystery sitter in the control room. It got a little confusing at times, as relatives and names started to overlap between the many sitters in classic "me, too" fashion.

> **Control room:** You can ask questions, and we'll pass them on.
>
> **John** (repeating): There's a connection to a brother or husband who had passed. There's a connection to two "J" names. There's an engagement or special announcement I'm feeling very excited about. I think this is happening within the year. And there's a connection to April as a birthday. The passing of this male isn't long ago . . . maybe two or three years. Do you understand that?
>
> **Control room:** Yep.
>
> **John:** There's a "me, too" thing here. One male figure to the side is connected to a Michael, and one wants me to acknowledge two nephews or two kids. And I think I'm supposed to say the name "Jeffrey." Is there a Jeff connected to you?
>
> **Erin:** Jeff is my cousin who passed, and his brother is Mark, not Michael.
>
> **John:** Mark might be the "MK"-sounding name I was getting. I get Michael, Mark, Mickey, names with strong "MK" sounds, the same way.
>
> **Control room:** That works in here, too, John.
>
> **John:** I knew I was going to get a "me, too." I have dueling brother/husband figures here. [To Erin]: Mark is your cousin? Is the Mark or Mike connected to the control room?

Then Doug, the stage manager, slips up. Or at least I think he does. He tells me he's going to check that last "Mark" validation in the control room "with him." I give Doug a dirty look. He just gave away that it was a man I was reading! And did he mean he was going to check with "Mark"? We have a "Mark" in the control room, so this must be for him, since his name was being thrown around. This must be for Mark, I'm thinking. Yep, I thought for sure it was . . . until . . .

Control room: No, the "Mark" doesn't make sense in here.

John: I want to be clear that the "MK" name is Mark. His mom is still here?

Erin: Yes.

John: You have his photo in your house, right?

Erin: I do . . . at home I do.

John: Is there snow in the background of the photo?

Erin: There might be . . . he visited us in Michigan during the winter.

John: I need to bring up the snow picture . . . does that make sense for the control room?

Control room: No.

John: Okay, I need to bring up some kind of . . . it looks like a ski lodge. There's a woodsy feeling. And . . . he might be to the side, but would you see him as older?

Erin: A little.

John: Is Jeff older than he is?

Erin: Yes.

John: Just let Jeff know he came through. Tell Jeff he sees the fact that he moved. With your cousin Mark, the spiritual event I'm getting that's coming up is more in connection with a child—as if a child is christened or had a confirmation.

Connected to the control room, I get an engagement, a wedding. And I'm seeing my cousin's birthday, August 19th, so there must be an August 19th connection in the control room?

Control room: Yes, August 20th.

John: The brother figure has someone who passed in a vehicle accident with him . . . unless that's how he passed.

There's a vehicle impact that takes place. Is this for the control room?

Control room: No.

Erin: Mark had a landscaping accident.

John: It has to be an impact. I feel like I'm being impacted.

Erin: No.

John: I need to be clear. Connected to the person in the control room, someone passes in a vehicle accident. They're not driving or responsible for this, but I feel like I'm supposed to say Marilyn or Mabel or Marabel, which is connected to this in some way. Some sort of unique "M" name.

Whoever passes with the impact . . . there's like a misprint in an obituary. Like the cause of how they passed was wrong, was incorrect. But it was rectified. But a big deal wasn't made about it.

The person with the impact isn't related by blood with the brother. The brother wants to bring this person through and acknowledge that there's some type of split happening in that family, where someone else in that family has passed or has left . . . or passed . . . an older male. The Jeffrey is connected to the control room, too, right?

Living?

Control room: Yes.

John: The brother figure wants me to say that people need to talk about this passing. It needs to be discussed. It's a sad passing, but they don't want to upset someone, so they don't talk about it. The guy is making me feel like *I want to be talked about!* I'm not getting that from your Mark [looking at Erin]. I'm getting it from the other energy who was the first one to get my attention.

I get the feeling that they're teasing that they could do this anytime. Like here at work when I'm walking down the hall and I can get pulled into an office. . . . "Oh, by the way, I've got your brother figure coming through." But they waited until I cannot *not* pay attention. For some reason, they chose today's date to do this. There must be something significant about the date today for the family.

I'm also supposed to acknowledge that Richard or Robert has to be connected to them as well. The "R" name . . . that's for the control room.

Control room: Not so far.

John: Absolutely, there's a Rick or Rich . . . a male "R" name connected to him. There's also a brain-tumor connection. This is for the control room as well. . . .

Control room: Yes . . . there's a Rick who died of a brain tumor.

John: Connected to the male figure to the side?

Control room: Yes, it is.

John: Okay, this guy is a *pain in the butt!* [laughing] I'm supposed to tease about eating pretzels. Right at this second, are they eating pretzels or something? If not, is there some kind of joke about the pretzels?

Control room: Not eating pretzels at this moment.

John: Then there has to be a pretzel reference that I feel has to be a joke. Is Dad there, too? Dad must be passed.

Control room: Yes.

John: And Dad passed *before* him. Dad wants to acknowledge the grandchildren. I also need to acknowledge four or five kids in the family. There's a reference to someone who's known for having issues with alcohol. And there's a reference to some sort of disconnect . . . it's either with the baby of the family, or the "one" . . . like if there are four boys and one girl, it's the girl. It's like they had to make their own space, and I need to compliment them on what they did. They came into their own by doing that, but never lost sight of the family at the same time. Does that make sense?

Control room: Yes, it does.

John: Mom has to have a brother as well there, besides Dad. There's got to be a brother or a brother-in-law for Mom there. It could also be a close family friend who lost a husband, but I feel it's connected to Mom.

Control room: Yes.

John: The father figure needs the family to know he's around. There's a wedding or engagement or birth of a child coming up . . . a family event that both the father and younger male want the family to know—this is really important that they're going to be there for this. The family needs to hear this. The brother is pushing the father figure out of the way, like, okay, you're done and now I'm back! And I need to talk about being on TV. This guy is such a ham. There's a total *I'm-messing-with-you* feeling . . .

He wants me to tease you about the shoes. [To Kristin]: Were you not going to wear those shoes today?

Kristin: Me? I wasn't . . . no, I wasn't!

John: Why would this person's brother be talking about your shoes? They're showing me fuchsia . . . hot pink. You don't have anything pink on except your lipstick.

Kristin: I had a hot pink, fuchsia heart on last night.

John: Well, they were with you last night then. Why this . . . this doesn't make any sense. But it's like the person in the control room, their brother, wants me to acknowledge you were wearing whatever this is. I don't understand this. It has to be a conversation you had—

Control room: John, this *does* make sense in here.

John: It *does?*

Control room: They were together last night.

Okay, so now I'm totally, *totally* confused. Why the heck would someone in my control room be hanging out with Kristin Chenoweth? There's just no way . . . this didn't make sense. I'm racking my brain trying to figure out what lucky guy had a hot date with Kristin the night before . . . and then it hit me. This was not for Mark or any other man—or woman, for that matter—on *Crossing Over*. This could only be for someone who knew Kristin well and who was with her last night at whatever glittery affair she was attending, and who was also in the control room today. . . .

I was baffled and couldn't figure it out (self-psychic amnesia?) when Doug, the stage manager, finally leaned over and let me in on the secret. "John, it's JILL!" I was shocked.

> **John** (pause): What? This is for *Jill?!*
> **Kristin:** Yes!

I was stunned—and totally excited. And I had to stop for a second and take a breath. Jill had totally "pulled a Natasha" and had purposely kept details of her family and their history from me. And now here they were, making an appearance. My heart just melted, and I couldn't stop smiling at the thought of Jill up there getting her own reading in secret. Especially after she'd watched me do hundreds of readings, and never once did anything come through for her. As soon as we finished up with Jill's relative coming through, I was able to finish Kristin's reading.

> **John** (to Kristin): On your dad's side, there's this woman—I don't know if you knew her in life, but I feel she's very strongly tethered to the energy of what you do. Is there anyone on your dad's side who used to do what you do?
> **Kristin:** I'm not sure.
> **John:** I would love for you to find out. Because there's such a strong feeling of "she's following in my footsteps." Like someone else did this.
> **Kristin:** I've wondered about that.
> **John:** There had to be, in your development, some type of overwhelming standing ovation. Like you got out in front of thousands of people at a very young age. But it's spiritual to me . . . like you were asked to sing in church.
> **Kristin:** I did—it was in front of 10,000 people when I was nine or ten.
> **John:** That event was a pivotal experience. You already had a taste early on of what if feels like to be known and appreciated. And you're now blending the two worlds

again. What you did in front of 10,000 people, you're now moving it forward.

Kristin: My next album will be "Faith and Inspiration."

John: Remember how Natalie Cole did the Nat King Cole overlay? Either you're doing an overlay or doing a duet with yourself. As if there were two separate Kristins singing . . . there are two of you. And I'm supposed to tell you that what's not being handed to you today on a professional level probably isn't going to happen for another three years. But it's a positive, not a negative. Something you're going to do will be different from what you're known for, and you'll go in a different direction. Maybe it's publishing or writing music . . . something different, an adjunct, another outlet of the same thing. There's something about going to Europe. I don't know if maybe you're planning to go to Vienna? There's a large international feeling, and you'll be asked to sing in a different language or do something different from what I know you as doing. . . .

And, the pull you already have in your leg? Stay on top of it. It's always a warning, so be careful. This is muscle related; it feels like you had a tear. Normally, it wouldn't be a problem, but if you do something like this, it will be an issue.

Now . . . did you get the cat yet? They want to know if you got the cat yet.

Kristin: I'm giving him my cat! [She points to Denny.]

John: These are the trivial little things to show you they know what's going on.

They're pulling their energy back. . . .

When the reading was over, we all had a laugh at how Jill's brother had "messed with me," as he put it—and I was amazed and more than a bit freaked out at how the reading for Jill had come about.

"Boom, boom, *boom*—you had everything right," Jill said as she ran down from the control room excitedly listing off the validations: "My dad and my brother have both passed. I'm from Pennsylvania, and you said that. The "JE" and the "JL" . . . I'm Jill, my brother is Jeff, and my brother who passed is Joe. His birthday is August 20th, and he died in May . . . you said there was a May connection . . . and the two-year anniversary is coming up . . . and it was a sudden passing, like you said.

"My mother had talked to him the day before, and he said he wasn't feeling well, and he said he was going to go to sleep and we didn't hear from him for two days . . . and he had passed in his apartment of a heart problem. He was here one day, gone the next. And then you said April for a birthday . . . my birthday is April. You called my brother a ham, and it's true . . . he used to tease me all the time like the way *you* tease me. And then last night, with the pink heart . . . we were laughing because Kristin was going to wear something with a pink, fuchsia heart on it, and we were like; wear it . . . don't wear it . . . wear it . . . don't wear it . . . take it off . . . put it on . . . I never told you any of this stuff, and you nailed it. Except . . . I don't know what the pretzel thing is. . . . "

It was such a rush of emotion and elation that I saw coming out of my friend, and I was so happy that her family had come through for her. And once again, I was amazed at the timing of it all. Why didn't her family come through earlier, during all of our business trips and seminars and lunches and long drives in the car?

"I guess, for whatever reason, it had to take that long—maybe so I could understand the process better," Jill told me. After she explained more about her family, I realized that there was more of a "timing" thing happening than I thought. Remember when I told you earlier that when I first met Jill I felt that there was an important reason she needed to be connected with this work?

Well, when her friend and client Aaliyah died in that plane crash, I thought that was the reason she would be questioning mortality. But I had no idea that the first time I had called her for a meeting, it was almost to the day of her brother's death.

"Actually, that's another strange story," Jill told me. "You called me the first or second day after he passed, and I pretty much freaked out because I was like, why is he calling me *now?* What does he know?"

It wasn't until over a year later in conversation when she casually mentioned that she'd lost a brother. I thought it was odd that she'd never mentioned it before, and I asked her why she hadn't.

"John, you *always* tell me not to tell a medium *any* information," she laughed, "and if he ever showed up, I'd want to know I hadn't told you *anything* about it." And for that reason, we dropped the subject right away without her telling me any more. I was shocked at how professional she'd been—never taking the opportunity as we worked together to try to arrange a reading for herself or anyone in her family.

At least she didn't try to arrange it *with me*. Jill had had a little chat with her brother before Kristin's reading. "The other day, I said to my brother out loud, 'By the way . . . if you are *ever* going to come through, why don't you come through on Tuesday when I'm going to be in the studio? Wouldn't that be funny? Ha, ha!' But I still didn't think it would happen. When I was in the greenroom, they wanted me to sign the release form in case I was read, and I told them, 'Look, I don't need to sign the form. I'm with John all the time! Believe me, I'm not going to be read. I talk to him a hundred times a day, and *no one ever comes through for me.'*"

But let me reiterate: People come through in their own time and in their own mysterious ways. Kristin had to be there that day so that Jill's brother and father could come through.

"And I was glad it was me," piped up Kristin, who was thrilled about her own messages as well. I myself was most curious about Kristin's "international" singing reference and asked her what that was all about.

"I went to London this summer and sang, but I sing in other languages, too," she explained. "I've done *Phantom* in German—in Germany. And I was asked while I was in London to come back to do an international festival this summer and sing more of a religious type of music. My great-aunt Inez would always encourage me and come to church and hear me sing, so that's who I think came through on my father's side.

"I was asked to sing at the Southern Baptist Convention in Oklahoma in front of 10,000 people when I was nine or ten. It was huge.

When you said it was 'spiritually based,' it was so true, and my aunt was a part of that. It was a real turning point in my life and a big deal. You nailed that!

"Being a Christian, I know a lot of people don't look at this stuff as being 'of God.' But I believe that people who leave us are with us. For me, personally, the big freak-out moment was when you said I would be doing a 'blending' of what I did with a more spiritual aspect. That definitely hit home because I'm working on my next album with Sony Classical, titled 'Faith and Inspiration.' Then when you asked if I was wearing fuchsia or pink, that cracked me up. Last night I was at the movie premiere for *The Music Man,* and I had a big pink fuchsia heart on, and there was a big discussion about what to wear and what shoes to wear. I wanted to wear these because they're more comfortable, but Jill was like, 'You have to wear the dressy boots!'

"Jill was really adamant about what I wore last night, and that's why I'm laughing . . . because her brother was teasing about it. We didn't know Jill was in the control room during the reading, so we didn't think any of this had a connection to her, and all of a sudden, it hit us like a lightbulb. And then you asked about the pull in my leg? I have a really bad hamstring injury from my high school cheerleading days, and it bothers me still."

I NEVER TIRE OF WATCHING how hard the Other Side works to get their messages through to us, and I'm still amazed after all these years at their elaborate methods. In this case, Kristin's family acted as a link for opening for Jill's family to come through in such a way that I wouldn't know it was for her—thereby protecting the integrity of the experience, just as Jill had hoped.

When someone's getting a reading and they bring through family for a friend, I call that the widening of the "circle of love." And Kristin's circle opened up to include our friend Jill.

To repeat once more, the Other Side comes through to us when they're ready . . . but more important, when *we're* ready. Jill waited a year and a half for her family to show up, but they didn't arrive until all the elements were right. I can't control who comes through, and neither can you. It's up to them, and they know best.

"My mother was always saying to me, 'You work with John Edward. I don't understand why you can't just ask him to do a reading!'" Jill told me afterwards. "She didn't understand why you weren't having conversations with my brother all the time. And I told her, 'Mom . . . it doesn't work that way. If it's meant to be, it will happen. When the time is right, it will just happen.'"

CHAPTER SEVEN

Teachers

PSYCHIC PUBERTY

I HAD MY FIRST ENCOUNTER with psychic work in 1985 when I attempted to debunk a woman named Lydia Clar, who arrived at my home one afternoon to do readings for my mother and a bunch of other eager relatives. I, too, had my very first reading that day—reluctantly. I didn't believe in that kind of silly stuff, but I went along with it, at my cousin's urging, to prove that this woman was a fraud. But it was at that initial reading, at age 15, when I was told that I'd someday be an internationally known psychic, lecture around the world, and write numerous books on the subject of psychic phenomena. Ha! I laughed at this, thinking, *How psychic could this woman be if she can't even pick up that I think she's full of s—t?*

Lydia foresaw my career as a psychic medium 16 years before it began. And what did she get in return? About $35 and a whole lot of attitude from me. In life, there are many signposts and teachers along the way. Lydia, I didn't know it at the time, was the first person who pointed me in the right direction. As they say, when the student is ready, the teacher will appear. But I wasn't quite ready . . . yet.

One of my most important teachers was a stranger who was to become one of my best friends. My previous book, *CROSSING OVER: The Stories Behind the Stories*, is dedicated to the memory and energy of a psychic medium and astrologer named Shelley Peck, who was my dearest pal.

I want to talk about Shelley here for many reasons. One primary reason is because she and I shared much of the same philosophy and thoughts about our work, and even worked in a similar style. At times, it was downright shocking to us how alike we were. After events we did together, we'd talk for hours and compare the "Hey, me, toos" we shared.

I'm sure you'd be surprised to know that Shelley was almost 30 years older than I. One of the funniest moments in our friendship was when I'd call Shelley's home on a weeknight and one of her three kids would answer the phone. They were all around my age, but I'd be asking them if their mom could "come out and play." It was something her husband, Marvin, had to shake his head at. So, how did the Universe arrange for Shelley and me to meet?

After my reading with Lydia Clar that day in my house, I needed to know how she was able to do it. I figured that there had to be something to this psychic stuff because she was extremely accurate in my session, as well as with my other relatives who were read that day. I broke up her reading into three parts.

One part was the "You're going to be a famous psychic" part, where I had to restrain myself from laughing out loud right in her very serious face. Another section was where she came up with a bunch of specific information about my life that was right on tar-get—the classes I was taking and how I was doing in them, the teachers I had, and the girls I had crushes on. Okay, could she actu-ally have some ability? I rationalized most of what she said as stuff that would apply to any hormonally charged teenage boy.

Then came the last part, which made me sit up and take notice. Lydia brought up a private situation in my life that nobody—not even my family—knew about. She gave me details about a girl I liked, mentioned a few names related to this girl, and even predicted the outcome of the romance. After the session, my head was spinning as I tried to poke holes in the reading, but I couldn't do it. I felt out of control and even a bit . . . violated. That might sound absurd, but that's the feeling you sometimes get from a good reading when a stranger "exposes" your private life out loud like a grocery list is being read. In case you've ever had that experience, you should know that it's normal to feel that way.

Lydia didn't go out of her way to try to "teach" me anything that day. She was there to set me on course. After making her startling pronouncements, she didn't even recommend a book I should read on the topic of psychic phenomena. I think back to that reading and consider her more like the first "gardener" of my uncultivated psychic soil. She planted the seeds, and grow they did—my interest was like a weed spreading out of control.

I started out at the library with a few books. Soon, I was reading anything I could get my hands on that was written about parapsychology or metaphysics. Like many of you reading this right now, I had a lot of questions, such as: *What's it all about?* and *How does it work?* Soon, I was reading books on the deeper meanings of tarot cards during English class instead of focusing on *A Tale of Two Cities* or *Lord of the Flies*—much to my teacher's chagrin.

It was then that I realized I needed professional help. No, I don't mean a therapist who would examine me and dissect my inner psyche. I needed someone who actually did psychic work to explain it and help guide me through it. And since I was 15 and didn't have a driver's license yet, I needed that person to live close by (Lydia Clar lived in New Jersey, a whole other state). And I needed this person pronto. I mean, I was told that I had these "powers" and these highly evolved guides who were ready to work with me—words that sounded straight out of Yoda's mouth in the Jedi training camp. Great! I have these abilities? Where are the instructions? It wasn't like I could wiggle my nose or cross my arms like in *Bewitched* and blink up a prediction . . . or someone's grandpa from the Other Side.

The best analogy I can give you is that Lydia told me I can speak this "other language"—think of it as the language of energy. And like any other language, you had to develop an understanding and command of it. This is exactly what psychic development felt like for me—learning the language of a whole new world. But until I could find the proper teacher to tutor me, I continued to teach myself by reading and putting into practice anything I learned.

By the time I was 16, I was dabbling in readings of my own, and I'd met with moderate success. I'd started to meditate regularly, had taught myself how to read playing cards from a book, and was developing skills in psychometry—the reading of a person's energy while holding something that belongs to them—such as a watch or a ring. Soon, I was able to tell people details about their life, job, relationships, and past . . . and also make predictions that would come true a few days into the future. It felt like I was tapping in to a whole new reservoir of awareness. Of course, if I was to compare my abilities then to now, it's like the difference between a drip from a leaky faucet and Niagara Falls.

WHERE TO FIND A PSYCHIC TEACHER? The Yellow Pages, of course. . . .

Although I was experiencing moderate success, I knew there was so much more I needed to learn. Desperate to find someone—anyone—to guide me, I turned to the only resource I could think of—the phone book. I'm not kidding. I let my fingers do the walking and looked under "P" for psychic. There were only a few listings, and most of them were for the storefront, neon-palm-glowing-in-the-window types. You know, the ones that tell some poor, gullible soul they have a curse on them and it will cost $5,000 to make it go away. If you ever come across a scam like this, do yourself and everyone else a favor—call the police and turn that wacko in, because that's called fraud.

My mother had an experience with a woman like this whom I nicknamed "Madame Assola" (get it?). This woman told Mom that her marriage was really bad because there was a dark cloud looming over her head that had followed her since the day she was born . . . and if my mother didn't give her $1,000 per month to light candles and pray for her, the curse could be passed down to her children.

My mom, psychic junkie that she was, wasn't stupid. She politely ended the session by saying, "Thank you for your time, but I will light my own candles in church," and left. When she related this story to me as a young boy, I will admit that I thought about the many arguments she and my dad had, and I asked her if that black cloud was something I'd inherited. My mom calmed my fears and assured me that as long as you have a strong faith in God and surround yourself in prayer, no dark clouds would be on your back—words I still believe.

Characters like that manipulating fortune-teller and any of the 1-900-dial-the-dead psychic hotlines make me sick, because they prey on trusting people in a vulnerable condition. They're why I always say it's really important to have skeptics out there to raise the "opposing views" on the subject matter. These skeptics sometimes group me in the same category with the swindlers, which I don't particularly like, but nevertheless, I still appreciate their value.

So back to my search for guidance: I flipped through the Yellow Pages and came across a listing for the Astrological Institute of Integrated Studies (AIIS) which, at the time, was located in Bayshore, Long Island, and run by a husband-and-wife team, John Maerz and Sandy Anastasi. The first thing I did was to arrange to have a reading with Sandy, who was the resident psychic. Yes, I was looking to develop the skills Lydia said I was capable of, but I wanted to check out the psychic first. This would be like going to a gym and checking out the trainers, or going to a school and sizing up the teachers.

The only snag in this plan was my mother. The psychic junkie herself didn't want me venturing into fresh, new territory all alone. I couldn't figure out if she didn't want to miss out on a good reading opportunity or if this was genuine parental concern. I personally think it was a little bit of both. She insisted that we make two appointments with the psychic, and, because she was the "Grand Dame of Readings," she had to go first. Just in case Sandy was a nut job, she would protect me, her little cub, from the psychic predator.

On the day of the reading, as I waited out in the hallway, my mom emerged from the room and gave me "The Look," which meant that not only was Sandy very good, but I was next. Once in the room, Sandy immediately picked up on my abilities and then followed through with a spectacular reading. When it was over, we discussed the classes I should take for my new psychic school curriculum. As I was still in high school, I signed up for weekly sessions on Saturday mornings. My mother was ecstatic. Some mothers want their sons to be doctors. My mom? She couldn't believe her luck: Her son was going to psychic school. She envisioned a lifetime of free readings spread out before her.

I signed on for Basic Tarot with Sandy and Basic Numerology with John. I had made it through about half of Sandy's Psychic Development One class before she politely kicked me out. She was worried that I'd make the other students feel slow because of my above-average abilities. I remember her joking around, calling me "the up-and-coming Merlin."

My studies at AIIS helped me establish a good foundation that's evident in my work today. Recently, Sandy sent me her current Basic Development book, and I flipped through it, surprised by how similar her style of teaching is to the way I conduct my workshops on developing psychic skills. I e-mailed Sandy and asked how she thought that was possible—did we possess the same guides? She was polite in her response, reminding me that I was indeed her student at one time!

Instead of accusing me of "stealing" her style, Sandy took my nod to her teachings as a compliment—glad that I was able to learn from her and use it as a basis for my own work. Sandy and John—who still help others develop their psychic abilities and now run Starchild Books in Port Charlotte, Florida—were two of my earliest, most influential teachers.

PSYCHIC FRIENDS NETWORK

DURING ONE OF MY FIRST TAROT CLASSES, held in the basement of John and Sandy's Bayshore, Long Island, home, I noticed a list of recommended Long Island psychics pinned to the wall. One person on the list, Shelley Peck, was in the same phone exchange as me.

What? There was a psychic living in the Glen Cove area and my mother didn't know her?

I jotted the number down and telephoned Shelley that afternoon when I got home. She picked up the phone at 4:30 P.M. . . . and we hung up at 7 P.M., after a nearly three-hour intense chat. We had an amazing and instantaneous connection, so I booked an appointment with her for the following week. She was fully booked for months, but because she, too, felt a connection to the voice on the other end of the phone line, she squeezed me in on her day off.

That day could not have come soon enough for me. My mom's brother, Uncle Joey, went with me to make sure his 16-year-old nephew wasn't going to be taken in by some crystal-ball-wielding wacko. I will never forget our first meeting. Shelley opened the door, looked at my Uncle Joey, then at me, and extended her hand out to Uncle Joey.

"John? Very nice to meet you. . . . " And I thought, *This is the psychic? She didn't even know who I was!*

I jumped into the conversation: "No, no . . . Shelley, it's me . . . I'm John."

She looked at me and blurted out, "You're a kid! I had a three-hour conversation about metaphysics with a kid?" and she started to laugh. "Come on in and let's talk . . . but I'm not reading you . . . you're way too young," and she shook her head, laughing at herself.

I soon found that Shelley had this very down-to-earth, matter-of- fact, good ol' New York way about her. In later years, sitting in more Long Island diners that I can count, we often laughed about that first meeting. After every house party or psychic fair we did together, we'd make a beeline to nourish the body after the soul had been fed—hamburger deluxes for me, Chinese roast pork sandwiches for her . . . and make it heavy on the duck sauce, please, or "I'll send you back for more!"

Every Sunday, the psychic fair where Shelley and I worked would be in a different location on Long Island. One particular Sunday it was to be in Port Jefferson—-about an hour and 15 minutes from where we lived. We were early, and neither of us had eaten breakfast, so we were starved. We also both realized at the same time that we'd left our wallets at home. At least I had a full tank of gas, thanks to my father instilling that rule in me early on.

But we were lucky that morning, as I happened to be driving a new car at the time—well, a new *used* car—a Dodge Charger that I nicknamed the Old Alfer (after the furry alien on the TV show *Alf*. I always saw Alf as an acerbic cross between Don Rickles and an anteater). There's that tradition you might have heard about, where, when you get a new car, your friends and family throw fistfuls of change in the back seat for luck. Well, picture this scene: Outside the hotel where the psychic seminar was to be held, where people were already lining up for hours to book appointments with Shelley and me, where were we—these two dynamic psychics? We were on our hands and knees digging our fingers between the seat cushions and scrounging change off the floor of my car, trying to scrape together enough for a cheeseburger at McDonald's.

We shared a burger and fries that morning—which led to 17 years of friendship—where we shared everything about our families and professional experiences, even though we didn't belong to the same generation.

As we worked together over the years, we discovered that there were distinct similarities in how we conducted our readings. For us, it was all in the details. One night we were both booked for a group reading, and I was looking forward, as always, to watching Shelley work. During the reading, I made a connection with one participant's relative and was able to discern a very unusual combination of illnesses that he had passed from—a very specific cardiac condition and a rare blood disease.

Shelley couldn't control herself—she was so impressed that she blurted out, "Oh my God . . . how in God's name did you get that?!" It was my background working in the health-care field as a phlebotomist (a lab blood technician) that had really increased my awareness of medical issues.

Not five minutes later, Shelley was giving information to this same woman . . . details about the small town in Prussia that her family had come from. Shelley looked over at me and saw my jaw hanging close to the floor in amazement that she was relaying information about a country that no longer existed. And with this quiet confidence, she smiled, winked at me, and explained: "I majored in geography. "

Everyone laughed that night as they witnessed the chemistry between us. Shelley and I worked together often, and just like co-workers at any job, we'd vent to one another about clients. Yes, I will admit, every once in a while (just like in any other profession), a sitter would walk through our door who wasn't especially likable. Either they'd arrive with a whole lot of attitude that I'd have to deal with before we even got started, or they'd just be completely unappreciative of the process throughout the entire reading. Sometimes, as a medium, you're talking to the dead person on the Other Side and wondering why the heck they'd even *want* to talk to this living person sitting in front of you.

Another favorite evening for us that will live forever in our shared history was the night of the "perhaps lady." Shelley invited me to her home in Roslyn, Long Island, for a group she was reading, and I brought my aunt Roseann, "Big Ro," with me. We sat on Shelley's U-shaped sofa with a dozen others as everyone waited for Shelley to bring through their loved ones. To everyone's dismay, Shelley spent a good portion of the night locked in on one woman who'd lost her husband. What made it dismal was that this woman who was hogging the reading was a hardcore cynic.

"Your husband has passed . . . yes?" Shelley directed the statement to the woman sitting next to my aunt. The woman said nothing and just stared at Shelley as if she hadn't spoken to her.

"Ma'am, I'm talking to you," Shelley said, a bit louder. "Your husband is here . . . he's the man with the colon cancer?"

"Puuuurhaaaps . . . " was the answer.

"He's telling me he's been gone for the last five years . . . "

"Puuuurhaaaps . . . " was the answer.

Shelley went on with this woman, reciting solid facts coming from this deceased husband, and every incredible piece of information she brought through was received with this sing-song

"Puuuurhaaaps." After nearly an hour of this, the other people in the room were rolling their eyes and shaking their heads. Her husband was working so hard at coming through, but instead of acknowledging the information, she was responding with all this "perhaps" crap. Then came the breaking point.

"He's telling me that there's a major orange connection," Shelley continued, " . . . and to me, I think it's the orange groves in Florida . . . but I feel it's work related in some way."

Of course, we all silently mouthed with her: "*Perhaps.*"

Shelley just lost it. "Look . . . either this does or does not make sense to you. *You either do or don't understand what I'm telling you . . . YES OR NO?!*"

Finally, the one-word woman spoke. "Well . . . I don't know if I'm reaching to make this fit . . . but my husband was affiliated with orange and vitamin C products, which were all derivatives of the orange groves in Florida . . . but I'm not sure if that's it. . . . "

Shelley just stared at her, speechless. And then got the biggest laugh of the night when she answered: "Perhaps!"

A PAIN IN THE BUTT

When my mom was diagnosed with cancer, Shelley would come to the hospital with me to see her. My mom would always perk up when she saw Shelley because she had a great respect for her and knew how much I respected her as well. On one of those visits, I remember telling Shelley as we walked through the parking lot of Syosset Hospital—one of the five or six hospitals my mom frequented from April 1989 to October 1989—that when I was a child, I used to tell my mom that if smoking ever kills her, I'd refuse to go the funeral. I was forever trying to get her to quit, and I remember making this funeral threat at least a hundred times—starting from the time I was in first grade and was taught about the dangers of cigarettes. But my mom would just shrug it off.

So now, it was indeed lung cancer that she was suffering from, and I guess you could say I was a bit high-strung during this time, with so many mixed emotions about it. I was 19 years old, and I was scared and angry. I realized the gravity of the situation, and I psychically "knew" the outcome. But at the same time, I was praying for a miracle like anybody else would whose loved one was dying of cancer.

But what happened next was like a scene straight out of a soap opera. I'd just finished telling Shelley about my childhood funeral vow as we made our way up to see my mother. The elevator doors opened, and Shelley and I walked out onto my mother's floor, down the hall, toward the lounge area. And there, sitting next to a half-open window, was my mother, in a wheelchair, *smoking*.

My father, Little Ro, and Big Ro were there . . . but I didn't know which one of them was her willing cigarette accomplice. It didn't matter. I had a complete meltdown and went ballistic. I'd love to recount for you exactly what I said, but all I remember is screaming like a lunatic. I guess that everything I was holding in—my fear of losing my mom and my hatred for smoking, the evil villain that was taking her—erupted from within. Shelley grabbed me and pushed me out of the lounge and back into the hall, but I was totally out of control.

My father stepped out of the lounge to try to calm me down, but he was about four feet away from me when I realized that *he* was the one who'd given Mom the cancer stick she was smoking. Even in my hysteria, I had the ability to process what brand of cigarette she was smoking—both Roseanns only smoked Parliament white tips . . . *he* smoked the orange Marlboros . . . and mom was smoking the *orange* one.

I felt betrayed by both of them. Back in the lounge, my mom got upset, started to cry, and was apologizing to me . . . but I didn't want to hear any of that. I was outraged and hurt that she would be smoking, and I saw it as a betrayal—like she was cheating on me and the rest of the family with her illicit nicotine. I wasn't thinking logically at the time that whatever damage the smoking was going to do to her was already done. I was just a kid, crazy and blinded with anger.

What happened next, nobody expected. *WHACK!* Shelley slapped me hard across the face in the hallway. And I assure you—she didn't hold back.

"This is not about one cigarette . . . you know that!" She shook me. "Don't make your mom feel any worse than she already does. I'm sorry I had to slap you . . . but . . . "

I was a bit stunned, but not too dazed to notice my father getting all riled up that this strange, small, blonde woman had the audacity to slap his son around—and in front of him, no less. Shelley didn't really have a fondness for my father, and she completely ignored the fact that he was standing there. She excused herself from me, walked right past my dad, went over to my mom, and told her not to worry about me—Shelley would calm me down and bring me back in to see her in a bit. Later, as we left the hospital, I burst out laughing at the whole scenario.

"Do you realize that you slapped me pretty damn hard?!" I asked her.

"Yes, I do. But I had to do something to get your attention. I think I *got* your attention, didn't I?"

"Oh . . . you got my attention all right."

Then, as we walked toward my car, Shelley pulled out a cigarette from her purse like nothing had just happened and started to light it up. I stopped dead in my tracks and looked at her. *"Are you kidding me?!"*

"I'm quitting . . . I'm quitting . . . I know . . . don't say it . . . you want to smack *me* now, right?"

Right. Maybe I should have.

My mother crossed on October 5, 1989, at 3:54 a.m. I didn't have to call Shelley to tell her my mother had officially left this world. Mom did it for me. Around ten o'clock that morning, before I had a chance to call her, Shelley phoned me to extend her condolences. To some of you this might sound strange, but for us it wasn't . . . we had that type of connection.

I didn't have to ask how she knew—I assumed that her guides had told her. But in this case, I was wrong—my *mom* had told her.

I was lying on my bed when the phone rang and Shelley asked how I was holding up. I was kind of numb, but was mentally preparing myself to get ready for a family wedding two days later, in which I was part of the bridal party. It was my mom's wish that if anything happened to her, her nephew's wedding would go on as planned, and I was instructed to make sure that her family didn't use her death as an excuse to bail out.

When Shelley called me that morning, I was trying to figure out just how to accomplish this.

"John," she said excitedly, "I have all these messages for you!"

We knew so many of the same people from our seminars that I figured she had condolences for me from our colleagues. Not exactly. Shelley had pages and pages of notes that had come directly from my mother, she said, that morning. It seemed that my mom had barely crossed over, and already she was a force to be reckoned with on the Other Side! After being sick for so many months, I'm sure that she desperately wanted me to know she was okay as soon as she was able. But was I able to hear this now?

"Your mom wanted me to tell you," Shelley began, "that she appreciates what everybody did for her and that— "

"*Whoa . . . stop! Wait a minute!*" I interrupted, mid-sentence. "I don't know if I want to hear this yet." Remember what I said earlier about waiting a certain amount of time after a loved one's passing before seeking out a medium? Well, it was true for me, too. I was only human, and I didn't feel ready. At that moment, I wasn't a psychic—I was a son who had lost his mother and was in the initial, shocking stages of mourning.

Shelley had no patience for that.

"John, I know how difficult this is," she said firmly, "but I also know how hard your mother worked to get these messages through to me to let you know that she's all right. *So I know that you're gonna get your ass up outta bed and get a piece of paper and a pen and write all this stuff down,* because I *also* know that I didn't work my butt off at seven o'clock this morning doing this for someone *who's not going to appreciate everyone's efforts . . . right?!*"

I never told her this, but at that moment she was downright getting on my nerves.

There I was, indulging in a well-deserved moment of wallowing, and that's all I wanted to do! The invitations for the pity party were out, and I was going to be the guest of honor. But my mother and Shelley wouldn't be RSVP-ing for that kind of get-together, Shelley informed me. So I dragged myself off the bed, fetched a pen and paper, and dutifully began writing.

"There's something that was in your mom's room," Shelley began, "and she told me to tell you it's now in *your* room. It's something of a religious nature . . . I think it might have a *Mary* connotation . . . and she also wants you to know that there's going to be some sort of mix-up with the flowers, the pink carnations . . . in the next few days. And also, she's showing me hand-carved Jesus faces made of wood, and I think they're from Italy . . . she likes them. . . . "

I was listening, but in my head I had another whole mental commentary going on that was worthy of the most stubborn cynic. As I sat in bed, I scanned my room from floor to ceiling. Nope, there was *nothing* of a "religious nature" in here, I told her. Shelley was just plain wrong. Then this whole mix-up with the flowers . . . how would I know if there was going to be a mix-up at the wake? I'd have to wait. And the hand-carved, wooden, Italian Jesus references? I just laughed at that one. I used to tease Shelley, who was Jewish, that she had "Catholic envy." She didn't, of course, but she was fascinated with the religion. I told her to lay off the Catholic references because she was *all wrong.* I could tell by her voice that she was getting a bit indignant at my reaction. I'm sure she was thinking that I wasn't appreciating her time and energy, especially since she had hernia surgery pending the next day.

Two days later, we all dressed up and went to my cousin's wedding. An hour before the ceremony, there was indeed a mix-up with the flowers for the wedding party. The flower shop was supposed to send white carnations for us to wear, but instead sent pink—which clashed with the bouquet. That was validation hit number one.

The next day was the first day of the wake. What I remember most vividly was the vision of Shelley hobbling into the funeral home that day. I say "hobble," because she had just had her surgery, and upon being discharged from the hospital, she forced her husband to take her to the funeral home instead of going straight home like the doctor ordered. It wasn't so much to pay respects to my mother because, as far as Shelley was concerned, the two ladies had already had their private "visit" with each other the morning Mom crossed. Instead, it was to check in on me and make sure I was hanging in there.

After my mother passed, Shelley insisted that I call her every night and "download" the events of the day because she wanted to make sure I didn't bottle up my emotions. She wanted me to know I had a friend who was ready to talk and who was just a phone call away.

As everyone gathered together at the wake, I noticed a string of rosary beads hanging on the inside of the casket and leaned in to take a closer look. They were hand-carved, Italian-made, wooden rosary beads, each bead shaped in the face of Jesus. I immediately investigated where they'd come from and found out that they'd been sent by my mother's older sister, Rachel, who'd picked them out on a whim. Validation hit number two.

Later that night when I returned home, I walked into my bedroom, turned the light on, and gasped at what I saw.

The day Shelley had called me with my mom's messages, I'd been sitting up in bed leaning up against my headboard as we talked on the phone. But it wasn't really a headboard . . . it was the mirror from the bureau in my mother's room that used to be positioned directly opposite her bed. Due to her deteriorating condition, the family had thought it best to take the mirror down so she didn't have to stare at herself all the time and constantly be reminded of how sick she was. The only other place the mirror would fit was right behind my headboard, and oh, yeah, taped up to the mirror was a picture of the Sacred Heart of Jesus and a photo that was taken at an apparition site of the Blessed Mother in Medjugoria, Yugoslavia.

I couldn't see any of these things when I was talking to Shelley on the phone because they were behind my head as we spoke. Standing in the doorway of my bedroom, I looked at those photos and wept uncontrollably. I called Shelley at around 2 A.M. and told her about all the validations that day and apologized to her for not being appreciative of her time and friendship that morning on the phone. She told me it was all right, not to worry—that's what friends were for.

ENGAGEMENT DAY

SHELLEY PROVED TO BE A CONDUIT between my mother and me again and again, passing along her messages. It was like she was my mom's personal secretary here on this side. Why didn't my mother just come directly to me, you ask? That would seem the simpler way, but really it isn't. Before she passed, I distinctly instructed my mother that when she wanted to connect with me from the Other Side, to go through someone like Shelley. I knew that if I got things psychically from my mom, I wouldn't trust the information because I was too close to her. I would worry that what I was getting would be jumbled up with my emotions and memories, and brought on because I missed her.

When it comes to anyone close to me coming through from the Other Side, I trust the process better if the information is coming via another psychic, especially Shelley, who always let me know that Mom was around me during the most intimate, joyous occasions of my life.

IT WAS THE FALL OF 1993, and I'd just picked up Sandra's engagement ring—a pear-shaped diamond with three small chips on each side. I'd bought it from friends of friends who worked in Manhattan's diamond district.

I was very excited about popping the question a few weeks later, but first I had to make sure that Mom knew of my purchase. I got into my car, opened up the ring box, and held it up: "Mom, you're the first one to see the ring!" I said out loud. I drove home with a smile on my face, and when I got there, I had two blinking messages on my answering machine.

"John . . . it's Shelley. If you're there, pick up. Your mother won't let me get any work done today. Call me back as soon as you get this message." *Click.*

"John . . . it's me again . . . all right, I know this can't be true, and what your mom is telling me must be far off, because I know we're such good friends that you would have told me about this . . . but she's so damn excited . . . call me back!" *Click.*

In the back of my mind, I was hoping that Shelley had gotten a message about the ring from my mother, but I didn't want to think about it and get my hopes up. I dialed Shelley's number, and when she answered, she told me that my mother had been "hanging out" with her all morning and was very excited to tell her I was getting married. Shelley was perplexed by this message, because even though she'd accurately (and eerily) predicted that I'd end up with Sandra in a reading she'd done about seven years earlier, I hadn't told her yet about my potential engagement.

"Your mother is all excited, and she said you showed her the ring 'first'? Does this make sense to you? What's she talking about? Am I cracking up or what?"

Please imagine that you're me and you're sitting on the edge of the bed, listening to Shelley deliver this message—confused but with spot-on precision—all the while staring at the ring in your hand. This was just another moment of my being wowed and amazed by her uncanny accuracy.

I confessed to her that it was true . . . and we went out and celebrated over a hamburger deluxe and a roast pork sandwich with extra duck sauce (of course).

Shelley was to astound me with her accuracy again and again during our friendship. Shortly after I moved to Huntington, Long Island, Sandra asked me to do a small group reading for her mother and a few of her mom's friends. I called Shelley and invited her over for dinner. What she didn't know was that she was going to work for her supper that night as well. I sprang it on her at the last minute when I picked her up at her house, telling her I had this group to do . . . would she mind participating? She laughed and said she already knew she was going to be working that night—her guides had told her, and she'd meditated in preparation before I picked her up (yes . . . she was *that* good).

We started the group, and some amazing details started to come through about my mother-in-law's family. The funny part of it, though, was that Sandra had to act as "guest medium" during the group because the women we were reading only spoke Portuguese. Shelley and I joked that we would say a sentence, and Sandra would translate what seemed like four paragraphs. We were convinced that Sandra was adding in a bit of her own "translation" of the Other Side as well. But it was during this group that Shelley rendered me speechless for the second time in the almost 15 years that I'd known her.

The first time was when my Uncle Carmine had died. I'd asked her to do a reading for my cousin, his daughter, Little Ro, and she agreed. A few hours before the session, Little Ro and I were having a bite to eat at a local diner, and I saw Shelley across the room in another booth. (Yes, both of us practically *lived* at diners.) I went over to her table to say hello and to tell her I really, really appreciated that she was squeezing my cousin in for a session instead of putting her on her long waiting list. And then I made the gravest error possible.

"I just hope," I continued, "that her dad . . . my Uncle Carmine . . . comes through for her and . . . "

"*Damn it, John!*" I thought she was going to hit me. "I can't believe you just told me her father died and that's who she wants to connect with . . . *and you told me his name!*" What was I thinking? One of the first things you learn in Basic Mediumship 101 is to never divulge anything ahead of time so the integrity of the experience won't be violated. That doesn't mean you should be cagey and evasive. Quite the contrary, you should validate what does or doesn't make sense . . . but don't offer information, which is what I'd just done. Shelley immediately wanted to cancel the session.

I stood up and firmly told her that if I had to march back to my table and tell my cousin I just messed up her chance to talk to her dad—whom she missed and loved so desperately—because of a stupid mistake on my part . . . well, I just couldn't do it. Shelley begrudgingly agreed to go on with the session, but she was clearly annoyed with me.

About an hour and a half later, we arrived on Shelley's doorstep. She welcomed my cousin and me into her beautiful home and directed us to sit in the breakfast nook off her kitchen. Little Ro sat there waiting, nervous—but I assure you, not more nervous than I. For the entire car ride over, I was praying to her father to come through, despite my pre-reading faux pas.

When it was time, Shelley invited my cousin into the den for the reading. Ro asked Shelley if I could sit in on the session, and Shelley said that was fine, even though she was still a bit ticked off at for me for making her job more difficult than it needed to be. Now, both she and Uncle Carmine were going to have to work twice as hard since I'd already given away some prime validating information.

The reading lasted over an hour, and Shelley came through with dozens upon dozens of accurate details about my uncle—from the clothes he wore to the location where he lived—it was like she was reading from a list compiled by Uncle Carmine himself. She even "embodied" him at one point during the session by mimicking what he'd do and say, capturing his gestures. My cousin laughed and cried, and I took notes so she wouldn't forget a word. Then, near the end of the reading, Shelley looked over at me, her face beaming.

With a burst of confidence, she declared: "Why . . . his name isn't Carmine . . . it's *Carmen!*"

Oops, strike one for Shelley, I thought. I put a big "X" down on the piece of paper where I was keeping a tally of validations. Or, wait . . . maybe there was another energy on the Other Side Shelley was going to bring through who also had a "C" name. I was racking my brain trying to think of another "C" name, when I heard my cousin reply, "Yes!"

"What?!" I asked, totally interrupting the session (another no-no).

"His real name is Carmen, not Carmine," Ro explained.

"But . . . Carmen is a woman's name!"

Little Ro explained that it was the Italian way to spell it like that, and that Carmen really *was* his official name, I just didn't know it. My big error at the diner gave Uncle Carmine an opportunity to come through with an even more detailed and obscure validation about himself that only intimate family members knew. Hurray for him. That night, I saw a change in my cousin, as if a weight had been lifted. She knew that her daddy was still with her.

The group session in my living room with Sandra's relatives was about to be an instant replay of that kind of *Wow!* validation. Shelley and I were delivering messages as a team, alternating like a relay duo passing the baton as we brought them through. Then, as I was finishing one message, I felt Shelley staring at me. She was sitting in a chair to my left and had turned to fully face me with this inquisitive look on her face.

"You wore your mother's nameplate under your tuxedo on your wedding day?"

Pow!

My jaw hit the floor. The day I got married, as I was getting dressed, I looked at my mother's picture and told her out loud that I was going to keep her with me that day by wearing her nameplate that said "Princess" under my tuxedo shirt. Nobody, not even Sandra, knew I did this, and quite honestly, up until that moment when Shelley made that statement, I'd almost forgotten about it. But at that second, the emotions I felt so long ago came back to me, and I couldn't speak. My eyes welled up, I looked down, then I looked over to Sandra and smiled—then back to Shelley.

"I did . . . I did wear that nameplate!" I told her. "Thank you for that."

THE GREETING COMMITTEE

OVER THE YEARS, I watched as Shelley developed an uncanny ability to connect with extremely recent passings during her readings, whether it was during a private session or a group reading. Neither of us could figure out exactly how she was able to do this, but I think it was just part of who she was and what her job was here in this world. One evening in 1994 when she and I were giving a talk at a seminar called "Gifts of Love" at the Smithtown Sheraton in Long Island, she made a connection with a man who'd lost his wife a few days before. Everybody in the audience was shocked and very moved—not the least being Shelley herself, who at one point (in her trademark, blunt, mother-from-Queens fashion) asked the man, "What are you *doing* here? So recently after your wife's passing? You should be at home!"

Another night when Shelley accompanied me on one of my group readings in New Jersey, she also brought through a woman's son who had crossed a few days earlier. Then there was a benefit I organized for Hospice Care of Long Island where I asked Shelley and Lydia Clar (the woman who'd given me my first reading) to read the audience. We all did good work that evening, but I must say, Shelley's messages were so detailed and specific that on more than one occasion she brought the entire room to tears. I was standing in the back of the room, listening, admiring, and watching my friend do her thing when she connected with the spirit of a grandmother of one person, and then another woman's son, both of whom had passed within the month.

"John . . . where are you? Are you still in the room?"

"I'm back here, Shelley. . . ."

"Here I go again . . . what is it that you call me?"

"The Greeting Committee!"

Shelley told the entire room how I tease her with that nickname at these events because you could put her in a room full of people and she'd connect with the most recent passing. I decided that one of her purposes in having this ability was to be the first one to say *hello* to people who were new to the Other Side. I kept threatening to get her a sweatshirt that said "Greeting Committee" on it. She made me promise in front of everyone at that benefit that I *would* finally buy her that shirt after all these years. I wish I had.

In June of 2001, the friend and teacher I had known for half my life made her transition to the Other Side after succumbing to cancer. In a way, it was like a déjà vu of losing my mother. I'd been keeping tabs on Shelley's condition throughout her illness, since we always spoke with each other two to three times a day at length.

Then I noticed that our calls were becoming shorter and less frequent, usually ending with Shelley asking if she could call me back later because she was feeling tired. When she asked me if I thought her diagnosis was terminal, I could not—would not—answer. I knew it was because I was shown this by my guides. But even when her family pressed me to answer that question, I was evasive in my response—perhaps because I held out hope and faith that she could beat this, despite what my guides told me. I didn't want to it to be true.

Shelley split her time between her apartment in Bayside, Queens, and her house in Vermont. (Her husband, Marvin, had passed about ten years before.) Shelley's daughter would graciously call me and give me updates about what was happening and what the doctors were saying.

One afternoon I got a message on my answering machine from her daughter with the usual update, but this time I stopped in my tracks when I heard it. There wasn't anything emotional or urgent about this particular message, but there was something about her daughter's tone that made me feel I needed to see Shelley right away and that this visit would be our last.

I called the *Crossing Over* producers and cancelled two tapings I was to do that day, and within minutes, Carol had printed up driving directions to the hospital in Vermont off the Internet. An hour later, I was heading north on the freeway without a suitcase or a change of clothes or even a toothbrush . . . and without telling my wife. I called Sandra from the car and told her I was somewhere in New England and I wouldn't be home for dinner.

She completely understood—Sandra and Shelley had struck up a great connection of their own, and we'd spent many a Jewish holiday together, with Sandra always teasing Shelley that one of these days she was going to have to feed her a big bowl of matzoh ball soup like a proper Jewish mother should. That was their little joke together.

The entire drive to the hospital, I listened to an Enya CD. I've always loved her voice and music, but when she released the song "Only Time," it immediately reminded me of Shelley. And here I was, months later, driving up to see my friend for the last time . . . realizing that the song is correct. In life, we have only time. But how long, we never know.

According to my Internet directions, my drive to the hospital should have taken me about four hours. But when I got to the hospital, after getting lost (please, no psychic jokes about that), it was seven hours later. Still, I was able to spend a couple of hours with Shelley alone, even though she slept through most of my stay. When she did wake up, I think she was a bit alarmed to see me. Not that she thought she had crossed over or anything . . . but seeing me would have tipped her off that the time was near.

I put her mind at ease and even got her to smile a few times. At this stage in her illness, Shelley had lost mobility and wasn't able to speak. At one point, she was trying to tell me something, and she was mouthing it, but I couldn't understand her. I didn't realize it, but one of the nurses had walked into the room and was standing behind me when I said, "Shell, look at me. Whatever you're trying to say . . . *send* it to me. . . . " Meaning, telepathically send me the message and see if I can get it. Immediately, my head began to itch . . . and I asked her if she wanted me to scratch her head. She nodded and I scratched, much to her relief.

"Wow! How cool was that?" the nurse standing behind me piped up. "What is that, some psychic thing? I heard that Mrs. Peck is a psychic. Is that really true?"

I smiled, looked at the nurse, and then back at Shelley, and said, "Not only is Shelley Peck one of the country's top psychic mediums, but she's also a great astrologer and numerologist. But to me, she's my buddy." I winked, and Shelley smiled. I stood there for a couple of hours watching her, going over our relationship and my memories in a weird, fast-forward kind of way. I waited for her to fall asleep before I left after midnight, way past official visiting hours.

Shelley crossed over just a few days later.

I WANT YOU TO KNOW that while writing this chapter, I had to stop a number of times because the memories opened up my emotional floodgates. I could barely type through my smiles and tears. I always say that our tears are a tribute to the feelings we have for our loved ones, so we should never hold them back. It's not a sign of weakness or sadness, but instead, a physical sign of our appreciation and affection for them.

People ask me all the time if I've heard from Shelley since she passed. Because of the connection I had with her, she falls into the same category as my own family. She was so close to me that I can't be objective about whether she's coming through to me or if I'm just thinking about her. But there was a connection one night three months after she passed that I'm certain of.

I had just come back from a group reading in New Jersey, and I was to meet Sandra at the home of our good friends, Jon and Stacy. The whole car ride there, I couldn't get Shelley out of my mind, and I knew it was her way of letting me know that she was around. Our teachers, our friends, and our spirit guides on the Other Side are always around us, sending signals that they're taking care of us and guiding us on our path. And the guidance and love we get from our teachers and friends on this earth doesn't stop once they cross over, but continues on a higher plane.

On the way to meet Sandra, I decided to stop by my office in Huntington to use the rest room because the drive was a bit longer than I had anticipated. When I walked into my empty office, there was a video on my desk marked "Shelley"—it was a taped interview she'd given the year before for a cable-TV special called *Messages from the Dead*, which launched my show, *Crossing Over*. The producers of that show had heard that Shelley had crossed over and had sent me her entire, unedited interview to keep.

I slipped the tape into the VCR and sat on my couch in the office, watching and hearing my old friend laugh and speak about our relationship. There were moments on that tape I'd never seen before.

"What makes John special?" the interviewer asked her. My ears perked up at this one.

"What *doesn't* make John special is a better question," she answered. "He's the type of person who would drop everything he's doing and run to wherever you are if you needed him. I know he would do that for me if I ever needed him. "

To me, it was as if she'd made a psychic prediction during that interview and was now showing it to me from beyond the grave. In that interview, she basically recounted my rush to the hospital a few days before she left this world. And as I listened to her, I couldn't help but cry. Even though I'm a medium and I know she's all right and still around . . . I miss her.

CHAPTER EIGHT

The 9/11 Factor

I BELIEVE THAT WE ALL DECIDE when to leave our physical body and "go home" or "join God." I don't think most of us are aware of this choice on a conscious level, although some people who are highly attuned to the spiritual world, including children, sometimes are. But mostly, it's a subconscious "knowing" of the soul that it's time to leave this realm and move onward to the next one. Perhaps we've learned all we're capable of learning or need to learn here, and understand it's our time to "graduate." Or perhaps our leaving also involves teaching other people left behind important lessons of their own that they'll learn as a result of our departure.

But although I believe we choose *when,* I'm not necessarily sure if we choose *how*—that is, I don't know if we can decide upon our method of departure. If we could, I'd guess that most people would pass on in a loving and pain-free manner . . . maybe drifting off to sleep in a loved one's arms. Then there would be the adventurous types who'd want to do it while jumping out of a plane or scaling Mt. Everest.

But the reality of life is that death is rarely peaceful, pretty, or fun for that matter. Even with my strong belief that we choose when we cross over, like anyone else I still have trouble coming to terms with the fact that so many people die violent or cruel deaths—which brings up this question for many: If there *is* a God, how could He or She make us suffer unduly? And what about tragedies we endure, such as earthquakes or volcanoes or plane crashes that kill hundreds at a time?

The most recent tragedy still on all of our minds, which has become part of the fabric of our lives in New York City, is the terrorist attack on the World Trade Center on September 11, 2001. In a few horrible moments, thousands of innocent lives were taken, and scores of families were left heartbroken and stunned, wondering why. It's difficult for me to answer that question except to say that, in keeping with what I believe and as hard it is to hear, all the people who crossed over in the attack that day needed to go on to the next spiritual level at the same time. In fact, since the attack, I've probably conducted hundreds of readings that are September 11-related, and many energies have come through saying as such—that it was their "time," and they had to move on to other work at the next level.

After September 11, I received countless letters, e-mails, and phone calls from people who had lost loved ones that day, anxious to get a reading. Normally I'm a stickler about anyone skipping ahead on the long waiting list I have for personal sessions, but in this case, I felt I had to make an exception. First, I needed to feel that I was doing my part, like everyone else, to help the country heal after the disaster. Second, I figured that giving out socks or canned goods at Ground Zero wouldn't be using my abilities to their best advantage. I needed to do what *I* do—make connections for these people who were in pain and let them know that their loved ones were safe and well on the Other Side. My staff and I randomly chose families to come in for sessions, and I saw them on my personal time on evenings and weekends. I insisted that these families speak to grief counselors both before and after a reading since it was still so soon after the tragedy.

As I've said earlier, I don't usually remember the readings I do after they're over. By the next day, any details are wiped from my memory forever. But there have been a handful of sessions, especially in the last two years, that have left an indelible impression on me. During one seminar in Long Island, about six weeks after the World Trade Center attack, I was doing a reading on one side of the room when I was suddenly seized by a new energy coming through. It was a firefighter calling out the name of his wife, Nancy. I felt a forceful pull toward a pretty woman sitting in the second row.

Nancy Carroll had come to the seminar from Ridgewood, New Jersey, in the hopes of connecting with her husband, Michael, a firefighter who had died on 9/11. She was given a ticket to the seminar by a friend who had bought it in July—two months before the attack. Not only did Michael come through that day with details of Nancy's life since he'd passed (and details of events still to happen), but he also came through with his signature sense of humor.

John: I have a rescue worker coming through [looking at one woman, then pointing directly at her]. Are you Nancy?

Nancy: Yes, I am.

John: I have a Michael coming through. Do you understand this? He passed on September 11th.

Nancy: Yes . . . yes, I do.

John: I don't know if he's a fireman or a cop, but here we go. He's showing me a gavel, but I have no idea what it means.

Nancy: I do. His friend was killed with him . . . his name was Michael Judge. He was a chaplain for the fire department.

John: Wow. Okay—and he wants to acknowledge Robert.

Nancy: That's his friend, a firefighter, who gave his eulogy at his memorial.

John: And he's telling me there's another Nancy he wants to acknowledge. Not you . . . a different Nancy.

Nancy: Yes . . . his sister.

John: Connected with her . . . there's a changing of companies or something.

Nancy: Yes! Nancy and I have been running Michael's small business since he died . . . and we're selling the business this week.

John: He also says a very special hello to Billy.

Nancy: That's his brother . . . he's a retired fire captain.

John: He says Billy isn't doing well, and the family needs to know that . . .

Nancy: Yes, I think that's true. He's very upset about Michael.

John: He says he's glad you "turned down the reporter," whatever that means. He says the reporter didn't have the children's best interests at heart. That they were only interested in the story. Do you know what this means?

Nancy: Yes, I do! A news show called me and wanted to do a story on my kids . . . but I didn't feel right about it and I said no . . .

John: Okay. Now, do you have a picture of Michael that was in the newspaper? He's says it's a picture of him rescuing a girl.

Nancy: Yes! I was just looking at this!

John: Because Michael says he was with you when you were looking at this picture. He also says they'll give you what you want that's connected with you. You will get it . . . whatever this means. . . .

Nancy: Okay . . .

John: He says the Florida trip is postponed, not cancelled.

Nancy: We were supposed to go to Florida a month after he was killed.

John: Did your daughter have a dream recently that was very shocking to you?

Nancy: Yes!

John: Michael was with her in that dream, he wants you to know that. And he says he enjoyed his memorial. He says that Mayor Giuliani was there.

Nancy: Yes, he was!

John: And he's telling me that right now . . . there are people at the site who are being injured in some way.

Nancy: I'm not sure what you mean.

John: I don't know either, but he's saying people at the site are injured, and there's a "DN" connection to you involving that. Okay . . . [pause, then sarcastically], he says, "Now aren't you glad I didn't wear my ring to work?"

Nancy: Yes! Because I get to have his ring now!

John: Michael tells me he's a Catholic and you pray for him. He thanks you for his prayers. He says they help him tremendously. He tells me you carry his rosary beads with you.

Nancy: I do!

John (laughing): Oh . . . hold on. He also tells me you carry a 5-by-7 picture of him!

Nancy: Well, I don't usually . . . but it's in my purse now!

John: And [laughing] he tells me he's such a good-looking guy!

Nancy: Yes! He looks like JFK, Jr.

John: It's very important for his family to know that he's still doing what he did here. He's still a rescue worker on the Other Side. And Michael tells me there's something important happening this weekend in the town you live in.

Nancy: Yes, 12 people in our town were killed on 9/11. We're having a special ceremony for all of them. I'm going to that.

John: He wants you to look out for a bird on that day. He says it's a validation that he's always with you. There's going to be some kind of a sign with a bird.

Nancy: Okay.

One week later, on the morning of the ceremony, Nancy was awakened by loud noises in the house and her mother shaking her by the shoulders. "She said, 'Nancy, wake up . . . there's a giant bird flapping around in the bathroom!" The two women raced down the hall to find that a stray bird had somehow gotten through a crack in the open window and was now trapped in the bathroom, flailing about, with no intention of leaving. Nancy was shocked. Could the "sign" have been more obvious? She didn't think so. After trying to usher the bird out the window themselves, Nancy and her mother called Animal Control to come and get it.

"I told my mom, 'Well . . . I guess this is my bird!'" But even without such a dramatic signal, Nancy had no doubt that her husband had come through "like gangbusters" in the reading the week before, and he'd be with her on this day and always.

By the time Nancy had come to the seminar, the hope she'd held on to for days—that her husband had survived the World Trade Center collapse—was gone. Together since they were teenagers and married for 13 years, she described their relationship as soul mates who "couldn't wait for the other to walk through the door at the end of the day." As Nancy explained some of the details her husband came through with during the reading, the rest of the seminar attendees gasped.

"The photo of my husband in the newspaper was a picture of him coming out of a building, holding his hat over a woman's head to protect her. I had framed it and put it up in the living room. And Michael said to me at the time, 'Why would you frame this one? It's not like it's a rescue or anything! It's ridiculous!' But I really liked the photo. The night before I came to the seminar, I was looking at the picture, and I was feeling really annoyed at him . . . annoyed that he had 'left' me. And I flung the picture across the room and said out loud, 'How could you leave me?!'" But as Nancy found out, he hadn't really left her. In fact, he was with her at that moment when she'd been in such pain. Similarly, he'd been at home to comfort their three-year-old daughter, Olivia, through the pain of missing her daddy. In a vivid dream just three weeks after September 11, Olivia had a "play date" with her dad who was on the Other Side.

"My daughter had been very sad, and she really missed her father playing with her," recalled Nancy. "Michael had just put up one of those wooden play gyms in the yard, and he loved to play with Olivia on it. She was so sad. But one morning she came downstairs and was so happy. She told me, 'I had a dream that Daddy came into my room, got me dressed, took me out to my new play gym to play, and then took me to McDonald's!' She was in a great mood." Nancy didn't know it at the time, but her daughter had experienced a "visit" from her daddy, which he confirmed in the reading.

Not only did Michael come through with specifics that only Nancy knew about, but she was struck by the *way* he had come through with them—for example, his joking about her having his wedding ring. "Michael had been a fireman for 16 years, and when he went to the academy, they were taught to never wear jewelry on the job," said Nancy. "He'd come home from work and say, 'Darn, I left my ring and watch in my locker!' Then he wouldn't be due in to work for another two days, and it would drive him crazy because he didn't have his ring or watch on. I used to always tell him, 'Why don't you just wear them while you work?' but he wouldn't do it. Three days after September 11th, when I realized that he probably wasn't coming home, I went to his locker to get his backpack. And there were his wedding ring and his watch sitting there. I was so happy to have these things—I was so happy he'd left them there. I put his wedding ring around a long chain, and I wear it around my neck." Nancy pulled the ring out from under her sweater and showed the group.

There were a few details in the reading that didn't make sense to Nancy at the time, but which were validated in the weeks to come. She couldn't figure out what Michael meant when he said people were being hurt down at Ground Zero, so she called up Michael's station the next day to check on it.

"I called up and asked the guy who answered, 'What happened down there last night?' and he said, 'Oh, the cops were telling us we couldn't dig.'" As it turns out, the night of the seminar was a very tense, violent night down at Ground Zero. The firemen had been digging nonstop to find people in the rubble, including their comrades, and wanted to continue, "but the police were harassing them and roughhousing them," the firefighter on the phone said.

After Nancy hung up, she realized that the name of the fire-fighter she'd just been speaking to was connected to the message. This firefighter, who was a buddy of Michael's, was in the famous photo that appeared in the media all over the world—the picture of three firefighters hoisting a flag up at the disaster site. His name is Danny—the "DN" connected to the message in the reading. The final mystery, when Michael said that Nancy would receive what was "connected" to her, was solved a few weeks later. Michael's body was recovered from the disaster site and returned home for a hero's burial.

"When I went home after the reading," Nancy remembered, "I felt such peace. Michael and I had so much together, and something like that just doesn't go away. Even now, I still feel very connected to him. Since the reading, I talk to him constantly. I don't know why September 11th happened . . . I guess I'll know when I get to the Other Side myself. Maybe I have my own life lessons to learn. And sometimes I wonder . . . if 2,000 people were going to die at once, maybe God needed 400 good firefighters up there to help them all with the transition. Firefighters are such good people, such help-ful souls, who only want to help others. That's the kind of man my husband was—and *is*. I know he's out there and listening to me, and I know this because of the reading."

Michael Carroll was one of the first firefighters to come through to me so soon after September 11, and it was a very emotional night for me, for Nancy, and for everybody in the room. I still remem-ber how brave and proud Nancy was as she sat up straight in the chair, taking in the information and validating it with such pride and love for her hero husband.

When the seminar was over, Nancy approached me up front and gave me her husband's mass card—which had his picture on it for remembrance.

Then, as further validation to me that Michael was still around, two days later I was given another token of this firefighter's brav-ery. At another, separate seminar, a young man approached me who had heard about the September 11-related readings I'd been doing and wanted to say a general thank you from all the families I was helping. As a gift, he handed me a T-shirt that was made in honor of the firefighters. At that time, the firehouses were making up shirts with individual names of their brothers and sisters they'd lost on the back. This man handed me a navy blue T-shirt with a firefighter emblem on it, and as he did, I felt a twinge of familiarity.

As soon as I got home, I raced to my desk to check the name on the Mass card Nancy had given me with the name on the shirt. Sure enough, it was the same name. On the back of the T-shirt were the words in bold: *In Loving Memory of Michael T Caroll* [sic]. It was yet another hello from Michael, who was now rescuing and helping others on the Other Side on a grand scale.

To this day, I keep that Mass card and the T-shirt at home—the card is on my work desk, and the shirt is carefully folded in my "special" drawer of items that have great meaning to me. Each time I sit at my desk, I see the card, and I think of Michael and Nancy and their ongoing love that transcends the boundaries of the human body.

My link with Nancy and the Other Side continues. Last May, Nancy was roaming through a bookstore and saw the new paperback version of *CROSSING OVER: The Stories Behind the Stories*, on the bookshelf with the added 9/11 chapter. "I bought it and took it home and leafed through it, wondering if my reading was mentioned," Nancy said. She fell asleep a bit disappointed, with the book on her lap, open to the 9/11 chapter. Her reading wasn't in there. The very next day, she got a telephone call from Natasha—who'd been trying to track her down for weeks—asking if she'd be a part of this book, *After Life*. "I couldn't believe it!" Nancy exclaimed.

Looking back, the link between Nancy and the man who gave me the T-shirt may have surprised me then, but doesn't now. In the two years since the terrorist attacks, I've witnessed a sort of spiritual phenomenon I've never seen before—a banding together of families linked to 9/11 on the Other Side. During my group readings in the New York-New Jersey area and my many tapings of *Crossing Over*, anytime there's someone in the room who suffered a loss due to 9/11, their loved one who comes through for them will then bring through other 9/11 losses. Even if these people who died didn't know each other at all in life, their mutual bond in how they passed is so intense that they act as "family" and link up to help each other.

I've done a number of seminars and groups where for the first two hours only 9/11 energies have come through. It kind of feels like they take me hostage and won't let me go. Once one of them gets my attention, they form a chain of sorts and bring in the rest of their 9/11 "family" to dominate the group. Now bear in mind, this phenomenon doesn't happen all the time. So if you're sitting in a seminar where all these 9/11 families are showing up left and right and your loved one who also passed in 9/11 doesn't come through, please don't be upset. Although I see it happen often, the 9/11 factor isn't a given at every event. It doesn't mean your loved one isn't okay or doesn't want to talk to you. It just means I cannot, as always, get to every person and each energy that wants to make a connection.

After many months of experiencing this banding together of souls, I had to admire their tenacity. And because this exclusive "family" pushes everyone else's family aside and holds me hostage, I began calling them a nickname—"The 9/11 Factor." And if anyone out there is offended by this nickname, please know that I use the phrase with humor, and with that humor is respect and a bit of awe. And make no mistake—that's how the other energies on the Other Side feel about The 9/11 factor, too. Because as they strong-arm their way and cut to the front of the line, the families on the Other Side who are *not* 9/11-related dutifully bow their heads and stand aside.

LAST DECEMBER 2002, I conducted several group readings in New York overrun by this 9/11 tag team. I didn't know it at the time, but in one group in Secaucus, New Jersey, Nancy Carroll had returned and was sitting in the back. With her, she had brought along some extended members of the her new 9/11 family—other women who had also lost their husbands at the World Trade Center. These five women had been strangers to one another one year earlier. They met in a 9/11 support group in New Jersey and had since become friends.

Nancy had told the group about her first reading when Michael came through with flying colors, but the women were very skeptical, to say the least. Here's an example of how the 9/11 family on the Other Side passes the baton from member to member. In this case, it was a situation involving five husbands, all on the same team, trying to get hold of the ball and shoot. They were coming through to me so fast that I could barely keep up and match the husbands to the corresponding wives. The wives, too, were getting confused.

John: I have an older female who passes from cancer. Helen, Ellen, Eileen. And there's a March connection. Someone's coming through claiming to be a mother figure, and there's a connection to March.

Woman #1: I have a birthday in March . . . my husband has an Aunt Helen.

John: Your husband has passed, right?

Woman #1: Yes.

John: Did you lose someone on 9/11?

Woman #1: Yes.

John: Helen is telling me . . . wait . . . .

I then felt the pull move to two other women sitting nearby. It switched gears and pointed to them . . .

John: Wait . . . you two also lost someone on 9/11?

Woman #2 and Woman#3 (together): Yes.

John: Where's the Michael?

Woman #2: My son.

Woman #3: . . . and my husband.

John: There is an "A" connection. And someone's birthday is coming up in January.

Woman #2: Yes.

John (pointing to Woman #3): You have two kids?

Woman #3: Yes.

John: Who has the ongoing heart problem?

Woman #2: My dad.

John: Your husband is saying he has to watch it . . .

I felt a new energy try to get my attention. To a fourth woman sitting with them, I posed a question.

John: Did you lose a husband on 9/11, too?

Woman #4: Yes.

John: I'm bringing through someone connected to the number six.

Woman #4: My son is connected to a six.

John: Does someone have a Steve?

Woman #4: I'm connected to a Steve.

John: Is he a smartass? If he was here, would he be making jokes about all of this?

Woman #4: Oh, yeah.

John: I have to acknowledge that someone wrote his name in cement.

Woman #4: Yes, we did.

John: I also have to acknowledge you have his chain.

Woman #4: Yes . . . I do.

John: Does he have a major connection to the name Britney? I'm seeing Britney Spears. Or does he have a huge affinity with Britney Spears.

Woman #4: My daughter loves Britney. She's going to the Jingle Ball tomorrow night.

John: I wouldn't be surprised if Britney shows up there.

Again, I felt a new energy joining the team on the Other Side and was pulled to yet another woman in the group here on this side.

John: Where's the Chris [pointing to Woman #5]? Are you connected to the Chris?

Woman #5: My husband is Chris.

John: He's making me feel like I need to talk about your clothes. Did you just go on a spending spree? Did you change sizes? He's making me feel like your skirt doesn't fit you anymore.

Woman #5: I'm three sizes smaller now.

John: He says two days before September 11th, you had a very special day.

Woman #5: Yes, it was our anniversary.

John: He says he'll never forget it.

Once again, I felt another new energy arrive on the scene. . . .

John: Where's John?

Woman #6: My husband is John.

John: He's apologizing for the mortgage. What does that mean?

Woman #6: We moved just two months before he passed.

John: Is he the one who would pick you up and throw you over his shoulder?

Woman #6: Every night, he did that with my little one.

John: Do all these guys know each other?

All the women in unison: No.

John: Were you all taking bets before you got here as to which husband would come through tonight?

All women in unison: Yes . . . we were!

The reading continued in this way, bouncing around from wife to wife, with each woman getting a snippet of information before a new husband butted in. At one point, it felt like that scene in the movie *Ghost,* when Whoopi Goldberg was surrounded by a crowd of spirits all trying to talk to their relatives at the same time. If I didn't know better, I would have guessed that all these husbands coming through were brothers because of the kinship feeling I was getting attached to them, and because they kept bringing through each new energy like they were introducing a new family member into the equation. But while the husbands were working hard to get through to their wives, not all of the women were appreciative of their efforts. At one point, one wife who had gotten a few details during the reading put up her hand.

"When are you going to say something specific?" she demanded. "When are you going to say something that will make me, or any of us, know this is for real? I mean . . . do you all believe this?"

There was a hush in the room. At that moment, part of me wanted to grab this woman by the collar and slap her silly. I was working my ass off trying to reunite her with her family, and I knew that the energies were working their asses off, too. And through it all, she sits there wearing "The Face" (what I call the arms crossed/mouth-pinched look that skeptics sometimes give me), making me feel that she was insulting the process.

I must admit that I'm intolerant of this type of behavior. I don't believe that the loss of a loved one gives someone the right to be mean or to make demands, especially of someone who's trying to help. If you ever find yourself in a situation where you're lashing out at people because you're suffering a loss, take a moment to think about what you're doing. Maybe the people you're lashing out at are those closest to you, and those who are trying to help you deal with the tragedy or loss.

Initially, I reacted to her question out of ego. *"I know you must be kidding! I thought that's what I was doing."*

She just shook her head and folded her arms as the rest of the room stared at her in disbelief. I'm not going to identify which woman this was, but I will say that she had several validations throughout the reading that were accurate and specific.

Nancy Carroll, who had come with the woman, acknowledged these validations: "She was getting some good information that I knew was right, but she still wasn't buying it," Nancy said. "Then I realized that maybe these women didn't have the background I had. I had read your books and watched *Crossing Over*, and I knew how it all worked, so when the information started flying at me like that, I could decipher it. These women walked in with certain expectations. They were like, 'I want John to come through with my nickname,' but it doesn't work that way." During a break in the seminar, Nancy came up to me and apologized for her friend's behavior.

"You've got to tell your friends that they can't be like this when the energies come across," I said. "Because if they are, the energies will never come through again." And it's true. If these energies are not "welcomed" or think we're taking their attempts to make contact as a joke, they won't bother to come back. Why should they? Would you visit a friend or relative who slammed a door in your face?

This is why I always, always warn people at the beginning of a session that they can't enter into this process with fixed expectations or wearing blinders. I can't stress this point enough. If you approach a session with a closed mind, you'll miss the messages and be disappointed no matter what happens.

After this woman gave me "The Face" and "The Tone," I took a deep breath and counted to five, trying to suppress my rising anger. I reminded myself that this woman was still wrestling with her loss and had a long way to go before she came to terms with it. To her, by validating what was going on in the room that day, she'd have to acknowledge the death of her husband—something she didn't want to do. I believe that she channeled her anger at the loss toward me, and through her pain, she lashed out.

That same month, I was doing a seminar in Long Island, and the 9/11 factor was working overtime. I had already done at least five 9/11-related readings that night and assumed my hostage situation was over . . . until I was hauled over to the back of the room. There, five kids—Marie, Kathy, Chuck, Ray, and Joey—and their mom, Rosalie, were spread out across two rows of seats with expectant, hopeful looks on their faces. As I zeroed in on them, I'm sure they didn't expect to hear the first thing that flew out of my mouth. How was I to know that I was about to reveal a well-kept family secret? Blame it on the Other Side:

> **John:** Someone here is pregnant. I have a father figure coming through who's saying congratulations.
> **Kathy:** I am!
> **Chuck, Ray, Joe:** What?!
> **Kathy:** My brothers didn't know yet!

John: You have a dad who's passed. He claims he was in uniform—like a policeman or postman or military person or fireman.

Kathy: Yes.

John: He's telling me he had a nickname like "Duke" or . . . something like . . . I see some sort of grand title.

Kathy: His nickname was "God"! And he has "Dutch" tattooed on his arm.

John: Oh, how I wish he got me to say that to you! *"God is coming through to you!"* He says his passing is recent. He's complimenting you on a wreath . . . as if there was a wreath in his honor with red and white on it. And he's claiming his sister and wife would look at his passing in the way Jack Kennedy passed. And he says his wife was stoic and strong like Jackie Kennedy. I need to compliment her for doing that—she kept everyone together. And he had a flag burial.

Rosalie: Yes.

John: He's acknowledging a celebration in May.

Rosalie: His daughters' birthdays are in May. And that's when we had his funeral.

John: I'm asking him to describe his passing, and he won't. Is he one of three boys? Or does he have three boys?

Rosalie: Both. He has three brothers . . . and he has three sons.

John: Does he have a son with him? Did he lose a son or lose someone he looked at as a son? A friend's son. Is there a Michael living?

Rosalie: That's a friend's son. And yes, there was always a joke, just kidding around, that Michael was his illegitimate son.

John: Michael was there before him, to help him over. Also, he's making me feel like he didn't get enough face time. Did this man have a really, really healthy ego?

All of them: *Oh, yeah!*

John: I don't wanna say he's cocky, but . . . he's confident. He's saying, "HERE I AM!"

Is there a reason why he wants me to go to Jersey? He wants me to go through the Lincoln tunnel. Did he get in a massive accident in the tunnel?

Marie: He was stuck in the tunnel for a long time.

John: And someone was born right after he passed. Where's the "P"? Pat. Paul.

Marie: Yes, his grandson.

John: He says there's a police officer in the family.

Kathy: Yes, my husband.

John: What does he mean that he's on the "other" team?

All (laughing): We understand that!

John: He's claiming that "J" passed.

Kathy: That's his brother, Joe.

John: He brings up his uniform again. Is it on display somewhere? He's telling me 11 . . . so that's either the 11th month, November . . . or the 11th of a month.

Rosalie: Yes, that makes sense.

John: Who has his hat? He's showing me his hat. This is a work hat.

Chuck: I have it.

John: And . . . one of you is in school. Does one of you teach something to do with balls?

Ray: Yes, I teach phys. ed.

John (to Chuck): And you have his ring, too? You have his ring in your pocket?

Chuck: Yes! [Chuck pulls out his dad's ring from his front pocket.]

John (to Ray): And what about you? Do you have the ring yet?

Ray: Not yet. My mom says I'm supposed to get his other ring, but I don't have it yet.

John (to Joey): He says your skepticism is good. That is how he would be. He also says one of you has his name.

Ray: I do!

John: He's also acknowledging Mickey Mouse. And I see a boat . . . I see fishing.

Marie: Oh my God! We're going on the Disney Cruise. We just booked it.

John: And what does he mean that they gave him a page? Someone wrote about him in a book?

Kathy: He wrote a book.

John: No, he . . . he only has one published . . . well, as far as he's concerned, it's two. And the second one can be finished. He says someone in the family has a talent for writing and can write a kickass ending. His passing seems extremely fast to me. He's going back to the wreath.

Rosalie: I just saw a wreath I wanted to get for him.

John: Was it red and white?

Rosalie: Yes. For Christmas.

John: He says your house is like Grand Central Station, with people coming and going. He puts a spotlight on your house. I see famous people coming over. I see Giuliani?

Rosalie: Yes, that's right.

John: Wait . . . your husband passed on September 11th, too?

Rosalie: Yes.

John: He's pulling me forward . . . I think there's going to be a "me, too" connection coming up. . . .

Deputy Chief Ray Downey, Chief of Special Operations, was a New York firefighter known across the country for developing innovative rescue techniques to save people's lives. He had directed rescue efforts after the bombings in Oklahoma City and at the World Trade Center (WTC) in 1993, and after hurricanes in the Dominican Republic. So it was sadly ironic on the day of September 11, 2001, that this time he was one of the thousands missing beneath the rubble.

Chief Downey was making his way over to the Trade Center when the first tower collapsed, stalling him in a tunnel en route to

Manhattan. Before the second tower came down, he had reached the WTC and had joined the rescue efforts. He was last seen running to help others as the debris from the second tower began falling.

For days after, Chief Downey's two firefighter sons—Chuck, a lieutenant; and Joe, a captain—dug through the rubble where his car had been parked in the hopes of finding their dad alive. They found the crushed car, but not their father. In the car, though, was the favorite hat he always wore—a fire-department baseball cap with the words "Special Operations" on the front, which is now cherished by his sons.

Less than two months before the disaster, Downey had been honored at a party given for him at Gracie Mansion by New York Mayor Rudy Giuliani, where he was bestowed the Crystal Apple award for his contribution to the city. It was no wonder then that the guys at the firehouse called him "God"—a nickname the family didn't know about until son Joe joined the department.

"He came home one day and said to my mom that all the guys were calling him 'Jesus' because he was 'the son of 'God,'" recalled Kathy, "and that's when we discovered what they called him. He could be very intimidating because he'd accomplished so much, but my father was the first person at your side if you needed help." At his funeral, attended by the mayor and decorated with flags, "people told my mother she reminded them of Jackie Kennedy because of the way she was so dignified," Kathy said.

The whole family was shocked when Chuck stood up in the middle of the reading and pulled their dad's lieutenant ring from deep inside his pocket—no one knew he'd brought it that day. And they had a good laugh at their dad's ribbing about one family member being a cop.

"My husband was a police officer, and my whole family were firefighters, and they had that rivalry." Kathy laughed. "That was the big joke. And the funny thing is, now he's a fireman, as of last month. He graduated in April!"

Since September 11, dozens of newspaper articles have been written about Chief Downey, and tributes including scholarship funds have been established in his name. But the family would also like to continue on with his work. He had written one book, *The Rescue Company,* and after he died they discovered he'd been working on a second.

"I hope we can finish it for him," said Marie, "since he says it can be done." The Downey family always knew that their dad was special to them, but didn't realize how many lives he touched when he left for work each day.

"Ten thousand people came to his funeral service," recalled Marie. "We were amazed. They closed the schools in town, they closed the roads. It was overwhelming. And so was the reading we had. We left the seminar that night feeling differently about 'death.' It doesn't bring him back, but to know he's still there somewhere makes our hearts feel good."

And just to top off the evening, the Other Side went for number eight. I was pulled over to another family, two sisters, sitting in the front row . . .

John: I'm being pulled over here . . . who's the Jeff?
Woman: That's with me.
John: Someone passes from an impact. And I think . . . wait. You have a 9/11 connection, too?
Woman: Yes.
John: I'm getting a feeling of honor. So he was working? Was he a fireman?
Woman: Yes.
John: And . . . they called him in the bombing in 1993, too, right? He was there the other time, he's telling me.
Woman: Yes.
John: He wants me to say "Tiger."
Woman: Another fireman he worked with, that's what he called him.
John: And who's Nick?
Woman: That's him . . . that's my husband.
John: Wait . . . and . . . [to the woman sitting beside her] . . . *you* have a 9/11 connection, too?
Woman #2: Yes.

At this point, the rest of the room could barely contain themselves. The atmosphere was so highly charged that everyone was sitting on the edge of their seats.

> **John:** He's acknowledging a "Kate" or a "Katey."
> **Woman #2:** Kitty. We have an Aunt Kitty who's passed.
> **John:** He says there's a male one level above who's with him.
> **Woman #2:** Uncle Ben.
> **John:** He says that when the terror attack happened . . . you knew he'd be gone. . . .
> **Woman #2:** I knew. I knew it when he called me.
> **John:** He called two people. Wait [to the two women] . . . you two are related?
> **Woman #2::** Yes, she's my sister-in-law. I lost my two brothers.
> **John:** They were literally together? In the same building?
> **Woman #1:** Yes.
> **John:** One of them is making me feel like . . . your mother, she'd be fine if she didn't wake up tomorrow.
> **Woman #2::** She's a very spiritual person, but she's tired. . . .
> **John:** Your mom lost two other children before this. I don't know if she had two miscarriages?
> **Woman #2:** I know she had one for sure.
> **John:** I'm getting that there are five kids in the family.
> **Woman #2:** Yes.
> **John:** He wants me to acknowledge Ted.
> **Woman #2:** My brother, Ted.
> **John:** And what's your Pennsylvania tie?
> **Woman #2:** My mother lived in Pennsylvania.
> **John:** Where's Julia? Julie?
> **Woman #1:** Julie, that's me.
> **John:** They're okay. They were very high up in the building, right?

Woman #1: Yes. On the 95th floor.

John: They passed very fast. On the phone . . . did he say something to you like he was afraid?

Woman #1: He said to me, "It doesn't look good. This is bad."

John: Please, please know that they're okay.

A 9/11 passing is no different from any other passing to the people left behind. Each person who has lost a loved one experiences their own personal tragedy, and we all must find a way to deal with the loss and grief. I would hope that in dealing with that grief, you would honor those around who are trying to help you through it. And if a loved one on the Other Side attempts to make contact with you, please don't dismiss the experience. They're reaching out with love, and if you respond with anger, you'll cut off the communication because they'll see that you're not ready and willing.

Yes, it *is* important to have certain expectations about the process . . . and that means you should expect solid validations that will assure you that it is indeed your loved one coming through. At the same time, you can't expect only validations that *you* decide upon to come through—and if they don't, decide the process isn't real. That's like going to a concert and expecting a performer to sing only your favorite songs, and when they don't, deciding that the concert didn't exist at all.

As this generation becomes more aware of the open lines of communication between our world and the next one, you yourself will become more a part of this process. I think that talking to our loved ones on the Other Side on a daily basis—and without the use of a medium—will become commonplace.

WHEN I THINK OF THE SPIRITUAL EVOLUTION we've already seen in the last few years—the drastic changes in societal views about life after death—I can't help but think of Shelley, who would have flourished in this new environment. Her death was a major personal and professional loss for me, and when she died I couldn't understand why God would take such a gifted medium and teacher who could have helped so many more people here in this world. But now, I wonder if God took her so she could expand her work elsewhere. Remember when I said that Shelley was always the queen of the "Greeting Committee" here on Earth? Well, I believe that Shelley is still acting as the Greeting Committee, but on the Other Side.

Shelley died two months before the attack on the World Trade Center, and the timing of her death is uncanny to me. The way I figure it, she crossed over, had a few weeks to acclimate herself, and then she got to work doing what she does best—acting as Grand Dame of the Greeting Committee. And trust me, if your loved ones needed to be met on the Other Side, they couldn't be in more loving hands. It's not a coincidence that Shelley passed when she did, and it's also not coincidental that a TV show like *Crossing Over*, which deals with death and communicating with our loved ones, was put on the air one year before such a tragedy. I think it was part of the Universal plan, to prepare the consciousness of our country for what was to come and what we would need to endure.

And to be a part of that preparation and healing has been the greatest honor for me.

CHAPTER NINE

Mama Mia!

MY MOTHER LEFT THE PHYSICAL WORLD NEARLY 14 YEARS AGO, and I still hear her talking to me almost every day. I don't mean I hear her in the "psychic" sense, but in the regular mother-son sense. Her love and parenting are so deeply ingrained in my soul that I hear her teaching words and sometimes just her Mom-like remarks ringing in my ear as I go about my daily routine.

Especially now that I'm a dad, I experience flashbacks of my mother from my childhood—songs she sang to me, funny voices she used in order to amuse me (she'd make me laugh by doing Ernie's laugh—of the Bert and Ernie duo on *Sesame Street*). I consider all these small moments validations that my mother is still with me.

The reading in this chapter, with model Mia Tyler, demonstrates how one mother's love and connection to her daughter is still strong and very much alive on the Other Side. When we began this book, Natasha immediately thought of Mia—daughter of Aerosmith's Steven Tyler and sister of actress Liv Tyler—as someone who would be interested in this process.

As usual, I had no idea whom I was reading the day I walked into the hotel suite in midtown Manhattan. And, since I'm not a subscriber to *Vogue* magazine, I didn't recognize Mia on sight. Arriving 30 minutes late, I was met at the door by Natasha's smiling and excited face, and my first thought wasn't about the "client" I was about to meet, but about Natasha. She'd organized this session and felt a sense of obligation, which the planner of a reading often takes on—as if they're responsible for who comes through during the session (when even the psychic cannot take on that responsibility!). And there was something else on my mind. Ever since we began this project, and particularly since I discovered in our earlier reading with Norris Mailer that Natasha had lost her own mother, I'd been seeing that the sessions were having a personal effect on her. Especially during readings involving mothers and daughters, it was as though she was vicariously experiencing a reading herself, and hearing her own mother's words of love and validation.

That has always been true for me, too, with each and every one of the thousands of readings I've done. I've always maintained that I do this work selfishly, because with each connection I make for a stranger, I'm indirectly validating for myself that my own loved ones are alive and well on the Other Side.

Mia came to the reading with her cousin, Julia, and as I found out after the fact that she (Mia) was hoping to connect with *her* mother, who had passed away six months earlier. Mia's reading is an example of a daughter finding out her mom is still watching over her—and a reminder to us all that our parents look out for us even after they're gone.

> **John:** I've got an older female coming through that I'd look at as being either a mother or being like an aunt or a grandmother. The connection is intense. And the emotion that comes up around this feels split, as if there's a dual type of relationship, where two people are within one in some way. And I feel like it's something that has unfinished business attached to it.

Now, I don't know if there's a connection to somebody who crossed themselves over, where their actions bring about their passing, but there's somebody who's claiming that they're responsible for how they got there.

I'm being shown drums, so I don't know if there's some type of drum connection to this woman, if there's a drum relationship to you, or it's you. But they're banging on drums for me. It's a way of either telling me that somebody is known for their drums, somebody has the drums, somebody's taking drum lessons, somebody's a drummer, but there's a drum reference that they want me to come up with.

Mia: Should I tell you what—

John: Nope, nope. This woman who's claiming to be like the mother has a male figure to her side who's with her. So, this is actually a biological mom that we're talking about?

Mia: Yes.

John: Then I'm talking about either her brother, a brother figure, or somebody who would be on the same level . . . an uncle or another male figure like that who's with her.

Mia: Okay.

John: Now, I just want to say something else, and I'm sorry to say it like this, but there's an issue of abuse that comes up here in a big way. So I feel like I don't know if this is physical abuse or sexual abuse, but there's a lot of abuse here.

Mia: Yes.

John: This is connected to your mom?

Mia: Yes.

John: I think she feels that there were dead ends in places for her. And, I don't know if she gave you up, or if she chose not to raise you, or if she chose to shirk responsibility of being the nurturing, maternal energy that you would like to convince yourself you had—

Mia: Yes.

John: But she's making me feel like, you need to understand that we both know you didn't have that, okay?

Mia: Yes.

John: But she wants you to know that doesn't mean that she doesn't love you. And it doesn't mean that she doesn't look at you as being a friend, because I think she does. And I also feel like your connection to her is probably even stronger now than it was when she was here, and that she has influenced your creativity, and she's influenced your self-worth. So I feel like you actually now look at things in a very, very different way.

Mia: Yes.

John: She knows that in her death she's altered your life in the biggest way possible, but you have to know that that doesn't come without paying a price. And the price is huge. And she's making me feel like you have to understand that there are a lot of issues within your family that you won't be able to fix or control, you won't be able to get the answers, you won't be able to understand, and some things just have to be taken at face value, and you have to know this is what it is.

Mia: Yes.

John: Now, she's also claiming you [pointing to Julia]. So, I don't know if you're not her daughter, if you are her daughter, I don't know what your connection is to her, but she's making me feel like I need to thank you for being supportive, and for—you come across with words at times when people couldn't actually give the words. And I don't know if you guys know each other from being three years old, or if there's some type of really strong bond right underneath the age of five, like in kindergarten, or if you were split up in some way. . . .

Mia/Julia (laughing in unison): *Yes!*

John: . . . but she's making me feel like it's important for her to address that you're here. And I don't know if you're the artist or if somebody is known for their painting, or you're supposed to acknowledge the painting reference to you. Like you painted on her walls when you were a child or took nail polish and made pretty little faces on whatever this is.

I also want to tell you that she's got her mother with her. So to me there's a female figure above her I'd see as being her mother, her aunt. You're looking at me like I'm crazy, but I'm still going with this—

Mia: No, I think—

John: Wait, wait . . . let me do this. There's a unique "G" name connected to this family, so somebody might be Gloria, somebody might be Gwen, there's like a "GA" sound, there's a hard "G." But I really believe her mom passed, so if it's not her mother she's got, then I believe it's the oldest female that's with her. . . .

Mia: Yes, yes.

John: Who I believe passed before her.

Mia: Yes.

John: Who wants me to let you know she was there to greet her on the Other Side. Now, there's a magazine connection that I'm supposed to bring up connected to your mom.

Mia: Yes.

John: But I'm supposed to acknowledge the magazine connection to you *with* your mom. So does she mean she was in it? Or on it?

Mia: Yes, both of us.

John: And she's making me feel like there's one shot of your mom that looks like you, or that you paralleled her in some way.

The other thing she wants me to talk about is a frame. And she's making me feel like it's—it looks like a brassy-looking, gold metal frame, but it's not an old-fashioned frame, it's a . . . I don't know what you call it. Imagine having a frame and hammering the crap out of it so that it would have circles banged into it, like bent. She's telling me to acknowledge that.

Now was she adopted?

Mia: No . . .

John: Why would she bring up adoption? She's telling me to talk about Carol. Or Carolyn, or Kara, Carol . . .

Mia: Carol? I don't know a Carol . . .

John: Did Carol live near you when you were kids?

Mia: Well, yeah, when we were little, across the street.

John: She might want to get me to go back to that time frame. So if you try to take us back to that place—that might be where the adopted thing goes, to that time period. So at that age, when there was that Carol person around, that might be the time period when someone was either given up for adoption or that might have been the time when she took care of somebody else's child, or somebody else took care of her child.

She's showing me pink roses. That's her way of expressing her love for you. You wanted to know if she had the dog with her?

Mia: Oh, yeah!

John: She says yes.

Mia: Oh my God.

John: You have a camera of hers? She's showing me an actual camera, and it's an old-fashioned-looking camera to me. Like a Polaroid camera.

Mia: She gave me one she found. It wasn't hers; it was something she got when she was sick.

John: It might just be her way of describing what was happening around you at the time. She says to bring up October. There's gotta be a connection to October as well. And I'll tell you I think it's around the 17th. Write this down. There's a connection to October 17th. Now . . . she said you were hoping to hear from her today?

Mia: Oh, yeah.

John: I love when that happens.

She's making me feel, though, that there's a . . . I just want to go on record, you said she was sick, but she's making me feel like there's maybe a three-day period where everyone thought she was gonna be okay, or there was a three-day period where everything was fine, or there was a three-day period where she just felt awesome. Or maybe a three-day period where she was on very heavy medication and that's why she would feel awesome, I don't know.

Mia: Yeah.

John: She's telling me to talk about upstate. She wants me to tell you about upstate?

Mia: Yeah.

John: And I don't know if you're her only child? Okay, you are. Because she's making me feel like you're *it* . . . you're the world. But I don't know if she was ever really able to say that to you. I don't know if she was ever able to verbalize to you your importance. You know the feeling that I have is . . . it's very hard to describe it when they give me this feeling, but I feel if I'm your mom, I'm in awe of you.

Mia: [nods]

John: Like you're mine—I made this—how did this happen? I don't feel like I deserve this because I didn't really do this, you know, it's like I can't take credit for this. That's the feeling, that's how it's coming across to me. And there's silent praise. She wants to know if you kept the barrette. To me a barrette would be a hair tie or something that goes in the hair, so I don't know if it's something you have from your childhood or if it's something of hers that you kept. I don't think she means you kept her hair, but there's something about the barrette or the hair thing.

Mia: I don't know. I've got so much of her stuff. . . .

John: She's also telling me to talk about . . . are you going to California, are there any California connections? Because I'm hearing the song "California Dreaming" in my head.

Mia: Yeah! I'm going to move there. Is it a good thing? [laughing]

John: They'll never tell us what to do, but she's showing me that this is what's here. [To Julia:] Did you come into the city especially to do this? [To Mia:] So you're supposed to take her out to dinner tonight because of this?

Mia and Julia (laughing and in unison): Yes! We're going right after this!

John: Okay, when they do that, that's just their way of letting you know they know what's what.

Mia: We just decided this, like a half hour ago!

John: Just know that she's very happy to be able to do this. She's happy to be able to come through for you. And I don't know if you come from a Catholic background, but she's showing me St. Patrick's Cathedral.

Mia: Yeah, of course she is, yeah.

John: But St. Patrick's Cathedral is a big deal.

Mia: Yes. I was baptized there.

John: You were? Wow. Okay . . . she's pulling her energy back.

Mia's mother, actress/model Cyrinda Foxe Tyler, died on September 7, 2002, at age 51, after battling a stroke and a brain tumor, but she came through to me that day bursting with intensity and energy. "Yep, that's my mom," said Mia, "She was intense. She was a ball of fire."

Cyrinda, I learned, was born Kathleen Hetzekian, was the inspiration for the David Bowie song "Jean Genie," and was also a regular of Andy Warhol's avant-garde scene of the '60s. After Mia filled me in on her and her mom's history, the drum references I got during the reading made perfect sense. As well as Cyrinda's obvious music connection, Mia told me that her boyfriend, Dave (who became her fiancé a few months after the reading), is a drummer and that her father started out as one, and then Julia added that her father and brother were also drummers—"so there are all kinds of drummers in the family," they laughed. Also, since Mia's dad is a celebrity, it may have been a way for Cyrinda to show that connection without letting me know who Mia's dad was, thereby protecting the anonymity of the reading.

Some of the information that came through was very personal to Mia and her family. Her mother revealed the abuse she'd endured growing up, which Mia acknowledged. Linked to that abuse was Cyrinda's perception of herself as a "dual personality."

"Oh God, yeah, because her real name was Kathleen," Mia explained, "and when she ran away from home from the abuse and everything, she changed it to Cyrinda Foxe . . . so there are two personalities. She left that other person behind."

I assured Mia that her mother was going through a healing process on the Other Side about her past troubles growing up and the conflicts she had as a mother. "I'm glad she acknowledges what she did here and that she doesn't feel that way there," Mia replied. "As sad as I was to watch her suffer, I kept saying after she died that she's in a better place, and maybe she's not feeling all that there. That was the one thing I wanted to know . . . if she's still angry or not, and since that was the first thing you said, it makes me feel a lot better."

The girls were also giddy that Mia's mom came through with their own spotted history. The two of them, Mia and Julia, had been very close as little kids and then were separated for many years and lost contact until Mia tracked Julia down again. Since their reunion, the two have been as close as sisters, which came through in the reading as well.

Mia's mother also picked up on a lot of events happening in her daughter's life today, such as her upcoming move to Los Angeles from New York to jump-start her music career, and a recent photo shoot that was a special nod to mom.

Mia recalled, "I just did a thing in *Vogue* magazine where I'm wearing this outfit, and I've been saying for weeks that it's the exact same outfit she'd wear and that she would *love* it if I was in this outfit because it's *exactly* how she wanted me to dress. And I keep saying, 'That's her!' It's me, but it's also her."

Both Mia and Julia have felt Cyrinda's presence around them since she passed, and asked me if some of the "strange" occurrences—a missing phone, a temperamental, flickering stove—were her ways of trying to communicate with them. I checked in with my guides, who were still keyed in to Cyrinda's energy, and asked them. "No, she didn't do any of that," I told them, "but . . . she *will* take credit for the computer thing. . . . "

At that, the two young women got excited. Mia explained that right after her mom passed, she was in Chicago with her boyfriend, and his computer kept going on and off as she was thinking about her mother. And then, in our discussion, she discovered yet another computer communication.

"Oh my God . . . there was something else I never even told you," Julia excitedly told Mia. She described how she and her boyfriend were at their computer late one night when all of a sudden he looked at the screen and saw words there that he didn't write. "It was your mother talking to me!" Julia also promised to print out and send the message to her cousin as soon as she got home.

One validation Mia was hoping to hear, but didn't, was a reference to a necklace she'd brought with her that day. Her mother had sold most of her jewelry when she ran out of money at one point, but had saved one favorite necklace that Mia had inherited. Mia pulled the necklace out of her pocket—it had a coin-sized golden mandolin player on the end of the chain—and as soon as I saw it, I recognized the hammered metal with the little circles on it.

"That's what I was seeing in the reading . . . when I described the frame . . . it looked like this!" I exclaimed. I asked Mia if she'd ever hung the necklace on the edge of a frame and, indeed, she's kept the necklace hanging on a frame in her bathroom for months. It's the first thing she sees every morning. Mia was very thrilled by this final validation, and the fact that her mother was not alone on the Other Side. The male figure who came through to her side who might be the one who crossed himself over, she suspected, was Mom's old pal, singer Johnny Thunder, who'd died from an overdose in 1991 at the age of 38.

"She always said he was waiting for her; she knew he was waiting," Mia recalled. Also on the Other Side keeping mom company is Mia's childhood pet, a German shepherd. But most of all, Mia was heartened to know that her mother had let go of old, angry feelings from her past. "I just wanted to know that wherever she is, she's not bitter . . . she's happy."

Before we left each other, I told Mia that while I was driving to the reading that day I'd gotten stuck behind a bus painted with a giant advertisement for the Broadway play *Mamma Mia!,* so I should have known I had an appointment with a Mia and her mama.

"I was her baby." Mia smiled. "She would always call me 'my baby, my baby.' She would definitely always say I was her world, and she was definitely in awe of me."

With Mia's reading, we can see that even though our loved ones may have been troubled and in pain in this world, they find peace on the Other Side. And they send that peace our way, too, trying to heal relationships they have with us and trying to give us the strength to face our own challenges. With the support they send us, we can carry on in directions they may not have been able to. So in a sense, we continue to take their unfinished dreams forward, as well as our own.

After the reading, Natasha and I were both in that missing-Mom mode once more, but we were also elated that Mia had left the hotel room that day certain she'd connected with her own mother. "She wanted it so badly," Natasha told me. "I was afraid it wouldn't happen."

Judging by Cyrinda's intense energy during the session, I told Natasha that she was obviously very ready to come through for Mia. And her daughter was prepared and eager to hear encouraging, healing words from her mom. It was the right time for both of them.

CHAPTER TEN

Papa, Can You Hear Me?

WHEN SANDRA AND I DISCOVERED THAT SHE WAS PREGNANT in January 2002, thanks to the granny in Vegas, we were overjoyed. I had always wanted to be a dad and imagined having a big, loud brood of kids sitting around the kitchen table. Maybe it's because I was an only child and had always wanted brothers and sisters, or maybe it's because I loved every second of the large, crazy Italian family that has surrounded me my whole life.

Before Justin was born, I tried to imagine what kind of father I'd be, and there was one thing I knew for sure: I didn't want to be a father like mine—emotionally distant. So since the day Justin was born, every morning and night I hold my little "monster"—as I affectionately call him—and whisper into his ear, "Daddy loves you. Daddy loves you, Justin. . . . " These are words I never, ever heard from my own father.

Throughout my entire life, the relationship between my father and me alternated between two extremes—turbulent and non-existent. Most people outside my family don't know this, because I never speak about him in public. While many of you can probably recite ad nauseum the family stories I've told over and over in my books and on *Crossing Over* about Mom's side of the family, I'm sure you've noticed that I don't mention Dad or his side. At one seminar a few years ago in San Francisco, a woman in the audience stood up during the question period and asked me why I never mentioned my dad . . . did I even have one?

Well, yes and no, I told her.

For years I've kept quiet about our lack of relationship for fear of embarrassing him. But it has become more difficult to keep it under wraps with reporters wanting to unearth some juicy, scandalous tidbits about the man who talks to the dead. How about this one: In the last seven years, I've barely had one conversation with my own father. Now, I know what many of you are thinking: How can I preach about communicating, appreciating, and validating the people in your lives when I don't do this myself? Simple: I believe you should try as best you can to value your family and friends, but I also believe that if you've tried your utmost and the relationship remains unhealthy for you, you should let it go.

My father, Jack, was known to most people as one of the most honest, loyal, respectful people you would ever meet. To the outside world, he was a great guy. But to me, he was an emotional stranger. I heard for years from other people that my dad loved me but had a difficult time demonstrating his feelings and couldn't show it. My mother and father would constantly argue about his lack of emotional support for me, his only son. When did our relationship go wrong? Well, to be honest, when I was born. Part of me thinks I was born too quickly into my parents' young marriage—within their first year together.

Perhaps my father wasn't ready or emotionally equipped to be a father at the age of 26. Or maybe he resented the attention my mother gave me and took away from him. But I also believe that my mother didn't allow herself to fully detach from her somewhat overwhelming family. They were a tight-knit group, always into everybody else's business and very open, whereas my dad's family was very quiet and didn't discuss anything.

In the midst of this rambunctious Italian family, my father stood alone, the odd man out. My dad's background was Irish—which is kinda like the opposite of Italian when it comes to expressing emotion. How the two sides communicated was worlds apart: Mom's side wore their hearts on their sleeves; Dad's side kept them tightly sewn up. To top it all off—and I know I'll be pissing off many people in his family for revealing this—my father wrestled with a severe drinking problem.

As long as I can remember, he had two personalities—the one that was *not* drinking and the one that *was*. Unfortunately, the one that *didn't* drink wasn't a communicator. My father was a New York City police officer and a career military man who had a strong demeanor that came across as almost gruff. He would often make my mother cry, and then she had to tell me, this five-year-old kid, not to be angry at Daddy for making her cry. I heard at least once a day that my father loved me . . . from my mother. She would constantly tell me that I had to be understanding of him, and patient, that he just could not be like her brothers, who would hug me and play with me and throw me over their shoulders.

When the *other* Jack showed up—the *drinking* Jack—it was a little different. His eyes would be a bit glassy, and his speech a bit slurred, but he would be more attentive to me. Still, I always shunned that Jack because he scared me. I would run to my room and close the door, praying that he wouldn't come in. At night, when my parents thought I was sleeping, I would hear my mom complain to him about how he should tell me he loved me and not just stare at me while I was sleeping. Apparently, he would come into my bedroom and watch me sleep, amazed that I was his. One night I woke to find him petting my hair, and I remember smiling and then rolling over, wishing he'd continue. But then left.

THE GAP WIDENS

MY PARENTS SEPARATED WHEN I WAS IN THE SIXTH GRADE, and my mother and I went to live with my grandmother in Glen Cove to save on rent. I'd come home for lunch every day and watch soap operas with my grandmother and eat leftover macaroni and meatballs smothered in warmed-up gravy. (I don't mean to offend other Italians out there, but in my house, the red stuff simmering in the pot all day was called "gravy," not "sauce.") I was an independent kid who never wanted to accept an allowance from my mom because I saw how hard she worked and didn't want to contribute to her burden. So from age 12 on, *I* worked—nabbing my first job at a local hair salon, Foxy Lady, as a "go-fer" boy. I would go for coffee, tea, bagels, dry cleaning—whatever they wanted, I went and got it.

Because of this job, I also never had to go to my dad for money, which exasperated him. He told me once that he was always waiting for the day I'd come to him and need him for something. But I'd inherited his stubbornness. I never wanted to ask him for anything, especially cash, because I always knew that the price for asking would be too high.

Besides his problem with alcohol, another major issue I had with my father was that he attached "conditions" to everything—nothing happened in his life unless it was on his terms. If I asked for help (which I rarely did), it was a big production. Yet he was always there for his friends, whether it was some police buddy who needed a favor or a friend with a military training camp who needed Dad's expertise. My father helped other people but was absent for my mother and me.

When I was in elementary school, I took my Uncle Joey to Father-and-Son Day because Dad was busy at a military meeting. He didn't show up for any of my piano competitions or recitals either—I'm guessing because they weren't macho enough for him. Ditto with my high school graduation. Like that lady in San Francisco, the other kids I went to school with didn't think I *had* a father—just a mother and a grandmother.

I remember the one time I gave in on the money issue, and only served to prove myself right. I was about 14, and VCRs had just became popular. My Aunt Theresa, my mother's older sister, was one of the first to buy one from the local video store. By this time I'd graduated from my job at the beauty salon to washing dishes at the nearby deli, a definite promotion. Even so, I knew I couldn't afford a VCR on my own.

Aware of what a TV and movie buff I was, Aunt Theresa convinced the manager of Video Quest to purchase one wholesale for me if I wanted it. The cost? Only $700 (it's hard to believe you can buy one today for something like 50 bucks). Well, it might as well have been seven *thousand*. I was making $3.35 an hour scrubbing plates for 20 hours a week, so it would have taken me more than a year to save that much. My mother had a job as an executive secretary for Columbia Ribbon and Carbon, and while her paycheck put food on the table, it wasn't enough for such luxuries.

"Johnny, I'd love to buy it," my mother told me, "but we can't afford it." And then she said it: "Why don't you ask your father?"

There she goes again, was all I could think—trying to get me together with Dad any way she could. There was no way I was going to ask him to buy it for me. But after much thought, I decided I'd ask him for a loan. I figured if I was paying him back, he couldn't hold it over my head. It was one of the only times in my life I ever asked him for anything at all. I called him up, gave him my big pitch, and was shot down.

He told me he'd only lend me the money if, after he had a "meeting" with his three other siblings, they all agreed I was "worthy" of the loan. No joke. Well, all my 14-year-old brain could register at that moment was the word *worthy*, and I felt empty inside. I was standing in my grandmother's kitchen, with the receiver to my ear, silent and numb. And when I could finally speak, I thanked my father for teaching me an important lesson that day: to never ask anyone for anything ever again for as long as I lived.

I can only think of one occasion when my father did something for me that was completely unconditional. In my junior year of high school, he showed up unannounced on my doorstep dangling a pair of car keys . . . for me. On the driveway was a cherry-red, second-hand 1979 Chevette—a gift I was not expecting and, of course, didn't ask for. He handed me the keys to this old, beat-up car—which to me was as precious as a Mercedes-Benz—and on the key chain were the words *My Keys*. He asked me if I understood what that meant, and I nodded yes. He didn't want anyone else driving this car—it was mine. And for once, his "condition" wasn't a control issue. He wanted this to be something special between the two of us, and also, he was concerned for my safety if someone else was at the wheel.

I got in the driver's seat with my dad in the passenger seat beside me, and I turned on the ignition. Before I stepped on the gas pedal, he put his hand on my shoulder.

"Son . . . *be careful,*" he told me, " . . . and never let the gas gauge get too low." And with that advice, we took a spin in my new wheels. We drove around for hours—to the beach, to the McDonald's drive-thru for lunch, across town and back with the windows open and the wind whipping against us. It was so great. To this day, I still have my keys on that key chain because it symbolizes the only time I ever felt us really connect . . . and I cherish it.

When my mother was near the end of her battle with cancer, she left the hospital to spend her last days at home. About eight of her ten siblings came over to see how my mom—and their mom (my grandma)—were holding up. In the midst of this family congregation, in walked my dad. He saw what looked like this big family meeting, pulled me aside, and demanded I speak with him upstairs in my room *in private.* It was the first time in my entire life that I thought he was going to hit me; he was furious because he felt left out once again.

By this stage in the game, I wasn't really sleeping or eating much and didn't have an ounce more of energy or patience in me. After what was probably the biggest, loudest argument we ever had, he stormed out of the house. The next few days were tough, and every morning and night my cousin Roseann (Little Ro) came over to help me take care of my mom—feeding her, bathing her . . . everything.

One night the phone rang and it was my dad's sister, Gwen. I'd like to say she was calling to find out how my mom was doing, or even me for that matter, but that wasn't the case.

"I just want you to know that if your father goes back to drinking over this, *it's your fault. . . . *"

"What are you talking about?"

"I just spoke to him, and he told me what happened at your grandmother's house, and—"

In total shock, I cut her off mid-sentence. "The only person I have a responsibility to is the woman who's in the next room dying, and to her mother, my grandmother, who's watching this take place. My father is an adult and will have to act accordingly. This conversation is *over*." I slammed down the phone.

CYCLE INTERRUPTED

MY MOTHER LEFT THIS WORLD on October 5, 1989, and up until the end, she was hoping that I'd mend my relationship with my dad and his family. So I continued to try, but I kept getting blindsided. In one of our last conversations, my father telephoned and began with, "Congratulations! I'm a new uncle . . . what does that make you?"

"Uh . . . how about *confused?*" I answered. "Did someone adopt a baby?"

"No . . . no one was adopted," he said. "My sister had a baby boy! Isn't that great?"

"Are you kidding me?"

"Why would I joke about that?"

"You're calling me up to tell me that she gave birth? What happened to the phone call . . . oh . . . I don't know, maybe six months ago, announcing the fact that she was expecting?"

"Well, it's her business," he said.

"Ookaaaaaay, then, if I wasn't good enough to know about it then, why am I good enough to know about it *now?*" I don't think he kept the pregnancy news from me to hurt me or ignore me on purpose. But what I was feeling was a big buildup of so many frustrations, and it was all linked to the way his family dealt with everything—under wraps, shrouded in secret, don't discuss it.

And I was also feeling like that teenager again, being told I wasn't "worthy" enough.

My father immediately became defensive and went on the attack. He claimed that my mother was too possessive of me as a

195

child and because of her, I never truly understood the way "his" family thought and acted. He told me I was too Italian.

"Too Italian?!" I repeated. Who knew there could be such a thing? His attack on my mom's parenting skills and half my heritage sent me into orbit. We went a few rounds on the phone until The Boys butted in and started feeding me information. (Recently, my guides had started to show me insights about my dad and our relationship.)

"Wait! Stop! I have to say something," I told my father. "My guides are shedding some light on what's happening here, and I want to tell you—"

"Your *what?*" he interrupted, in an Archie Bunker-ish tone. He wasn't amused.

"My *guides*," I repeated, with pride. "The unseen energies that work with me when I do my psychic work, remember? *Your son is a psychic medium.* He talks to dead people." I said it as if I were speaking to a deaf person, very loud and very deliberately, and also very sarcastically.

Ever since I'd begun this work, my father hadn't been supportive of it—he wanted me to follow in his footsteps and become a police officer. In my early 20s, when I was doing psychic readings as a sideline while working as a phlebotomist, he wondered why I was wasting my time. So when I decided to pursue my abilities as a medium full-time, all he said was: "Just don't use my name." Which is why I never used my original last name, McGee—Dad didn't want me to "tarnish" his good name, so my middle name, Edward, became my last name professionally—and now personally.

"And *what,*" my father continued to ridicule me, "do these *unseen scholars* have to say?" I took a deep breath and told him what I was shown.

"They show me . . . you . . . on the phone arguing with *your* dad," I told him, "and then he died. Then they showed me the arguments you and your mother had at night on the phone. I used to ask Mom all the time why you and Grandma fought like that, and why you spoke with her like that, and Mom tried to minimize the fighting. . . . "

There was silence on the other end of the phone line. I knew he hated how personal I was getting, but I wasn't about to stop.

"And after Grandma died, the arguments were turned to home. You and Mom argued all the time—day, night, weekend . . . it was constant."

"I *loved* your mother," Dad insisted.

"I don't doubt you both loved each other," I replied. "I think that was clear. But after Grandma died, Mom was next in line for you to argue with. And now that she's gone, it's me."

My guides showed me that, because of how my father was raised, he needed to create conflict with someone to feel that he was relating to them. Unfortunately, the person he'd be "relating" to would end up wanting to choke the crap out of him. I told him all this, and made it very clear that this pattern of conflict was stopping right here, and if he wanted to have a relationship with me, I had my own communication rules and they were simple: "Respect me and treat me like the adult I am. Let's try to have a friendship."

Silence.

"You're just as sick as your mother," was my dad's response, "and I should have taken you away from her and her family a long time ago." *Click.*

If my guides, or even my mother, were trying to transmit messages from above on how to mend this painful relationship, our lines were sure getting crossed.

In light of the above, the big question on everyone's lips when I was planning my wedding a few years later was would I invite my dad? Yes, I invited him and his family—I wanted them there, if only to honor my mother's wishes and have the family together. Unfortunately, none of them responded to the wedding invitations. I remember talking about this with my cousin Phyllis. I told her that not only did I think they wouldn't come, but I knew they wouldn't even respond, and they proved me right. Phyllis was so baffled by their actions that I had to laugh.

"Now you finally understand what I've been talking about," I told her, "but my father will just say I didn't give him or his family proper respect for one thing or another, and that's why they're not coming." Phyllis, not the shy type, telephoned my father shortly after the wedding to get to the bottom of it. When he answered the phone, she asked him point blank why he hadn't come to the wedding. His response was verbatim what I'd guessed he'd say à la Rodney Dangerfield: *No respect, can't get no respect.*

I didn't talk to my father for years after that. I'd finally decided, as I mentioned earlier, that the relationship was too toxic to continue. No matter what my mother's hopes were for us, our relationship seemed too messed up to fix—at least, not in *this* lifetime or on *this* plane. We couldn't seem to get it right. Trying to work it out was more painful than beneficial, so I let it go.

Or so I thought. Three years ago Sandra got into a heavy discussion with two of her female friends—students at her dance studio—who are psychologists. The topic for that afternoon's Girl Talk session? John and his profound "dad issues." Both of these women had seen *Crossing Over* and noticed I rarely mentioned my dad or his family in my endless homespun anecdotes. In fact, they pointed out, Sandra and I barely mentioned my dad or his family even in conversation among friends. "John has a lot of father issues to resolve," they told her, in that serious-toned, therapist-speak.

When Sandra got home that night, she relayed their professional opinion to me over dinner, and I have to say, their comments really bothered me. I'd worked hard on these so-called issues, and as far as I was concerned, I'd reached a pretty good place about the whole thing, thank you very much. My dad and I kept our distance, and it worked fine for both of us that way.

I knew that my father followed what was happening in my life through the show and my media appearances and had come to respect my work somewhat. We e-mailed sporadically, and when Miss Cleo, the infamous 1-900 psychic hotline lady, was embroiled in all that scandalous fraud and court trouble, my father sent me an e-mail saying he hoped people wouldn't lump me into the same category as *her,* since I was providing a service that helped people, and not ripping them off. I had to pick myself off the floor after reading *that!*

Then there was the time I was paged off the set of *Crossing Over* with an urgent message. In total "Jack" style, my father had elicited the help of the police station around the corner from our studio to get the private studio phone number. The reason? A writer from *Details* magazine who'd interviewed me had located my dad in Florida and wanted to interview *him* for the story to get the goods on this "mystery" father and our relationship—or lack thereof.

My father was frantic and didn't know what to do, but at the same time, I could hear in his voice how excited he was that this journalist wanted to talk to him. I told him to do the interview if he wanted, but that the intrepid reporter would probably ask him about things he might not want to discuss—namely, the difficulties in our relationship. And I told him that the reporter would most likely also ask about the development of my psychic abilities—one of many questions my father wouldn't be able to answer since he wasn't around for that . . . or for a lot of things.

My dad decided not to do the interview, later telling my Aunt Theresa that he didn't want to do anything that would hurt me or my work. Each e-mail he sent to me, he signed "Daddy," and that felt a bit strange. There was still a thin, thin thread between us that hadn't been severed yet—which held the promise of one day getting stronger. But at this point, I felt that I'd dealt with our past and was beyond it all.

FATHER TIME

TWO NIGHTS AFTER SANDRA TOLD ME about her therapist friends' diagnosis of my lingering father issues, we went to see the movie *Frequency*, starring Dennis Quaid. The plot centers around the relationship between a firefighter father and his son, and how different the son's life might have been if his father hadn't died an untimely death and been absent during the kid's formative years. In a kind of supernatural *Field of Dreams* twist, the father is sort of brought back to life, and the two are given a second chance to work on their relationship.

The film really got to me, and I was mush by the time the credits rolled. Afterwards, as Sandra and I silently walked through the parking lot to the car, I looked at her and started laughing through my tears. What, she asked, was so funny?

"Not funny," I corrected her, *"ironic!"*

Watching that movie opened up a big emotional well in me and made me realize that I'd done a good job ignoring this relationship without dealing with those primal, core childhood feelings of not having a dad in my life. Even though I had my Uncle Joey and my cousin Glenn as great father figures, I didn't have a dad. And that realization hit me strong. Sandra's friends were right . . . I still had my dad issues. It was a startling realization for a grown man of 30. How was I supposed to fix this? The idea of instigating a heart-to-heart with dear ol' Dad like families do on all those *Afterschool Specials* felt totally foreign to me, and I knew that neither of us was up for any major surgery like that. We just weren't ready to deal with each other yet. We didn't have the tools to do it.

I kept my revelations at bay until two years later, when we found out Sandra was pregnant. The prospect of becoming a dad brought all those feelings up in me again: feelings of being abandoned by him, of being "unworthy," concerns that as a dad myself, the cycle would continue. Well, at least I could work on that last part by myself. I figured if I could devote myself to being a good father and explore the father-son dynamic from a dad's point of view, that would help me heal whatever issues I had, and they might transfer over to my relationship with my own father. So I vowed that I'd show my love to my son, would verbalize it, and would love him unconditionally.

During the pregnancy, I waffled back and forth with the thought of calling up my father to tell him about it, but each time I brushed it aside. I didn't want to deal with any negative stuff just yet when I was feeling so happy. Maybe later. But every month, as her belly grew, Sandra asked me the same question: *"When are you going to call your father and tell him he's going to be a grandfather?"*

At one point I told her *she* should call him. "I would," she said, "but I think you're the one who needs to do it." I must admit, I might have been delaying telling him the news because part of me wanted the satisfaction of calling him up and saying, "Congratulations! I'm a father! *You know what that makes you . . . ?*" like he'd said to me in one of our last conversations.

By the time Justin was born in September 2002, I still hadn't called my father. I still wasn't "ready." But I was beginning to understand him a bit more. I found myself staring at Justin's little face as he slept (just like Dad had) with so much awe and love, and I empathized with my own father because I now knew he must have loved me. And it must have tortured him that he couldn't show it. This realization was a start.

MYSTIC PIZZA

WITH THE NEW ADDITION TO THE FAMILY, Sandra and I settled into being Mommy and Daddy. Weekends at our house became like an Italian-Portugese convention, with tons of family and friends passing through; and lots of food, games, and loud conversation.

One Saturday night last November, we were having a pizza party with my Aunt Theresa; cousin "Little Ro" and her husband Glenn; my aunt Roseann ("Big Ro"); and the new cozy family threesome of Sandra, myself, and six-week-old Justin, when Aunt Theresa decided to get all psychic on me.

"John, look . . . all I've been dreaming about lately is dead people," she told me. "They come to talk to me about this or that. Why are they coming to me and not you?"

I laughed and told her I'd been working so much lately they were probably getting a busy signal trying to reach me and the psychic operator redirected them to her . . . *ha, ha, ha,* I laughed.

But Aunt Theresa wasn't laughing with me. All joking aside, she could be extremely psychic and often picked up on family stuff. Yes, I do believe psychic ability can run in families. In fact, I'd venture to say that *both* sides of my family have a kind of pre-genetic disposition for it—which is really ironic since my father always shunned the whole psychic world. I never knew he had other connections to it until one day, after I'd been doing this work for a few years and had decided he would never fully accept it.

My father and I were having a brief conversation about my work on the phone, and he casually dropped a bomb. "You know, " he said, just before hanging up, "I was sort of hoping that 'it' was going to skip your generation. . . ."

"What?" I said into the phone. Did I hear him right? "*What?!* What are you talking about?"

In his roundabout way, Dad all but admitted that his own mother—who had a knack for reading tea leaves among her circle of friends—had her own psychic abilities, which were frowned upon in the family and never, ever discussed. Except for seeing her on my birthday or at Christmas, I rarely saw my grandmother on Dad's side. I surely don't remember ever having any "psychic" connection with her.

"Now you tell me this?" I demanded. *"Now this comes out?!"*

It would have been nice to know earlier, that's for sure. It might have explained a lot about my own abilities and also about my father's distaste for the whole subject.

Either way, psychic ability is a family trait. So when one of my relatives tells me they're having dreams or visions or whatever, I listen. I asked Aunt Theresa to tell me more about these dreams she was having.

"Well, that's just it," she continued, puzzled. "I'm dreaming about all these dead people . . . and then I had a dream about your father last night. In the dream he was in a real rush—like he was going someplace and couldn't stay. But he specifically told me I was to call him in case there was anything wrong with Justin. Is Justin okay? And why would I be dreaming about your father?"

Big Ro, who was stacking up the empty pizza boxes, interrupted with her own psychic analysis: "John, you *did* call your father to tell him he was a grandfather, didn't you?"

I chose to answer Aunt Theresa's question first. I could explain the Other Side much easier than I could explain my relationship with my father.

"I think the energies know you're receptive to their messages," I told her, "and it's their way of letting you know they're around. But I have no idea why you're dreaming about my father . . . maybe you're going to hear from him soon. And Justin is fine." And then came the more difficult answer about my dad.

"I know I should call him . . . but I just haven't been able to do it yet," I admitted.

At that, the topic became a hot debate, with Sandra and Big Ro voting that I should call my father, and Little Ro and me vetoing the idea. "If I were you, I wouldn't call him," my cousin said. "After all, he was never around for anything else . . . why give him the honor?" Before an all-out battle erupted with me in the middle of the tug-of-war, I changed the subject and broke out the Pictionary.

At about six o'clock the next morning, I got up to change Justin's diapers and give him his first bottle, and the two of us settled into the rocking chair, swaying back and forth. It was such a peaceful moment, all alone with my son—complete tranquility as the sun rose through the curtains. Justin, on the other hand, was having an entirely different experience. He was cooing and gurgling and looking straight ahead, past me, and laughing as if someone was playing with him. I turned around and looked in the direction of his gaze, and all I saw was a wall.

"Who are you playing with, you little monster?" I asked him in baby-talk. "Justin, do you see Grandpa? Are you playing with Grandpa? *Where's Grandpa?*" I was thinking of Sandra's dad, Fernando, who lived about 20 miles away in Queens, whom Justin simply adored. And once I said it, I thought it was odd that I was asking Justin where Grandpa was. My grandmother used to say that when babies played and cooed at nothing in front of them, they were playing with the angels.

I do believe that babies are directly connected with the spirit world because they have no prejudices about the existence of the Other Side and its inhabitants. In a nervous tone, I said out loud, "Justin, Grandpa better be in Queens . . . or your mommy is going to be one upset cookie. Justin, *who are you playing with?*" But my son just nodded back into dreamland, and I thought whoever Justin's angelic playmate was, he or she would have to join him in his dreams now.

I carefully put him in his crib with his little *ShooSha* (Portuguese for "pacifier") to keep him company on *this* Side, and the phone rang. I jumped to answer it before it woke Justin.

"I know it's early," Aunt Theresa whispered apologetically, on the other end of the line, "but I thought I should call you right away. You're not going to believe this . . . but I think your father has died. . . ."

MAKING AMENDS

YOU COULD SAY THAT THE NEWS of my father's death reached me via a trail of coincidences, if you believe in them. You already know that I don't. My cousin James, Big Ro's son, had been chatting on-line with a girl he'd met the night before who lived in Florida, where my dad had moved about three years before. During the e-mail conversation, he mentioned to the girl that he was related to me, and oh, what a small world it is . . . this girl's aunt happened to work in the hospital where my dad had been a patient and had just died of complications from diabetes and throat cancer. She told my cousin that my dad's funeral was the next day.

I was a bit stunned. I hadn't "officially" known that my father was even sick, but the last time I spoke with him years before I'd felt a weird health vibe. I told him he'd better check it out, and he blew me off, telling me not to worry about it or about him. He hated when I got all "psychic" with him.

I tried the old phone number I had for my dad, but it was out of order. I called my Aunt Theresa back, and she said she had a more recent number. I called and got my dad's brother, Thomas, on the phone. Uncle Thomas said he'd called me the day before and left a message that my father had passed, yet I'd never gotten it—my voice mail just didn't record it.

My cousin Phyllis, who also lived in Florida, e-mailed me my father's obituary from the newspaper. I must say it was weird to read it. First of all, I wasn't mentioned as a surviving family member, and that final disconnection just made me shake my head. Of all the mixed emotions I felt—sadness, relief, shock—the one I felt the most was *defeat*. Reading his obituary, I had to finally acknowledge that in this lifetime I wouldn't be able to make our relationship better.

ALL OF THIS LEADS ME to one of the most important points I want to make in this book. I realized with my father's death that I was not able—and could now never—mend our differences while we were both still alive. But I also suspected that, in a strange way, with his death we might actually begin to have a relationship for the very first time.

How do I see this happening? Well, I know from my guides and from all the energies that have come through to me in the last two decades that when a person crosses over, their first task on the Other Side is to reflect on the life they've led here and understand why they made the choices they did, see how their actions affected others, and realize what they still need to work on while on the Other Side.

Our learning doesn't stop once our body does—in fact, it's probably hastened because we're no longer being dragged down by Earthly obstacles. I've said before that I see this life and the afterlife kind of like school: On Earth, it's like we're in kindergarten, running around in circles and getting distracted with the toys and not knowing how to do things. When we get to the Other Side, we graduate straight to college because we immediately have more understanding, more skills, and more smarts. It's still us, but it's like a wiser, *better* us.

Now if you understand that the exchange of energies between two people doesn't stop just because the body stops, and we can continue to "exchange energy" or communicate with our loved ones even after they've crossed over, it stands to reason that if you had a troubled relationship with someone and they crossed over, and then, in reviewing their life, they learned of their misguided ways and cleared their energy of negative patterns, then you both can continue to work on and improve your relationship even though they're not standing in front of you. You may not be able to communicate in the way you used to—talking on the phone, writing letters, or meeting for a cup of coffee—but you can adapt the old ways into new ones. I often suggest to people that they sit down and write letters to their loved ones who have passed because I know they're looking over our shoulders, reading our words as we write them (the Other Side is even faster than e-mail).

And why should you stop talking to your loved ones just because you can't see them? I do believe that they can hear our words and feel our feelings, and then respond by sending us their own feelings in return. Often, we might not be aware of it. For many people, this exchange happens during dreams, or with a "feeling" that we brush off and think is a figment of our imagination. But believe me, it's happening.

One woman I know, Sandy Goodman, author of *LOVE NEVER DIES: A Mother's Journey from Loss to Love*, talks to her son every day. Jason, 18, died in an electrical accident in 1996.

"From almost day one, I began talking to him," said Sandy. "Sometimes out loud and sometimes just in my head. I needed to know he was still around and hadn't just ceased to exist. And so a ritual began. On a daily basis, sometimes three or four times a day, I would say to Jason, 'I need to hear from you. If you can't get through to me, go to someone else and tell them to CALL YOUR MOM!'"

I "met" Sandy soon after on the Internet, when she was organizing a group seminar in Philadelphia with several mediums and she invited me to participate. Although I ended up not being able to attend, we exchanged a couple of short but friendly e-mails in which we discovered, of all things, a mutual appreciation for those gooey, orange slices of candy. Little did I know that from that day onward, Sandy began telling Jason to come to *me*.

A month later, I was lying on a beach one lazy Saturday afternoon getting some much-needed rest when a young male came through to me. He gave me the names "Jason" and "Sandy." I was trying to figure out whom I knew by those names when the clincher came through: "Orange slices." And then, an urgent message: *"Call my mom!"* After searching high and low for her phone number, I called Sandy for the first time ever and told her I thought I had a Jason coming through for her. After I gave her the rest of the messages that came through to me by the pool, Sandy was ecstatic. To her, this was proof that her son indeed had heard her and continues to do so.

Six years later, Sandy is still talking to Jason. And their open lines of communication have made it possible for their relationship to continue to develop.

"Jason was not a kid you would have met and thought he was a wise old soul," Sandy explained. "He acted like your typical rowdy teenager. But now, since crossing over, he's grown, and our roles have changed. I've had to accept that he's no longer my teenage son who needs my protection, guidance, and direction. Instead, he seems to be offering *me* guidance and direction when I need it."

THIS EVOLVING OF THEIR RELATIONSHIP doesn't surprise me at all. I think once people get the hang of communicating with their loved ones who have crossed over, we'll have a new generation who will consider it commonplace to work on relationships with loved ones who are on the Other Side and see them grow. At the same time, I want to point out, as I did early on in this book, that while I encourage this building of relationships, I don't advocate creating a *dependency* on communicating with the Other Side. We're still here to live our lives and shouldn't wait for a sign just to get us out of bed in the morning. A balance of both worlds is healthy so we can resolve past issues while still living in the present.

"So many people think that once a loved one dies, the opportunity to transform the relationship they had with that person ends," says Dr. Jane Greer, author of THE AFTERLIFE CONNECTION: *A Therapist Reveals How to Communicate with Departed Loved Ones* (to be published by St. Martin's Press in October 2003). "However, in life, this person may have given all they could in terms of love and support within their own earthly limitations. When they cross over, the spiritual transformation they go through, I believe, enables them to finally give and respond on an energy plane in a way they may never have been able to do before."

In her book, Dr. Greer guides readers on how to effectively resolve their anger and form the relationship connections they couldn't make while a loved one was alive. "So if you had a troubled relationship with someone when they were here, and after they pass you have an open heart and a willingness to still mend that animosity—you can. Without a doubt, a healing interaction can still take place."

In the five months since my father passed away, I've often spoken to him out loud and in my thoughts. I ask him daily to help me avoid making the mistakes with Justin that he and I made, and I also ask him to learn from *my* experiences as a loving, understanding father. I'm certain that my father hears me. Already, I feel a different vibration between our energies . . . as if he sees and understands our relationship differently now. I feel a lessening of anger, and more empathy and compassion for him.

If you're wondering if I've had any direct, dramatic psychic visitations from my dad yet, as of the time of this writing this book I have not. But I consider my Aunt Theresa's dream a true visit from my father, and confirmation that both he and my mother are watching over their grandson from where they are. My father had already passed when my aunt had that dream, and shortly after that, Justin did have a minor health problem that needed to be treated. I believe that was my dad's way of letting me know he was (finally) aware of my son and was watching out for him . . . perhaps in a way he never could for me. (I keep teasing Aunt Theresa that she's now going to have to guest-host a few episodes of *Crossing Over*.)

But as I told you in Chapter 1, when I talked about watching my son being born and waiting for my relatives to show up in the delivery room, I've learned to stop looking for the grandiose, psychic billboard, or the big *"Surrender Dorothy"* writing in the sky, because that's not always the way it happens. Sometimes the signs our loved ones send us are subtle, like hearing their favorite song on the radio, or getting a whiff of the scent of their perfume, or the smell of their cigarettes in the air.

So if you have a difficult relationship with a parent, child, or someone who has crossed over, please know that you still have a chance to work on that relationship after they're gone. However, I'm not saying you shouldn't try to work on your relationships when your loved ones are still *alive*. Please don't wait for them to cross over, thinking that this is the easier road to take.

I tried as much as I possibly could to honor my dying mother's wish that I reconcile and have a better relationship with my dad. It just didn't work. In life, my father's soul inhabited a vehicle that had a physical ailment—an addiction to alcohol that would often overtake him. I truly believe and live by my "communicate, appreciate, and validate" mantra, but I'm not Pollyana-like about it. If something isn't working when you've tried your best, should you continue to beat yourself over the head about it? I don't think so.

I believe that now, every day, I move forward and will develop a better relationship with my father—maybe not with the *man* who was here on Earth, but instead, with the *energy* that was inside that man, which still exists. I may not be able to erase the past, like Dennis Quaid could in that film *Frequency,* and bring him back to do it all differently. But I can have a future that's more peaceful and complete where he's concerned. The major feeling I have is that the struggle between us is over—like it's disintegrated in some way, even though there are days when I'm reminded of that old struggle.

A few weeks after he passed, a friend of my father who only knew my dad's version of our relationship sent an angry letter to my office about how I hadn't been "a good son" and that I was being a hypocrite when I told people to "communicate, validate, and appreciate" their loved ones. Carol read the letter out loud to me, and I sighed. There are still little minefields planted all around me, reminders of the "old Jack" I once knew, but I'm dealing with them one by one as I walk on this journey of self-discovery and healing.

Sometimes I feel that my dad is sending me encouragement from above. Just last week I got together with my Uncle Thomas and his wife, Anne Marie, and they told me that my father was so proud of me when he was alive. He used to turn on *Crossing Over* and show me off to his friends, saying, "That's my son!"

It's funny that, just like before, my father is telling me he's proud of me through other people. But I know it's true, and I know he hears me, and I believe that with him up there and me down here, we're both trying to bridge the gap inch by inch.

When I first heard the news that my father died, I must admit that for the first time in my life I felt . . . free. Not free *of* him, but free to *love* him.

And now, he, too, is free to love me.

I really do believe in my mantra of validating, appreciating, and communicating with our loved ones while they're still here. But I also believe that we all have our human limits and can only go as far as those boundaries will allow. We can continue working on our troubled relationships after someone has crossed. By the same token, if we had a loving relationship with someone who has crossed over, that relationship also continues onward and grows in its love. Remember, your loved ones are around you and always with you. The love never dies.

After 20 years of doing this work and helping countless people (including myself) through grief, I'm still grateful for the constant validations the Other Side gives us. They occur quietly and unexpectedly, like the delivery-room moment when Justin was born and the staff uttered five names of my family who had passed. On that day, I learned to focus on life happening in front of me. And the validations also appear on a grand scale. Soon after Justin was born, I made a seemingly impossible request of the Other Side. During a meditation one night, I asked my mother to validate once again that she saw Justin and knew she was a grandmother. "If you see this happening," I requested of my mother, "send me a rosary blessed by the Vatican."

A few weeks later, I received a letter at the office from a viewer of the show. It read, "I don't know why I'm sending this to you . . . but for whatever reason, I felt I had to. Here it is."

Out of the envelope a string of rosary beads dropped on my desk. They were blessed by the Vatican . . . with a card attached to it stamped with the date they were blessed: September 25th. *Justin's birthday.*

We're all still searching for answers. But when I think of my father and my son, of my mother and my grandmother, of my wife, and of all the people who have connected with the ones they love on the Other Side, I think deep down that we already know the answer:

The circle of love goes on and on and on. . . .

About John Edward

JOHN EDWARD IS AN INTERNATIONALLY ACCLAIMED PSYCHIC MEDIUM, and author of the *New York Times* bestsellers *ONE LAST TIME, CROSSING OVER,* and *WHAT IF GOD WERE THE SUN?*. In addition to hosting his own syndicated television show, *Crossing Over with John Edward,* John has been a frequent guest on *Larry King Live* and many other talk shows, and was featured in the HBO documentary *Life After Life.* He publishes his own newsletter and also conducts workshops and seminars around the country. John lives in New York with his family.

For more information regarding John Edward, see his Website at: **www.johnedward.net**.

About Natasha Stoynoff

NATASHA STOYNOFF IS A STAFF CORRESPONDENT FOR *PEOPLE* MAGAZINE, and this is her third book collaboration following *Life's Little Emergencies: Everyday Rescue for Beauty, Fashion, Relationships, and Life* with supermodel Emme; and *Never Say Never: 10 Lessons to Turn You Can't into Yes I Can* with former Miss America and CBS sportscaster Phyllis George. Natasha has worked as a news reporter/photographer for *The Toronto Star* and has been an entertainment columnist for *The Toronto Sun.* Her work has also appeared in cover stories for *Time* magazine and Germany's *Der Spiegel.* She lives in Manhattan with her husband, journalist Stephen Erwin, and is currently working on her first screenplay.

THE JOHN EDWARD NEWSLETTER
"BRIDGES"

The John Edward newsletter, "Bridges," is a quarterly magazine-style publication that includes:

- Inspirational stories
- A Q & A "Ask John" section
- Spiritually related areas
- Reader validations and experiences
- Special subscriber offers
- Guest contributors
- Other related material

To order your subscription of the "Bridges" newsletter, just fill out the order form. In addition, as a special gift from John for purchasing **both** the book *After Life* and a *"Bridges"* newsletter subscription, you will receive three (3) *free* John Edward Appreciation Pins (a $20.70 value).

Due to overwhelming demand, you must send the original form below, not a copy:

Name_____

Street Address_____

City_____State_____Zip_____

Phone_____E-mail address_____

Check appropriate box:

❑ 1-year subscription $24.95*   ❑ 2-year subscription $39.00*
*Please include $2.95 for shipping and handling. Thank you.

*Plus 3 **Free** John Edward Appreciation Pins*

Please make check payable *(in U.S. dollars only)* to **Get Psych'd, Inc.**, and mail your order to:

Get Psych'd, Inc.
P.O. Box 383
Huntington, NY 11743

Allow 4–6 weeks for delivery.

Visit our official Website at: **www.johnedward.net**

Coming in June 2004:

FINAL BEGINNINGS: The Tunnel

(fiction)

by John Edward

P

We hope you enjoyed this Princess Books publication. If you would like more information about Princess Books, you may contact the company through their distributor, Hay House, Inc.:

Hay House, Inc.
P.O. Box 5100
Carlsbad, CA 92018-5100

(760) 431-7695 or (800) 654-5126
(760) 431-6948 (fax) or (800) 650-5115 (fax)
www.hayhouse.com

Distributed in Australia by:
Hay House Australia Pty Ltd, 18/36 Ralph St., Alexandria NSW 2015
Phone: 612-9669-4299 • Fax: 612-9669-4144 • www.hayhouse.com.au

Distributed in the United Kingdom by:
Hay House UK, Ltd. • Unit 202, Canalot Studios • 222 Kensal Rd.,
London W10 5BN • *Phone: 44-20-8962-1230 • Fax: 44-20-8962-1239*
www.hayhouse.co.uk

Distributed in Canada by:
Raincoast • 9050 Shaughnessy St., Vancouver, B.C. V6P 6E5
Phone: (604) 323-7100 • Fax: (604) 323-2600

Sign up via the Hay House USA Website to receive the Hay House online newsletter and stay informed about what's going on with your favorite authors. You'll receive bimonthly announcements about: Discounts and Offers, Special Events, Product Highlights, Free Excerpts, Giveaways, and more!